VISUAL QUICKSTART GUIDE

NETSCAPE COMMUNICATOR 4

FOR MACINTOSH

Elizabeth Castro

Visual QuickStart Guide
Netscape Communicator 4 for Macintosh
Elizabeth Castro

Peachpit Press
1249 Eighth Street
Berkeley, CA 94710
(510) 524-2178
(510) 524-2221 (fax)

Find us on the World Wide Web at: http://www.peachpit.com
Or contact Liz directly at lcastro@cookwood.com

Peachpit Press is a division of Addison Wesley Longman

Cover design: The Visual Group

ISBN: 0-201-68886-7

0 9 8 7 6 5 4 3

Printed on recycled paper

Printed in the United States of America

For Becky and Jenny who taught me my multiplication tables,
my Uncle Myron Pollyea who taught me exponential powers,
and Stephen Ucich, my first (and only) computer teacher.

Special thanks to:

Nancy Davis at Peachpit Press. Her encouraging words and excellent edits were essential in helping me get through this book one more time, and instrumental in making the book worth reading.

Kate Reber at Peachpit Press for her careful and professional production work.

The folks who frequent the netscape.navigator newsgroup, like **Frank Tabor**, who seem to know all the answers.

Andreu, for expert Photoshop tips, hundreds of screenshots, most of the Preferences chapters, and strawberry milkshakes.

Table of Contents

Table of Contents

Introduction

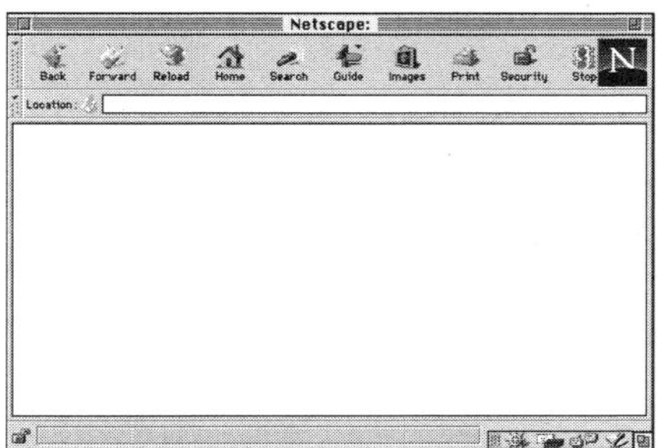

Figure i.1 *This is the new Navigator window.*

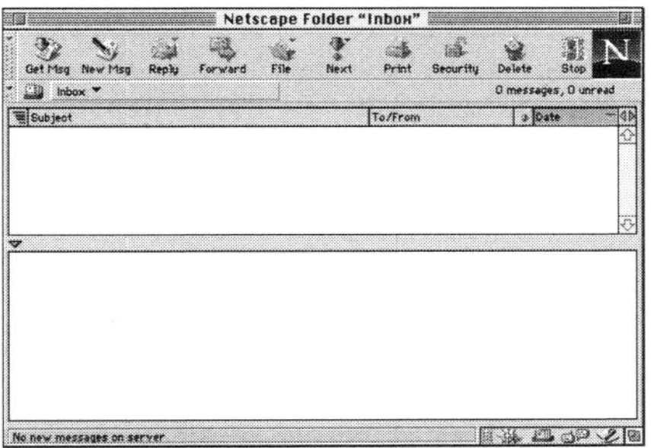

Figure i.2 *Although the Communicator menu includes an item called Messenger Mailbox, there is no window called Messenger* per se. *Rather, Messenger refers to a set of functions that manage e-mail and discussion groups, like the Inbox, shown here.*

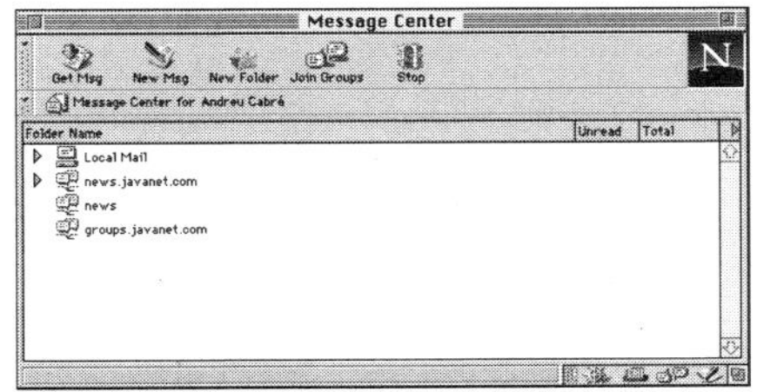

Figure i.3 *The same way that there is not a visible program called Messenger, there is none called Collabra (I wonder if they were thinking about a car here). When you choose Communicator > Collabra, you go to the Message Center, whose functions are intertwined with Messenger's functions.*

Netscape Navigator, the predecessor of Netscape Communicator 4, was designed to allow people to surf the World Wide Web. Although Navigator continues to serve this function, it now forms part of a set of components that, besides surfing the Web, let you write electronic mail, participate in electronic discussion groups, use the Internet as a telephone, and finally, create Web pages of your own.

Communicator

There are a few special tools that help integrate all of Communicator's modules. These are described in detail in *Netscape Communicator*, starting on page 17.

Navigator

Navigator, while losing some ground to the increasingly popular Microsoft Internet Explorer, is still the most popular browser used to surf the World Wide Web. Although it used to be known simply as Netscape (and *not* Navigator), its integration into Communicator has meant, among other things, that it has gotten its own name back. I refer to it in this book as Navigator **(Figure i.1)**. You'll learn how to use Navigator in *Part II: The World Wide Web*, starting on page 21.

Messenger and Collabra

Messenger is Communicator's component for reading and writing electronic mail **(Figure i.2)**. Collabra is for reading and writing messages to discussion groups **(Figure i.3)**. Because the two kinds of messages are almost identical, Messenger and Collabra overlap in many respects. You'll learn about messages in *Part III: Mail, Discussion Groups, and Conference*, starting on page 117.

Conference

Conference is new to version 4 of Netscape's software **(Figure i.4)**. You can use Conference as a special telephone. It not only lets you talk to other folks on the Internet, but lets you exchange files, write notes back and forth, share a common whiteboard with images, and surf the Web together. I explain how to use Conference in Chapter 16, *Using Conference*.

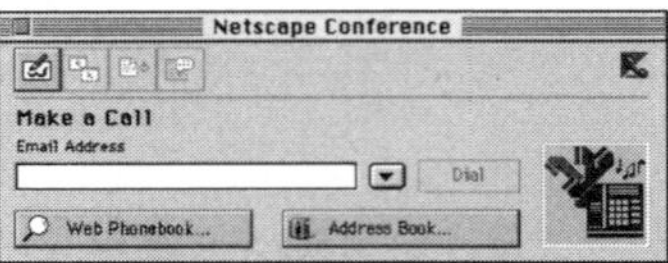

Figure i.4 *This is the Conference main window. Conference, new in this version of Communicator, can be used to communicate directly with another person and exchange files with him or her.*

Composer

Communicator also contains a module, called Composer, that helps you create your own Web pages without having to learn HTML **(Figure i.5)**. Composer is the new reincarnation of the Editor from Netscape Navigator Gold 3. I'll explain how to use Composer in *Part IV: Creating Web Pages*, starting on page 217.

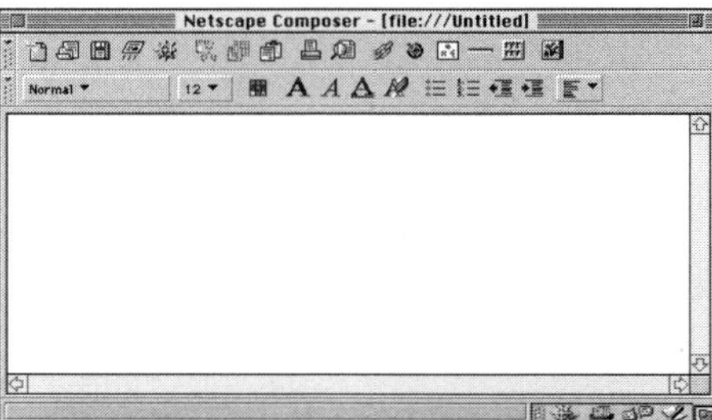

Figure i.5 *This is Composer's window. Composer is the module of Communicator that lets you create your own Web pages. It is the direct descendant of the Editor from Netscape Gold 3.*

Preferences

The final section, *Preferences*, that starts on page 309, details all the settings that you can adjust to make each of Communicator's components work better for you.

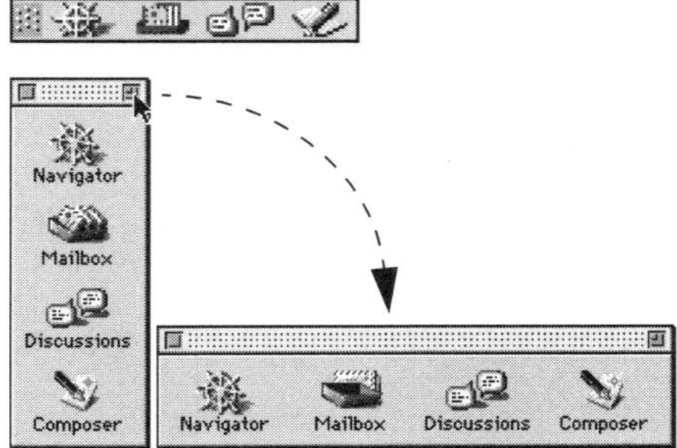

Figure i.6 *By default, the Component bar is located in the lower-right corner of most windows (top). You can expand it and have it float above everything else. Click on the zoom box to toggle between the horizontal and vertical position.*

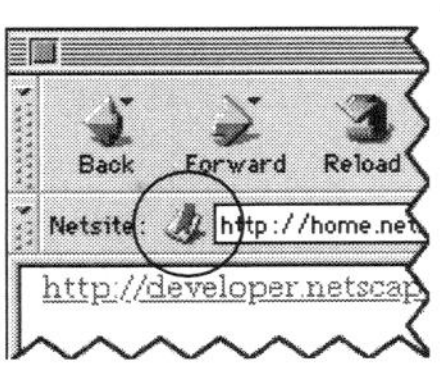

Figure i.7 *The new page proxy icon can be used to create bookmarks and shortcuts to Web pages from your hard disk.*

What's new in version 4?

This book has been completely updated to take into account the changes from Netscape 3 to Communicator 4, both minor and major.

Communicator-wide changes

- The Component bar has been added to the lower-right corner of most windows **(Figure i.6)**. Use it to jump from one component of Communicator to another. To learn how to use it, see *The Component bar* on page 18.
- Netscape has changed all the icons and many of the menus. Although most of the commands and options in Netscape 3 still exist, many have new names.
- You can create individual user profiles so that people with different user names, bookmark files, and address books can all use the same copy of Communicator on a given computer. For more details, consult *Creating user profiles* on page 19.

Browser changes

- The page proxy icon **(Figure i.7)** lets you create shortcuts and bookmarks, among other things. For more information, consult *Using the page proxy icon* on page 26 and *Creating bookmarks* on page 88.
- The Back and Forward buttons not only tell you where "back" and "forward" might be, but also let you choose to go further back and forward via a pop-up menu. (See *Going back and forward* on page 37.)

- The new Search button gives you access to certain Netscape-approved search engines **(Figure i.8)**. To find out how, consult *Searching vs. finding* on page 71.
- The new Guide button shows you what Netscape considers to be interesting on the Internet **(Figure i.9)**.
- The contextual Help system attempts to answer your queries depending on what you're doing when you make them.
- Navigator 4 includes support for dynamic fonts, cascading style sheets, floating objects, fixed placement, and other advanced HTML features.

Figure i.8 *The new Search button on the Navigation toolbar leads you to several Web search services.*

Figure i.9 *The new Guide button shows a list of places that Netscape considers interesting.*

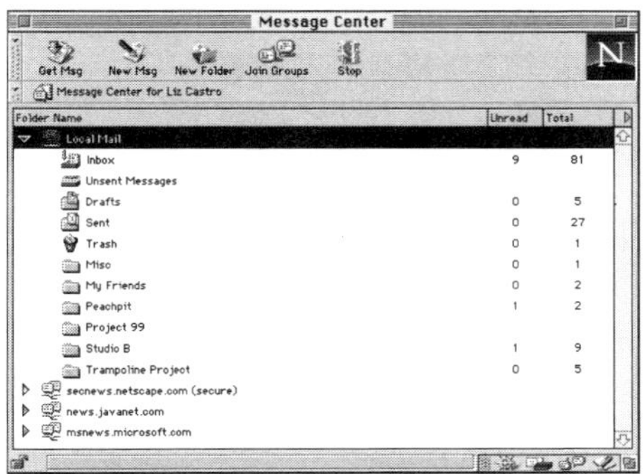

Figure i.10 *This is the new Message Center, which shows all the folder in which your e-mail is stored as well as the discussion groups and their servers.*

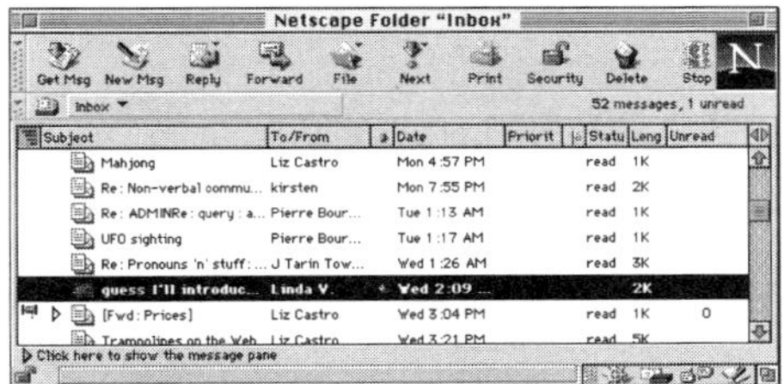

Figure i.11 *The Message List window is used for displaying lists of e-mail and discussion groups messages.*

Mail and News changes

- Newsgroups are now called discussion groups.
- The Message Center **(Figure i.10)** and Message List **(Figure i.11)** windows combine electronic mail and discussion group messages. I'm not so sure this is an improvement. Frankly, I find it a bit confusing. To learn more about how they work, see *Part III: Mail, Discussion Groups, and Conference* on page 117.
- The Go Offline command lets you download news and mail messages for offline reading (although it does not disconnect you from your ISP). For more information, consult *Downloading mail for offline reading* on page 123 and *Getting news messages for reading offline* on page 134.
- You can mark certain threads that you want to watch and then view just these, or ignore certain threads and have them disappear *(see page 144)*.
- You can spell check messages before sending them *(see page 193)*.
- You can save messages and then edit them at a later date *(see page 158)*.
- You can add Web page formatting to messages *(see page 154)*.
- You can specify the priority of outgoing mail *(see page 155)*.
- You can request a receipt for outgoing mail *(see page 156)*.
- You can filter incoming messages directly into the appropriate folders *(see page 188)*.
- You can search for addresses in online directories *(see page 177)*.

Conference

- Everything is new! For more information on placing telephone calls, writing notes, exchanging files, using a common whiteboard **(Figure i.12)**, and collaborative browsing, consult Chapter 16, *Using Conference*, starting on page 199.

Figure i.12 *The Whiteboard is one of the most interesting new tools included in Conference. It is used to send images and annotations.*

Editor changes

- You can add font information to the text on your page **(Figure i.13)** *(see page 234).*
- You can drag and drop images *(see page 252)* and links *(see page 268)* from the Desktop and the Navigator window.
- You can add HTML manually, either to existing tags *(see page 298)* or as independent tags *(see page 296).*

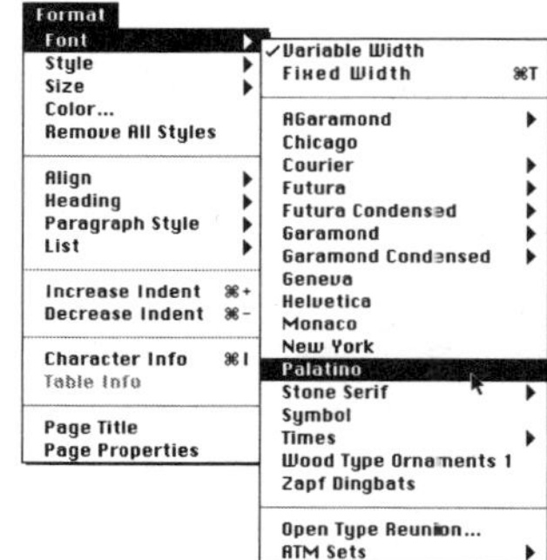

Figure i.13 *You can now choose a font to format your Web pages, which makes for greater flexibility when designing your pages.*

Part I:
Netscape Communicator

Netscape Communicator

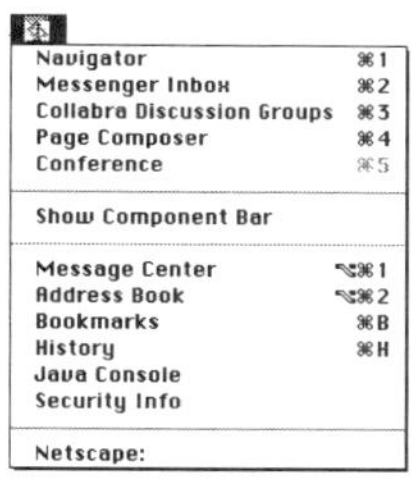

Figure 1.1 *The (Communicator) menu is used to switch from component to component.*

There are three principal features that are common to all of Communicator's components. First, you can create individual user profiles for each person who will use Communicator on a particular computer. Second, the Communicator menu enables you to switch easily from one component to another. Finally, the Component bar makes it even easier to move to and from the desired module.

Using the Communicator menu

The (Communicator) menu is the only menu that stays constant, no matter what component of Communicator you're using **(Figure 1.1)**. Select options from the Communicator menu to move from component to component, to access smaller modules, such as the Address Book and History windows, or to bring specific open windows to the front of the screen.

The Component bar

The Component bar lets you switch between Navigator, Messenger, Collabra, and Composer with just a click of the mouse. You can dock the Component bar at the bottom of each window, or let it float anywhere on the screen.

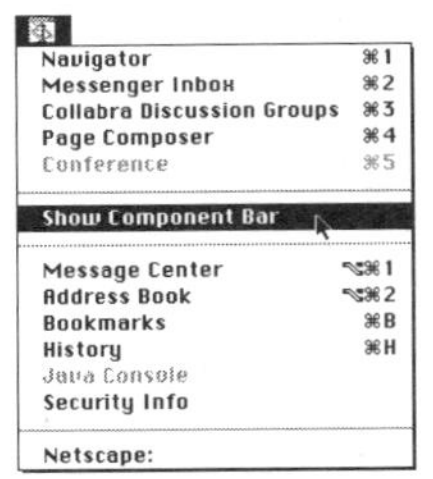

Figure 1.2 *Choose (Communicator) > Show Component Bar to display the palette with the main components of Communicator.*

To float the Component Bar:

Choose (Communicator) > Show Component Bar **(Figure 1.2)**. The Component bar floats on your screen.

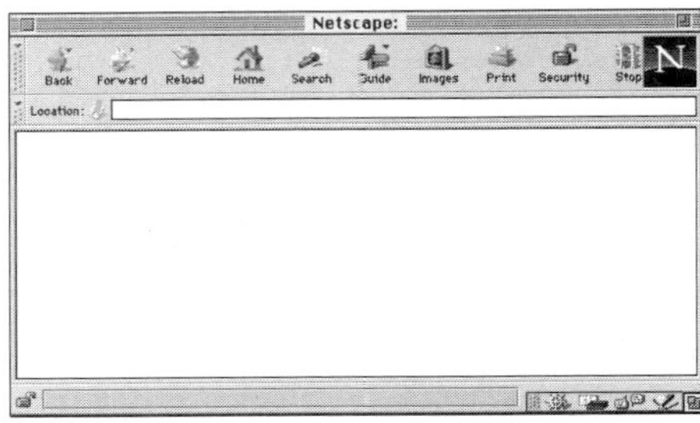

Figure 1.3 *The Component bar can also be docked in the lower-right corner of the window.*

To view the Component bar at the bottom of each window:

- Click the Close box in the upper-right corner of the floating Component bar.
- Or choose (Communicator) > Dock Component Bar.

Figure 1.4 *This is what the Component bar looks like when it's floating.*

To use the Component bar:

Click the component that you want to use to make it active.

✔ Tips

- The size of the floating Component bar icons depends on the settings chosen in the Appearance Preferences dialog box *(see page 312)*. You can't change the size of the icons when the Component bar is docked at the bottom of the window.
- The Component bar is always available, either at the bottom of the window, or floating on your screen. You can't hide it entirely.

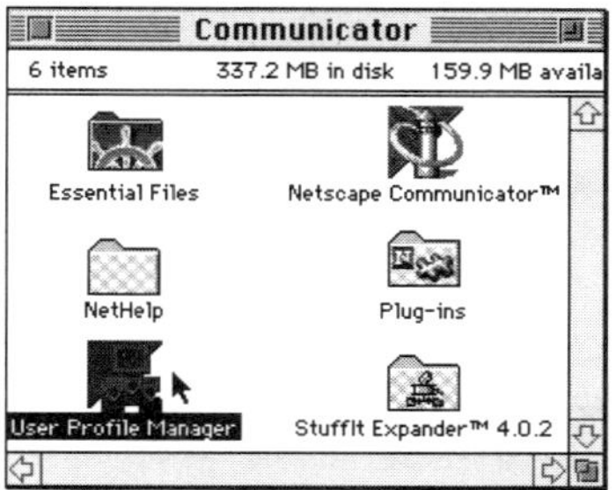

Figure 1.5 *Double-click the User Profile Manager icon in the Communicator folder to open the User Profile Manager.*

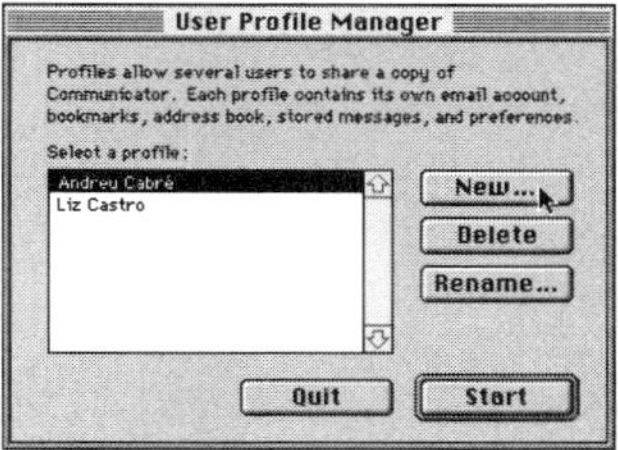

Figure 1.6 *Click New to create a new profile.*

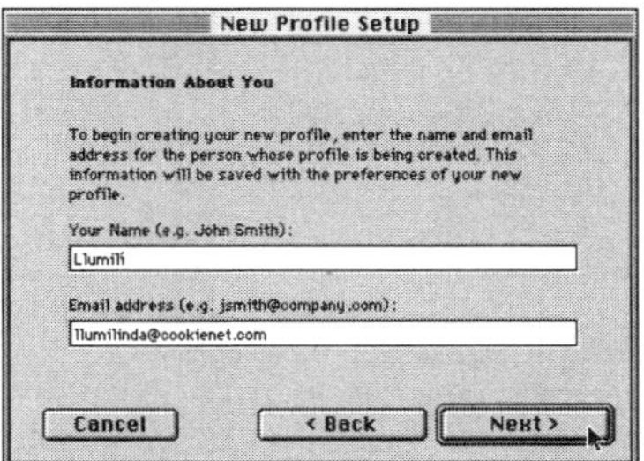

Figure 1.7 *Enter the information in each screen and then click Next to continue.*

Creating user profiles

If there is more than one person who uses the copy of Communicator on your computer, or if just one person has several accounts and wants to access them individually, you can create individual user profiles so that each user's e-mail address, bookmarks, address book, stored messages, and preferences are kept separated.

To create a user profile:

1. Open the User Profile Manager by going to the Communicator folder and double-clicking the User Profile Manager icon **(Figure 1.5)**. The User Profile Manager window appears.
2. Click New to create a new profile **(Figure 1.6)**. The New Profile Setup dialog box appears.
3. Read the instructions, enter any necessary information, and click Next until you've finished creating the profile **(Figure 1.7)**. The User Profile Manager quits automatically when it's finished gathering information.

✔ Tips

- A user profile is created automatically the first time you run Communicator.
- You can change a profile's settings by opening Communicator with that profile and choosing Edit > Preferences *(see page 309)*.
- Rename a profile by opening the User Profile Manager, selecting the profile, and clicking Rename.
- Delete a profile by opening the User Profile Manager, selecting the profile, and clicking Delete.

Choosing a user profile

You have to select a user profile each time you open Communicator so the program knows which e-mail address, bookmarks, and other personalized settings it should offer you.

To choose a user profile:

Once you've created more than one profile, Communicator automatically asks you to choose one when you launch the program. Simply choose the desired profile and click OK **(Figure 1.8)**. Your personal settings will be loaded.

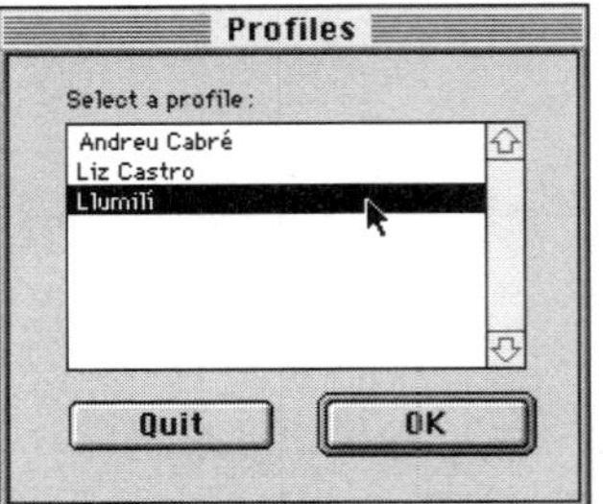

Figure 1.8 *When Communicator starts up, it asks you which profile you want to use. Select the desired profile and click OK to start Communicator.*

✔ Tips

- You can use the arrow keys to select a user profile in the list, and then press Enter to start Communicator.
- Each user has their own folder in the Netscape Users folder inside the Preferences folder in the System folder on the startup disk **(Figure 1.9)**. The folder has the same name as its corresponding profile and contains a Netscape Preferences file (see next tip), the address book, the bookmarks file, the cache, etc.
- You can double click the Netscape Preferences file for a particular user to launch Communicator without having to go through the Profiles dialog box. In fact, you can make aliases of each user's preferences file and leave them out on the Desktop. Just make sure you change the name of the alias (but not the original) to identify which user profile it belongs to.

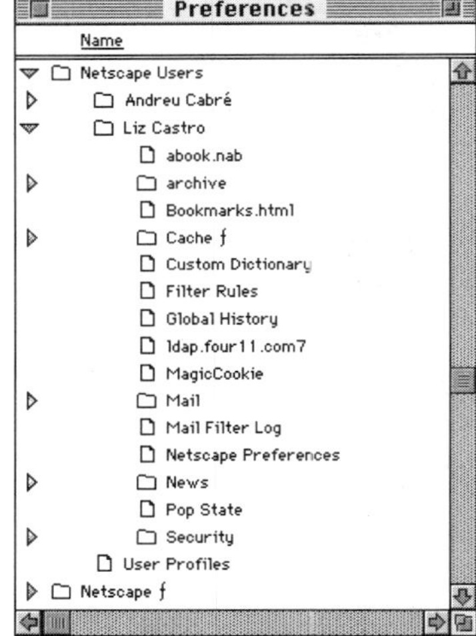

Figure 1.9 *The preferences for each user are stored in the Netscape Users folder inside the Preferences folder. Of special interest is the file "Netscape Preferences" which can be double clicked to launch Communicator with that particular user's preferences.*

Choosing a user profile

Part II:
The World Wide Web

Many-to-One Communication

The World Wide Web lets anyone publish material, called Web pages, that you can read and view. It is "many-to-one" communication. Each month thousands of new pages are added, by huge companies and private citizens alike. Some pages are serious collections of commercial information. Others are personal accounts of travels, history, and life itself. Still others attempt to fill the void that the paper publishing industry is unable to answer. Perhaps the nicest thing about the Web is that there are pages about everything, from cancer research to bowling, from solar panel design to hot new bands.

What is the Web, really?

The Internet is a huge collection of computers that are connected to each other. Some computers are connected to the Internet through a modem (and are only *on* the Internet when they are connected). Other computers (at universities and large companies) are permanently connected.

There are different ways of communicating over the Internet, called *protocols.* E-mail is the most common protocol, but you may have heard of FTP, Gopher, Usenet, and HTTP, as well. This last protocol, HTTP, is the method computers use to connect to each other and view Web pages. The World Wide Web, then, is the subset of computers on the Internet that communicate with each other using the HTTP protocol, in order to view and display information in the form of Web pages.

What is a Web page?

A Web page is nothing more than a text document with special tags called HTML or *HyperText Markup Language.* HTML allows you to format text, add rules, graphics, sound, and video and save it all in a text-only ASCII file that any computer can read. (Of course, to project video or play sounds, the computer must have the necessary hardware.) The key to HTML is in the tags, keywords enclosed in less than (<) and greater than (>) signs, that indicate what kind of content is coming up.

HTML is not just another way to create beautiful documents, however. Its key ingredient is in the first part of its name: Hypertext. HTML documents can contain links to other HTML documents or to practically anything else on the Internet. This means that a page can link to several other pages, either at the same site or at any other site in any part of the Internet.

Of course, HTML just looks like a lot of text sprinkled with greater than and less than signs until you open the file with a special program called a browser. A browser can interpret HTML tags and then show the formatted document on screen. Communicator's browser component is called Navigator and is discussed at length in this section of the book.

The Navigator Window

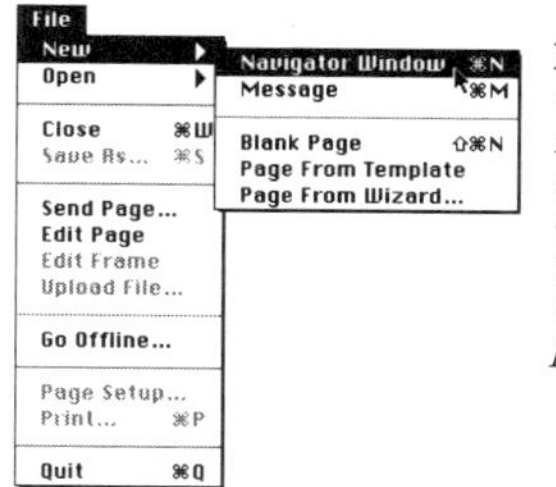

Figure 2.1 *Choose File > New > Navigator Window to open a new window for browsing Web pages.*

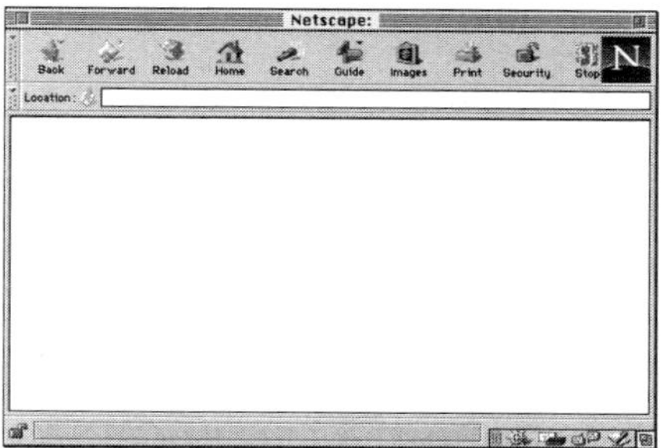

Figure 2.2 *A fresh Navigator window opens. It may or may not be empty, depending on the settings specified in the Navigator panel of the Preferences dialog box (see page 25).*

Figure 2.3 *Choose File > Close to make the Navigator window disappear.*

The Navigator module within Communicator is where you surf the World Wide Web—connecting to all those *www* addresses suddenly popping up in every company's advertisements—and to FTP and Gopher sites. This chapter explains how to take advantage of the Navigator window's features. To start exploring the Web right away, skip to page 31.

Opening or closing a Navigator window

You may open as many Navigator windows as your computer's memory will permit in order to display several different Web pages at once. This is useful if you want to follow a link on one page without losing track of the original source page.

To open a Navigator window:

Choose File > New > Navigator Window **(Figure 2.1)**. A fresh Navigator window appears **(Figure 2.2)**.

To close a Navigator window:

Choose File > Close **(Figure 2.3)** or click the window's close box in the upper-right corner.

✔ Tip

- Communicator automatically opens a new Navigator window upon launch. You can choose to display a specific page—including a blank page—*(see page 25)*, or skip Navigator altogether and begin with a different Communicator component *(see page 312)*.

The parts of the Navigator window

Each Navigator window has a number of elements that help you view the pages on the World Wide Web.

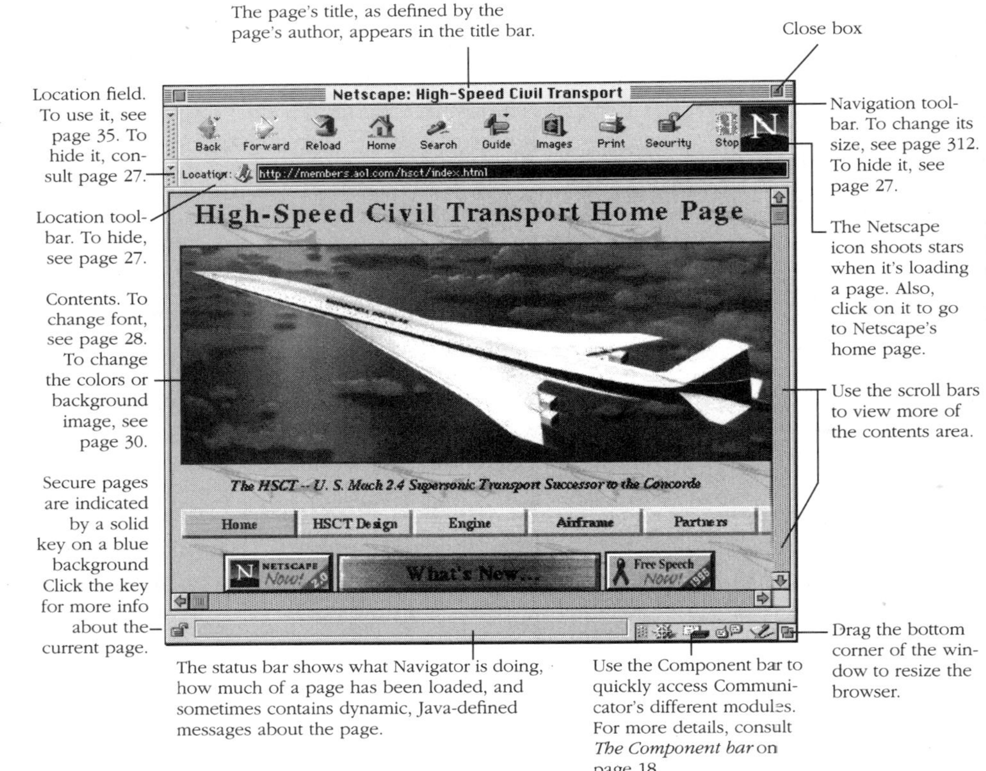

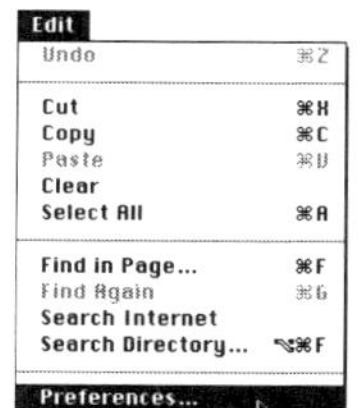

Figure 2.4 *Choose Edit > Preferences.*

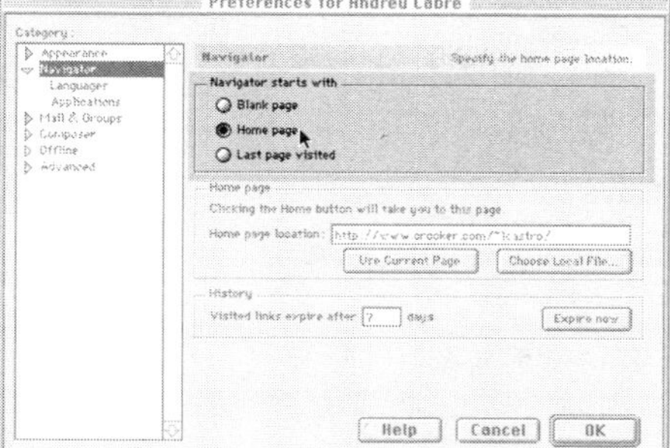

Figure 2.5 *Choose Blank page, Home page, or Last page visited in the Navigator starts with section to determine what is shown in the Navigator window upon launch. To have Netscape open without connecting to a particular page, click Blank Page.*

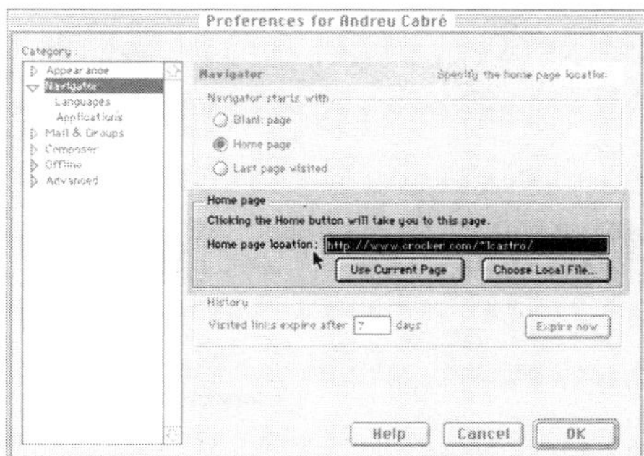

Figure 2.6 *For your home page, you can choose any page on the Web or any HTML file on your hard disk.*

Choosing the startup page

Navigator can begin with a blank page, with the last page that you browsed in the previous session with Navigator, or with any page you choose, either from the Web or your hard disk.

To choose the startup page:

1. Choose Edit > Preferences **(Figure 2.4)**. The Preferences dialog box appears.
2. Click Navigator in the Category list. The Navigator panel of the Preferences dialog box appears.
3. In the Navigator starts with section, choose Blank page, Home page, or Last page visited **(Figure 2.5)**.
4. If you chose Home page in step 3, in the Home page section, either click Use Current Page, type the desired home page's URL in the Home page location field, or click Choose Local File to choose a Web page saved on your hard disk **(Figure 2.6)**.
5. Click OK to close the Navigator preferences dialog box.

✔ **Tip**

■ You can save your bookmarks file *(see page 85)* as an HTML file and then use that file as your home page. Then click the Choose Local File button in the Navigator preferences dialog box to choose the bookmarks file as your startup page. For more information on how to save the bookmarks file as an HTML file, consult *Saving a bookmarks file* on page 99.

Using the page proxy icon

To the left of the Location field you'll find a small icon, called the *page proxy icon*, that looks like a bookmark on top of a book. This icon represents the URL of the page that you're currently browsing. You can use the icon to save or copy the current page's URL into other documents.

To use the page proxy icon:

- Drag the page proxy icon to the Bookmarks window—which has to be open and visible—to create a bookmark for the current page. You can drag the bookmark to any folder you wish. (This is a great feature!)
- Drag the icon to a Web page that you are creating in Composer to add a link to the current page **(Figures 2.7 and 2.8)**. For more information on creating links, consult Chapter 20, *Creating Links in a Page*.
- Drag the icon to any Navigator window to open the page in that particular window.
- Drag the page proxy icon to the Desktop to save the page to your hard disk **(Figure 2.9)**. Note that the page's images are not saved. You will be able to double click the file to open Navigator and view the page, but you will be viewing the file saved on your hard disk, not the current page out on the Web.
- If you can't see the page proxy icon, it's probably because the Location toolbar is hidden or collapsed **(Figure 2.10)**. To expand or reveal the Location toolbar, consult *Maximizing Web page viewing area* on page 27.

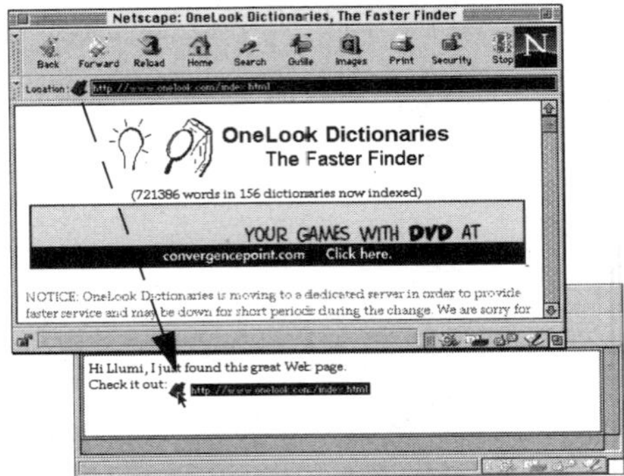

Figure 2.7 *Drag the page proxy icon at the left of the Location field to the document where you want to copy the page's URL.*

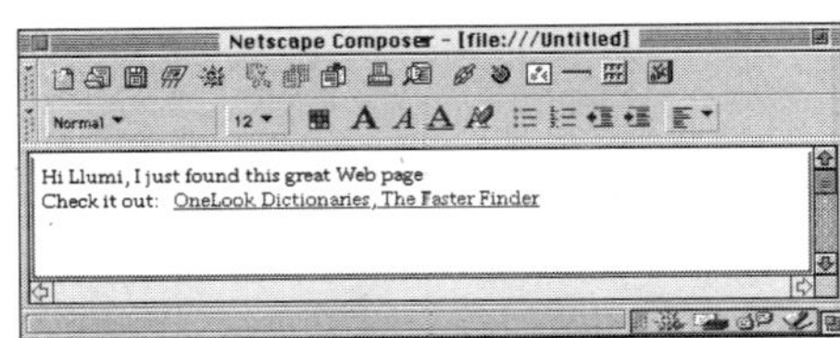

Figure 2.8 *The page's title becomes a link in the page that you are composing.*

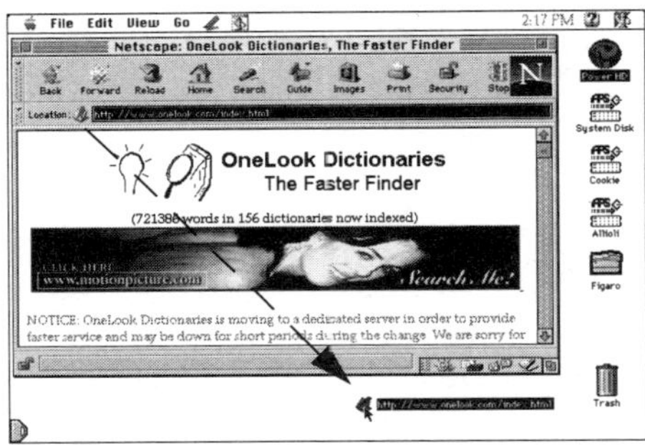

Figure 2.9 *Drag the page proxy icon to the Desktop to save the page (not including its images) as an HTML document.*

Figure 2.10 *If you can't see the page proxy icon, it's probably because the Location toolbar is hidden or collapsed.*

Figure 2.11 *Both the Navigation and Location toolbars are showing, by default.*

Figure 2.12 *Choose the appropriate command from the View menu to hide (or reveal) the corresponding toolbar.*

Figure 2.13 *This window is the exact same size as the one shown in Figure 2.11. Once you hide the extra window items, you see more of the actual page.*

Figure 2.14 *Click the thin bar at the extreme left end of a toolbar to collapse it.*

Maximizing Web page viewing area

By default, Navigator displays two toolbars at the top of each window **(Figure 2.11)**. You can collapse them—or hide them completely—to get more room for viewing Web pages.

To hide (or reveal) the toolbars:

Choose a View > Hide command to hide a toolbar **(Figure 2.12)**. The corresponding toolbar will disappear **(Figure 2.13)**. Choose the appropriate View > Show command to make the toolbar reappear. The next time you open Navigator, the toolbars will remain hidden (or revealed).

To collapse (expand) a toolbar:

To collapse a toolbar, click the bar at its left end **(Figure 2.14)**. The toolbar shrinks down and only the thin bar is visible. To expand the toolbar, click the thin bar.

✔ Tips

- To resize the buttons on the toolbar, use the Appearance panel of the Preferences dialog box *(see page 312)*.
- To change the appearance of the text within Navigator, consult *Controlling text in the Navigator window* on page 28. To change the color scheme or background, consult *Controlling colors and background images* on page 30.
- You can expand the status area by floating the Component bar *(see page 18)*.

Controlling text in the Navigator window

You can choose which font and size you wish to use for displaying proportional text and which font and size should be used for displaying fixed width text. You can also choose to let Navigator download fonts that the designer intended for the page—or to ignore them.

To choose fonts and size for Web page text:

1. Choose Edit > Preferences **(Figure 2.15)** and then click Fonts in the Category list to display the Fonts preferences **(Figure 2.16)**.
2. Choose a font and size in the pop-up menus next to Variable Width Font to decide how the principal text in your Web pages (and messages) should be displayed and printed.
3. Choose a font and size in the pop-up menus next to Fixed Width Font to decide how text in forms, block quotes, and other special areas should be displayed and printed.
4. Choose an option for Dynamic fonts:

   For the quickest viewing that might not always match the designer's font choices for the page, select Use my fonts, overriding page-specified fonts.

   To maintain quick viewing times while making an attempt to display the page in the fonts chosen by the page's designer, choose Use page-specified fonts, but disable Dynamic Fonts.

Figure 2.15 *Choose Edit > Preferences.*

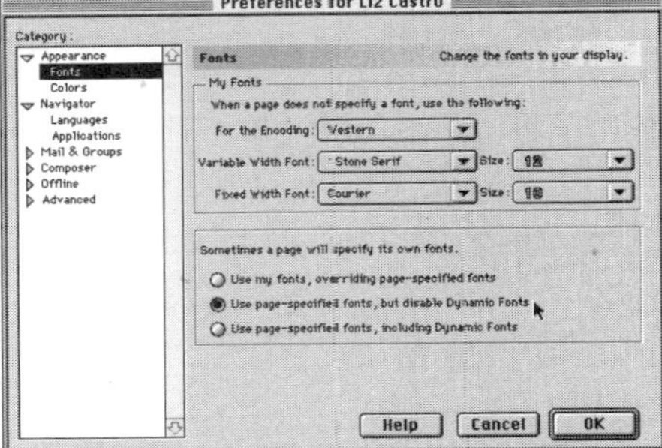

Figure 2.16 *The Fonts panel in the Preferences dialog box allows you to choose fonts for display and whether to use your own fonts or the fonts included in the design of the page.*

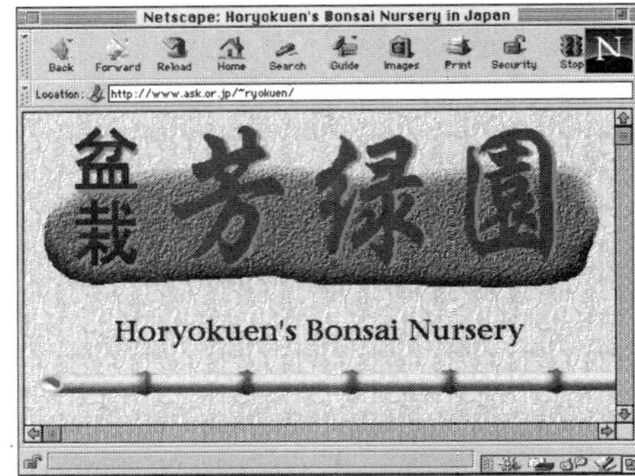

Figure 2.17 *Here is a page displayed with Navigator's default settings.*

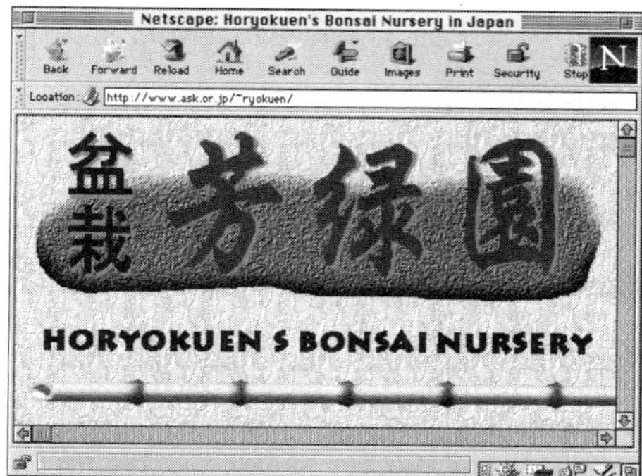

Figure 2.18 *Here's a new look at the page shown in Figure 2.17, but with Lithos 12 as a base font.*

To ensure that the page is displayed with the fonts that the designer selected, choose the last option: Use page-specified fonts, including Dynamic Fonts.

5. Click OK to close the dialog box.

✔ Tips

- Don't be surprised if your whole page is not displayed in the font and size you've chosen. The fonts and sizes you choose in the Preferences dialog box are just a base font. Navigator may add formatting as necessary—like increasing the font size for headings, adding bold formatting to table headers, etc.
- You don't have to pick a fixed width font (like Courier) in the Fixed Width font pop-up menu. Pick any font you like. (Windows users don't have this flexibility. Ha ha.)

Controlling colors and background images

You may find pages that, in an attempt to catch your attention, bowl you over with background images, colored text, and links. The result is often impossible to read. You can hide background images and choose different colors to make the page legible again.

To control colors and background images:

1. Choose Edit > Preferences **(Figure 2.19)** and then click Colors in the Category list under Appearance. The Colors preferences appear **(Figure 2.20)**.
2. In the Colors section, click the color boxes next to Text and Background to choose custom colors for each.
3. In the Links section, click the color boxes to decide how links should appear. Click Underline Links to show all links with an underline, regardless of their color.
4. Check Always use my colors, overriding page to apply the colors you've chosen to all pages, regardless of the colors already specified in those pages by their designers. Leave the option unchecked to apply your colors only when the designer has not done so.
5. Click Use Default Colors to use the default colors defined by Communicator.

✔ Tip

- Only text that has *not* been specifically colored by the designer (with the FONT tag) is affected by the color you choose.

Figure 2.19 *Choose Edit > Preferences.*

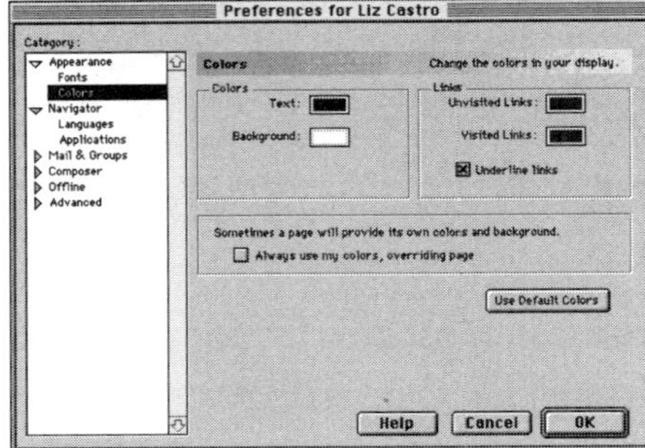

Figure 2.20 *In the Colors panel of the Preferences dialog box, choose one color for the background and another for the text or accept the defaults. Choose a color scheme for links on the right side of the dialog box.*

3

Surfing the Web

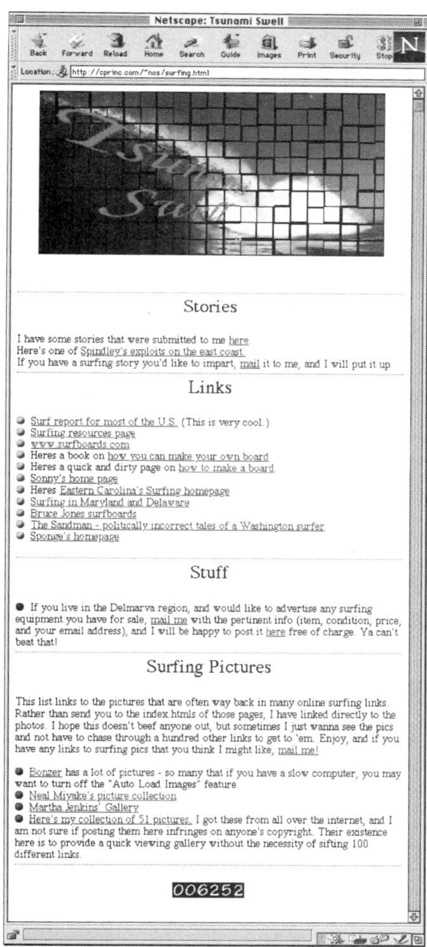

Figure 3.1 *There are millions of Web sites that you can surf to, each one different from the next.*

This is what you've been waiting for: actually getting to surf the World Wide Web. Although *surf* seems like a strange way to describe your activities as you sit in front of a computer, probably some distance from the beach, it does capture the idea of jumping from one Web page to another, perhaps reading and exploring as you go along, perhaps just enjoying the spray of information.

From its navigation buttons and keyboard shortcuts for getting from one place to another, to its clever new frames and history menu for remembering where you've been, Navigator makes surfing the Web as easy as it's ever been.

There are millions of Web sites across the Internet, and several thousand more are added daily. You could spend your whole life wandering from page to page and never get to the end (although you might circle around to where you started). It's something like reading an encyclopedia from *Aardvark* to *Zen*: you'd learn a lot, but it would take you a long time.

In this section, we'll talk about how to get around on the Web with Navigator, assuming you already know where you want to go, or, on the other hand, that you don't really care where you end up. For more information on finding specific topics or pages, see Chapter 7, *Finding Stuff on the Web*.

What is a Web page?

So what are these things that you surf to? A Web page is nothing more than a text file with special tags that format the contents, point to other pages, and insert images and sounds **(Figure 3.2)**. The tags are called *HyperText Markup Language*, or HTML, and are quite easy to learn **(Figure 3.3)**. For details on creating your own Web pages, consult *Part IV: Creating Web Pages* on page 217.

With millions of Web pages in existence, there is an incredible variety of designs and approaches, and of the kinds of information presented. It is probably safe to say that you can find a Web page about any topic you might choose to research—from Contra dancing to the Ethernet, from a subway map of major cities of the world to a database of every language spoken at each turnstile.

Some Web pages are personal, designed by a single individual with information about themselves, their family and friends, perhaps their dog or cat, and their hobbies—as well as links to their favorite pages at other sites. Personal does not mean sloppy. As you'll find out, many of the best pages are created by people with no economic interest in the Web.

Other pages are strictly (or more subtly) commercial, created by or for a company in order to offer promotional information, technical support, upgrades, special tips, and other benefits to the public. Often, a commercial page's mission is simply to impress—with dazzling graphics, sounds, or videos.

Each Web page has a unique address, or *URL,* which indicates its location on the Internet. For more information about URLs, consult *Links and URLs* on page 267.

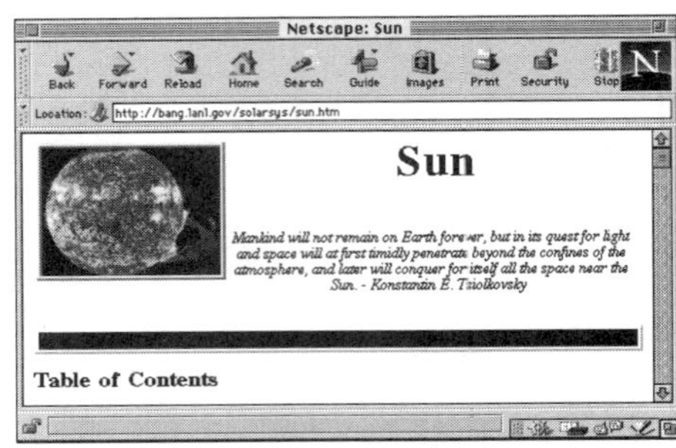

Figure 3.2 *This is a typical Web page, although perhaps more attractive and better organized than most. It was written by Calvin Hamilton, a private citizen like you or me, with the sole intention of sharing information and resources across the Internet.*

```
<HTML><HEAD>
<META http-equiv="PICS-Label" content='(PICS-1.0 "http://www.rsac.org/
<TITLE>Sun</TITLE></HEAD>

<BODY>
<IMG SRC="thumb/sun/sun.gif" WIDTH=150 HEIGHT=112 ALT="" ALIGN=LEFT>
<CENTER>
<FONT SIZE=+4><B>Sun</B></FONT><P>
<I>Mankind will not remain on Earth forever, but in its quest for ligh
and space will at first timidly penetrate beyond the confines of the
atmosphere, and later will conquer for itself all the space near the
Sun. - Konstantin E. Tsiolkovsky</I>
</CENTER>
<BR CLEAR=ALL>
<BR>
<P><TABLE BORDER=2 WIDTH=100% BGCOLOR="#0"><TH><FONT SIZE=-2> </F

<H2>Table of Contents</H2>
<UL>
<LI><B>Sun Introduction (This Page)</B>
<UL>
<LI><A HREF="#intro">Introduction</A>
<LI><A HREF="#stats">Sun Statistics</A>
<LI><A HREF="#movie">Eclipse &amp; Sun Movies</A>
<LI><A HREF="#views">Views of the Sun</A>
</UL>
<LI><A HREF="edu/convect.htm"><B>Educator's Guide to Convection</B></A
<LI><A HREF="edu/eclipses.htm"><B>Educator's Guide to Eclipses</B></A>
<LI><A HREF="edu/sunspots.htm"><B>Educator's Guide to Sunspots</B></A>
<LI><A HREF="craft2.htm#sun"><B>Chronology of Sun Exploration</B></A>
<LI><A HREF="sohopr1.htm"><B>
Thought-Provoking Imagery Shows Sun's Place in the Galaxy</B></A>
<LI><B><A HREF="raw/sun/index.htm">Sun Image and Animation Index</A></
</UL>
```

Figure 3.3 *This is the actual text that creates the page shown in Figure 3.2. The HTML codes are shown in less than and greater than signs "<>".*

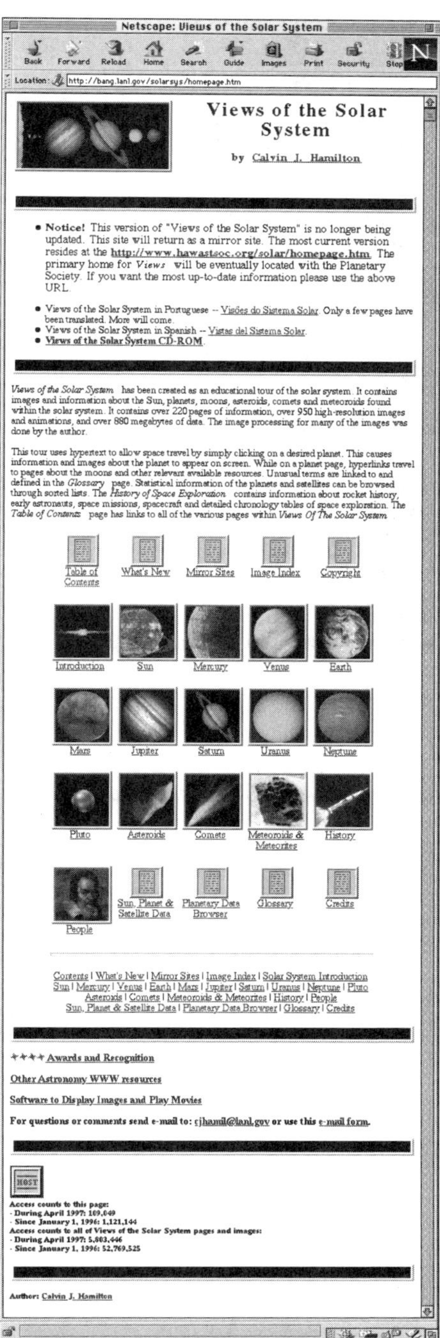

Figure 3.4 *This is the home page for the Solar System site. It contains an introduction, links to other pages at the site, and links to related sites.*

Sites, home pages, and servers

A Web *page* is a single text file written in HTML. A Web *site* is a collection of Web pages that belong to a single individual or company. Most Web sites have a special page, called a *home page,* that serves as a door to the rest of the site **(Figure 3.4)**. A home page generally has a banner explaining what the site contains—commercial sites usually include their company logo on the home page—as well as links to the other pages available at the site.

Beware: Although Netscape Communications knows exactly what a home page is, they've chosen to use the same term to denote the page that you jump to automatically upon launching the program *(see page 25)*. The page you choose may or may not be a *real* home page.

Web pages, including any graphics, sounds, videos, or other external files, are stored on *servers*, dedicated computers that are connected to the Internet 24 hours a day—so that anyone, in any part of the world, can reach the Web page at any time.

Although you might think a server looks like something out of a movie—a huge, hulking thing with those reel-to-reel tapes—any kind of computer can be a server, including Macs, PCs running Windows, and most often, Unix machines. The most important criterion for a server is not size or speed, but rather that it have a high-speed connection to the Internet so that it can efficiently handle the incoming requests for the Web sites it contains.

In addition to Web sites, servers can also contain FTP and Gopher sites, and manage e-mail, Usenet newsgroups, and internal discussion groups.

Following links

A Web page's most distinguishing characteristic, and certainly the feature that has made Web surfing so popular and exciting, is its *links*. By clicking a link, you jump to another page, either at the same site or at a different site—which can be on the same server or, just as easily, at a site halfway around the world. You may also use links to jump to FTP and Gopher sites and to write e-mail or join in discussions.

Links may either be text or images. Generally, new links—that is, the ones you have not yet visited—appear underlined and in blue (or in gray on monochrome monitors). Once you have followed a link to its destination, it will appear in purple so you can quickly distinguish new links from those you've already visited.

To follow a link:

1. In the current Web page, decide which link you wish to follow. Point to the link with the mouse. The link's URL appears in the status area at the bottom of the window **(Figure 3.5)**.
2. Click the link. Navigator takes you to the link's destination **(Figure 3.6)**.

✔ Tips

- Open the link in a new window by clicking the link and choosing New Window with this Link from the pop-up menu that appears, or by dragging the page proxy icon to a different window *(see page 26)*.
- You can always tell if a link is really a link by pointing at it with the mouse. If it is a link, the pointer will change into a pointing finger, and the link's destination will appear in the status area at the bottom of the window.

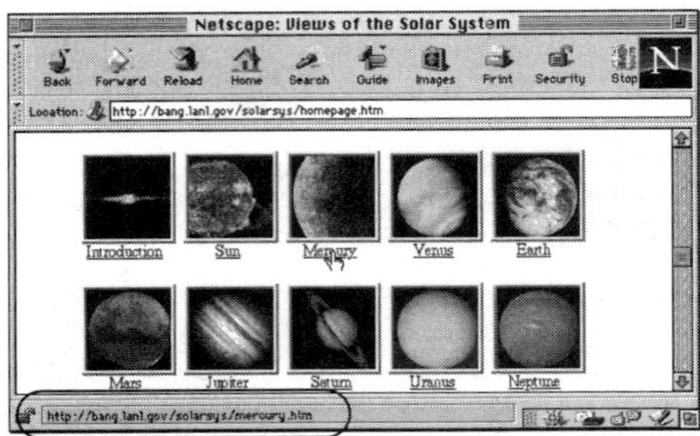

Figure 3.5 *When you place the pointer over a link (usually the blue, underlined items), the URL for the destination page appears at the bottom-left corner of the browser.*

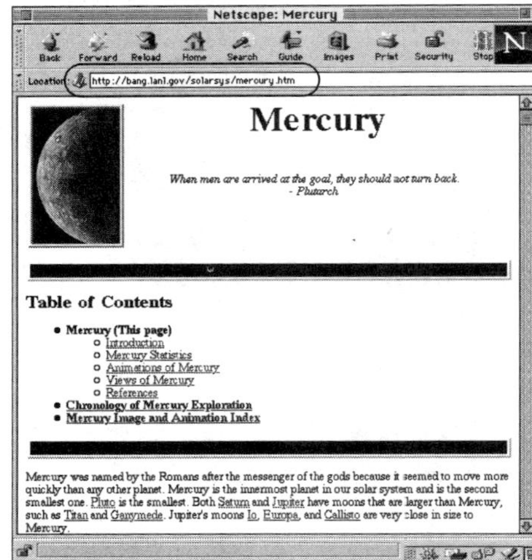

Figure 3.6 *When you click a link, Navigator loads the corresponding page. Notice how the URL in the Location field above matches the URL at the bottom left of Figure 3.5.*

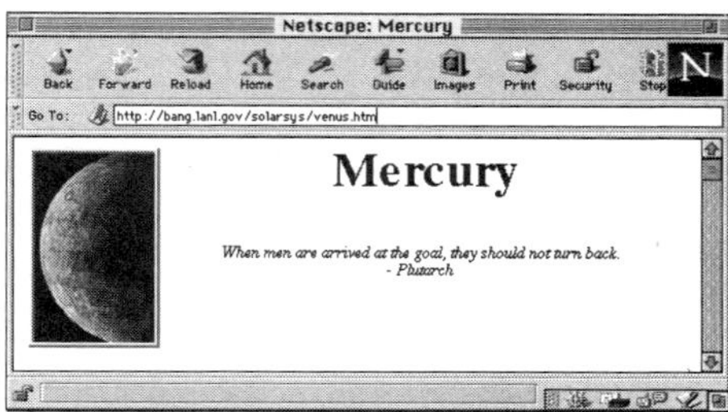

Figure 3.7 *In the Location field between the toolbar and the content area, type the URL of the desired page. As soon as you begin to type, the label changes from Location to Go To.*

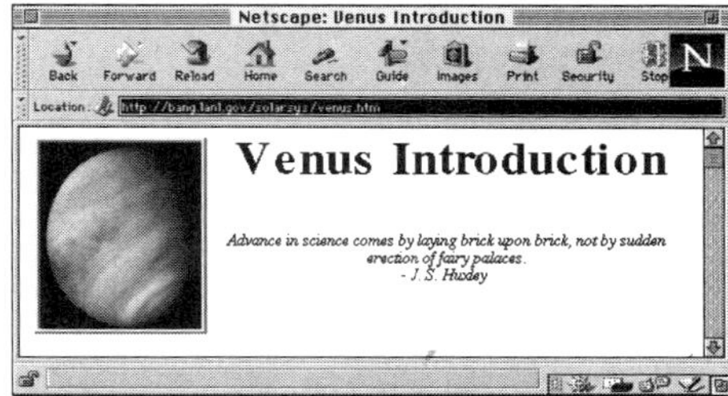

Figure 3.8 *Navigator loads the specified page.*

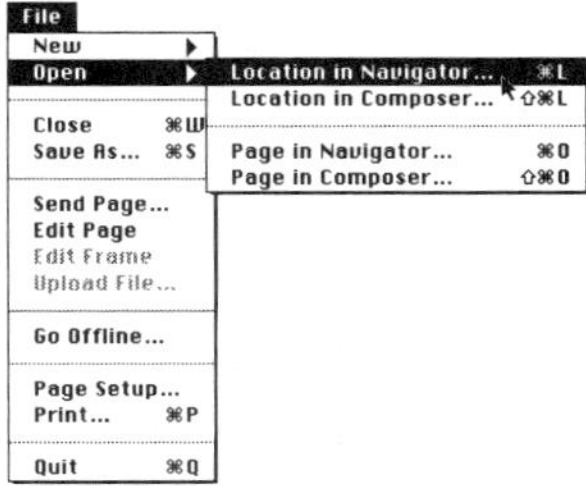

Figure 3.9 *Choose File > Open > Location in Navigator to reach a known page.*

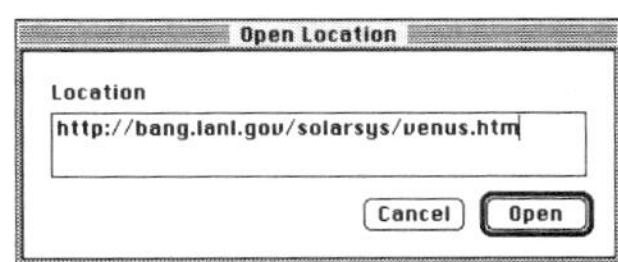

Figure 3.10 *In the Open Location dialog box that appears, type the URL of the page that you wish to jump to.*

Surfing with URLs

You see them on billboards, magazine advertisements, even on television: "Visit our Web site at www.visit-us.com." That string of unpronounceable gobbledygook is called a URL, or Uniform Resource Locator and is the page's *address* on the World Wide Web. If you already know the URL of the Web page that you want to visit, the best way to get to the page is to be direct: tell Navigator.

To surf with a URL:

1. Make sure the Location field is showing on the screen *(see page 27)*.
2. Type the URL of the page you want to visit in the Location field **(Fig. 3.7)**.
3. Press Return. The new page appears **(Figure 3.8)**.

✔ Tips

- For more information about URLs, consult *Links and URLs* on page 267.
- If a URL begins with *www (ftp, gopher)*, you don't need to type the protocol (**http://**, **ftp://**, or **gopher://**). Further, if a Web page address is in the form of *www.site.com*, you only need to type **site**.
- Choose File > New > Navigator Window before going to a new page to open the page in a new window.
- You can also use the Location field to jump to FTP and Gopher sites, or to open a discussion group.
- Another way to reach a known page is to choose File > Open > Location in Navigator **(Figure 3.9)** and type the URL in the Open Location dialog box that appears **(Figure 3.10)**.

Surfing with URLs

Going to *your* home page

You can return to the home page that you specified in the Preferences dialog box at any time with a simple click. For information on how to set your home page, consult *Choosing the startup page* on page 25.

To go to your home page:

Click the Home button in the toolbar **(Figure 3.11)** or choose Go > Home **(Figure 3.12)**. Navigator loads the home page specified in the Navigator preferences dialog box **(Figure 3.13)**.

✓ Tips

- Remember, the Home button and Home menu command bring you to *your* specified home page, not to the home page of the site that contains the page you are currently viewing (which would be much more useful, if you ask me).
- Further, even if you have specified that Navigator *start* with a blank page, the program will still jump to the page specified in the Preferences box when you use the Home button or command.

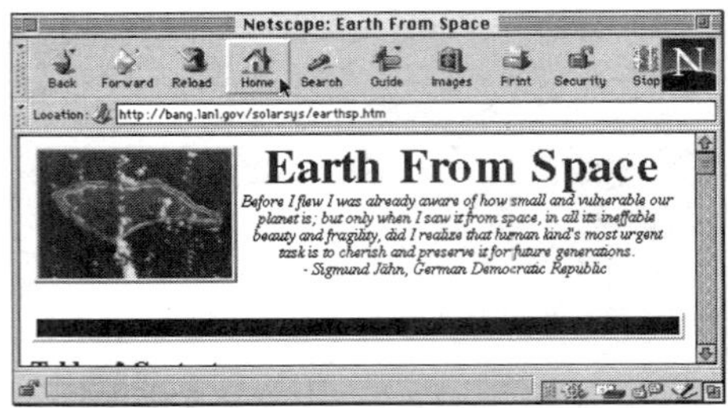

Figure 3.11 *Click the Home button to load the page specified in the General dialog box (not the site's home page).*

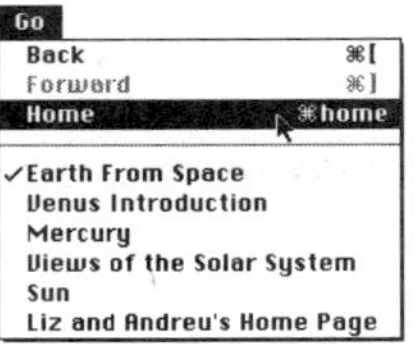

Figure 3.12 *You can also choose Go > Home to load your home page.*

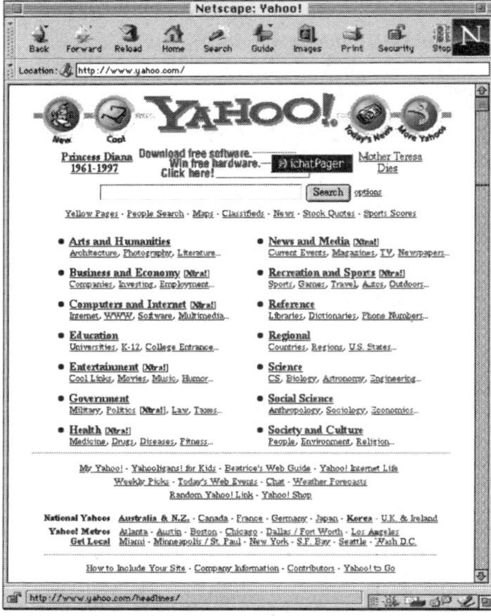

Figure 3.13 *A home page should either be a page that you consult often, or a page with a lot of links to other pages. Yahoo is a good choice.*

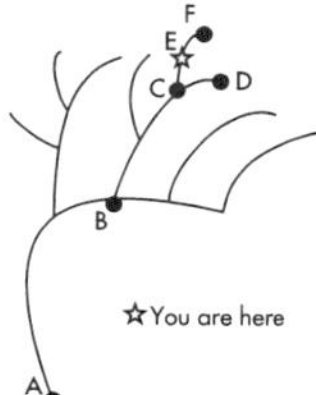

Figure 3.14 *Supposing you are at point E, the Go menu will contain points F, E, C, B, and A, in that order. D (and all the other branches) will be forgotten. Going forward will bring you to F. Going backward will bring you to C. Going backward again will bring you to B.*

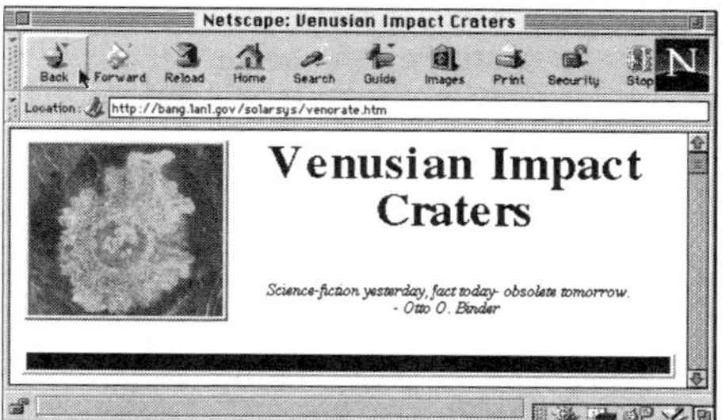

Figure 3.15 *Click the Back button to return to the last page you were browsing.*

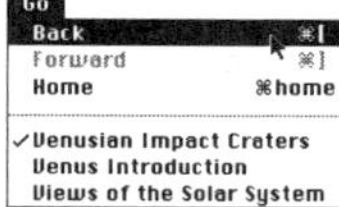

Figure 3.16 *You can choose Back from the Go menu to get the same result.*

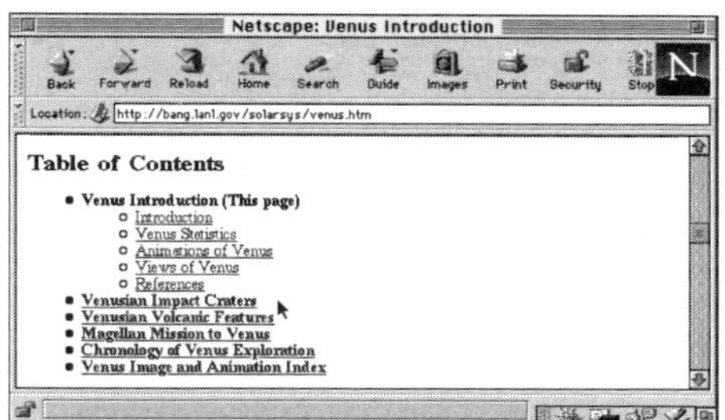

Figure 3.17 *Here, Navigator goes back to the Venus Introduction page, which as you can see in Figure 3.16 is the next page below the current page (Venusian Impact Craters) in the Go menu.*

Going back and forward

Perhaps one of the most difficult problems you'll have on the Web is following all of the links that interest you. Typically, you will find one Web page with several links that you want to follow. It's important to know how to get *back* to the page with the important links, once you've explored one or more of them **(Figure 3.14)**.

To go back to the previous page:

Click the Back button on the Navigation toolbar **(Figure 3.15)** or choose Go > Back **(Figure 3.16)**. Navigator will load the page that you visited immediately before jumping to the present page.

Going back means returning to the pages that brought you to the present page. *Going forward* is turning around once again and continuing on the original path.

There are two conditions to going forward. First, you have to have already gone back. Second, you must not have chosen a new link on an earlier page that brings you in a new direction. Since Navigator only remembers one path at a time, if you switch paths, all the most forward pages are forgotten.

To go forward:

Click the Forward button or choose Go > Forward. Navigator will bring you to the corresponding page.

Going further back or further ahead

As you wander around the Web, Navigator records the title and URL of each page that you visit and stores it in the Go menu. You can go back and revisit a page by choosing its title in the menu.

To go further back or further ahead:

Select the desired page from the Go menu **(Figure 3.18)**. Navigator jumps to the corresponding page **(Figure 3.19)**.

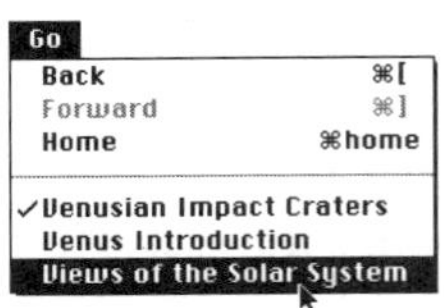

Figure 3.18 *You can choose any page in the Go menu to jump to that page.*

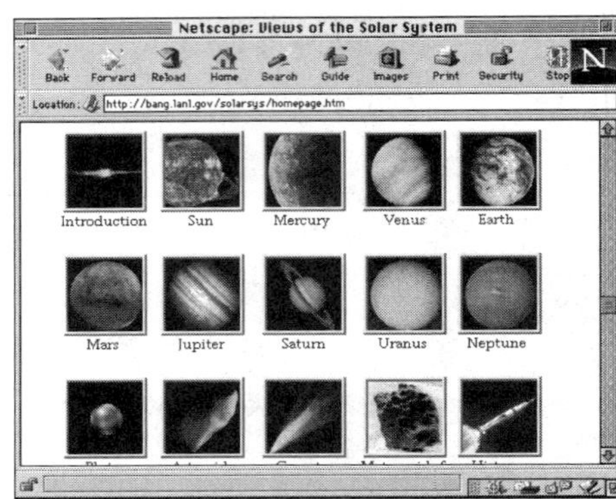

Figure 3.19 *A page that is loaded from the Go menu often appears faster than a brand new page since Navigator has already saved a copy of the page in its memory cache. In addition, when using the Go menu or Back and Forward buttons you always return to the area of the page that you last visited.*

✓ Tips

- Navigator stores up to fifteen URLs in the Go menu.
- Hold down the pointer over the Forward or Back buttons to reveal a list of destinations **(Figure 3.20)**.
- The Go menu only keeps track of the path of pages that has brought you to the current page. So if you backtrack (with the Back command or the Go menu) and then choose a link that leads you in a different direction, the references to the *later* pages will be lost **(Figure 3.21)**. The History window works the same way *(see page 39)*.
- One way to make sure the Go menu keeps track of *every* page you visit is to avoid using the Back and Forward commands and even the Go menu itself. If you need to go back to a page you have already visited, use the Open Location command instead.
- To record a page's URL permanently, create a bookmark for it. For more details, see Chapter 8, *Bookmarks*.

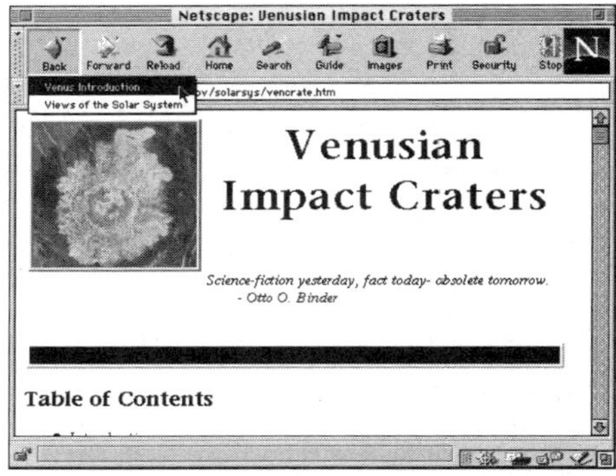

Figure 3.20 *Click and hold over the Forward or Back buttons to choose exactly which page you wish to return to.*

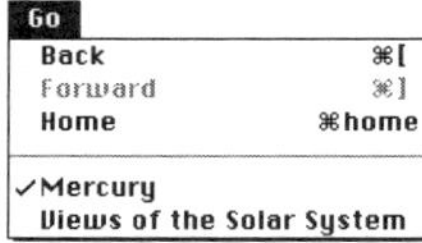

Figure 3.21 *If you backtrack and then set off in a new direction (as in this case, going back from Venus to the home page and from there, on to Mercury) and then view the Go menu, the old path (that led to the Venus page) will no longer be shown.*

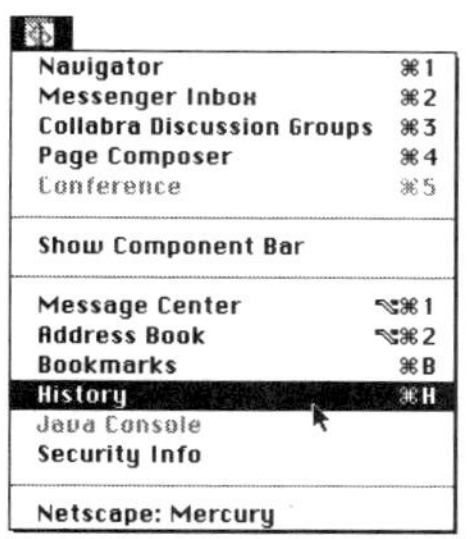

Figure 3.22 *Choose* (Communicator) > *History to display the History window on your screen.*

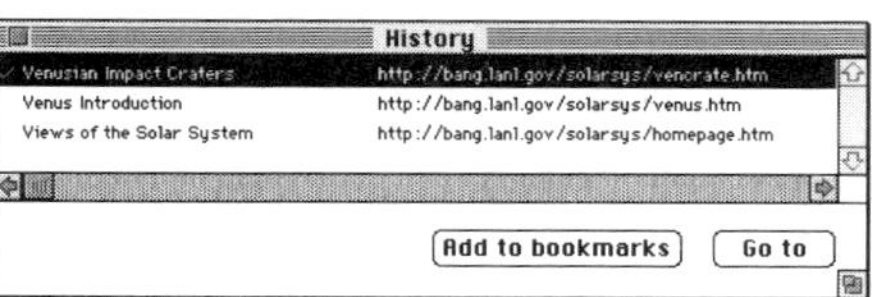

Figure 3.23 *The History window lets you see the pages that you have visited in the current session. You can jump to any page by double clicking it, and add a bookmark by choosing the Add to bookmarks button.*

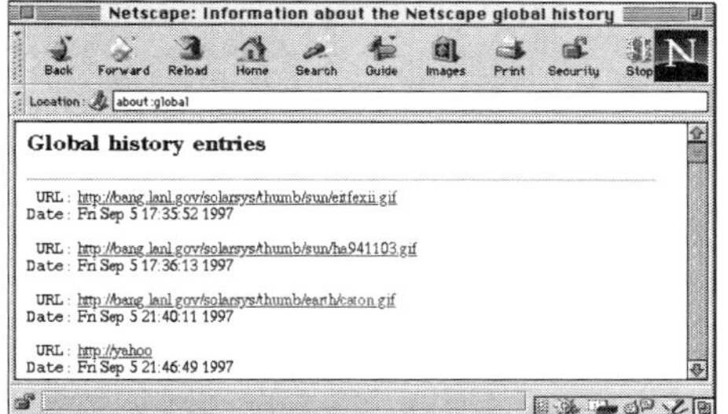

Figure 3.24 *Type* **about:global** *in the Location field to see all the URLs that you've accessed recently. (The number of URLs shown is determined by the Visited links expire after option in the Navigator panel of the Preferences dialog box.)*

Seeing where you've been

Navigator's History window keeps track of your travels on the Web. Each time you jump to a new page, the page's URL and title are added to the History window. However, the History window, like the Go menu, only keeps track of one path of pages at a time. That is, if you backtrack and then follow a new link in a new direction, all the pages after that page will be erased from the History window.

To see where you've been:

Choose (Communicator) > History **(Figure 3.22)** to view the History window **(Figure 3.23)**.

✔ Tips

- Double click on a page to jump to that page. You can also click once and then click the Go to button.
- Click on a page and click Add to bookmarks to add a bookmark for that page to your Bookmarks window.
- If you have the History window open as you backtrack, a checkmark appears next to the current page in the History window, while the pages further ahead on the path remain visible.
- If you want to see all the files that you've visited recently, including images, type **about:global** in the Navigator window's Location field and press Return. Navigator will show the URLs for every file that you've recently surfed to **(Figure 3.24)**. You can specify how many are remembered in the History panel of the Preferences dialog box *(see page 40)*.

Controlling what Navigator remembers

You can choose how many pages you want to remember when you type **about:global** in the Location field in the Navigator window (as described in the Tips on page 39). This can be useful to find a page that you visited a few days ago but didn't create a bookmark for. It's also handy for seeing where others (like your kids, maybe?) may have surfed recently.

To control what Navigator remembers:

1. Choose Edit > Preferences **(Figure 3.25)**. The Preferences dialog box appears.
2. Click Navigator in the Category list to display the Navigator preferences **(Figure 3.26)**.
3. Type a number in the days field in the History section at the bottom of the dialog box to determine how long pages will be remembered when you type **about:global** in the Location field.
4. Click OK to close the Preferences dialog box.

✓ Tip

- To erase what appears when you type **about:global**, click the Expire now button.

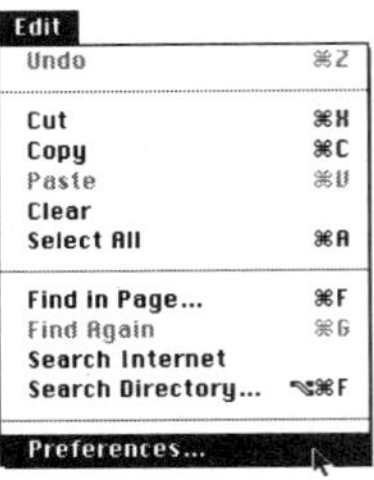

Figure 3.25 *Choose Edit > Preferences.*

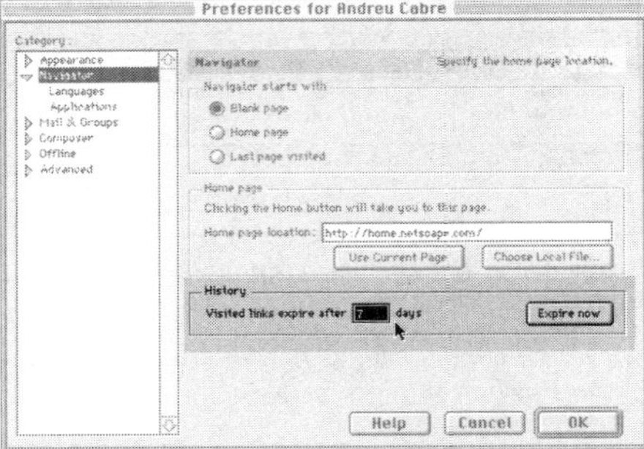

Figure 3.26 *Click once on Navigator in the Category list to display the options related to the History window. Then, in the History section, type the number of days that pages should be remembered.*

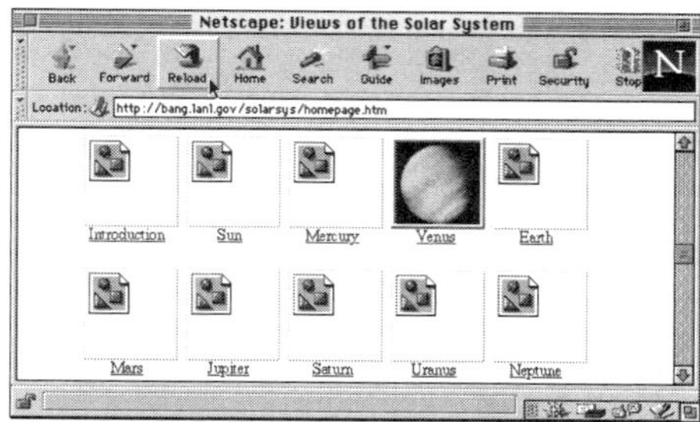

Figure 3.27 *Click the Reload button to have Navigator consult the server for any changes and update the page accordingly. The Reload button also comes in handy if you've stopped the page in mid-transfer, as shown.*

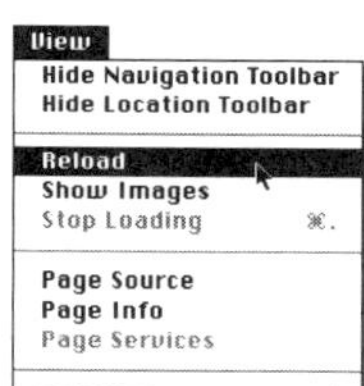

Figure 3.28 *You can also choose View > Reload to have Navigator update a page.*

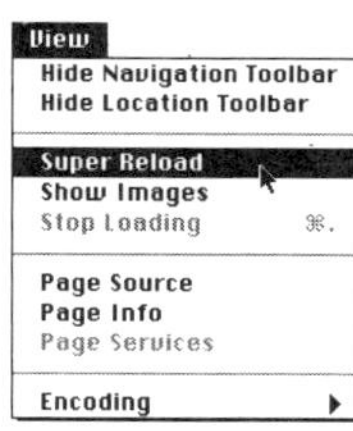

Figure 3.29 *Hold down the Option key to get access to the Super Reload command.*

Reloading a page

When you jump to a page, Navigator automatically loads a copy of the page into its memory cache *(see page 337)*. The *next* time you jump to the page, instead of asking the server for the information (which might be rather slow, depending on the type of connection you have and the type of server that contains the page), it loads the page from memory.

However, if you suspect (or know) that the contents of the page have changed, if the page has not loaded completely, or if it has not loaded properly, you will want Navigator to load the page from the server and not from memory.

To reload a page:

Click the Reload button **(Figure 3.27)** or choose View > Reload **(Figure 3.28)**. Navigator updates the page's contents.

✔ Tip

- You can force a reload, regardless of the status of a page, by holding down the Option key and selecting View > Super Reload **(Figure 3.29)**.

Stopping page loading

There are three principal reasons why you might want to abort a jump to a page. First, you may simply have changed your mind or made an errant click. Second, the page may be taking so long that you decide to go somewhere else. Finally, you may notice, as you watch the status bar, that it takes an unusually long time to connect to the host. This is a good clue that either the server is busy or that the page is no longer located where you thought it was. Just abort the jump and move on.

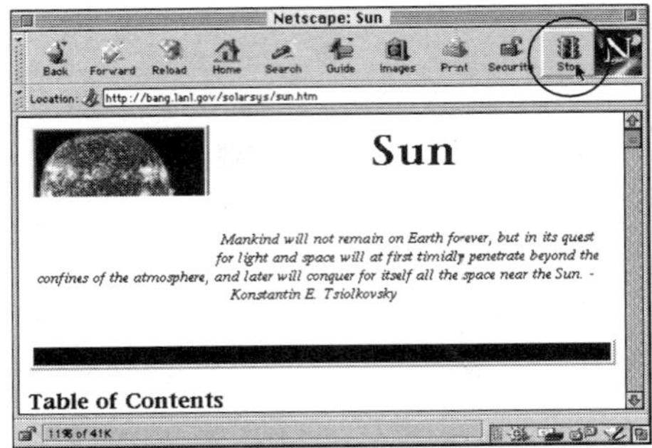

Figure 3.30 *You can stop loading a page at any time. Notice the progress information in the status area at the bottom left of the window and the half loaded image.*

To stop a page from loading:

1. Click the Stop button on the toolbar **(Figure 3.30)** or choose View > Stop Loading **(Figure 3.31)**. Navigator immediately stops trying to load the page and shows you what it's come up with so far, if anything.

2. If part of the page has already loaded, and if you decide you really do want to continue loading the page, click the Reload button, or choose View > Reload, to load the entire page *(see page 41)*.

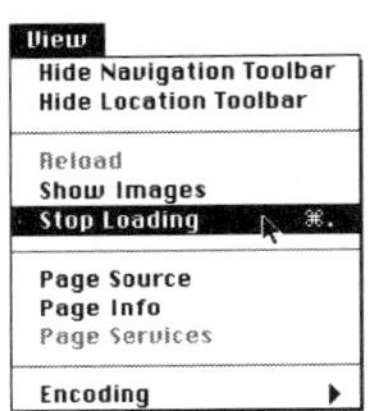

Figure 3.31 *You can also choose View > Stop Loading to break Netscape's link to the server.*

✔ Tips

- You can also press Command-Period to stop loading a page.
- Sometimes, different elements on the page are loaded independently and you'll have to click the Stop button several times to completely halt the loading process.

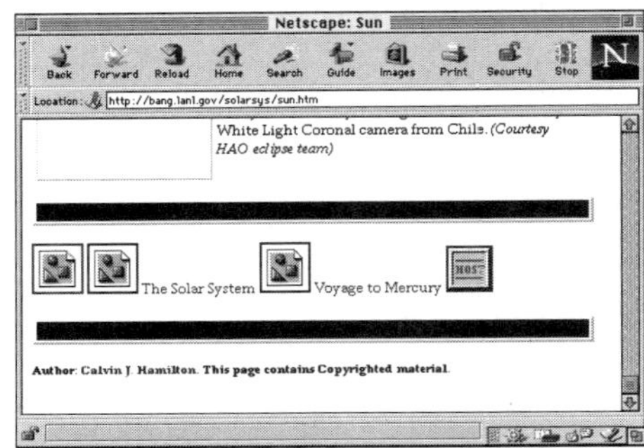

Figure 3.32 *This is another view of the page that I stopped loading in Figure 3.30. The images shown here never got a chance to begin loading and so the image placeholder icon is displayed in their place. You can load individual images by clicking them. For more information, consult* Viewing images on the Web *on page 43.*

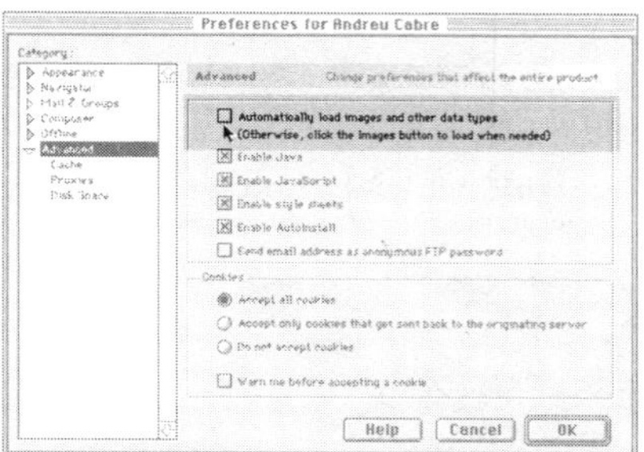

Figure 3.33 *Check the option Automatically load images and other data types in the Advanced panel in the Preferences dialog box to control whether the images are loaded or not.*

Figure 3.34 *With the Automatically load images option off, the images are replaced with icons.*

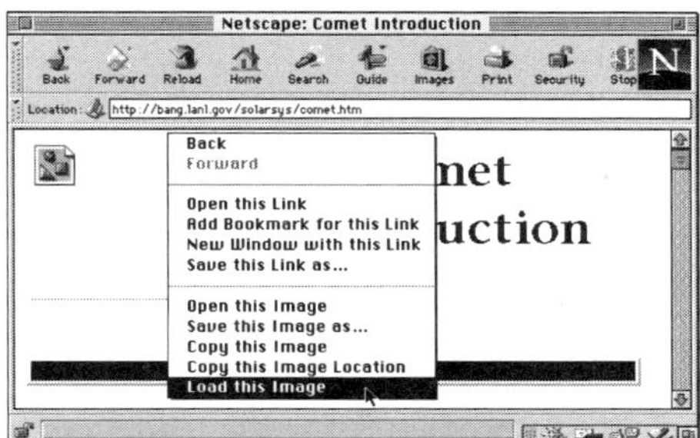

Figure 3.35 *Load an individual image by clicking it and choosing Load this Image in the menu.*

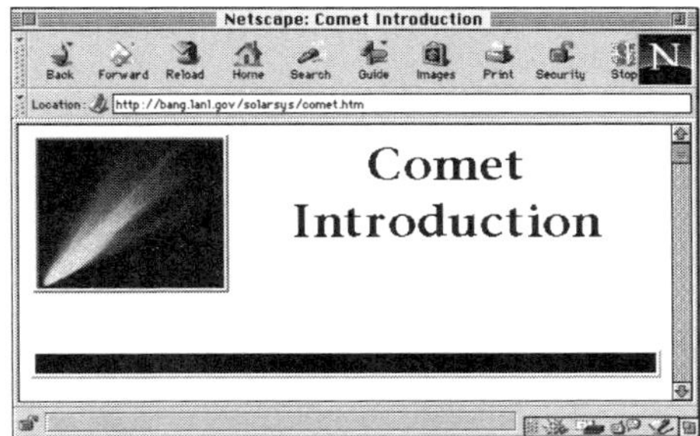

Figure 3.36 *The selected image is loaded.*

Viewing images on the Web

The most common kinds of images that you'll find on the Web are GIF and JPEG images. Both can be viewed automatically in Navigator. However, since images tend to be large (and are always larger than text), they can take a long time to download and view. By default, Navigator automatically downloads all the JPEG and GIF images on the pages that you jump to. If you have a particularly slow connection, you may want to view only the text.

To deactivate automatic image download:

1. Choose Edit > Preferences and then click Advanced in the Category list. The Advanced preferences appear.
2. Check Automatically load images and other data types to remove the checkmark from the command **(Fig. 3.33)**. The next time you jump to a page, the images will be displayed with placeholders **(Figure 3.34)**.

If you've chosen not to automatically load images, you can manually load images individually or all at once.

To load a particular image:

Click the desired image and choose Load this Image in the pop-up menu **(Figure 3.35)**. Navigator displays the corresponding image **(Figure 3.36)**.

To load all the images on a page:

Choose View > Show Images. All of the placeholders are replaced by the corresponding images. You can also click the Images button on the toolbar to load all the images at once.

Viewing information about a document

You may want to get more information about a page, including the images it contains, its MIME type, when it was last modified, how big it is, what character set was used to create it, and what its security level is. You can find out all this information with the Page Info command.

To view information about a document:

1. Navigate to the desired page **(Figure 3.37)**.
2. Choose View > Page Info **(Fig. 3.38)**. Navigator displays a window with information about the document **(Figure 3.39)**.

✔ Tips

- You can copy information from the Document Info window using the keyboard shortcut (Command-C).
- You can jump to the images and links shown in the Document Info window by clicking them the regular way *(see page 34)*.

Figure 3.37 *Navigate to the desired page.*

Figure 3.38 *Choose View > Page Info.*

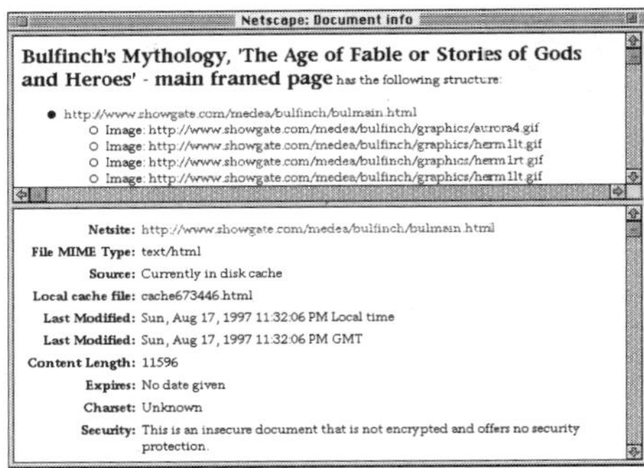

Figure 3.39 *Navigator displays information about the current page.*

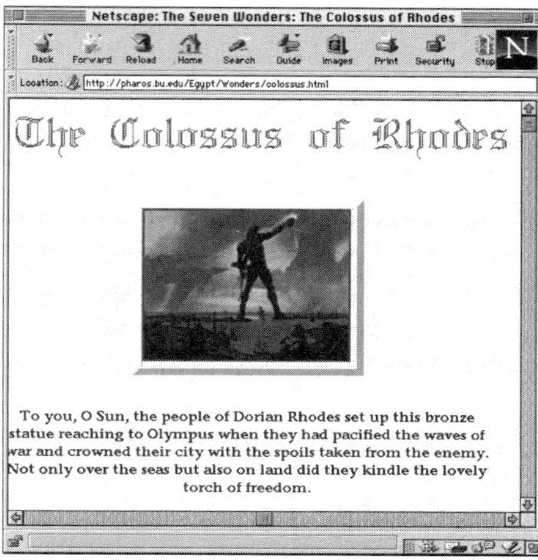

Figure 3.40 *Navigate to the desired page.*

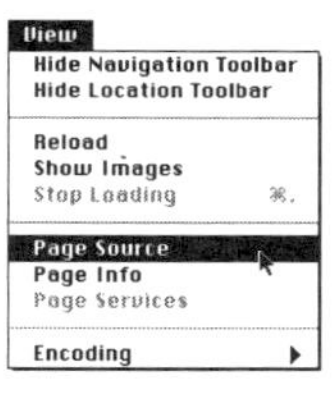

Figure 3.41 *Choose View > Page Source.*

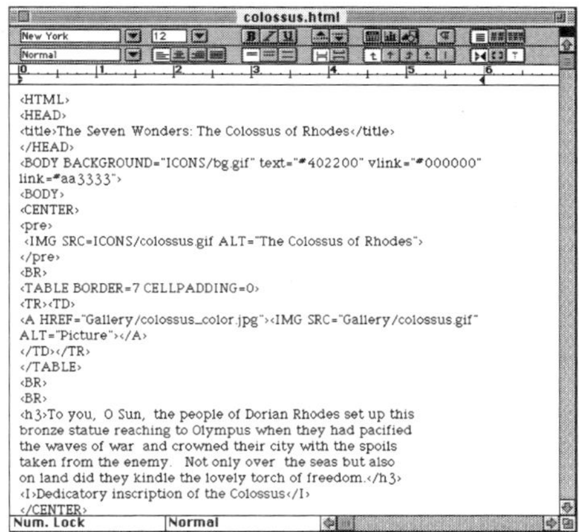


```
<HTML>
<HEAD>
<title>The Seven Wonders: The Colossus of Rhodes</title>
</HEAD>
<BODY BACKGROUND="ICONS/bg.gif" text="#402200" vlink="#000000"
link="#aa3333">
<BODY>
<CENTER>
<pre>
 <IMG SRC=ICONS/colossus.gif ALT="The Colossus of Rhodes">
</pre>
<BR>
<TABLE BORDER=7 CELLPADDING=0>
<TR><TD>
<A HREF="Gallery/colossus_color.jpg"><IMG SRC="Gallery/colossus.gif"
ALT="Picture"></A>
</TD></TR>
</TABLE>
<BR>
<BR>
<h3>To you, O Sun, the people of Dorian Rhodes set up this
bronze statue reaching to Olympus when they had pacified
the waves of war and crowned their city with the spoils
taken from the enemy. Not only over the seas but also
on land did they kindle the lovely torch of freedom.</h3>
<I>Dedicatory inscription of the Colossus</I>
</CENTER>
```

Figure 3.42 *The page source is displayed in the program that you have specified (in this case, Word).*

Viewing a page's HTML code

As you surf, you may find pages that make you wonder just how they were created. Wonder no longer. You can look at the HTML code behind the page. For more information on HTML, consult *Part IV: Creating Web Pages* on page 217.

To view a page's HTML code:

1. Navigate to the desired page **(Figure 3.40)**.
2. Choose View > Page Source **(Figure 3.41)**. The page's HTML code is displayed in the default window or with the program you've selected **(Figure 3.42)**.

✔ Tip

- For information on viewing HTML in your favorite word processor, consult *Choosing a program for viewing HTML* on page 46.

Choosing a program for viewing HTML

You can use *any* word processor—including SimpleText—to view (and then edit) HTML code.

To choose a program for displaying HTML code:

1. Choose Edit > Preferences. Then click Applications under Navigator in the Category list. The Applications preferences appear.
2. Choose View Source in the Description list **(Figure 3.43)**.
3. Choose Edit. The Edit Type dialog box appears.
4. Under Handled by, click Application.
5. Click Choose to locate a word processor on your hard disk **(Figure 3.44)**.
6. Click OK to close the Edit Type box.
7. Click OK to close the Preferences box. The next time you choose View > Page Source, the HTML code will be displayed in the program you've selected. (See Figure 3.42 on page 45.)

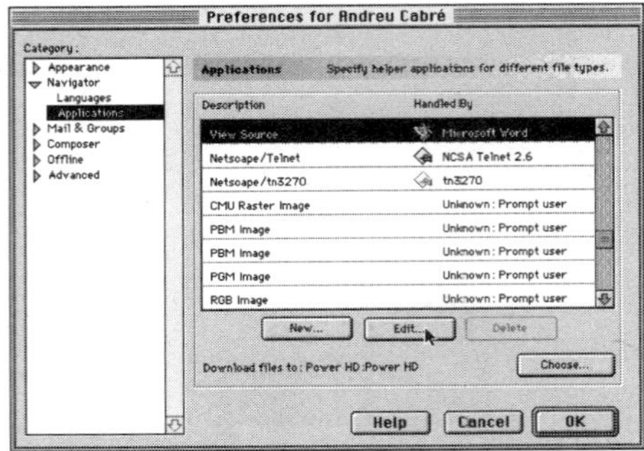

Figure 3.43 *In the Applications panel of the Preferences dialog box, choose View Source in the Description list and click Edit.*

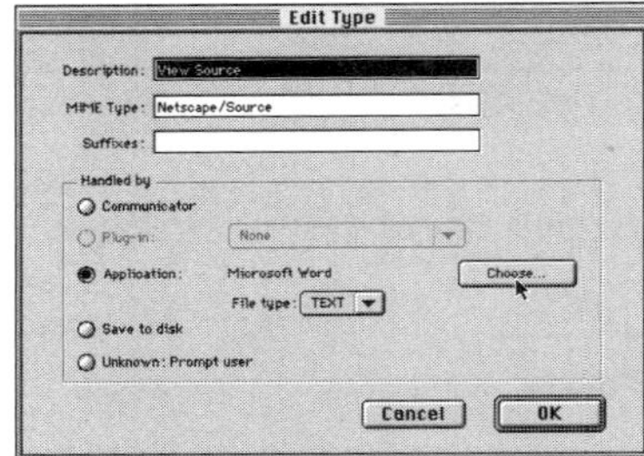

Figure 3.44 *Click Application and then click Choose to locate the word processor you want to use to view and edit the HTML of particular pages.*

Frames

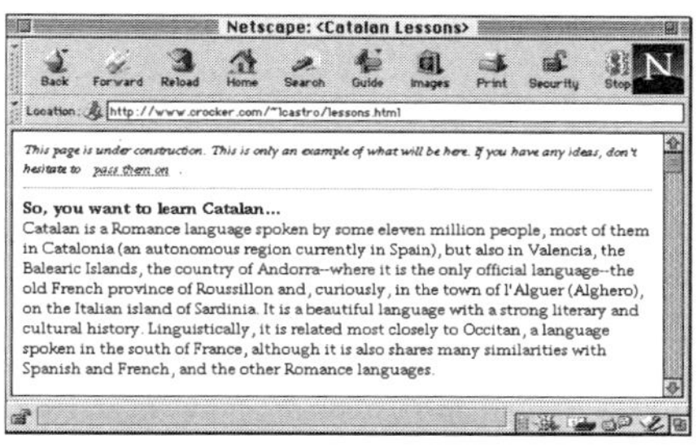

Figure 4.1 *A frame is a regular page with its own URL (like the one above) that is fit into a frameset like the one shown in Figure 4.2.*

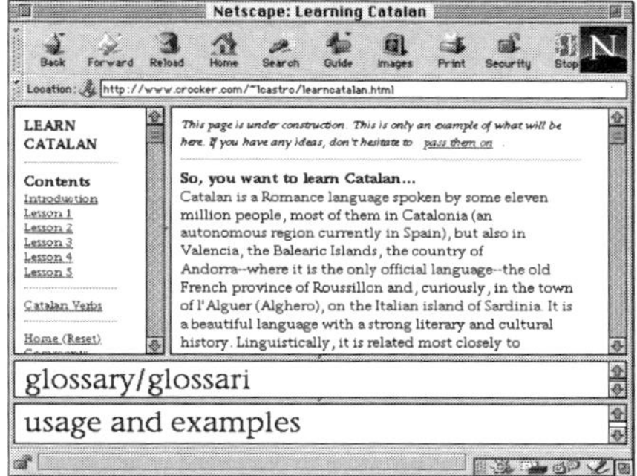

Figure 4.2 *A frameset is a page that is divided into individual frames, each of which displays the information from its own URL.*

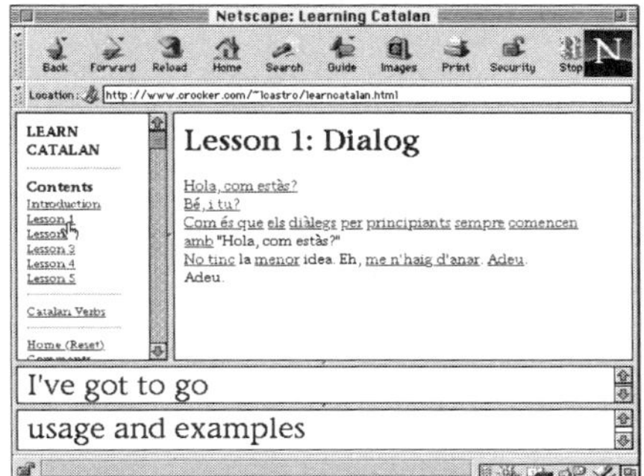

Figure 4.3 *Oftentimes when you click a link in one frame, the corresponding URL is shown in one of the other frames, while all the remaining frames stay constant.*

Frames are an ingenious feature that divide each window into individual panes that each contains its own URL. Frames make it easy to hold on to one page (maybe a table of contents with a series of links) while viewing a whole series of others (where the links lead). Navigating such sites can be confusing. This chapter should make it easier to get around.

Frames and framesets

A *frame* is nothing more than a regular Web page **(Figure 4.1)** that has been shoe-horned into a smaller area within another Web page, called a *frameset* **(Figure 4.2)**. The frameset contains information about the size of the frames within it, including their sizes, names, scrolling qualities, and URLs.

When you click on a link inside a frame, one of two things can happen. If the link is to a page at the same site, it will usually appear inside the currently open frameset, replacing the contents of one of the existing frames. The other frames remain unchanged so that you can still see the information that they contain **(Fig. 4.3)**.

If the link is to a page at a different site, the page will usually open up in a new window. If it doesn't and you want it to, consult *Opening a frame in a new window* on page 49.

Perhaps the most important thing to remember is that only the Web page designer can create or add frames to an existing page. You, the Web surfer, can only navigate the frames that are already there.

Following a link in a frame

Following a link on a page with frames is practically identical to following links on regular pages *(see page 34)*—simply click and go. The difference is in where the result will be displayed. When you click on a link in a frameset, the link is usually opened in one of the frames, while the other frames remain unchanged.

To follow a link in a frame:

1. Place the pointer over the link that you wish to jump to **(Figure 4.4)**. You may have to scroll around in the frame to make the link visible.

2. Click the link. Navigator brings you to the link's destination **(Figure 4.5)**. Many times, the page will be displayed inside one of the frames in the current frameset.

✔ Tips

- You can't open a link in a specific frame unless the designer has allowed for it, but you can open the link in a new window *(see page 49)*.
- Usually, a frameset contains a narrow frame with links, a central frame where those links are displayed and sometimes a static frame that contains a logo or toolbar.
- You can often resize frames to better suit your needs. For more information, consult *Resizing and scrolling around a frame* on page 50.
- Not all frames have visible borders. Just because you can't see borders doesn't mean they're not there.

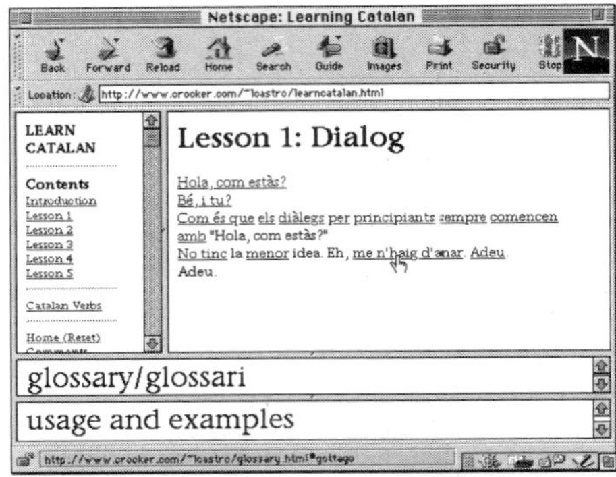

Figure 4.4 *Follow the link in one of the frames in the usual way, by positioning the cursor over the link until it turns into a hand. Then click the mouse.*

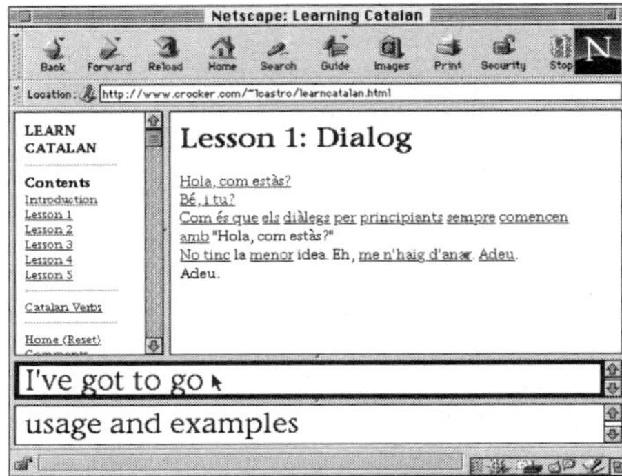

Figure 4.5 *In this example, the corresponding URL is displayed in the first of the two lower frames. The other frames remain unchanged.*

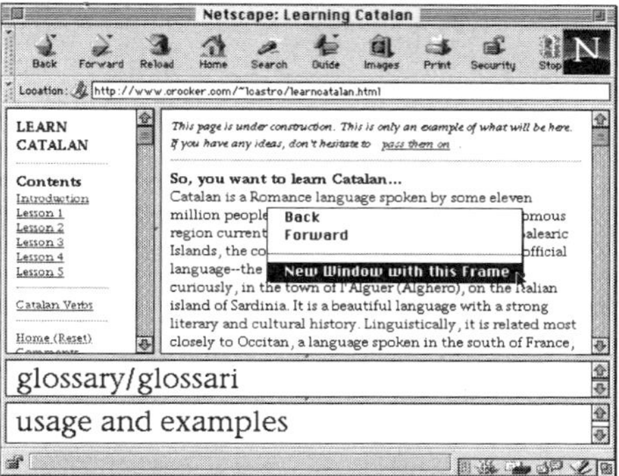

Figure 4.6 *Navigate to a page with the desired frame. Click in the frame and hold the mouse button down until the pop-up menu appears. Then choose New Window with this Frame.*

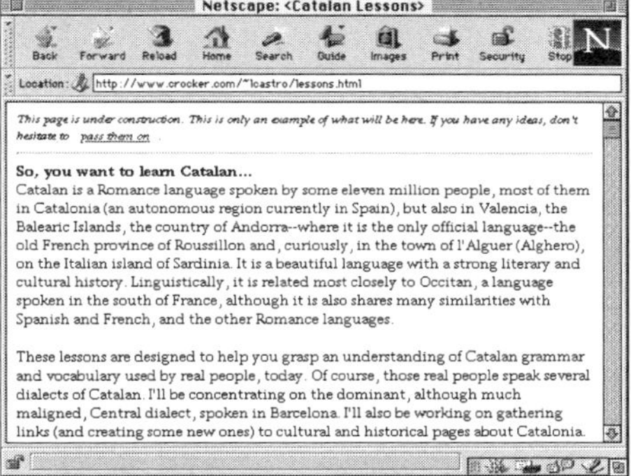

Figure 4.7 *The selected frame is opened in a new Navigator window.*

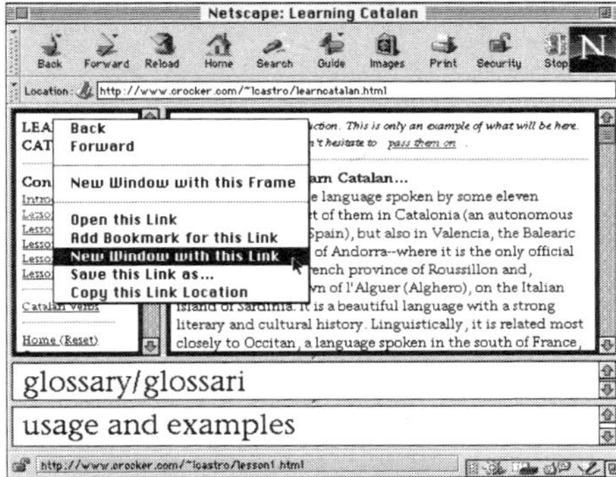

Figure 4.8 *You can also click a link and hold down, and then choose New Window with this Link in the pop-up menu that appears.*

Opening a frame in a new window

Often, links are *targeted* to particular frames. That means that when you click the link, the corresponding URL appears within a specific frame. If the frame is too small or too unwieldy, you may wish to open the link in a separate, independent window.

To open a frame in a new window:

1. Navigate to a page that has the desired frame **(Figure 4.6)**.
2. Place the pointer in the frame (anywhere except over a link) and hold down the mouse button until the pop-up menu appears.
3. Choose New Window with this Frame. The frame is displayed in a new Navigator window **(Figure 4.7)**.

✔ Tips

- If there is a link to the frame that you want to open in a new window, you can click and hold the link and then choose New Window with this Link in the pop-up menu that appears **(Figure 4.8)**. If you choose New Windows with this Frame, the selected frame—but not the link to the frame—is opened in a new window.
- Sloppy Web page designers sometimes make links to external sites appear inside a frame. If the external site happens to have its own frames, the whole frameset will be stuffed into the frame on the original page. The best thing to do is go back *(see page 51)* and then open the link in a new window as described above.

Resizing and scrolling around a frame

Depending on how the Web page designer has written the HTML for the frameset, a frame can either have a fixed size (in pixels), a relative size (that depends on the size of the whole Navigator window), or be adjustable by the user.

Since there is no way to foresee what size window a user will have, designers should always make frames adjustable. Unfortunately, not all Web page designers agree.

To resize a frame:

1. Place the pointer over one of the borders of the frame **(Figure 4.9)**. If it changes into a double-pointed arrow, you can change the size of the frame.

2. Drag the border to the desired new position **(Figure 4.10)**.

Similarly, a designer can create a frameset so that a frame has scroll bars all the time, none of the time, or only when necessary.

To scroll around a frame:

- If the scroll bars are visible, click on the up or down arrows to see more information at the top or bottom of the frame, respectively. Drag the scroll box to move more quickly. Click in the gray area to move one frame area at a time **(Figure 4.11)**.

- Or, select the frame (by clicking in it) and use the arrow keys to move around the frame.

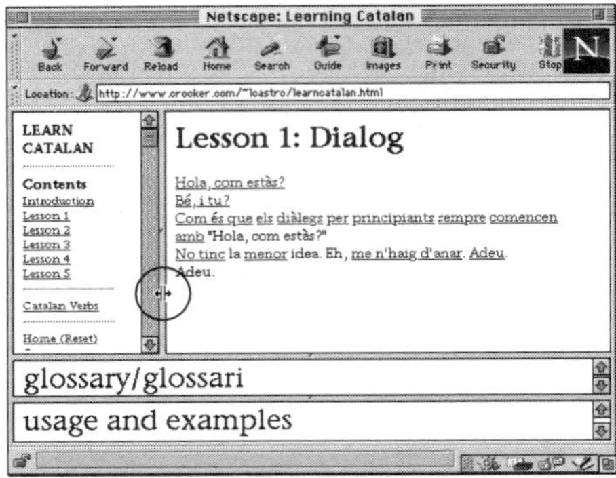

Figure 4.9 *Place the cursor between the frames. When it changes to a double-pointed arrow, drag it to resize the frames.*

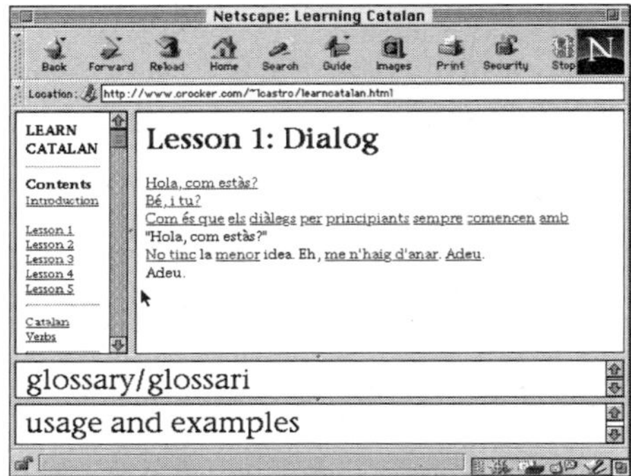

Figure 4.10 *The left column is narrower now.*

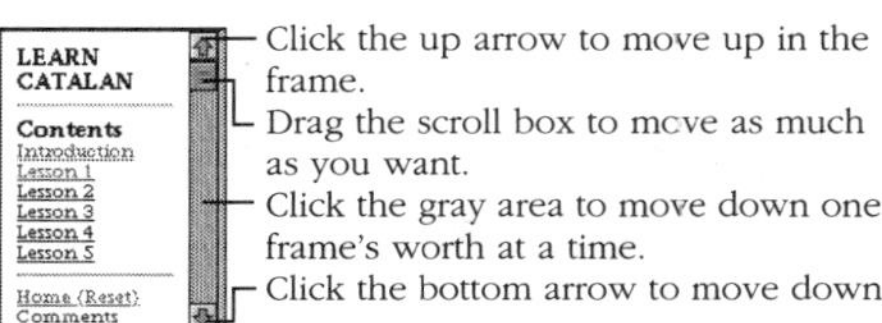

Figure 4.11 *The scroll bars (if they're visible) let you move around the frame to see additional information.*

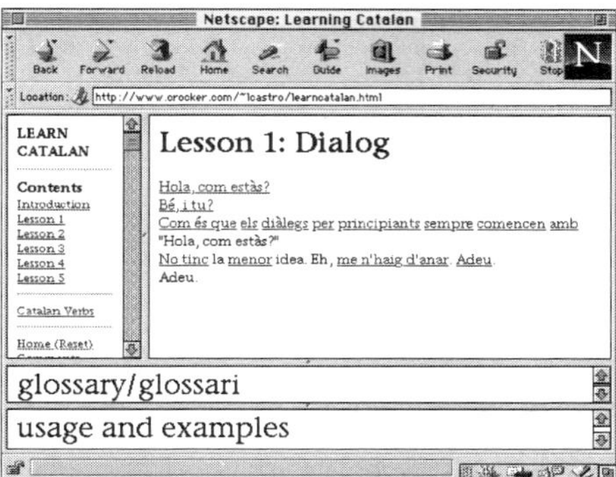

Figure 4.12 *After clicking on Lesson 1 and showing the corresponding frame, you may want to go back to the information previously contained in that frame.*

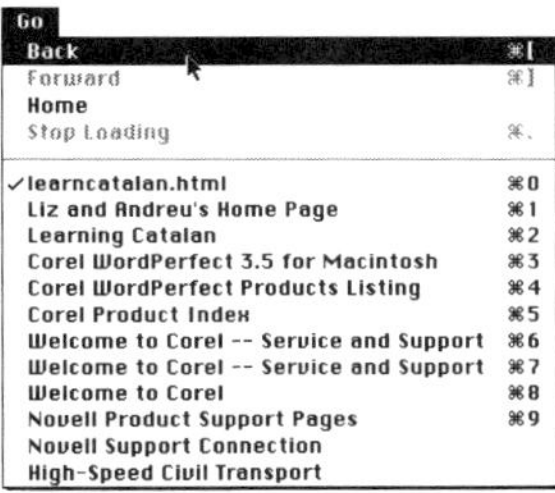

Figure 4.13 *Choose Back or Forward in the Go menu to navigate from frame to frame. Note that the individual frames are* not *listed at the bottom of the menu.*

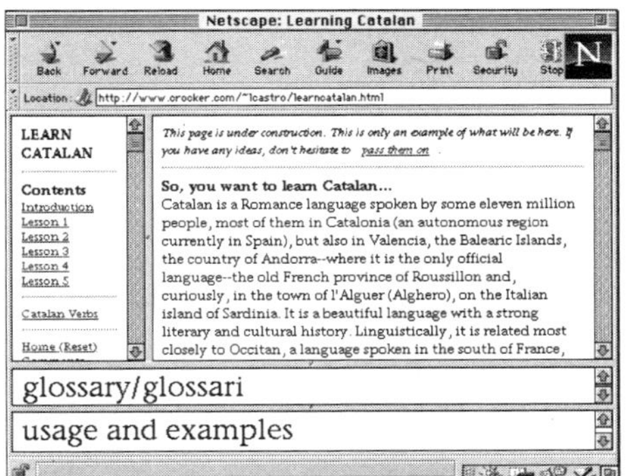

Figure 4.14 *The previous contents of the selected frame are shown. The other frames remain unchanged.*

Going back or forward in a frame

Navigator's Back and Forward buttons affect the last frame that has changed, and not just entire Web pages or framesets. Thus, if you have viewed several different pages in a particular frame, you can use the Back button to see the previous ones (and the Forward button to see later ones).

To go back or forward in a frame:

Choose Go > Back or Go > Forward **(Figure 4.13)**. Navigator changes the last changed frame to its previous contents **(Figure 4.14)**.

✔ Tips

- You can also use the Back and Forward buttons on the toolbar to go backward and forward in a frame. In fact, if you hold down either of these buttons, you'll see (and be able to choose from) a list of all the pages and framesets you've been viewing, but not individual frames.
- Or click and hold down in the frame and choose Back or Forward in the pop-up menu that appears.
- Neither the Go menu nor the History window displays the addresses for individual frames, so you cannot jump to a specific frame directly.
- To go directly back to the *page* before the frameset, choose the desired page in the Go menu or click and hold the Back button and choose the page from the pop-up menu.

Getting information about a frame

In the same way you can get information about an entire page, you can get information about an individual frame. In addition, you can get information for a frameset—and see all the frames it contains.

To get information about a frame:

1. Select the frame by clicking it. The frame is outlined with a black border **(Figure 4.15)**.
2. Choose View > Page Info **(Fig. 4.16)**. Navigator displays the information for the selected frame **(Figure 4.17)**.

✔ Tip

- To get information about the entire frameset, choose View > Page Info *before* selecting a frame **(Fig. 4.18)**. For more information about the Page Info command, consult *Viewing information about a document* on page 44.

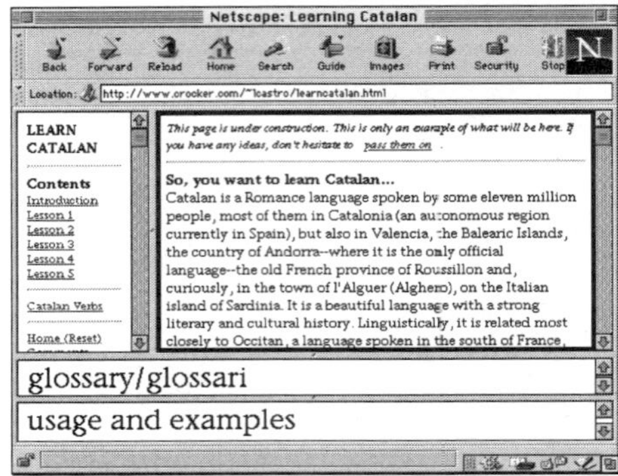

Figure 4.15 *Select the frame that you want to get information for by clicking it. The heavy black outline shows which frame is selected (upper-right, in this case).*

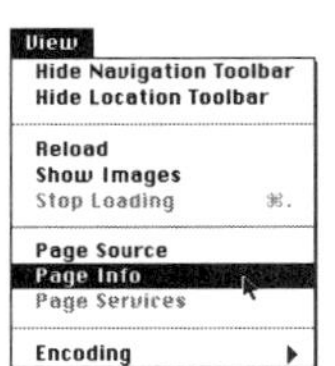

Figure 4.16 *Choose View > Page Info.*

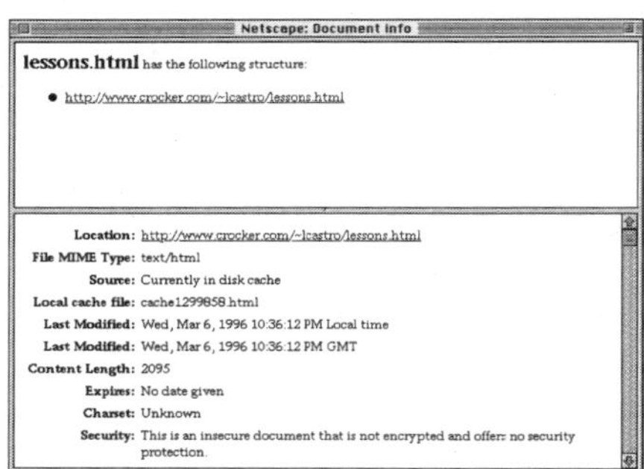

Figure 4.17 *Navigator displays the information about the frame in a new window.*

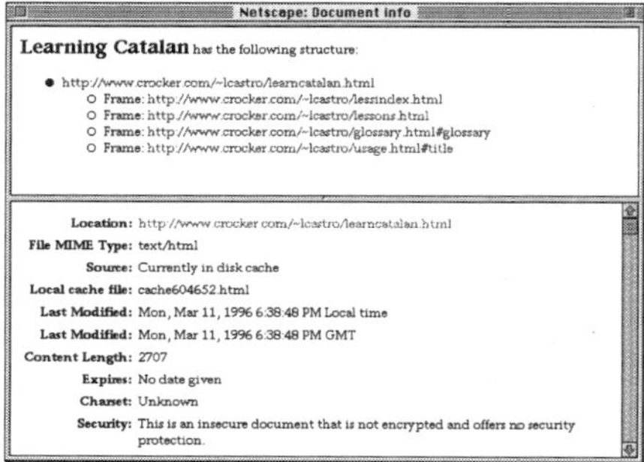

Figure 4.18 *If you choose Page Info for a frameset, you'll get information on all the frames.*

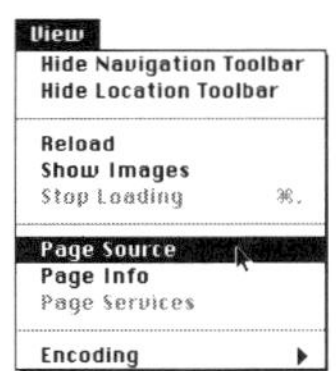

Figure 4.19 *Choose View > Page Source.*

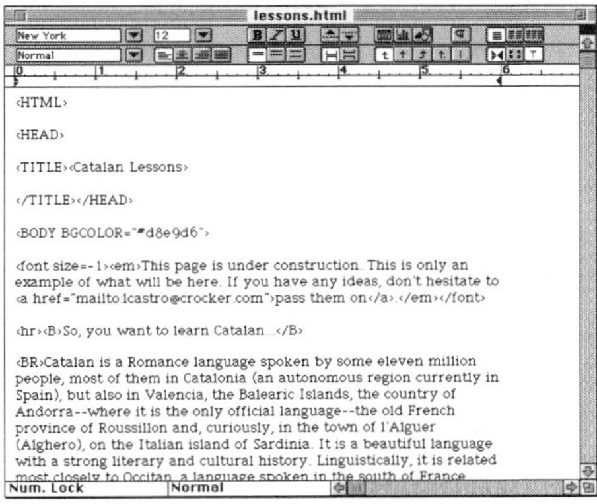

Figure 4.20 *The HTML code for the frame is displayed. You can display HTML code in any word processor. This is Microsoft Word (OK, OK, it's version 5.1. I admit it.)*

Viewing a frame's HTML code

Frame's are a little bit tricky to set up. If you find a good frameset and want to see how it was constructed, you can view its HTML code. For more information on HTML, consult *Part IV: Creating Web Pages* on page 217.

To view a frame's HTML code:

1. Select the frame by clicking it.
2. Choose View > Page Source **(Figure 4.19)**. The HTML code for the selected frame is displayed in the program that you chose in the Applications panel of the Preferences dialog box **(Figure 4.20)**.

✔ Tips

- Remember that imitation is flattery and that copying is plagiary.
- To view a frameset's HTML code, choose View > Page Source *before* selecting a frame.
- For more information on choosing the application in which to display HTML code, consult *Viewing a page's HTML code* on page 45.

5 Transferring Files

In order to transfer files from one computer to another, for example, from a server in New Jersey to your house, the two computers need to speak to each other the same way—by using the same communication system or *protocol*. Before the Web, the most common protocols for downloading files were FTP (which stands for *file transfer protocol)* and Gopher. And even though today it's quite simple to download files from a Web page, most servers continue to offer files through the two older systems.

Navigator allows you to access FTP or Gopher servers in much the same way as you would regular Web servers by displaying their contents as a series of hierarchical folders.

FTP and Gopher servers do not have links to other sites, and generally they don't include explanatory text. They are dedicated to file transfer. Some sites are open to the public, while others are restricted to particular users.

To transfer files to another person or company via e-mail, consult *Attaching files to a message* on page 165.

Accessing an FTP site

Many servers offer either anonymous or private FTP. Universities, Internet service providers, and computer manufacturers typically offer anonymous FTP access to their files, which may be doctoral dissertations, Web software, or program updates, respectively, among many other possibilities. In addition, you may have access to a private FTP site at your own server.

To access an FTP site:

1. Choose File > Open > Location in Navigator **(Figure 5.1)**. The Open Location dialog box appears.
2. For an anonymous FTP site, type **ftp://ftp.site** where *ftp.site* is the URL address of the desired FTP site **(Figure 5.2)**. To access a private FTP site, you'll have to type **ftp://user name:password@ftp.site**.
3. Click Open. Navigator contacts the FTP server and displays the contents of the FTP site **(Figure 5.3)**.

✔ Tips

- You can also type the FTP address in the Location field in the Location toolbar, if it is showing *(see page 27)*.
- If the anonymous FTP address begins with the word *ftp*, you don't need to type the initial **ftp://**; Navigator will add it automatically **(Figure 5.4)**.
- Some anonymous FTP sites require that you log in with your e-mail address as your password. It is also considered proper Internet etiquette. To do so, choose the corresponding option in the Advanced preferences box *(see page 336)*.

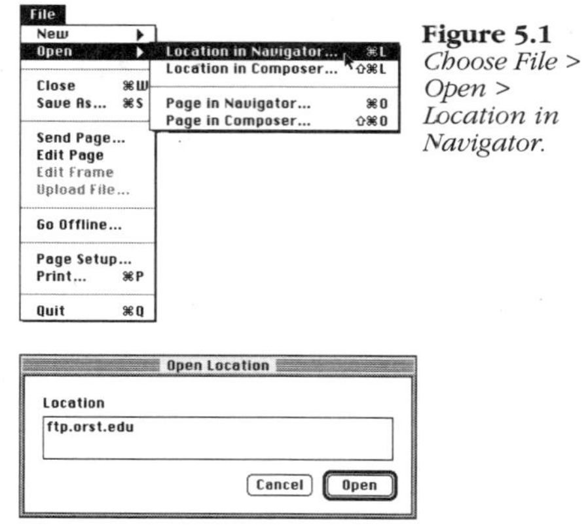

Figure 5.1 *Choose File > Open > Location in Navigator.*

Figure 5.2 *Type the FTP address in the Open Location dialog box and click Open.*

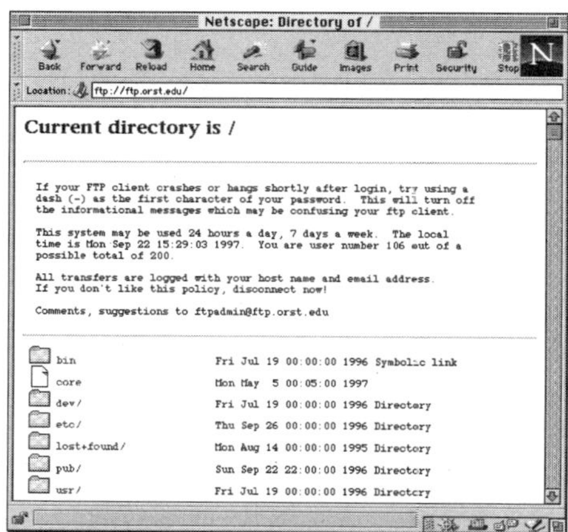

Figure 5.3 *The FTP site is displayed in the browser. Click on a folder to see its contents. Click on a file to download it.*

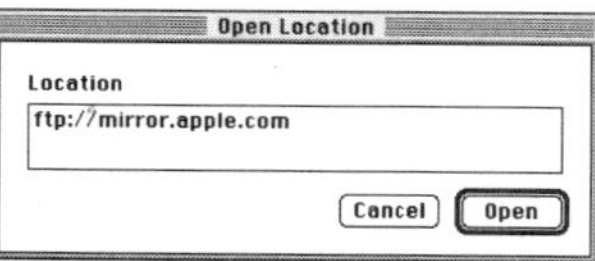

Figure 5.4 *You only have to type* ftp:// *at the beginning of the URL if the FTP address itself does not begin with the letters* ftp.

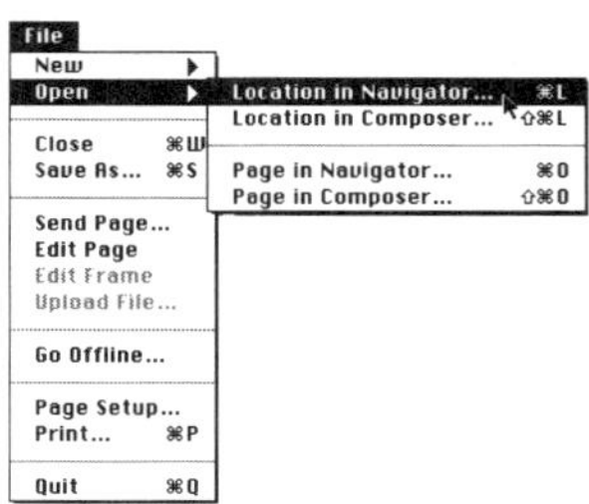

Figure 5.5 *Choose File > Open > Location in Navigator.*

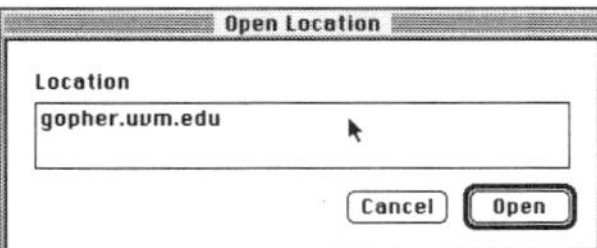

Figure 5.6 *Type the URL of the desired Gopher site in the Open Location dialog box.*

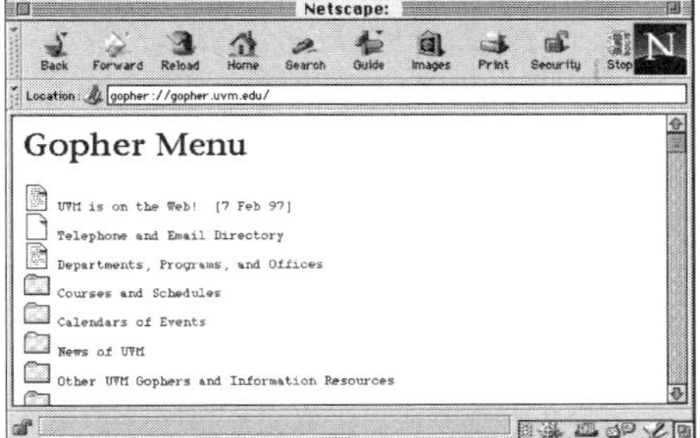

Figure 5.7 *The Gopher site is displayed. Click a folder to access its contents. Click a text file to display it.*

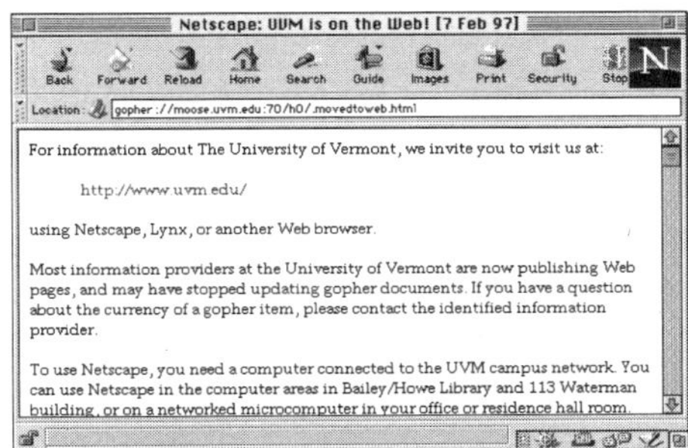

Figure 5.8 *When you click a text document, it is displayed in the browser.*

Accessing a Gopher site

The Gopher protocol, supported by many university sites, lets you search databases and retrieve files. Although there continues to be wide support for Gopher, it has been generally supplanted by the Web.

To access a Gopher site:

1. Choose File > Open > Location in Navigator **(Figure 5.5)**. The Open Location dialog box appears.
2. Type **gopher://gopher.site** where *gopher.site* is the URL address of the desired Gopher site **(Figure 5.6)**.
3. Click Open. Navigator contacts the Gopher server and displays the available files on screen **(Figure 5.7)**.
4. Click on a folder to see its contents. Click on a text file to display it **(Figure 5.8)**.

✔ Tips

- If the Gopher address begins with the word *gopher*, you don't need to type the initial **gopher://**; Navigator will add it automatically.
- You can also type the Gopher address in the Location field in the Location toolbar, if it is showing *(see page 27)*.

Downloading files

Once you have accessed the desired FTP, Gopher, or Web site, actually downloading a file is only a click away.

To download a file:

1. Access the desired site.
2. Click on the appropriate folders until you find the file you wish to download **(Figure 5.9)**.
3. Double click the desired file. Navigator may ask you what to do with the file **(Figure 5.10)**. Click Save File to save it to your hard disk.
4. In the Save As dialog box that appears, choose the directory in which to save the file and click Save **(Figure 5.11)**.
5. Navigator initiates the transfer and shows the Save file dialog box which indicates the size of the file and how long it will take to download **(Figure 5.12)**.
6. If you change your mind about downloading the file, click the Cancel button in the Save file dialog box.

✓ Tips

- Navigator automatically displays text files in the browser instead of saving them. To *save* a text file, click the link to it and choose Save this Link as in the pop-up menu. For more information, consult *Saving a page without jumping to it* on page 63.
- You can set up Navigator so that it uncompresses certain kinds of files automatically. For more information, consult *Applications* on page 318.

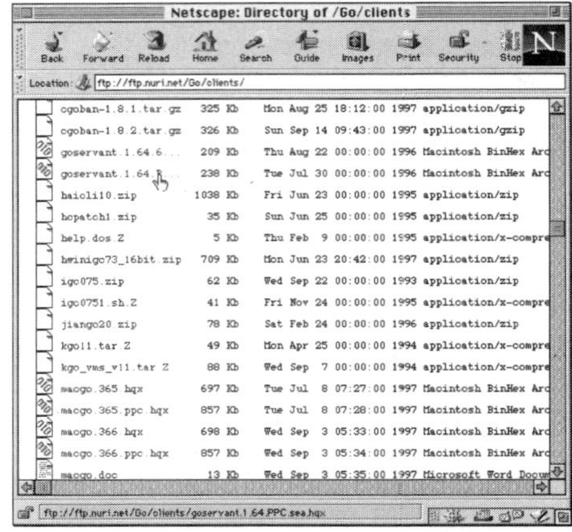

Figure 5.9 *Find the file that you wish to download from an FTP or Gopher site, or from a Web page. You may have to wade through several layers of folders. Click the file to download it.*

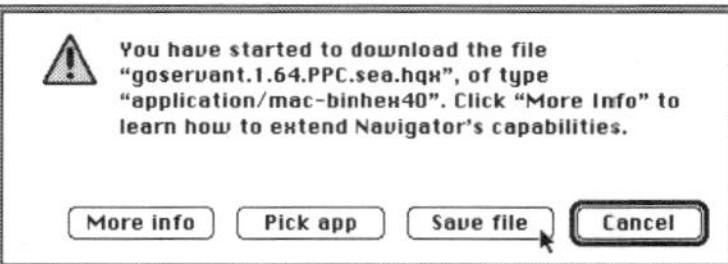

Figure 5.10 *Depending on your settings in the Applications category in the Preferences dialog box, you may have to choose what to do with the file you are about to download.*

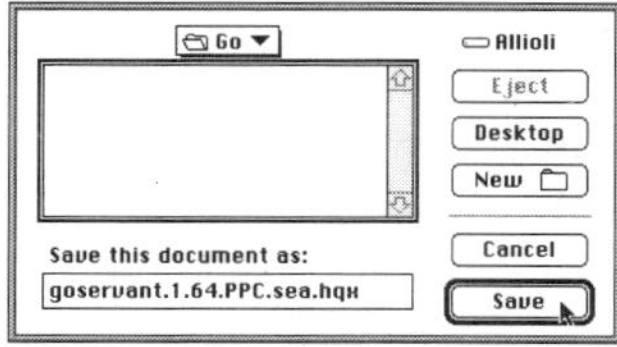

Figure 5.11 *Communicator shows you the Save As dialog box. Give the file a name (if it doesn't have one already), choose a location, and click Save.*

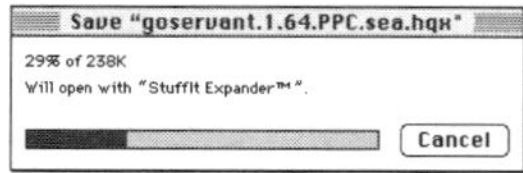

Figure 5.12 *The Save file dialog box shows how large the file is and how much of it has been downloaded. You can click Cancel to abort the download at any time.*

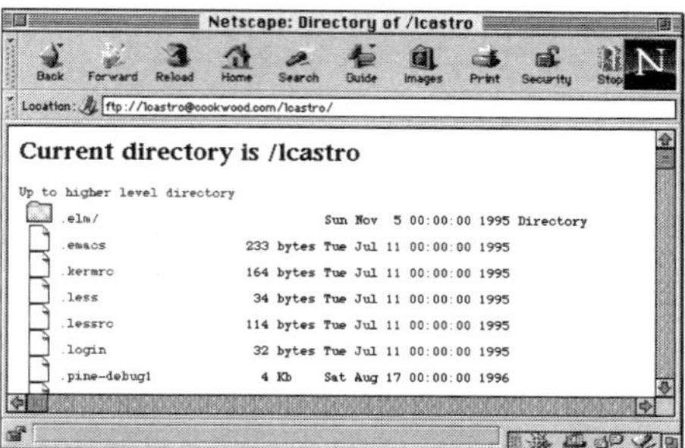

Figure 5.13 *Navigate to the FTP site where you want to upload the file.*

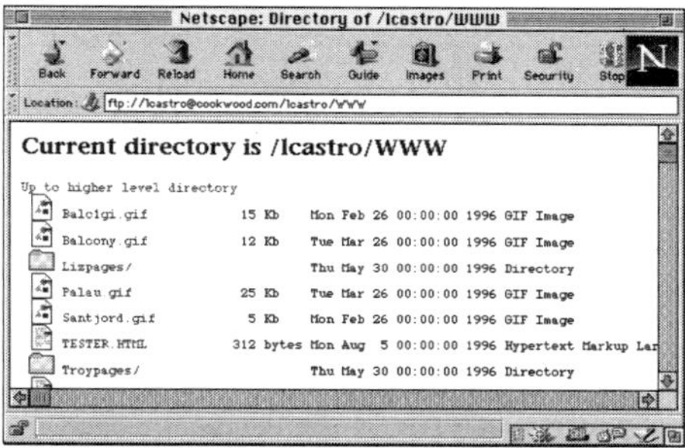

Figure 5.14 *Choose and open the folder (WWW, in this case) in which you wish to save the file.*

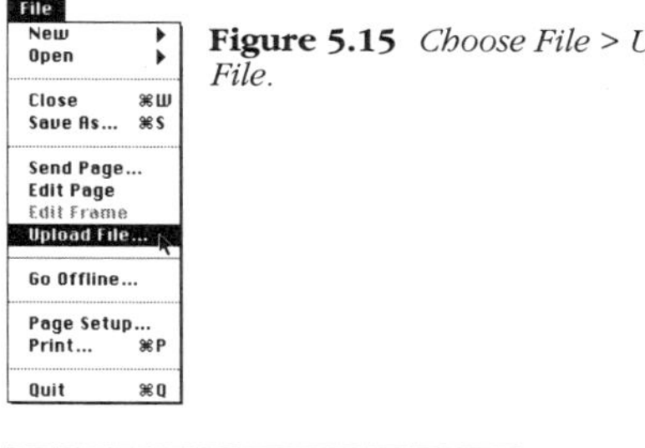

Figure 5.15 *Choose File > Upload File.*

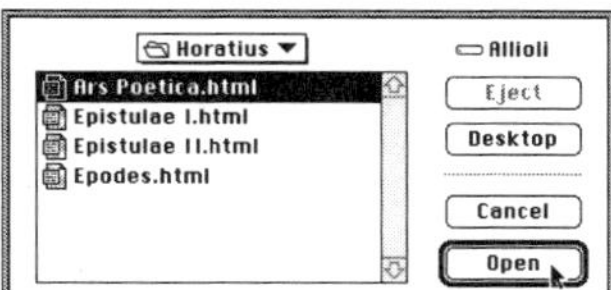

Figure 5.16 *In the dialog box that appears, select the file on your hard disk that you wish to upload. Click Open.*

Uploading a single file

Although you can download a file from an FTP, Gopher, or Web site, you can usually only upload a file to an FTP site. You might want to upload a Web page that you've created to your Internet service provider's server so that other users can have access to it. Or a software manufacturer might ask you to upload a file that lists your system extensions so that they can help you with a bombing program.

To upload a file:

1. Access the FTP site *(see page 56)* and navigate to the desired folder in which you wish to upload the file **(Figures 5.13 and 5.14)**.
2. Choose File > Upload File **(Figure 5.15)**.
3. In the dialog box that appears—that displays the contents of your hard disk—choose the desired file and click Open **(Figure 5.16)**. The file is transferred to the FTP site.
4. If you change your mind about uploading the file, click the Cancel button in the dialog box or the Stop button on the toolbar.

✔ Tips

- You may continue using Communicator while you are uploading a file. Of course, it won't be as fast as if it were dedicated to the one task.
- Be careful when you upload files. Once you've uploaded them, you can't change their location with Navigator. Of course, you can use a dedicated FTP client like Fetch to move files around on the FTP server.

Uploading multiple files

You can upload several files at once to an FTP site using drag and drop. To do so, you drag files from the desktop directly to the Navigator window which you've previously opened to your FTP site.

To upload multiple files:

1. Connect to your FTP site *(see page 56)* and navigate to the desired destination directory **(Figure 5.17)**.
2. Select the desired files on the desktop **(Figure 5.18)**.
3. Drag the files to the Navigator window showing the FTP site **(Figure 5.19)**.
4. Click the Navigator window to make it active. An alert appears asking if you wish to upload the dragged files to the FTP site **(Figure 5.20)**.
5. Click OK in the alert. The files are uploaded.

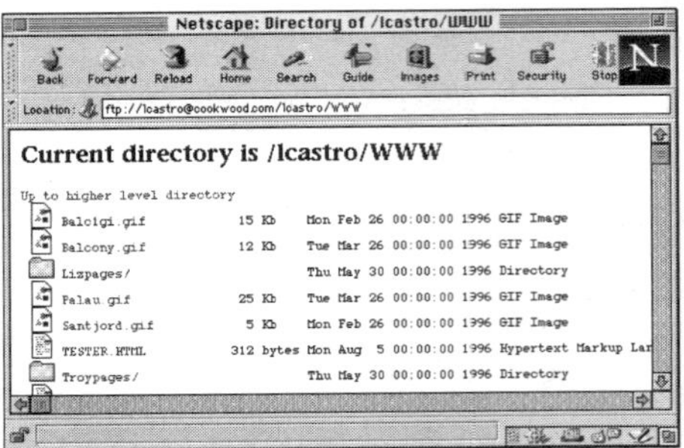

Figure 5.17 *Connect to the FTP site and navigate to the desired destination directory.*

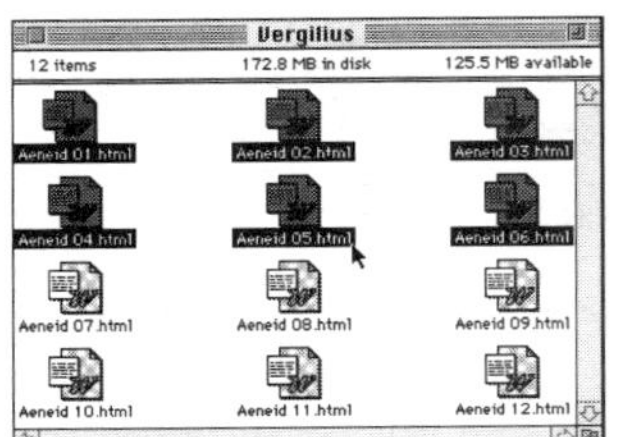

Figure 5.18 *In the Finder, select the files that you wish to upload.*

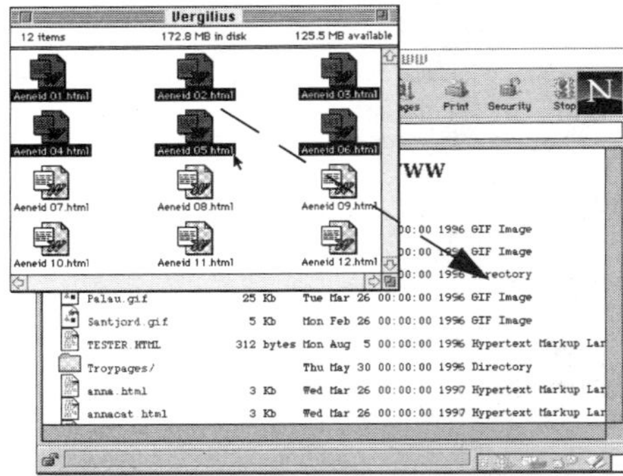

Figure 5.19 *Drag the files to the Navigator window which will be inactive but visible behind the Finder.*

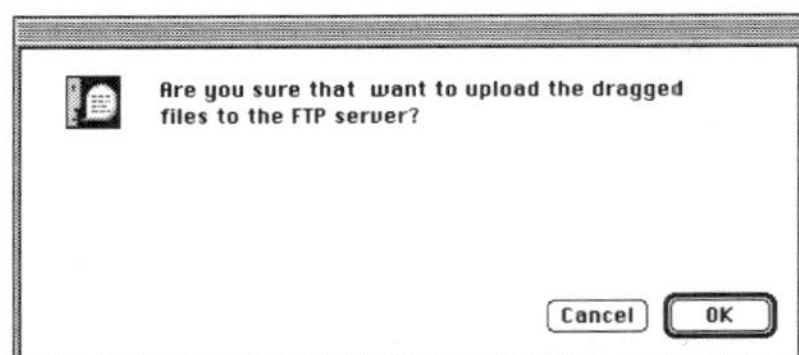

Figure 5.20 *When you click on the Navigator window, this alert appears. Click OK to upload the files.*

Saving and Printing

6

As you surf, you may find images and text that you would like to save. Although much of the material on the Web is copyrighted, you are allowed to save files for your own use—for example, to read a page or view an image after you have disconnected from your online service.

The images that you find on Web pages can only be saved in their original format. You will have to use a separate program like GraphicConverter or Adobe Photoshop to convert them to other formats.

If you find a particularly interesting page and you want to keep a copy of it, or share it with someone who's (gasp) not on the Web, you can print out a copy.

Saving a Web page

Navigator can save a Web page with or without its HTML tags. To open the file with a word processor and work with the data in some way, you should save the page *without* HTML tags—Navigator calls this "Text" format.

To read the page with Navigator once you've disconnected from your online service, or to study other peoples' HTML, you should save the file *with* HTML tags—Navigator calls this "Source" format.

To save a Web page:

1. Jump to the desired page **(Fig. 6.1)**.
2. Choose File > Save As **(Figure 6.2)**. The Save As dialog box appears.
3. In the Format submenu at the bottom of the dialog box **(Figure 6.3)**, choose Source to save the page with HTML tags, or Text to save the page without HTML tags.
4. Give the file a name and click OK. A progress bar indicates how long it will take to save **(Figure 6.4)**.

✔ Tips

- Don't be confused by Navigator's use of *Text*. All Web pages—even those saved with HTML tags in Source format—are text files.
- Images are not downloaded unless you save a page with Composer *(see page 227)*. To save images with Navigator, see page 64.

Figure 6.1 *First, navigate to the page that you want to save.*

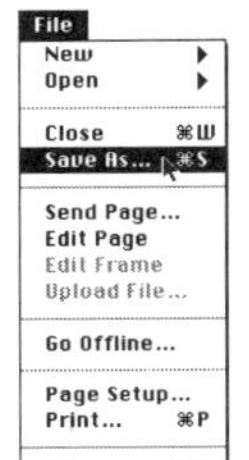

Figure 6.2 *Choose File > Save As.*

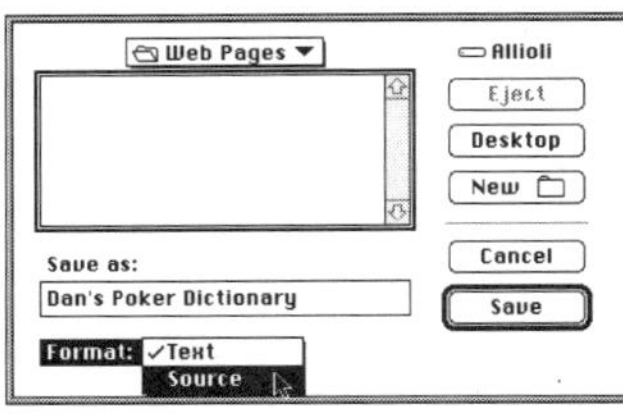

Figure 6.3 *Choose either Source or Text in the pop-up menu, give the file a name (or use the existing one), and then click Save.*

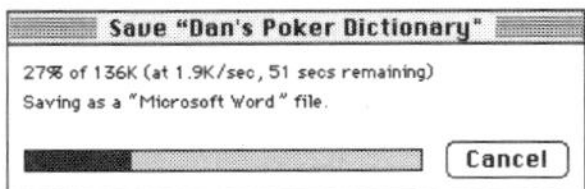

Figure 6.4 *A progress bar will appear telling you how long it will take to save the file to disk.*

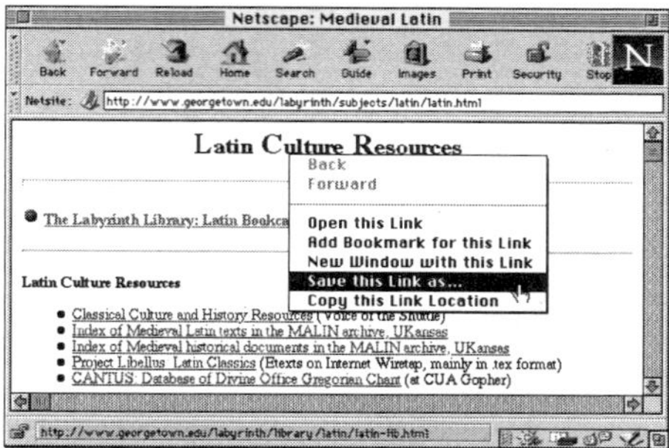

Figure 6.5 *First, navigate to a page that contains a link to the page you want to save. Place the pointer over the link. Press down the mouse button until the pop-up menu appears and then choose Save this Link as.*

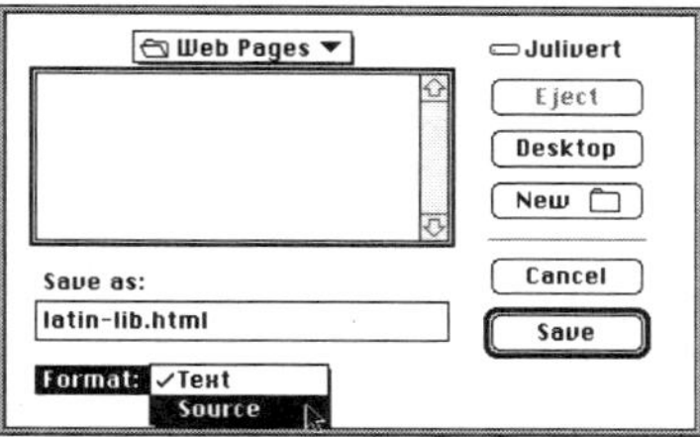

Figure 6.6 *Choose either Source or Text in the pop-up menu, give the file a name (or use the existing one), and then click OK.*

Saving a page without jumping to it

You can save a Web page without even navigating to it. This is convenient when you are on a page with several links to other interesting looking pages, since you can save each of the other pages without leaving the main page that has the links.

To save a page without jumping to it:

1. Jump to a page that contains a link to the page you wish to save.
2. Click the link and choose Save this Link as in the menu **(Figure 6.5)**.
3. In the Format submenu at the bottom of the Save As dialog box that appears, choose Source to save the page with HTML tags, or Text to save the page without HTML tags **(Figure 6.6)**.
4. Change the file name if desired and click OK.

✓ Tips

- Hold down the Option key and click (just click, don't click *and* hold) a link to save the corresponding page without using the pop-up menu.
- When you save a Web page with the Save As command *(see page 62)*, the default file name is the title of the Web page. When you save a *link* to a page, the default file name is the original file name. Use the original file names if you want the internal links between a set of related pages to work offline.

Saving an image

Inline images are not downloaded automatically when you save a Web page. You must save each image separately.

To save an inline image:

1. Navigate to the page that contains the image.
2. Click the image and choose Save this Image as in the pop-up menu **(Figure 6.7)**. The Save As dialog box appears **(Figure 6.8)**.
3. Click OK to save the image with the name and extension given. The Saving Location dialog box shows you how long the download will take to finish **(Figure 6.9)**.

✓ Tips

- Although you can change the extension of an image file when you save it, this will *not* magically change its format. To change an image's format, you need to use an application like GraphicConverter or Adobe Photoshop.
- If you choose File > Edit Page, and then choose Save in the Composer window, you *will* be allowed to save all the images it contains in one fell swoop *(see page 227)*.
- External images—that is, those that are displayed when you click a link to them—can be downloaded by clicking and holding the link and choosing Save this Link as.
- A much more Mac-like way to save an image is to just drag it from the Navigator window onto the Desktop (as easy as that!).

Figure 6.7 *To save an inline image, click on the image and hold down the mouse button until the pop-up menu appears. Then choose Save this Image as to save the image.*

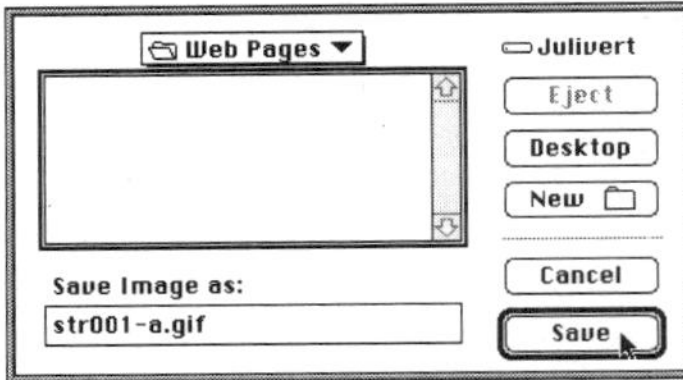

Figure 6.8 *In the Save image dialog box, choose a file name (or use the existing one) and click Save.*

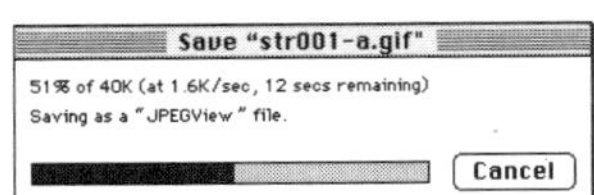

Figure 6.9 *A progress bar appears to show you how long it will take to download the image. You may continue browsing by clicking the main window.*

Saving an image

Figure 6.10 *Navigate to a Web page whose background you definitely want to have.*

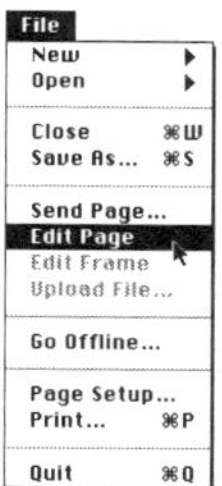

Figure 6.11 *Choose File > Edit Page.*

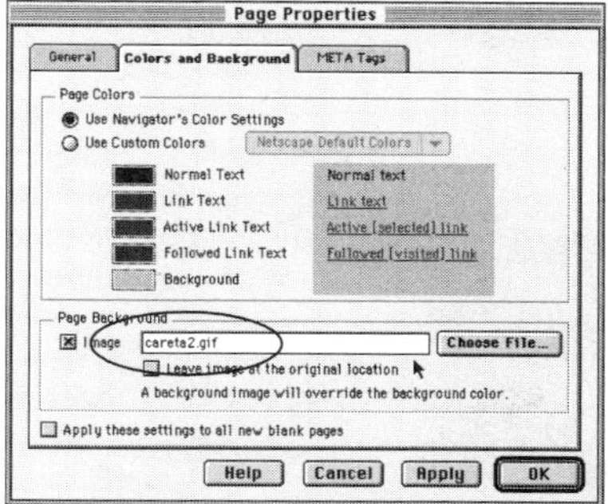

Figure 6.12 *Note the name of the background image used in the page in Figure 6.10.*

Figure 6.13 *Chose File > Save As. This action not only saves the background image, but also all the other files related to the Web page.*

Saving a background image

A background image is duplicated as necessary to fill the Navigator window and serves as the backdrop for the page's contents. You can copy a background image but be aware that when it's not used as a background (that is, when it's not repeated across the window), it may look different than you'd expect.

To save a background image:

1. Navigate to the desired page **(Figure 6.10)**.
2. Choose File > Edit Page **(Figure 6.11)**.
3. Once in the Composer window, choose Format > Page Properties. Click the Colors and Background tab in the Page Properties dialog box, and note the name for the background image in the Page Background section **(Figure 6.12)**.
4. Still in Composer, choose File > Save As **(Figure 6.13)**. Choose a destination for the files. This action copies the whole Web page with all its related files.
5. Go to the folder where you have saved the files, and locate the image file for the background.

✔ Tips

- To change an image's format, you need to use an application like GraphicConverter or Adobe Photoshop.
- To use a background image in one of your own pages (having gotten permission, if necessary), consult *Adding a background image* on page 265.

Copying an image

If you want to copy a single inline image, just selecting it with the mouse won't be enough.

To copy a single inline image:

1. Place the cursor over the desired image and press the mouse button until the pop-up menu appears.
2. Select Copy this Image in the pop-up menu **(Figure 6.14)**. The image is copied to the clipboard.
3. Switch to the application and document into which you wish to paste the copied image.
4. Choose Edit > Paste from that application. The image is pasted in the desired document **(Figure 6.15)**.

✔ Tip

- Many images on the Web are copyrighted. It is against the law to use copyrighted images without permission of the author. On the other hand, you probably won't get thrown in jail for using them in strictly personal documents like the one in Figure 6.15.

Figure 6.14 *Place the pointer over the desired image (and who has a more carefully designed image than Madonna?) and hold down the mouse button until the pop-up menu appears. Then choose Copy this Image from the menu.*

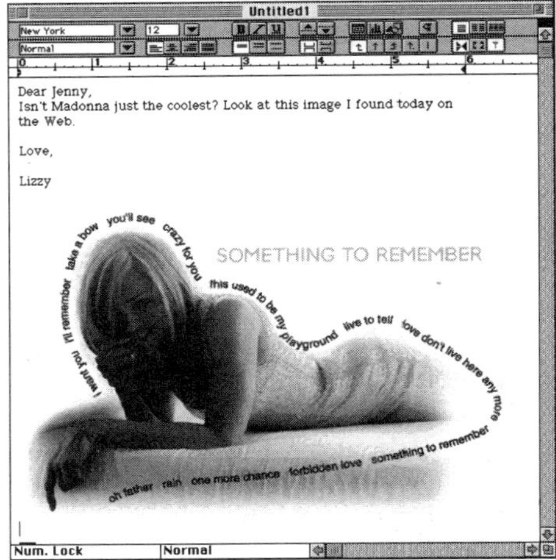

Figure 6.15 *Then paste the image into the desired document with the Paste command.*

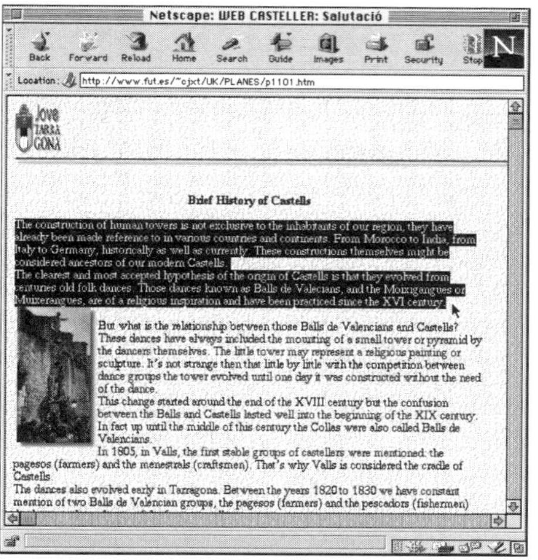

Figure 6.16 *Select (with the mouse) the part of the page that you wish to copy.*

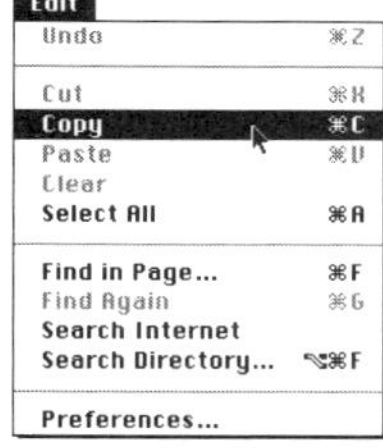

Figure 6.17 *Choose Edit > Copy.*

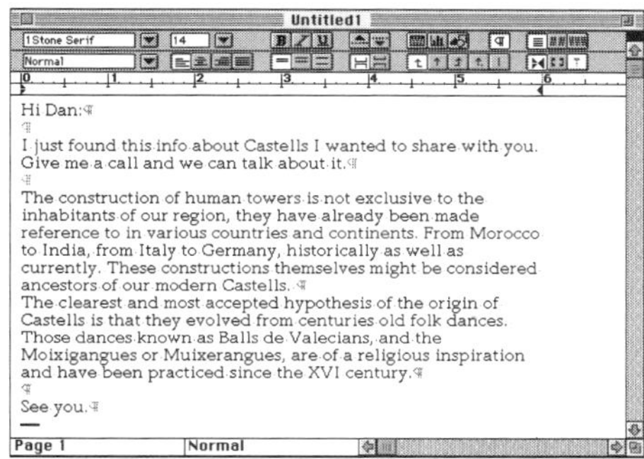
Untitled1

Hi Dan:

I just found this info about Castells I wanted to share with you. Give me a call and we can talk about it.

The construction of human towers is not exclusive to the inhabitants of our region, they have already been made reference to in various countries and continents. From Morocco to India, from Italy to Germany, historically as well as currently. These constructions themselves might be considered ancestors of our modern Castells.
The clearest and most accepted hypothesis of the origin of Castells is that they evolved from centuries old folk dances. Those dances known as Balls de Valecians, and the Moixigangues or Muixerangues, are of a religious inspiration and have been practiced since the XVI century.

See you.

Page 1 Normal

Figure 6.18 *Here I've pasted the copied material into a letter (in Microsoft Word).*

Copying and pasting parts of a page

There is no law that says you must save an entire page when you are only interested in one portion of it. In addition, copying the page as described below is a fast and easy way to transfer information to other files in other applications.

To copy and paste part of a page:

1. With the mouse, select the part of the page that you wish to copy **(Figure 6.16)**.
2. Choose Edit > Copy or press Command-C **(Figure 6.17)**.
3. Place the cursor where you want to paste the material (perhaps in an e-mail note, in another application, or wherever).
4. Choose Edit > Paste or press Command-V. The text is pasted into the current window **(Figure 6.18)**.

✓ Tips

- HTML tags and images cannot be copied using this technique. To save a page with HTML tags, consult *Saving a Web page* on page 62. To copy images, consult *Saving an image* on page 64 or *Copying an image* on page 66.
- You may not paste anything into an existing Web page in the Navigator window. Instead, open a Web page (saved with HTML tags) with a word processor—or in the Composer window *(see page 227)*—and then paste parts of other pages into it there.

Reading a saved page offline

If you've found an interesting but long page that you would like to read without hearing the connect-time clock ticking anxiously at your back, you can save the page, disconnect from your online service, and then open the page to read.

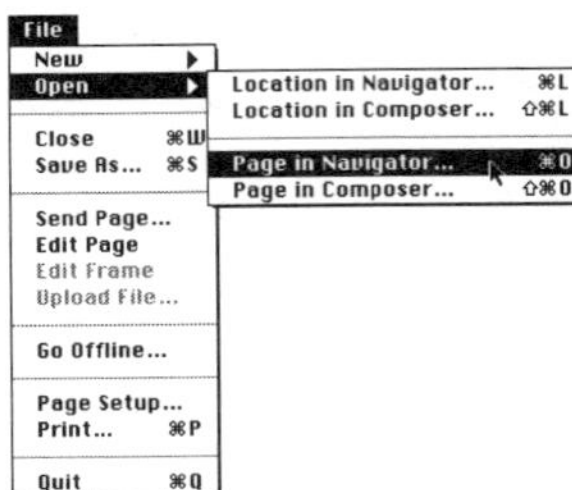

Figure 6.19 *To open a saved file, choose File > Open > Page in Navigator.*

To read a saved page offline:

1. Save the page *with HTML tags* using the techniques described on page 62 or page 63.
2. Disconnect from your online service.
3. Choose File > Open > Page in Navigator **(Figure 6.19)**. The Open dialog box appears.
4. Choose the file you saved in step 1 and click Open **(Figure 6.20)**. The page will appear in the Navigator window **(Figures 6.21 and 6.22)**.
5. Read at your leisure.

Figure 6.20 *In the Open dialog box, choose the desired file and click Open.*

Figure 6.21 *This is the original file.*

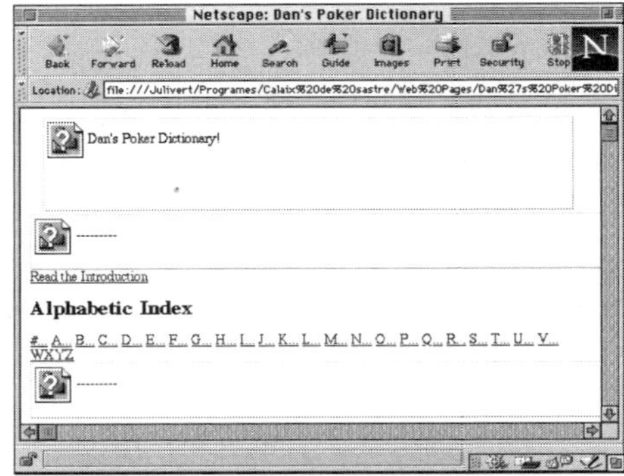

Figure 6.22 *This is the file in Figure 6.21, saved as Source. Notice how the hypertext links are intact, but all the images are substituted with placeholders. You have to save the images separately in order for them to appear.*

✔ Tips

- For another way to browse the Web offline, consult *Using Netcaster to surf offline* on page 116.
- You can also view saved GIF or JPEG images offline. Simply choose the image in step 4 above. The image appears by itself in the window.
- If you saved the page in Text format, it appears without formatting, images, or links.
- If you save the images from the page *(see page 64)*, they will appear when you browse the page offline—as long as the images are located in the same relative position on your hard disk as they occupied on the server.

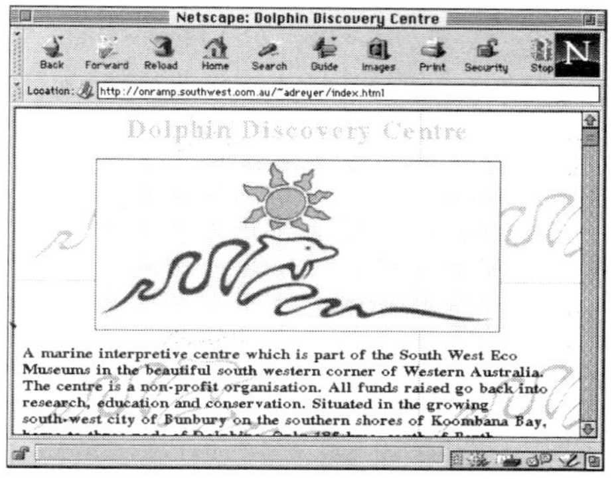

Figure 6.23 *Navigate to the page that you want to print.*

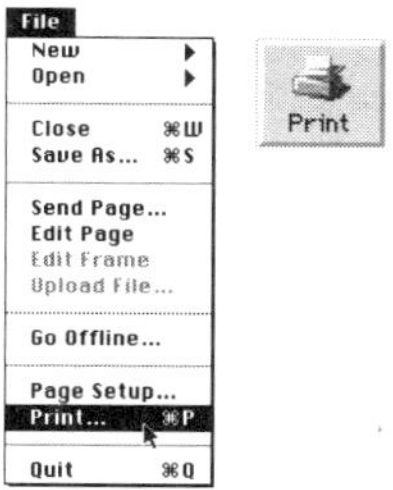

Figure 6.24 *Choose File > Print or click the Print button on the Navigation toolbar.*

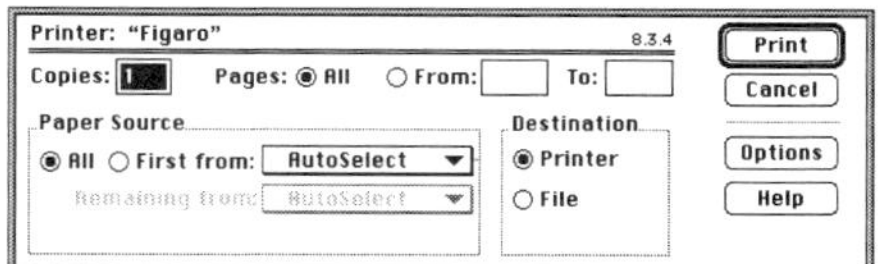

Figure 6.25 *In the standard Print dialog box, choose the desired options and then click Print.*

Printing a page

You may want to create a hard copy of one of the pages that you find on the Web for future reference. Navigator automatically resizes the information on the Web page to fit on the printed page.

To print a page:

1. Navigate to the page that you wish to print **(Figure 6.23)**.
2. Choose File > Print or click the Print button on the Navigation toolbar **(Figure 6.24)**. The standard Print dialog box appears.
3. If desired, change the printing options.
4. Click Print **(Figure 6.25)**. The page will be printed.

✔ Tips

- You can also print messages or your own pages created with Composer. Simply view the desired item before choosing File > Print.
- Print an individual frame by clicking in the frame before choosing File > Print Frame.
- A page's contents are automatically arranged according to the paper size you have selected. The width of the Navigator window is not reflected in the printout. The size of the text will be the one selected in the Fonts preferences panel *(see page 28)*.

Setting up printing options

When you print a document, you can choose to include the page number, date, location of the page (i.e., its URL), or title in the header or footer of each printed page. You can also choose to print a page's background.

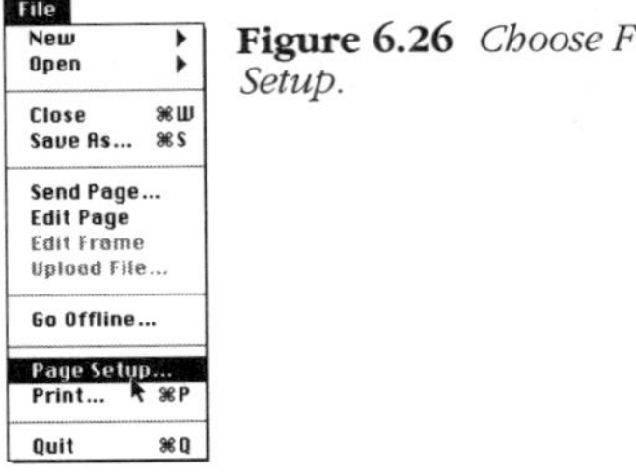

Figure 6.26 *Choose File > Page Setup.*

To set the printing options:

1. Choose File > Page Setup **(Figure 6.26)**. The Page Setup dialog box appears **(Figure 6.27)**.
2. In the Header section, select the item (Page Number, Date, Location or Title) in the pop-up menu under the desired area where you want that item to be printed in the header.
3. Repeat step 2 for the Footer section.
4. Click Print Backgrounds if you want to include colorful or image-based backgrounds when you print a Web page. Leave the option unchecked to print pages with a white background.
5. Click OK to save the options.

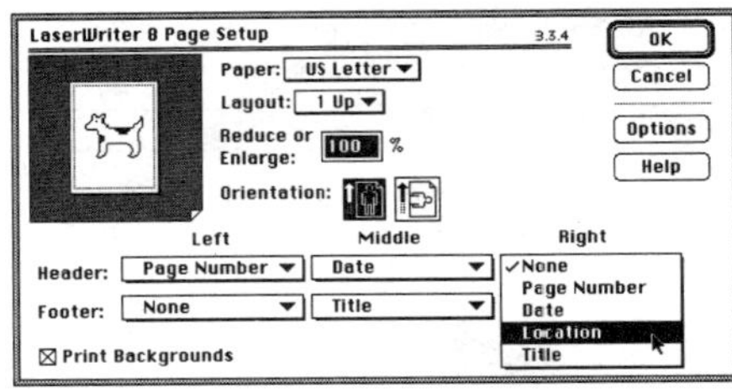

Figure 6.27 *Choose the element from the pop-up menu that represents the desired position where you want to print that element on the page. In the example, I've chosen Location in the top right pop-up menu—in the Header row under Right. Therefore, when I print this page, the Location will be printed at the right side of the header.*

✓ Tip

- The options in the Page Setup dialog box affect all the pages you print from that moment onwards, not just the current document.

7 Finding Stuff on the Web

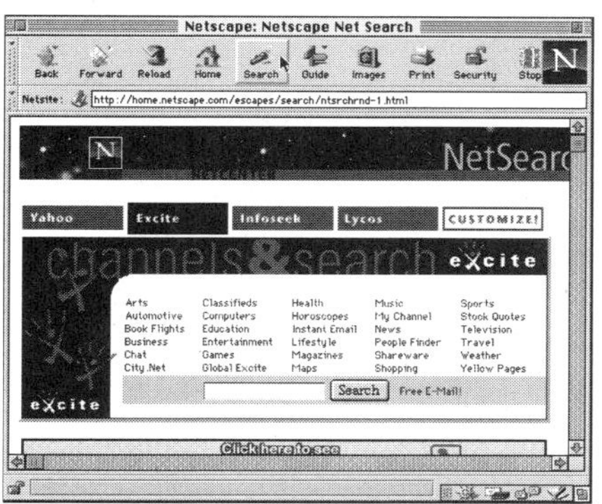

Figure 7.1 *The Search button brings you to a page created by Netscape Communications with links to several Web-wide search services.*

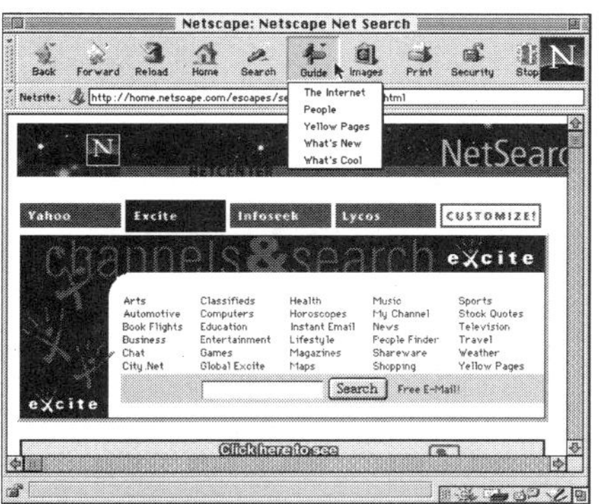

Figure 7.2 *Click the Guide button and choose an item from its menu to see the pages that the folks at Netscape Communications think might be of interest to you.*

With millions of Web pages, fourteen thousand newsgroups, and countless e-mail users, it is sometimes a challenge to find the information that you're looking for. There are many companies that offer Internet search services in exchange for a glance at their advertisers' promotions.

There are services that search Web pages, services that search newsgroups, services that search for e-mail addresses, and even services that catalog shareware. You simply jump to the service that is most likely to have the information you need.

Searching vs. finding

Navigator distinguishes between searching the Web and finding text on a particular page. The new Search button on the toolbar **(Figure 7.1)** connects you to several Web-wide search services, some of which are discussed on the following pages. There is also a new Guide button that points you to several pages that Netscape Communications thinks might be of interest to you **(Figure 7.2)**.

To find something on a page, instead of using the Find button that was available on the toolbar in earlier versions of the software, use the Find in Page command in the Edit menu. For more information, consult *Finding information in an open page* on page 80.

Finding Web pages by subject

One of the best known Web page search indexes is Yahoo!. Yahoo! sorts its Web index by topic, and creates a kind of Table of Contents for the Web. If you want to see several pages about the same or related general topics, or if you just want a place to start surfing, Yahoo! is a good place to begin.

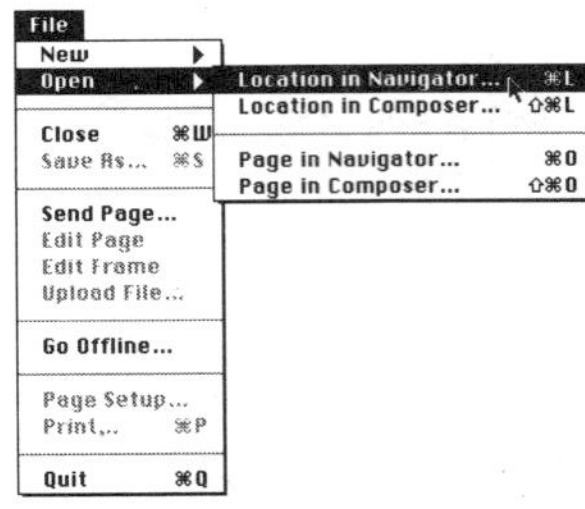

Figure 7.3 *Choose File > Open > Location in Navigator.*

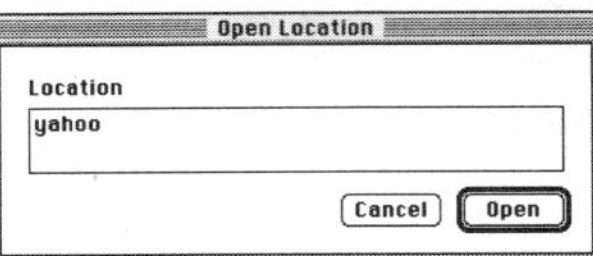

Figure 7.4 *Type Yahoo's URL in the Open Location dialog box.*

Figure 7.5 *You can also type the address (or just plain* **yahoo***) right in the Location toolbar and then press Return.*

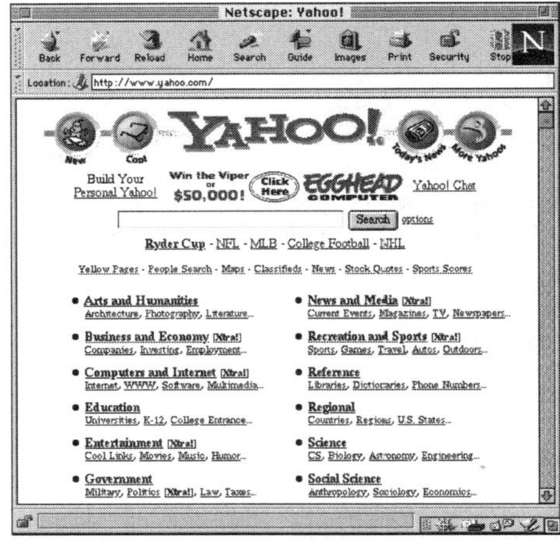

Figure 7.6 *The Yahoo! home page is divided into categories and subcategories, according to topic, all of which contain links to related articles.*

To use Yahoo! to find Web pages by topic:

1. Choose File > Open > Location in Navigator **(Figure 7.3)**. The Open Location dialog box appears **(Figure 7.4)**.
2. Type Yahoo!'s URL address (or just **yahoo**) in the text box and click Open. Navigator displays the Yahoo! home page **(Figure 7.6)**. Each main topic is divided into clickable subtopics.
3. Click any topic or subtopic of interest. Yahoo! displays a set of related links **(Figure 7.7)**. The links may be divided into indices (lists of related links), subtopics (which when clicked on reveal a list of links to pages about the subtopic), or Web pages (that fit the general topic but none of the subtopics listed).
4. Click the desired link **(Figure 7.8)**. The page is displayed.

✔ Tip

- You can also search for keywords through Yahoo! by entering the words in the text box and clicking Search. However, there are other services that are better at straight word searches.

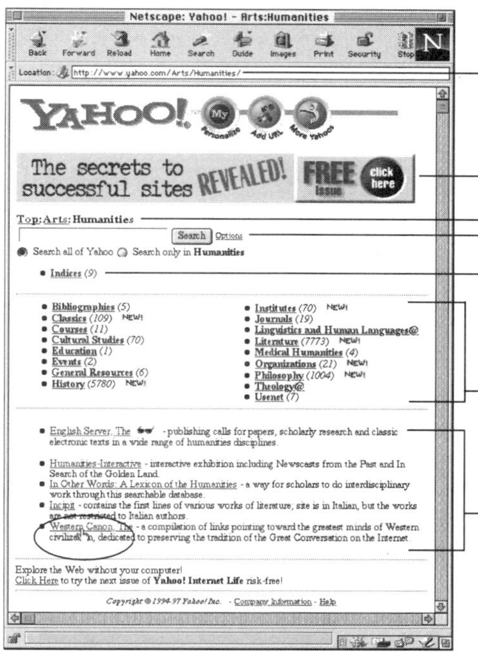

Figure 7.7 *A click on Humanities brings up this page of related links, divided into subcategories.*

Yahoo's address is displayed in the Location text box.

Advertisements are sprinkled liberally throughout the Yahoo! site. This is how Yahoo! makes money, but you don't have to pay attention.

Yahoo! always lists the path that you have taken. You can click on the links to the earlier pages to go back (up) in the hierarchy of categories.

You can also choose to search for a keyword, either in the entire Yahoo! index, or just in the pages that are in the currently selected category.

The Indices are pages that contain a collection of links to the main topic (Humanities, in this case).

Yahoo! divides all the articles into subcategories. The number after each category indicates how many articles it contains. An @ symbol means that the subcategory is further divided into smaller subcategories.

The articles that are related to the main category (Humanities) but that don't fit into any subcategories, are listed at the bottom of the page.

Figure 7.8 *A click on a link in Figure 7.7 brings you to the corresponding article out on the Web. You are no longer at the Yahoo! site.*

The selected page is not part of the Yahoo! site; Yahoo! just helped you find it. This page is just like any other Web page on the Net created from some individual's effort.

Searching for Web pages by keyword

There are two or three good search services that have indexed as much of the Web as they can find—by sending out automatic robots called *spiders* that go from server to server looking at all the Web pages and recording their addresses, titles, and sometimes even their contents. One comprehensive service I've found is AltaVista (by Digital), that claims to include some 30 million pages in its index.

Figure 7.9 *AltaVista's home page (at the time this was written).*

To search for Web pages by keyword with AltaVista:

1. Choose File > Open > Location in Navigator. The Open Location dialog box appears.
2. Type **altavista.digital.com** and click Open. Navigator displays AltaVista's home page **(Figure 7.9)**.
3. Type a word or phrase in the text box **(Figure 7.10)**.
4. Choose where you wish AltaVista to search in the left pop-up menu. Choose the Web for Web pages and Usenet for newsgroup articles.
5. If desired, click the Preferences link to choose how results should be displayed, as well as the languages you want to include in your search. Click on Set Preferences **(Figure 7.11)**.
6. Click Search or press Enter to start the search. AltaVista shows the links to the pages that satisfied the search criteria **(Figure 7.12)**.
7. If desired, click Next or the page numbers to see more matches.
8. Click on one of the links to display the corresponding page **(Figure 7.13)**.

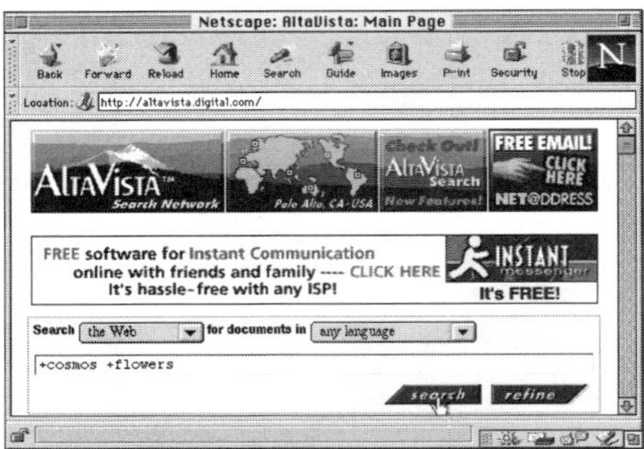

Figure 7.10 *Type the criteria (first,* cosmos, *and then,* flowers*). Use plus signs before the words to ensure that every page includes that word.*

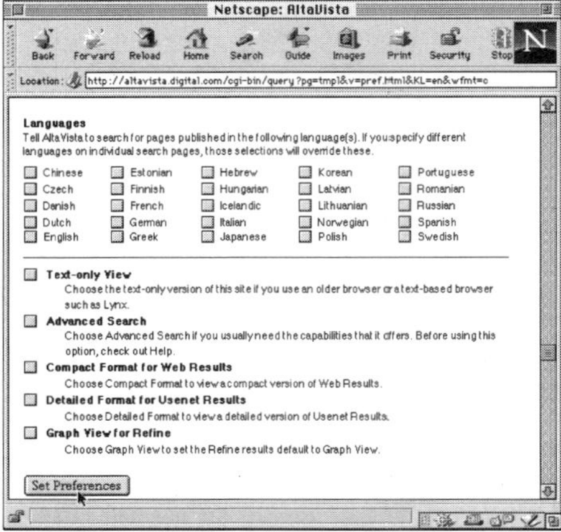

Figure 7.11 *On the Preferences page, select the desired default settings for your searches.*

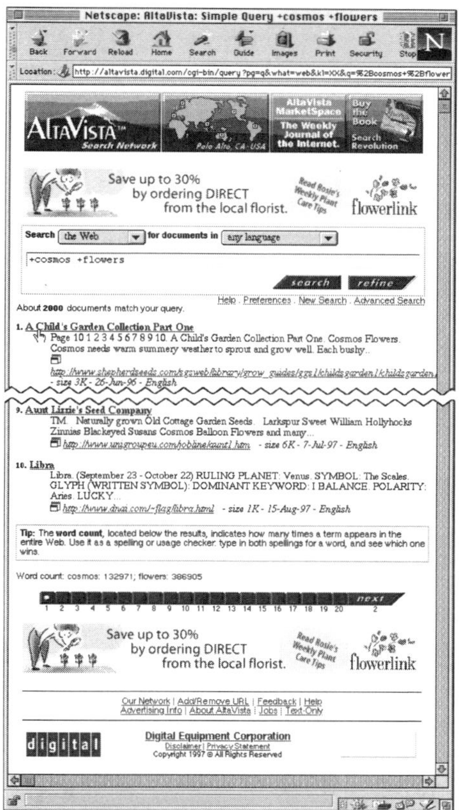

Figure 7.12 *AltaVista lists the pages that meet the criteria. Click on a page to jump to it (as in "A Child's Garden Collection Part One," here). Click on Next or on a particular page number at the bottom of the list to see that page of links.*

Figure 7.13 *The desired page is shown in the browser.*

✔ Tips

- Make sure you spell the keyword(s) correctly. If you type "Catchmear" when looking for lush, goat fiber, you are likely to be disappointed.
- Precede words that *must* appear on the page with a plus sign (+) and words that you wish to *exclude* with a minus sign (-).
- Use the asterisk (*) as a wild card to find alternate spellings. For example, type **theat*** to find both *theater* and *theatre.*
- Search for a contiguous phrase in a page by inserting the words in double quotes: **"The New York Times"**.
- Use uppercase letters to restrict the search to words with those uppercase letters. Lowercase letters are case-insensitive. (**Frank** finds only *Frank*; **frank** finds both *Frank* and *frank.*)
- To find pages with links to *your* page, type **link:url**, replacing *url* with the URL of your page. To omit links to your pages from your own pages (you've already seen those!), add **-url:yoursitesname.com**.
- In AltaVista's advanced query area, you can use operators like *Near* to find people like Ronnie Schwartz (type Ronnie NEAR Schwartz).
- Lycos *(http://www.lycos.com)*, Excite *(http://www.excite.com)*, and HotBot *(http://www.hotbot.com/)* are three other word-based Web search services.
- Review AltaVista's Help pages (click on the Help link) to get more information on refined searches.

Searching for people and organizations

Remember Marina Laboy from high school? Haven't talked to her lately? Maybe you can find her. There are several services that give you access to most white page directories in the US, and even some from abroad. Some services also point you to e-mail and postal addresses.

To search for a person's phone number or address:

1. Choose File > Open Page.
2. Type **four11** in the text box and click Open to display Four11's home page **(Figure 7.14)**.
3. Click Telephone under Directories in the left column.
4. Type the person's name in the text boxes at the right.
5. If desired, enter information about the person's address.
6. Click Search. Four11 displays the results as links, and gives city information to help you choose **(Figure 7.15)**.
7. Click a name to see the full address and phone **(Figure 7.16)**.

✔ Tips

- Although you can use Four11 (and others) to search for e-mail addresses in Navigator, Communicator has a built-in search system *(see page 177)*.
- Other good search services for finding long lost friends are Bigfoot (www.bigfoot.com) and WhoWhere? (www.whowhere.com).

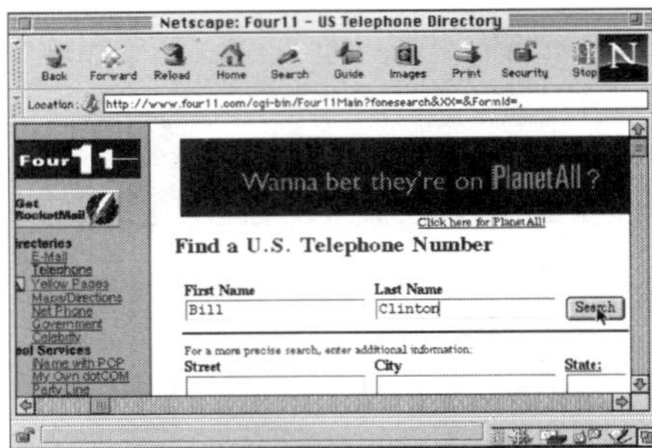

Figure 7.14 *Click Telephone to find a person's phone number or postal address. Then type the person's name. Finally, click the Search button.*

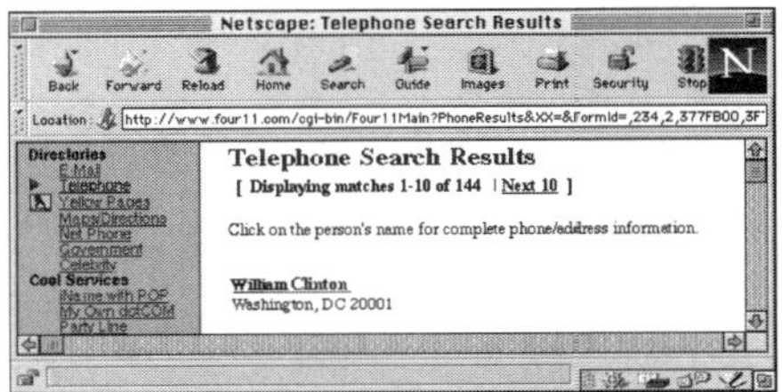

Figure 7.15 *Click on a name to see the full address and phone. Four11 does a smart search on names, finding* William *even though I typed* Bill.

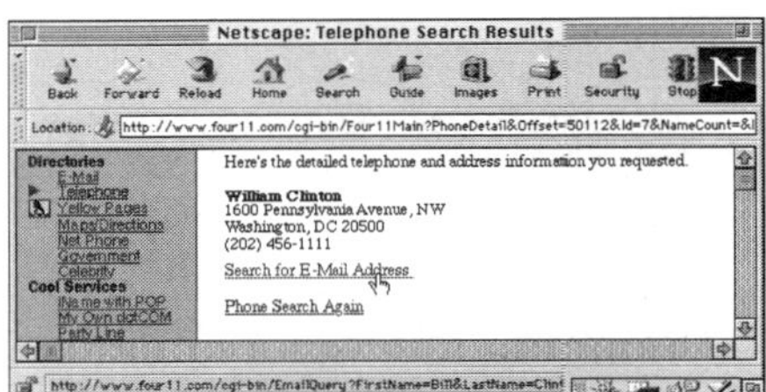

Figure 7.16 *The full address of the person is listed. Click Search for E-Mail Address to use the same criteria to find the person's electronic address.*

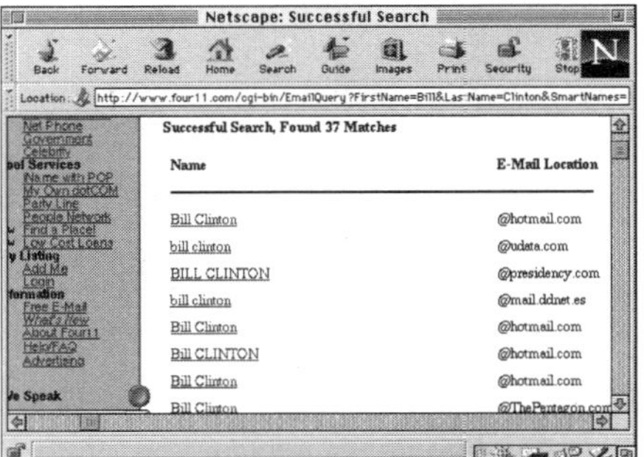

Figure 7.17 *Four11 lists the e-mail addresses that match all the criteria shown.*

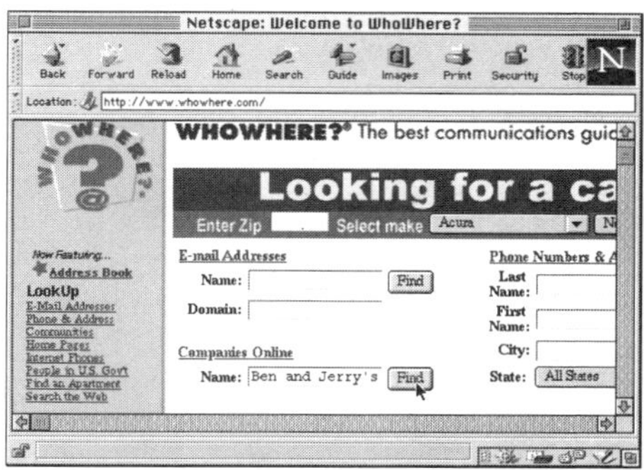

Figure 7.18 *Type the name of the organization in the text box under Companies Online and click Find.*

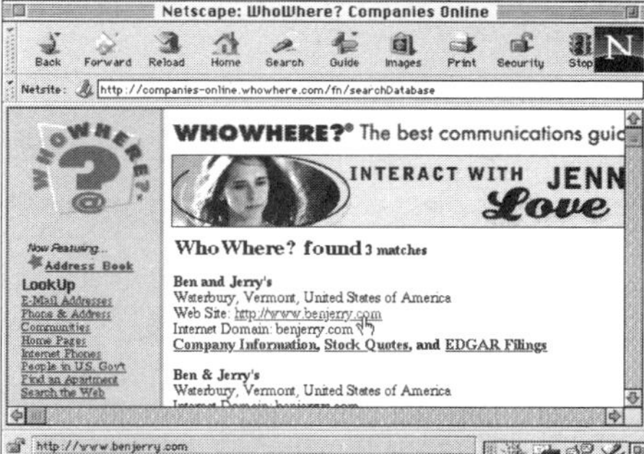

Figure 7.19 *In the list that appears, click the organization that you were looking for.*

Figure 7.20 *The organization's home page is displayed in the browser.*

You can also use Navigator to find a company's or organization's Web site. Though many organizations have guessable URLs in the form of *www.organization.com,* others do not. Services like WhoWhere? bridge the gap.

To find an organization:

1. Jump to WhoWhere?'s site (http://www.whowhere.com).
2. Type the name of the company under Companies Online **(Figure 7.18)**.
3. Click the Find button or press Return. WhoWhere? shows you the links to the pages that satisfy the search criteria **(Figure 7.19)**.
4. Click on the desired link. (Links to organizations tend to be Web pages as opposed to e-mail addresses.) The newly found page is displayed **(Figure 7.20)**.

✔ Tip

- Before doing a search, try typing **www.organization.com** in the Open Page dialog box or in the Location field, where *organization* is the name of the company you're looking for. Theoretically, you could just type **organization** *(see page 35)* but I've had better luck typing the whole thing. If the name has a space (like Ben and Jerry's), you'll have to search for the proper address, since URLs cannot contain a space.

Finding an article in a discussion group

There are over 14,000 discussion groups, and each of them receives from several to several hundred messages a day. Finding a message that deals with a particular topic can be difficult. You can use Deja News to search for discussion group messages.

To do a quick search for an article in a discussion group:

1. Choose File > Open > Location in Navigator.
2. Type **dejanews** in the text box and click Open.
3. In the Deja News home page that appears, type the search criteria, and click the Find button **(Figure 7.21)**.
4. Deja News lists the articles that fit the criteria **(Figure 7.22)**. Click an article that interests you to view that message. The message is shown in the Navigator window, not the Message window **(Figure 7.23)**.
5. If desired, you can reply to the posting by clicking Post Message. Deja News has its own system for posting messages to discussion groups.

✔ Tips

- You can also refine requests further by clicking Power Search on Deja News' home page.
- You can also use AltaVista *(see page 74)* and other search services to search for discussion group articles.

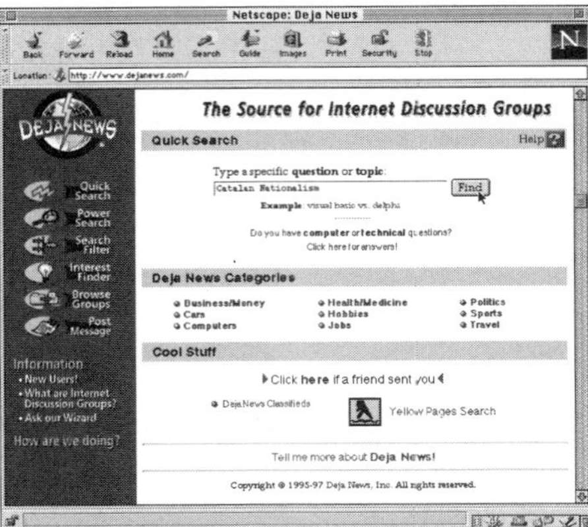

Figure 7.21 *In Deja News' home page, type the search criteria and click Find.*

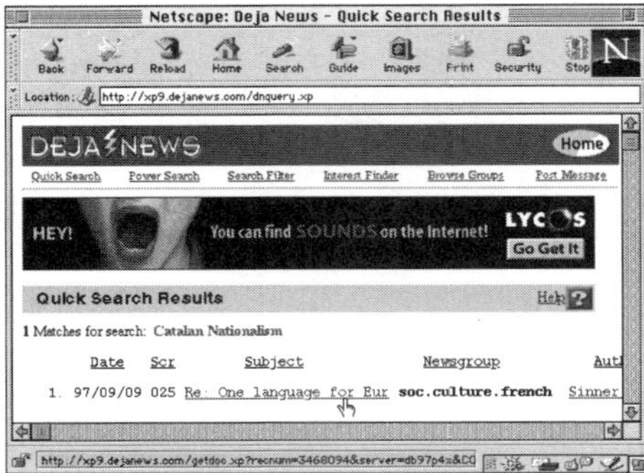

Figure 7.22 *By default, the articles are listed in abbreviated form. Click the desired article to read it.*

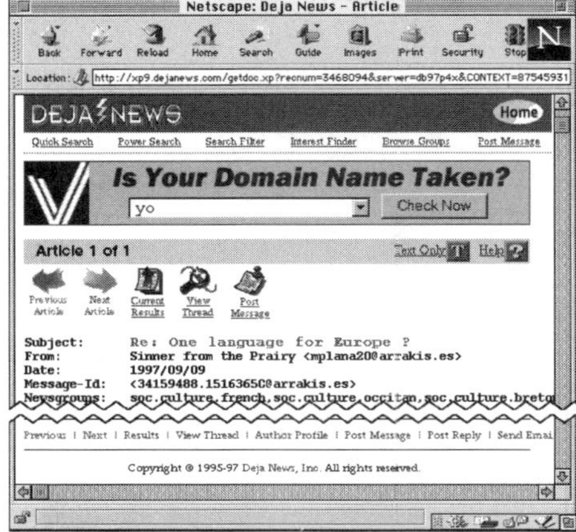

Figure 7.23 *The news posting appears in the Navigator window. To reply, click Post Message.*

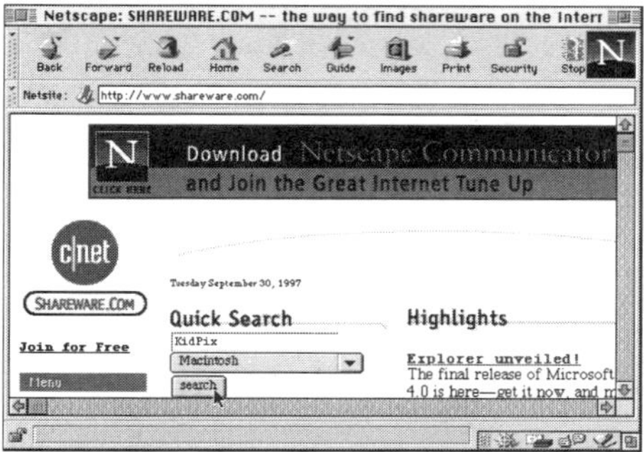

Figure 7.24 *In C/net's home page, choose the appropriate platform (I've chosen Macintosh) and the keywords (in this example, KidPix). Click the search button.*

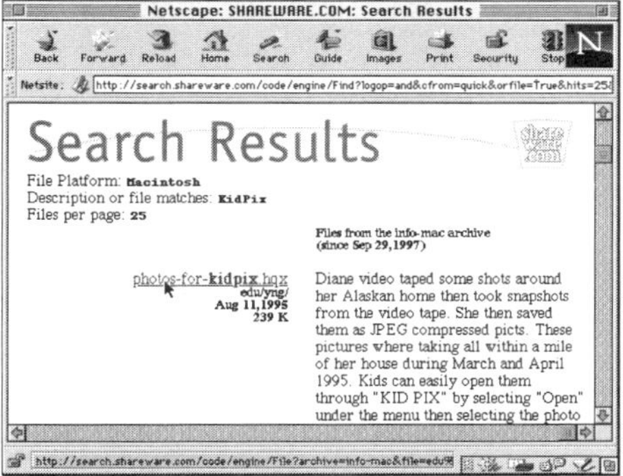

Figure 7.25 *The shareware programs or updates that satisfy the criteria given in the Search window (Figure 7.24) are listed. Click one to see the available FTP sites.*

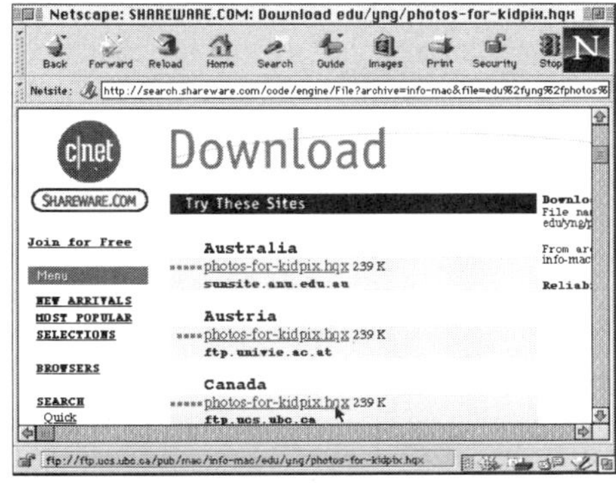

Figure 7.26 *When you click a file to download, shareware.com lists the FTP sites where you can find it. Click an FTP site to download the file to your computer.*

Finding shareware through the Web

Sometimes, the hardest part about downloading a file is finding it. One service that provides you with the FTP addresses for over 160,000 shareware programs (as well as commercial software updates) is shareware.com by C/net.

To find shareware through the Web:

1. Choose File > Open > Location in Navigator.
2. Type **shareware** in the text box and click Open. The C/net home page appears.
3. Choose the desired platform in the pop-up menu **(Figure 7.24)**.
4. Type the appropriate keywords in the text field.
5. Click search. The shareware files that satisfy the criteria given are listed **(Figure 7.25)**.
6. Click the desired file to list the FTP sites where it can be found **(Figure 7.26)**.
7. Click the desired FTP site to download the file to your computer. For more information on FTP transfers, consult *Downloading files* on page 58.

Finding information in an open page

Once you've searched the Web with the services described on the preceding pages, you may find a page that contains the information you want—somewhere in there. If the page is very long, you can use the Find in Page command to jump directly to the desired word or phrase.

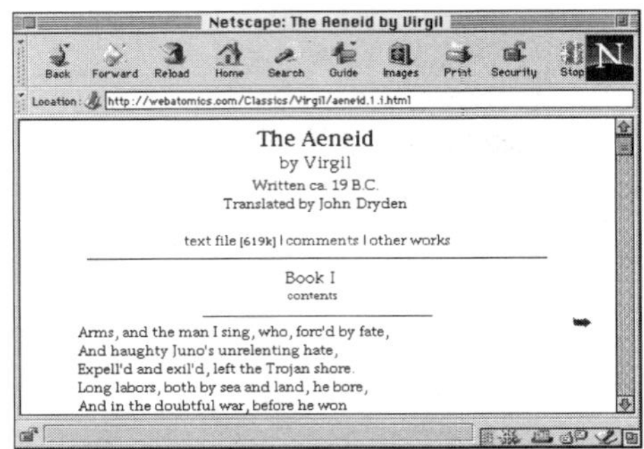

Figure 7.27 *Jump to the page where you want to perform your search.*

To find information in an open page:

1. Jump to the desired page **(Fig. 7.27)**.

Figure 7.28 *Choose Edit > Find in Page.*

2. Choose Edit > Find in Page **(Figure 7.28)**. The Find On Page dialog box appears.

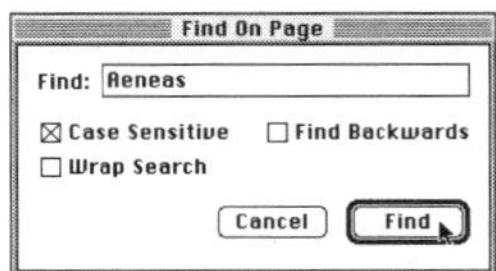

Figure 7.29 *Type the text you're looking for and click Find.*

3. Type the word or phrase that you wish to look for and click Find **(Figure 7.29)**. Navigator will highlight the first occurrence of the word, if any, in the currently open page **(Figure 7.30)**.

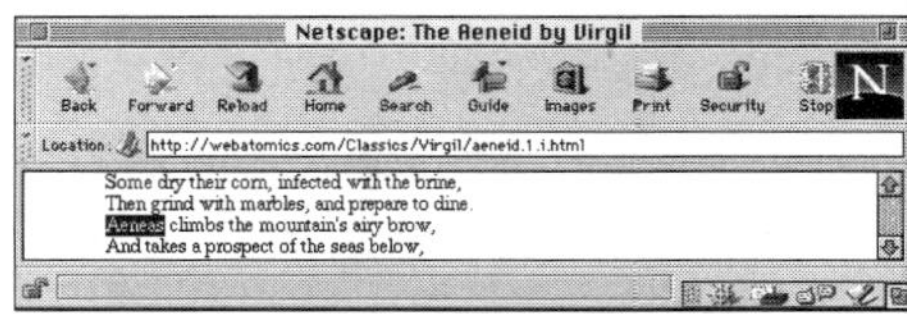

Figure 7.30 *Navigator highlights the found text. If this is the text you want, click on the page to work with it.*

4. If desired, choose Edit > Find Again to find the next occurrence of the search word or phrase **(Figure 7.31)**.

Figure 7.31 *Choose Edit > Find Again to find the next occurrence of the text in the open page.*

Figure 7.32 *Click Netscape's logo to jump to Netscape Communication's home page.*

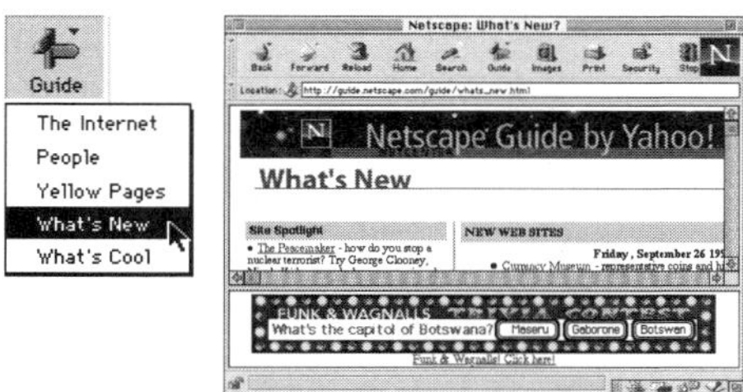

Figure 7.33 *Choose What's New to see which sites Netscape has discovered lately.*

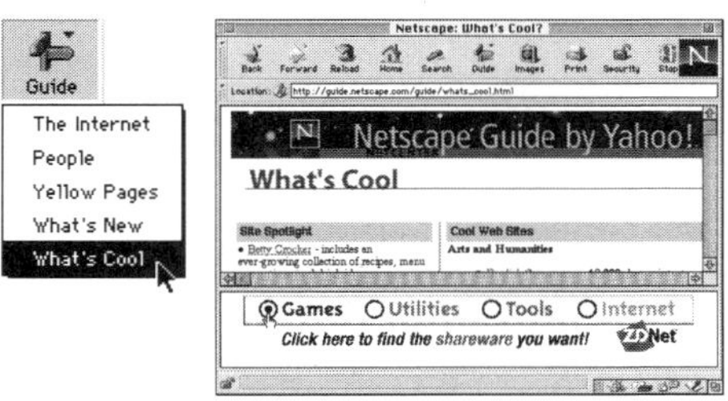

Figure 7.34 *Choose What's Cool in the Guide menu to see what Netscape Corporation considers a "cool" page.*

Figure 7.35 *Click the Guide button on the Navigation toolbar and then choose The Internet, People, or Yellow Pages in the pop-up menu.*

Checking out Netscape's pages

Some of Navigator's menu commands take you to particular pages on the Web (mostly on Netscape's own site). Some of these sites are kind of helpful. Some are less so.

To find Netscape's home page:

Click the Netscape icon at the right side of the Navigation toolbar **(Figure 7.32)**. Netscape Communications' home page is displayed in the Navigator window (as long as you're connected to the Internet).

To find new pages (according to Netscape):

Click the Guide button on the Navigation toolbar and then choose What's New in the pop-up menu **(Figure 7.33)**.

To find cool pages (according to Netscape):

Click the Guide button on the Navigation toolbar and then choose What's Cool in the pop-up menu **(Figure 7.34)**.

To use Netscape's links to Web search services:

Click the Guide button on the Navigation toolbar. A pop-up menu appears. Choose The Internet to see Netscape and Yahoo's collaborative effort at providing a customizable guide to the Internet. Choose People to find links to services specializing in white pages searches. Choose Yellow Pages for links to sites that sell and distribute advertising space to businesses across the United States **(Figure 7.35)**.

Getting help with Navigator

Navigator has a contextual help system that works just like a system of Web pages.

To read Navigator's documentation:

Choose Help > Help Contents **(Figure 7.36)**. Navigator's help file is displayed **(Figure 7.37)**. You can also access the help file by clicking the Help button in any dialog box that has one. The file automatically displays help for the dialog box where you started.

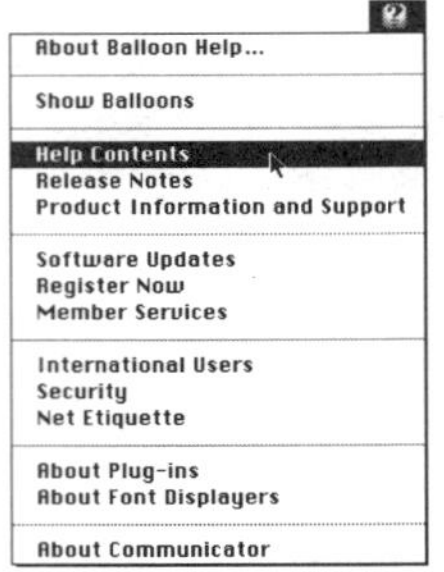

Figure 7.36 *Choose Help > Help Contents.*

Figure 7.37 *If you open the Help file by clicking on a Help button, the file automatically jumps to the appropriate section.*

FAQ, which rhymes with *smack*, stands for Frequently Asked Questions. The *Netscape UFAQ* is an unofficial list of such questions, compiled by many of the folks who frequent the Netscape newsgroups (see Tip). It's pretty helpful.

To find the Netscape UFAQ:

1. Choose File > Open > Location in Navigator **(Figure 7.38)**.
2. Type **http://www.sousystems.com/faq/default.htm**. The UFAQ page is displayed **(Figure 7.39)**.
3. The UFAQ is divided by platform. Browse through until you find what you need.

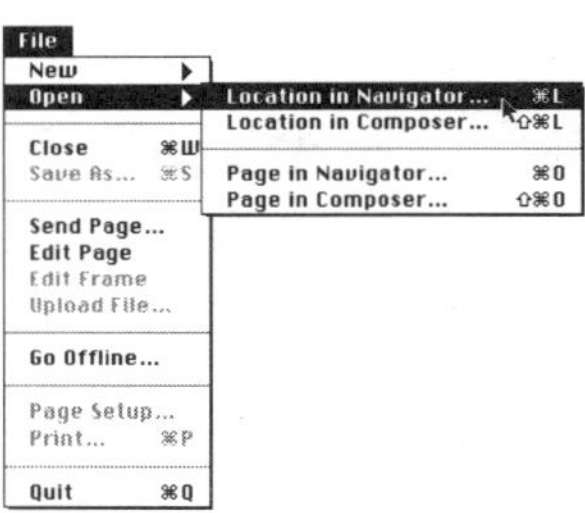

Figure 7.38 *Choose File > Open > Location in Navigator.*

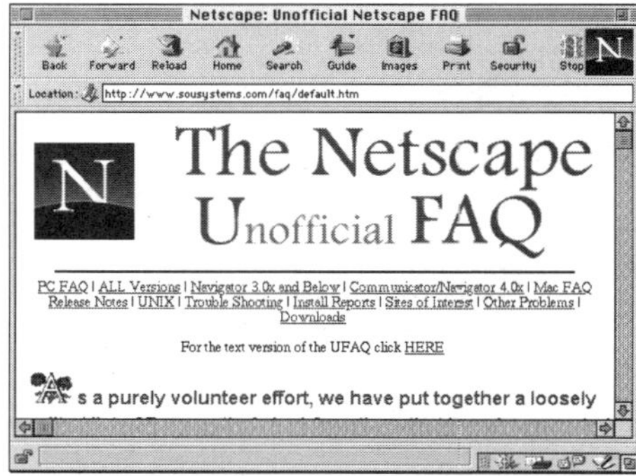

Figure 7.39 *The Netscape Unofficial FAQ page contains many common questions (and answers!) about Netscape Navigator and Communicator.*

✔ Tip

- One more good source for help on specific Navigator functions is the Netscape Communicator newsgroup (snews://secnews.netscape.com/netscape.communicator.mac). For more information on joining discussion groups, consult *Subscribing to a discussion group* on page 131.

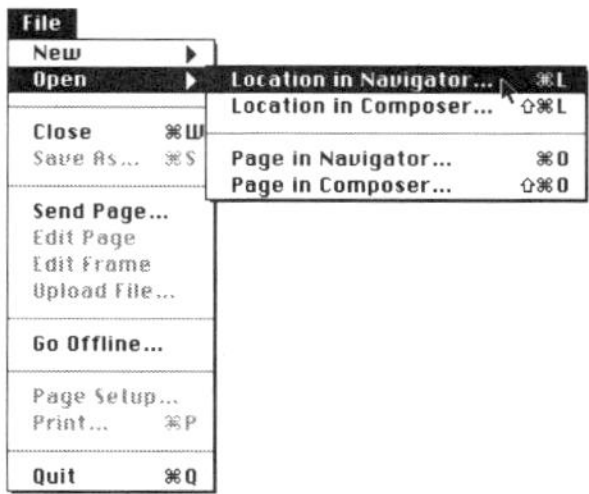

Figure 7.40 *Choose File > Open > Location in Navigator.*

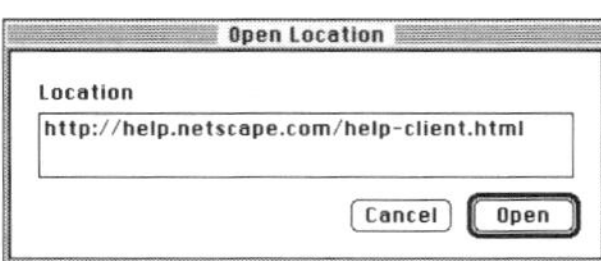

Figure 7.41 *Type the URL address for the support request form in the Open Location dialog box.*

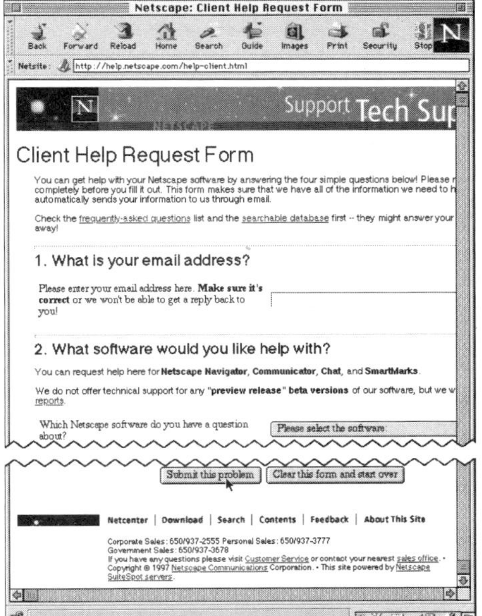

Figure 7.42 *Fill out the Client Help Request Form (it's long) and then click the Submit this problem button at the bottom of the page.*

Finding technical support

Netscape is pretty stingy with technical support. It offers free telephone support to registered users for installation only. If you have questions on any other topics, it'll cost you $25 per "incident."

To get free installation help by telephone:

Call 1-800-639-0939. For more information on pricing, consult *http://help.netscape.com/contact.html.*

Once you begin paying Netscape for support, you can also request help via e-mail.

To send a message to Netscape technical support:

1. Choose File > Open > Location in Navigator **(Figure 7.40)**. The Open Location dialog box appears **(Figure 7.41)**.
2. Type **http://help.netscape.com/help-client.html**.
3. Fill out the form **(Figure 7.42)**.
4. Click Submit this problem at the bottom of the page. As long as you are a registered user, you should receive a notification in a couple of hours and a response within a few days.

✓ Tip

- Choose Help > Product Information and Support to get complete information on the technical support solutions that Netscape sells.

Finding info about your Netscape software

Navigator's menus offer ways to get information about the software itself. You can find out what version you have, what plug-ins you have installed, what your registration number is, what upgrade options you have, and what new features have been added to the program since your version was released.

To get information about your Netscape software:

1. Choose Help > About Communicator. The version number of your software is displayed **(Figure 7.43)**. (You can also choose this command in the Apple menu.)

2. Choose Help > About Plug-ins. A list of the currently installed plug-ins is displayed **(Figure 7.44)**.

3. Choose Help > About Font Displayers. Information about the plug-in specifically designed to display fonts in your Web pages is shown. Choose the desired displayers and click OK.

4. Choose Help > Register Now. The registration options and benefits are displayed **(Figure 7.45)**.

5. Choose Help > Software Updates. Navigator displays the various upgrade options for your version of Communicator **(Figure 7.46)**. Although the command is called *Software Updates,* Netscape refers to the feature as *SmartUpdate.*

6. Choose Help > Release Notes. A list of the new features included in your copy of Communicator appears **(Figure 7.47)**.

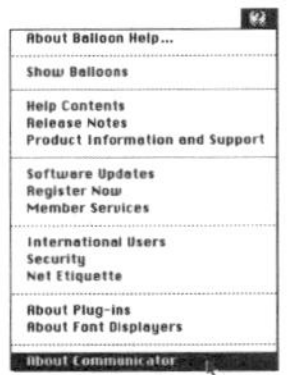

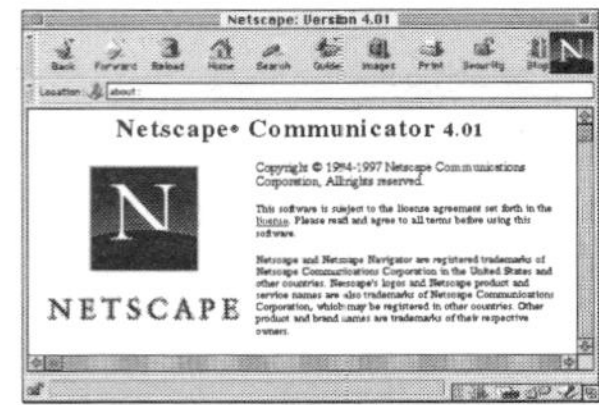

Figure 7.43 *Choose Help > About Communicator to see what version of the program you are using.*

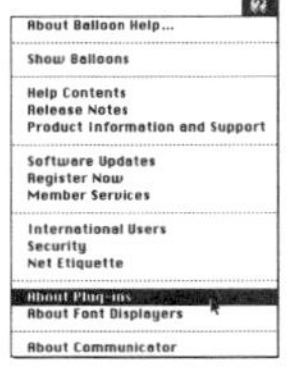
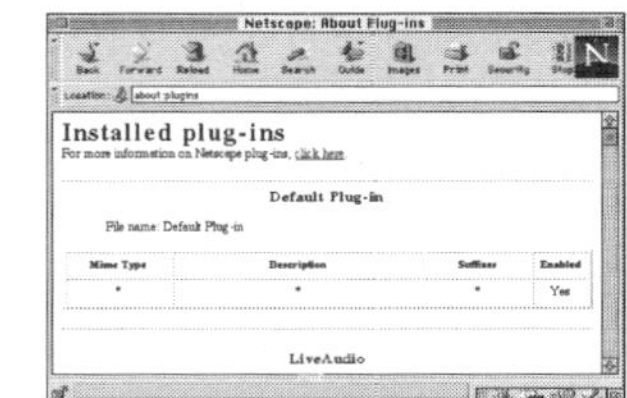

Figure 7.44 *Choose Help > About Plug-ins to see which plug-ins you have installed.*

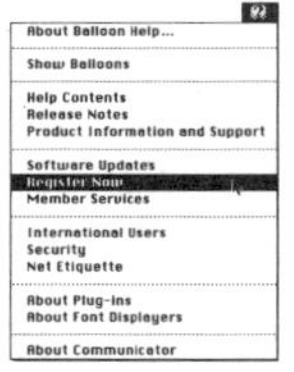
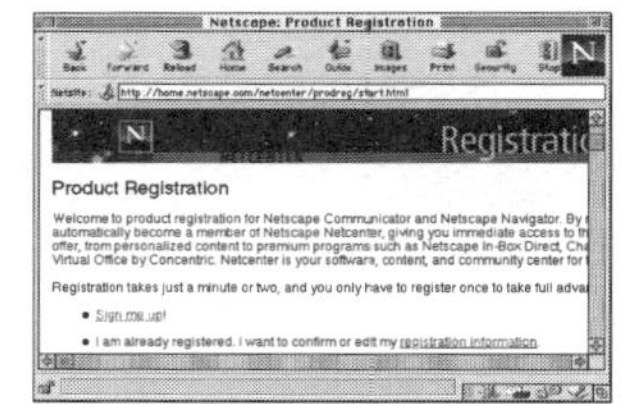

Figure 7.45 *Choose Help > Register Now to register the program or see your registration ID.*

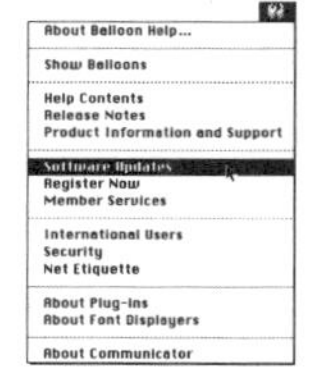

Figure 7.46 *Choose Help > Software Updates to see the upgrades for your version of Communicator.*

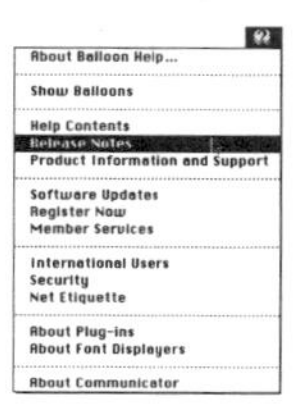
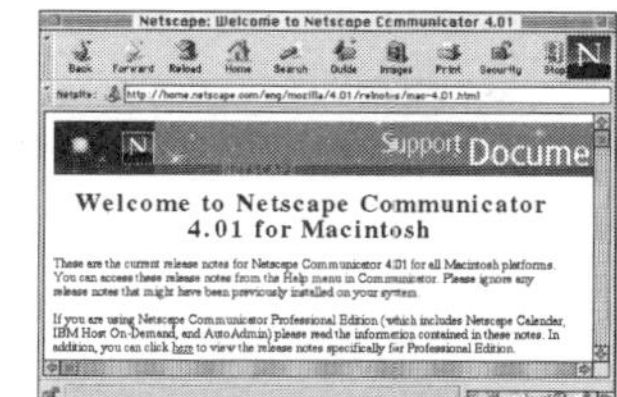

Figure 7.47 *Choose Help > Release Notes to see a list of new features for your version of Communicator.*

8

Bookmarks

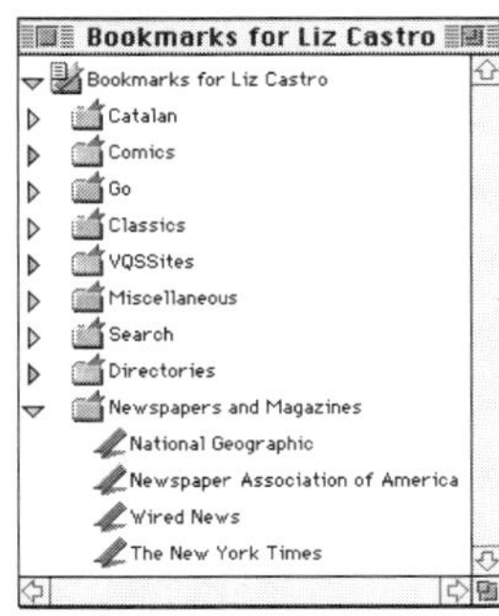

Figure 8.1 *The Bookmarks window helps you organize your favorite sites and get back to them with a simple double click.*

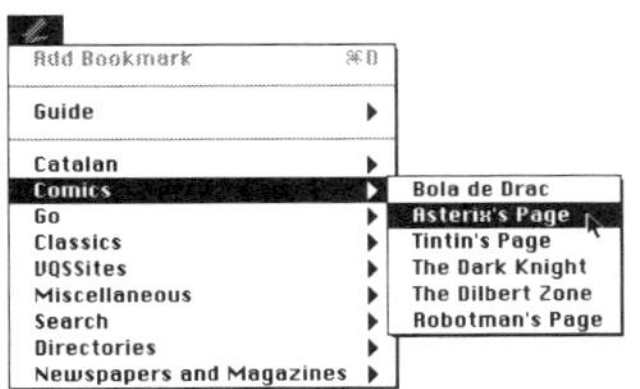

Figure 8.2 *In the Bookmarks menu, choose the page you wish to jump to.*

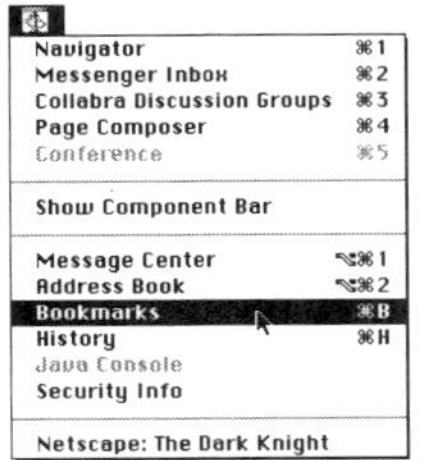

Figure 8.3 *To open the Bookmarks window, choose Communicator > Bookmarks.*

What is a bookmark?

There are millions of Web pages already in existence. If someday you should find a link to a gem of a page, you won't want to lose it. With Communicator you can store the URL addresses to your favorite sites as *bookmarks*. The next time you want to jump to that site, instead of trying to remember the circuitous route you took the first time, simply pull down your Bookmarks menu, choose a bookmark, and sail in. Or surf. Whatever.

Bookmarks are edited and organized in the Bookmarks window which you can display on screen or hide at your convenience **(Figure 8.1)**. They are also listed at the bottom of the Bookmarks menu ( ) for easy access **(Figure 8.2)**.

To open the Bookmarks window:

Choose (Communicator) > Bookmarks **(Figure 8.3)**. The Bookmarks window appears.

Using bookmarks to navigate the Web

Bookmarks make it easy to find your way back to favorite sites. The truth is, typing URLs is a pain. It's easy to mix up lower- and uppercase letters, leave off a forward slash, or simply misspell part of the address. Navigating with bookmarks is a breeze—select a location and you're there.

To navigate with the Bookmarks menu:

Pull down the Bookmarks menu in the menu bar ( ) and then choose the desired Web page from the list **(Figure 8.4)**. The page is loaded into the Navigator window **(Figure 8.7)**.

To navigate with the Bookmarks window:

1. Open the Bookmarks window *(see page 85)*.
2. Double click a bookmark to jump to the corresponding Web page. You may also click once on a bookmark and choose File > Go to Bookmark **(Figures 8.5 and 8.6)**. The page is displayed in the Navigator window **(Figure 8.7)**.

✔ Tip

- Double click a folder in the Bookmarks window to open it and see its contents or to close it and hide its contents. You can tell that a folder is open by the arrow to its right. If the arrow points to the folder, the folder is closed. If the arrow points down, the folder is open.

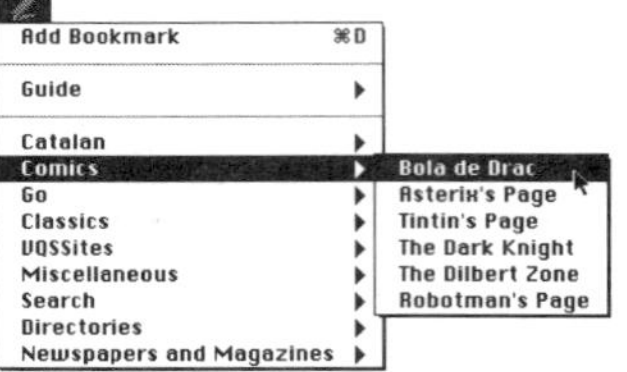

Figure 8.4 *If you don't have the Bookmarks window open, it may be faster to use the Bookmarks menu. Simply select the page desired to jump to it.*

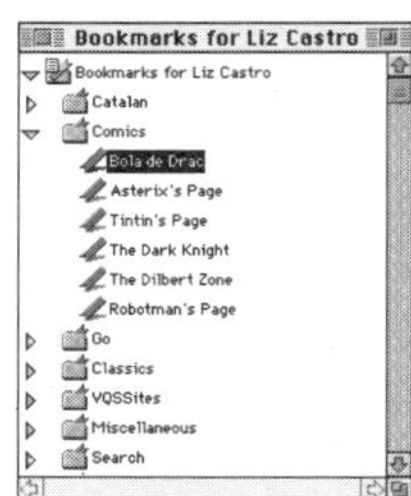

Figure 8.5 *Select a bookmark in the Bookmarks window.*

Figure 8.6 *Choose File > Go to Bookmark.*

Figure 8.7 *The chosen page is displayed in the browser.*

Figure 8.8 *With the Bookmarks window active, choose View > What's New?.*

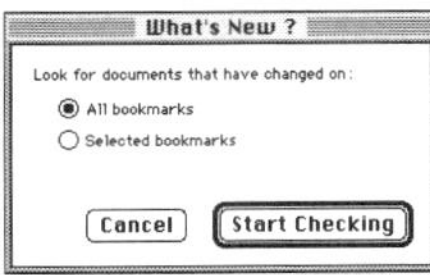

Figure 8.9 *Choose All bookmarks or Selected bookmarks and then click Start Checking.*

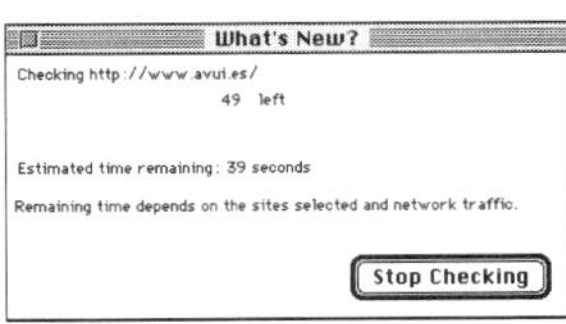

Figure 8.10 *While Navigator connects to each of the sites in your bookmarks file, it gives you a progress report. Click Stop Checking to cancel the search.*

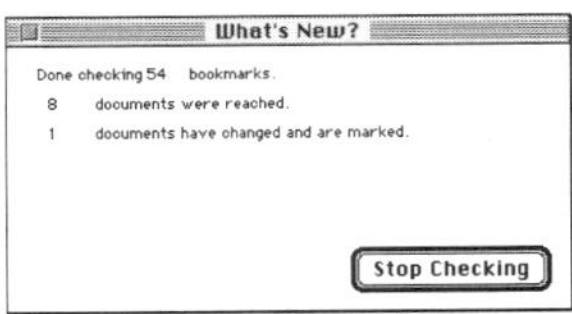

Figure 8.11 *Once Communicator has finished checking each of the sites in your bookmarks file, it gives you a final report.*

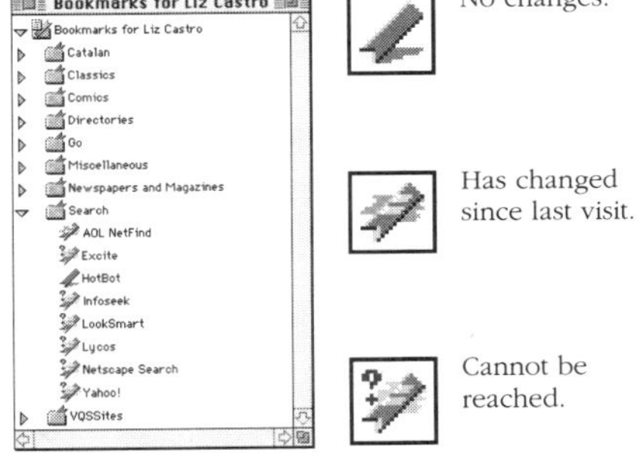

Figure 8.12 *Changed pages have a shiny teal band across the bookmark (the first one here). Pages that have not changed appear as usual. A question mark means the program can't tell if there have been any changes or not (as most of the bookmarks in this window).*

Checking what's new

Navigator can look through all your bookmarks, or through a selected group of them, and tell which pages have been changed or updated since your last visit.

To check what's new:

1. Open the Bookmarks window *(see page 85)*.
2. If desired, select the bookmarks that you wish to check.
3. Choose View > What's New? **(Figure 8.8)**. The What's New? dialog box appears.
4. If you made a selection of bookmarks, click the Selected bookmarks option. Otherwise, leave All bookmarks checked **(Figure 8.9)**. Click Start Checking. Navigator connects to each of the pages listed in your bookmarks file to see if they've changed since your last visit.
5. A dialog box appears that charts Navigator's progress **(Figure 8.10)**. Click Stop Checking if you get tired of waiting. Navigator gives you a final report **(Figure 8.11)**. Click Stop Checking to close the dialog box. Navigator displays changed bookmarks with a teal band **(Figure 8.12)**. Bookmarks that Navigator was unable to analyze are indicated with a question mark.

✔ **Tip**

- When you create a bookmark manually *(see page 89)*, Navigator marks it with a question mark, indicating that you have not visited it.

Creating bookmarks

The hardest part about creating a bookmark is finding a page that is worth going back to. Once you are there, adding a reference to the page is a snap.

To add a bookmark:

1. Navigate to the page whose URL you wish to save.
2. Choose (Bookmarks) > Add Bookmark **(Figure 8.13)**. The title and URL of the Web page that you are currently browsing will be saved in a bookmark in the New Bookmarks folder *(see page 90)* and will be automatically appended to the Bookmarks menu **(Figure 8.14)**.

✓ Tips

- You can also drag the page proxy icon to the Bookmarks *window* to create a bookmark for the current page **(Figure 8.15)**. This is a great new feature since it lets you choose what folder to put the new bookmark in.
- Control-click a link and then choose Add Bookmark for this Link in the pop-up menu to add a link from a page without going to the page **(Figure 8.16)**.

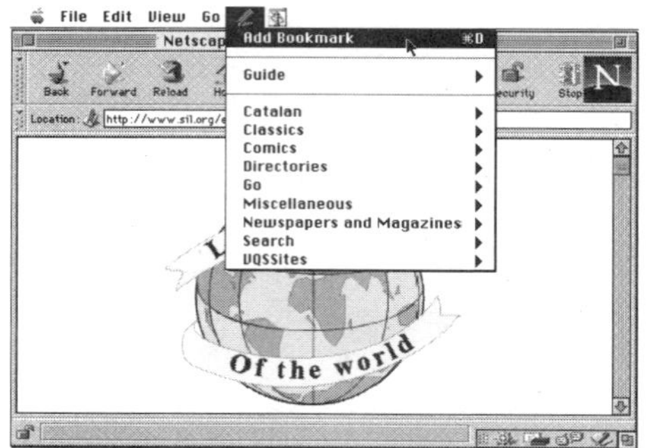

Figure 8.13 *Once you have found a good page, simply choose Bookmarks > Add Bookmark (Command-D) to add the page to your bookmarks file.*

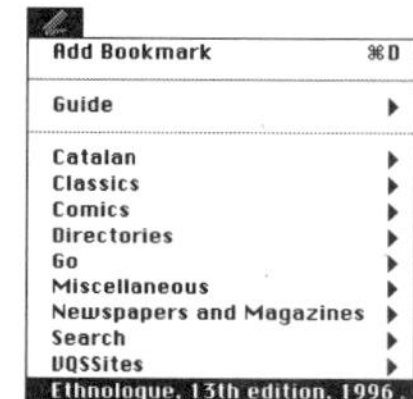

Figure 8.14 *The current page's title and URL are immediately added to the Bookmarks menu (as shown) and to the Bookmarks window.*

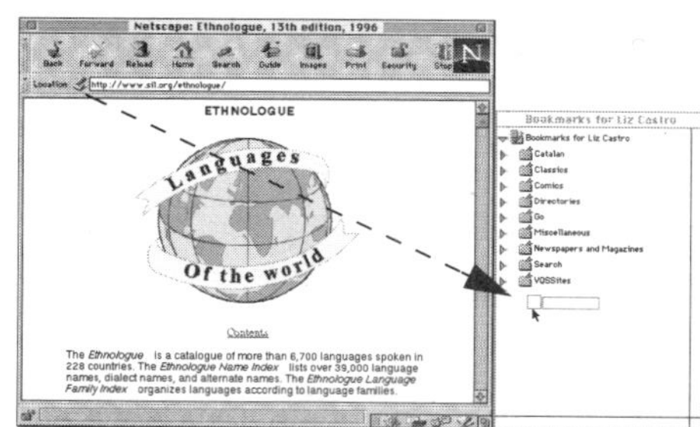

Figure 8.15 *Drag the page proxy icon to the open Bookmarks window to create a bookmark for the page you're currently viewing.*

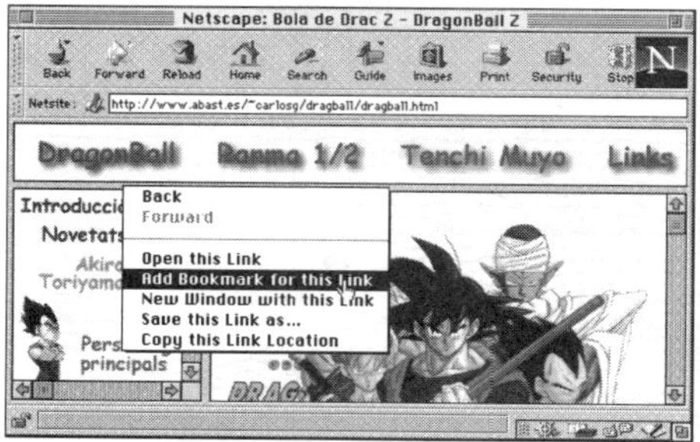

Figure 8.16 *Control-click the link and choose Add Bookmark for this Link from the pop-up menu to add a bookmark without visiting the page.*

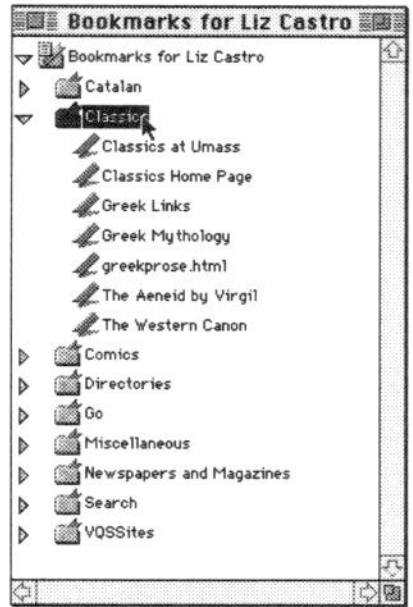

Figure 8.17 *Select the folder in which you wish to create the bookmark.*

Figure 8.18 *Choose File > New Bookmark to open the New Bookmark dialog box.*

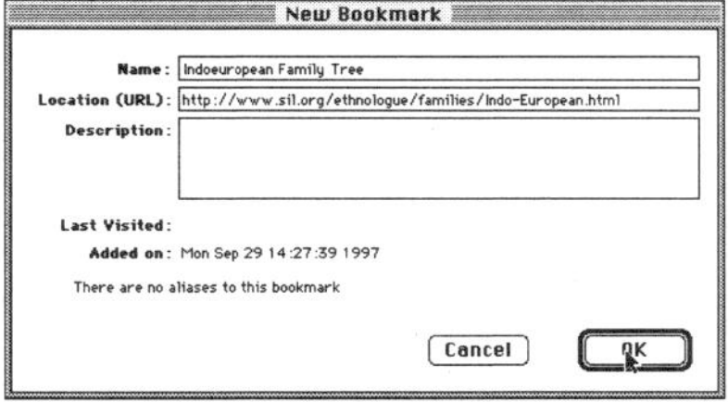

Figure 8.19 *Type the name, URL, and comments for the new bookmark. Then click OK.*

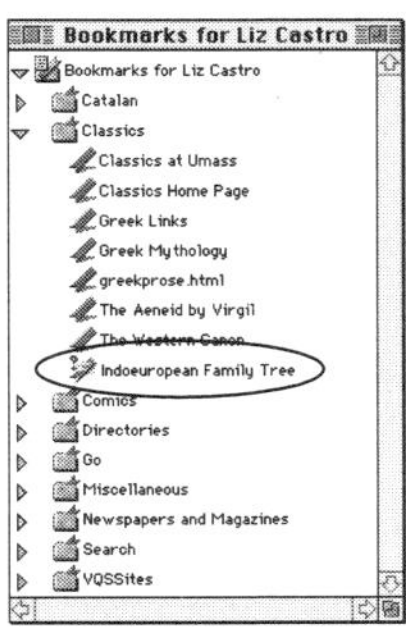

Figure 8.20 *The new bookmark appears in the Bookmarks window with a question mark on the icon. The question mark means the bookmark has not yet been visited. The bookmark also appears in the Bookmarks menu.*

Creating bookmarks manually

You don't need to connect to a page in order to add it to your bookmark file. As long as you know a page's URL—perhaps you've found a reference in a magazine—you can create a bookmark for the page manually.

Adding a bookmark by hand:

1. Open the Bookmarks window *(see page 85)*.
2. Select the folder *(see page 93)* in which you wish to create the bookmark **(Figure 8.17)**.
3. Choose File > New Bookmark **(Figure 8.18)**. The New Bookmark dialog box appears **(Figure 8.19)**.
4. Type a name (that will appear in the Bookmarks menu and window), URL, and description, if desired.
5. Click OK. The new bookmark appears in both the Bookmarks menu and the Bookmarks window **(Figure 8.20)**.

✔ Tips

- Type upper- and lowercase letters in URLs exactly as they were, and beware of typos.
- You can add bookmarks manually without connecting to the Internet thereby saving connect time and phone charges.

Setting the New Bookmarks folder

When you create a bookmark with the Add Bookmark command, the bookmark is automatically appended to the New Bookmarks folder in the current bookmarks file. By default, Navigator sets up the principal folder to receive new bookmarks. However, you can choose any folder as the receiving folder, making it easy to add several bookmarks at a time to a particular category.

To set the New Bookmarks folder:

1. Click once on the folder to which new bookmarks should be added when you use the Add Bookmark command **(Figure 8.21)**. You may choose any folder at any level in the Bookmarks window.

2. Choose View > Set as New Bookmarks Folder **(Figure 8.22)**. The new New Bookmarks folder is indicated by a folder with a bright tealish-green bookmark icon on it **(Figure 8.23)**.

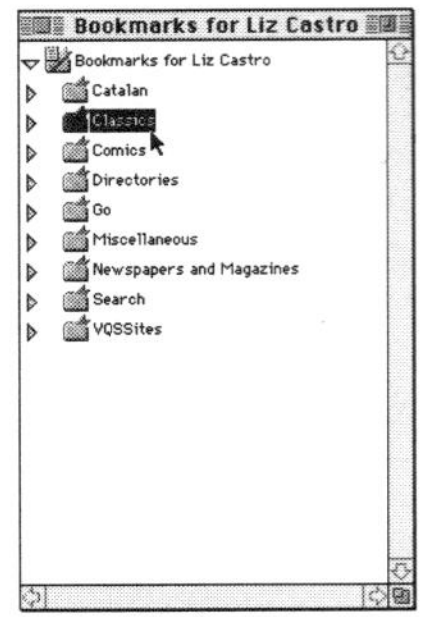

Figure 8.21 *Choose the folder that you want to add new bookmarks to when using the Add Bookmark command.*

Figure 8.22 *Choose View > Set as New Bookmarks Folder.*

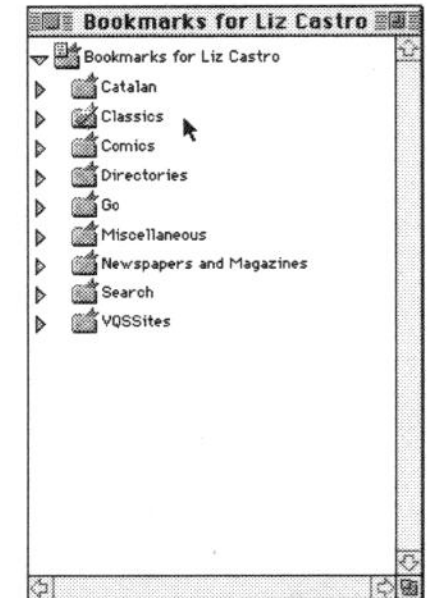

Figure 8.23 *A small icon of a tealish-green bookmark appears on the folder that you have designated as the "New Bookmarks folder."*

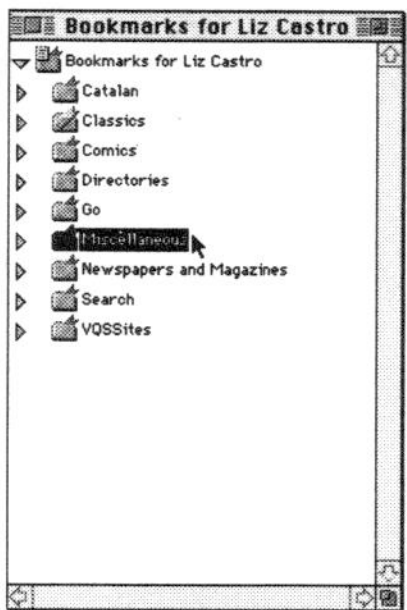

Figure 8.24 *Select the folder from which you wish the Bookmarks menu to be generated.*

Figure 8.25 *Choose View > Set as Bookmark Menu Folder.*

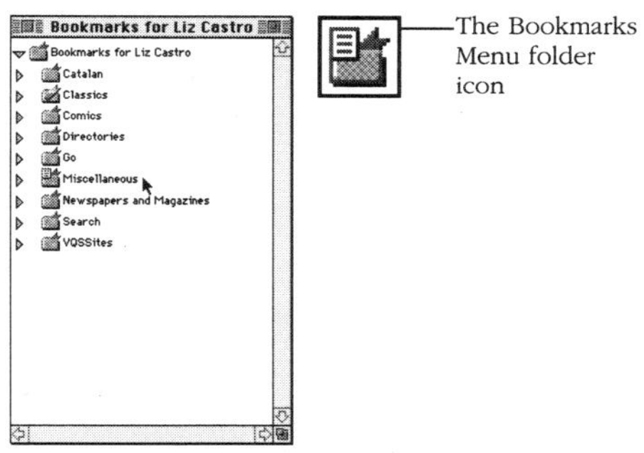

Figure 8.26 *The new "Bookmarks Menu folder" has a small page icon on top of the folder icon.*

Figure 8.27 *The Bookmarks menu shows only those bookmarks that are contained in the folder that you've designated as the Bookmarks Menu folder (in this case the* Miscellaneous *folder in Figure 8.26).*

Setting the Bookmarks menu folder

The Bookmarks menu is generated from the bookmarks in the Bookmarks window. You can choose which folder in the Bookmarks window is used to create the menu.

To set the Bookmarks menu folder:

1. Click once on the folder from which you want to generate the Bookmarks menu **(Figure 8.24)**. You can choose any folder at any level of the Bookmarks window.
2. Choose View > Set as Bookmark Menu Folder **(Figure 8.25)**. A small page icon is shown on top of the folder **(Figure 8.26)**.
3. Display the Bookmarks menu to see the new configuration **(Figure 8.27)**.

✔ Harrumph

- OK, this isn't really a tip, just a complaint. The menu is called "Bookmarks" not "Bookmark" so why is the option called "Set as Bookmark Menu Folder"? Ask Netscape.

Organizing your bookmarks

A bookmark is only useful if you can find it. There are several ways to organize them so that they are easier to find, and thus easier to use.

To organize bookmarks:

- Drag the bookmark to a new position or to a new folder. As you drag, a gray outline and a short horizontal line show where the bookmark will end up **(Figures 8.28, 8.29, and 8.30)**. Categorize your bookmarks by creating new folders *(see page 93)* and then dragging bookmarks to those folders.
- Edit the bookmark's name (which comes from the title embedded in its HTML code) so that it better reflects the contents of the page *(see page 94)*.
- Create aliases of your most used bookmarks and place them in several folders *(see page 94)*.
- Add separators between groups of bookmarks within folders *(see page 96)*.
- Sort your bookmarks *(see page 97)*.

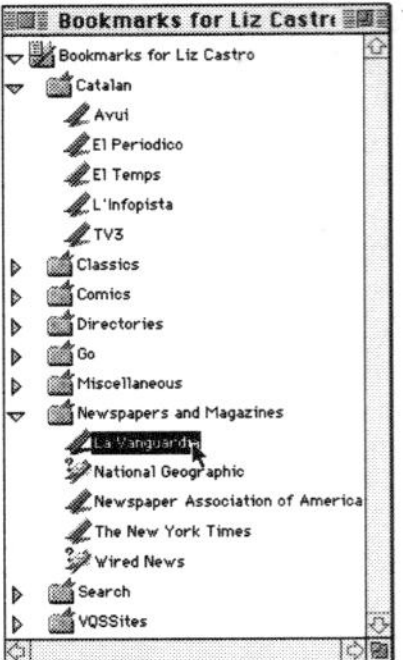

Figure 8.28 *Select the bookmark that you want to move.*

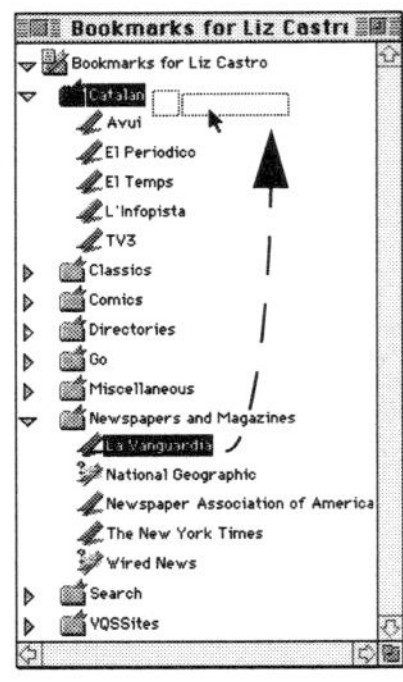

Figure 8.29 *Drag it to its new location. A gray outline indicates where the bookmark will be inserted.*

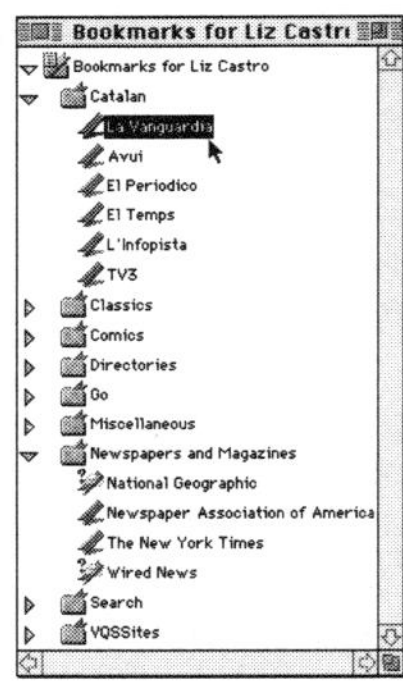

Figure 8.30 *The bookmark appears in its new location.*

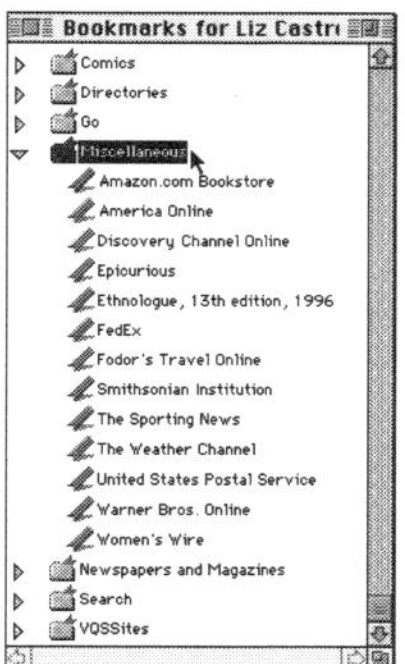

Figure 8.31 *Select the folder in which you wish to create the new folder.*

Figure 8.32 *To create a new folder for organizing your bookmarks, choose File > New Folder.*

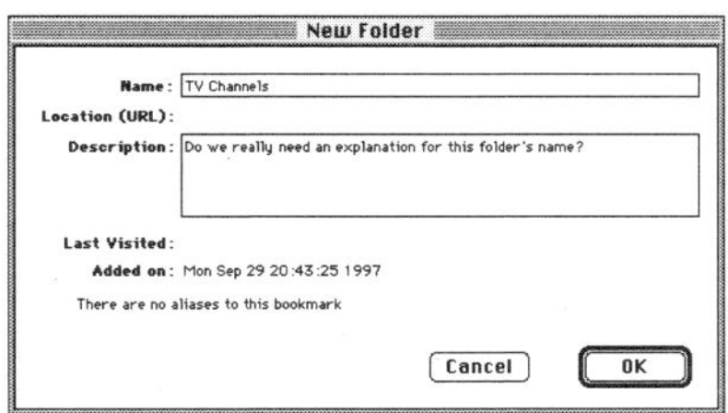

Figure 8.33 *Use the New Folder dialog box to change the Name and Description of folders as well as bookmarks. You cannot associate a URL with a folder. (It wouldn't make sense anyway.)*

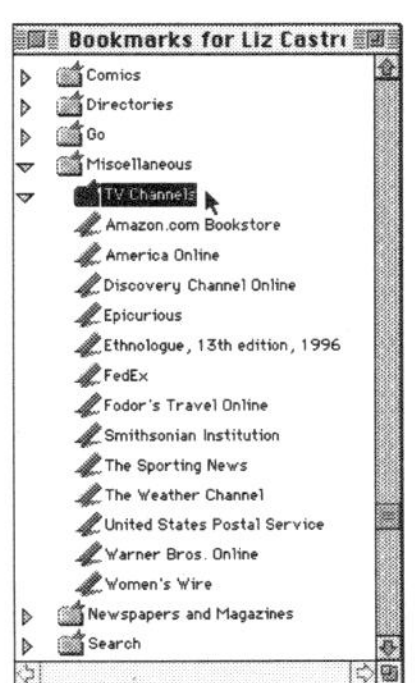

Figure 8.34 *The new folder appears directly below (and inside) the selected one.*

Creating a bookmark folder

If you have a lot of bookmarks, sooner or later you will find that searching through your list is almost as troublesome as searching through the Web. The solution is a little organization. You can categorize your bookmarks and separate them into named folders.

To create a bookmark folder:

1. Open the Bookmarks window *(see page 85)*. If you haven't created any folders yet, all the bookmarks will be in the default folder that Navigator creates for you.
2. Select the folder in which you wish to create the new folder **(Figure 8.31)**.
3. Choose File > New Folder **(Figure 8.32)**. The New Folder dialog box appears **(Figure 8.33)**.
4. In the Name field, type the name for your new folder.
5. In the Description field, enter a few words that define your category. This is a good way to help you remember what goes in this folder which, in turn, makes the folder more useful.
6. Click OK. The new folder appears in the Bookmarks window below—that is, *inside*—the folder you selected in step 2 **(Figure 8.34)**.
7. Drag bookmarks or other folders to the new folder.

Editing a bookmark or folder

When you add a bookmark with the Add Bookmark command, the title of the page is automatically used in the Bookmarks window to identify the bookmark. You may wish to give the bookmark a name that more clearly identifies its contents. In addition, you can change a bookmark's URL (perhaps, the creators of the page have moved it to a new server) or change its description.

To edit a bookmark or folder:

1. Open the Bookmarks window *(see page 85)*.
2. Click once on the bookmark or folder that you wish to edit.
3. Choose Edit > Get Info **(Fig. 8.35)**. The Bookmark Properties dialog box appears **(Figure 8.36)**.
4. Change the Name, URL, and Description in the corresponding text boxes as desired **(Figure 8.37)**.
5. Click OK to save the changes. The information is automatically updated in the Bookmarks menu and window.

✔ Tips

- To delete a bookmark or folder (or separator), select it and choose Edit > Clear **(Figure 8.38)** or press Delete.
- Hold down the Option key while you double click a bookmark to open the Bookmark Properties dialog box.

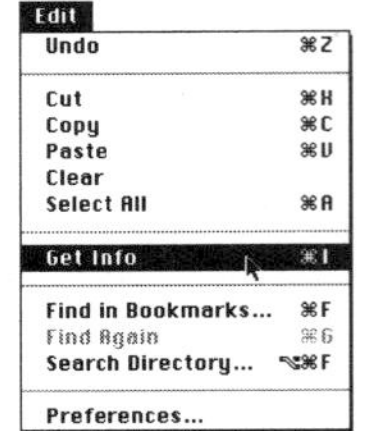

Figure 8.35 *Choose Edit > Get Info to display the Bookmark Properties dialog box (which will have the title of the folder or bookmark you selected).*

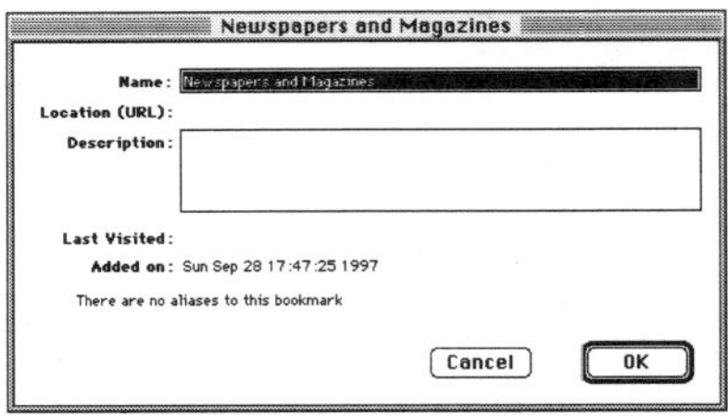

Figure 8.36 *In the Bookmark Properties dialog box (whose name changes depending on the name of your bookmark or folder), you may change the Name to better identify the page's contents, update a page's URL, or add a description for the page.*

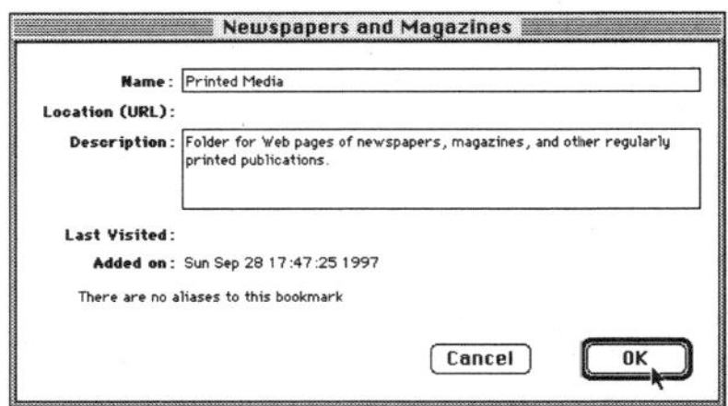

Figure 8.37 *Once you click OK to save the changes, the new data is automatically updated in both the Bookmarks window and the Bookmarks menu.*

Figure 8.38 *To delete a bookmark, select it in the Bookmarks window and then choose Edit > Clear. You can also select the bookmark and then press Delete.*

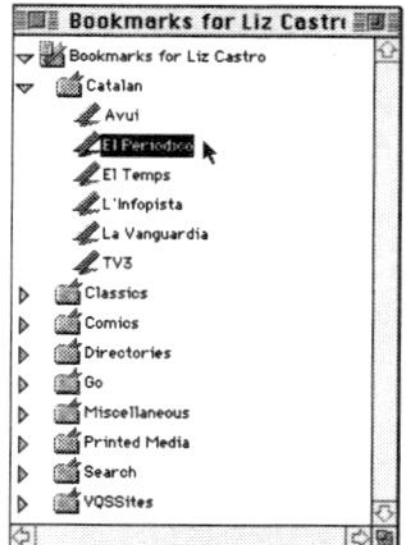

Figure 8.39 *In the Bookmarks window, select the bookmark you wish to create an alias of.*

Figure 8.40 *Choose File > Make Alias.*

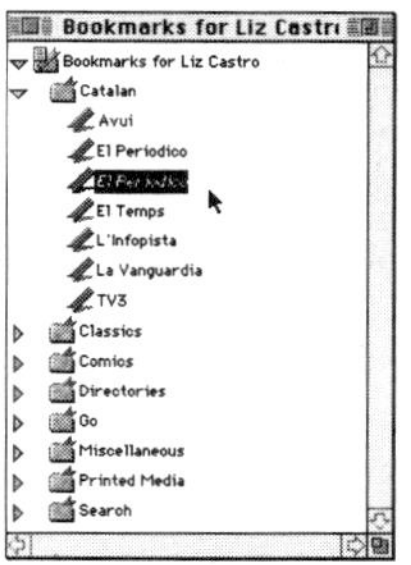

Figure 8.41 *The alias is created and placed below the selected bookmark. The alias appears in italic text.*

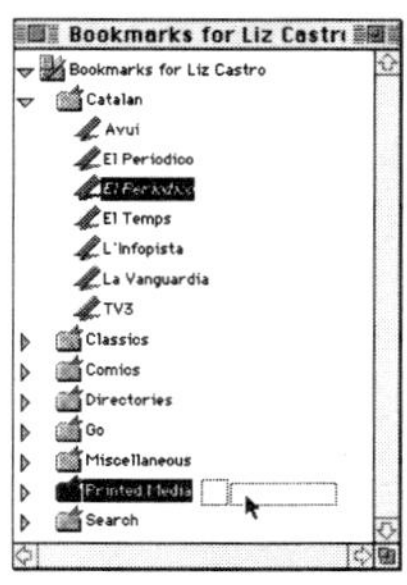

Figure 8.42 *Drag the new alias to another folder so that you can access the corresponding page from more than one place.*

Creating aliases of bookmarks

An alias is a sort of remote control. You can create aliases of your bookmarks in order to have access to your favorite sites in several locations in your bookmarks file. You use an alias exactly the same way you use a regular bookmark. The big difference is that if you change the URL or description of the original bookmark, the corresponding aliases are updated automatically.

To create an alias:

1. In the Bookmarks window, select the bookmark that you wish to create an alias of **(Figure 8.39)**.
2. Choose File > Make Alias **(Fig. 8.40)**. The alias appears below the original bookmark **(Figure 8.41)**. Aliases are shown in italics in the Bookmarks window to distinguish them from regular bookmarks.
3. Drag the alias to the new location **(Figure 8.42)**.
4. If desired, edit the alias to give it a new name or description. For more information, consult *Editing a bookmark or folder* on page 94.

✓ Tip

- The original and the alias are equal partners. Change either of them and the other is automatically updated.

Adding a separator

If you have several bookmarks or folders, it may be helpful to have a visual clue that separates them. Since the Bookmarks menu is generated from your Bookmarks window, the separators that you include in the window will also appear in the menu.

To add a separator to the Bookmarks window:

1. Click once on the folder or bookmark directly above the place where you wish to insert a separator **(Fig. 8.43)**.
2. Choose File > New Separator **(Figure 8.44)**. A dashed line appears in the desired location **(Figure 8.45)**.
3. Click on the Bookmarks menu to see your new separator **(Figure 8.46)**.

✔ Tips

- You are not limited to adding separators only between folders. You can insert a separator between any two objects in the Bookmarks window, regardless of their levels.
- Add separators after sorting *(see page 97)* to avoid having them moved around.

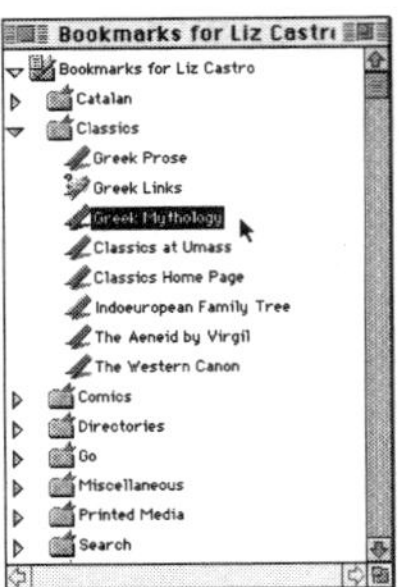

Figure 8.43 *Click once on the folder directly above the place where you wish to insert a separator.*

Figure 8.44 *Choose File > New Separator.*

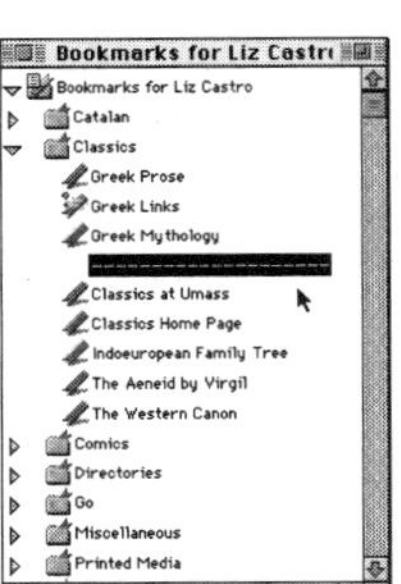

Figure 8.45 *The separator appears below the currently selected item. You may insert separators at any level of the Bookmarks hierarchy.*

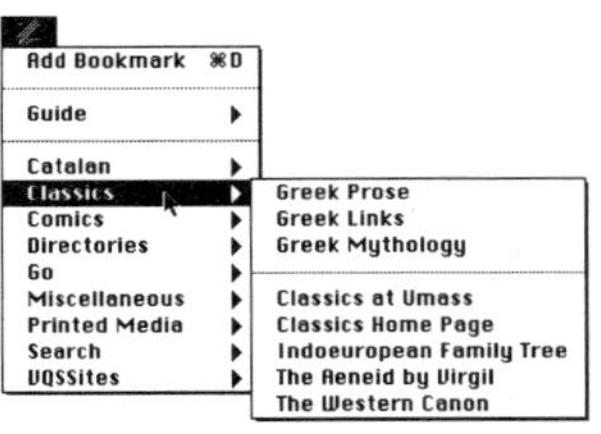

Figure 8.46 *The separator appears as a solid line in the Bookmarks menu.*

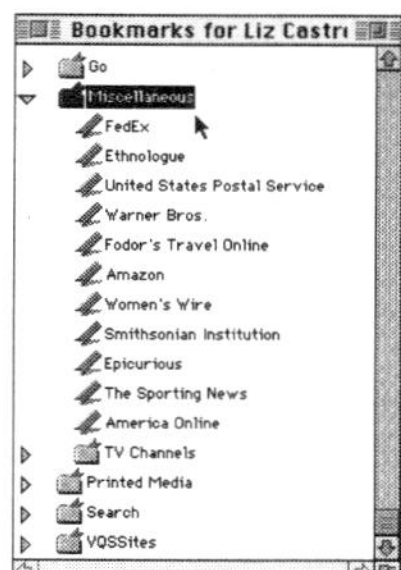

Figure 8.47 *Click once on a folder to select it for sorting.*

Figure 8.48 *Choose View > Alphabetize Bookmarks.*

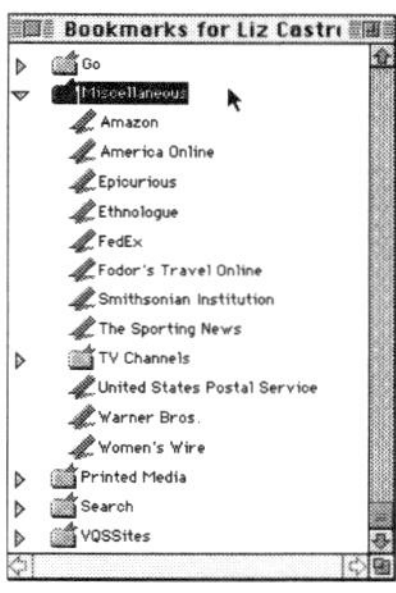

Figure 8.49 *The bookmarks are sorted alphabetically, in descending order, without losing the organization in folders.*

Sorting your bookmarks file

If you have more than five or six bookmarks in a folder, or more than five or six folders in your bookmarks file, you may wish to alphabetize the items to make them easier to find—on the menu and in the window.

To sort your bookmarks:

1. Click once in the folder whose bookmarks or subfolders you wish to sort **(Figure 8.47)**.
2. Choose View > Alphabetize Bookmarks **(Figure 8.48)**. All of the folders and bookmarks in the selected folder are sorted alphabetically **(Figure 8.49)**. Items within folders other than the selected folder are *not* sorted.

✔ Tips

- Add separators *after* alphabetizing to avoid having them moved around.
- When you save a bookmarks file with the Save As command *(see page 99)*, and open it again *(see page 100)*, all the bookmarks appear alphabetized, which may be what you need. But if you have spent a whole afternoon sorting your bookmarks exactly as you want, you'll loose the result of your efforts.
- You can undo a sort; simply choose Edit > Undo. (Be sure you choose the Undo command in the *Bookmarks window's* Edit menu and not the Navigator window's Edit menu.)
- Apparently, the Alphabetize Bookmarks command has been removed in the latest version of Communicator (4.03), although it still was there in version 4.01. Stay tuned!

Searching for a bookmark

Even if your bookmarks are not quite as well organized as you might like *(see page 92)*, there is still a way to find an elusive page that you know is archived *somewhere* in your bookmarks file: Search for it.

To search for a bookmark:

1. Open the Bookmarks window *(see page 85)*.
2. Choose Edit > Find in Bookmarks **(Figure 8.50)**. The Find Bookmark dialog box appears **(Figure 8.51)**.
3. Type what you want to look for in the Find box. Then check the Name, Location, and/or Description boxes to identify the text you are searching for.
4. Click Match Case or Whole Word to narrow the search.
5. Click OK. Navigator shows the first bookmark that satisfies the search criteria **(Figure 8.52)**.
6. If desired, choose Edit > Find Again to find the next occurrence of the search text.

Figure 8.50 *Choose Edit > Find in Bookmarks.*

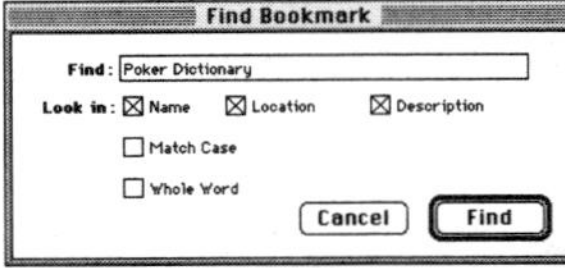

Figure 8.51 *The Find Bookmark dialog box allows you to look for bookmarks with a given name, location (that is, URL), or description.*

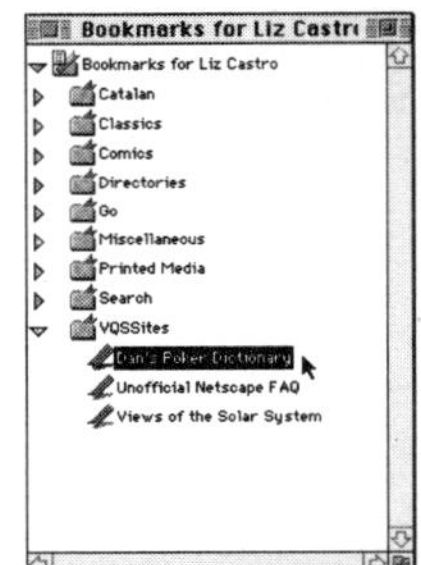

Figure 8.52 *The first bookmark that satisfies the criteria is highlighted in the Bookmarks window.*

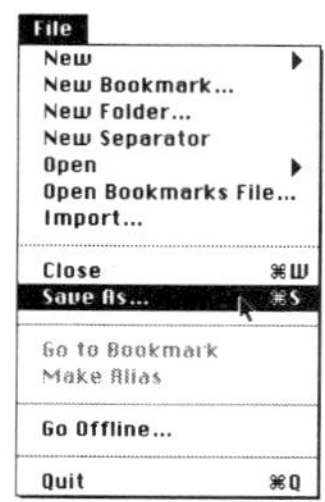

Figure 8.53 *To save a bookmarks file, perhaps to share with friends or as a backup, choose File > Save As with the Bookmarks window active.*

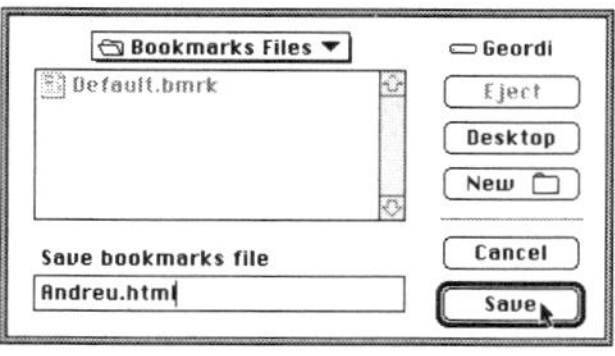

Figure 8.54 *In the Save As dialog box, give the file a name, choose the folder in which you wish to save it, and click Save.*

Saving a bookmarks file

You can save a bookmarks file to give to friends, or simply to make a back-up copy. In fact, a bookmarks file is nothing more than an HTML page that you can browse as you would any other local file.

To save a bookmark file:

1. Choose File > Save As **(Figure 8.53)**. The Save bookmarks file dialog box appears.
2. Give the file a name and choose the folder in which to save it **(Fig. 8.54)**.
3. Click Save to save the file.

✓ Tips

- Your main bookmarks file is saved automatically in the Netscape folder in your Preferences folder. You only need to use Save As if you want to change its name or location.
- If you add the .html extension to the end of the bookmarks file's name, you'll be able to open the file as a regular Web page *(see page 101)* and share it with other Mac and Unix users or use it as your home page *(see page 25)*. If you give it the .htm extension, you'll be able to read the file with a browser on a PC.

Opening a different bookmarks file

Although your bookmarks file is hidden from view when you close the Bookmarks window, it is not gone. Simply open the window again to see the bookmarks file again. If, however, you wish to open a *different* bookmarks file, you must follow these steps.

To open a different bookmarks file:

1. Open the Bookmarks window *(see page 85)*.
2. Choose File > Open Bookmarks File **(Figure 8.55)**. The Open bookmarks file dialog box appears.
3. Navigate to the bookmarks file that you wish to open, and double click it to open it **(Figure 8.56)**. The new bookmarks file will replace the current one in the Bookmarks window **(Figure 8.57)**. The old bookmarks file will remain intact in its former location.

✔ Tips

- Saving and opening multiple bookmarks files is an ideal way to share links to cool pages. Since the bookmarks file is nothing more than a simple HTML file, you can also open it directly with Navigator—on PCs, Macs or even Unix machines—no matter what kind of computer the bookmarks file comes from.
- The next time you open Communicator, the old bookmarks file is there again. If you wish to add the bookmarks from another bookmarks file permanently, use the Import command instead *(see page 102)*.

Figure 8.55 *To open a different bookmarks file, choose File > Open Bookmarks File.*

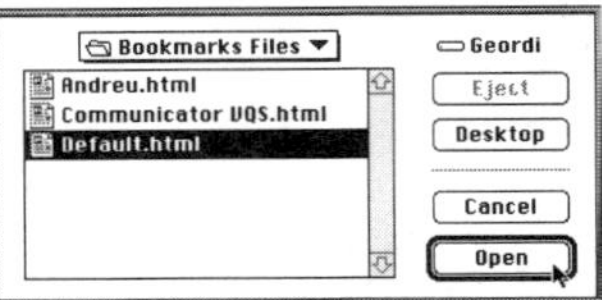

Figure 8.56 *In the Open dialog box that appears, choose the bookmarks file that you want to open and click Open.*

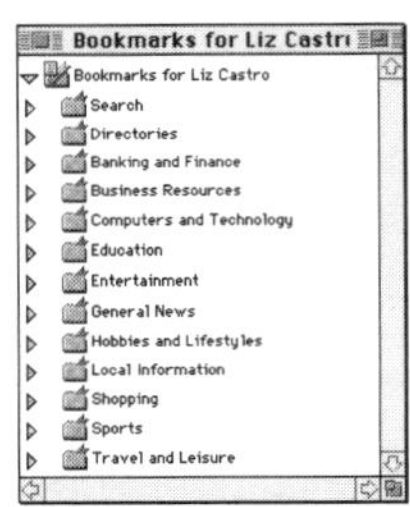

Figure 8.57 *The bookmarks in the new bookmarks file that you've just opened replace the ones from the old bookmarks file. The old bookmarks file remains intact on your hard disk.*

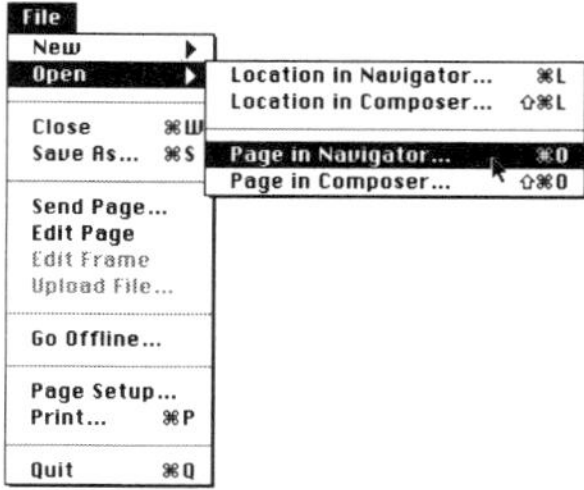

Figure 8.58 *To open a bookmarks file as a Web page, choose File > Open > Page in Navigator.*

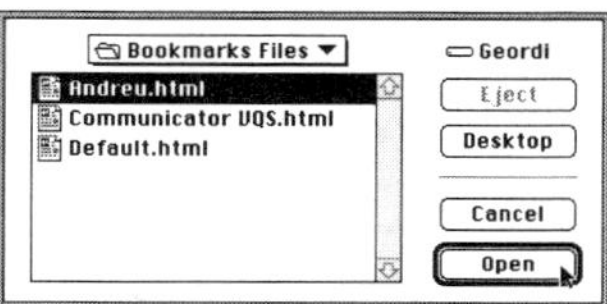

Figure 8.59 *In the Open dialog box that appears, choose the bookmarks file that you want to open as a Web page and click Open.*

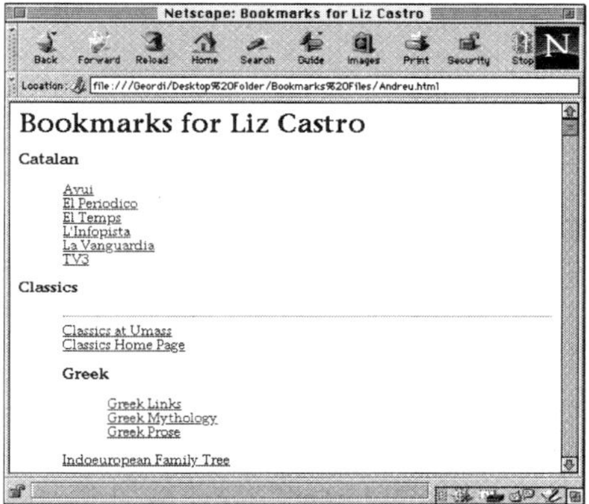

Figure 8.60 *The bookmarks file, complete with links to your saved sites, appears as a regular Web page.*

Opening a bookmarks file as a Web page

An easy way to see a bookmarks file without changing your regular bookmarks file is to open it as a Web page. Since the bookmarks file is in HTML format, like any other Web page, Navigator knows how to interpret it correctly, displaying folders in a large font, and making your bookmarks into links—automatically.

To open a bookmarks file as a Web page:

1. Save your bookmarks file. For more information, consult *Saving a bookmarks file* on page 99.
2. Choose File > Open > Page in Navigator **(Figure 8.58)**. The Open Page dialog box appears.
3. Choose the desired file and click Open **(Figure 8.59)**. The bookmarks file is displayed just like any other Web page **(Figure 8.60)** with each bookmark converted into a link.

✔ Tip

■ You can also designate a bookmarks file as the page that Navigator displays automatically every time you launch the program, giving you immediate access to frequently visited sites. For more information, consult *Choosing the startup page* on page 25.

Importing bookmarks

If you wish, you may *add* the bookmarks in a bookmarks file to your current bookmarks file instead of replacing the existing bookmarks.

To import bookmarks:

1. Open the Bookmarks window *(see page 85)*.
2. Choose File > Import **(Figure 8.61)**. A standard Open dialog box appears.
3. Choose the bookmarks file that you wish to import and click Open **(Figure 8.62)**. The bookmarks in the imported file are added to the current Bookmarks window **(Figure 8.63)**.

✔ Tip

- The Import command permanently adds the new bookmarks to the default bookmarks file (the one that is created automatically when you launch Communicator, and that resides in the Netscape folder inside your Preferences folder in the System folder). To just open a bookmarks file for that session (until you quit Communicator), use the Open Bookmarks File command *(see page 100)* or open the file as a Web page *(see page 101)*.

Figure 8.61 *Choose File > Import.*

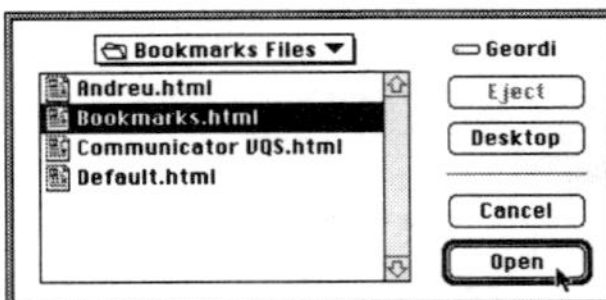

Figure 8.62 *Choose the bookmarks file that you wish to import and click Open.*

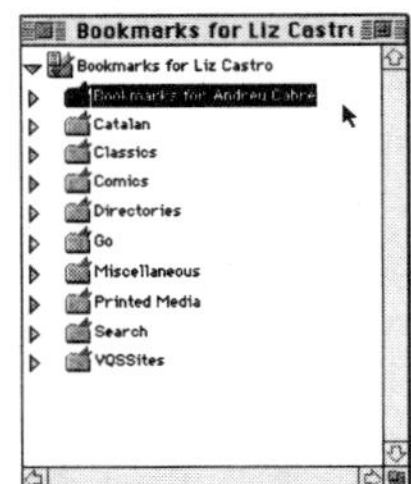

Figure 8.63 *The new bookmarks are added below the main folder in the current bookmarks file.*

Using Netcaster

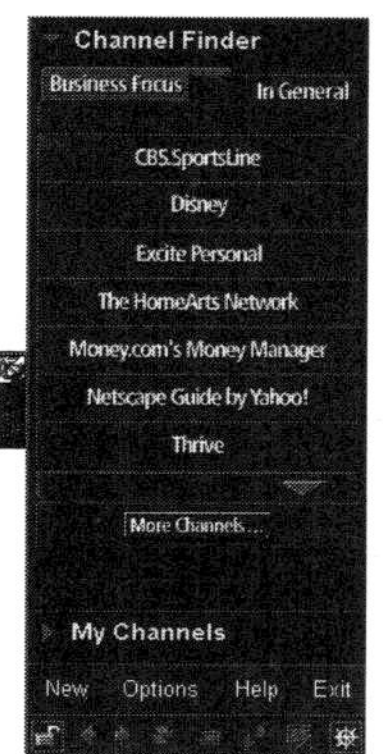

Figure 9.1 *The Netcaster drawer is a floating palette containing a list of channels and Netcaster controls. The drawer floats over anything else you may have on your screen at that moment, including other programs' windows, unless you collapse it by clicking the Netcaster tab (shown on the left side in this illustration).*

Netcaster is the component of Communicator that lets you view special Web sites called *channels*. The main difference between channels and regular Web sites is that channels are periodically updated. Further, instead of you having to go check if the page has changed, or use the Reload button, the new information is sent (or *pushed*) to you automatically from the site. Channels are perfect for providing up-to-date information, like news, weather, and even sports scores.

Netcaster's main controls are contained in a sort of remote control called the Netcaster drawer **(Figure 9.1)**. The drawer has two lists of channels: those channels that Netscape suggests are listed in the Channel Finder, those that you have subscribed to are listed in the My Channels list. Subscribing to a channel simply means that Netcaster will receive the information from the channels automatically and will store the data in your hard disk until you are ready to view it. Information from the channels in the Channel Finder is not automatically saved to your hard disk.

Opening and using Netcaster

Once you've installed Netcaster, you can open it up and start receiving Web pages.

To open Netcaster:

Choose Communicator > Netcaster from any Communicator component **(Figure 9.2)**. Netcaster's main window called the *drawer* and shaped rather like a television remote control, appears. The default channel, if any, is loaded *(see page 108)*.

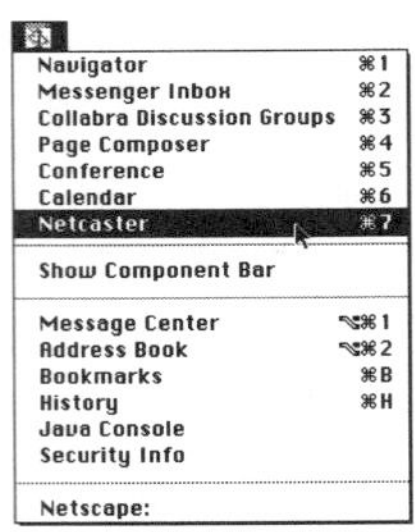

Figure 9.2 *Choose (Communicator) > Netcaster to start Netcaster.*

To close Netcaster:

Click the Exit button in the Netcaster drawer **(Figure 9.3)**. Netcaster closes.

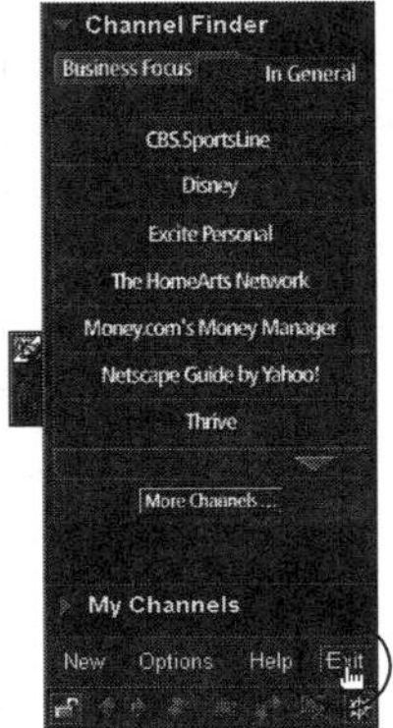

Figure 9.3 *Click the Exit button in the bottom-right corner of the Netcaster drawer to close Netcaster.*

✔ Tips

- Netcaster automatically closes when you close Communicator.
- You can't completely minimize Netcaster.
- To hide or reveal the Netcaster drawer, click the tab on the side of the Netcaster drawer to slide the drawer under the window (well, that's what it looks like). The drawer disappears and only the tab remains. Click the tab again to bring the drawer back.

Figure 9.4 *Click on the My Channels area in the Netcaster drawer to display a list of your channels.*

Figure 9.5 *Click the name of the channel you want to open.*

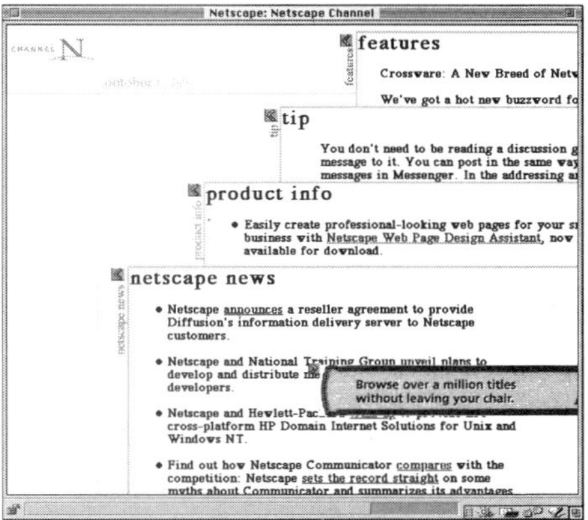

Figure 9.6 *The channel is displayed as a full-sized window.*

Opening a channel

Once you've chosen the channels that you want to have access to, opening them is just a question of clicking them.

To open a channel:

1. Click on the My Channels area in the Netcaster drawer if the My Channels list isn't already visible **(Figure 9.4)**. The My Channels list appears and displays your channels.
2. Click the name of the channel you want to open in the My Channels list **(Figure 9.5)**. The channel is displayed **(Figure 9.6)**.

✔ Tip

■ To add new channels to your My Channels list, consult *Adding channels to your list* on page 110.

Previewing Netscape's suggested channels

Netscape manages a list of available channels and lets you preview them and decide whether or not to add them to your own more permanent channel list.

To preview Netscape's suggested channels:

1. Click on the Channel Finder area in the Netcaster drawer if the Channel Finder is not already visible **(Figure 9.7)**. The current suggested channels are listed.

2. Click on one of the tabs that divide the channels into categories.

3. Click the channel that you would like to preview **(Figure 9.8)**. It expands in the Channel Finder **(Figure 9.9)**. The Add Channel and/or Preview Channel buttons may be available.

4. Click on Preview Channel to preview the channel **(Figure 9.10)**.

✓ Tips

- If desired, click the Add Channel button to add the channel to your personal list.

- Netscape promises to update the list of channels. You might want to periodically check the Channel Finder for new channels.

Figure 9.7 *Click in the Channel Finder area to get a list of the suggested channels.*

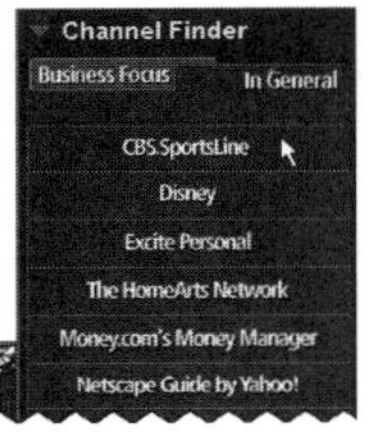

Figure 9.8 *The list of the current suggested channels appears. Click a channel to expand it.*

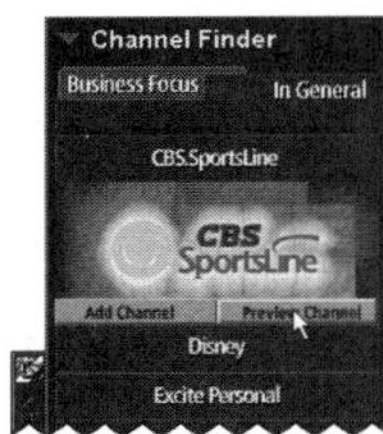

Figure 9.9 *The channel expands and Netcaster shows you its logo. Click Preview Channel to preview the channel.*

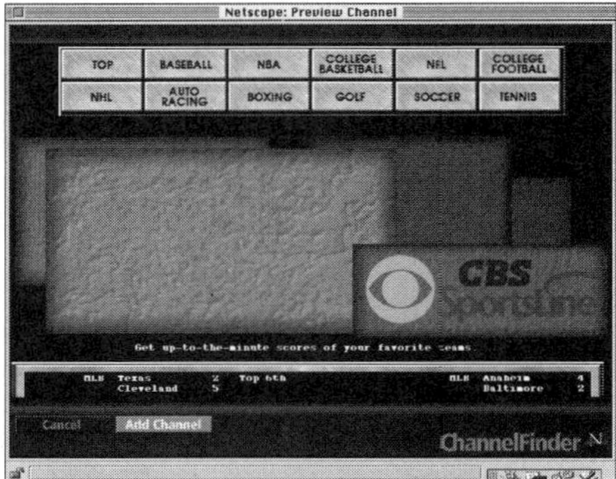

Figure 9.10 *Netcaster shows you a preview of the channel.*

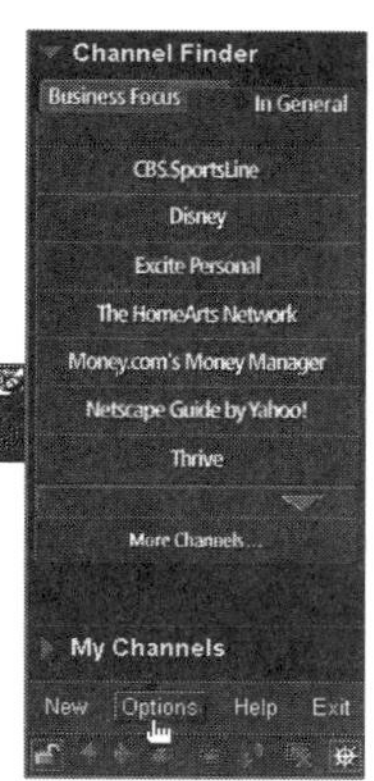

Figure 9.11 *Click the Options button on the Netcaster drawer.*

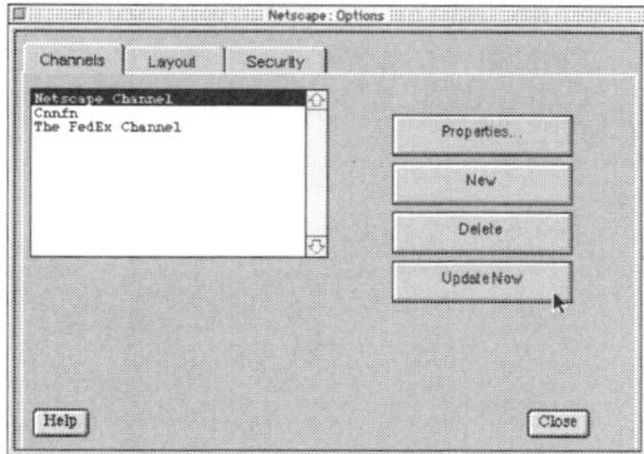

Figure 9.12 *Click the name of the channel that you want to update and click the Update Now button.*

Updating channels

You can either set a channel to be automatically updated—which is the point of channels in the first place—or you can update them manually. You can also manually update channels when you want to make sure you have the latest information from the channel, regardless of the regularly scheduled update.

To update channels:

1. Make sure you are connected to the Internet. You must be online to update a channel.
2. Click the Options button on the Netcaster drawer **(Figure 9.11)**. The Options dialog box appears.
3. From the list in the Channels tab of the Options dialog box, choose the channel that you want to update **(Figure 9.12)**.
4. Click Update Now. The newest information available for the channel is immediately downloaded from the server and displayed on your screen.

✔ Tip

- You can also simply adjust the channel so that it is updated as regularly as you need. For more information, consult *Adding channels to your list* on page 110.

Setting a default channel

You can specify which channel in your personal My Channels list should appear when you start Netcaster.

To set the default channel:

1. Click the Options button on the Netcaster drawer **(Figure 9.13)**. The Options dialog box appears.
2. Click the Layout tab. The Layout options appear.
3. Choose the desired channel in the pop-up menu at the bottom of the dialog box **(Figure 9.14)**. The next time you start Netcaster, this channel will be automatically loaded.

   Or click the None radio button so that no channel is automatically loaded upon starting Netcaster.

✔ Tip

- By default, Netcaster is set up to load Netscape's own channel at startup.

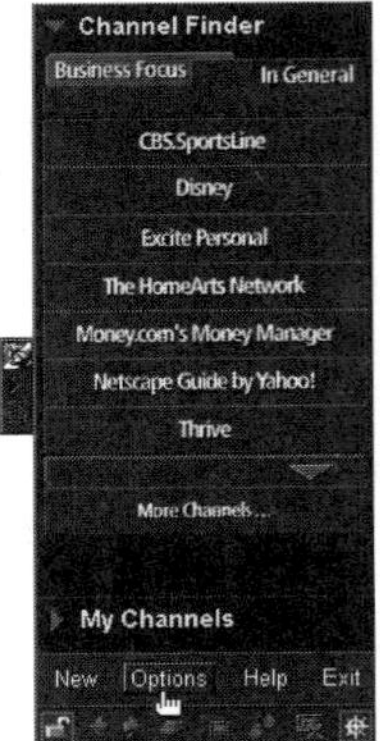

Figure 9.13 *Click the Options button on the Netcaster drawer.*

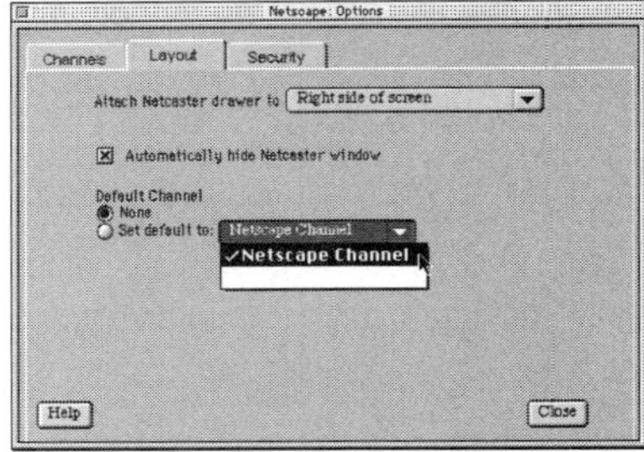

Figure 9.14 *In the Layout tab under Default Channel, choose the channel you want to open automatically each time you launch Netcaster.*

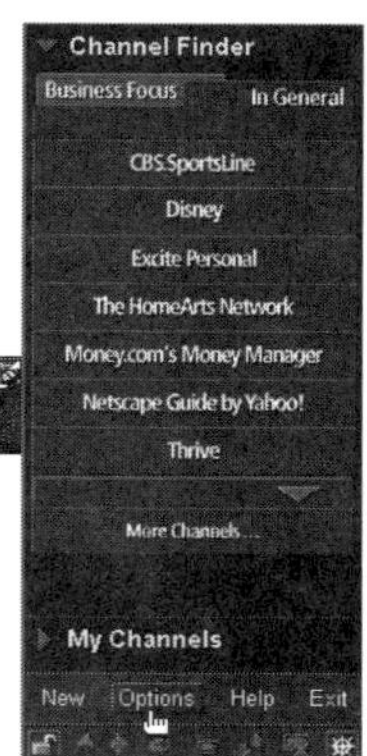

Figure 9.15 *Click the Options button on the Netcaster drawer.*

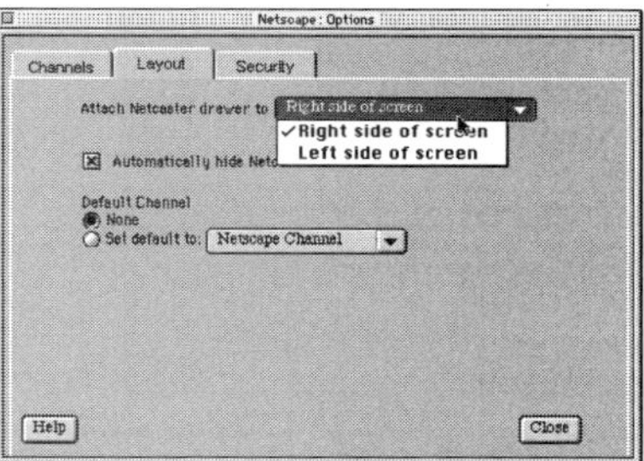

Figure 9.16 *In the Layout section you can choose the drawer preferences that have to do with Netcaster's appearance and behavior.*

Setting drawer preferences

You can have the drawer slide out of the right or the left side of the window, as you prefer. You can also hide the drawer automatically when you view a channel.

To set drawer preferences:

1. Click the Options button on the Netcaster drawer **(Figure 9.15)**.
   The Options dialog box appears.
2. Click the Layout tab **(Figure 9.16)**.
3. Next to Attach Netcaster drawer to, choose the side of the screen where you want the drawer to appear.
4. Check the Automatically hide Netcaster window box to have the Netcaster *drawer* (not window) disappear when you open a channel.
5. Click Close to close the Options dialog box.

Adding channels to your list

You can add both channels and regular Web sites to your My Channels list.

To add a channel from the channel itself:

If there is an Add Channel button available, simply click it to add the channel to the My Channels list.

To add a channel manually:

1. Click the New button at the bottom of the Netcaster drawer **(Figure 9.17)**. The Channel Properties dialog box appears.
2. Enter the name and location (URL) for the channel.
3. If you want to have the channel updated automatically, click the check box in the bottom half of the dialog box and choose a time interval in the pop-up menu.

Figure 9.17 *Click the New button to open the Channel Properties dialog box.*

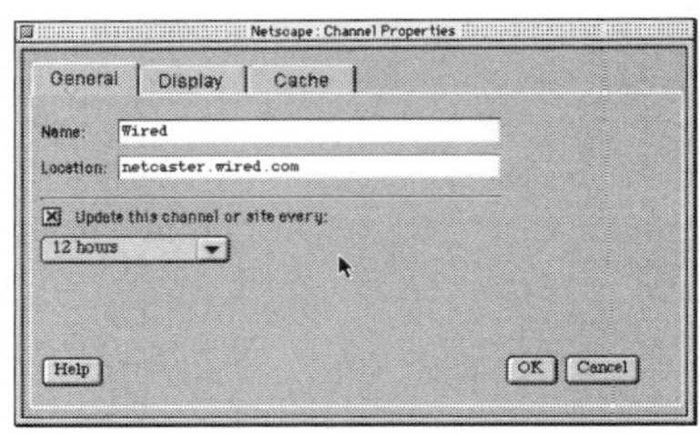

Figure 9.18 *Enter the name and location (URL) for the channel and click Update the channel or site every. Then check the Update box and choose the frequency with which you want the channel to be updated in the pop-up menu.*

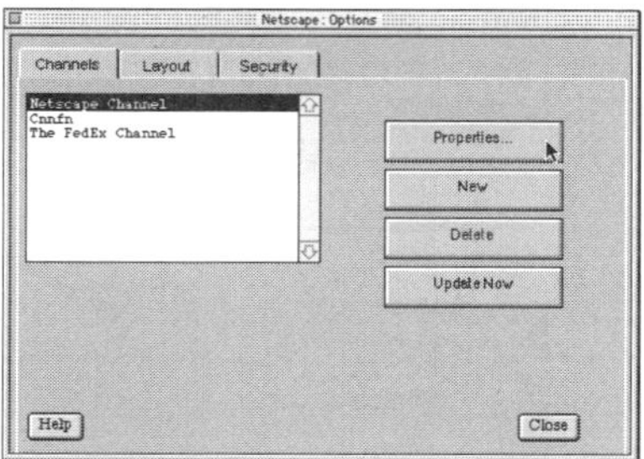

Figure 9.19 *Select a channel from the list and click the Properties button.*

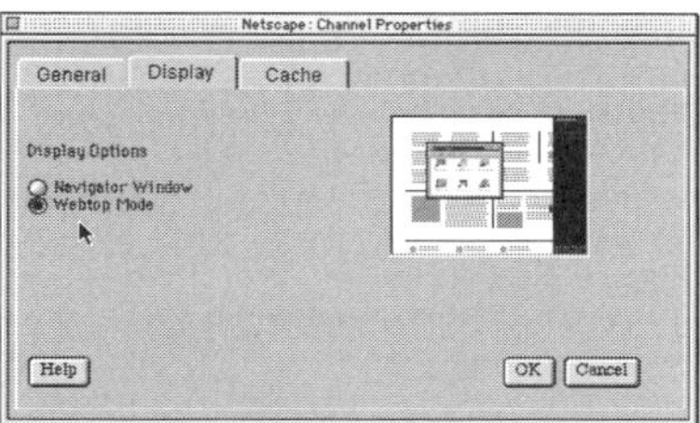

Figure 9.20 *In the Display tab, click the Webtop Mode option to fill the screen with the selected channel.*

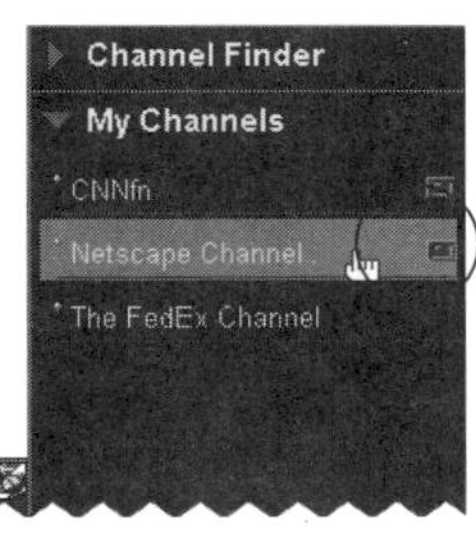

Figure 9.21 *Notice the little square that appears next to the name of the channel you have set up as a webtop.*

Figure 9.22 *The webtop covers the entire screen and is placed behind everything—including other windows, as can be seen here.*

Creating a webtop

A webtop is a channel that fills the back of your screen, like wallpaper. Creating a webtop is not much different from creating a regular channel.

To create a webtop:

1. Click the Options button in the Netcaster drawer. The Options dialog box appears.
2. Select the channel in the list and then click the Properties button. The Channel Properties dialog box appears.
3. Click the Display tab. The Display properties appear.
4. Click the Webtop Mode option to display the channel as a webtop—covering the entire screen.
5. Click OK and then Close to close both boxes of settings. A small square appears next to the names of webtops in the My Channels list **(Figure 9.21)**.

✔ Tip

- You can also right click a channel to access the Channel Properties dialog box.

Using webtops

Webtops work like regular channels and always contain the Netscape logo and the regular channel controls in the lower-right corner of the window **(Figure 9.23)**.

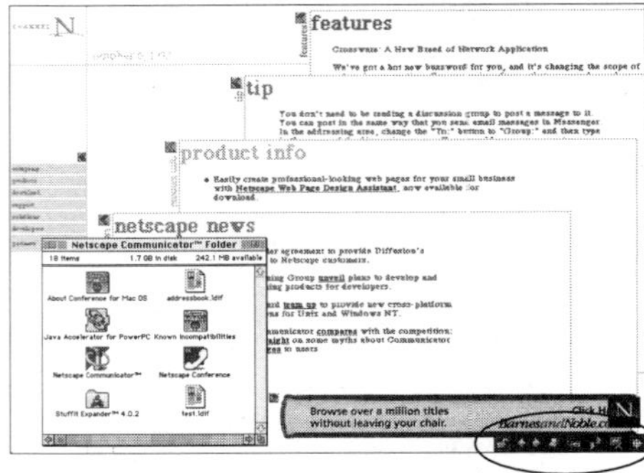

Figure 9.23 *Use these icons to work with the webtops.*

To work with webtops:

- Click the left arrow (Back) to go back to the previous webtop page **(Figure 9.24)**.
- Click the right arrow (Forward) to go forward to the next webtop page **(Figure 9.25)**.
- Click the printer icon (Print) to print a copy of the webtop **(Figure 9.26)**.
- Click the green square (Desktop/Webtop) to hide or reveal the webtop **(Figure 9.27)**.
- Click the up and down arrows (Front/Behind) to move the webtop in front of or behind the other windows on the screen **(Figure 9.28)**.
- Click the icon of a screen with an X on it (Exit) to close the webtop **(Figure 9.29)**.
- Click the ship's wheel (Navigator) to open a new Navigator window above the webtop **(Figure 9.30)**.

Figure 9.24 *Click the left arrow to go back to the previous webtop page.*

Figure 9.25 *Click the right arrow to go forward to the next webtop page.*

Figure 9.26 *Click the printer icon to print a copy of the webtop.*

Figure 9.27 *Click the green square icon to hide or reveal the webtop.*

Figure 9.28 *Click the up and down arrows to move the webtop in front of or behind other windows on the screen.*

Figure 9.29 *Click the screen with an X icon to close the webtop.*

Figure 9.30 *Click the wheel icon to open a new Navigator window above the webtop.*

✔ Tips

- You can display any channel as a webtop *(see page 111)*.
- Opening and closing webtops is the same as opening and closing any other kind of channel *(see page 105)*.

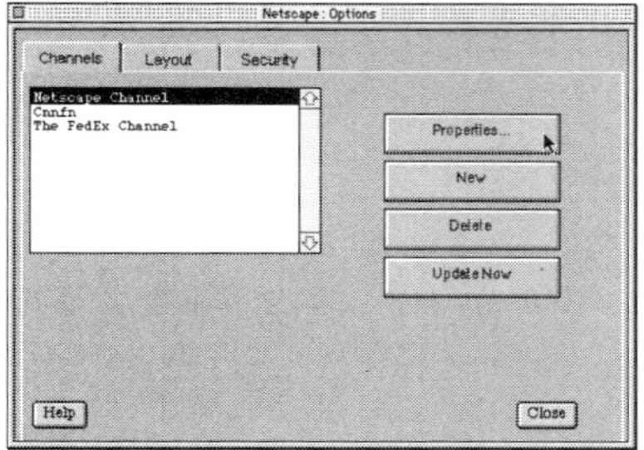

Figure 9.31 *In the Channels tab of the Options dialog box, select the channel you want to modify and click the Properties button.*

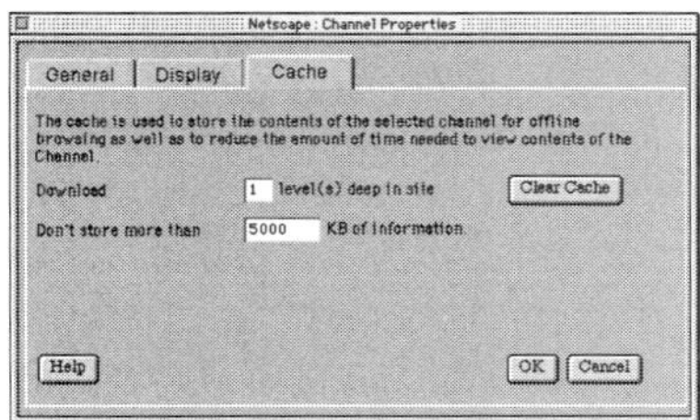

Figure 9.32 *In the Cache tab of the Channel Properties dialog box, choose how many levels of the channel you want to have copied to your hard disk.*

Setting limits for the channel

A channel (and the links it contains) is something like a family tree. The top channel may have two links that lead to two other pages. Those two pages may contain four links each; and those linked pages may contain their own links. It is easy to see that there may be many, many "great-grandchildren links" all related to the first page. Each generation is called a level. Of course, the more pages you download, the more space they'll take up on your hard disk. You can decide how many levels you want to have automatically updated, and set an upper limit for space on your hard disk at the same time.

To set limits for the channel:

1. Click the Options button in the Netcaster drawer.
2. Click the Channels tab.
3. Select the channel in the list at left and then click the Properties button **(Figure 9.31)**. The Channel Properties dialog box appears.
4. Click the Cache tab to view the Cache properties **(Figure 9.32)**.
5. Choose how many levels of the channel that you wish to have copied to your hard disk.
6. Set the maximum space available for this channel on the hard disk.
7. Click OK to save the cache settings.

Editing channels

You can change a channel's properties at any time, converting it into a webtop or changing the frequency with which it is updated.

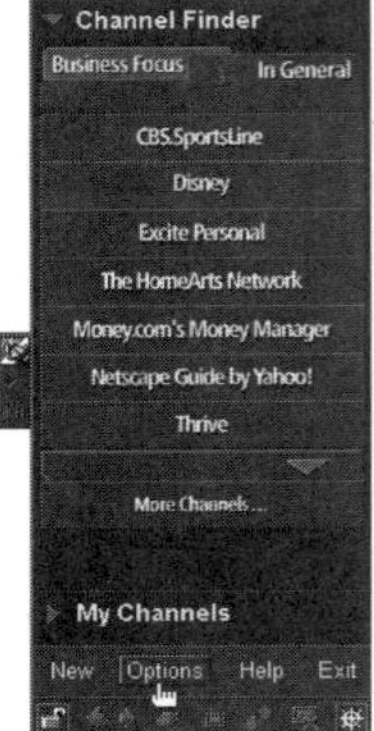

Figure 9.33 *Click Options at the bottom of the Netcaster drawer.*

To edit channels:

1. Click the Options button at the bottom of the Netcaster drawer **(Figure 9.33)**. The Options dialog box appears.
2. Click the Channels tab.
3. Select the channel in the list at left that you want to edit.
4. Click the Properties button. The Channel Properties dialog box appears **(Figure 9.34)**.
5. Make the desired changes, clicking the Display and Cache tabs as needed.
6. Click OK to save the changes.

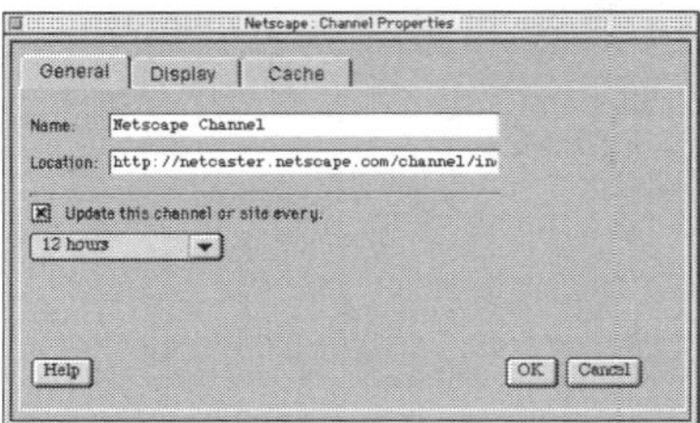

Figure 9.34 *Enter the desired changes in the three tabs of the Channel Properties dialog box.*

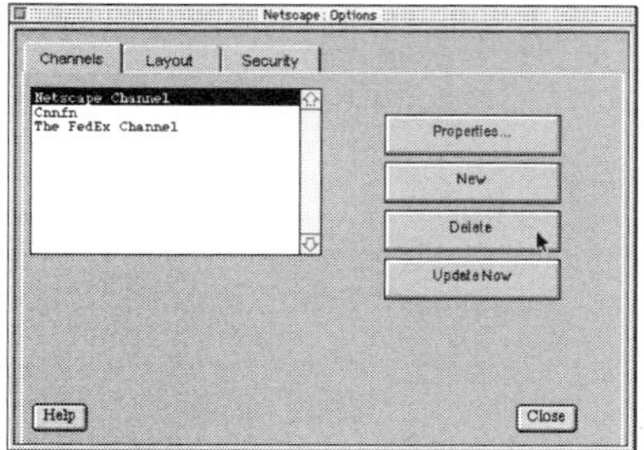

Figure 9.35 *In the Options dialog box, select the channel that you wish to delete.*

Deleting channels

If you find that you have a channel in your list that you're no longer interested in, you can delete it so that it doesn't take up unnecessary space on your hard drive.

To delete channels:

1. Click Options in the Netcaster drawer. The Options dialog box appears.
2. Click the Channels tab, if necessary.
3. Choose the channel that you want to delete from the list **(Figure 9.35)**.
4. Click the Delete button. The channel disappears from the My Channels list.

✔ Tip

- You can't eliminate channels from the Channel Finder. Netscape controls these channels.

Using Netcaster to surf offline

When Netcaster updates a channel, it copies it to your hard disk. If you want to browse a site offline, you can use Netcaster to update the channel. Then disconnect from the Internet and view the site.

To use Netcaster to surf offline:

1. Add the site to the My Channels list *(see page 110)*.
2. Determine how many levels of the site you want to be able to browse *(see page 113)*. The first level is the initial page. The links on the initial page lead to the second level pages. The links on the second level pages lead to the third level pages, and so on.
3. Update the channel *(see page 107)*. The channel is downloaded to your hard disk.
4. Disconnect from the Internet.
5. Open the channel *(see page 105)* and browse as usual.

✔ **Tip**

- Once the site is downloaded, you should be able to open it with Navigator, as well.

Part III: Mail, Discussion Groups, and Conference

One-on-One Communication

This section of the book is devoted to those components of Communicator that enable us to communicate one-on-one with other Internet users. This might be writing personal messages (mail), posting messages to a group (discussion groups), or speaking to another person directly (conference).

Mail vs. Discussion Groups

In earlier versions of Netscape Communication's software, a distinction was made between electronic mail and news postings. Although some of the windows (namely the Message Composition window) were shared by the Mail and News components of Netscape 3, most functions were performed in separate spaces: the Mail window and the News window, respectively. As a result, it was not so obvious that the two types of messages were so similar.

The truth, however, is that e-mail and news postings are practically identical. There are only two important differences. First, e-mail is sent to one person while a news posting is sent to an entire group. The second difference has to do with how Communicator treats each kind of message. Generally, e-mail messages are downloaded in their entirety to your hard disk while only a news posting's *header* is downloaded. Although you can download the contents of news messages if you want, you usually just read the contents online when you're connected to the server.

Conferencing

One of the more exciting additions to Communicator 4 is Conference, the module that lets you speak to anyone on the Internet, through your computer. That means you can call Australia without having to grapple with the choice of a long distance carrier. Conference also lets you draw on a shared whiteboard, exchange files, write notes back and forth, and browse together on the World Wide Web.

Getting Messages

10

As discussed in the introduction to this section, e-mail and discussion group (news) messages are practically identical. You read, create, send, and even file them the same way. However, the way you set up Communicator to retrieve these messages from the server is slightly different. You'll learn how to get messages, both individual messages (e-mail) and group messages (news postings), in this chapter.

Note: Netscape calls its e-mail component *Messenger* and its discussion group component *Collabra*. It is solely in this chapter, where the two modules overlap the least, that these terms have the most meaning. However, since it is not always clear where one component begins and another ends, I almost always use the more general term *Communicator*.

Getting ready to receive mail messages

Generally, Communicator sets you up to receive mail messages the first time you open the program. However, you can enter or update your settings at any time.

Figure 10.1 *Choose Edit > Preferences.*

To set up mail:

1. Choose Edit > Preferences **(Figure 10.1)** and then click Identity in the Category list. The Identity preferences appear **(Figure 10.2)**.
2. Enter your name and e-mail address in the first two boxes.
3. If desired, enter the e-mail address where you wish to receive replies (it need not be the same as your e-mail address).
4. If desired, enter the name of your organization. If you don't enter anything here, Communicator inserts the name of your service provider.
5. Click Mail Server in the Category list. The Mail Server preferences appear **(Figure 10.3)**.
6. Enter your mail server user name (usually the part of your e-mail address before the @ sign).
7. Enter your outgoing and incoming mail servers. Check with your ISP if you're not sure what to enter here.
8. Click OK to close the Preferences dialog box and save the changes. You're now ready to receive mail.

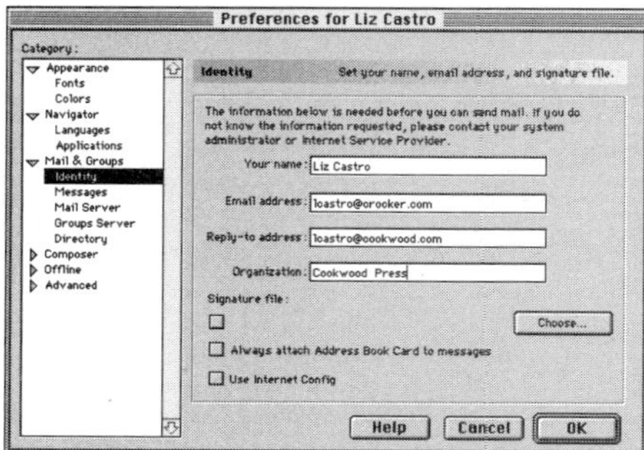

Figure 10.2 *Click Identity in the Category list under Mail & Groups to access the Identity preferences with which you specify your e-mail address.*

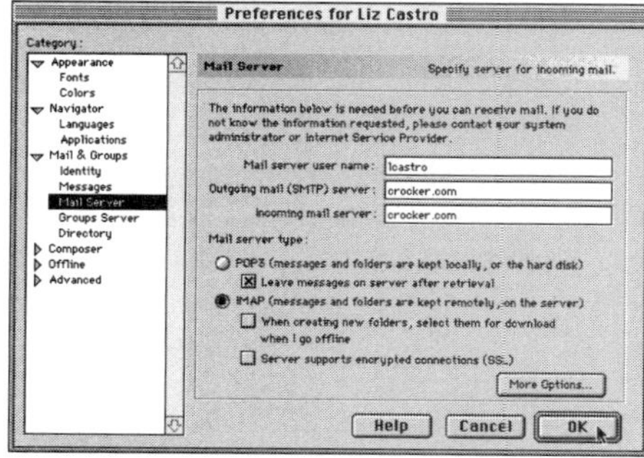

Figure 10.3 *The Mail Server category is used to specify your user name and your e-mail server.*

✔ Tip

- If you have trouble receiving mail, check with your ISP to help you adjust any special settings.

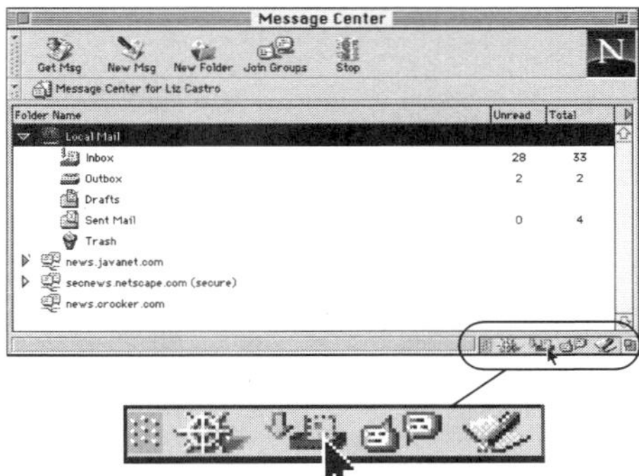

Figure 10.4 *To retrieve your mail from the server, click the letter icon on the Component bar, usually found in the lower-right corner of any main Communicator window.*

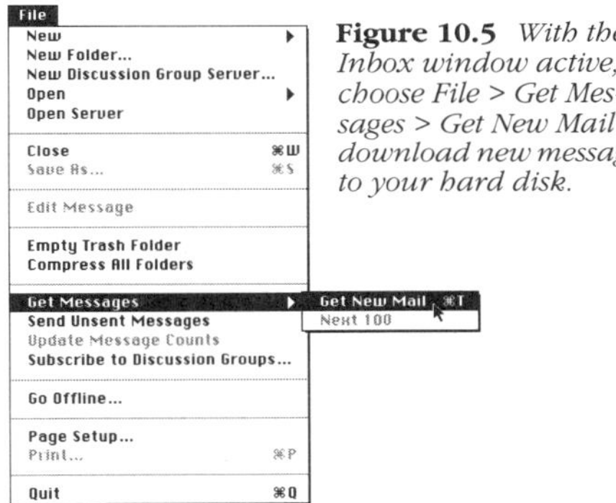

Figure 10.5 *With the Inbox window active, choose File > Get Messages > Get New Mail to download new messages to your hard disk.*

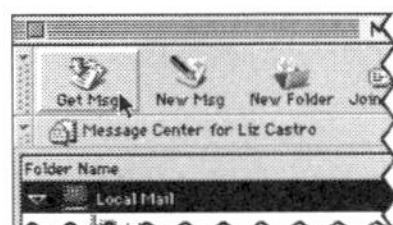

Figure 10.6 *You can also click the Get Msg button at the left end of the toolbar to check your mail.*

Getting new mail messages

Once you have a new e-mail address, checking to see if someone has actually sent you something becomes almost an obsession. Luckily, Communicator gives you several ways to check your electronic mailbox.

To get new mail messages:

- From any Communicator window, click the Mailbox button in the Component toolbar **(Figure 10.4)**. Communicator will display the Inbox, ask you for your password if necessary, consult your server, and finally show you your new mail—that is, if you have any.
- If you already have the Inbox window open, you can also choose File > Get Messages > Get New Mail **(Fig. 10.5)** or click the Get Msg button at the left end of the toolbar **(Figure 10.6)**. New messages, if there are any, will be displayed in the Inbox folder.
- For information on retrieving news messages from the server, consult *Getting new news messages* on page 133.

✔ Tip

- The Mailbox icon changes depending on whether you have mail or not. In Figure 10.4, the down arrow indicates that there is new mail waiting on the server. For more information, consult *Checking for mail messages periodically* on page 122.

Checking for mail messages periodically

When you are connected to the Internet, you can have Communicator check for mail every few minutes and alert you when you've received something. Of course, if you're not connected, Communicator won't be able to tell if you have mail.

To check for mail messages periodically:

1. Choose Edit > Preferences and click Mail Server in the Category list at left. The Mail Server preferences appear **(Figure 10.7)**.
2. Click the More Options button. The More Mail Server Preferences box appears **(Figure 10.8)**.
3. Check the box next to Check for mail every and enter a number to determine how often Communicator will check the server for mail.
4. Click OK twice to close both preferences boxes.

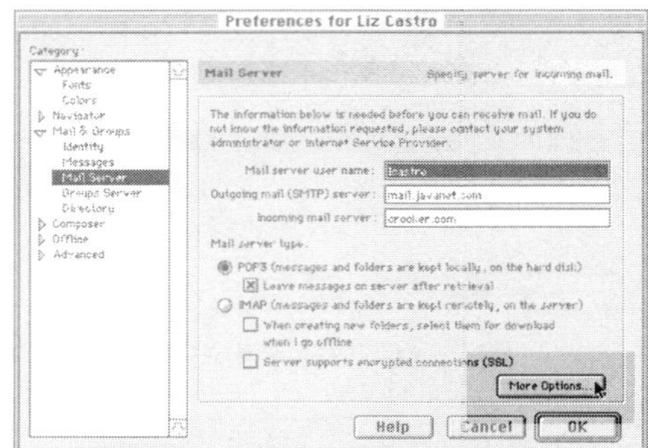

Figure 10.7 *Choose Mail Server under Mail & Groups in the Category list. Then click the More Options button.*

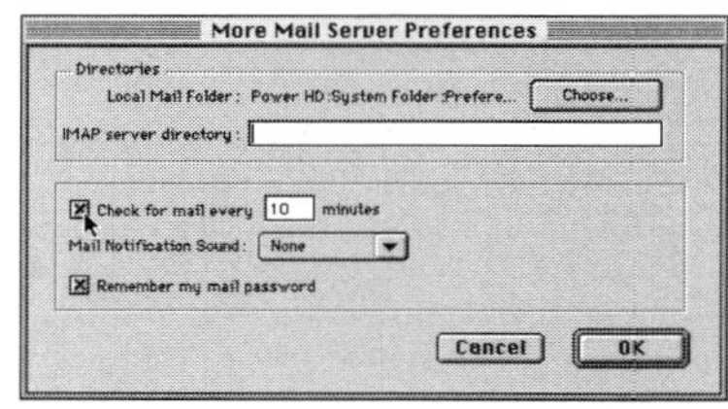

Figure 10.8 *Enter how often you want Communicator to check the server for new messages.*

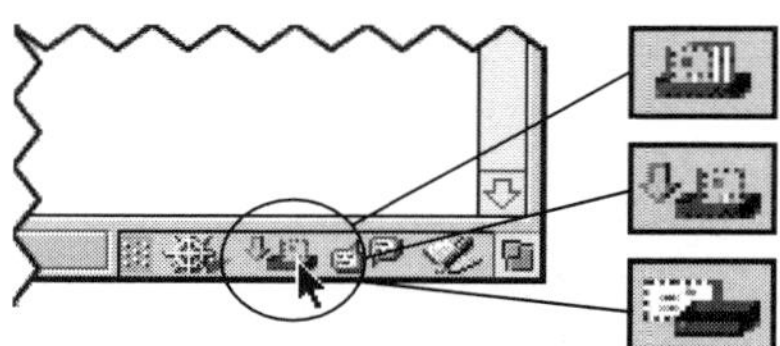

Figure 10.9 *A plain letter icon (top) means you have no letters waiting on the server. An arrow pointing down (middle) means you have mail waiting on the server. An icon of envelopes outside of the bin (bottom) means that Communicator can't tell whether there are messages for you or not (you're probably not connected).*

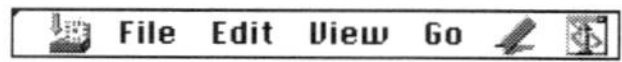

Figure 10.10 *Even if Communicator is hidden, a flashing inbox over the Apple menu will notify you when mail has arrived.*

✔ Tips

- Communicator doesn't automatically *copy* mail from the server—it just checks to see if there is any. If there is, it notifies you with an arrow pointing down next to the letter icon both in the Communicator window **(Figure 10.9)** and at the top of the Apple menu **(Figure 10.10)**. You still have to *get* your mail *(see page 121)*.
- If you only want to check for mail manually, remove the checkmark from the option in step 3.
- Communicator will only check for mail automatically if you have saved your mail password *(see page 323)*.

Figure 10.11 *Choose File > Go Offline.*

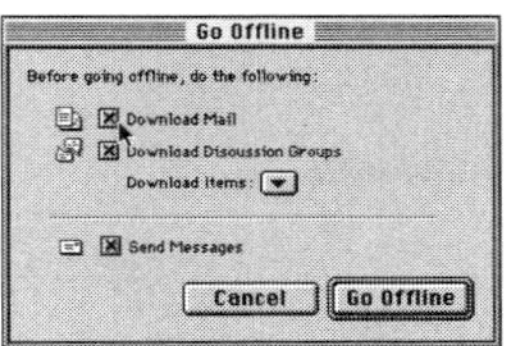

Figure 10.12 *Check the Download Mail option in the Go Offline dialog box.*

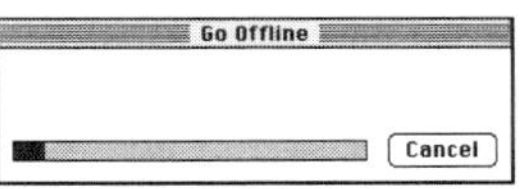

Figure 10.13 *A progress bar shows you how long it will take to download all the messages.*

Figure 10.14 *When you are offline, Navigator shows the line "You are offline..." in the status bar to indicate that you will not be able to connect to Web pages, get new mail, or read discussion groups until you go online again.*

Downloading mail for offline reading

Every time you get your e-mail *(see page 121)*, it is automatically downloaded to your hard disk. You can always choose to disconnect from the Internet before reading it. However, Communicator has a one-step command that lets you download your mail starting from any window.

To download mail for offline reading:

1. Choose File > Go Offline **(Fig. 10.11)**. The Go Offline dialog box appears.
2. Check the Download Mail option **(Figure 10.12)**.
3. Click Go Offline. Your e-mail is downloaded and placed in your inbox.
4. If desired, disconnect from the Internet. Communicator does not complete this step, whatever it may imply.
5. Choose Communicator > Messenger Mailbox to see any new messages in your Inbox.

✔ Tips

- The Go Offline and Go Online commands do precisely the same things: download e-mail and news messages and send any queued messages. Neither has any effect whatsoever on your Internet connection. However, the Go Offline command makes it impossible to connect to Web pages, check your mail manually, or read discussion group messages.
- For more information on downloading *news* messages for offline reading, consult *Getting news messages for reading offline* on page 134.

Setting your discussion groups server

Figure 10.15 *Choose Edit > Preferences.*

Most ISPs give you access to at least one discussion groups server. In general, the server's name is *news.serviceprovider-name.com* (or .edu). If you're not sure, contact your ISP. Before you can read discussion group messages, you'll have to give Communicator the name of your principal discussion groups server.

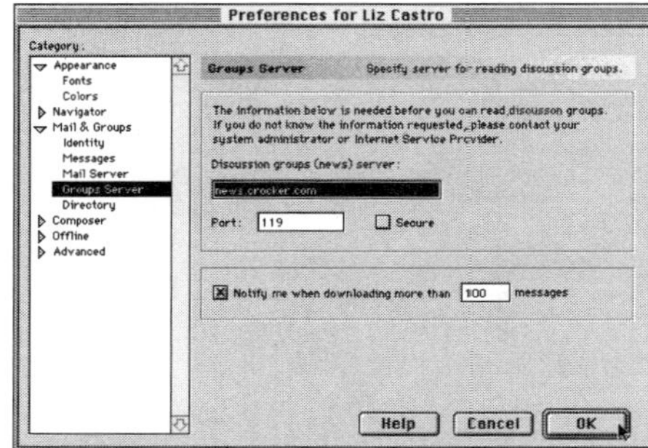

Figure 10.16 *In the Groups Server category of the Preferences dialog box you can specify the principal discussion groups server from which you wish to get your discussion groups messages.*

To set your discussion groups server:

1. Choose Edit > Preferences **(Figure 10.15)**.
2. Click Groups Server in the Category list. The Groups Server preferences appear at right **(Figure 10.16)**.
3. Enter the name of the discussion groups server. If you are not sure, contact your ISP. They will be able to provide you with this information.
4. If necessary, enter the port number.
5. If you are accessing a secure server, check the Secure box.

✔ Tips

- You can have Communicator contact more than one discussion groups server for news messages. For more details, consult *Adding and deleting groups servers* on page 125.
- Netscape uses the term "discussion groups" to refer to both Usenet newsgroups (that is, those that are publicly available) and intranet discussion groups (those that are available only from your private server). In earlier versions of the software, both were called *newsgroups*. Now both are called *discussion groups*. Keeping up?

Figure 10.17 *Choose File > New Discussion Group Server.*

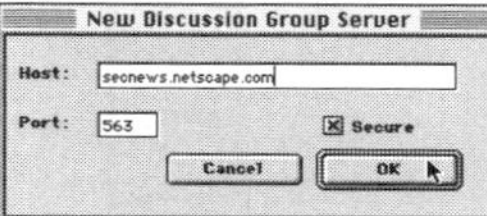

Figure 10.18 *In the New Discussion Group Server dialog box, type the name of the server you want to add. If necessary, enter the port number and check the Secure box.*

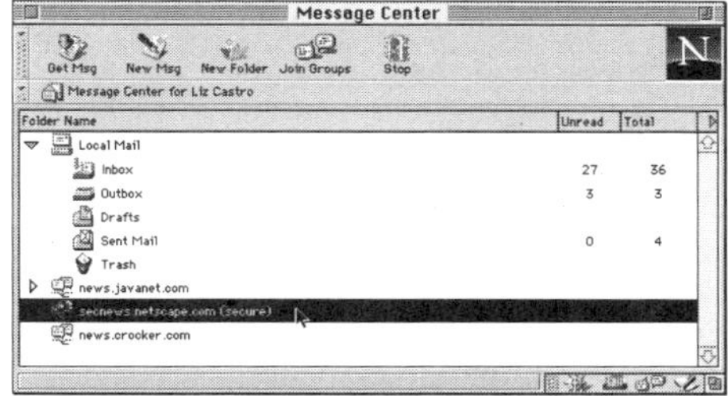

Figure 10.19 *The new discussion groups server appears in the Message Center window.*

Adding and deleting groups servers

You can get discussion groups from as many servers as you have access to, simply by connecting to additional discussion groups servers. For example, you can connect to Netscape's secure news server to join discussions about Communicator, as shown in this example.

To add a new discussion groups server:

1. Choose Communicator > Collabra Discussion Groups. The Message Center appears.
2. Choose File > New Discussion Group Server **(Figure 10.17)**. The New Discussion Group Server dialog box appears.
3. In the Host box, type the name of your news server—something like **news.provider.com (Figure 10.18)**. Consult your Internet provider if you're not sure.
4. If necessary (usually, it's not) type the port number in the Port box.
5. Check the Secure box if it is a secure server (Netscape's is).
6. Click OK. Communicator contacts the discussion groups server and, if you have the proper access privileges, shows the server in the Message Center window **(Figure 10.19)**.

Continued...

To delete a discussion groups server:

1. Choose Communicator > Collabra Discussion Groups. The Message Center appears.
2. Select the discussion groups server that you want to delete **(Figure 10.20)**.
3. Press the Delete key. An alert appears asking if you really want to remove the server and the discussion groups it contains, if any, that you had subscribed to **(Figure 10.21)**.
4. Click OK. The discussion groups server disappears **(Figure 10.22)**.

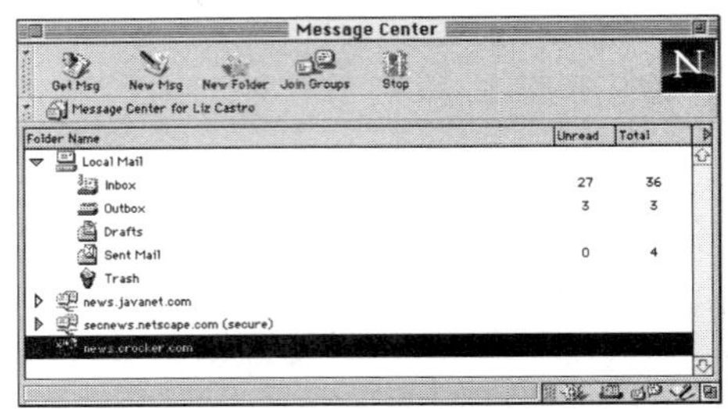

Figure 10.20 *Choose the discussion groups server that you want to delete.*

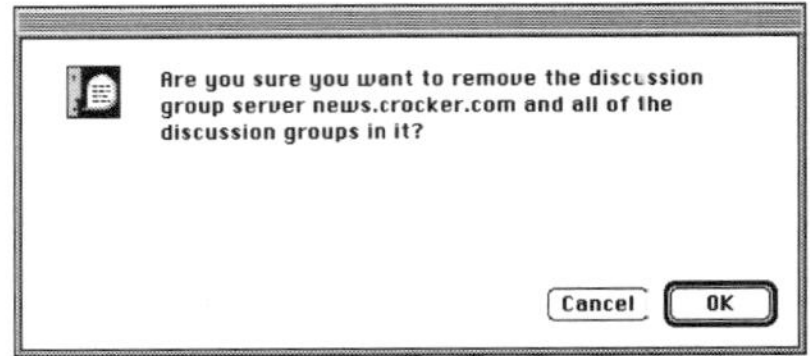

Figure 10.21 *Read the alert and click OK to remove the discussion groups server.*

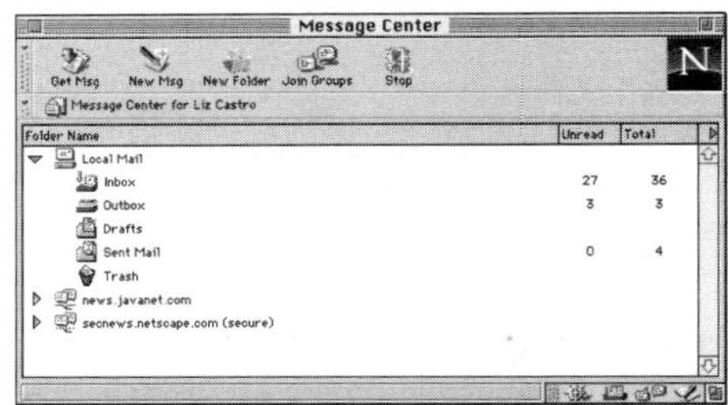

Figure 10.22 *The discussion groups server is removed from the list of servers in the Message Center.*

✓ Tips

- Some discussion groups servers restrict access to certain users. Others let anyone connect to see the groups it contains. For example, to see the discussion groups offered to the public by Netscape Communications, open the server **secnews.netscape.com**. (The name of the Communicator group is **netscape.communicator.mac**.)
- Microsoft Corporation also lets the public access its discussion groups server: msnews.microsoft.com.
- You can open as many discussion groups servers as you have access to.
- Secure servers' names begin with *secnews*, as in Netscape's discussion groups server: secnews.netscape.com.
- You can also add a discussion groups server by clicking Add Server in the Subscribe to Discussion Groups dialog box *(see page 131)*.

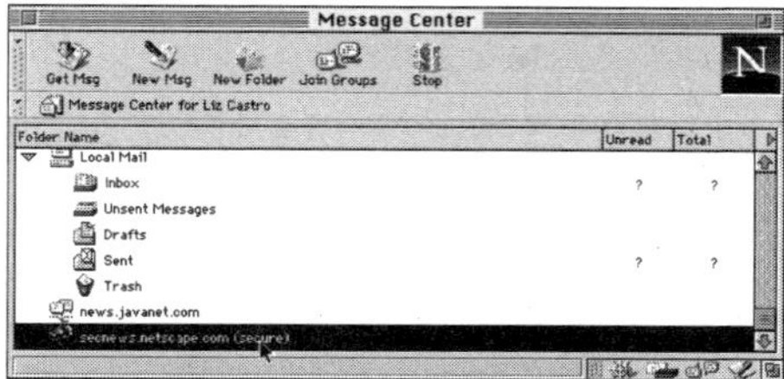

Figure 10.23 *Select the discussion groups server.*

Figure 10.24 *Choose File > Subscribe to Discussion Groups (left) or click the Join Groups button on the toolbar.*

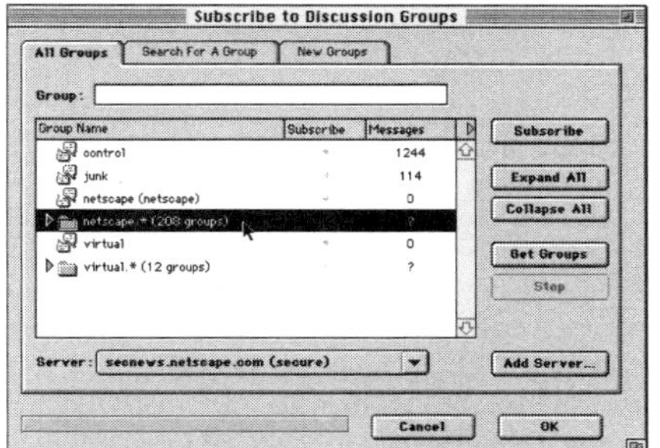

Figure 10.25 *All of the discussion groups available from the selected server are displayed, divided into categories. Click a triangle next to a discussion group folder (which has an asterisk in its name) to see the discussion groups it contains.*

Viewing a list of all discussion groups

Your Internet service provider decides which discussion groups you have access to and which you don't. Some commercial online services like CompuServe and AOL have gotten a bit of press about their efforts to censor certain groups. By getting the full list from the server, you can see exactly what you have access to.

To view a list of all discussion groups:

1. Select a discussion groups server **(Figure 10.23)**.
2. Choose File > Subscribe to Discussion Groups **(Figure 10.24)** or click the Join Groups button on the toolbar. After what might be a good long while, a list of available discussion groups is downloaded from the server and shown in the Subscribe to Discussion Groups dialog box **(Figure 10.25)**.

✔ Tips

- Once you view all the discussion groups, you can scroll through them to see if there are any you like. You can subscribe to the groups that interest you so that they appear in the Message Center window. For more information on subscribing to discussion groups, consult *Subscribing to a discussion group* on page 131.
- Click the triangle next to a folder name (with an asterisk) to see all the discussion groups in that category. Click it again to hide them. Select a set and click Expand All to view all of the individual groups it contains. Choose Collapse All to hide them.

Where discussion group names come from

There are several major categories of discussion groups: alt (*alternative*, includes a wide variety of groups from alt.sex to alt.appalachian), comp (*computer*, with every program and operating system imaginable), news (*newsgroups*, most contain information about discussion groups themselves), rec (*recreation*, from rec.arts.cinema to rec.games.go to rec.sport.fencing), sci (*science*, from sci. archaeology to sci.virtual-worlds), and soc (*society*, includes the soc.culture discussion groups that discuss different countries and their customs). Your server will probably have access to several more categories, including specialty or local groups **(Figure 10.26)**.

One good way to find out what a discussion group is about is by reading its FAQ or *frequently asked questions* file, if it has one. Each discussion group's FAQ is generally posted to the group once a month. You can find many of them at **ftp://rtfm.mit.edu/pub/usenet/discussiongroup.name** where *discussiongroup.name* is the full name of the group in question **(Figure 10.27)**.

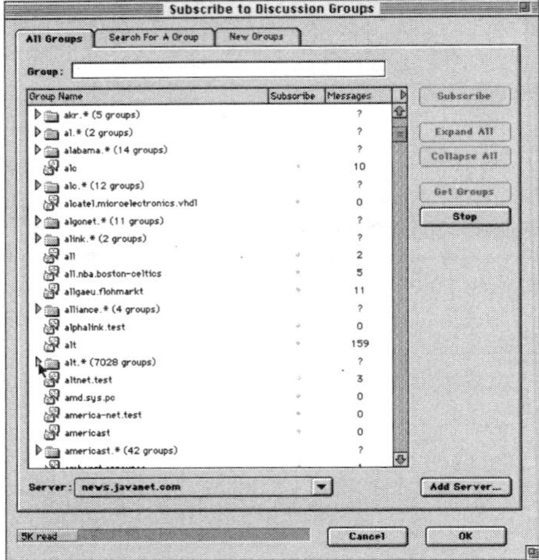

Figure 10.26 *A server may offer several different categories of discussion groups. Click a triangle to see the individual groups in a category.*

Figure 10.27 *A FAQ (this one is from the discussion group* rec.games.go*) tells what topics are discussed in a particular group and gives general information about those topics.*

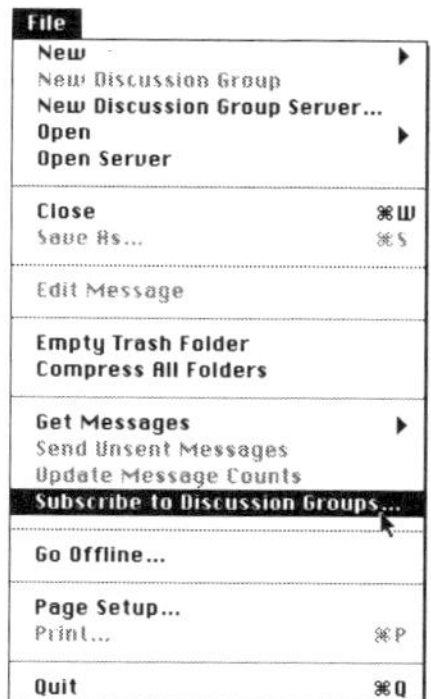

Figure 10.28 *With the desired discussion groups server selected, choose File > Subscribe to Discussion Groups (left) or click the Join Groups button on the toolbar.*

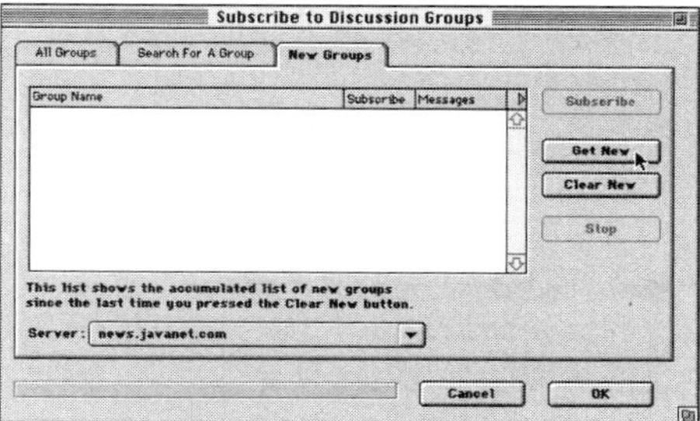

Figure 10.29 *Click the Get New button in the New Groups tab.*

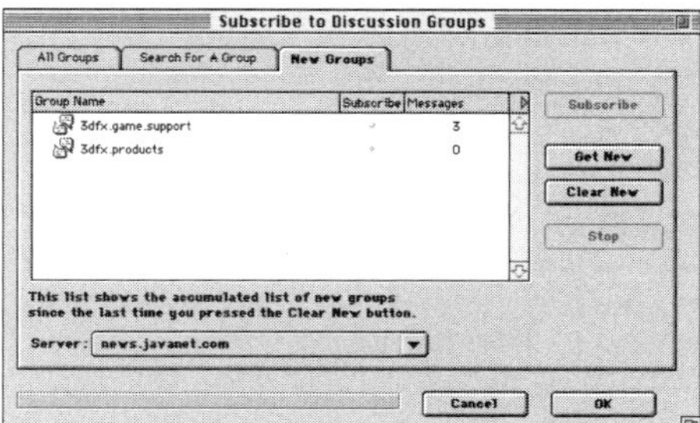

Figure 10.30 *If new discussion groups have been created since the last time you checked, Communicator will display them in the New Groups window list.*

Getting a list of new discussion groups

New discussion groups are created all the time. For public discussion groups on Usenet, all it takes is a group of people who write a charter, elicit votes from the potential public, and then distribute the new discussion groups to the Internet. Discussion groups on your local intranet are even easier to set up. You can search for and display the groups which have been added since the last time you checked.

To get a list of new groups:

1. Select the desired discussion groups server.
2. Choose File > Subscribe to Discussion Groups **(Figure 10.28)** or click the Join Groups button on the toolbar.
3. Click the New Groups tab at the top of the dialog box.
4. Click Get New **(Figure 10.29)**. A list of new discussion groups appears **(Figure 10.30)**.
5. Click OK.

✔ Tips

- Subscribe to a new group by selecting it and clicking the Subscribe button or by clicking in the Subscribe column next to the group's name.
- The new groups remain in the New Groups list until you click the Clear New button. At that point, they disappear from this list and join the full list *(see page 127)*.
- Abort the search at any time by clicking the Stop button.

Finding a discussion group

Some servers carry so many discussion groups that it's hard to find the one you're looking for. There are two ways to quickly find an elusive discussion group.

To find a discussion group when you know the whole name:

1. Choose File > Subscribe to Discussion Groups **(Figure 10.31)** or click the Join Groups button on the toolbar.
2. Type the name of the discussion group in the Group box at the top of the All Groups panel **(Figure 10.32)**. As you type, Communicator will display the discussion group that matches your entry, if possible.

To find a discussion group when you only know part of the name:

1. Choose File > Subscribe to Discussion Groups or click the Join Groups button on the toolbar.
2. Click the Search For A Group tab.
3. Type the key word(s) that you want to search for **(Figure 10.33)**.
4. If necessary, select the server that you wish to search in.
5. Click Search Now. All the discussion groups in the selected server that contain the given key words appear in the list in the lower part of the dialog box **(Figure 10.34)**.

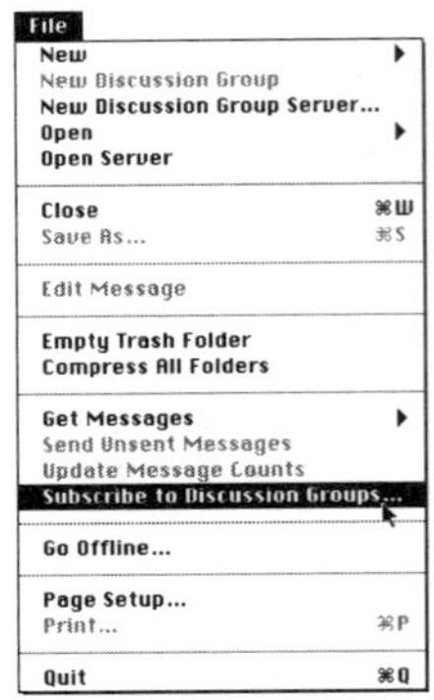

Figure 10.31 *With the desired discussion groups server selected, choose File > Subscribe to Discussion Groups (left) or click the Join Groups button on the toolbar.*

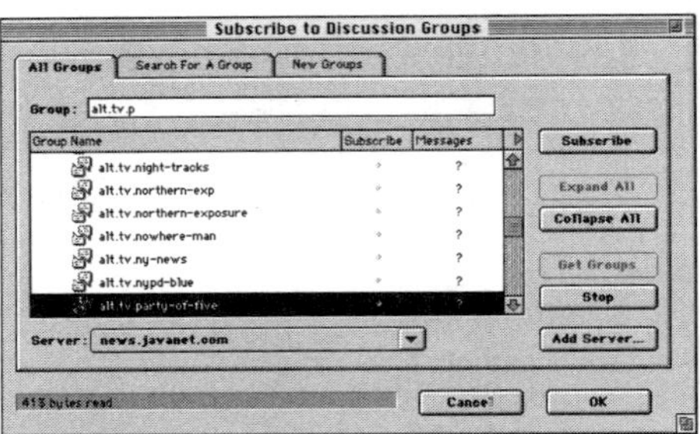

Figure 10.32 *Type the name of the discussion group that you want to subscribe to in the Group field. As you type, Communicator displays the discussion group that matches your entry.*

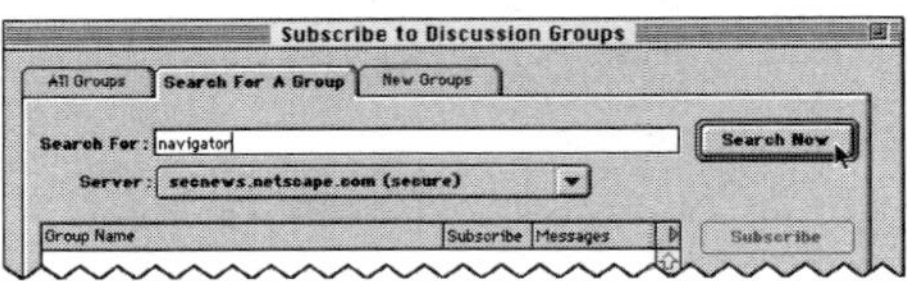

Figure 10.33 *Type the key words in the Search For box. If necessary, select the server that you want to search in the Server pop-up menu.*

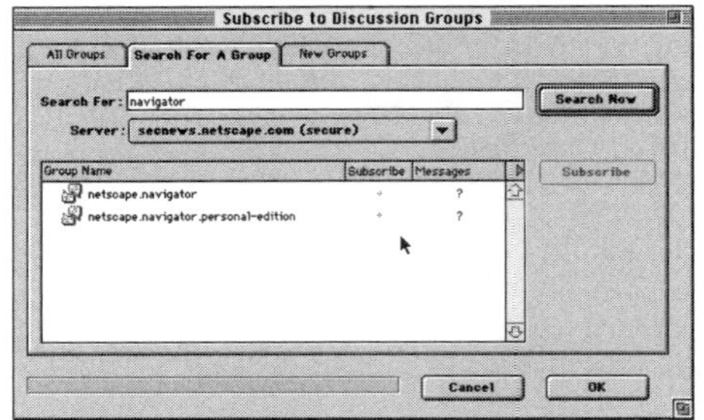

Figure 10.34 *All the discussion groups that meet the search criteria are shown in the list box in the Search For A Group panel.*

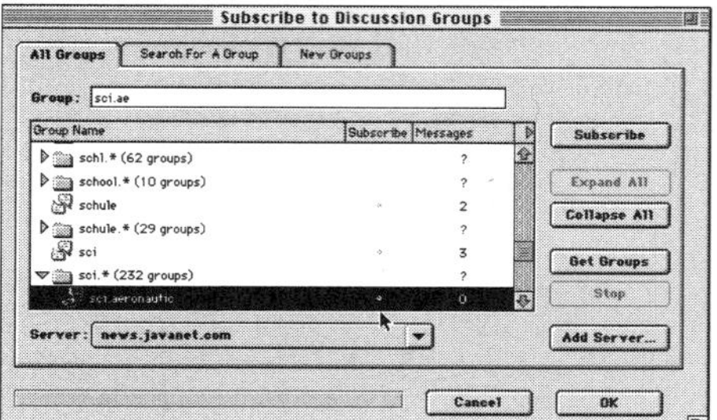

Figure 10.35 *Scroll around in the list of discussion groups until you see the one that you want to subscribe to. Click the triangle next to folders to expand them or collapse them.*

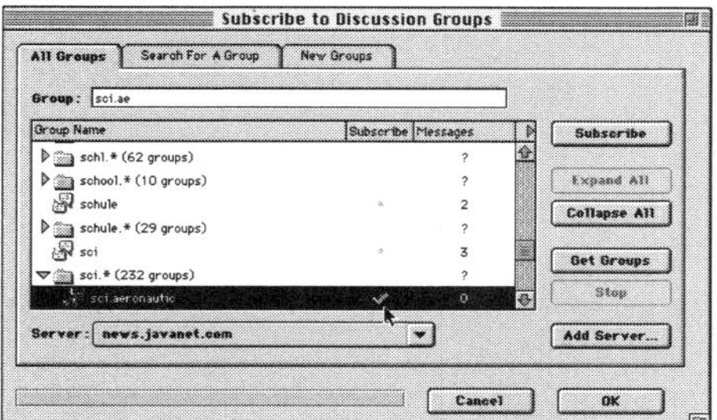

Figure 10.36 *Click in the column next to the discussion group's name to subscribe to it. A checkmark will appear.*

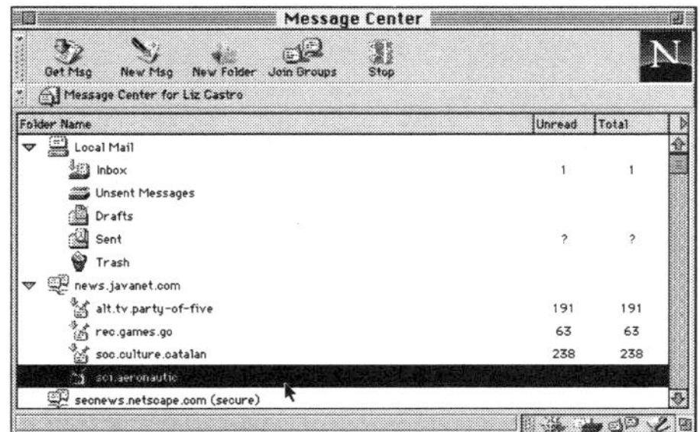

Figure 10.37 *The group appears inside the discussion groups server in the Message Center.*

Subscribing to a discussion group

You have to subscribe to a discussion group before you can read the messages it contains. Once you've subscribed, you can open the discussion group in the Message Center, see how many messages there are, and read and respond to them.

To subscribe to a discussion group:

1. Choose File > Subscribe to Discussion Groups or click the Join Groups button on the toolbar.
2. Use the techniques described on the preceding pages to show the desired discussion group in any of the panels of the Subscribe to Discussion Groups dialog box **(Figure 10.35)**.
3. Click in the Subscribe column, to the right of the discussion group's name **(Figure 10.36)** or click Subscribe. A checkmark appears next to the discussion group to show that you have subscribed to it.

To cancel a subscription to a discussion group:

1. Select the discussion group in the Message Center window.
2. Press the Delete key. An alert appears asking you to confirm the deletion.
3. Click OK. The group disappears.

✔ Tip

- You can subscribe to as many discussion groups as you like. The idea, of course, is to subscribe to the ones that you will actually read, and then hide the rest. You can always go back to the main list.

Jumping to a group from Communicator

You can view, and then subscribe to, a discussion group from other components of Communicator. If you know the group's name, you can type it in the Location field in Navigator. Or, if you come across a link to the group, either on a Web page or in a message, you can click the link to view the discussion group.

To jump to a discussion group from other Communicator components:

1. In Navigator, type **news:discussion group.address** in the Location field, where *discussion group.address* is the complete name of the discussion group that you wish to view **(Figure 10.38)**.
2. Or, click the link on a Web page or message **(Figure 10.39)**.
3. The discussion group's messages are displayed in the Message List window **(Figure 10.40)** and the discussion group itself is listed in the Message Center **(Figure 10.41)**. Browse through the messages as desired.

✔ Tips

- You are automatically subscribed to a discussion group when you view it this way. For more information on subscribing, consult *Subscribing to a discussion group* on page 131.
- You can only open groups this way if they can be accessed through your principal news server. Groups at other servers must be accessed in the conventional way *(see page 131)*.

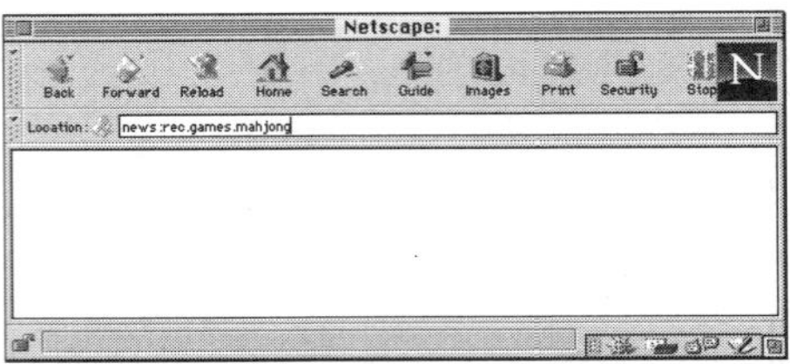

Figure 10.38 *Type* **news:** *followed by the discussion group's name in Navigator's Location field.*

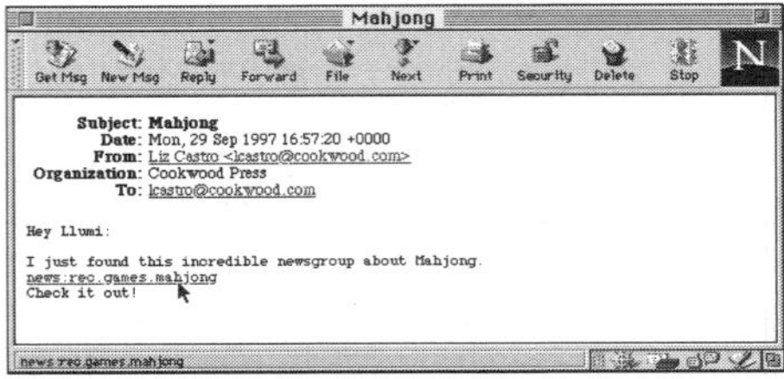

Figure 10.39 *Or click a link to a discussion group from a Web page or an e-mail message.*

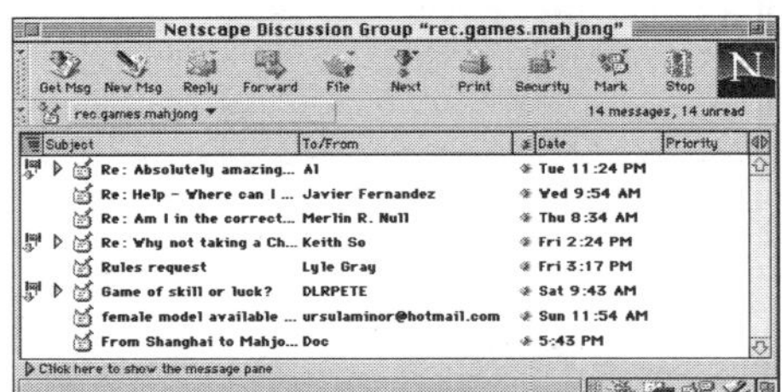

Figure 10.40 *The discussion group's messages are displayed in the Message List window.*

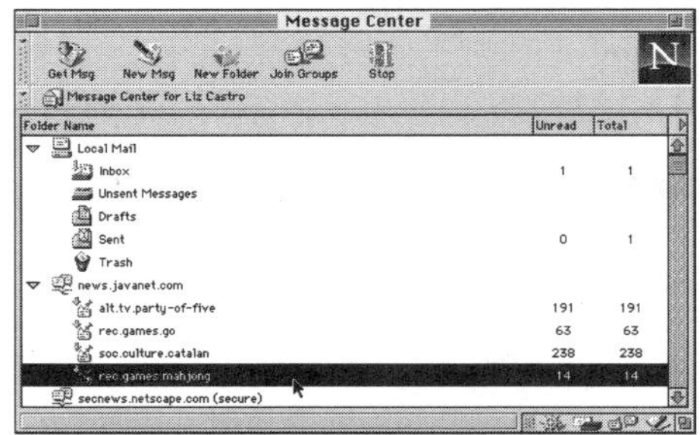

Figure 10.41 *You are automatically subscribed to the discussion groups that you jump to from other components of Communicator.*

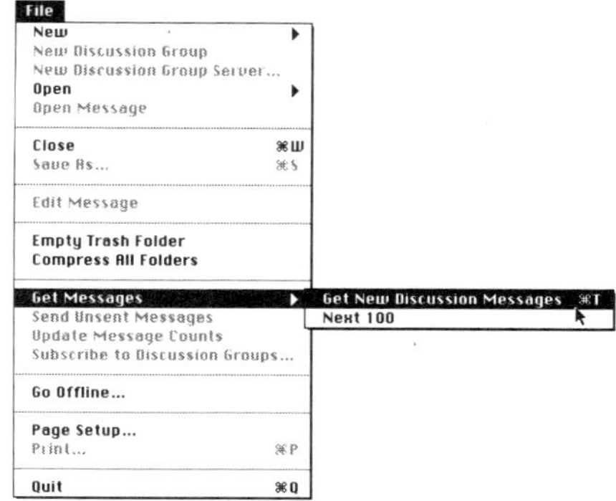

Figure 10.42 *After double-clicking on a discussion group and reading all its messages, choose File > Get Messages > Get New Discussion Messages to download any messages that have been posted since you started reading.*

Figure 10.43 *Click the Get Msg icon from within a discussion group to download more new messages from the server, if there are any.*

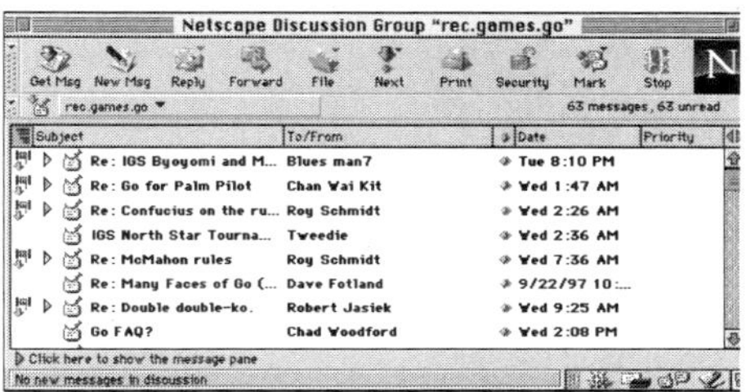

Figure 10.44 *The new messages are displayed in Communicator's Message List window. Notice that only the headers are downloaded to your hard disk, and that messages that you have not read yet have a green diamond next to them.*

Getting new news messages

Discussion groups can have hundreds of new messages posted daily—or none. There are several ways to see if the discussion groups that you've subscribed to have any new traffic.

To get new news messages:

- Double click the discussion group in the Message Center. The group opens in the Message List window. Communicator automatically contacts the server to see if there are any new messages. The message *headers* are downloaded to your hard disk.
- From the Message List window, get more new messages by choosing File > Get Messages and then one of the options in the submenu **(Figure 10.42)**, or by clicking the Get Msg button on the toolbar **(Figure 10.43)**.

✓ Tips

- Generally, the contents are not downloaded with the headers. Instead, when you open a message, Communicator contacts the server and retrieves the contents at that time. This means that you cannot use these techniques for reading news offline. For reading offline, consult *Getting news messages for reading offline* on page 134.
- If there are too many new messages, Communicator asks you how many you want to download. How many is "too many" is determined in the Groups Server panel of the Preferences dialog box *(see page 324)*.

Getting news messages for reading offline

If you have a dial-up account and a limited amount of hours each month, you may want to download messages from the discussion groups you have subscribed to and then read them offline. Even if you do have unlimited access, reading offline is also a great way to keep a single telephone line free.

Figure 10.45 *Choose File > Go Offline.*

To get new news messages for reading offline:

1. Choose File > Go Offline **(Fig. 10.45)**. The Go Offline dialog box appears.
2. Check the Download Discussion Groups option **(Figure 10.46)**.
3. In the Download Items pop-up menu, choose the discussion groups whose messages you wish to download before going offline **(Figure 10.47)**. Selected discussion groups are marked with a bullet.
4. Click Go Offline from the Download dialog box. Communicator downloads the headers *and contents* of each message in each group that you selected in step 3 **(Figure 10.48)**.
5. Disconnect from the Internet, if desired, and read your messages.

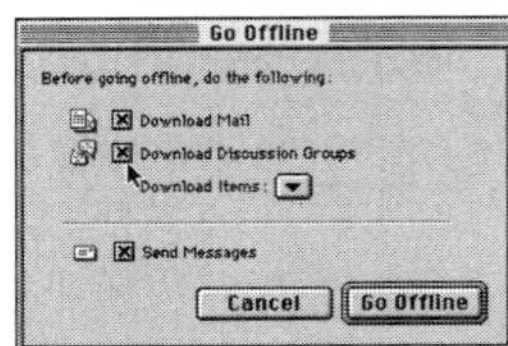

Figure 10.46 *Check Download Discussion Groups.*

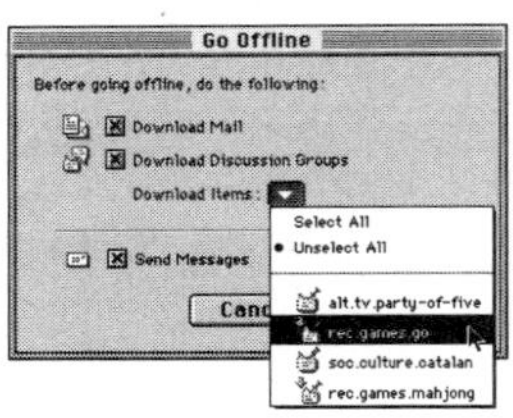

Figure 10.47 *From the pop-up menu, choose the discussion groups whose messages you want to download before going offline.*

Figure 10.48 *Communicator shows a progress bar dialog box as it downloads the messages from the selected discussion groups.*

✔ Tip

- Discussion group messages take up space. You may not want to download too many. You can also adjust Communicator to eliminate old messages in order to save space *(see page 339)*.

11 Reading Messages

Once you get the messages via e-mail or discussion groups, you can open them and read them. Communicator has several features that help you find the messages that you want to read—from viewing particular groups of messages, to putting them in threads, to reorganizing the columns—so that you can see the information that most interests you.

Reading messages

Once you have gotten new messages *(see page 121)*, you can open them and read them. You can also re-read mail received earlier, or read mail that you have sent to others.

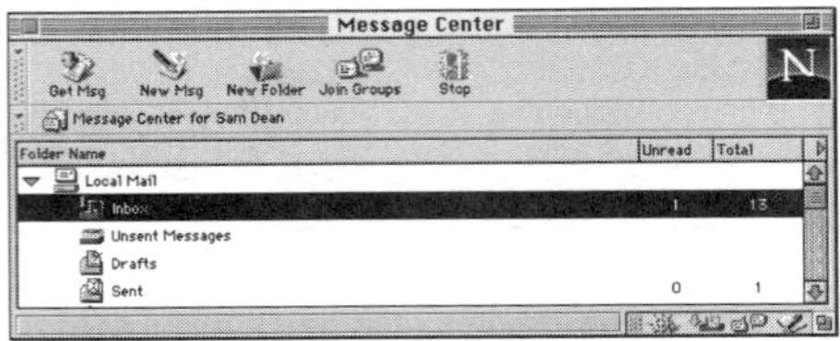

Figure 11.1 *Double click any folder in the Message Center to see the messages it contains.*

To read messages:

1. From the Message Center, double click any folder or discussion group **(Figure 11.1)**. You'll find new mail messages in the Inbox folder. The folders contents are listed in the Message List window **(Figure 11.2)**.

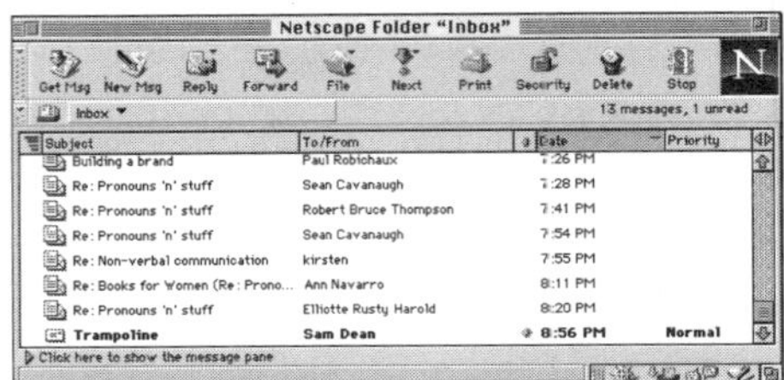

Figure 11.2 *The messages in the selected folder are listed. New messages are shown in bold and are marked with a green diamond. Select a message and click the triangle in the bottom-left corner to display its contents.*

2. To read messages in the same window as the list, click a message and choose View > Show Message or click the triangle at the bottom-left corner of the window. The message is revealed in the lower half of the window **(Figure 11.3)**.

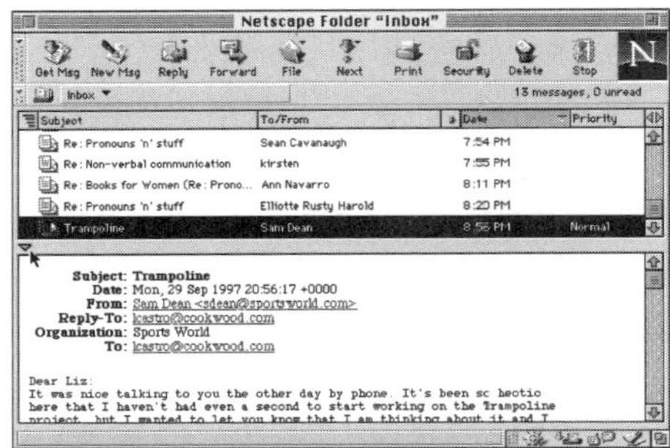

Figure 11.3 *The message is revealed. Click the triangle again to hide the message.*

✔ Tips

- Hide the bottom half of the window (i.e., the contents of the message) by clicking the triangle, or by choosing View > Hide Message.
- To read messages in the Message Contents window, double click the message header **(Figure 11.4)**. You can display each message in a separate window or "reuse" windows each time you view a new message. (See *Mail & Groups* on page 320.)

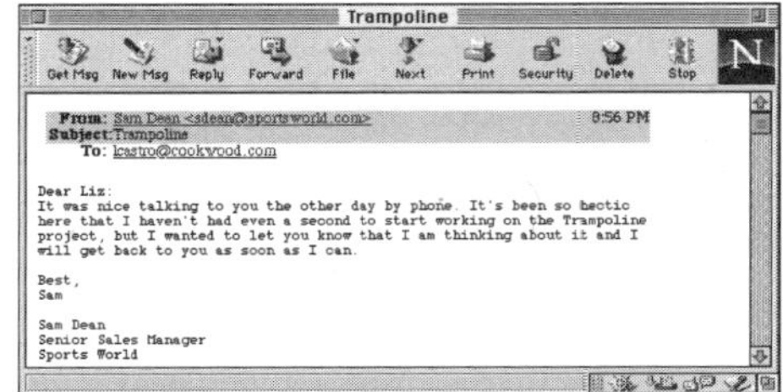

Figure 11.4 *Or double click the message to show its contents in the Message Contents window.*

- You can display only those messages that you haven't read yet *(see page 138)*.
- You can show additional information about a message, including the route it took to get to you—which is sometimes useful for exposing fraudulent messages *(see page 140)*.

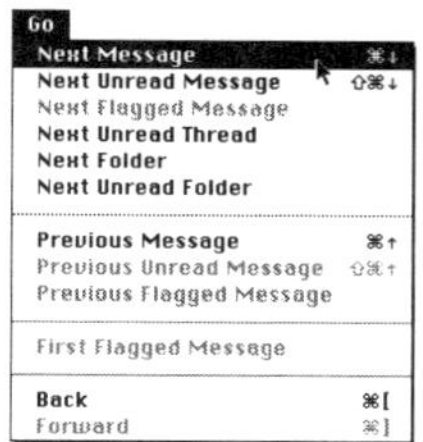

Figure 11.5 *Use the commands in the Go menu to move from one message to another.*

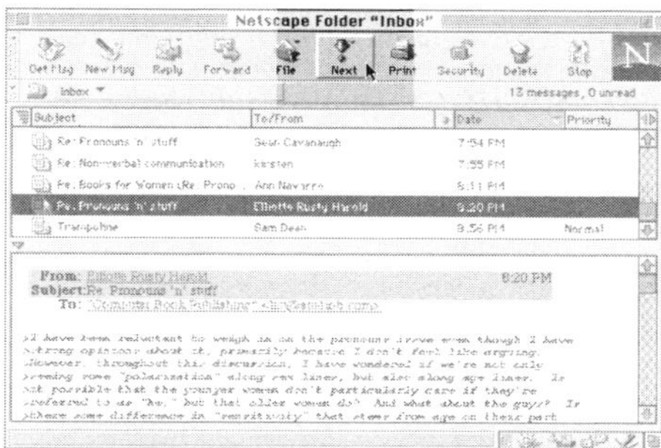

Figure 11.6 *Or click the Next button to view the next message in the folder or discussion group.*

Navigating through your messages

Netscape's Go menu makes it easy to move from one message to the next.

To navigate through your messages:

Choose a command from the Go menu to see the next or previous message of whatever type you wish **(Figure 11.5)**.

✔ Tips

- You can also click the Next button on the toolbar to advance to the next message **(Figure 11.6)**.
- The up and down arrows work for navigating from message to message if the cursor is in the upper half of the window. If you've clicked in the lower pane, the up and down arrows simply navigate you through that particular message.
- Choose Go > Back and Go > Forward to navigate through the messages that you've read, in the order that you've read them.

Viewing messages

New messages are shown in bold with a green diamond in the Read column. However, sometimes you have so many messages, that the new ones get lost in the shuffle. You can choose exactly which messages you want displayed in the Message List window. If you have a lot of messages in a folder, viewing only the new ones, or only the new ones in a particular thread, can help make messages of interest stand out.

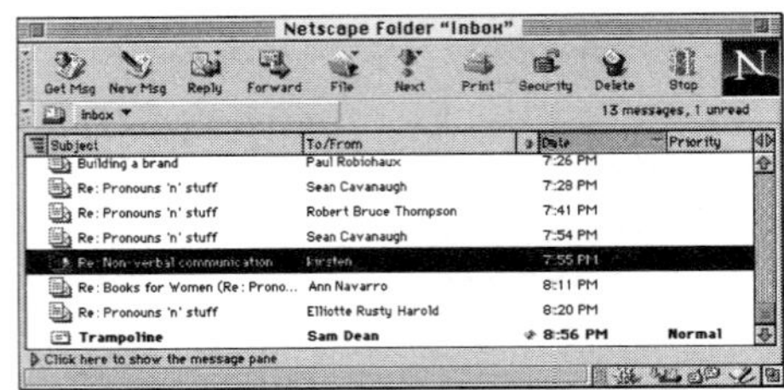

Figure 11.7 *In this example, we can see several messages, some of which have been read already. (New messages are shown in bold with a green diamond. Messages you've already read are in normal text with no diamond at all.)*

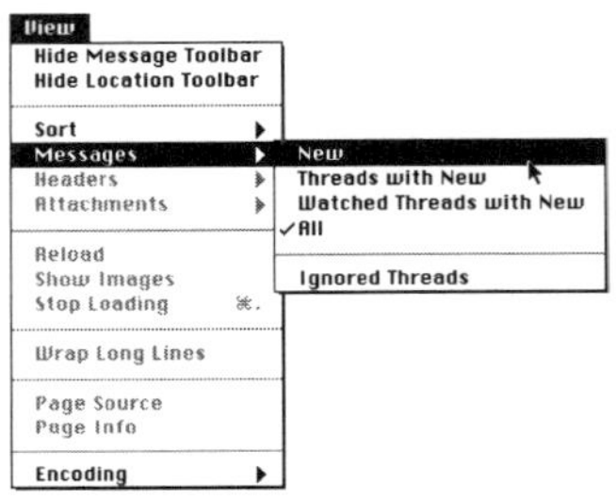

Figure 11.8 *Choose View > Messages > New.*

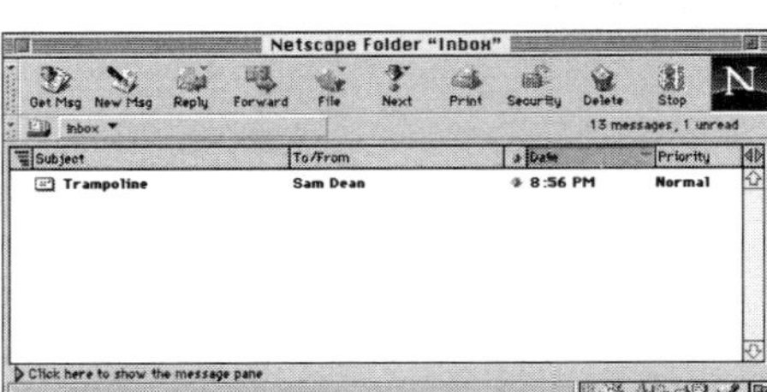

Figure 11.9 *The Inbox now shows only the messages that have not yet been read.*

To view new messages:

- Choose View > Messages > New to display only those messages that you have not read or that are marked as unread **(Figure 11.8)**.
- Choose View > Messages > Threads with New to display only those threads that contain new messages. Messages that you've already read in the thread will also be displayed.
- Choose View > Messages > Watched Threads with New to display only those threads that you've chosen to watch *(see page 148)* that have new messages. Messages that you've already read in the watched thread will also be displayed.
- Choose View > Messages > All to display both new and old messages.
- Choose View > Messages > Ignored Threads to display the messages that you previously had marked to ignore.

✓ Tip

- If a message is displayed in the bottom half of the Message List window, it will remain visible when you choose a View > Messages option, whether or not it belongs to the selected group.

Figure 11.10 *Choose Edit > Preferences.*

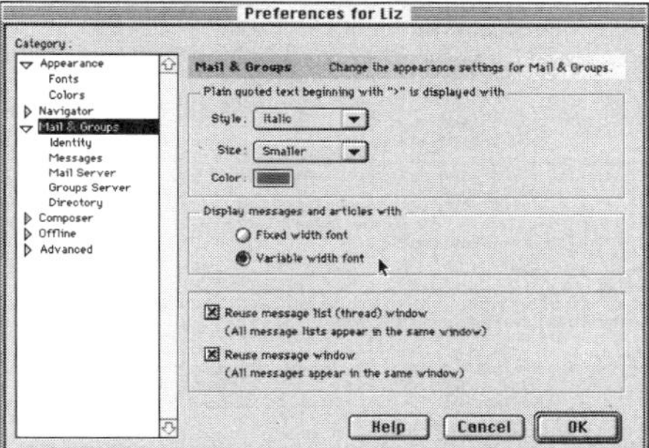

Figure 11.11 *Click Mail & Groups in the Category list. Then choose a style, size, and color for quoted text, and a type of font for regular text.*

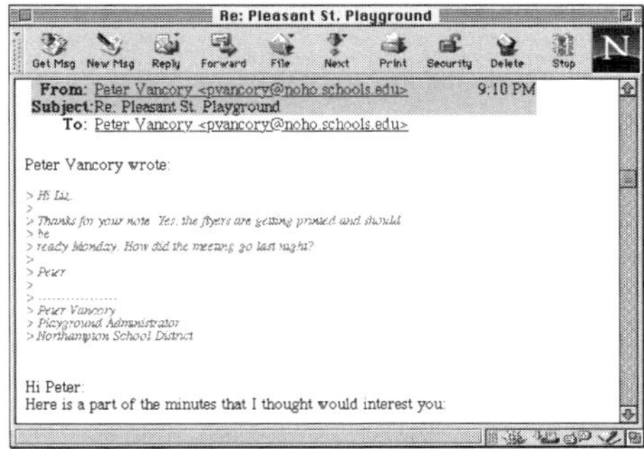

Figure 11.12 *Notice how the entire note is displayed in a Variable width font (Times, in this case) and that the quoted part of the note is in a smaller size, in italics, and red.*

Changing your messages' appearance

You can change the appearance of messages in the Message List and Message Contents windows to make them easier to read.

To change your messages' appearance:

1. Choose Edit > Preferences **(Figure 11.10)**.
2. Click Mail & Groups in the Category list. The Mail & Groups preferences appear **(Figure 11.11)**.
3. In the first section, choose a style, size, and color for the quoted text in your messages.
4. In the second section, choose Fixed width font to show your messages in a font like Courier or Variable width font to show your messages in a font like Times or Helvetica.
5. Click OK. Messages will now appear with the type of font selected. Quotes will appear with the style selected **(Figure 11.12)**.

✔ Tips

- You can specify the actual fonts in the Fonts panel of the Preferences dialog box *(see page 313)*.
- Unfortunately, these options have no effect on the Message Composition window (where they would be particularly handy).

Viewing more or less header information

A message's header contains information about where the message was sent from and can be used to determine if the sender is really who she says she is. On the other hand, all that information takes up a lot of screen space. You can choose to view varying amounts of the header information.

To view more or less header information:

1. Choose View > Headers and then an option in the submenu **(Fig. 11.13)**:

   Choose > All to view all the available header information, including the complete information about where the message was received from, the full date, sender, recipient, Subject, Message ID, MIME-Version, Content-Type, Status, and X-Mozilla Status, among others **(Figure 11.14)**.

   Choose > Normal to view only the Subject, Date, From, and To lines **(Figure 11.15)**.

   Choose > Brief to view the Subject, From, and To lines, with an abbreviated date—all on a gray background **(Figure 11.16)**.

✔ Tip

- Unfortunately, you can't hide the header information altogether.

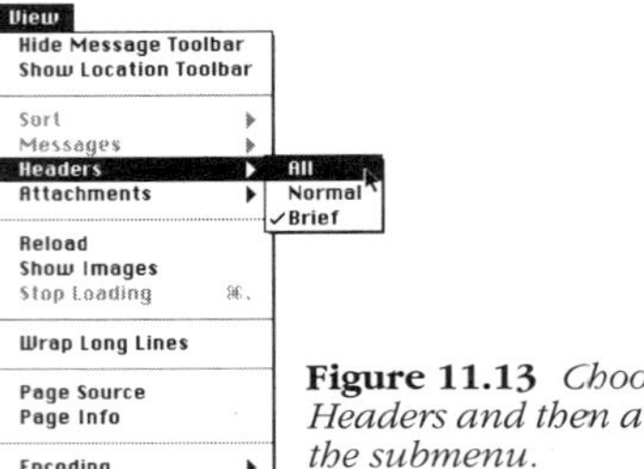

Figure 11.13 *Choose View > Headers and then an option in the submenu.*

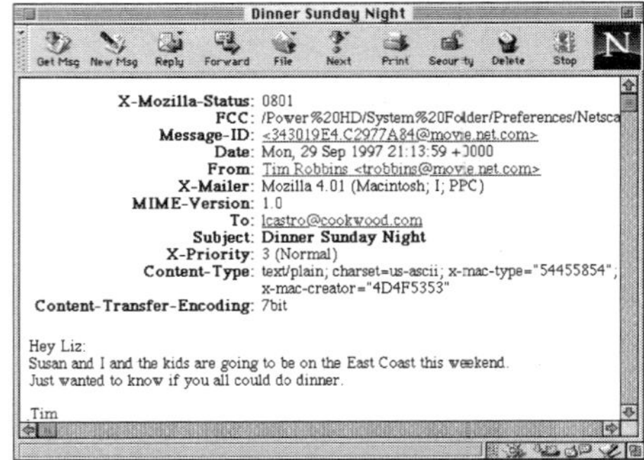

Figure 11.14 *Showing all the headers can take up a considerable amount of window space.*

Figure 11.15 *A "Normal" header contains the Subject, Date, From, and To lines.*

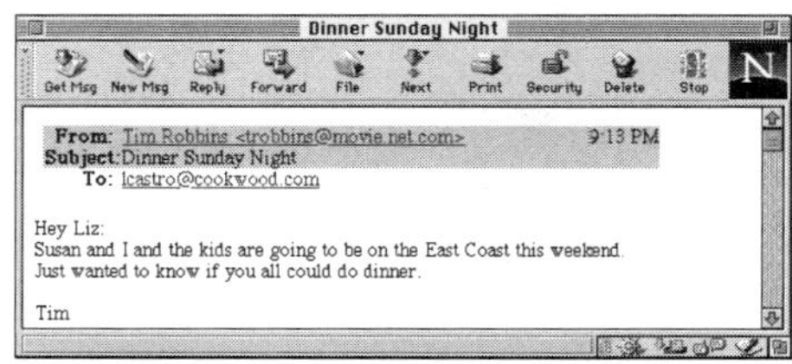

Figure 11.16 *Choose "Brief" headers in order to abbreviate the date and position it in the upper-right corner, and then shade the From and Subject lines. Frankly, it's not that much more brief than Normal (Figure 11.15).*

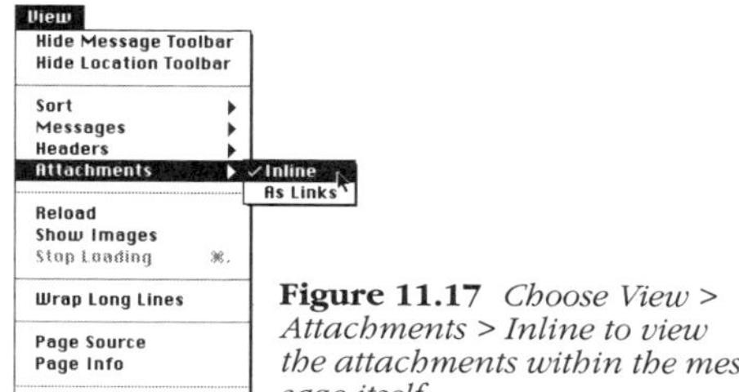

Figure 11.17 *Choose View > Attachments > Inline to view the attachments within the message itself.*

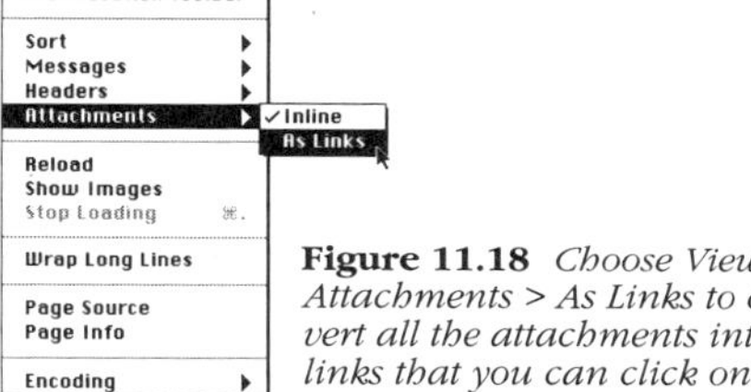

Figure 11.18 *Choose View > Attachments > As Links to convert all the attachments into links that you can click on.*

Figure 11.19 *Viewing attachments as links (as shown here) is faster than viewing them inline.*

Viewing attachments

If you receive an attachment, you can choose to view it within the message itself (for convenience), or to view a placeholder (for speed).

To view attachments within the message:

Choose View > Attachments > Inline **(Figure 11.17)**. Attachments like images, text files, and Web pages will be shown within the body of the message itself.

To view attachments as a link:

Choose View > Attachments > As Links **(Figure 11.18)**. All attachments are converted into links **(Figure 11.19)**. Click a link to see the attachment.

Wrapping long lines

Not all e-mail programs include returns in their messages. For example, earlier versions of Netscape inserted returns in outgoing messages according to the width of the Message Composition window when the message was created. If you receive a message whose lines are too long to read comfortably on screen, you can choose to add additional returns to make it easier to read.

Figure 11.20 *Choose View > Wrap Long Lines.*

To wrap long lines to view messages better:

Choose View > Wrap Long Lines **(Figure 11.20)**. Additional returns will be added to the viewed messages in order to view them in entirety on screen.

✔ Tip

- The Wrap Long Lines option in the Message List window's View menu is *not* the same as the Wrap Long Lines on Send option in the View menu when a Message Composition window is active *(see page 153)*. The former controls only the appearance of incoming messages while the latter actually adds returns to outgoing messages.

Figure 11.21 *Choose Edit > Search Messages.*

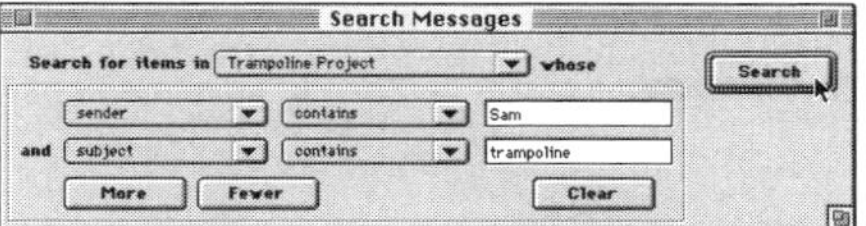

Figure 11.22 *Choose a folder to search in, choose a category for the criteria, and then type the search criteria. Finally, click Search.*

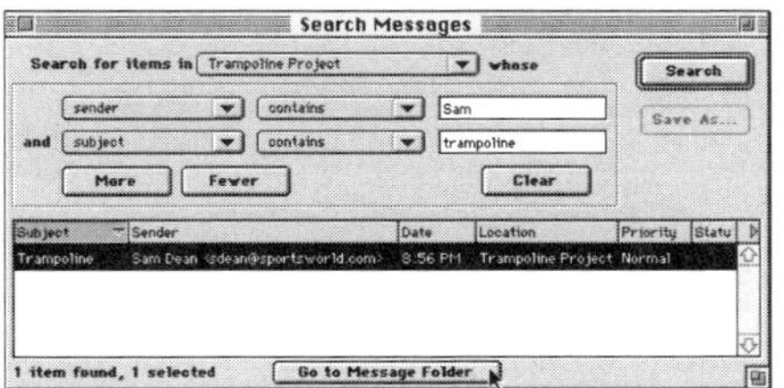

Figure 11.23 *Once the Search dialog box finds what you are looking for, select it and then click Go to Message Folder to display the message in its folder.*

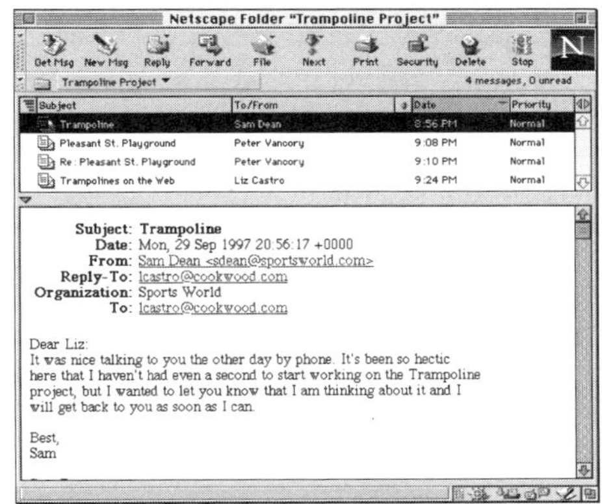

Figure 11.24 *The message is shown in its folder.*

Searching for a message

Ever file something so well that you can't find it? Now you can search for particular messages using the sender's name, subject, or other criteria.

To search for a message:

1. Choose Edit > Search Messages **(Figure 11.21)**. The Search Messages dialog box appears.
2. Choose a folder to search in from the pop-up menu at the top of the dialog box **(Figure 11.22)**.
3. Enter the criteria by choosing options in the first two pop-up menus and typing what you're looking for.
4. If desired, click More to add another line of search information. Items found will satisfy each line you add.
5. Click Search. A list of messages that satisfy the search criteria are shown at the bottom of the dialog box **(Figure 11.23)**.
6. Select the desired message and click Go to Message Folder. The message is displayed **(Figure 11.24)**.

✔ Tip

- Choose Local Mail in step 2 to search through all your e-mail folders. Choose a news server or discussion group to search through discussion group messages.

Threading messages

Communicator can relate all the replies (and replies to replies) that are generated from a single original message into a wonderful invention called a *thread*. This makes it easy to follow a particular conversation from start to finish even if you have a busy mailbox. You can choose to view your e-mail in threads or as individual messages.

To thread messages:

1. Choose View > Sort > by Thread **(Figure 11.26)**. The option will have a check next to it when it is active. Choose the option again to toggle it. Each message that is related to another will appear hidden underneath the parent message **(Figure 11.27)**.
2. Click the arrow to the left of a threaded message group to reveal the replies beneath it. Click the arrow again to hide the replies beneath it **(Figure 11.28)**.

✔ Tip

- Click the box to the left of the Subject column to thread messages. Click it again to view the messages in ascending or descending order. You can't use this box to unthread messages; instead, choose View > Sort and the desired option in the submenu.

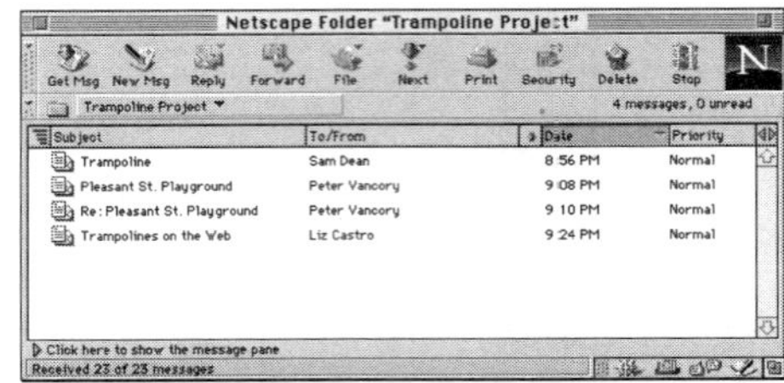

Figure 11.25 *Unthreaded messages appear independently.*

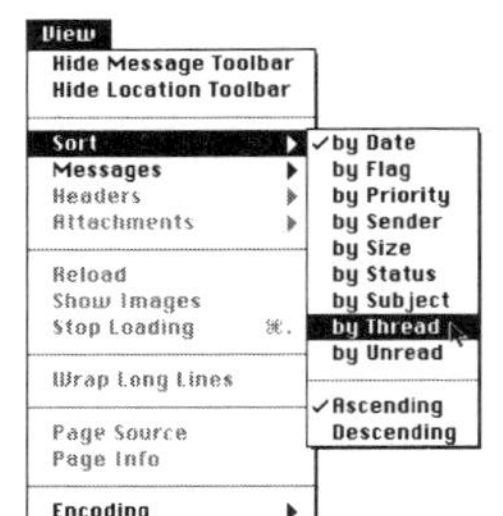

Figure 11.26 *Choose View > Sort > by Thread to relate messages with the same subject line.*

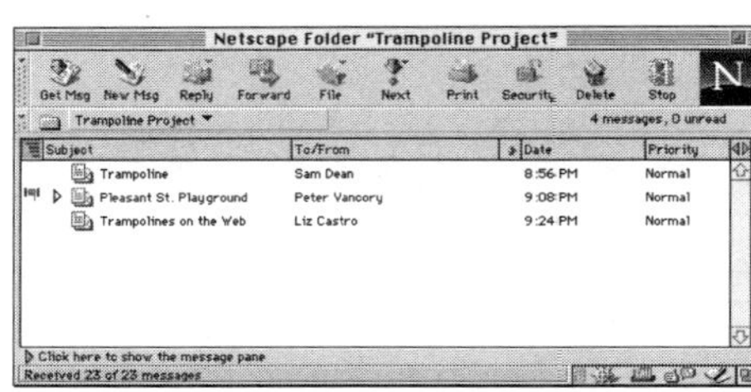

Figure 11.27 *The third message shown in Figure 11.25 is now hidden under its "parent."*

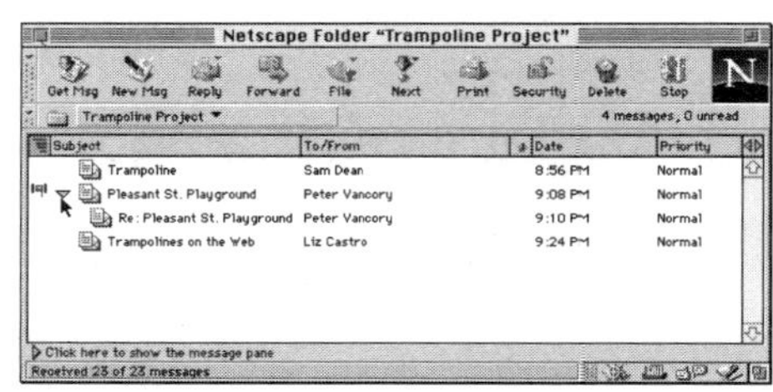

Figure 11.28 *Click the arrow to the left of the original message's letter icon to display the related messages. Click it again to hide them.*

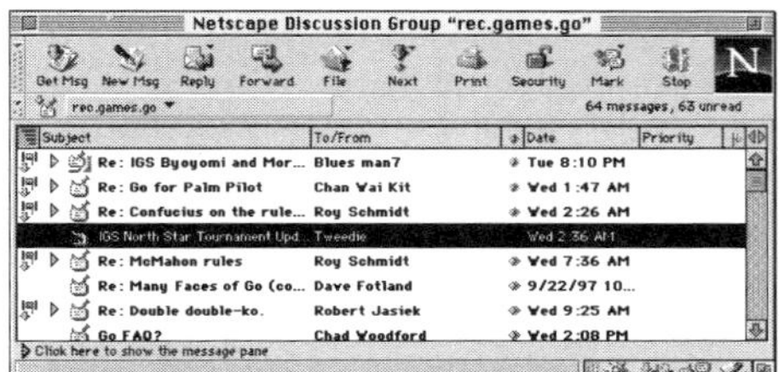

Figure 11.29 *Select the message you wish to flag.*

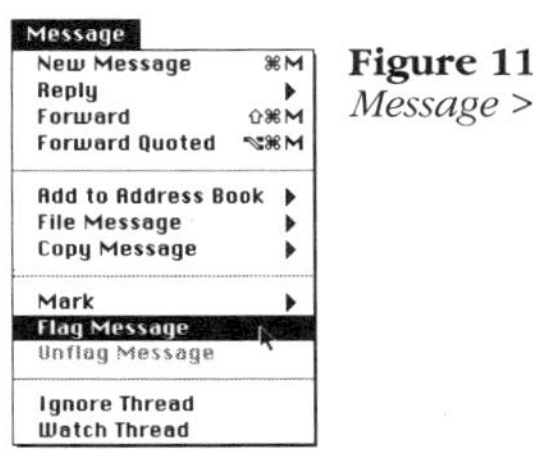

Figure 11.30 *Choose Message > Flag Message.*

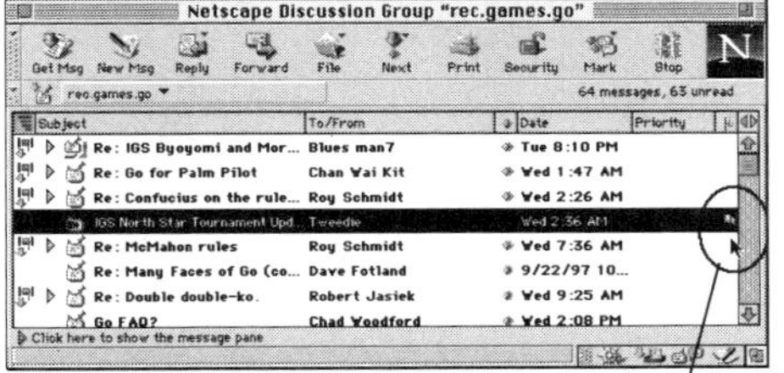

Figure 11.31 *A little red flag appears next to the message.*

Flagging messages

In a busy mailbox or discussion group, it's sometimes hard to keep your eye on an important piece of mail. One easy way to make a message stand out is to flag it.

To flag or unflag a message:

1. Select the desired message in the Message List window **(Figure 11.29)**.

2. Choose Message > Flag Message **(Figure 11.30)**. A checkmark next to the command indicates that the message is flagged. Choose the command again to toggle it. A little red flag appears in the Flagged column to the right of the flagged message **(Figure 11.31)**. The flag disappears when you unflag the message.

✔ Tips

- You can flag a message (or remove its flag) by clicking in the Flagged column next to the desired message.
- If you cannot see the Flagged column, click the left arrow in the upper-right corner of the list box until the column appears. For more information on revealing hidden columns, consult *Changing the columns* on page 150.
- You can navigate through only the flagged messages using the First Flagged, Next Flagged, and Previous Flagged commands in the Go menu. For more information on getting from message to message, consult *Navigating through your messages* on page 137.

Marking mail as read or unread

New messages are marked in bold and with a green diamond so that you know that they're new. Once you've read a message, the mark disappears. You can choose to restore the Unread mark to remind yourself to return to that message at a later date. You can also mark mail as read, even if you haven't read it—perhaps because you can tell from the Subject line that the message is not of interest to you.

To mark messages as read or unread:

1. Select the message(s) that you want to mark **(Figure 11.32)**.
2. Choose Message > Mark and then the desired option in the submenu **(Figure 11.33)**. A green diamond appears next to unread messages and disappears for messages that you've read or marked as read **(Fig. 11.34)**.

   • Choose > Mark Selected as Read or > Mark Selected as Unread to mark the selected message as read or unread.

   • Choose > Mark Thread Read to mark the entire thread to which the message belongs as read.

   • Choose > Mark All Read to mark as read all the messages in the current folder.

   • Choose > by Date **(Figure 11.35)** to open the Mark By Date dialog box. Choose a date, and click OK to mark all messages with that date or earlier as read **(Figure 11.36)**.

   • Choose > for Later to mark a message as read in the current session but have it appear as unread the next time you open Communicator.

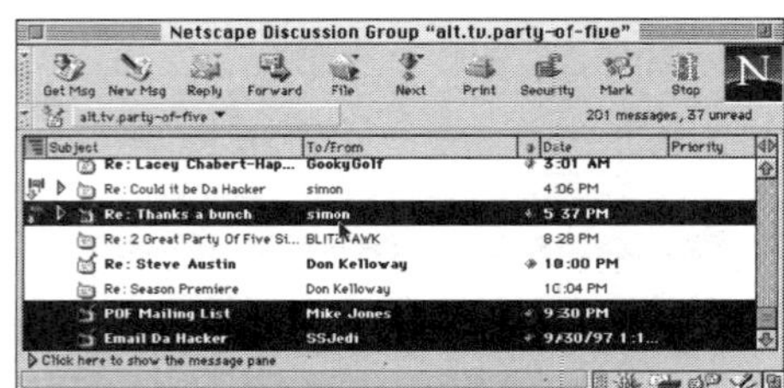

Figure 11.32 *Choose the unread messages that you wish to mark as read.*

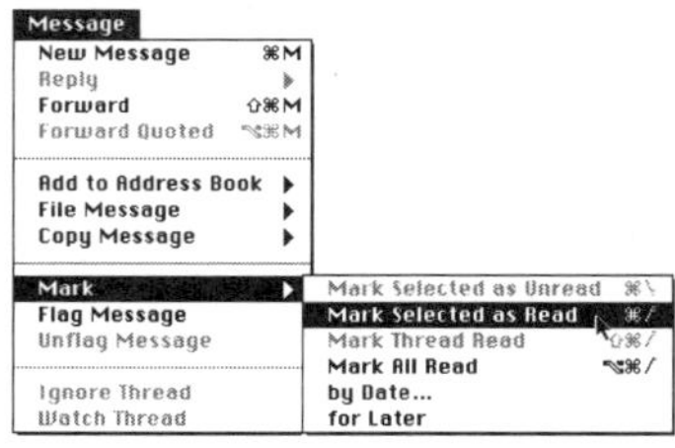

Figure 11.33 *Choose Message > Mark > Mark Selected as Read.*

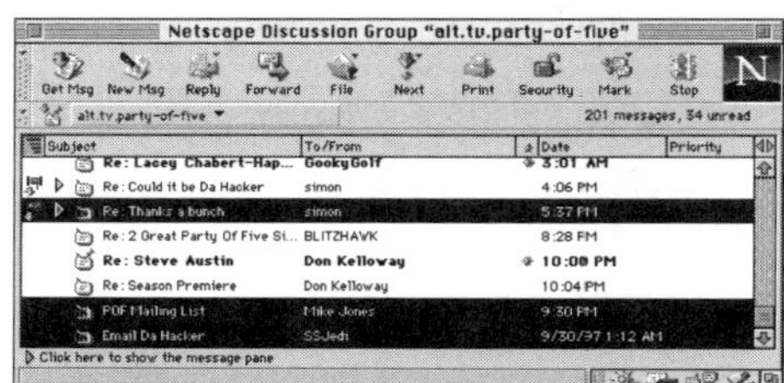

Figure 11.34 *The newly "read" messages appear in plain text and the green diamonds disappear.*

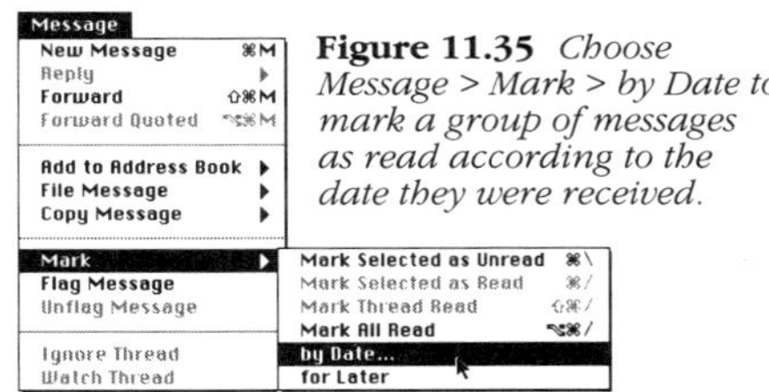

Figure 11.35 *Choose Message > Mark > by Date to mark a group of messages as read according to the date they were received.*

Figure 11.36 *In the Mark By Date dialog box, choose a date to mark as read all the messages received before that date.*

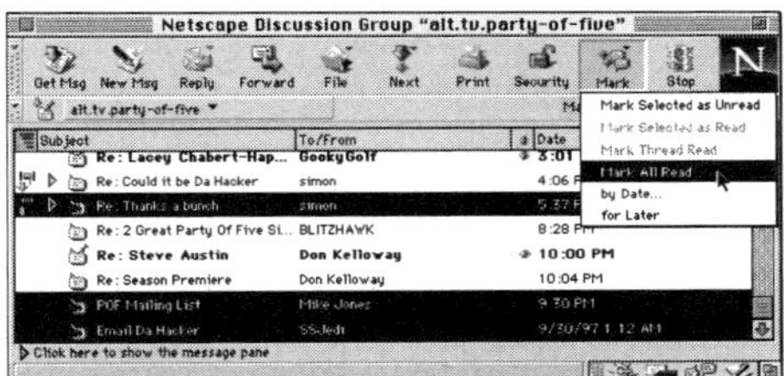

Figure 11.37 *If you're reading discussion group messages, you can mark messages as read by choosing an option in the pop-up menu that appears when you click the Mark button on the toolbar.*

✔ Tips

- You can also mark a message as read or unread by clicking in the Read column (the one with the green diamond) next to the desired message.
- You can hide read messages (or messages marked as read) so that the ones you haven't read are more obvious. For more information, consult *Viewing messages* on page 138.
- For more information about threaded messages, consult *Threading messages* on page 144.
- If you're reading a discussion group, you can also use the Mark button on the toolbar to mark messages as read. Click the button and hold down to choose an option from its submenu **(Figure 11.37)**. The Mark button is not available if you are reading e-mail messages. Use the menu.

Watching and ignoring threads

If you post a message to a busy discussion group, it's useful to mark the thread of interest and hide the others so that you can quickly see if anyone has responded to your message.

To watch a thread:

1. Select a message in the thread **(Figure 11.38)**.
2. Choose Message > Watch Thread **(Figure 11.39)**. A tiny pair of glasses appears next to the message name **(Figure 11.40)**.

To ignore a thread:

1. Select a message in a thread that you don't want to read. (A message with a header like "Make MONEY MONEY MONEY" is probably a good choice.)
2. Choose Message > Ignore Thread **(Figure 11.41)**. A No symbol appears to the left of the message name **(Figure 11.42)**. Ignored messages disappear.

✔ Tips

- You can hide all but the watched threads with new messages. For more information, consult *Viewing messages* on page 138.
- You can see ignored threads by choosing View > Messages > Ignored Threads. For more details, consult *Viewing messages* on page 138.

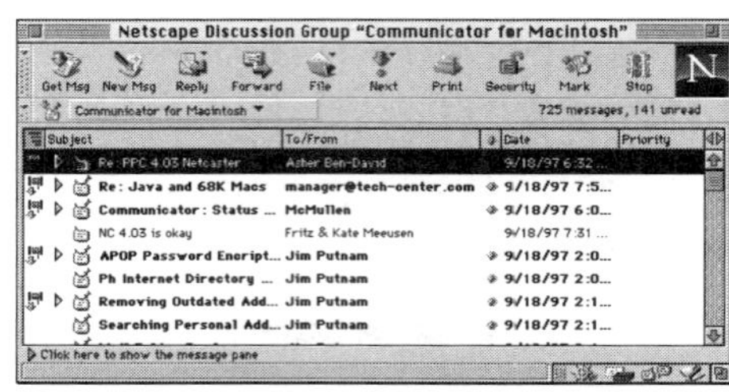

Figure 11.38 *Select a message in the thread.*

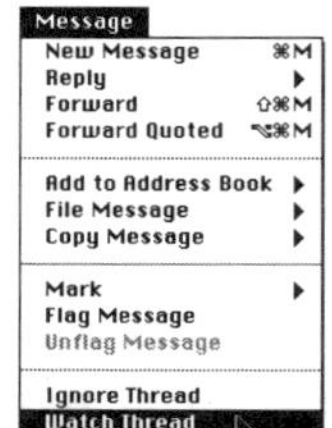

Figure 11.39 *Choose Message > Watch Thread.*

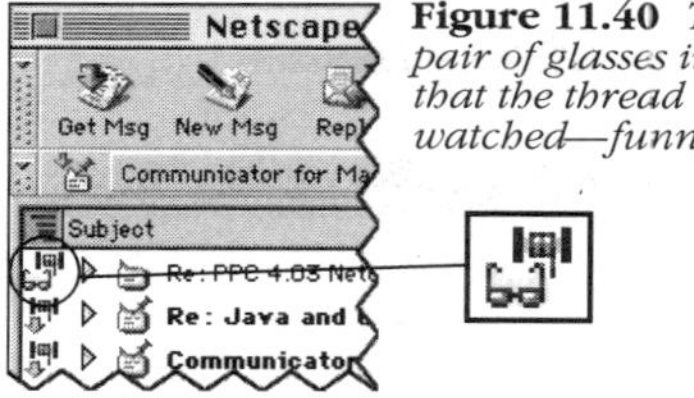

Figure 11.40 *The tiny pair of glasses indicates that the thread is being watched—funny, eh?*

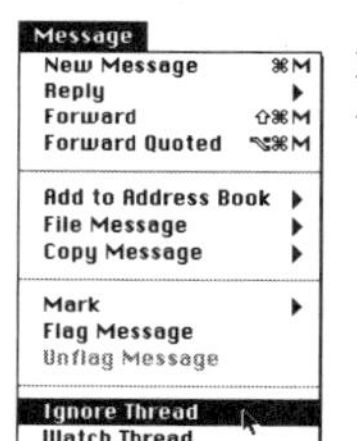

Figure 11.41 *Choose Message > Ignore Thread.*

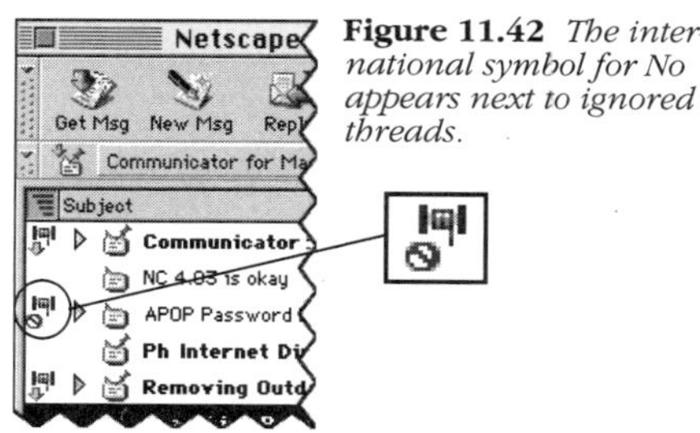

Figure 11.42 *The international symbol for No appears next to ignored threads.*

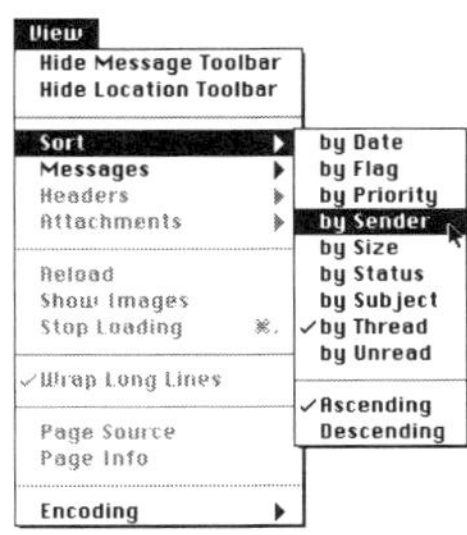

Figure 11.43 *Choose View > Sort and then the desired criteria in the submenu.*

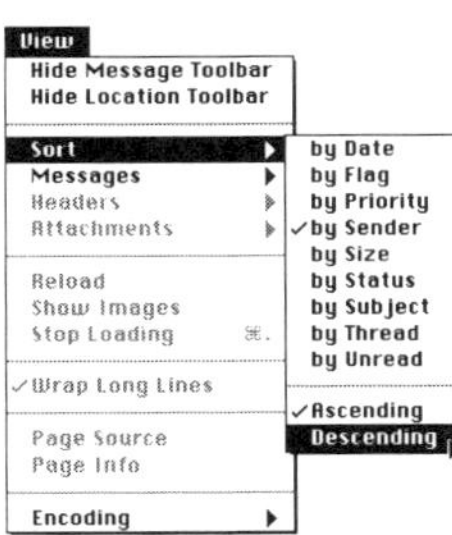

Figure 11.44 *Choose View > Sort > Ascending or Descending to choose the direction in which to sort.*

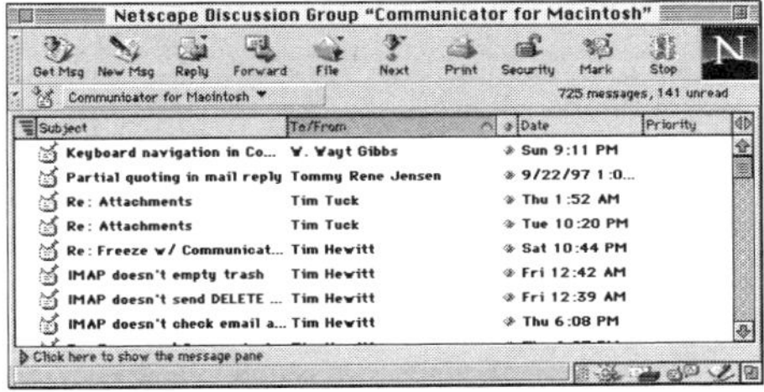

Figure 11.45 *Descending order, by sender.*

Putting your messages in order

You can sort your messages by date, sender, subject—or whatever criteria you choose. Regardless of the criteria chosen, they may be sorted in ascending or descending order. Mail *folders* (and discussion groups) are always displayed in alphabetical order.

To put your messages in order:

1. Choose View > Sort and then the criteria by which you wish to sort your messages **(Figure 11.43)**. The messages are sorted according to the criteria chosen.
2. Choose View > Sort > Ascending or Descending to list the messages in ascending or descending order **(Figure 11.44)**.

✔ Tips

- Ascending means the A's, 0's, and past dates are at the top and the Z's, 9's, and present dates are at the bottom of the window. Descending is just the opposite. Here's the confusing part: An up arrow in the column header indicates descending; a down arrow means ascending. Go figure.
- You can also click the column header to sort your messages by the contents of that column. Click the column heading a second time to reverse the ascending/descending option.
- The Re: is not taken into account when sorting by subject.
- Names are sorted by first name, not last.

Changing the columns

There are potentially eleven columns of information to display in a Message List window. You can adjust the width or order of the columns to suit your particular task. You can even hide columns you don't need.

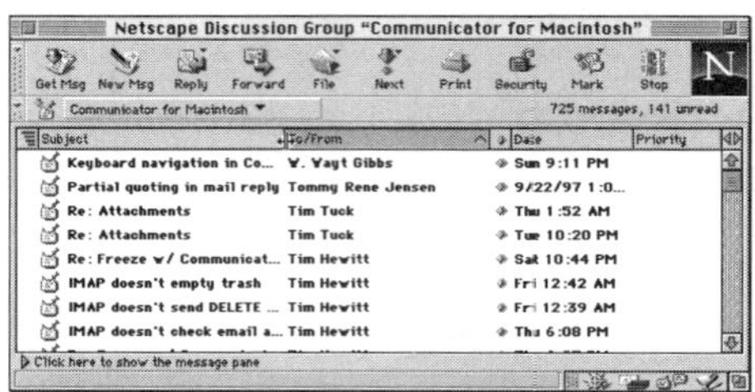

Figure 11.46 *Some of the subject lines are cut off. To make the Subject column wider, click the right border of the column (the cursor changes to a double-headed arrow) and drag to resize.*

To change the column width:

1. Place the cursor on the left border of the column's title **(Figure 11.46)**. The pointer changes to a double-headed arrow.
2. Drag to adjust the size of the column **(Figure 11.47)**.

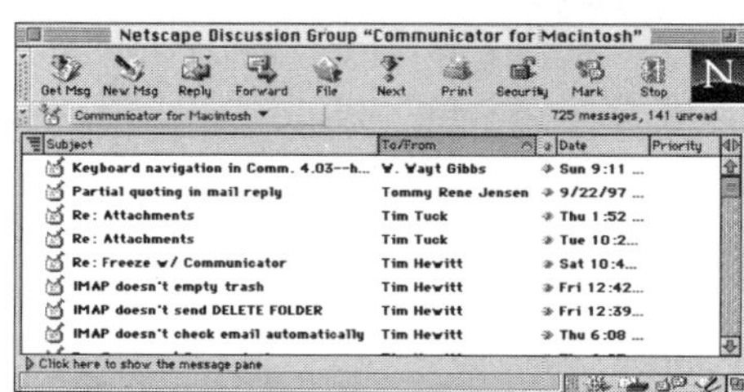

Figure 11.47 *Once the column is wider, the complete subjects can be seen.*

To add or remove columns:

Click the left and right arrows in the upper-right corner of the Message List window. The columns appear or disappear **(Figure 11.48)**.

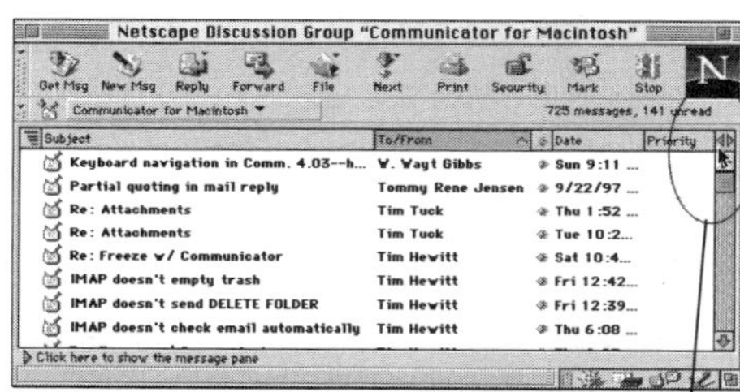

Figure 11.48 *Click the arrows in the upper-right corner of the window (right) to hide or reveal more columns of information. In this illustration, I've hidden all but four columns in order to have more space.*

To change the column order:

Click in the desired column's title and drag it to the new position. The other columns are adjusted accordingly.

✔ Tip

- If you aren't interested in a particular column's data, drag it to the right-most position in the pane. Then, use the right arrow in the upper-right corner to hide those columns.

12 Writing Messages

You can use Communicator to compose and send both e-mail and discussion messages, and to read or reply to messages that you've received from others. The important thing to remember is that whether you are composing a message for one person (e-mail) or for many (discussion group), the procedure is basically the same.

You can compose messages in two ways: you can create a new message from scratch, or you can reply to a message that somebody has sent to you or to a whole discussion group. In addition, when you reply to a message from a discussion group, you can also decide between responding to it in public (that is, posting your message to the discussion group, where everybody can see it) or in private (replying to the e-mail address of the person that posted the message, but not posting it in the discussion group). A friend of mine once posted a personal message intended for me to a discussion group—he had mistakenly selected the wrong option—and he was embarrassed by the fact that he was having a private conversation in public. So, be careful and aware of where you're sending your messages!

When you reply to a message, you can also automatically quote the words from the original message. This is quite customary in discussion groups and enables people to jump into a conversation even after it's begun. It's also helpful with e-mail to remind the other person just what you're responding to.

Composing a new message

Somehow, e-mail is a thousand times easier to write than a conventional letter.

To compose a new message:

1. Choose File > New > Message **(Figure 12.1)** or click the New Msg button **(Figure 12.2)**. A fresh Message Composition window appears.
2. Type the recipient's address in the To field **(Figure 12.3)**. Press Return to add multiple addresses.
3. In the Subject field, type a subject. As the most visible part of the message, it is often used as the criteria for filing—and sometimes even for reading.
4. Type the contents of the message in the area at the bottom of the window.
5. Now you have three choices:

   Choose File > Send Now **(Fig. 12.4)** or click the Send button on the toolbar **(Figure 12.5)** to send the message to its recipient immediately.

   Choose File > Send Later to store the message in the Unsent Messages folder until you're ready to send it **(Figure 12.6)**.

   Choose File > Save Draft to store the message in the Drafts folder until you're ready to finish writing it **(Figure 12.6)**.

✔ Tips

- Use the Save button on the toolbar to save a draft of your message.
- Choose File > Save As to save a copy of the draft message with a new name or in a new location.

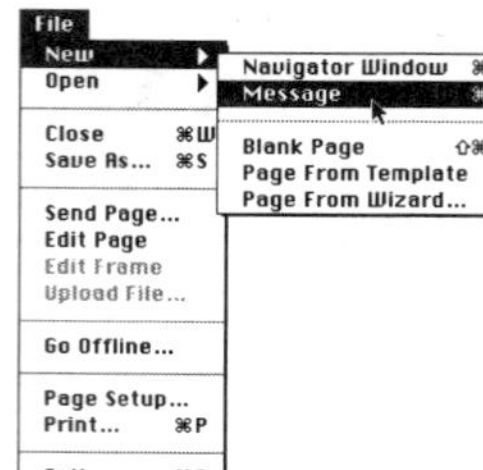

Figure 12.1 *Choose File > New > Message.*

Figure 12.2 *You can also click the New Msg button on the toolbar to start a new message.*

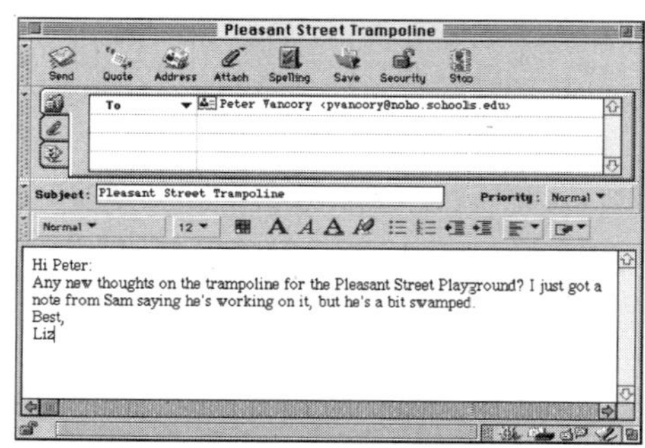

Figure 12.3 *In the Message Composition window, type the recipient's address next to the To button, type a Subject, and type the contents of the message.*

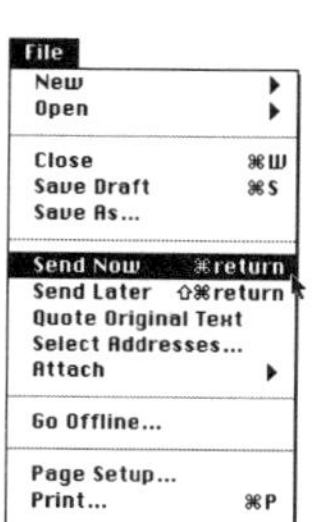

Figure 12.4 *Once you're satisfied with the message, choose File > Send Now to send the file immediately.*

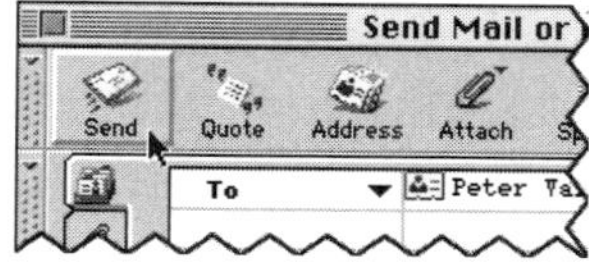

Figure 12.5 *In the Message Composition window, type the recipient's address next to the To button, type a Subject, and type the contents of the message.*

Figure 12.6 *Choose File > Send Later (left) to store the message in the Unsent Messages folder until you have connected to the Internet and decide to send it. Choose File > Save Draft (right) to store the message in the Drafts folder for further editing at a later time.*

Figure 12.7 *Choose one of the recipient types from the pop-up menu.*

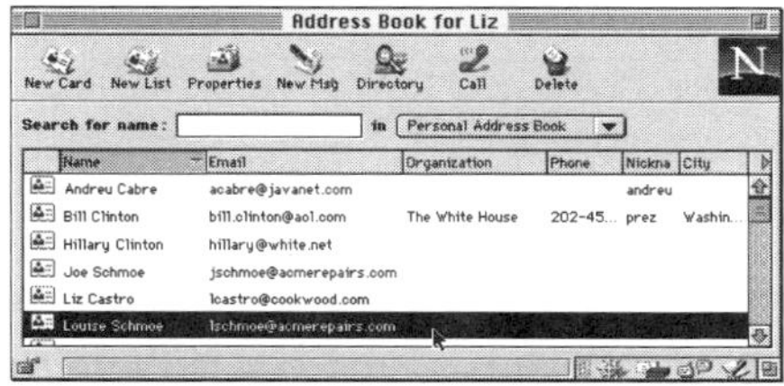

Figure 12.8 *Select a recipient's name from the Address Book.*

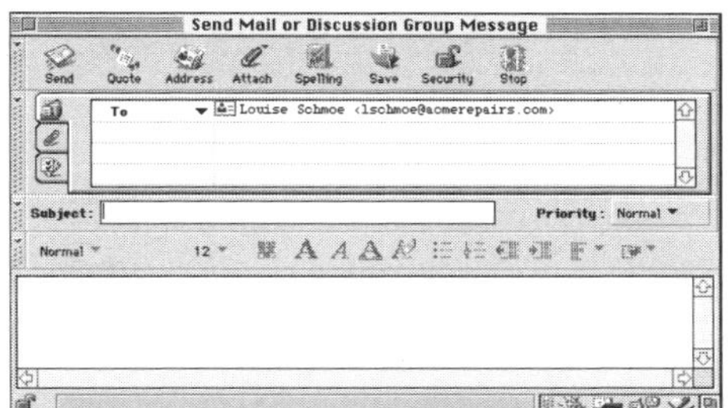

Figure 12.9 *When you select File > New > Message, the recipient's name appears automatically in the recipient field of the Message Composition window.*

- To finish writing saved messages, consult *Editing drafts of messages* on page 158.
- Click the Address button to get addresses stored in the Address book.
- The Message Composition's View menu includes the Wrap Long Lines on Send option, which when activated, ensures that outgoing messages have the proper line breaks. You should generally leave it active.
- The Subject line often determines whether or not a message is read; if you do not type a subject, you will be prompted to do so.
- For information on attaching files to your messages, consult *Attaching files to a message* on page 165.
- For information on attaching your address card to messages, consult *Attaching your address card to messages* on page 168.
- You can change the recipient type (To, Cc, Bcc, Reply, Discussion, Followup) by clicking the current option and choosing another from the pop-up menu **(Figure 12.7)**. Press Return to add additional recipient lines. To eliminate recipients, place the cursor on the field and press Delete.
- If you have a discussion group open or selected when you create a new message, the group's address will automatically appear in the Addressing area.
- Select a recipient in the Address Book before choosing File > New > Message to automatically address the message to the selected person **(Figures 12.8 and 12.9)**.

Adding images, links, and formatting

The Message Composition window contains the same formatting tools as Composer. You can use them to add images, links, and other typical Web page elements to your messages.

To add Web page formatting to your messages:

1. Use the Formatting toolbar in the Message Composition window to add images, links, and other formatting to your message **(Figure 12.10)**. The formatting tools are described in detail in *Part IV: Creating Web Pages*, starting on page 217.
2. Click the bottom icon in the central section of the Message Composition window. The Options section appears **(Figure 12.11)**.
3. Choose anything but Plain Text Only in the Format pop-up menu **(Figure 12.12)**.
4. Send the message as usual. As long as the recipient is using HTML savvy software like Communicator to read her mail, she'll see all the Web formatting that you've included in the message.

✓ Tips

- Check the Prefers to receive HTML option at the bottom of a recipient's Address Card to automatically send that person messages *with* Web page formatting *(see page 172)*.
- Choose "By default, send HTML messages" in the Messages section of the Preferences dialog box to always send outgoing messages with Web page formatting.

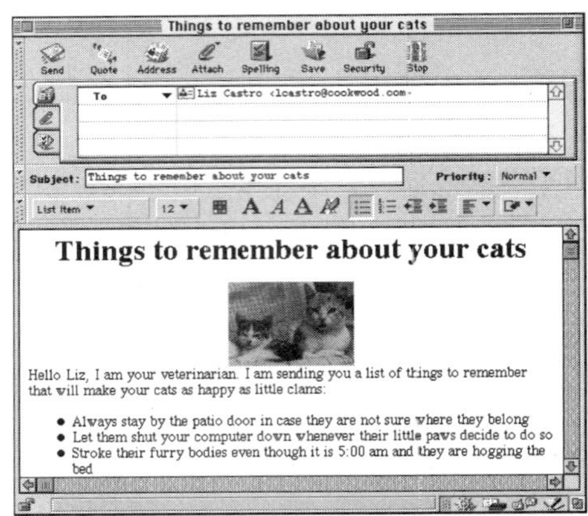

Figure 12.10 *Compose your message as usual. Use the Formatting toolbar to add images, links, and formatting. Notice, in particular the large, centered heading, the image, and the list.*

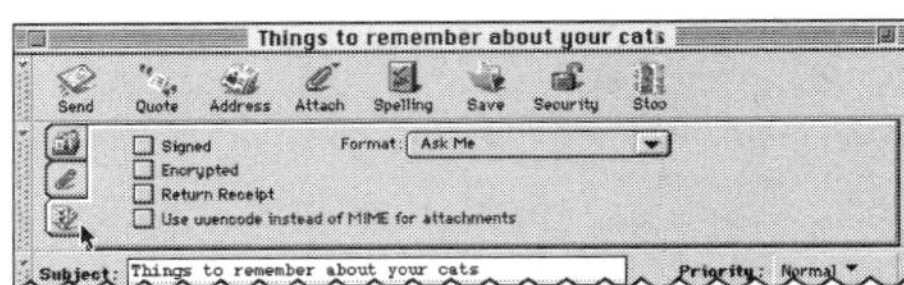

Figure 12.11 *Click the Options tab in the central part of the Message Composition window.*

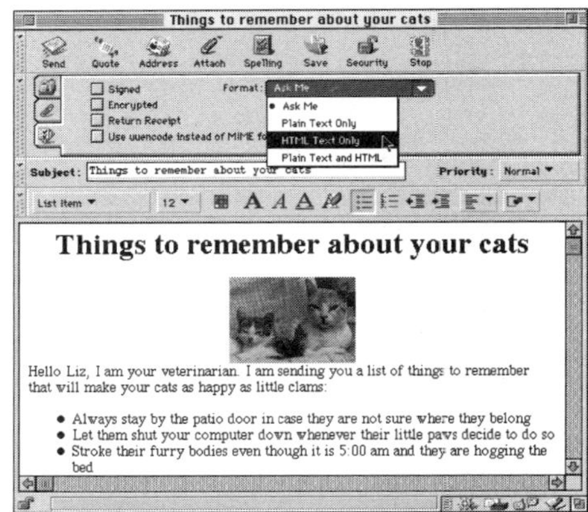

Figure 12.12 *Choose one of the HTML options in the Format pop-up menu in the Options section.*

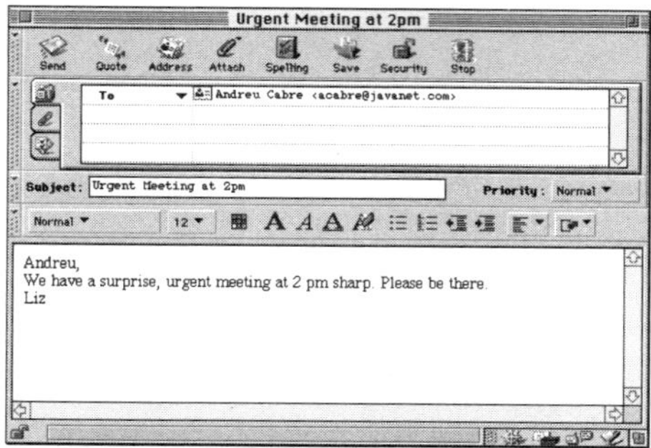

Figure 12.13 *Compose your message as usual.*

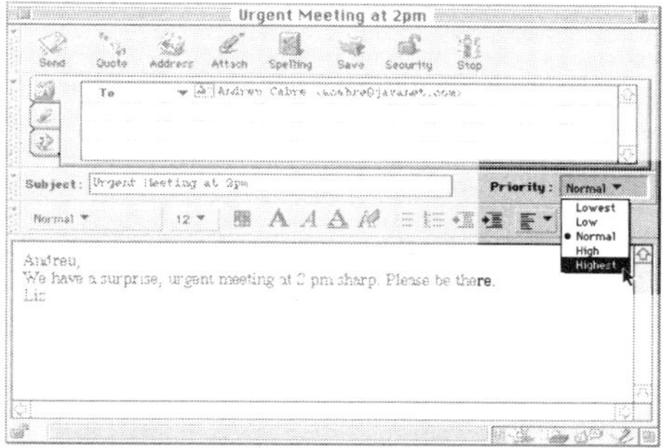

Figure 12.14 *Choose an option from the Priority pop-up menu at the right of the dialog box.*

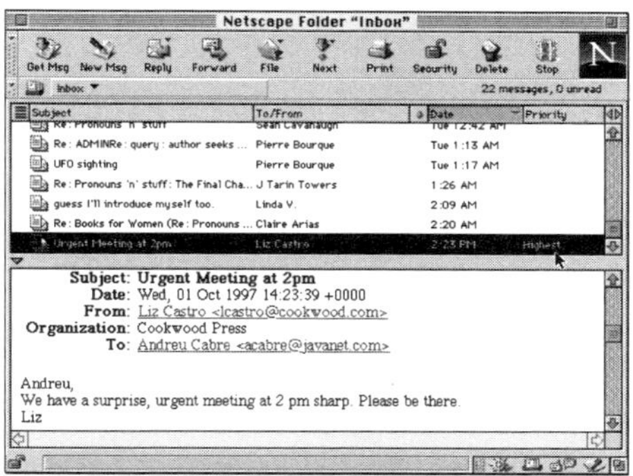

Figure 12.15 *When the message is received, the Priority information is displayed in the Priority column of the Message List window. Message headers of highest priority, like this one, are displayed in red.*

Setting a message's priority

If you want to call someone's attention to the urgency of a message, you can change its priority to high or highest. If you want someone to ignore your message, choose a low priority. OK, I can't imagine doing that either.

To set a message's priority:

1. Compose the message as usual **(Figure 12.13)**.
2. Choose the desired priority from the Priority pop-up menu **(Figure 12.14)**.
3. Complete the message as usual.

✓ Tips

- When the message is received, the priority will be shown in the Priority column in Communicator **(Figure 12.15)** or in other ways in other e-mail programs.
- In Communicator, highest priority message headers are shown in red, high priority message headers are shown in purple, normal priority message headers are shown in black, low priority headers are shown in blue, and lowest priority headers are shown in green.
- If you can't see the Priority column, click in the left arrow ◀▷ in the upper-right corner of the dialog box until the column appears.

Setting special options

Communicator lets you request a receipt, choose whether to send HTML formatting, encrypt messages, sign them, and choose what encoding to use for attachments.

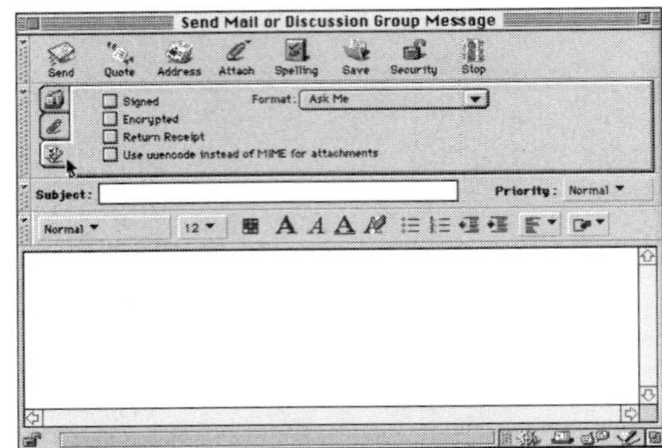

Figure 12.16 *To access the special options area, click the Options tab in the middle of the Message Composition window.*

To set special options for messages:

1. Click the Options tab in the middle of the Message Composition window. The addressing section disappears and the special options section is displayed **(Figure 12.16)**.
2. To shield messages from prying eyes, check the Encrypted box.
3. To ensure the recipient that the message really came from you, check the Signed box.
4. To change how attachments are sent, check the Uuencode instead of MIME for attachments box.
5. To get a receipt when your message reaches its recipient, check Return Receipt.
6. To decide on the spur of the moment whether or not to send HTML codes with your message (not all e-mail programs can handle them), choose an option from the Format menu.
7. Complete the message as usual.

✓ Tips

- You'll need a security certificate to use either the Encrypted or Signed options. For more information, click the padlock in the bottom-left corner of the window.
- You can record a recipient's preferences about how to receive HTML in her address card *(see page 172)*.

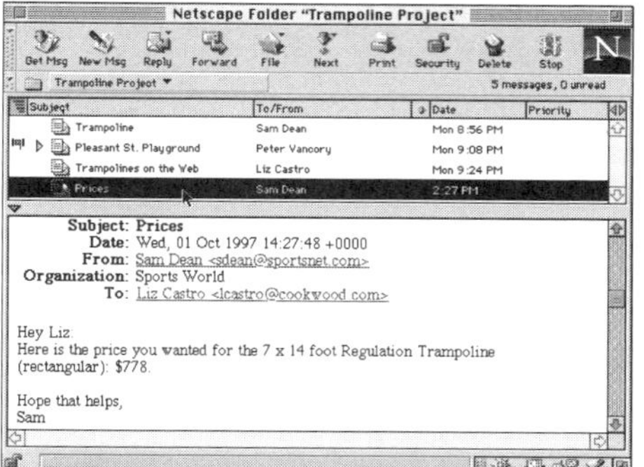

Figure 12.17 *Select the message to which you wish to reply.*

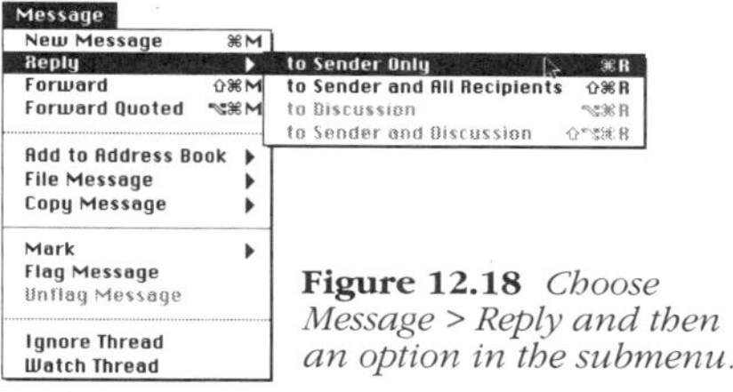

Figure 12.18 *Choose Message > Reply and then an option in the submenu.*

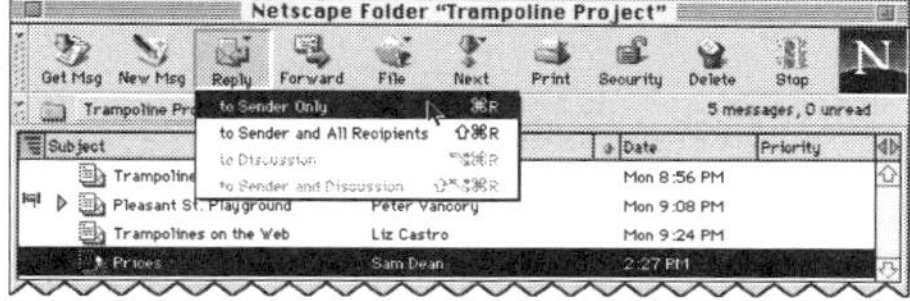

Figure 12.19 *Or click the Reply button on the toolbar and choose an option in its submenu.*

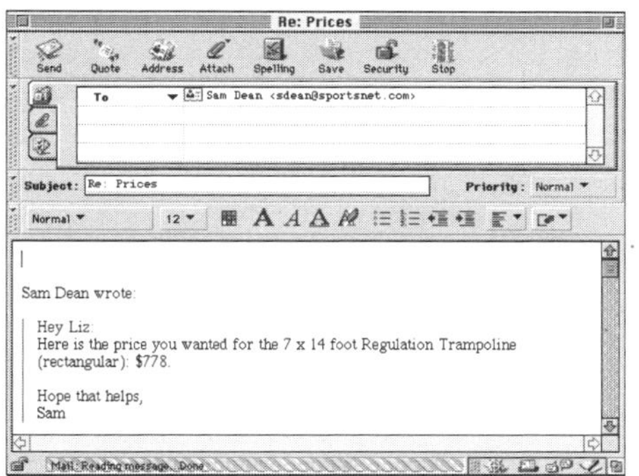

Figure 12.20 *The To and Subject fields are automatically filled in and the contents may contain a quoted version of the original message.*

Replying to a message you've received

Replying to someone else's message instead of creating a new message *(see page 152)* has certain advantages: the addressing is done automatically and you can choose to quote the original letter in your reply.

To reply to a message you've received:

1. Select the message to which you wish to reply **(Figure 12.17)**.
2. Choose Message > Reply and then an option in the submenu **(Fig. 12.18)** or click the Reply button on the toolbar and choose an option in *its* submenu **(Figure 12.19)**. The Message Composition window appears. The recipient area is automatically filled in. The original letter may or may not be quoted in the message area *(see page 160)*. The subject area contains the original subject preceded by "Re:" **(Figure 12.20)**.
3. Type the contents of the reply.
4. Choose File > Send Now or click the Send button on the toolbar to send the message immediately. Consult step 5 on page 152 for other choices.

✔ Tip

- If the original message was addressed to more than one person, you can reply to all of them at once by selecting to Sender and All Recipients in either of the Reply submenus. If the message is from a discussion group, you'll be able to reply both to the group and to the sender, or to either individually.

Editing drafts of messages

Once you find the time, you can go back and edit any saved messages (drafts). Then you can either send them immediately or store them in the Unsent Messages folder in order to send them all together once you've connected to the Internet.

To edit drafts of messages:

1. Select the Drafts folder in the Message List window **(Figure 12.21)**.
2. Select the message and choose File > Edit Message **(Figure 12.22)**. The message appears in the Message Composition window **(Figure 12.23)**.
3. Edit the message as necessary **(Figure 12.24)**.
4. If you're finished editing the message, choose File > Send Now or Send Later *(see page 152)*.

   If you want to save the changes again with the possibility of further editing, choose File > Save Draft or Save As.

✔ Tips

- You can also double click the message to open it for editing.
- If you've chosen Send Later and thus moved a message to the Unsent Messages folder, you can still edit it. Open the Unsent Messages folder and edit the message as described above. The main difference between the Unsent Messages and Drafts folders is that the messages in the Unsent Messages folder get sent when you choose File > Send Unsent Messages *(see page 159)*. Messages in the Drafts folder are not sent until you select them and choose File > Send Now (or Send Later).

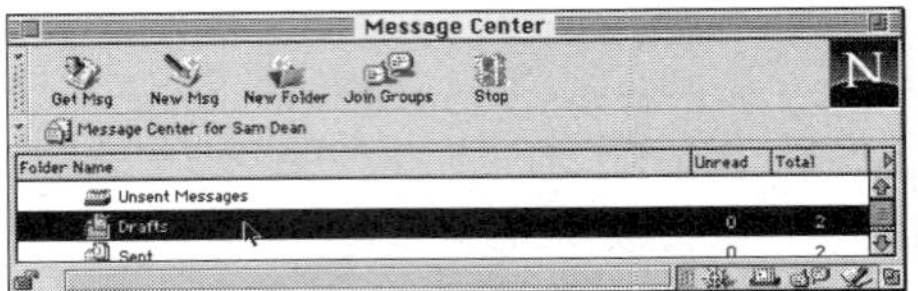

Figure 12.21 *Select the Drafts folder in the Message List window and then select the message that you want to finish writing.*

Figure 12.22 *Choose File > Edit Message.*

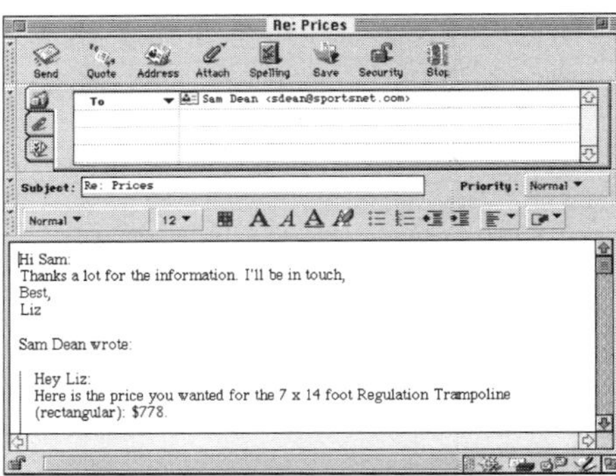

Figure 12.23 *The message reappears in the Message Composition window.*

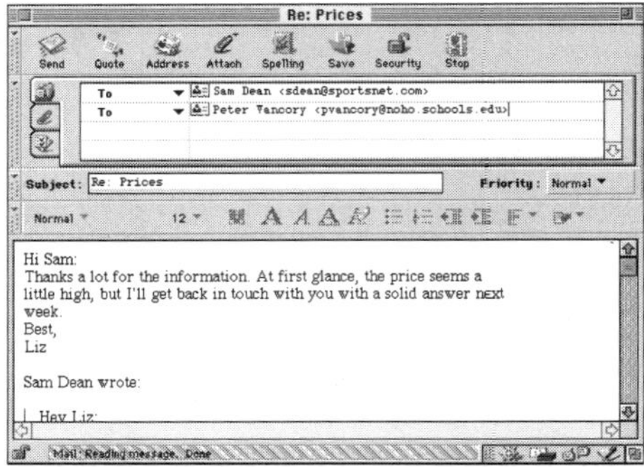

Figure 12.24 *Edit the message as necessary.*

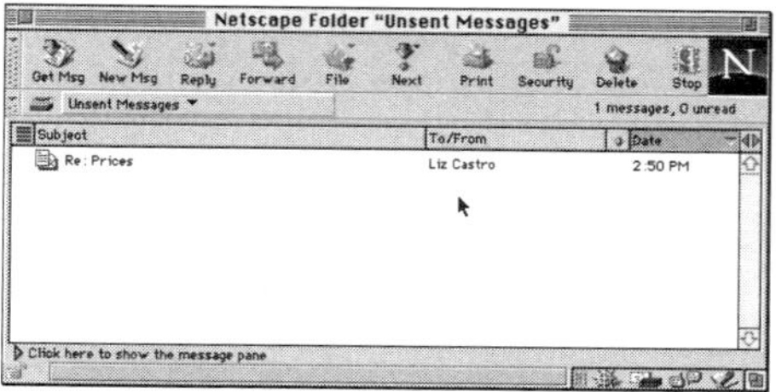

Figure 12.25 *As you compose messages offline and choose File > Send Later, as described in step 5 on page 152, they are stored in the Unsent Messages folder.*

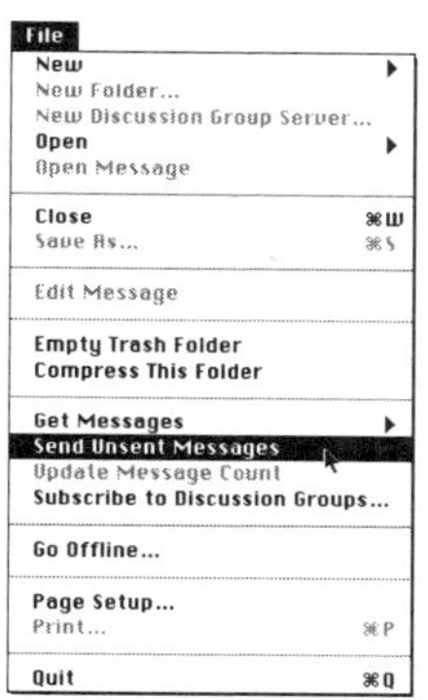

Figure 12.26 *Once you've connected to the Internet and are ready to send your messages, choose File > Send Unsent Messages.*

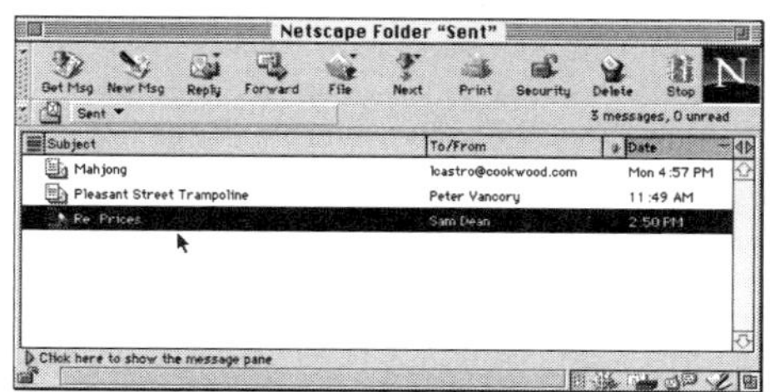

Figure 12.27 *Once you send the messages in the Unsent Messages folder, they are automatically moved to the Sent folder.*

Sending the unsent messages

If you've composed several messages offline—both e-mail and discussions *(see page 152)*—you can choose to send them when it is convenient for you.

To send the unsent messages:

1. If desired, open the Unsent Messages folder to see which messages you've stored for later delivery **(Fig. 12.25)**.
2. Open your Internet connection.
3. Choose File > Send Unsent Messages **(Figure 12.26)**. All your stored messages are sent. Sent messages are automatically transferred to the Sent folder **(Figure 12.27)**. For more information about the Sent folder, consult *The Message Center's five default folders* on page 182.
4. Close your Internet connection, if desired.

✔ Tips

- You can move files out of the Unsent Messages folder if you don't want to send them. For details, consult *Filing and copying messages* on page 186.
- As long as you haven't sent them yet, you can edit messages in the Unsent Messages by selecting the messages and choosing File > Edit Message or by double clicking the message. For more information, consult *Editing drafts of messages* on page 158.

Quoting every message

When you reply to a message, you can automatically "quote" the original correspondence, so that the recipient readily knows what you are responding to. Each line of a quoted message is preceded with a greater than sign (>), by Internet convention, and the original author's name is inserted at the beginning of the quote.

To quote every message:

1. Choose Edit > Preferences **(Figure 12.28)**.
2. Choose Messages under Mail & Groups in the Category list. The Messages preferences appear **(Figure 12.29)**.
3. Mark the option Automatically quote original message when replying at the top of the dialog box. Leave the option unchecked if you don't want to include a copy of the original message every time you reply.
4. Click OK to close the Preferences dialog box. From now on, each message you reply to will automatically include a copy of the original message.

✔ Tip

- You can choose how quoted material appears in the Message and Message Composition windows. For more details, consult *Changing your messages' appearance* on page 139.

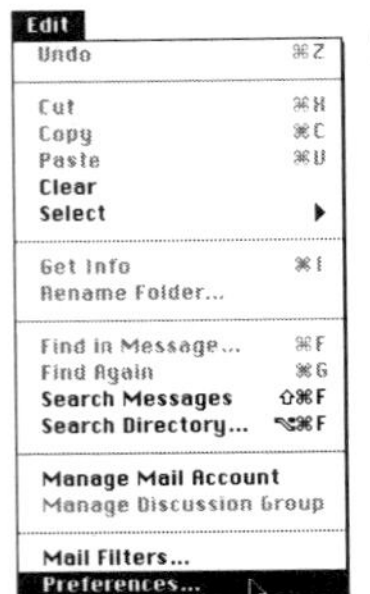

Figure 12.28 *Choose Edit > Preferences.*

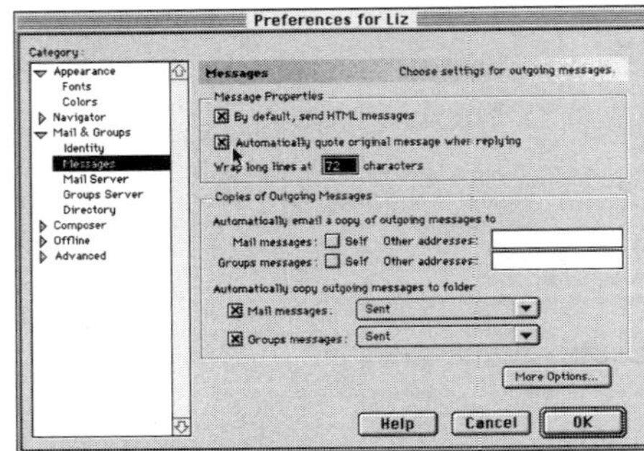

Figure 12.29 *Click Messages in the Category list at left. Then check the Automatically quote original message when replying checkbox.*

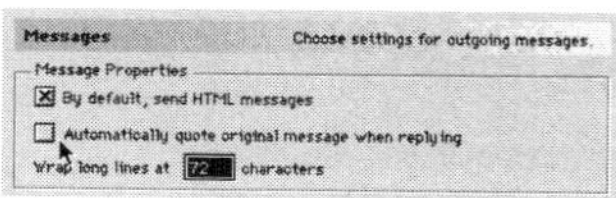

Figure 12.30 *Uncheck the Automatically quote original message option in the Messages panel of the Preferences dialog box (cf. Figure 12.29).*

Figure 12.31 *Select a message. Then click the Reply button and an option in the submenu.*

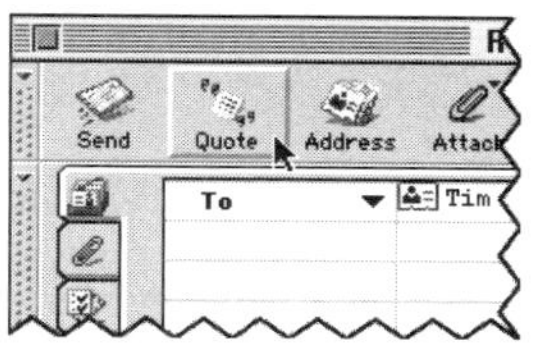

Figure 12.32 *Click the Quote button to quote the original message.*

Figure 12.33 *Or choose File > Quote Original Text.*

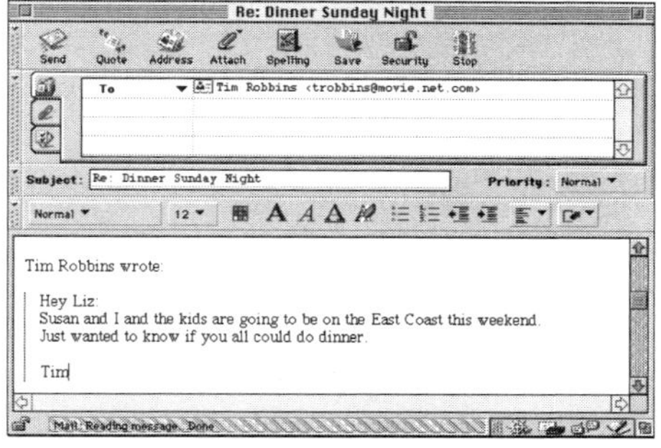

Figure 12.34 *The original message is quoted.*

Quoting individual messages

Quoting every message you reply to can get a little tiresome, especially if the original messages are long. You can turn off automatic quoting and then quote messages individually, when desired.

To quote individual messages:

1. Generally, you will have turned off automatic quoting, as described on page 160, unchecking the option in step 3 **(Figure 12.30)**.
2. Reply to a message in the normal way **(Figure 12.31)**. See page 157 for details. The Message Composition window appears.
3. In the Message Composition window click the Quote button **(Figure 12.32)** or choose File > Quote Original Text **(Figure 12.33)**. The original message appears in the message area, labeled with the original author's name. The quoted area is marked with a vertical blue line **(Figure 12.34)**.
4. You may cut out parts of the quote if you wish. Simply select them with the mouse and choose Edit > Cut, or press Delete.

✓ Tips

- With Communicator 4 comes the ability to change the way a quote is displayed in the Message Composition window. For more details, consult *Changing your messages' appearance* on page 139.
- Communicator highlights quoted material with a vertical blue line, by default. However, folks who do not receive HTML format will see conventional greater than signs.

Custom quoting

If you don't want to quote the entire message, or if you want to quote several parts of various messages, you can use the custom quoting feature to mark the quoted text, either with a vertical blue line (for HTML savvy e-mail clients) or with a greater than sign at the start of each line of text (which is the Internet convention).

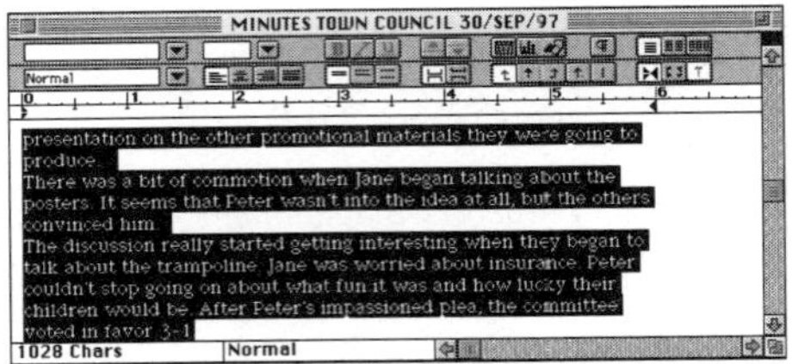

Figure 12.35 *Select the material you wish to quote in the original document. (This is from Microsoft Word.)*

Figure 12.36 *Choose Edit > Copy to copy the material to the clipboard.*

To quote a part of a message:

1. Select the text that you wish to quote **(Figure 12.35)**. The text may be from any file; it doesn't have to be from a message received with Communicator.
2. Choose Edit > Copy (Command-C) **(Figure 12.36)**.
3. With the Message Composition window active, choose Edit > Paste as Quotation **(Figure 12.37)**. The copied text will be highlighted with a vertical blue line **(Figure 12.38)**.

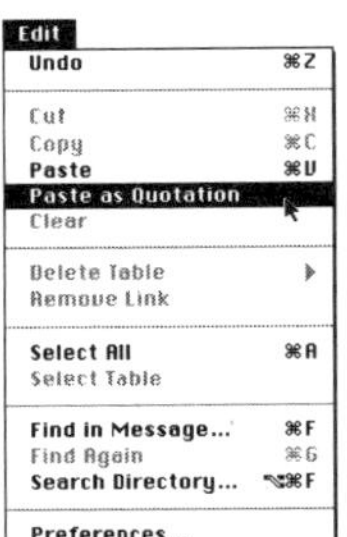

Figure 12.37 *Switch back to the Message Composition window in Communicator and choose Edit > Paste as Quotation.*

✔ Tip

- Communicator offsets quoted text in the Message Composition window with a vertical blue line. Depending on the software the recipient uses, he may see the quoted material highlighted in the same way, or more conventionally, with a greater than sign (the Internet-recognized symbol for quoted text) at the beginning of each paragraph.

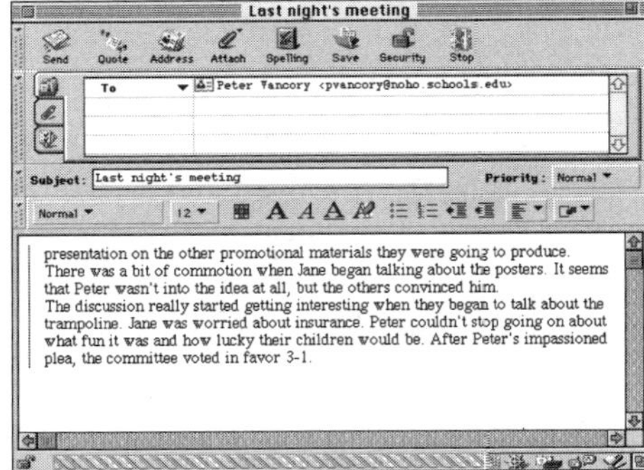

Figure 12.38 *The copied material is pasted in the contents area and is highlighted with a vertical blue line.*

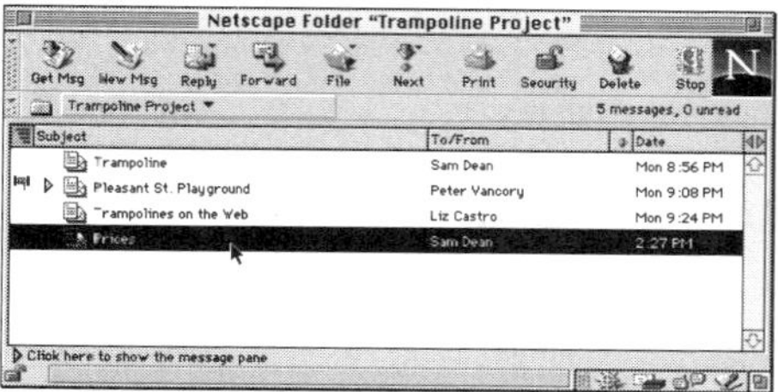

Figure 12.39 *Choose the message you wish to forward.*

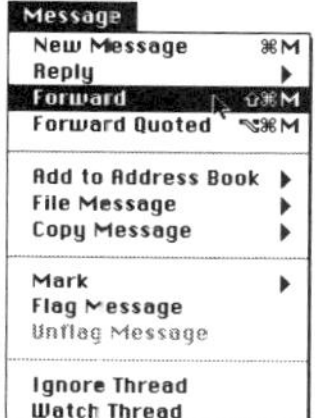

Figure 12.40 *Choose Message > Forward.*

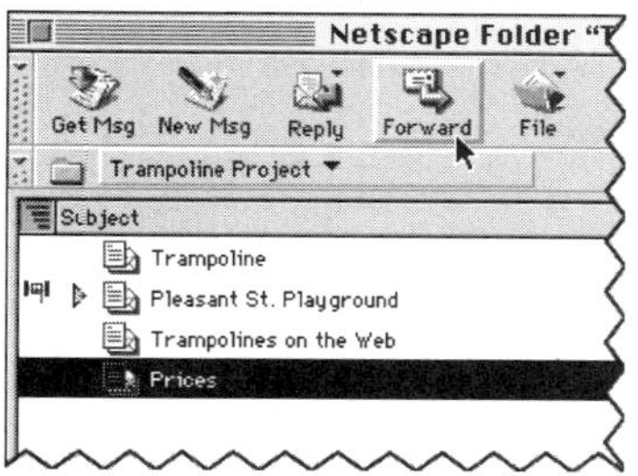

Figure 12.41 *Or, click the Forward button.*

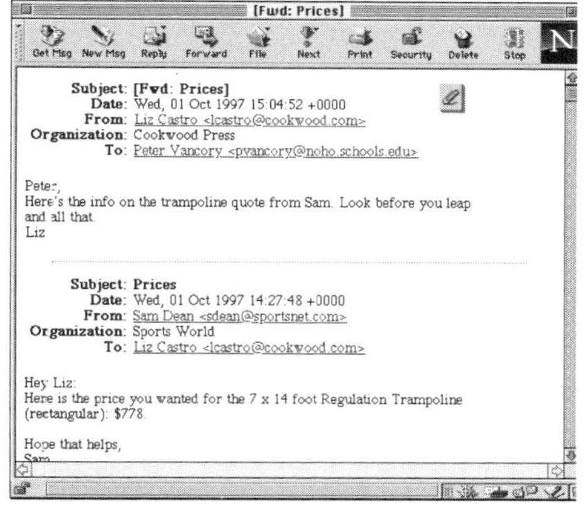

Figure 12.42 *A forwarded message appears below the new portion of the current message.*

Forwarding a message

Sometimes you will receive e-mail that either isn't for you or that you would like to share with others. The easiest way to share mail you have received with other people is to forward it.

To forward a message as an attachment:

1. Select the message that you wish to forward in the Message List window **(Figure 12.39)**.
2. Choose Message > Forward **(Figure 12.40)**. The Message Composition window appears. The Subject is automatically set to "[Fwd: title of original message]" and the original message is attached to the new message.
3. Enter the recipient's address next to the To button.
4. Fill in the other message parts as desired.
5. Add any personal comments about the forwarded material in the message area.
6. Click the Send button or choose a Send command in the File menu.

✔ Tips

- You can also click the Forward button on the toolbar to forward a message **(Figure 12.41)**
- A forwarded message appears below the main message, much like an attached document **(Figure 12.42)**.
- You can forward discussion group messages to yourself to keep a record of them.

Forwarding a message as a quote

You can also forward a message as a quote, that is with a vertical blue line (in HTML format) or with greater than signs (>) at the beginning of each line.

To forward a message as a quote:

1. Select the message that you wish to forward in the Message List window.
2. Select Message > Forward Quoted **(Figure 12.43)**. The Message Composition window appears. The Subject is automatically set to "[Fwd: title of original message]" and the original message is quoted in the message area **(Figure 12.44)**.
3. Enter the recipient's address in the To box.
4. Fill in the other message parts as desired.
5. Add any personal comments about the forwarded material in the message area above (or below) the quoted, forwarded message **(Figure 12.45)**.
6. Click the Send button, or choose a Send command in the File menu.

✔ Tip

- Users will see quoted material differently, depending on the software they use to read their e-mail. Text-only e-mail clients generally offset quotes with a greater than sign (>) at the beginning of each line. Communicator can handle HTML and highlights quotes with a vertical blue line **(Figure 12.46)**.

Figure 12.43 *Choose Message > Forward Quoted.*

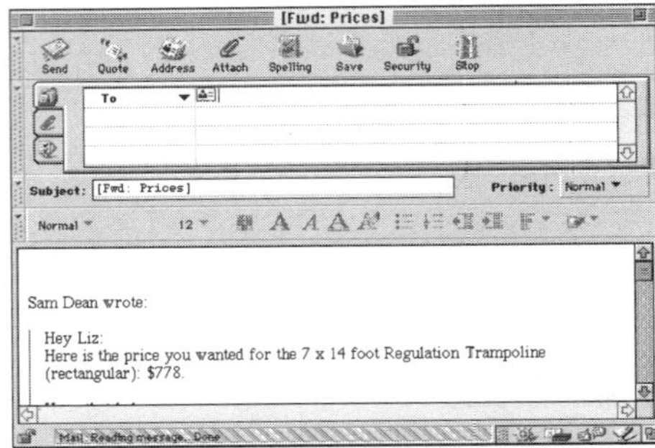

Figure 12.44 *The forwarded message appears as a quote (highlighted with a vertical blue line) in the contents area.*

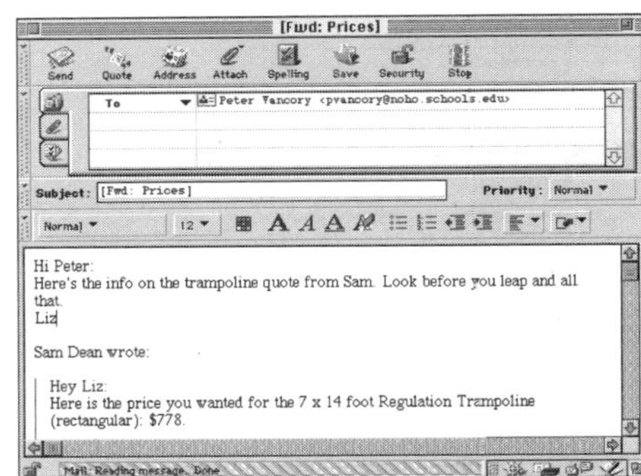

Figure 12.45 *Type the new material above (or below) the quoted message.*

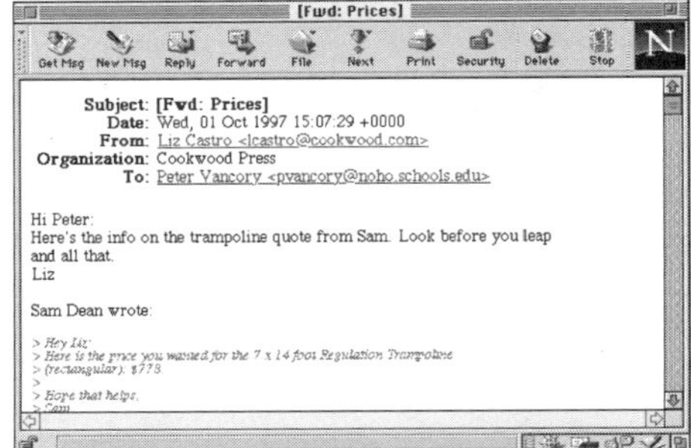

Figure 12.46 *The original message appears as a quote in the new message.*

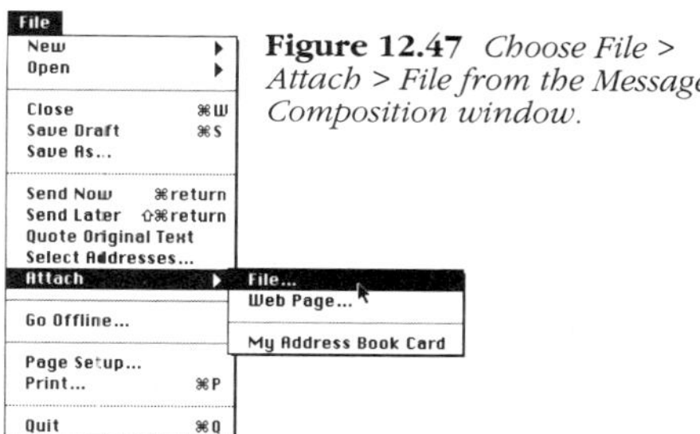

Figure 12.47 *Choose File > Attach > File from the Message Composition window.*

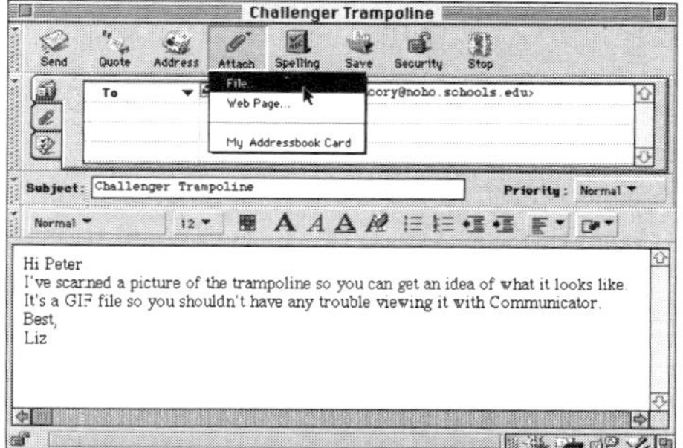

Figure 12.48 *Or click the Attach button and choose File in the submenu.*

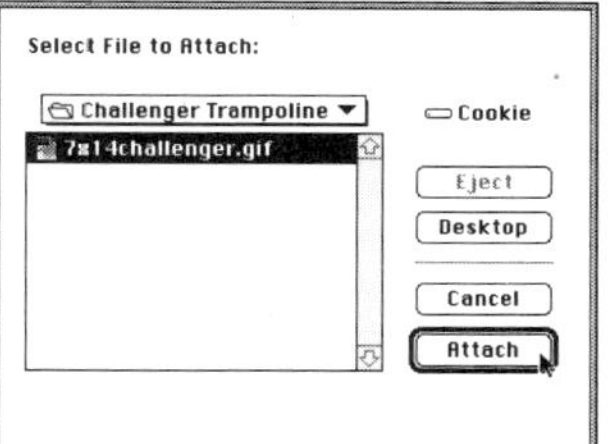

Figure 12.49 *Choose the desired file and click Attach.*

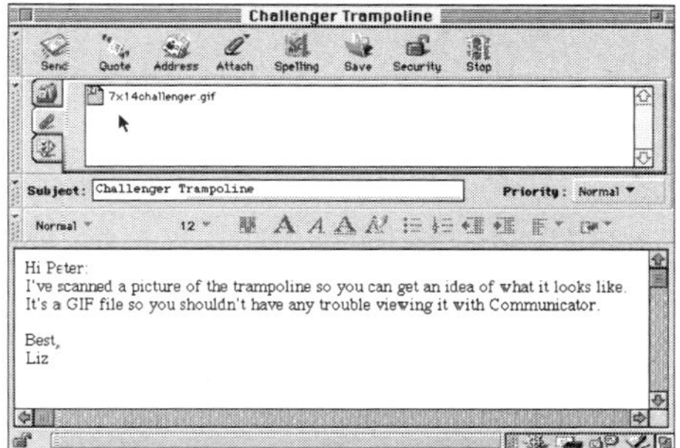

Figure 12.50 *The attached file appears in the Attachments field in the Message Composition window.*

Attaching files to a message

Electronic mail does not limit you to letters; you can send packages, too. You can attach any kind of file to a message—including images or even programs. You can also attach a URL to a message, giving the recipient direct access to a Web page *(see page 166)*.

To attach a file to a message:

1. Choose File > New > Message or select a message and choose Reply in the Message menu. The Message Composition window appears.
2. Choose File > Attach > File **(Figure 12.47)** or click the Attach button and choose File in the submenu **(Figure 12.48)**.
3. In the dialog box that appears, select the file that you wish to send with the message and click Attach **(Figure 12.49)**. The file's path appears in the Attachments section of the Message Composition window **(Figure 12.50)**.
4. Compose the rest of the message.

✓ Tips

- Attachments are indicated by a red paper clip on the Attachments icon in the middle of the Message Composition window.
- Reveal the Attachments area by clicking the Attachments icon in the middle of the Message Composition area.
- You can drag any file from the Desktop and drop it in the Attachments area in the Message Composition window.

Attaching a Web page

If you find a great Web page on the Net and want to share it with someone, instead of sending the page's address in text form, you can send them the actual page within your message. As long as they use Communicator to view your message, the page will appear just as if they had jumped to it themselves.

To attach a Web page:

1. From the Message Composition window, choose File > Attach > Web Page **(Figure 12.51)** or click the Attach button and choose Web Page in the submenu **(Figure 12.52)**.
2. In the dialog box that appears, type or paste the desired URL and click Attach **(Figure 12.53)**. The URL appears in the Attachments area of the Message Composition window **(Figure 12.54)**.
3. Compose the rest of the message.

✔ Tips

- You can drag the page proxy icon from a Web page in the Navigator window and drop it in the Attachments area. In fact, I find that this is the best way to ensure that images are properly included.
- As long as the recipient reads your mail with Communicator, the page will appear within the message itself **(Figure 12.55)**
- If you're not sure what program the recipient uses for e-mail, you may be better off sending the URL address in the body of the message instead of sending the page itself.
- Users can choose to display attachments inline or as links *(see page 141)*.

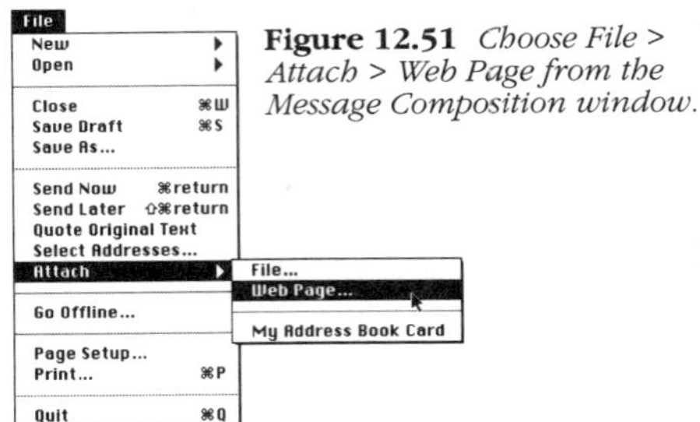

Figure 12.51 *Choose File > Attach > Web Page from the Message Composition window.*

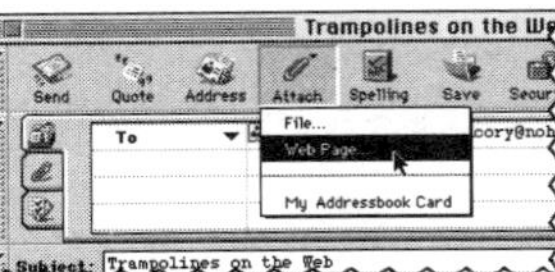

Figure 12.52 *Or click the Attach button on the toolbar and choose Web Page in the submenu.*

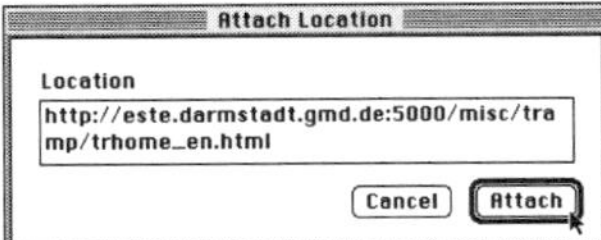

Figure 12.53 *Type or paste the URL and click Attach.*

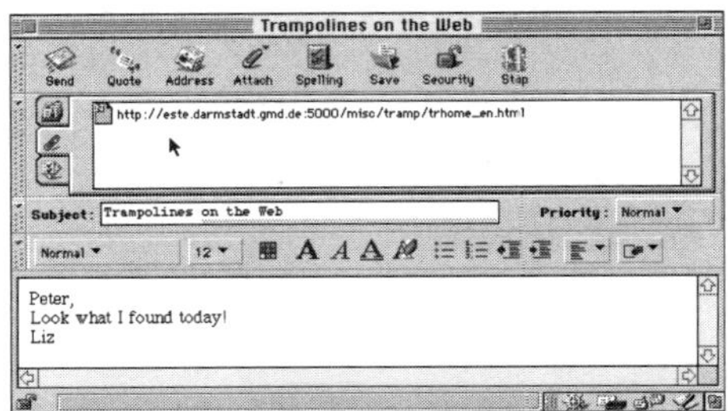

Figure 12.54 *The URL appears in the Attachments area of the Message Composition window.*

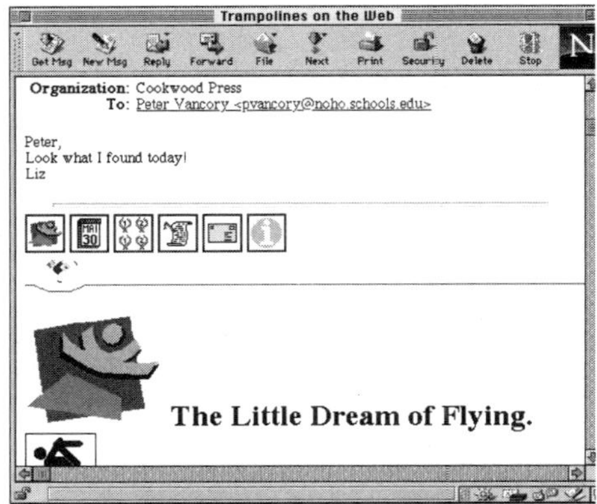

Figure 12.55 *This is how the message looks when it's received—as long as the recipient views attachments inline (see page 141).*

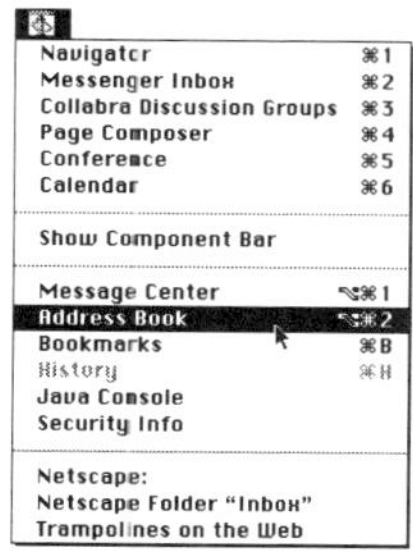

Figure 12.56 *Choose* (*Communicator*) > *Address Book to open the Address Book.*

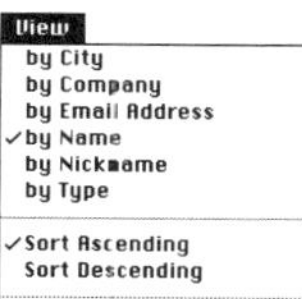

Figure 12.57 *Choose View > My Address Book Card to open your own address card.*

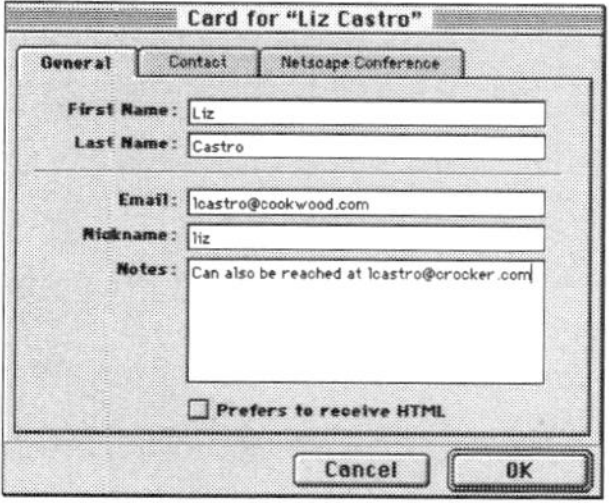

Figure 12.58 *Fill in the information that you want to appear on your address card.*

Filling out your address card

An address card—if you fill it out—works just like a business card, conveying pertinent business or personal information about you, like your e-mail address, postal address, phone, fax, and much more. You can attach your address card to any outgoing messages.

To fill out your address card:

1. Choose (Communicator) > Address Book **(Figure 12.56)**. The Address Book window appears.
2. Choose View > My Address Book Card **(Figure 12.57)**.
3. In the dialog box that appears, fill in any information as desired **(Figure 12.58)**.
4. Click each of the tabs at the top of the dialog box to access more areas that you can fill in.
5. Click OK to save your personal address card.

✓ Tips

- For more information on filling out the Address Card dialog box, consult *Storing an address* on page 172.
- To enclose your personal address card to outgoing correspondence, consult *Attaching your address card to messages* on page 168.

Attaching your address card to messages

Once you've filled it out, you can attach your address card to all or some of your outgoing correspondence—just like you might add your business card to a written letter.

To attach your address card to messages:

1. Create a new message or reply to an existing one.
2. Choose File > Attach > My Address Book Card **(Figure 12.59)** or click the Attach button and choose My Addressbook Card in the submenu **(Figure 12.60)**. A checkmark (or bullet) appears next to the option in both menus.
3. Complete the message as usual.

✓ Tips

- When the recipient receives your message, they will see the condensed version of your address card at the bottom of the message **(Fig. 12.61)**. They'll be able to click View Complete Card to see all of the data you entered **(Figure 12.62)**, or Add to Address Book to add your information to their address book file. Of course, all of this only works if they also use Netscape Communicator 4.
- Remove your personal address card from a message by selecting the option in step 2 again to toggle it. The checkmark (or bullet) will disappear.
- You can choose to add your address card to outgoing messages automatically. Set the option in the Identity preferences box *(see page 321)*.

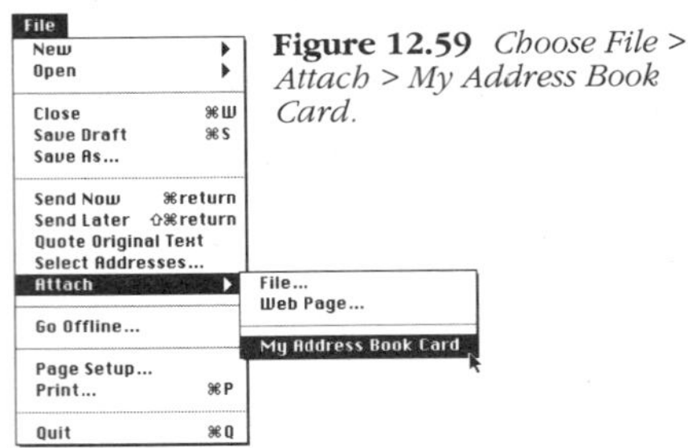

Figure 12.59 *Choose File > Attach > My Address Book Card.*

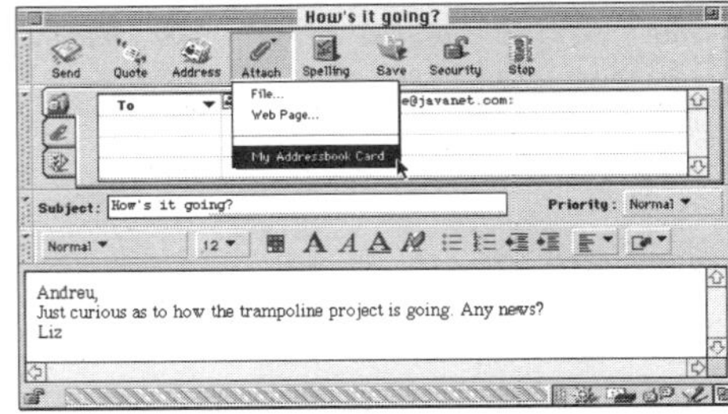

Figure 12.60 *Or click the Attach button and choose My Addressbook Card in the submenu.*

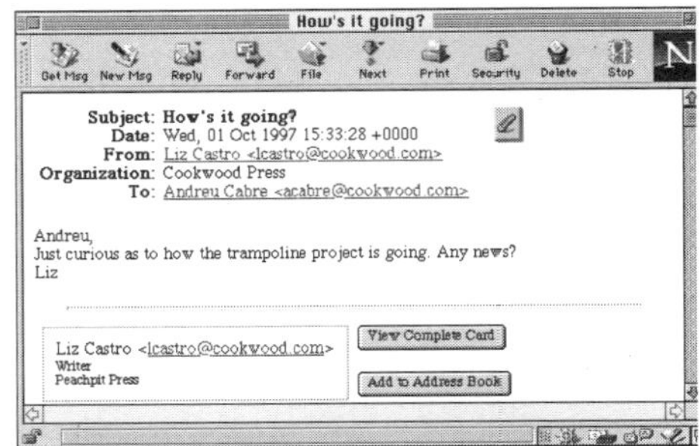

Figure 12.61 *The condensed version of the address card appears at the bottom of your message. To view the complete version, the recipient will click View Complete Card.*

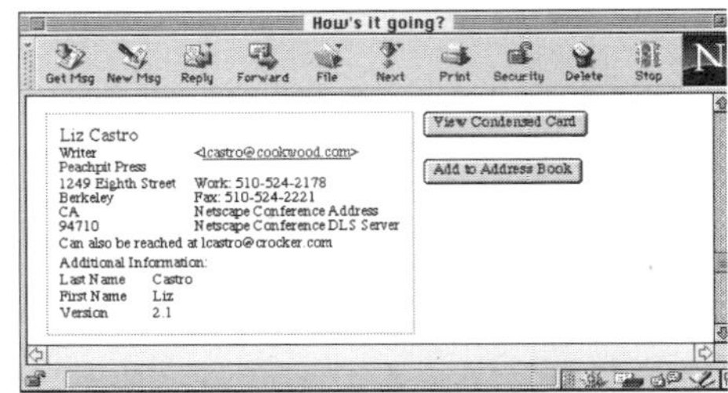

Figure 12.62 *Once the recipient clicks View Complete Card, all of the information on your address card is displayed at the bottom of your message.*

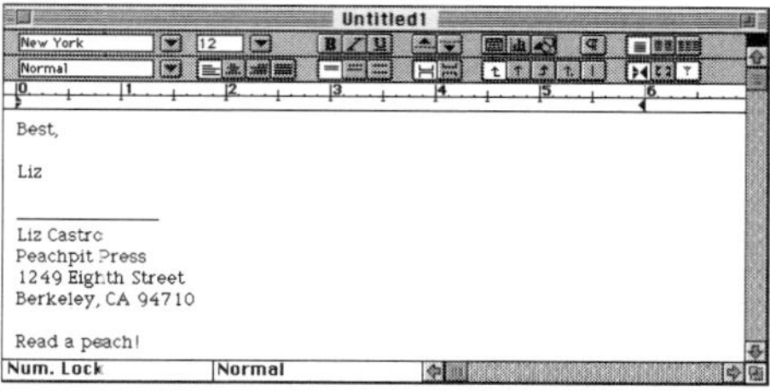

Figure 12.63 *A signature typically contains your name, e-mail and snail-mail addresses, and a pithy quote. This one was created with Word.*

Figure 12.64 *Choose Save As in the text editor's File menu.*

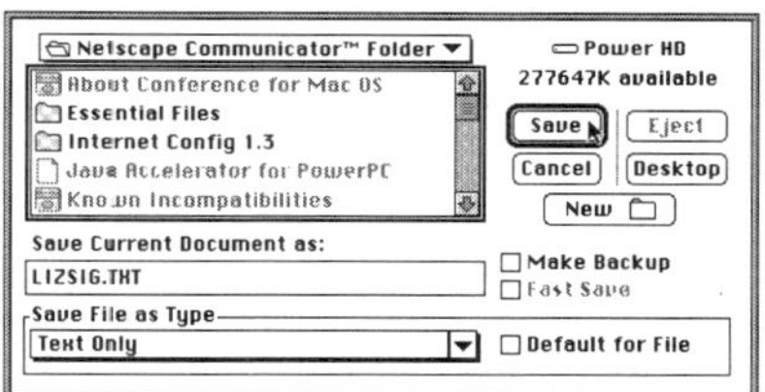

Figure 12.65 *Save the signature file in text-only format.*

Creating a signature file

One of the nice traditions of e-mail writing is adding a few lines at the bottom of each note that tell who you are, and sometimes what you do and where you're from. You can set Communicator up to add these few lines, called a *signature*, to all your outgoing correspondence. You can create a signature in any word processor, including SimpleText or TeachText.

To create a signature:

1. Open a word processor or text editor. SimpleText is fine.
2. Create your signature as desired **(Figure 12.63)**. A signature typically contains your name, e-mail and snail mail addresses, and a pithy quote. You can also add ASCII images.
3. Choose Save As in the text editor's File menu **(Figure 12.64)**.
4. Give the file a name and choose the text-only format in the Save As dialog box **(Figure 12.65)**. Click Save.
5. To use the signature file, consult *Using a signature file* on page 170.

✔ Tips

- Although a signature is limited to text characters, you can be creative about how to use them. Some people even make pictures out of text characters. Others simply add famous quotes and sayings to their signatures.
- Add your e-mail address in the format **mailto:name@server** and your address will appear as a link in most e-mail programs, including Communicator and Eudora.

Using a signature file

Once you've created a signature file *(see page 169)*, Communicator can automatically add it to each message that you send. All you have to do is tell Communicator where the signature file is.

To use a signature file:

1. Choose Edit > Preferences.
2. Click Identity in the Category list.
3. At the bottom of the Identity preferences panel, click the Choose button **(Figure 12.66)**.
4. Choose the desired signature file in the dialog box that appears and click Open **(Figure 12.67)**. The file's path will appear in the Identity preferences box **(Figure 12.68)**.
5. Click OK to close the Identity preferences box. The next time you write a message, your signature will be automatically included **(Figure 12.69)**.

✓ Tips

- If you want to send a particular message without the signature, simply delete the signature text from the Message Composition window.
- If the signature file does not appear in the Open dialog box when you try to choose it, you probably didn't save it in text-only (or ASCII) format *(see page 169)*.
- If you move the signature file, or change its name or the name of the folder it's in, Communicator won't be able to find it and will simply stop adding it to your messages. Unfortunately, Communicator won't tell you there's a problem, so you have to watch it.

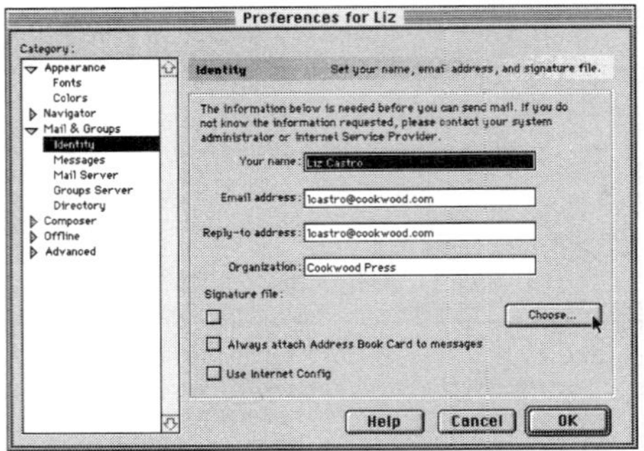

Figure 12.66 *Click the Identity panel and then the Choose button to choose a signature file.*

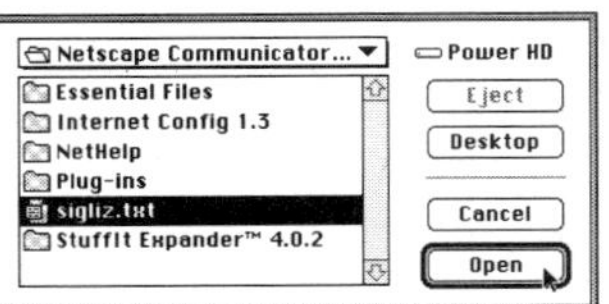

Figure 12.67 *Locate the desired signature file on your hard disk and click Open.*

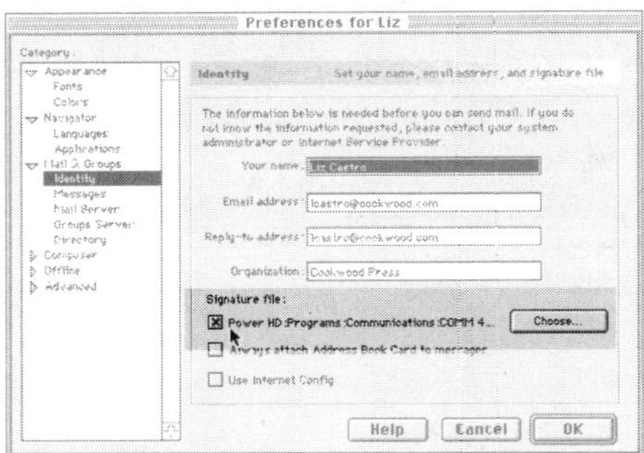

Figure 12.68 *The path to the selected signature file now appears in the Identity preferences tab.*

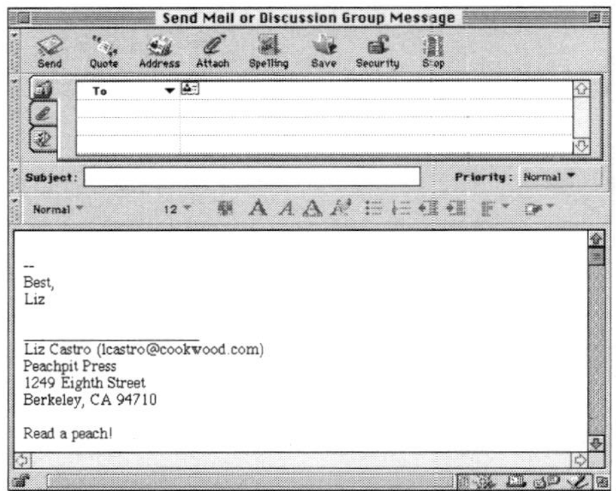

Figure 12.69 *The signature file is automatically copied to each new Message Composition window.*

The Address Book

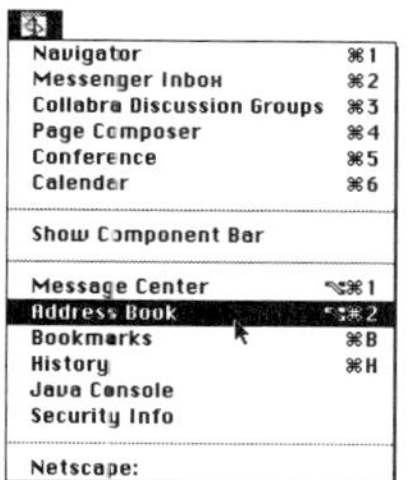

Figure 13.1 *Choose (Communicator) > Address Book to open the Address Book.*

Figure 13.2 *The Address Book helps you keep track of those long and complicated e-mail addresses.*

Figure 13.3 *Click the arrows in the upper-right corner of the Address Book window to hide or reveal additional columns of information.*

The Address Book window

Communicator lets you save e-mail addresses in the Address Book, a window that you can let float on the screen beside the message windows or hide at your convenience.

The Address Book includes not only the e-mail addresses themselves, but also the person's postal address, business information, and other data. The Address Book always lists addresses in alphabetical order, by first name.

An address book can also contain *mailing lists* that make it easy to send messages to more than one person at a time. You can include an address in as many mailing lists as desired.

To open the Address Book:

Choose Communicator > Address Book **(Figure 13.1)**. The Address Book appears **(Figure 13.2)**.

To hide or reveal additional columns in the Address Book:

Click the arrows in the upper-right corner to hide or reveal additional columns of information in the Address Book window **(Figure 13.3)**. The available columns of information are: Name, Email Address, Organization, City, and Nickname.

Storing an address

E-mail addresses tend to be long and hard to remember. You can store e-mail addresses in an address book together with the recipient's name, description, nickname, and other data.

To store an address in the Address Book:

1. With the Address Book window active, choose File > New Card **(Figure 13.4)** or click the New Card button on the toolbar **(Figure 13.5)**. The New Card dialog box appears **(Figure 13.6)**.
2. Enter the first and last name, organization, and title for the person **(Figure 13.7)**.
3. In the Email field, type the e-mail address carefully. One mistyped digit or letter can keep your mail from getting to its destination.
4. Enter a short, descriptive, easy-to-remember word for the Nickname. You can enter the nickname to call up the person's e-mail address in a message.
5. If desired, enter descriptive notes in the Notes field. Click the Contact and Netscape Conference tabs to add yet more information about the person.
6. Finally, check the option at the bottom of the General panel if the person wishes to receive HTML enhanced messages (with images, links, etc.).
7. Click OK. The address appears in the Address Book in alphabetical order by first name **(Figure 13.8)**.

Figure 13.4 *With the Address Book active, choose File > New Card.*

Figure 13.5 *Or click the New Card button on the toolbar.*

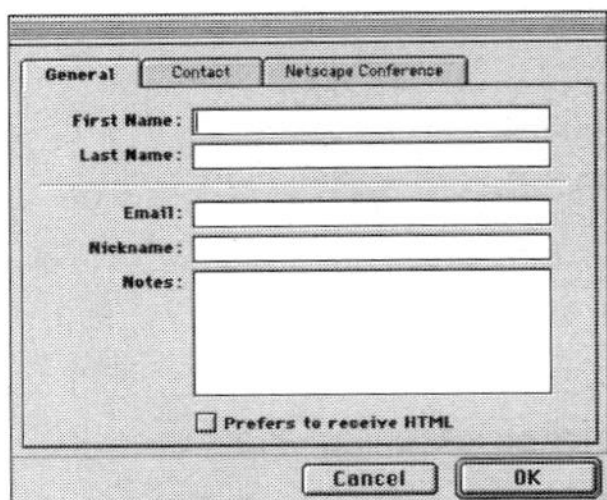

Figure 13.6 *Enter the desired information in the New Card dialog box.*

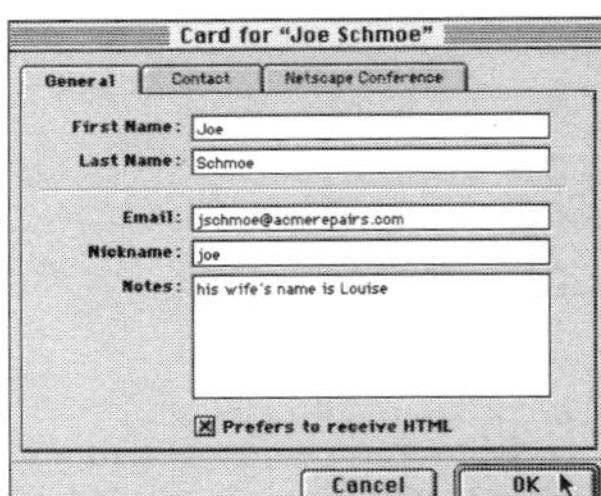

Figure 13.7 *Enter the information in each field and then click the Contact and Netscape Conference tabs to continue.*

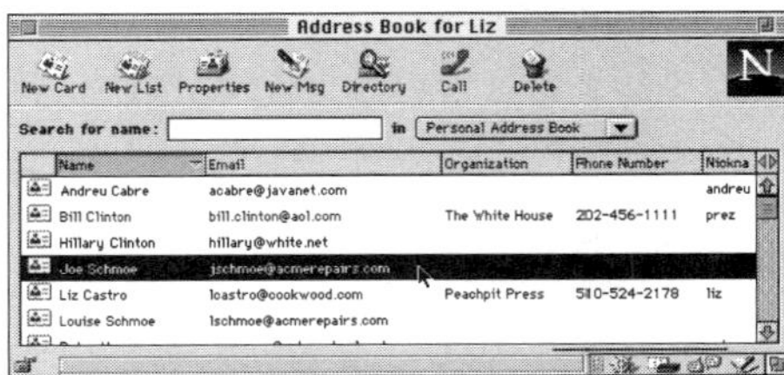

Figure 13.8 *The new address appears in the Address Book window.*

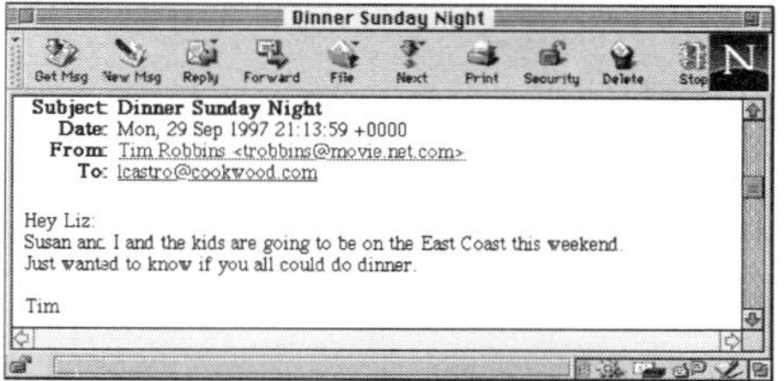

Figure 13.9 *Select the message from the person whose address you wish to add to your Address Book.*

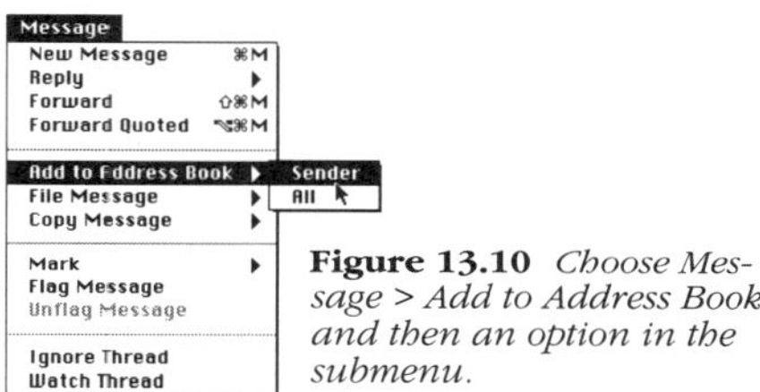

Figure 13.10 *Choose Message > Add to Address Book and then an option in the submenu.*

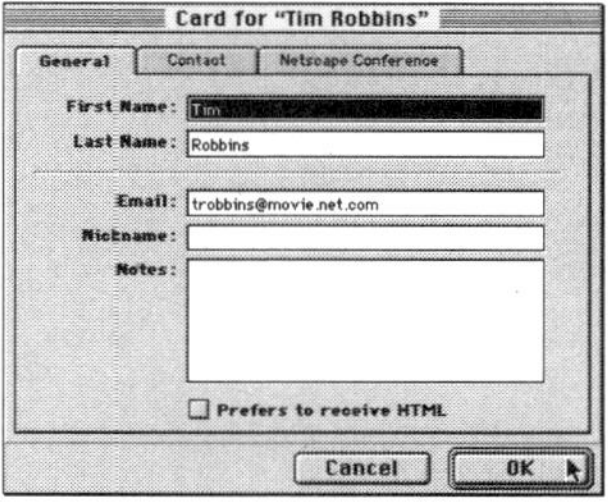

Figure 13.11 *The sender's name and e-mail address are entered in the New Card dialog box automatically. Enter a nickname and description, if desired, and click OK.*

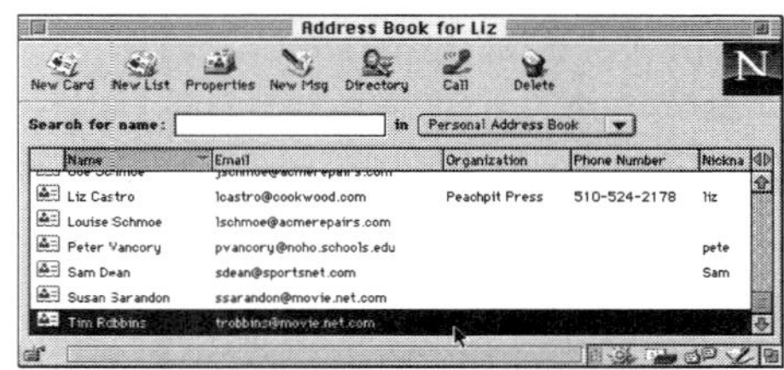

Figure 13.12 *The new address appears in the Address Book.*

Copying an address from incoming messages

You can add the addresses of anyone listed in an incoming message, including those cc'd or bcc'd. Adding an address in this way ensures that the address is not misspelled.

To copy an address from incoming messages:

1. Open the message from which you wish to copy the address **(Figure 13.9)**.
2. Choose Message > Add to Address Book > Sender **(Figure 13.10)**. The Card dialog box appears with the name and address automatically filled in **(Figure 13.11)**.
3. Add additional information if desired. For more information, consult *Storing an address* on page 172.
4. Click OK. The new address is added to your address book **(Figure 13.12)**.

✔ Tips

- Choose Message > Add to Address Book > All to add not only the sender's address but also those of any persons cc'd or bcc'd. An individual dialog box like the one shown in Figure 13.11 will appear for each address.
- You can also Control-click a message and choose Add Sender to Address Book or Add All Addressees to Address Book in the pop-up menu.
- It is possible (and not very hard, as you can see in Figure 13.9) to send mail with a false address. If the sender has not used a real address, you won't be able to use it to write them back.

Creating a mailing list

You can relate a group of addresses—called a *mailing list*—in the Address Book in order to send messages to a whole group of people at a time.

To create a mailing list:

1. From the Address Book, choose File > New List **(Figure 13.13)**. The Mailing List dialog box appears.
2. Enter a descriptive name for the list.
3. Type a nickname for the mailing list. You will be able to use the nickname to invoke the list.
4. Type a description of the list.
5. Drag the addresses that you wish to add to the mailing list from the Address Book to the List dialog box **(Figure 13.14)**. The names appear in the List dialog box's scroll box **(Figure 13.15)**.
6. Click OK. The mailing list is added to the Address Book and looks like a regular address **(Figure 13.16)**.

✔ Tips

- You can also click the New List button in the Address Book window to create a new list.
- A mailing list's name is like a nickname for *all of the addresses* the list contains. As such, it does not appear on any of your correspondence but instead is replaced by the addresses of each person on the list.
- Remove addresses from the mailing list by selecting them and choosing Edit > Clear or by pressing Delete.

Figure 13.13 *Choose File > New List.*

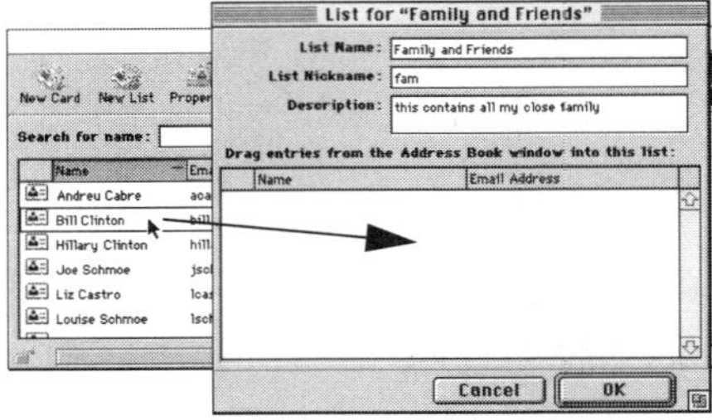

Figure 13.14 *Type the name, nickname, and description, if desired. Then drag names from the Address Book into the scroll box at the bottom of the List dialog box.*

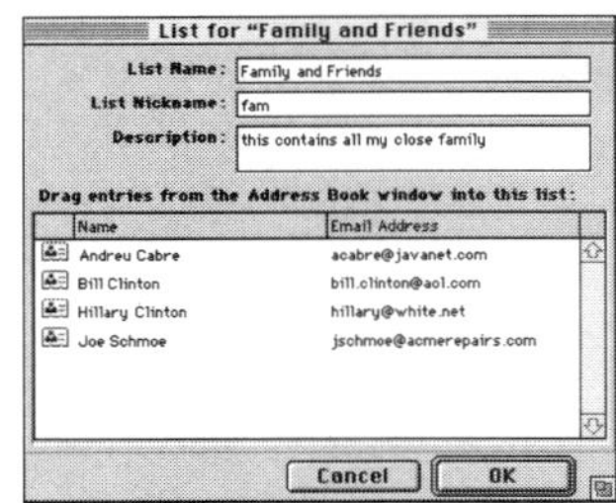

Figure 13.15 *The members of the mailing list appear in the scroll box once they've been dragged from the Address Book. When you're finished dragging names to the List box, click OK.*

Figure 13.16 *The new mailing list appears in the Address Book. Double click the list to open it for editing.*

Figure 13.17 *Select an address or list in the Address Book window.*

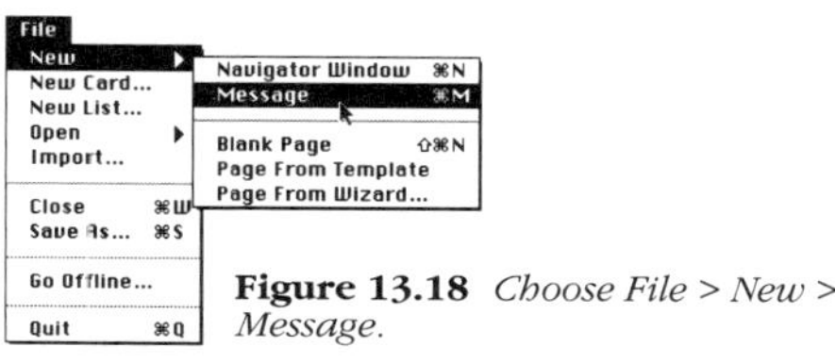

Figure 13.18 *Choose File > New > Message.*

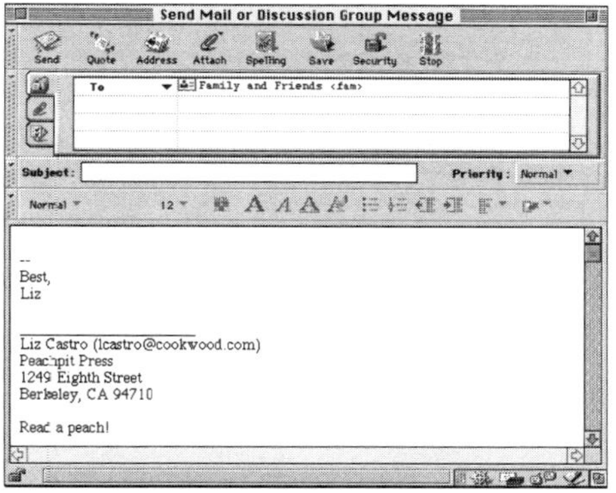

Figure 13.19 *A pre-addressed Message Composition window appears.*

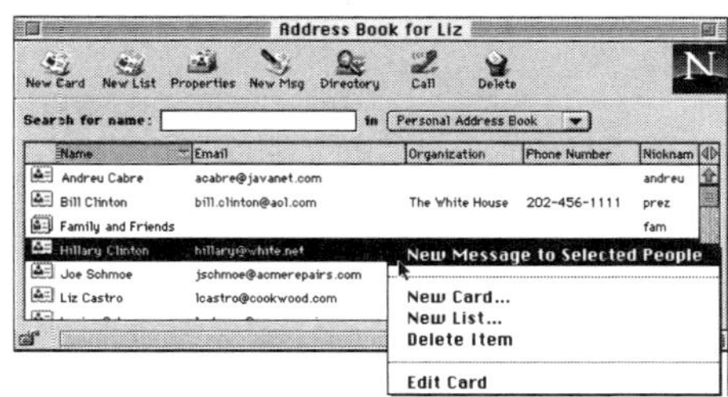

Figure 13.20 *You can also Control-click an address and then choose New Message to Selected People in the pop-up menu that appears.*

Using an address or list

The beauty of the Address Book is that you can send e-mail to someone without having to type his address. A list lets you e-mail *several* people at once.

To use an address or list:

1. Select the desired address or list in the Address Book **(Figure 13.17)**.
2. Choose File > New > Message **(Figure 13.18)** or click the New Msg button. The Message Composition window appears and is automatically addressed to the person or list of people selected in step 1 **(Figure 13.18)**.
3. Compose the message as usual.

✓ Tips

- Control-click an address and choose New Message to Selected People to open a new, automatically addressed Message Composition window **(Figure 13.20)**.
- Add one or more addresses or lists to an existing mail message by dragging them from the Address Book.
- Once in the Message Composition window, click the Address button to open and use the Address Book.
- You can also type a nickname in a field in the Message Composition window to add an address or list to that field. When you press the Tab key (to go to the next field), the nickname is replaced by the full address.
- When you type the first few letters of an address Communicator uses the Address Book to anticipate which address you want. Press Enter to accept its suggestion.

Changing or deleting an address or list

You may need to change an entry in your address book, for example, if the person changes online services, or to add descriptive information or a nickname.

To change an address or list:

1. Select an address or list and then choose Edit > Get Info **(Fig. 13.21)**.
2. In the dialog box that appears, change the values in the fields as desired **(Figures 13.22 and 13.23)** and then click OK to save the changes.

✔ Tips

- Select an address and then click the Properties button on the toolbar to view or edit it.
- Control-click an address and choose Edit Card in the pop-up menu to edit it **(Figure 13.24)**.

Getting rid of unused addresses or lists is simple. The cleaner you keep your address book, the easier it will be to find the addresses you *do* use.

To delete an address or list:

1. Select the item you wish to delete in the Address Book by clicking it once.
2. Choose Edit > Clear **(Figure 13.25)**, or press Delete. The address or list disappears.

✔ Tips

- Or click the Delete button on the toolbar to delete a selected address or list.
- No alert appears when you delete an address or list. And there is no Undo.

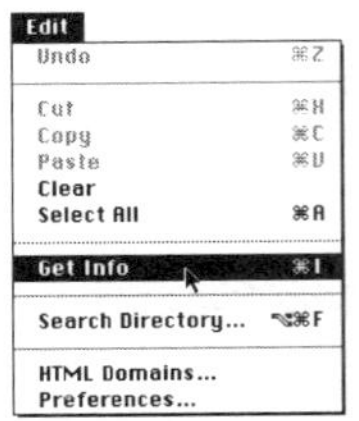

Figure 13.21 *Choose Edit > Get Info.*

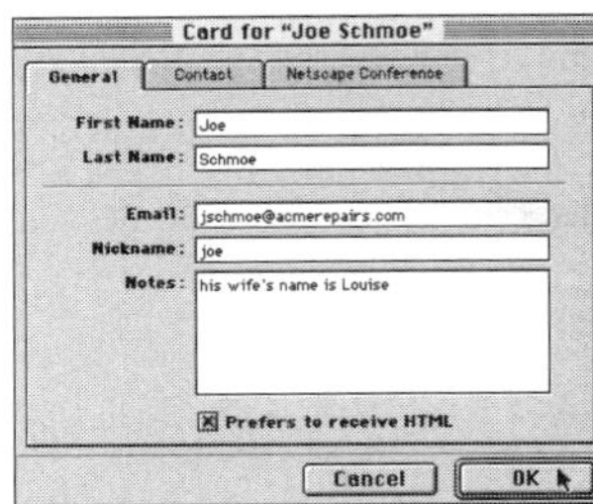

Figure 13.22 *If you've selected an individual address, the Card dialog box appears. Edit the address as desired.*

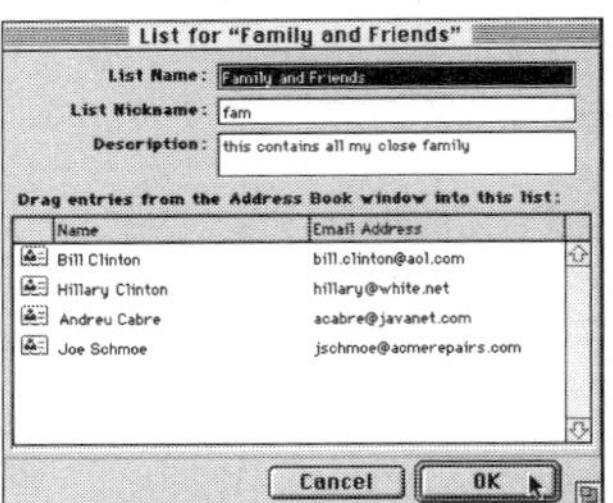

Figure 13.23 *If you've selected a mailing list, the List dialog box appears. Drag new addresses to the list box, or delete addresses as necessary.*

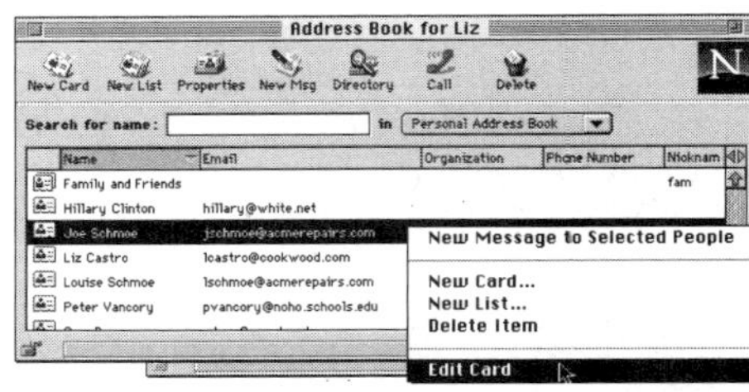

Figure 13.24 *You can also Control-click an address and then choose Edit Card to make any necessary changes.*

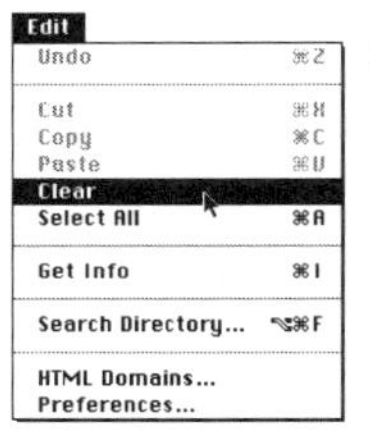

Figure 13.25 *To delete an address or mailing list, select it and then choose Edit > Clear.*

Figure 13.26 *Choose Edit > Search Directory.*

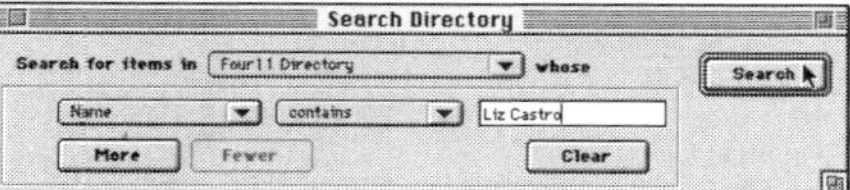

Figure 13.27 *Choose a directory and then type the search criteria. Finally, click Search.*

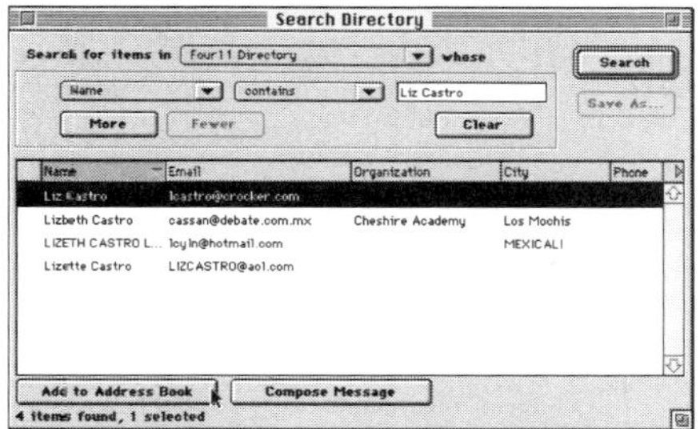

Figure 13.28 *Communicator contacts the server and lists all the addresses that match the search criteria. Select an address and click Add to Address Book to store the address. Or click Compose Message to begin a new message to the selected person.*

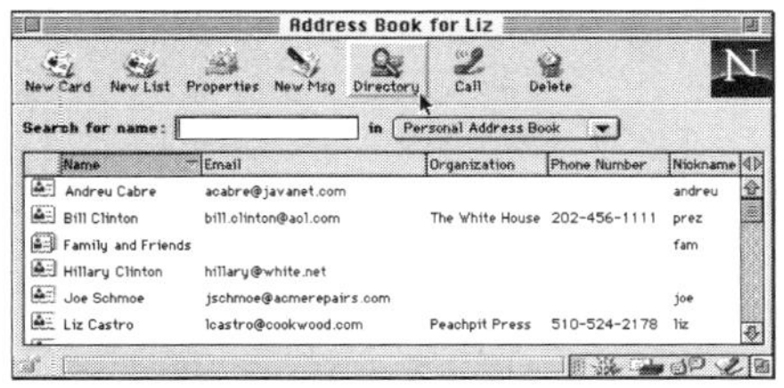

Figure 13.29 *Click the Directory button in the Address Book to open the Search Directory box.*

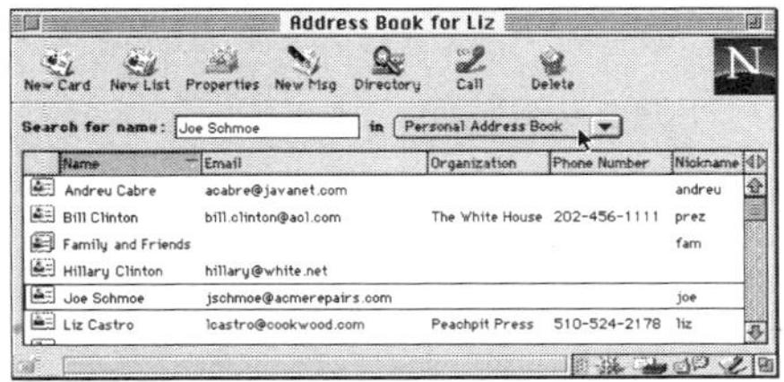

Figure 13.30 *To search your personal directory, use the Search line under the toolbar in the Address Book window.*

Searching for an address

Incorporated into the Address Book is a special search feature that uses commercial white pages services to locate e-mail addresses that you need. Once you've found the e-mail address, you can add it to your Address Book or create a new message addressed to that person.

To search for an address:

1. Choose Edit > Search Directory **(Figure 13.26)**. The Search Directory dialog box appears.
2. Choose which directory you want to search **(Figure 13.27)**. You can choose from several commercial white pages directories.
3. Enter the criteria that you wish to search for. Click More to add additional criteria.
4. Click the Search button. Communicator connects to the chosen directory and lists all matches **(Figure 13.28)**.
5. Select a match.
6. If desired, choose Add to Address Book to record the e-mail address in your personal Address Book.
7. If desired, click Compose Message to open a new Message Composition window already addressed to the selected person.
8. Click the close box.

✔ Tips

- Click the Directory button in the Address Book to open the Search Directory dialog box **(Figure 13.29)**.
- To search your personal directory, use the Search line in the Address Book window itself **(Figure 13.30)**.

Saving an address book

You can save an address book in order to share it with others or simply to make a back-up copy.

To save an address book:

1. Choose File > Save As **(Fig. 13.31)**. The Save dialog box appears **(Figure 13.32)**.
2. Give the file a name and choose the folder in which to save it.
3. Add the extension .ldif to the file name. For some bizarre reason, if you don't complete this step, Communicator will not save the file.
4. Click Save to save the file.

✔ **Tip**

- You used to be able to save an address book and then open it as a Web page. Unfortunately, Communicator 4's address book format has changed and this is no longer possible.

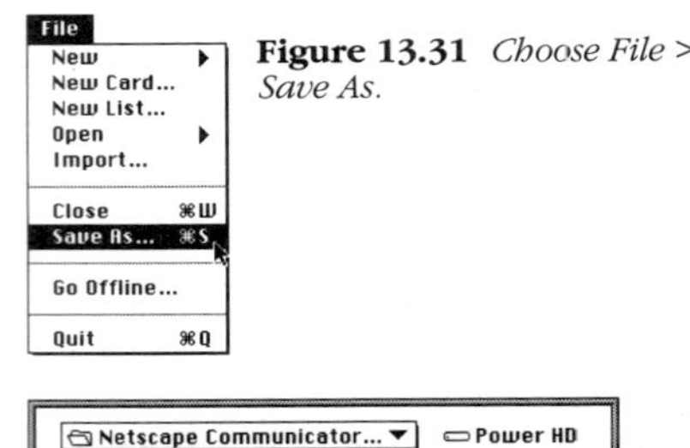

Figure 13.31 *Choose File > Save As.*

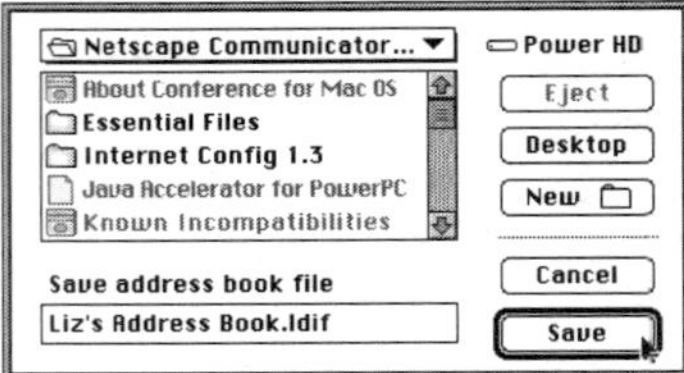

Figure 13.32 *In the Save dialog box, give the address book file a name. Add the .ldif extension to the name. Then click Save.*

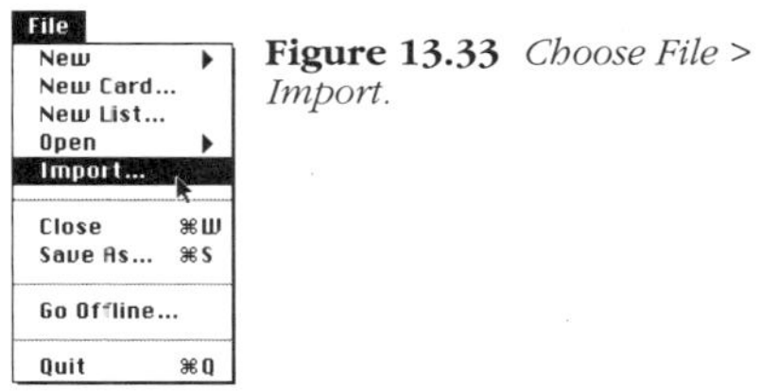

Figure 13.33 *Choose File > Import.*

Figure 13.34 *Select the desired address book file and click Open.*

Importing an address book

You can import the addresses from a saved address book file into your current address book. For example, you can save the address book file on your computer at work and then import it into your address book at your home computer.

To import an address book:

Choose File > Import **(Figure 13.33)**. The Import dialog box appears. Choose the address book file that you wish to import and click Open **(Figure 13.34)**. The addresses in the imported file are displayed in the current Address Book window.

✔ Tip

- Currently, Netscape does not replace or update names that already exist. It simply ignores any incoming address with the same name as an existing address.

14 Organizing Messages

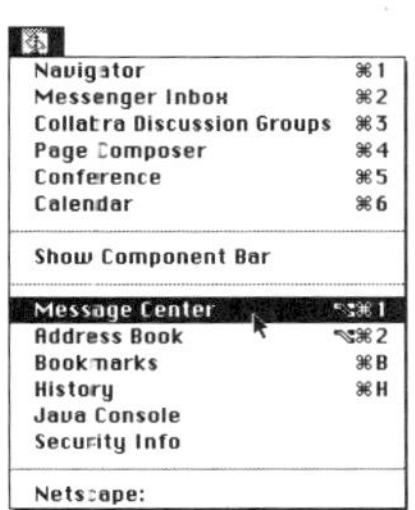

Figure 14.1 *Choose (Communicator) > Message Center to open the Message Center window.*

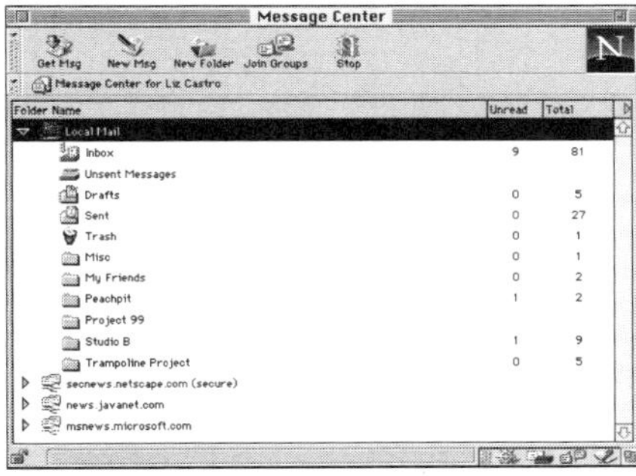

Figure 14.2 *The Message Center window is where you access the different e-mail and discussion groups folders.*

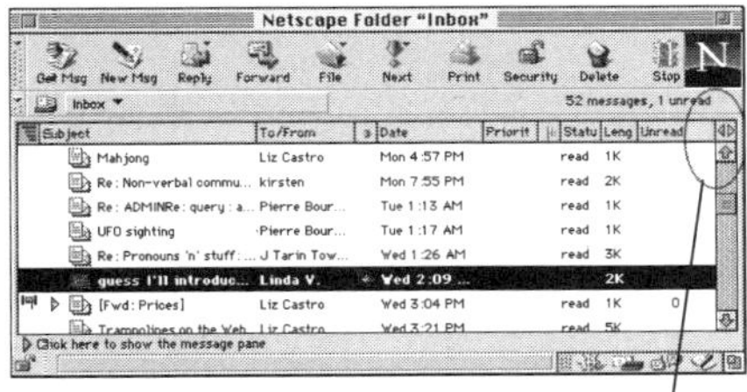

Figure 14.3 *From the Message List window, you can access all the different folders through the pop-up menu on the toolbar and read and move around messages. Click the arrows in the upper-right corner (right) to hide or reveal additional columns of information.*

Both e-mail and discussion group messages are organized in the Message Center and Message List windows. The Message Center lists each folder and gives an overview of your organizational system. The Message List window lists both folders and individual messages and lets you move items from one place to another.

The Message Center

When you click the Discussion Groups button on the Component bar, choose (Communicator) > Collabra Discussion Groups, or choose (Communicator) > Message Center **(Figure 14.1)**, the Message Center window appears **(Fig. 14.2)**. The Message Center contains the folders into which your e-mail messages are filed, as well as your discussion group servers and the discussion groups to which you have subscribed.

The Message List window

When you click the Mailbox button on the Component bar, choose Communicator > Messenger Mailbox, or double click any folder in the Message Center, the Message List window appears. The Message List window shows all the messages in each folder or discussion group. Display or hide columns by clicking the arrows in the upper-right corner of the window **(Figure 14.3)**. Display the contents of a message by clicking the arrow in the window's bottom-left corner.

The Message Center's five default folders

Communicator creates five default folders for filing messages: Inbox, Unsent Messages, Drafts, Sent, and Trash **(Fig. 14.4)**.

Communicator stores the new, incoming messages in the Inbox. Once you've read them, you can move them to a more specific folder *(see page 186)*. Or if you're lazy like me, you can just leave them there.

The Drafts folder holds messages that you've started to write, and have saved, but that you haven't yet decided to send. You can open the messages in the Drafts folder at any time to continue working on them or to send them off, either immediately or the next time you connect to the Internet.

The Unsent Messages folder holds messages that you've queued for later delivery. For example, you can write several messages without being connected to your Internet server and then send them all at once *(see page 159)*. If you change your mind about sending a message, simply move it from the Unsent Messages folder.

Once you've actually sent a message, Communicator transfers it to the Sent folder. You can choose to refile sent messages in another folder, or just leave them there.

Finally, the Trash folder holds messages that you've deleted. For more information on deleting files, consult *Deleting messages and folders* on page 190. You can retrieve messages from the Trash (it doesn't even smell bad) until you decide to empty it. Once you've emptied the trash *(see page 191)*, the messages are truly gone.

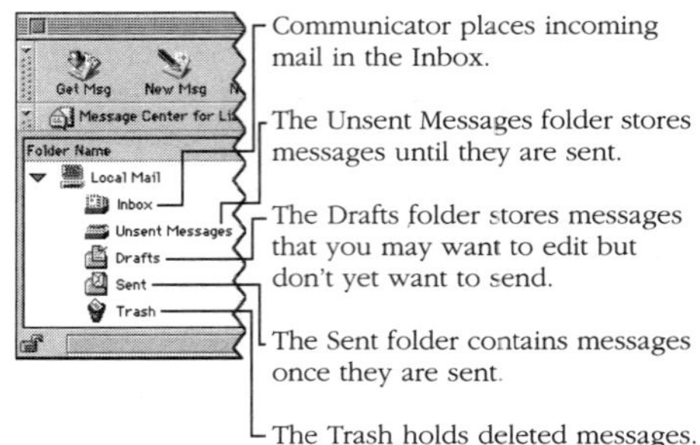

Figure 14.4 *The Message Center window contains five folders by default. You may add others as desired.*

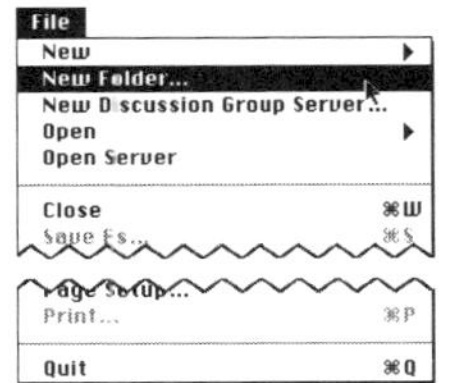

Figure 14.5 *Choose File > New Folder.*

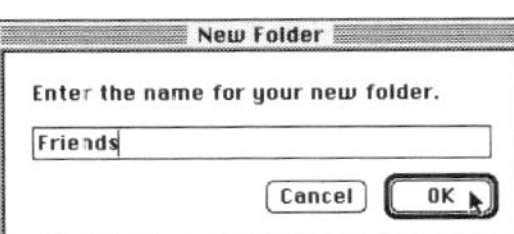

Figure 14.6 *In the New Dialog dialog box, type a name for the new folder and click OK.*

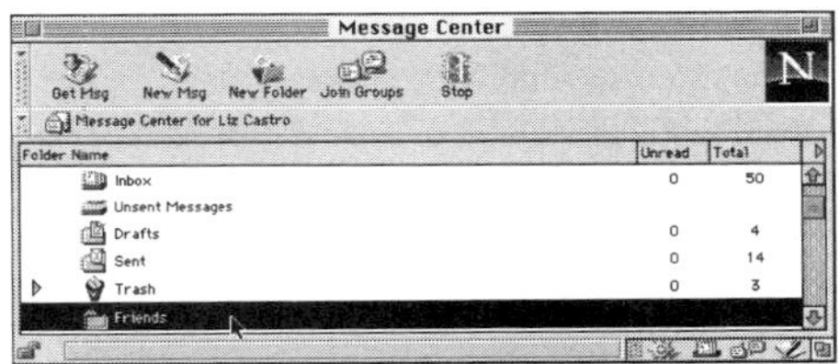

Figure 14.7 *The new folder appears in the Message Center window.*

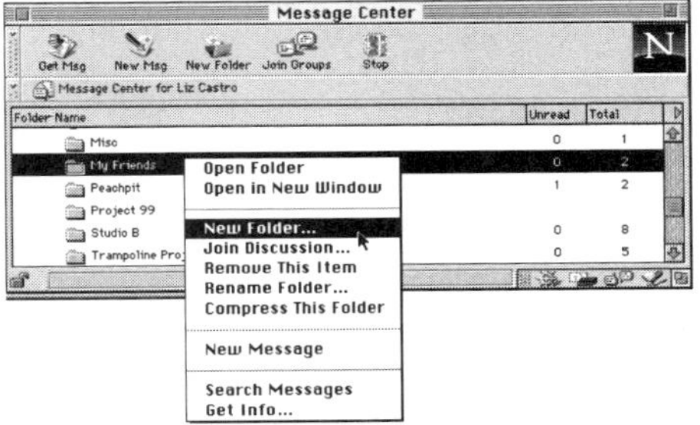

Figure 14.8 *Control-click a folder and choose New Folder in the pop-up menu to create a new folder in the selected one.*

Figure 14.9 *Select a folder and then choose Edit > Rename Folder to change its name.*

Creating new folders

In addition to the default folders *(see page 182)*, you can create as many of your own as your hard disk space will allow. Folders are helpful for organizing your mail once you've received or sent it.

To create a new folder:

1. Select the folder in which you wish to create the new folder.
2. From either the Message Center or the Message List window, choose File > New Folder **(Figure 14.5)**.
3. Enter a name for the folder in the New Folder dialog box that appears and click OK **(Figure 14.6)**. The new folder appears **(Figure 14.7)**.

✓ Tips

- You can also Control-click a folder and select New Folder in the pop-up menu **(Figure 14.8)**.
- To create a folder on an equal level as the five default folders, select Local Mail in step 1 above.
- You can't create folders inside discussion groups, but you can file messages from discussion groups into folders under Local Mail.
- Rename a folder by selecting the folder and choosing Edit > Rename Folder **(Figure 14.9)**. You can't rename the five default folders.
- You can drag folders into other folders.

Selecting messages

There are several ways to select messages that make it easier to file, read, or delete a particular group of messages. You always select messages in the Message List window, not the Message Center.

To select more than one message:

- Hold down Shift and click to add one or more messages **(Figure 14.10)**.
- Hold down Command and click to add one or more messages that are not next to the currently selected one **(Figure 14.11)**.

You can also select all the flagged messages in a folder, perhaps prior to moving them to another folder en masse. For more information about flags, consult *Flagging messages* on page 145.

To select the flagged messages:

1. Select the desired folder.
2. Choose Edit > Select > Flagged Messages **(Figure 14.12)**. All of the flagged messages in the currently selected folder are selected **(Figure 14.13)**.

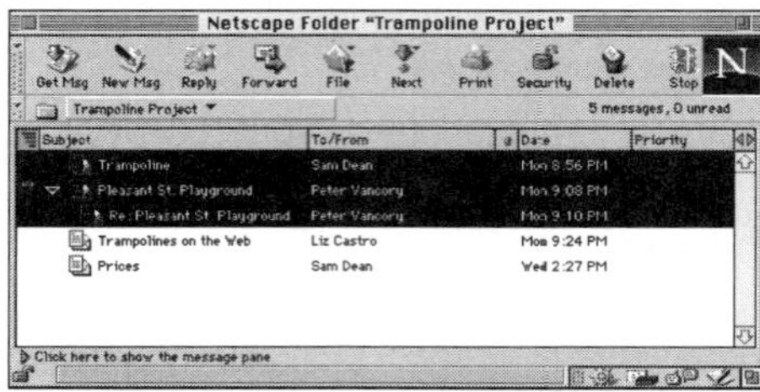

Figure 14.10 *Hold down Shift and click to select several messages in a row.*

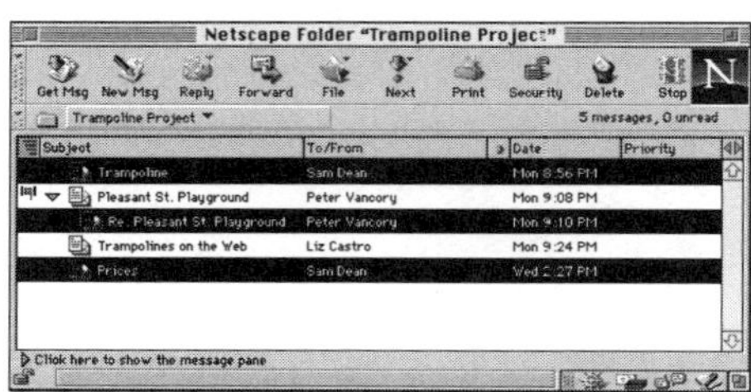

Figure 14.11 *Hold down Command and click to select several messages that are not in a row.*

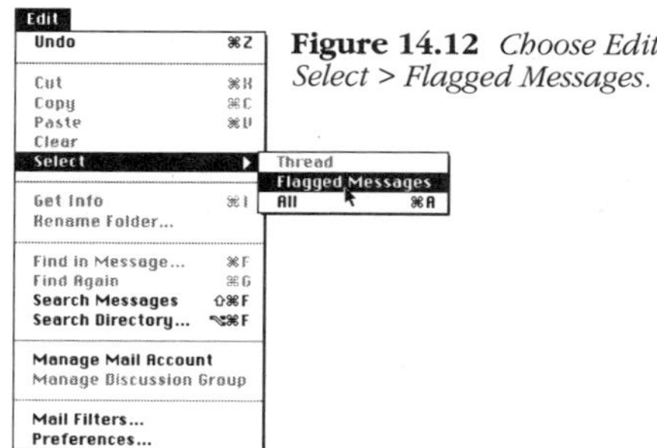

Figure 14.12 *Choose Edit > Select > Flagged Messages.*

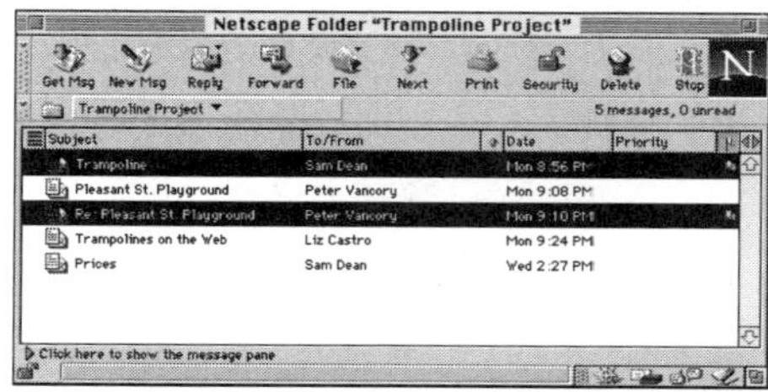

Figure 14.13 *All of the flagged messages in the current folder are selected.*

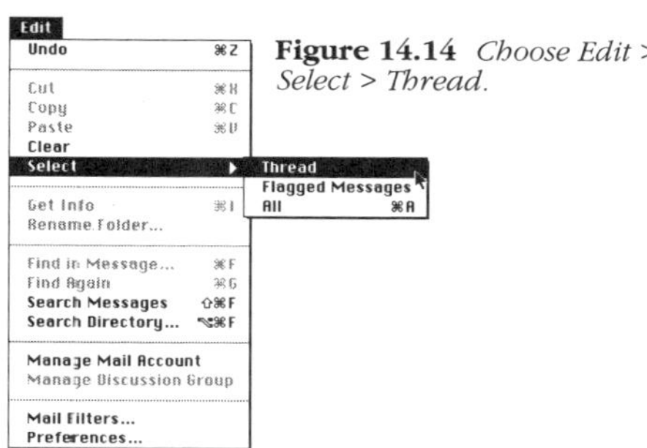

Figure 14.14 *Choose Edit > Select > Thread.*

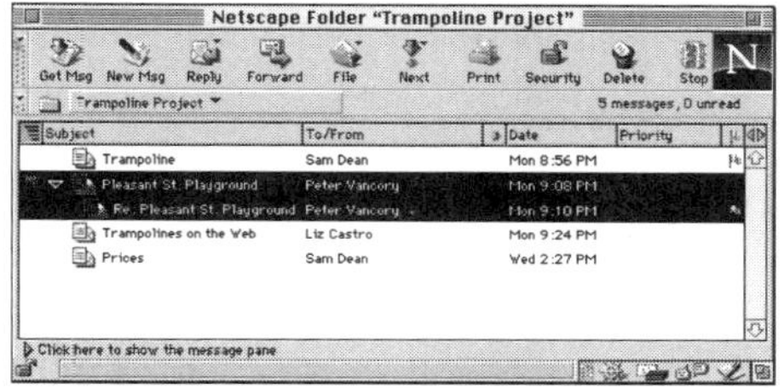

Figure 14.15 *All of the messages related to the original message—that is, in the message's thread—are selected.*

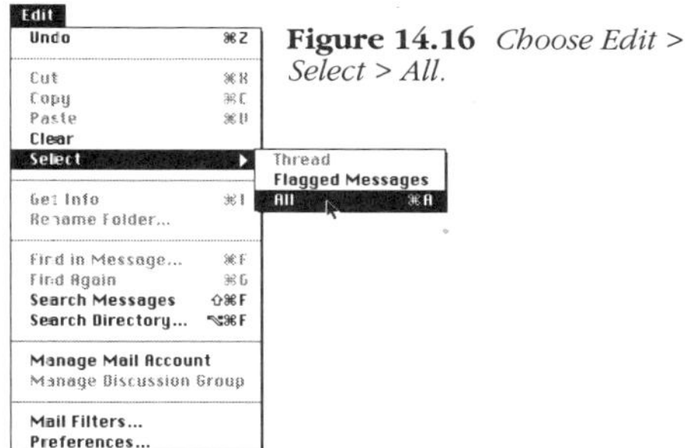

Figure 14.16 *Choose Edit > Select > All.*

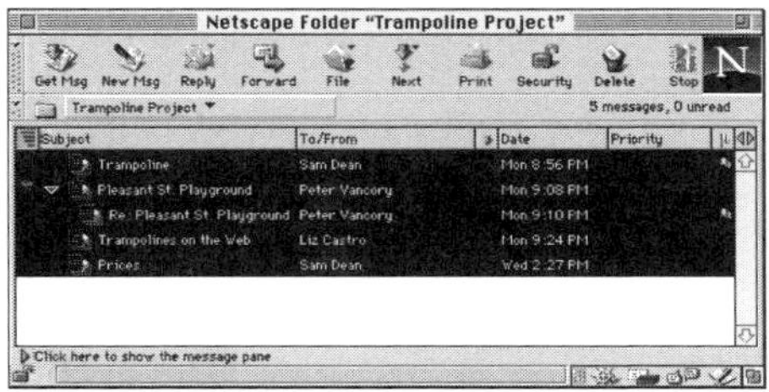

Figure 14.17 *All of the messages in the folder are selected.*

You can also select all the messages in a thread (in a given folder) in order to move, copy, or delete them at once. For more information about threads, consult *Threading messages* on page 144.

To select a thread:

1. Select one of the messages in the thread.
2. Choose Edit > Select > Thread **(Figure 14.14)**. Each message that belongs to the thread is selected **(Figure 14.15)**.

Last but not least, you can select all the messages in a folder.

To select all the messages in a folder:

1. Open the desired folder in the Message List window.
2. Choose Edit > Select > All **(Figure 14.16)**. All the messages in the chosen folder are selected **(Figure 14.17)**.

✔ Tips

- You can't select messages in more than one folder at a time.
- Once you've selected a group of messages, you can move or copy them to another folder, or delete them. For more information on moving and copying messages, consult *Filing and copying messages* on page 186. For more information on deleting messages, consult *Deleting messages and folders* on page 190.

Filing and copying messages

Generally, in order to keep things organized, you move messages from the default folders (e.g., the Inbox and Sent folders) to the folders you have created. *Copying* moves the message to the new folder and leaves a copy in the old one.

To file messages in a different folder:

1. Select the message(s) **(Figure 14.18)**.
2. Choose Message > File Message and then the desired destination folder in the submenu **(Figure 14.19)**. The message disappears from the current folder and is transferred to the selected one **(Figure 14.20)**.

To copy messages to a different folder:

1. Select the message(s).
2. Choose Message > Copy Message and then the desired destination folder in the submenu **(Figure 14.21)**. The message remains in the current folder and is also copied to the selected one.

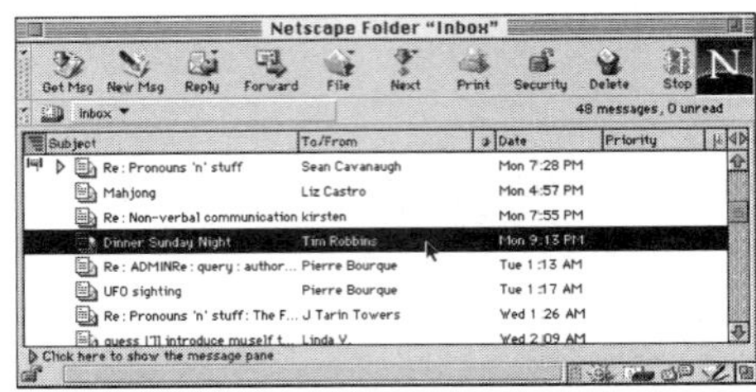

Figure 14.18 *Select the desired message.*

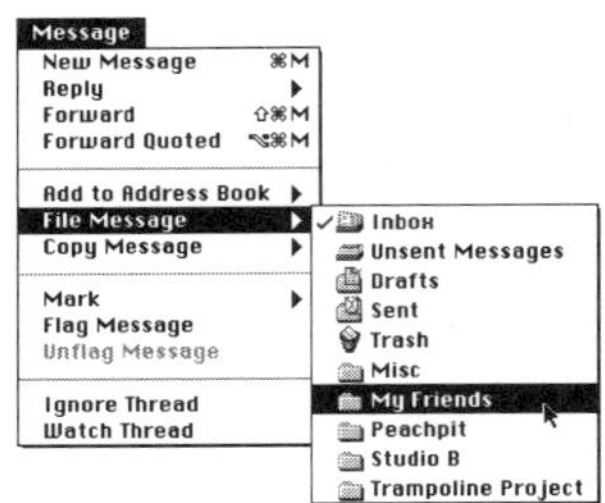

Figure 14.19 *Choose Message > File Message and then the destination folder in the submenu.*

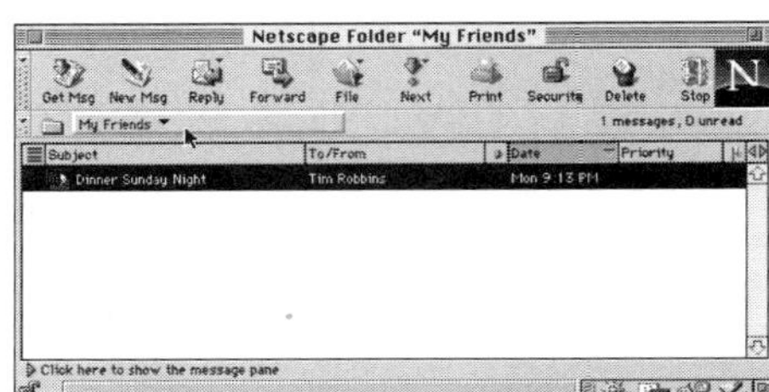

Figure 14.20 *The message now appears in its new location (the My Friends folder).*

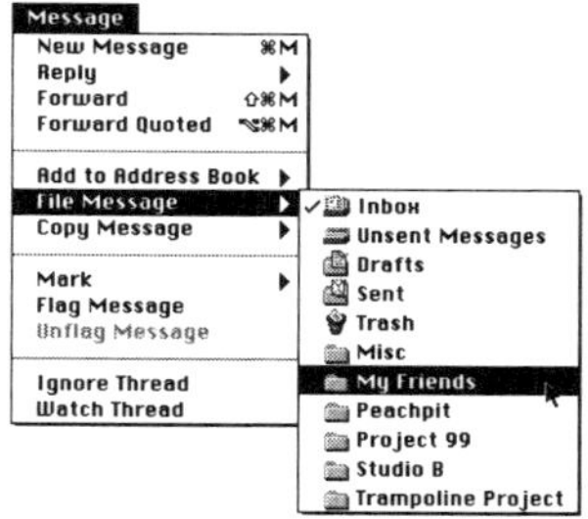

Figure 14.21 *Choose Message > Copy Message and then the desired folder in the submenu.*

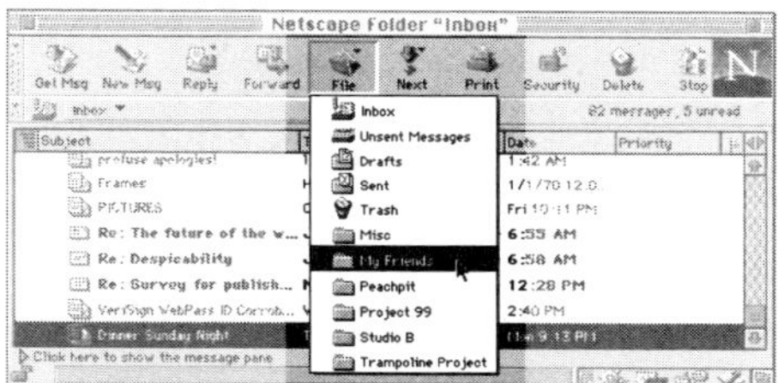

Figure 14.22 *You can also file a message by selecting the message, clicking the File button on the toolbar, and then choosing the destination folder in the submenu.*

✓ Tips

- You can also file messages by selecting the message, clicking the File button on the toolbar, and then choosing the destination folder in the submenu that appears **(Figure 14.22)**.
- You can also drag messages from one folder to another. To copy them, hold down Option while you drag.
- Use the special selecting commands *(see page 184)* to select more than one message before moving or copying.
- You cannot move or copy messages to the Unsent Messages folder. The only way to place messages there is by choosing File > Send Later. For more information, consult *Composing a new message* on page 152.
- You can resend a message by moving it from the Sent folder (or wherever you have filed it) to the Drafts folder. Then send it as usual by double clicking it and choosing File > Send *(see page 158)*. You can use this same technique to modify and send any message (including those you have received from other people).

Filtering messages

You can have Communicator analyze the messages you receive, according to certain conditions you define (is the subject line "Make MONEY MONEY MONEY"?), and then automatically perform actions on those messages (delete!). For example, imagine that you receive mail from your brother and you want to keep his messages separate from the rest. You can create a folder with his name and then use a filter to automatically store his messages in the folder that you have created.

To create a filter in order to file messages:

1. From the Message Center, choose Edit > Mail Filters **(Figure 14.23)**. The Mail Filters dialog box appears. Its main function is to change the order in which the filters are applied.
2. Click New to create a new filter **(Figure 14.24)**. The lower part of the dialog box is revealed **(Fig. 14.25)**.
3. In the Name field, enter a name for the filter. Use a descriptive name.
4. Choose one of the options from the "If an incoming message's" pop-up menu. These are the variables that Communicator takes into consideration when deciding which messages will be affected by the filter.
5. Choose an option from the next pop-up menu. These can be: contains, doesn't contain, is, isn't, begins with, ends with.
6. Type the filtering criteria in the text box at the end of the condition.

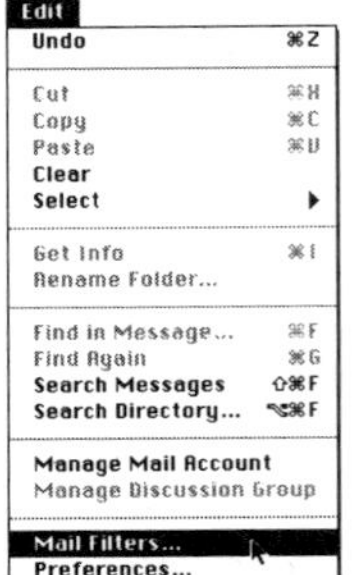

Figure 14.23 *Choose Edit > Mail Filters.*

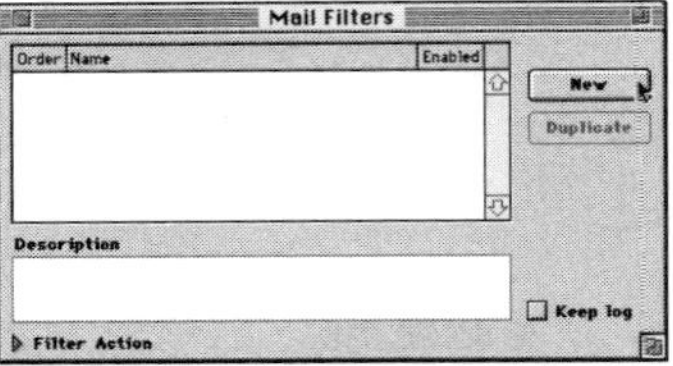

Figure 14.24 *Click New to create a new filter.*

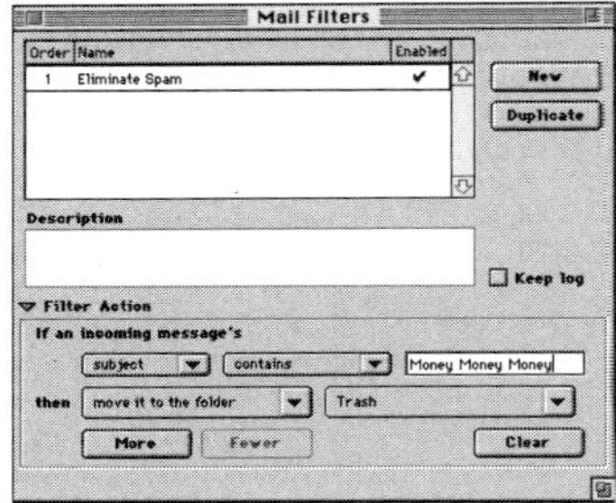

Figure 14.25 *The lower part of the dialog box is automatically revealed. Give the filter a name. Then, enter the criteria by which Communicator will decide which messages to act on. In this example, all messages that have "Money Money Money" in the subject line will be automatically dumped in the Trash.*

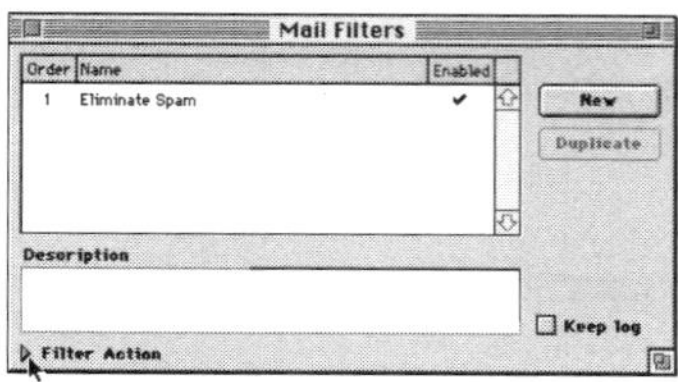

Figure 14.26 *You can click the triangle in the bottom left corner to hide the lower portion of the dialog box.*

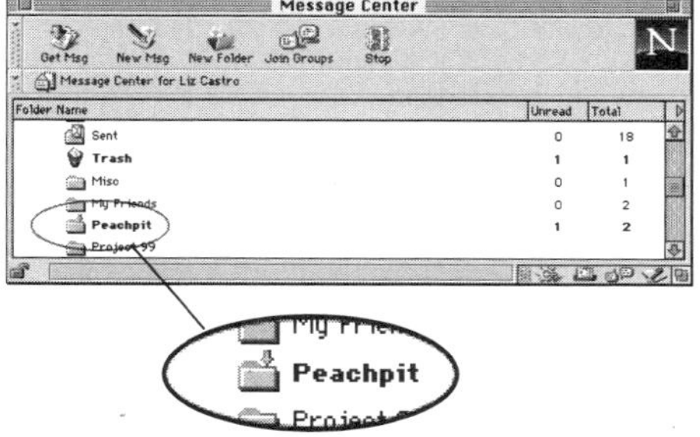

Figure 14.27 *When you receive new messages that satisfy the criteria of your various filters, the messages are automatically placed in the specified folders (or the Trash). Folders with new messages are marked in bold with a green arrow (as in Peachpit above). The Trash is just marked in bold.*

7. Click More to enter up to 5 conditions that Communicator has to match in order to perform the desired action. Click Fewer to eliminate conditions.

8. In the "then" area, choose what Communicator should do with the messages that match the given criteria. The action can range from moving the message to a specific folder, to marking it as read, to deleting it.

9. If desired, describe the filter so that you can remember what it does.

✔ Tips

- It's kind of strange, but there's no OK button in the Mail Filters dialog box. Instead, use the close box. Filters are automatically saved.
- No OK button means no Cancel button either. If you make changes to a filter, there's no way to go back to the old version.
- To turn a filter on and off, click the checkmark next to the filter's name in the Mail Filters box. A checkmark indicates that the filter is on.
- You can use filters to automatically delete spam (junk e-mail).
- Filters only affect incoming messages. Messages that you've already received cannot be filtered.
- Check the Keep log checkbox in the Mail Filters dialog box to keep a record of all the files that Communicator filters. You can view the log by choosing File > Open > Page in Navigator and then selecting the file called "Mail Filter Log" which you will find in your Netscape folder inside the Preferences folder inside the System Folder.

Deleting messages and folders

Once you no longer need a message, you can delete it in order to conserve space on your hard disk and keep your message windows reasonably neat.

To delete a message or folder:

1. Select the desired message(s) or folder(s) **(Figure 14.28)**.
2. Choose Edit > Clear **(Figure 14.29)**. The message or folder disappears from the current folder and is moved to the Trash folder **(Figure 14.30)**.

✓ Tips

- You can press the Delete key to delete messages and folders.
- You can also Control-click a message or folder and then choose Remove Message in the pop-up menu **(Figure 14.31)**.
- You can also drag a message to the Trash folder to delete it.
- To recover a message you've deleted, simply drag it out of the Trash folder or use the File and/or Copy commands *(see page 186)*.
- You can't delete messages from a discussion group. The Delete button won't even be available. But don't fret; all the messages will disappear on their own in a day or two.

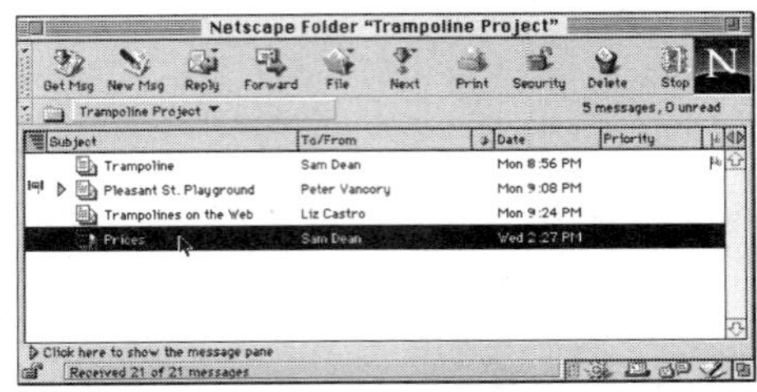

Figure 14.28 *Choose the message you wish to delete.*

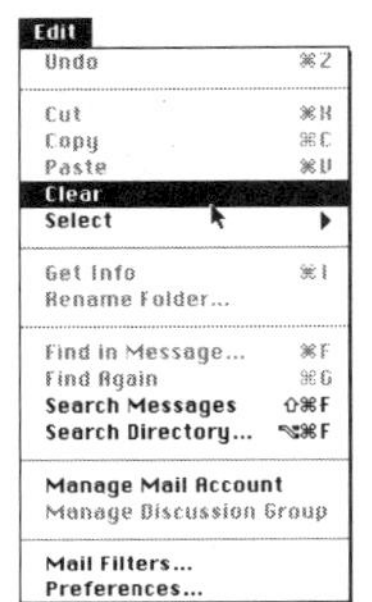

Figure 14.29 *Choose Edit > Clear.*

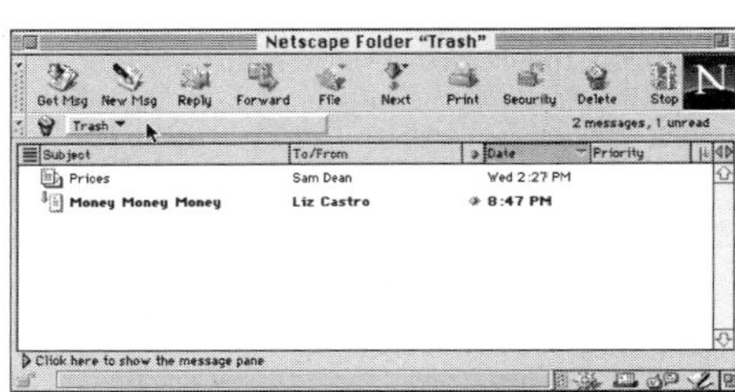

Figure 14.30 *The message disappears from the current folder and is placed in the Trash.*

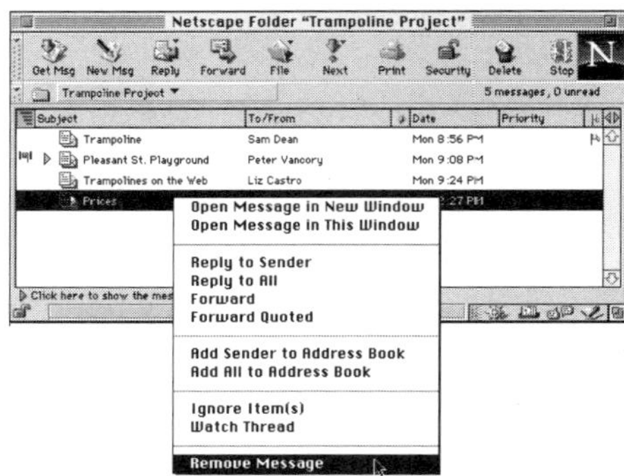

Figure 14.31 *Control-click the message you want to delete and choose Remove Message in the pop-up menu that appears.*

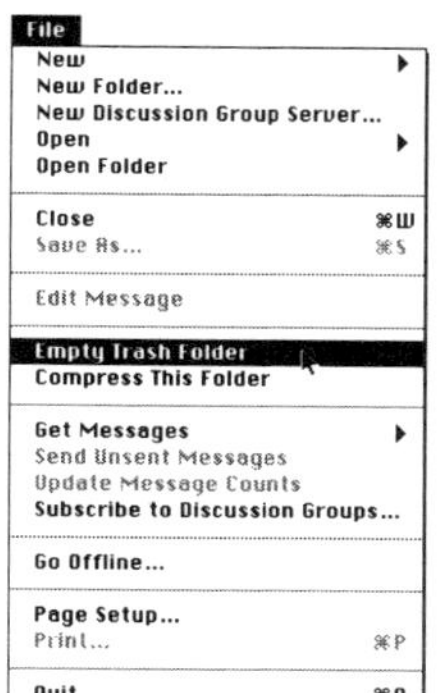

Figure 14.32 *To permanently remove the deleted messages, choose File > Empty Trash Folder.*

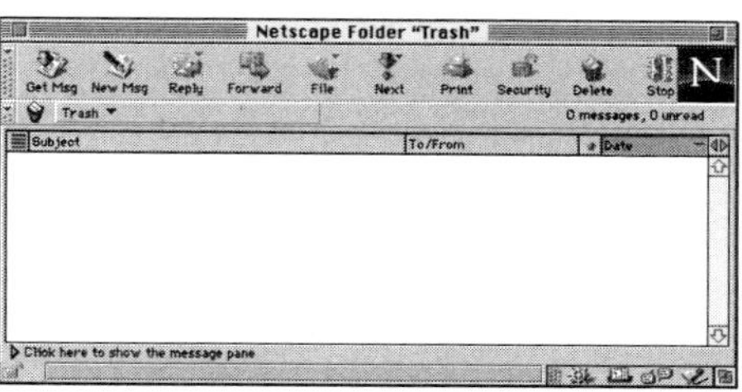

Figure 14.33 *The Trash folder is empty.*

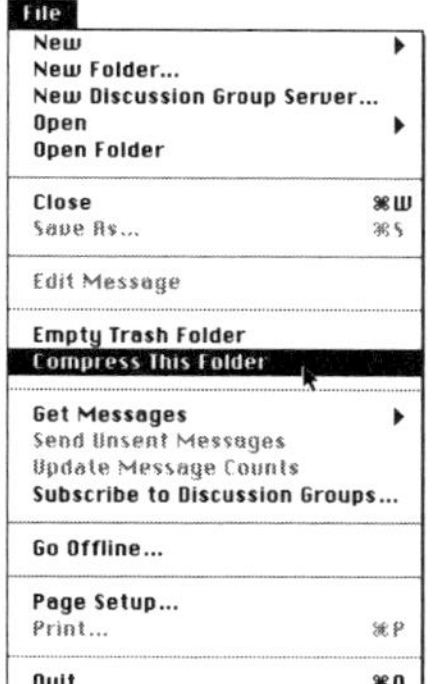

Figure 14.34 *Choose File > Compress This Folder.*

Conserving disk space

When you delete a message, it is not permanently deleted, but instead is placed in the Trash folder. You can retrieve an item from the Trash folder at any time before emptying it *(see page 186)*. Empty the trash to permanently remove the messages it contains.

To empty the Trash folder:

Choose File > Empty Trash Folder **(Figure 14.32)**. No alert box appears, and the Undo command is unavailable and cannot make your messages come back. The Trash folder simply appears empty **(Figure 14.33)**.

Another way to reduce the amount of space taken up by your folders and messages is by compressing your folders.

To compress your folders:

Choose File > Compress This Folder **(Figure 14.34)**. All of the folders are compressed.

✓ Tips

- Before emptying the trash, make sure you really want to delete all the messages that it contains. Once the trash is emptied, those messages are gone forever.
- Emptying the trash compresses all the folders automatically.
- Compressing a folder does not affect any of the messages it contains. It simply recovers wasted space that is generated when you move messages from one folder to another.

15 Checking Your Spelling

One of the most convenient new features in Communicator is the spell checker. Although we describe the spell checker here in the Messages section, you can also use it to proofread the Web pages you create with Composer.

Checking a whole message

Once you've finished writing your message (or Web page), you can run it through the spell checker to correct all your typos.

To check a whole message:

1. With your message open **(Fig. 15.1)**, choose Tools > Check Spelling **(Figure 15.2)** or click the Spelling button on the toolbar **(Figure 15.3)**. The Check Spelling dialog box appears. The first misspelled word, if any, is displayed in the Word box and possible replacement spellings may be listed below.

2. At this point you have several choices:

   Click Ignore or Ignore All to leave this or all instances of the word alone **(Figure 15.4)**.

   Choose the desired replacement word, if it is not selected already. Or type the correct spelling in the Word box. Then click Replace or Replace All to use the replacement word in this or all instances of the misspelled word **(Figure 15.5)**.

   Click Learn to add the word to your custom dictionary so that Communicator doesn't ask you about it again.

3. When the spell checker has finished going through your document, a Done button becomes available **(Figure 15.6)**. Click Done to close the Check Spelling box. To stop checking before reviewing the entire page, click the Stop button.

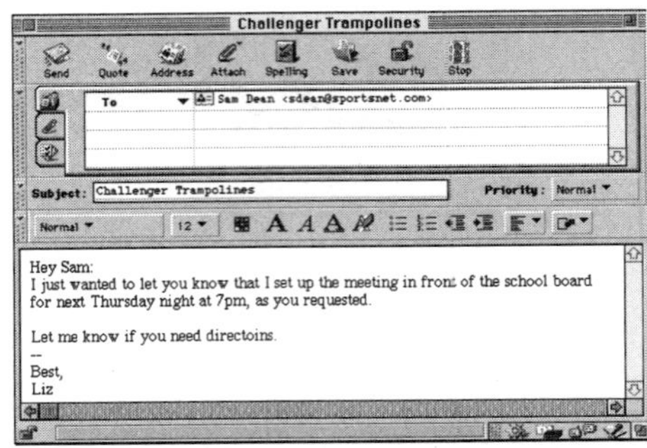

Figure 15.1 *Compose a message or Web page.*

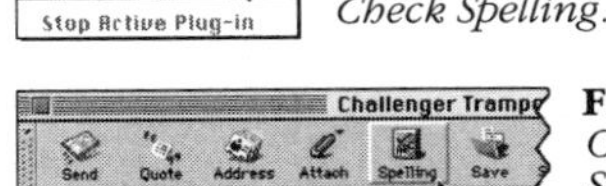

Figure 15.2 *Choose Tools > Check Spelling.*

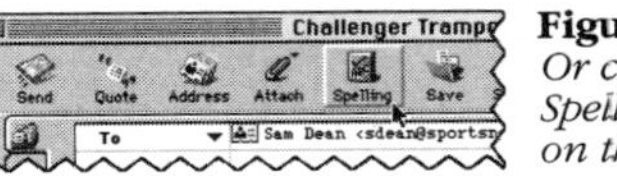

Figure 15.3 *Or click the Spelling button on the toolbar.*

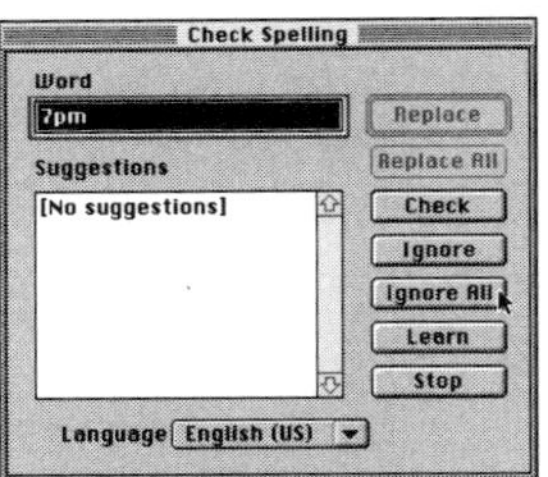

Figure 15.4 *The first unknown word is displayed in the Check Spelling dialog box. Click Ignore All to leave correctly spelled words alone.*

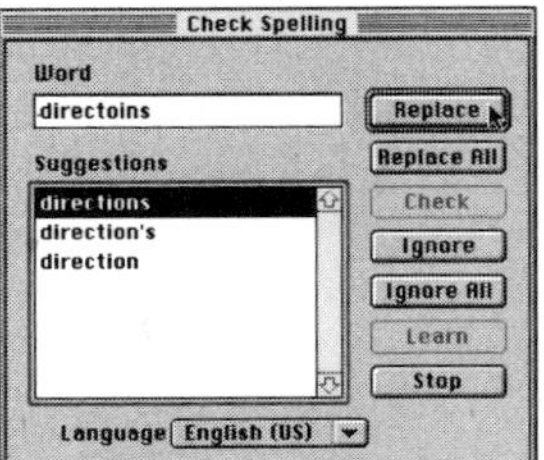

Figure 15.5 *If the spell checker finds a misspelled word, it attempts to offer correctly spelled replacements. Select the appropriate word in the list and choose Replace.*

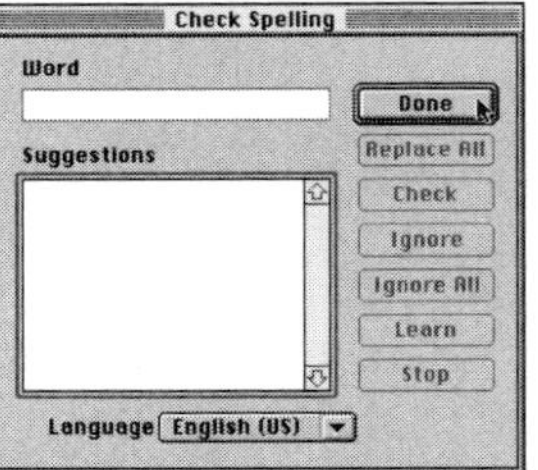

Figure 15.6 *When the spell checker can no longer find any questionable words, the Done button becomes available. Click it to close the dialog box.*

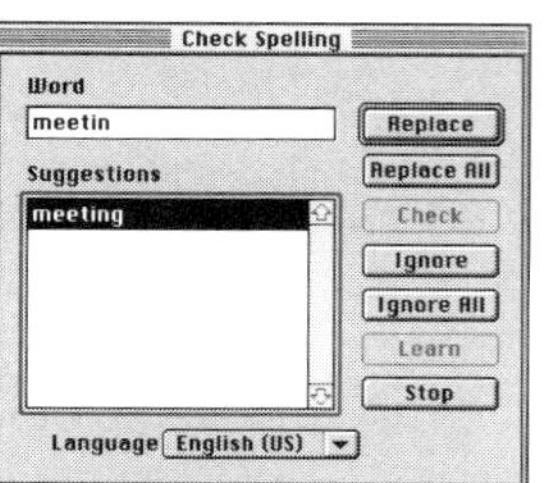

Figure 15.7 *The spell checker automatically suggests the words that most resemble the misspelled word.*

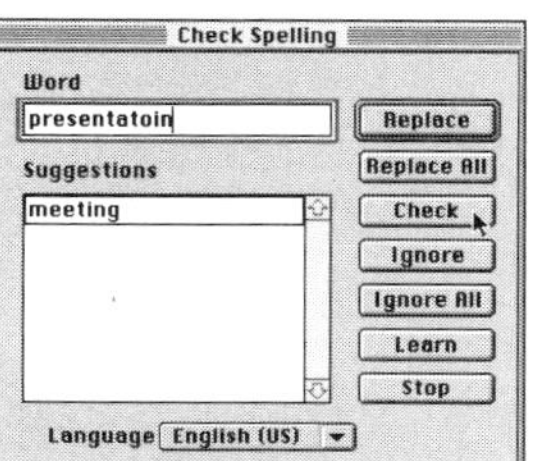

Figure 15.8 *You can type any word you want in the Word box. If you're not sure of its spelling, click the Check box.*

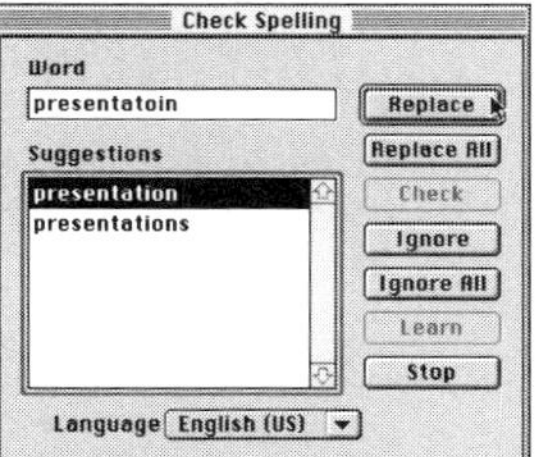

Figure 15.9 *The spell checker suggests the correct spelling for the manually entered word. Click Replace to use this word in your document.*

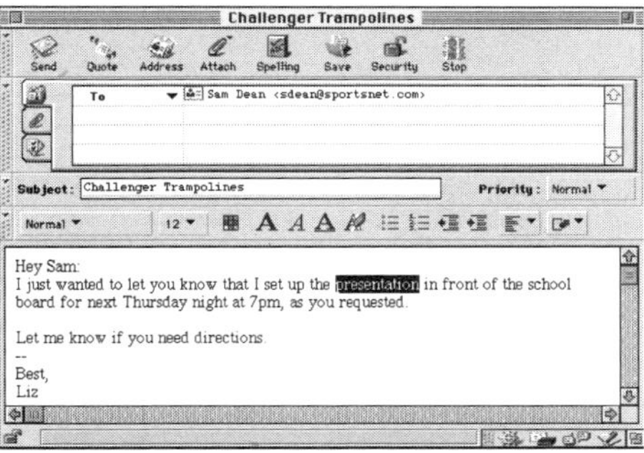

Figure 15.10 *The changes are reflected in the document. In this example, the misspelled "meetin" is replaced not with the correctly spelled "meeting" but rather with a new word—also correctly spelled—"presentation."*

Checking a single word

If you're doing a spell check and decide to use a completely different word (that is, one that is not available in the suggestions box), you can make sure it's spelled correctly before inserting it.

To check a single word:

1. While doing a spell check, the spell checker alerts you to a misspelled word **(Figure 15.7)**. Instead of accepting its suggestions, you decide to change the word completely. Type the new word in the Word box **(Figure 15.8)**.
2. Click Check. Communicator checks its dictionary for the word. If it is correct, the Suggestions box shows "correct spelling." If it is misspelled, the suggestions box contains possible correct spellings **(Figure 15.9)**.
3. Choose the correct spelling from the suggestions box, if necessary, and click Replace or Replace All. Communicator replaces the old word with the new one, now that you're sure it's spelled correctly **(Figure 15.10)**.

Adding words to the custom dictionary

Although Communicator's spell checker recognizes a fair amount of technical words, it doesn't know everything. In particular, it may be necessary to add personal or business names to your dictionary so that the spell checker doesn't ask you about them each time you check a page.

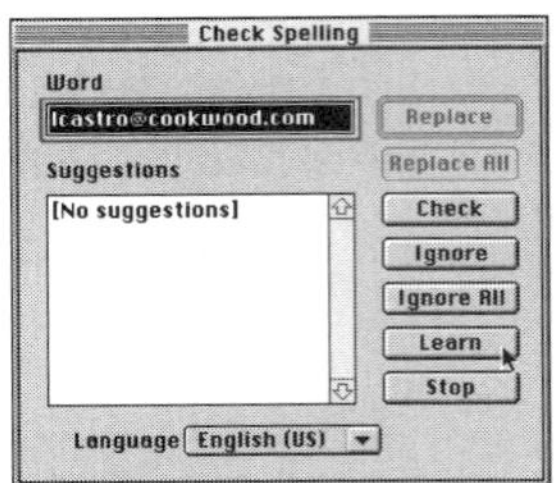

Figure 15.11 *Strangely enough, the spell checker does not recognize e-mail addresses. You'll have to add them to your custom dictionary by clicking the Learn button.*

To add words while you're doing a spell check:

When the spell checker pauses on an unknown word, click Learn in the Check Spelling dialog box **(Figure 15.11)**. The word is added to the custom dictionary and you won't be asked about it again.

✔ **Tip**

■ To edit or remove words from the dictionary, consult *Editing the custom dictionary* on page 197.

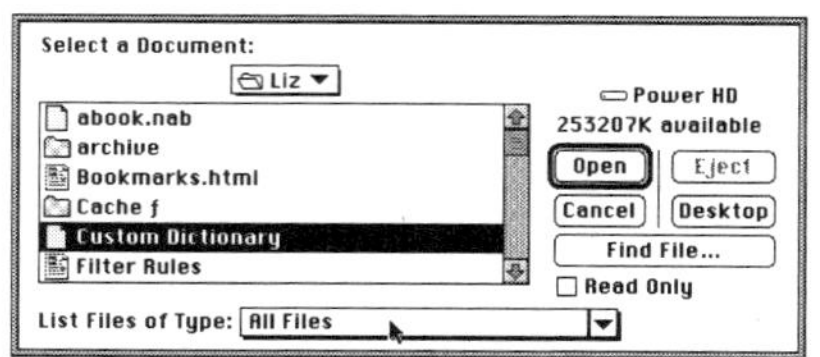

Figure 15.12 *After choosing File > Open in Microsoft Word, choose All Files in the List Files of Type pop-up menu at the bottom of the Open dialog box. Then find the Custom Dictionary file and click Open.*

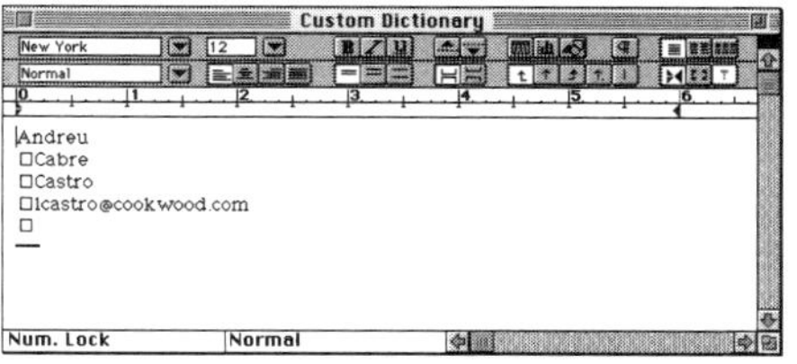

Figure 15.13 *The words that are currently in the custom dictionary are displayed one to a line in Word.*

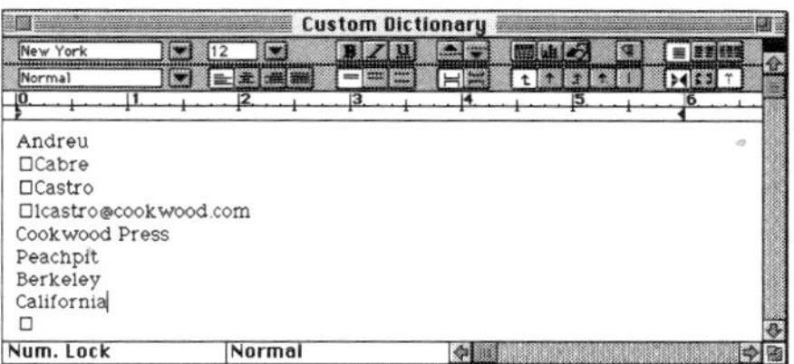

Figure 15.14 *Add, edit, or remove words from the dictionary. Don't worry about those strange little rectangles. Just ignore them.*

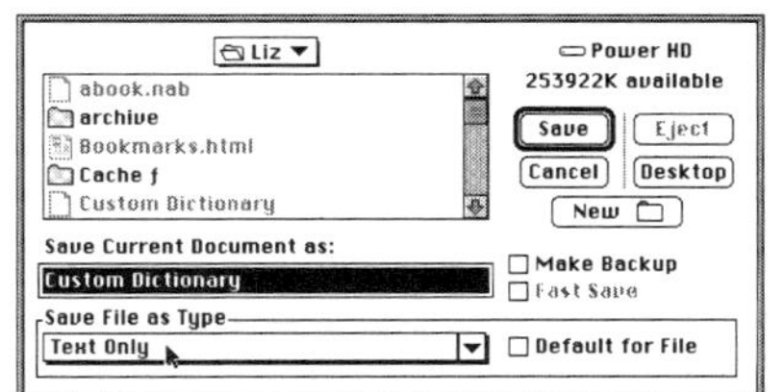

Figure 15.15 *In Word's Save dialog box, choose Text Only in the Save File as Type pop-up menu. Make sure you save the file with the same name and in the same folder as you found it.*

Editing the custom dictionary

Communicator ignores all the words in your Web pages that you have added to your custom dictionary. If you have added a misspelled word or one that you no longer use, you may wish to remove or replace it so that Communicator alerts you when it finds them in your page.

Unfortunately, there's no easy way to do this. I have, however, figured out a solution with Microsoft Word. It's a little bit crude, but it works.

To edit the custom dictionary:

1. Open Microsoft Word. Any version will do.
2. Choose File > Open. The Open dialog box appears.
3. Choose All Files in the List Files of Type pop-up menu at the bottom of the dialog box.
4. Find the Custom Dictionary file, in the System Folder, in the Preferences Folder, in the Netscape Users folder, in the particular user's folder. Click Open.
5. Add new words on additional lines, separating them with returns. Eliminate any words, as necessary.
6. Choose File > Save As.
7. In the Save dialog box, choose Text Only in the Save File as Type pop-up menu and save the Custom Dictionary in the same folder that you found it in.

✓ Tip

- You can use this technique to add a whole series of words at once.

Using Conference

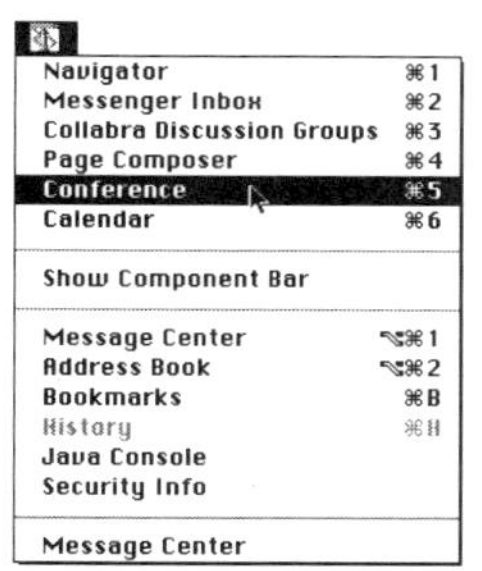

Figure 16.1 *Choose (Communicator) > Conference.*

Figure 16.2 *The Conference window appears.*

The Conference component of Communicator lets you connect to another person (just one, despite the sound of *conference*) in real time. Real time means that when you talk, the other party listens to you at that moment and when she responds, you hear her right away. Of course, this means that the person with whom you want to have a conversation has to be connected to the Internet (or your local intranet) and running Conference at the same time you are.

Conference lets you communicate with the person in several ways. You can talk to them using your microphone and speakers, write notes, exchange files, draw on the Whiteboard, or surf around the Web together.

Opening Conference

Although Conference is a separate program from Communicator, you can open it from within the latter program.

To open Conference from within Communicator:

Choose (Communicator) > Conference **(Figure 16.1)**. The Conference window appears **(Figure 16.2)**.

Getting ready to conference

Before you begin to conference with other folks across the Internet, you'll want to set up your preferences and fill out the information in your business card.

To get ready to conference:

1. From the Conference window, choose Edit > Preferences **(Figure 16.3)**. The Preferences dialog box appears **(Figure 16.4)**.
2. Click the Network tab, if necessary.
3. Choose your Network connection speed **(Figure 16.4)**.
4. Check the List My Name in Phone-book box if you want your name to be listed on a Web page each time you open Conference *(see page 202)*.
5. Click the Business Card tab and fill in the information about yourself as desired. This information appears to the other person when you make a connection **(Figure 16.5)**.
6. Click Open under the picture to load a picture (real or not) of yourself. An Open dialog box appears.
7. Choose the desired image file (in GIF, PICT, JPEG, or Adobe Photoshop format) from your hard disk and click Open **(Figure 16.6)**.
8. Click the Audio tab. The settings for your sound card and compression are displayed. Change them as needed.
9. Click OK to save the preferences. You're now ready to conference.

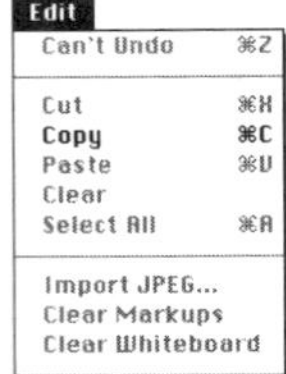

Figure 16.3 *Choose Edit > Preferences.*

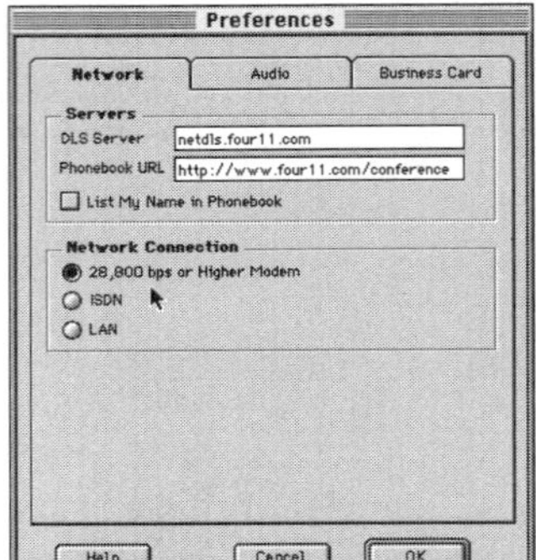

Figure 16.4 *Choose your network connection speed and server name in the Network tab of Conference's Preferences dialog box.*

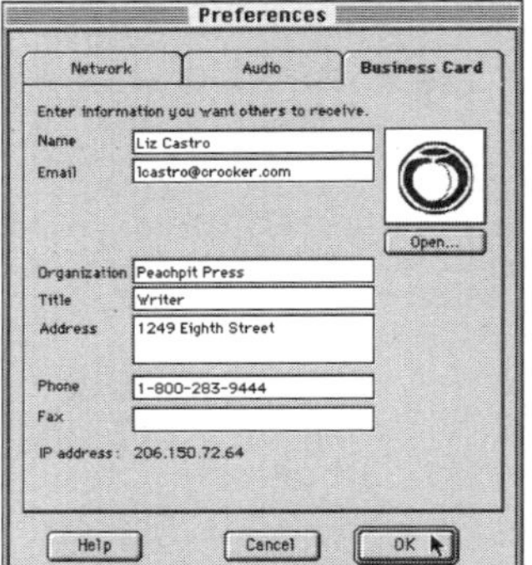

Figure 16.5 *Fill in the information that you want the other person to have about you. Click the Open button under the image to open an image file.*

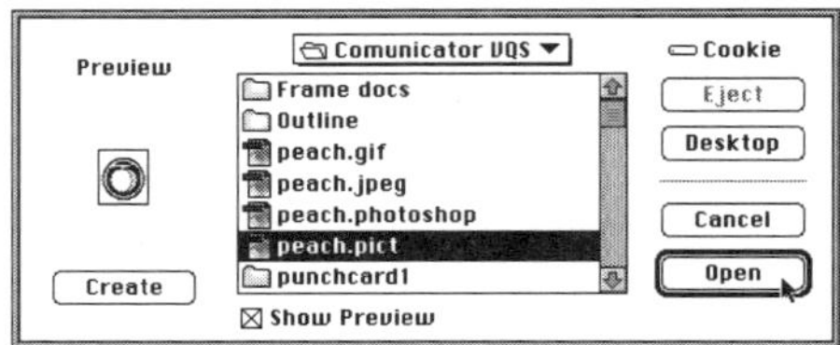

Figure 16.6 *After you click the Open button in the Business Card tab of the Preferences dialog box, choose any GIF, PICT, JPEG, or Adobe Photoshop file on your hard disk to choose the image that will identify you when you conference.*

Figure 16.7 *Type the e-mail address of the person you want to conference with and click Dial to connect. The person has to be connected and running Conference in order for the call to go through.*

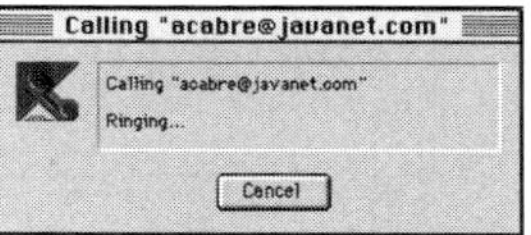

Figure 16.8 *A dialog box alerts you to the progress of your call.*

Figure 16.9 *Once you are connected, the image of your interlocutor appears.*

Figure 16.10 *Choose Tools > About "Name" to get information about the person you're conferencing with.*

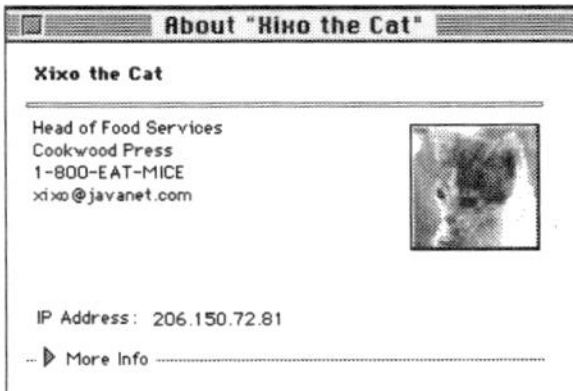

Figure 16.11 *The information the other person (or cat) entered into her business card (see page 200) is displayed in the About box.*

Making a call

Before you can conference with someone else on the Internet, you have to make a connection.

To make a call:

1. Choose (Communicator) > Conference. The Conference window appears.
2. Type the e-mail address of the person you want to conference with under Email address **(Figure 16.7)**.
3. Click Dial. A dialog box appears as the call goes through **(Figure 16.8)**. If the person is currently connected to the Internet and is running Conference, the connection is made. Her image will appear on your screen **(Figure 16.9)**.
4. If desired, choose Tools > About "Name" **(Figure 16.10)** to get information about the person you're conferencing with. The About window appears **(Figure 16.11)**.

✔ Tips

- Click the Web Phonebook button to see a list of people currently using Conference. This is rather like seeing a list of people in the world waiting by their telephones. You can call them, but what will you say?
- Click the Address Book button to access your Address Book and the e-mail addresses that you have stored there. For more information on saving names in the Address Book, see Chapter 13, *The Address Book*.

Answering calls

Once you open Conference, your name is automatically listed in the Web Phonebook described in the tip on the preceding page. People may begin to call. You can choose to answer all calls, not answer any calls, or have Conference ask you whether you want to answer or not. You can also remove your name from the Web Phonebook.

To screen your calls:

From the Conference window, choose Call > Always Prompt to have Conference ask you each time if you want to connect to the person who's calling you **(Figure 16.12)**. Choose Call > Auto Answer to answer all calls. Choose Call > Do Not Disturb to refuse all calls.

To remove your name from the Web Phonebook:

1. From the Conference window, choose Call > Preferences.
2. Remove the checkmark from the List My Name in Phonebook box **(Figure 16.13)**.
3. Click OK to close the Preferences dialog box.

To answer a call:

If someone calls you and you have chosen Always Prompt (see above), a dialog box will appear in which you can choose to accept or refuse an incoming call **(Figure 16.14)**. To accept the call, click Answer. Once you're connected, you can use the Whiteboard, file exchange, and other Conference components as usual.

Figure 16.12 *Choose Call > Always Prompt to have Conference ask you each time if you want to connect to whoever is calling you.*

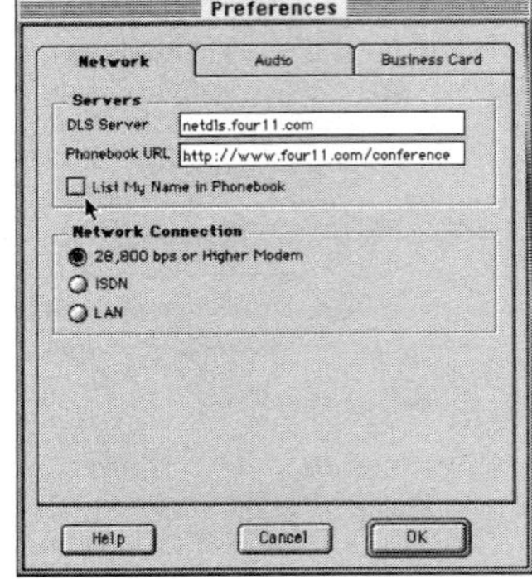

Figure 16.13 *Check the List My Name in Phonebook option to remove your name from the Web Phonebook.*

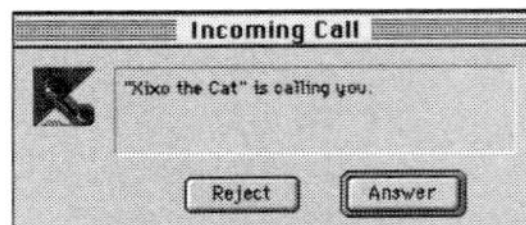

Figure 16.14 *An alert appears when someone calls you. Click Answer to accept the call.*

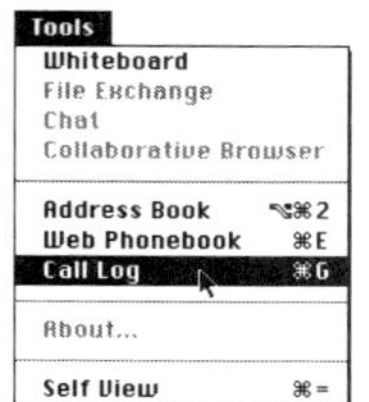

Figure 16.15 *Choose Tools > Call Log to access the Call Log dialog box with which you can keep track of all your call.s*

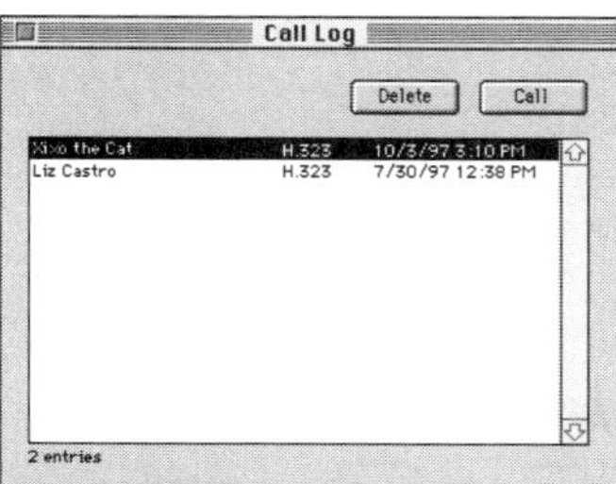

Figure 16.16 *The Call Log dialog box displays all the calls you've made. You can delete call records by selecting them and clicking the Delete button. Or call someone again by selecting their name and clicking the Call button.*

Keeping track of calls

Conference keeps a list of all the calls that you make. You can consult the list at any time to see who you've called and how long you were connected.

To keep track of calls:

Choose Tools > Call Log **(Figure 16.15)**. The Call Log dialog box lists all the calls you've made **(Figure 16.16)**.

To erase call records:

1. Select the call record that you wish to erase.
2. Press the Delete button. The record disappears.

Using speed dial

You can create up to six shortcuts which let you connect to your most frequent conference partners with a single click. The shortcuts can be in the form of speed dial buttons (found in the center area of the Conference window) or menu options (in the SpeedDial menu).

To create or edit speed dial buttons:

1. Choose one of the Speed Dial options from the SpeedDial menu and then Edit in the submenu **(Figure 16.17)**. The Edit Speed Dial dialog box appears **(Figure 16.18)**
2. Type in the name that you want to appear in the SpeedDial menu and on the button in the Conference window.
3. Type in the e-mail address and choose a server, if necessary.
4. Click OK. Both the menu option and the button reflect the new name **(Figure 16.19)**.

To use speed dial:

Either choose the desired person in the SpeedDial menu and then Call in the submenu or click the desired Speed Dial button in the Conference window.

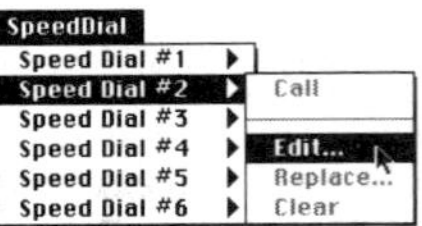

Figure 16.17 *Choose SpeedDial > Speed Dial # > Edit.*

Figure 16.18 *Type the name, e-mail address, and the DLS server name of the person you want to add to your Speed Dial menu.*

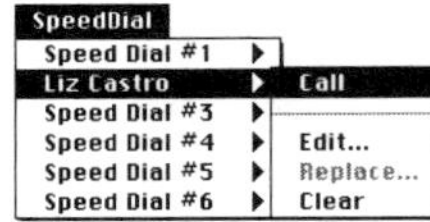

Figure 16.19 *Choose Speed Dial > (name) > Call.*

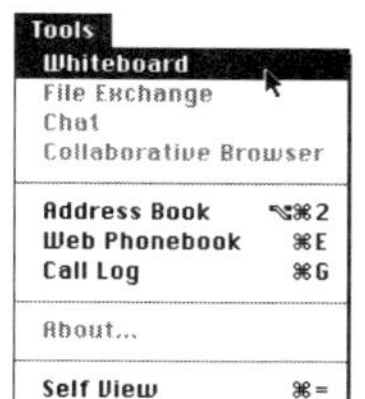

Figure 16.20 *Choose Tools > Whiteboard.*

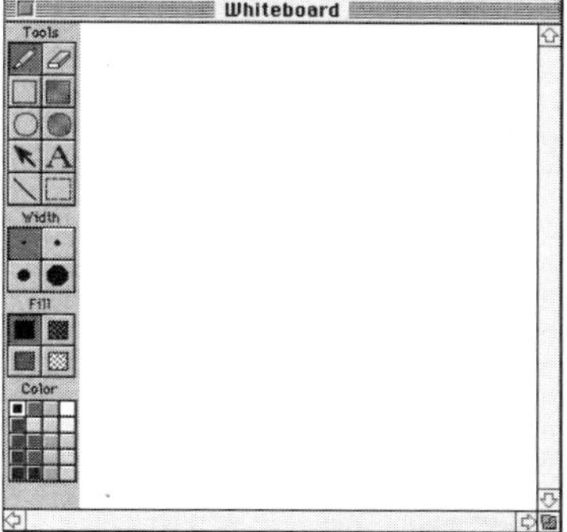

Figure 16.21 *The Whiteboard is like a (primitive) drawing pad shared between you and the other party. It allows you to visually demonstrate things to the other person.*

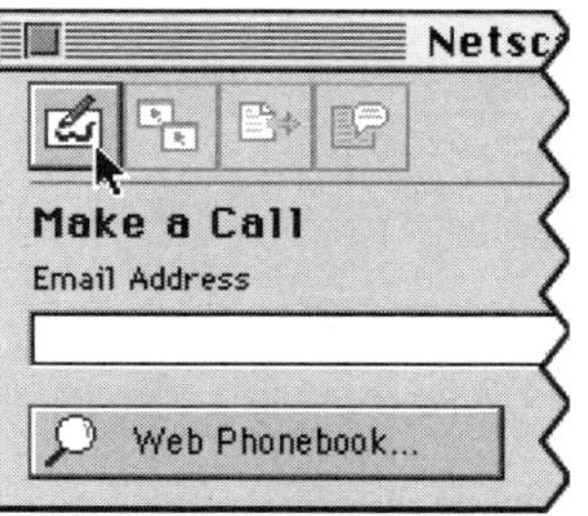

Figure 16.22 *You can also click the Whiteboard button on the toolbar in the Conference window to open the Whiteboard.*

Opening the Whiteboard

Conference's Whiteboard is like a drawing pad that you share with the other person. You can both draw on it and you can both see what the other is drawing.

To open the Whiteboard:

From Conference, choose Tools > Whiteboard **(Figure 16.20)**. The Whiteboard appears **(Figure 16.21)**.

✔ Tips

- You can also open the Whiteboard by clicking the leftmost button on the toolbar in the Conference window **(Figure 16.22)**.
- If the other party decides to open the Whiteboard first, your Whiteboard will open automatically. If you don't want it to open automatically, choose Whiteboard > Pop Up On Receive to remove the checkmark from that option.
- Print the contents of the Whiteboard by choosing Whiteboard > Print. Choose Whiteboard > Page Setup to adjust the printout.
- You can also save the contents of the Whiteboard for future viewing by choosing Whiteboard > Save as PICT.
- Copy the contents of the Whiteboard to the Clipboard by choosing Edit > Copy.
- Make the Whiteboard canvas bigger or smaller by choosing Whiteboard > Canvas Size and entering new dimensions in the dialog box that appears.
- Conference's Whiteboard has no undo. Once you've added or erased something, there's no going back.

Opening images in the Whiteboard

One of the Whiteboard's most useful features is sharing existing images. In fact, you can open any Bitmap, GIF, TIFF, or JPEG image in the Whiteboard. The person you're conferencing with will see the images right away.

To open an image in the Whiteboard:

1. With the Whiteboard open, choose Edit > Import JPEG. The Open dialog box appears.
2. Locate the desired image on your hard disk and click Open **(Figure 16.24)**. The image appears in the Whiteboard with a selection marquee around it **(Figure 16.25)**.
3. Click in the desired location in your Whiteboard to place the image **(Figure 16.26)**. The other party sees it immediately.

✔ **Tip**

- You can also fill the Whiteboard with screen shots. For more information, consult *Creating screen shots in the Whiteboard* on page 207.

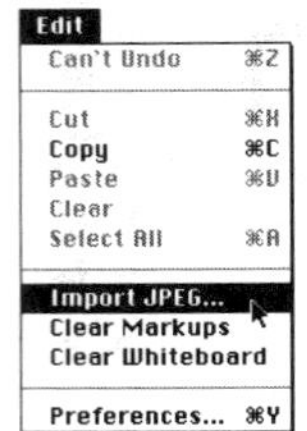

Figure 16.23 *Choose Edit > Import JPEG.*

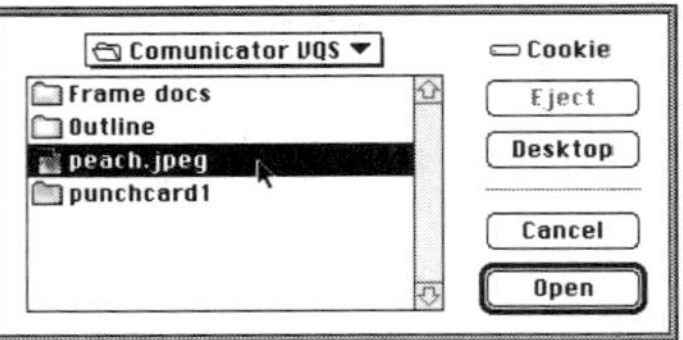

Figure 16.24 *Locate the image file that you want to share with the other party.*

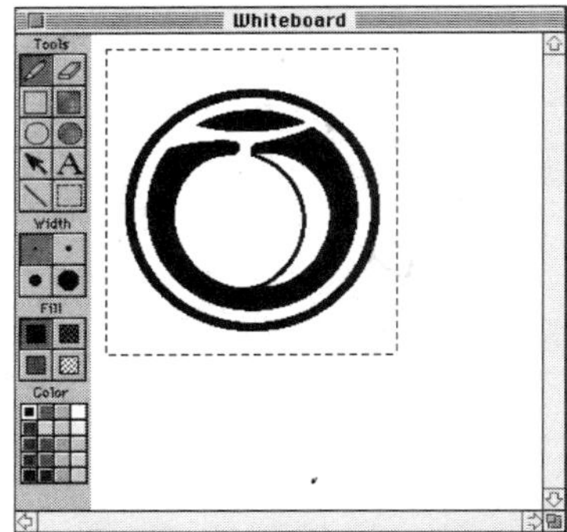

Figure 16.25 *The image appears with a selection rectangle around it in the upper-left corner of the Whiteboard.*

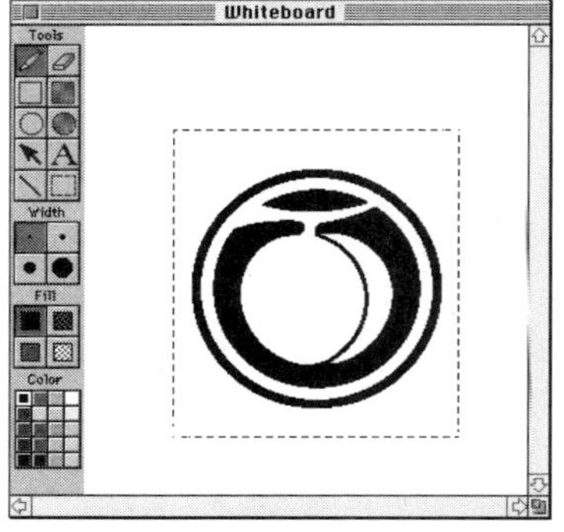

Figure 16.26 *You can move the image to any part of the Whiteboard.*

Figure 16.27 *Choose Whiteboard > Capture Region.*

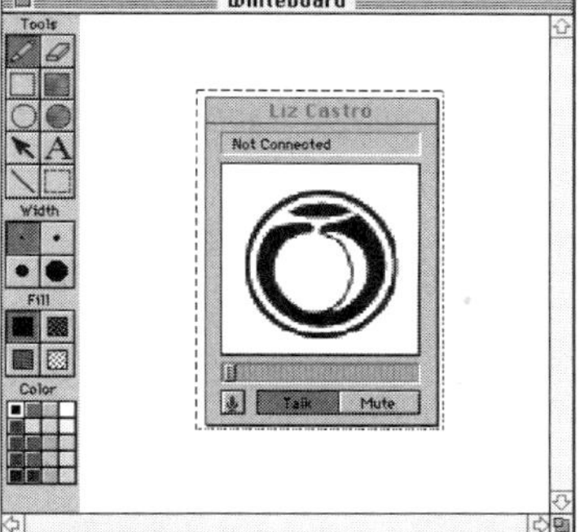

Figure 16.28 *The area that you select with the cursor is displayed in the Whiteboard. Unfortunately, since Conference stays active, mostly what you can capture is Conference itself.*

Creating screen shots in the Whiteboard

Sometimes it's useful to be able to precisely describe the contents of your screen to the person you're conferencing with. You can take a picture, or *screen shot*, of the entire screen or any portion of the screen and then share the picture through the Whiteboard.

To create a screen shot in the Whiteboard:

1. Choose Whiteboard > Capture Region or Whiteboard > Capture Desktop **(Figure 16.27)**.
2. Select the desired region that you wish to capture. (If you chose Desktop, skip to step 3.)
3. The screen capture floats with the pointer in the Whiteboard. Click in the place where you wish to place the image **(Figure 16.28)**. The person you're conferencing with sees it immediately.

✓ Tip

- As you might imagine, sharing screen captures with the person you're conferencing with is ideal for technical support situations: "*This* is the error message I get!" or "Press *this* button to solve your problem."

Drawing in the Whiteboard

You can use the Whiteboard's drawing tools to create freehand illustrations to share with the other person or to add to images that you've opened or copied in the Whiteboard.

To draw in the Whiteboard:

1. Select the desired tool from the Tools palette **(Figure 16.29)**.
2. Choose the width for lines and outlines, if necessary.
3. Choose the level of opaqueness in the Fill area.
4. Choose a color.
5. And draw!

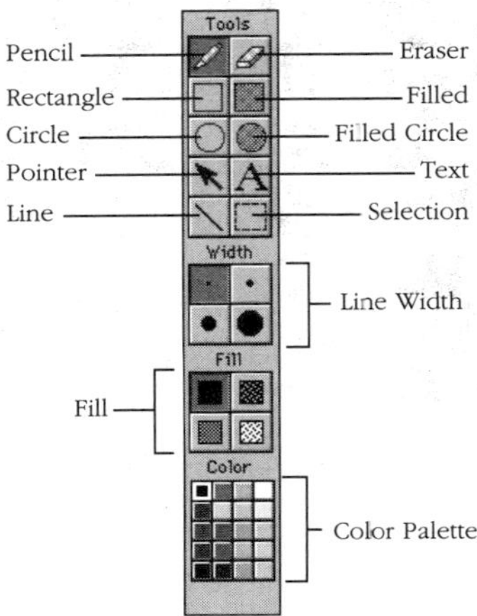

Figure 16.29 *This is the Tools palette. Select a tool by clicking it.*

✔ **Tips**

- Choose Whiteboard > Fill Solid to create filled circles and squares with opaque backgrounds. Choose Whiteboard > Fill Clear to make the backgrounds transparent. For some reason, these options also affect the color itself.
- To change the thickness of *text*, choose Whiteboard > Style, and choose Bold.
- Hold down Shift while using the Rectangle and Circle tools to restrain them to squares and circles, respectively.

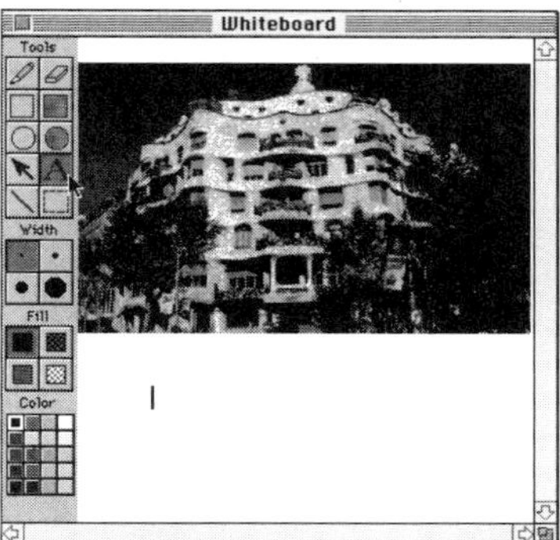

Figure 16.30 *Choose the Text tool (A) in the Tools palette.*

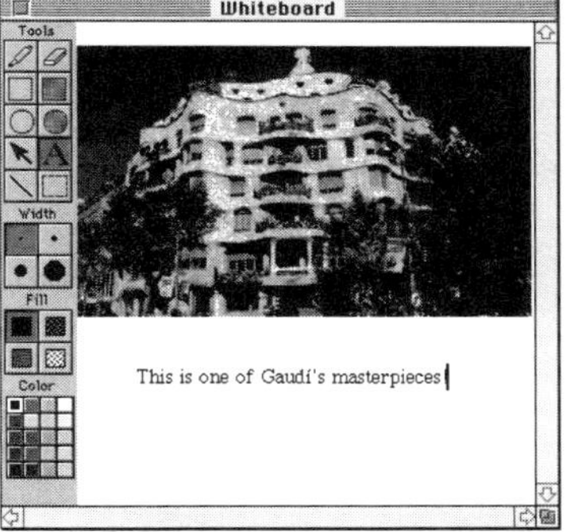

Figure 16.31 *The text is displayed in the font, size, style, and color attributes you have chosen.*

Creating text in the Whiteboard

Although the Chat area *(see page 212)* is more efficient for writing large quantities of text back and forth, you can add text to the Whiteboard to describe part of your image.

To create text in the Whiteboard:

1. Select the Text tool in the Tools palette **(Figure 16.30)**.
2. Click in the Whiteboard where you want to insert the text.
3. If desired, choose a font, size, and style (bold or italic) from the Whiteboard menu.
4. Make sure the Fill is set to the darkest level (the top left box).
5. Choose a color for the text.
6. Type the text **(Figure 16.31)**.
7. Press Enter to send the text to the other person.

✔ Tip

- Although you can't select text, you can change the font, size, and style after you've typed it. Simply choose the new option from the toolbar. Once you've sent the text, clicked somewhere else with the Text tool, or chosen a different tool, you can no longer change it.

Pointing out things in the Whiteboard

When you're discussing a complicated image or screen shot with someone long distance, having a pointer to mark areas of interest can come in handy. You can temporarily add a pointer to any part of your image and then move it to another part, as necessary.

To point out things in the Whiteboard:

1. Select the Pointer tool in the Tools palette.
2. Choose a color for the pointer, if desired.
3. Click in the Whiteboard where you want to point something out. The pointer is temporarily imprinted on the Whiteboard where both you and the other party can see it **(Figure 16.32)**.
4. Click in another area of the Whiteboard that you wish to highlight. The pointer moves to the new location **(Figure 16.33)**.

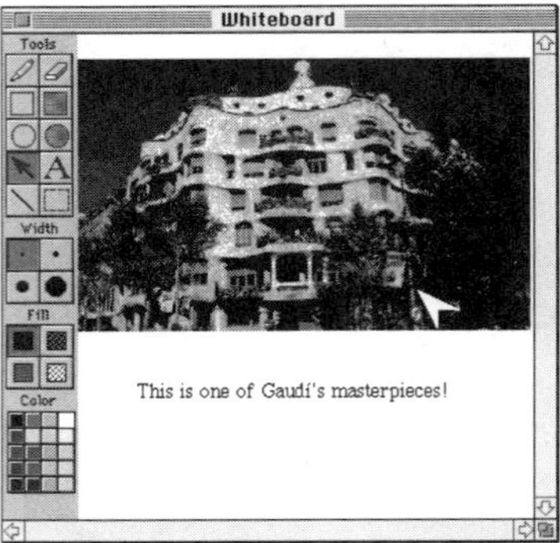

Figure 16.32 *The pointer is imprinted in the Whiteboard area.*

Figure 16.33 *Just by clicking again, you can move the pointer to another position.*

✔ Tips

- You can't change the size of the pointer.
- When choosing a color, go for the one that best contrasts with the image on your Whiteboard so that the pointer really stands out.
- If the pointer just isn't big or flashy enough, draw your own pointer with the drawing tools *(see page 208)*. You start to see why those sportscasters love to do this on television **(Figure 16.34)**.

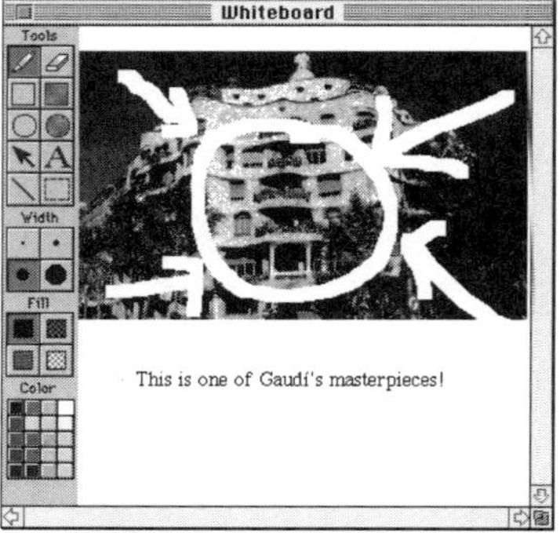

Figure 16.34 *You can draw handmade pointers to call attention to a part of your image (or to pretend you're one of those sports analysts on TV).*

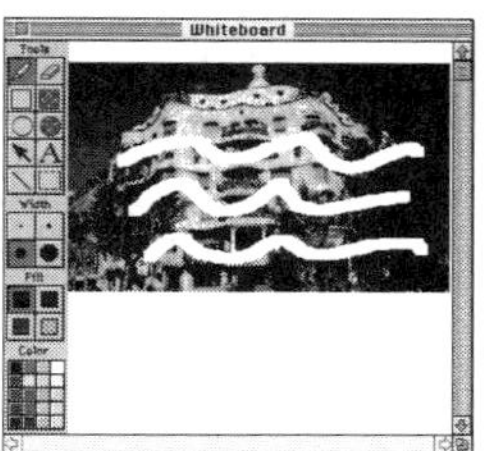

Figure 16.35
We've drawn on this image to call attention to its waviness.

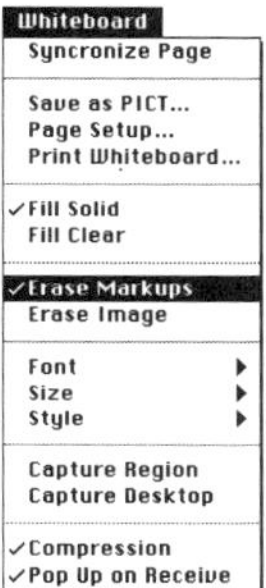

Figure 16.36 *Choose Whiteboard > Erase Markups to have the eraser affect only the elements on the Whiteboard that you have drawn yourself.*

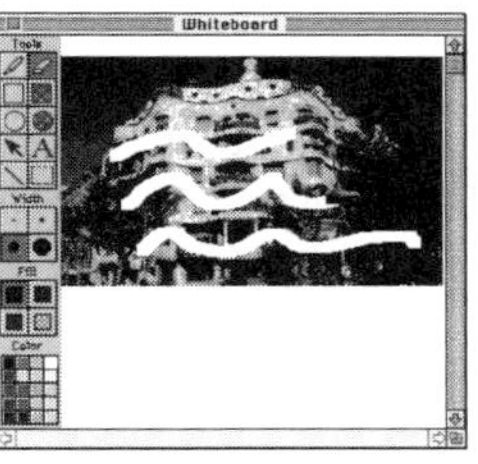

Figure 16.37
Notice that the wavy lines (the markups*) are erased while the image is left intact.*

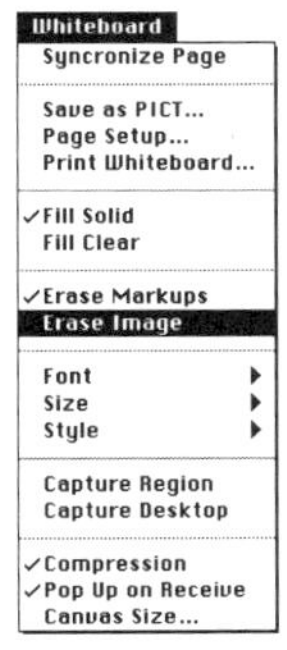

Figure 16.38 *Choose Whiteboard > Erase Image when you want the eraser to erase both the markups and the image.*

Figure 16.39
Choose Whiteboard > Erase Markups to have the eraser affect only the elements on the Whiteboard that you have drawn yourself.

Erasing the Whiteboard

When you erase the Whiteboard, copied and imported images are treated differently than anything you draw with the drawing tools. You can set the eraser to affect everything, or to affect only the items that you've drawn in manually, which Conference calls *markups.*

To erase the whole Whiteboard:

Choose Edit > Clear Whiteboard. Everything on the Whiteboard disappears.

To erase all of the drawn items:

Choose Edit > Clear Markups. Everything except imported images disappears.

To erase selectively:

1. Select the eraser in the Tools palette.
2. Choose Whiteboard > Erase Markups **(Figure 16.36)** to make the eraser only affect the items that you've drawn with the drawing tools **(Fig. 16.37)**.

   Choose Whiteboard > Erase Image **(Figure 16.38)** to make the eraser affect everything **(Figure 16.39)**.
3. Drag the eraser in the Whiteboard where you want to erase.

✔ Tips

- Conference's Whiteboard has no undo. If you erase something you wish you hadn't, you're stuck.
- The Width option on the Tools palette affects the size of the eraser.

Using Chat

Conference's Chat module is ideal for communicating in real time when you don't have sound capabilities, or you don't want to use them. Instead, you can write messages back and forth and get immediate feedback.

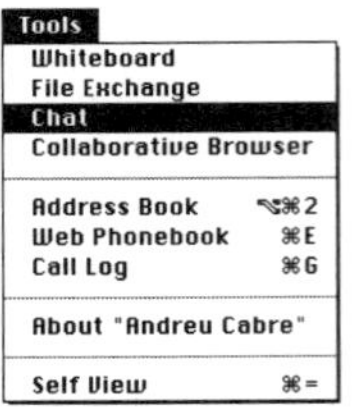

Figure 16.40 *Choose Tools > Chat.*

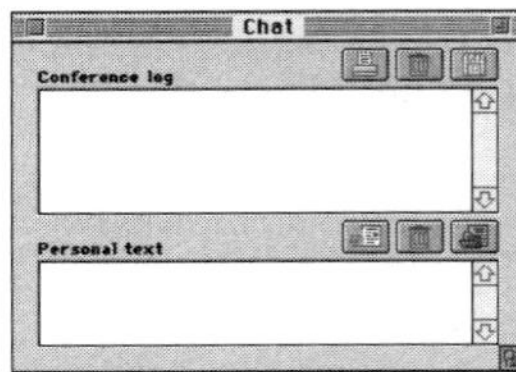

Figure 16.41 *This is the Chat window, with which you can "talk" to others in real time.*

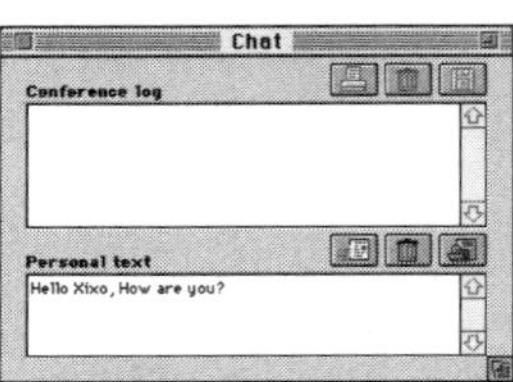

Figure 16.42 *Type the text you wish to send in the lower half of the Chat window.*

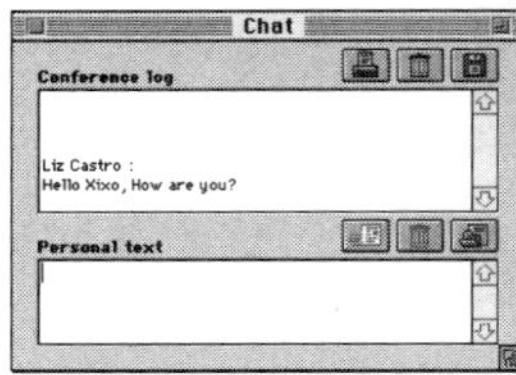

Figure 16.43 *After you send the text, it appears in the upper half of the window preceded by your name.*

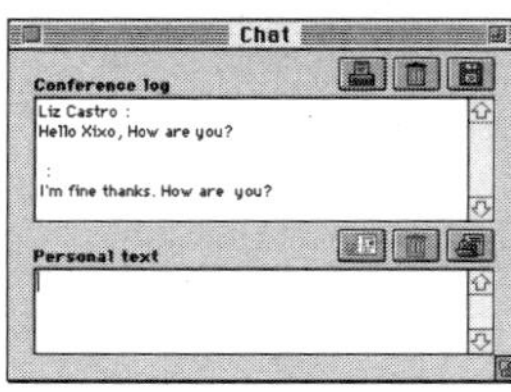

Figure 16.44 *The text that the other person responds with appears in the upper half of the window.*

To use Chat:

1. In the Conference window, choose Tools > Chat **(Figure 16.40)**. The Conference Chat window appears **(Figure 16.41)**.
2. Type the text that you want to send to the other party in the lower half of the Chat window **(Figure 16.42)**.
3. Edit the text, if necessary.
4. The text you've sent appears in the upper half of the window, preceded by your name **(Figure 16.43)**.
5. If the person responds, his message appears in the upper half of the window **(Figure 16.44)**.

✔ Tips

- The text being sent and received is stored in the Log file. You can save the file by clicking the disk icon, print it by clicking the printer icon, or copy and paste to and from it.
- The Chat window opens automatically if the person you're conferencing with begins to use it. Choose Options > Pop Up On Receive to control when the Chat window appears.

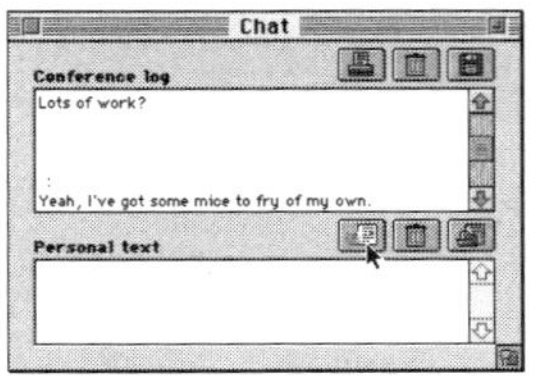

Figure 16.45 *Click the Include File icon to choose a file to include.*

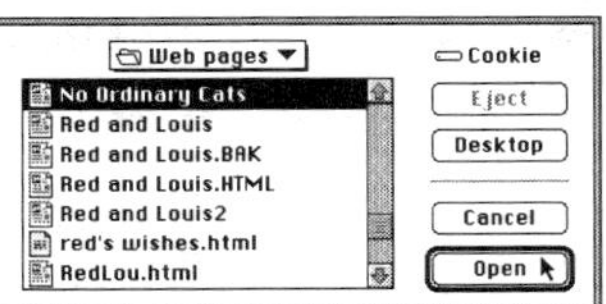

Figure 16.46 *Choose the text file you want to send from your hard disk.*

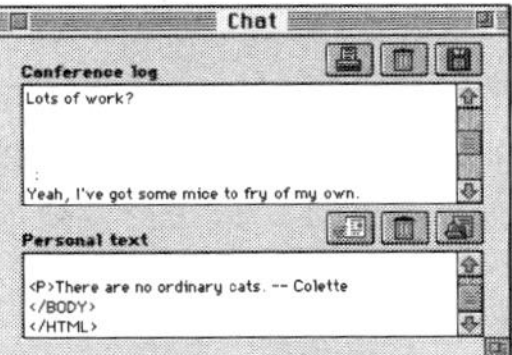

Figure 16.47 *The text of the file is displayed in the lower half of the Chat window.*

Including files in the Chat window

You can include an existing text file from any other program in your Chat session.

To include files in the Chat window:

1. Click the Include File button **(Figure 16.45)**. A standard Open dialog box appears.
2. Choose the text file that you want to send from your hard disk **(Figure 16.46)**.
3. Click Open. The text file is loaded into the bottom half of the Chat window **(Figure 16.47)**.
4. Press Ctrl+Enter to send the text file.

✔ **Tip**

■ Although Web pages are text files and can be sent through the Chat window, this doesn't mean that the other person will see the Web page's formatting. What they'll see are the *tags* that generate the Web page. For more information on looking at Web pages together, consult *Surfing in tandem* on page 216.

Sending files

You can use Conference's File Exchange module for sending and receiving text, images, or even programs without fussing with FTP or servers.

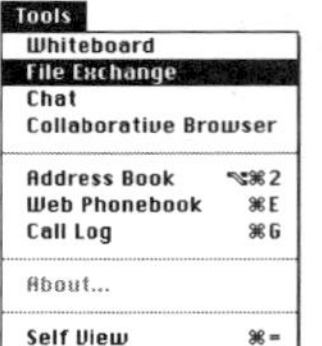

Figure 16.48 *Choose Tools > File Exchange.*

To send files:

1. Choose Tools > File Exchange **(Figure 16.48)**. The File Exchange window appears.
2. Click the first icon from the left **(Figure 16.49)**.
3. In the Open dialog box that appears, choose the file you wish to send **(Figure 16.50)**.
4. Click Open. The file is listed in the top half of the File Exchange window **(Figure 16.51)**.
5. Repeat steps 3 and 4 for each file you wish to send.
6. Click the Send button to send the files to the person you're conferencing with. The files are transferred. The progress bar informs you of how much of the file has been sent **(Figure 16.52)**

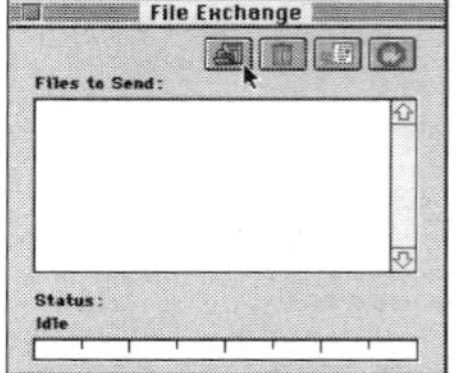

Figure 16.49 *Click the first icon on the left to select a file to send over.*

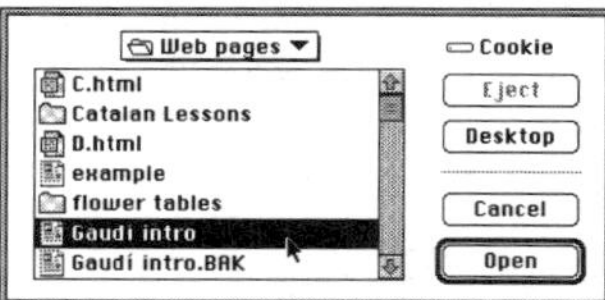

Figure 16.50 *Choose the file that you wish to send.*

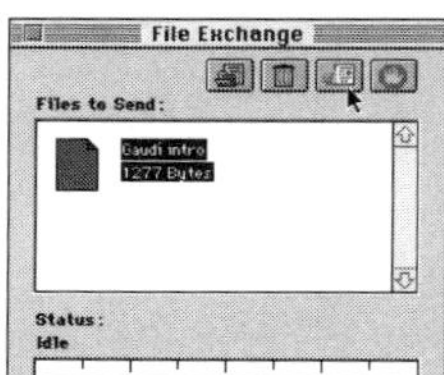

Figure 16.51 *The file you have chosen appears in the File Exchange window, together with a little icon of a file. Click the Send button (third from left) to begin the transfer.*

Figure 16.52 *The progress bar tells you how much of the file has been sent so far.*

✓ Tips

- You can also press Ctrl+Enter to begin the transfer of the files in the send list.
- Press the Stop button to cancel the file transfer without removing the file from the list.
- Select a file and then click the garbage can icon to remove it from the send list.

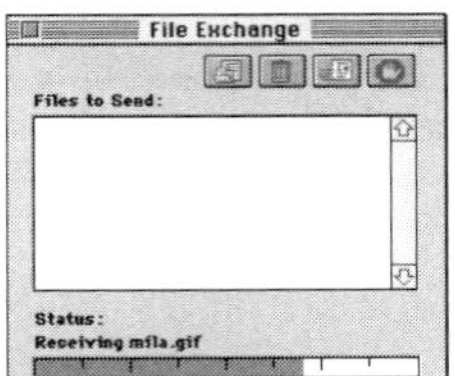

Figure 16.53 *Incoming files appear in the File Exchange window, with the progress bar indicating how much of the file is done.*

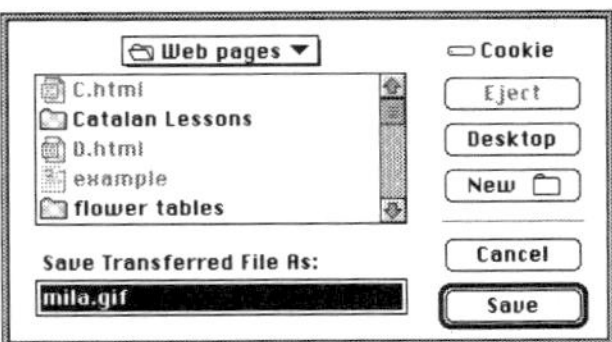

Figure 16.54 *Enter a name for the file, choose a destination, and click Save to save the file just received.*

Receiving files

Receiving files is somewhat simpler than sending them. The sender should follow the steps listed on page 214.

To receive files:

1. When the sender sends you a file, it will automatically appear in the bottom half of your File Exchange window **(Figure 16.53)**. A Save dialog box automatically appears.

2. Choose a filename, and click Save **(Figure 16.54)**. The file is downloaded to your hard disk.

✔ Tip

- The File Exchange window will automatically appear when the person you're conferencing with sends you a file. If you don't want the window to open, choose Options > Pop Up On Receive to remove the checkmark from the option.

Surfing in tandem

Conference also lets you surf the Web with another person. Both of you will see the same pages, but only one can click the links. Or you can take turns.

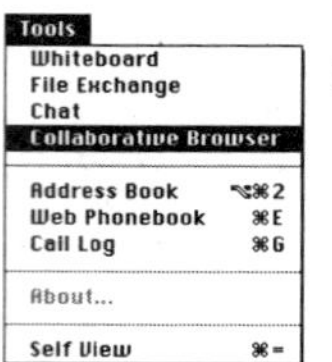

Figure 16.55 *Choose Tools > Collaborative Browser.*

To surf in tandem:

1. From the Conference window, choose Tools > Collaborative Browser **(Figure 16.55)**. The Collaborative Browser window appears.

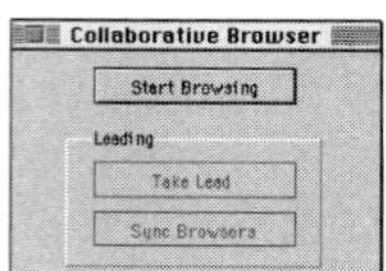

Figure 16.56 *Click Start Browsing.*

2. Click Start Browsing **(Figure 16.56)**. An alert appears in the other party's window, asking if they would like to surf with you **(Figure 16.57)**. If they accept, Navigator is automatically launched on both your system and the other party's system, if it was not already open. Whoever initiated the browsing session is the current "leader" and can travel around the World Wide Web as described in Chapter 3, *Surfing the Web.*

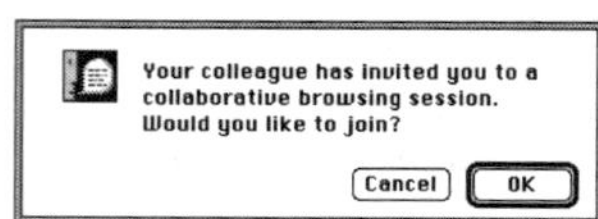

Figure 16.57 *An invitation appears on the receiving party's screen. If they accept, Navigator is launched on both computers and you can begin to surf together.*

Part IV: Creating Web Pages

One-to-Many Communication

Now comes your chance to communicate your ideas to others on the Internet. With your Web page, you can reach millions of people. It is "one-to-many" communication. Why would you want to publish your own Web page? Simply, to communicate with the world. The World Wide Web is the Gutenberg press of our time. Practically anyone can publish any kind of information, including graphics, sound, and even video, on the Web, opening the doors to each and every one of the millions of Internet users in every corner of the globe. Some are businesses with services to sell, others are individuals with stories to share. You decide how your page will be.

Communicator, and specifically the Composer component, makes creating Web pages relatively painless. You don't need to learn HTML, the language that pages are written in. Instead, you can format your page with buttons and pop-up menus similar to those found in any desktop publishing software. Import or drag images right onto your page. Create complex tables. Add sound and video.

One of the nicest things about Composer is that it shows you the page as you're creating it—which is somewhat harder to do if you're writing HTML by hand—so you can have a clear idea of how the page is coming out and if needs any adjustments.

Once you've finished tweaking your final page, Composer helps you publish the page, along with any images or other auxiliary files, right to your server. You'll be up on the Web in no time.

17 The Composer Window

The Composer window is where you create your own Web pages. The Composer window has two unique toolbars and some special menu commands.

The Composer window's toolbars

The Composer window has two toolbars: Composition and Formatting. The buttons on the toolbars are simply shortcuts to menu commands.

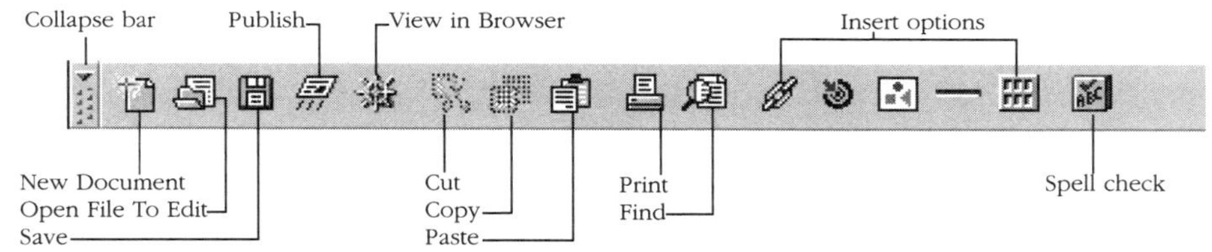

Figure 17.1 *The Composition toolbar contains many of the commands available in the File, Edit, and Insert menus, as well as the Spelling Checker.*

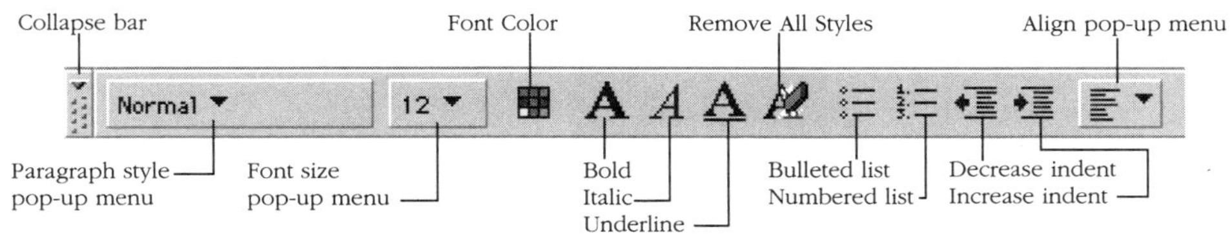

Figure 17.2 *The Formatting toolbar contains both character and paragraph formatting commands.*

Repositioning the toolbars

The Composer window's toolbars are very flexible. You can reorder them, collapse them, or hide them completely.

To reorder the toolbars:

Drag one toolbar below or above the other **(Figure 17.4)**.

To collapse a toolbar:

Click to the left of the toolbar to hide its buttons **(Figure 17.5)**.

To hide or show the toolbars:

Choose View > Show/Hide Composition Toolbar or View > Show/Hide Formatting Toolbar **(Figure 17.6)**. The toolbar is revealed or hidden **(Figure 17.7)**.

✔ **Tip**

- The configuration of one Composer window's toolbars does not affect the toolbars in other Composer windows that are already open. *New* Composer windows, however, will have the same layout as the current one.

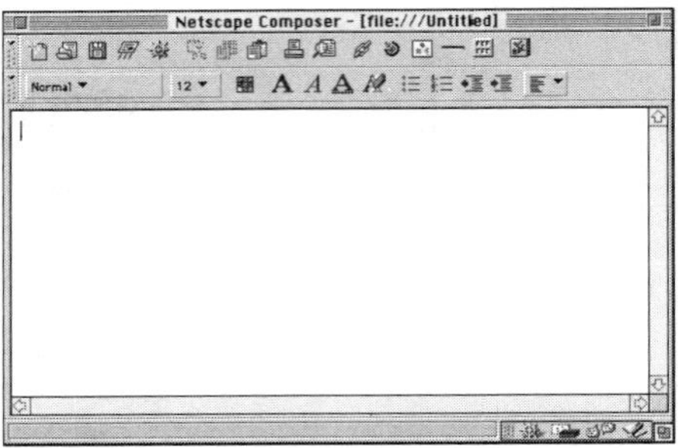

Figure 17.3 *By default, Composer displays both the Composition and Formatting toolbars.*

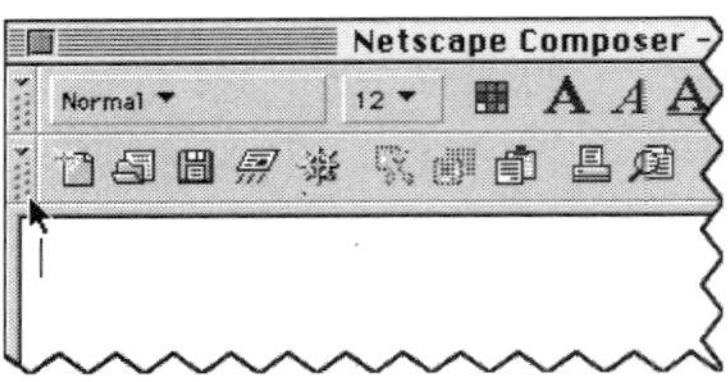

Figure 17.4 *You can change the position of the toolbars by dragging them.*

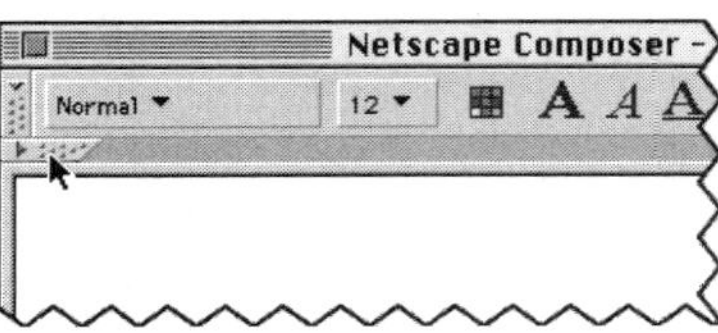

Figure 17.5 *Collapse a toolbar in order to have more room for editing by clicking in the bar at its extreme left.*

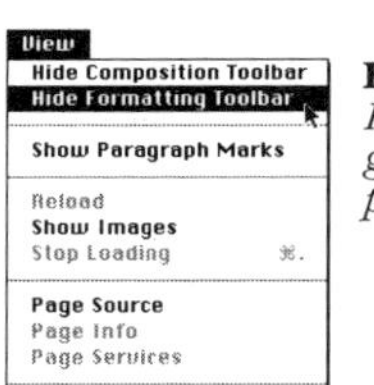

Figure 17.6 *Choose View > Hide Formatting Toolbar to gain more space in the Composer window.*

Figure 17.7 *The Formatting toolbar is hidden.*

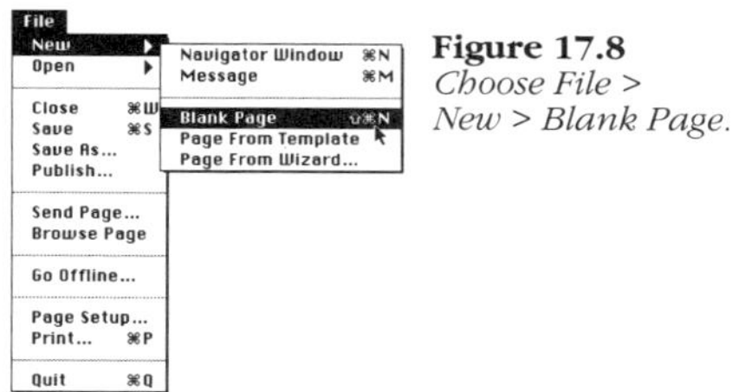

Figure 17.8 *Choose File > New > Blank Page.*

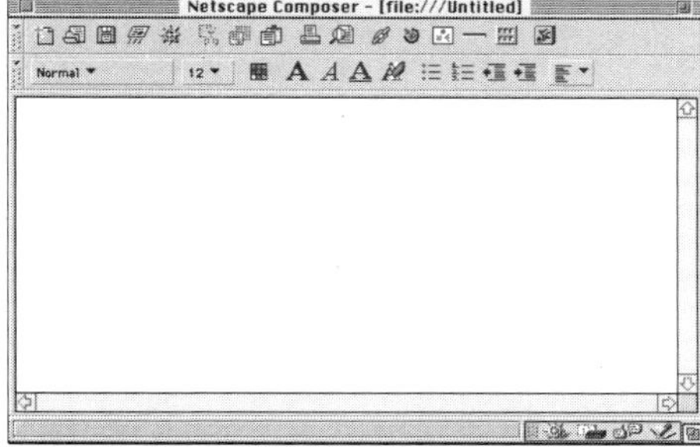

Figure 17.9 *An empty Composer window.*

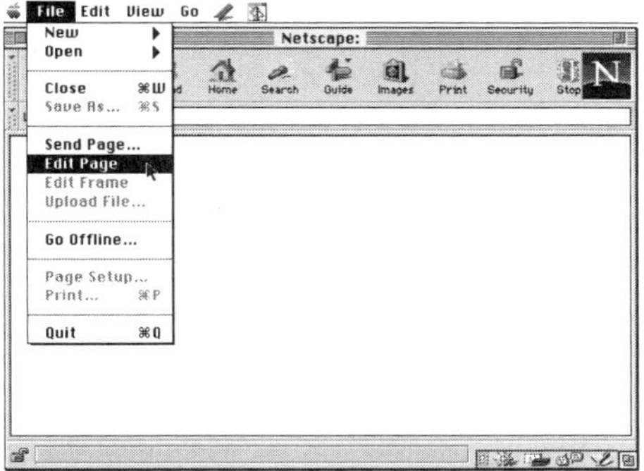

Figure 17.10 *If you've started up with a blank page in the Navigator window, you can choose File > Edit Page to convert the window into a blank page for composing.*

Creating a page from scratch

If you wish to start a Web page completely from scratch, you should open a blank Composer window. Then use the instructions in this and subsequent chapters to create your page.

To create a page from scratch:

1. Choose File > New > Blank Page **(Figure 17.8)**. An empty Composer window appears **(Figure 17.9)**.
2. Create the components of the page as described in the rest of this section of the book.

✔ Tips

- You can also open a blank page by clicking the New button on the Composition toolbar.
- Or, with a blank page showing in the Navigator window (perhaps that's your startup page?), choose File > Edit Page to open the page in Composer **(Figure 17.10)**.
- Choose File > Close or click the Close box to close the Composer window. You'll be prompted to save changes, if necessary.

Creating a new page from a template

If you have a large site and you want all of the pages to share a common format, you can create a master page, or template, to use as a base for all your Web pages.

To create a new page from a template:

1. Create the template page using the instructions in this chapter.
2. Choose File > New > Page From Template **(Figure 17.11)**. The Navigator window opens to the template page you've selected **(Figure 17.12)**.
3. Navigate to the page you wish to use as a template, if it is not already showing. If you are using Netscape's templates, this means choosing a template from the list on the main page. That page is then displayed in the Navigator window **(Figure 17.13)**.
4. Choose File > Edit Page **(Fig. 17.14)**. A copy of the template page is loaded into the Composer window **(Figure 17.15)**. The original template page is not affected.
5. Modify the template as needed.
6. Choose File > Save when you're ready to save the new page **(Figure 17.16)**. A copyright warning may appear. If so, click OK. For more information on saving Web pages, consult *Saving your Web page* on page 230.
7. In the Save dialog box, give the Web page a name (or accept the one that is offered), choose a folder, and click Save **(Figure 17.17)**.

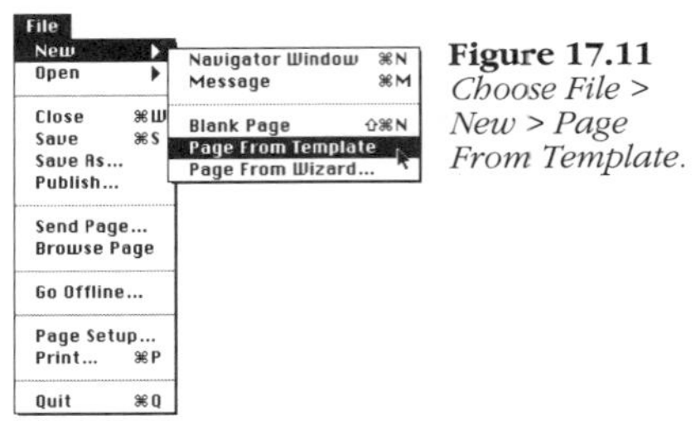

Figure 17.11 *Choose File > New > Page From Template.*

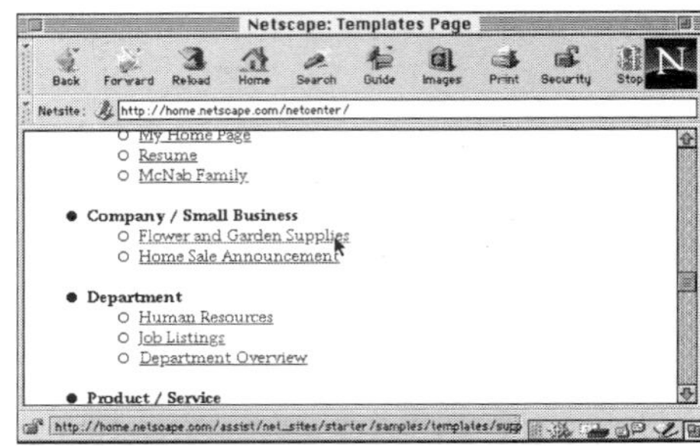

Figure 17.12 *Click the desired template's link.*

Figure 17.13 *The template appears in the browser. A template may include images, text, and links that you can replace with your own.*

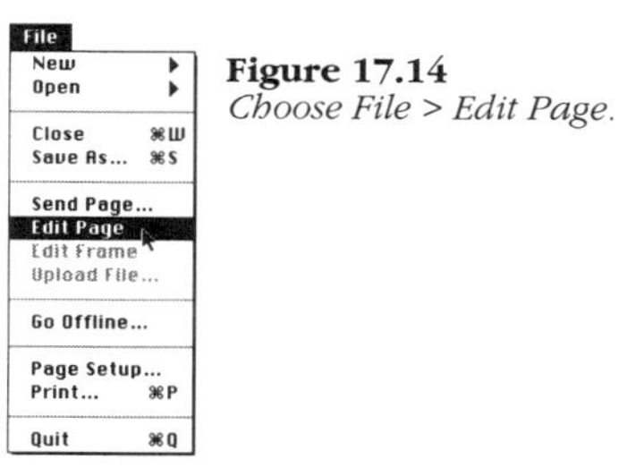

Figure 17.14
Choose File > Edit Page.

Figure 17.15 *A copy of the template appears in the Composer window. Make any desired changes.*

Figure 17.16 *Choose File > Save As (or File > Save).*

Figure 17.17 *Give the file a name (or accept the one that is offered), choose a folder, and click Save.*

✔ Tips

- By default, when you choose File > New > Page From Template, you'll jump to Netscape's own template page. But you can choose to open your own template page. For more information, consult *Using your own templates* on page 224.
- You must be connected to the Internet to access Netscape's templates.
- For more information on using your own templates, consult *Using your own templates* on page 224.

Using your own templates

You can set Composer up to open your own templates, instead of Netscape's, each time you choose File > New > Page From Template. This makes it easy to create an entire site with the same fundamental design structure.

To use your own templates:

1. Choose Edit > Preferences **(Figure 17.18)**. The Preferences dialog box appears.
2. Click Composer in the Category list, if necessary.
3. Type the URL of the desired template page under Template for new page or click the Choose Local File button **(Figure 17.19)**.
4. If you've clicked Choose Local File, an Open dialog box will appear in which you can choose the desired template page from your hard disk **(Figure 17.20)**. The path to the chosen file appears in the Preferences dialog box.

✔ Tip

- To use Netscape's templates again, click the Use default button in the Composer panel of the Preferences dialog box **(Figure 17.21)**.

Figure 17.18 *Choose Edit > Preferences.*

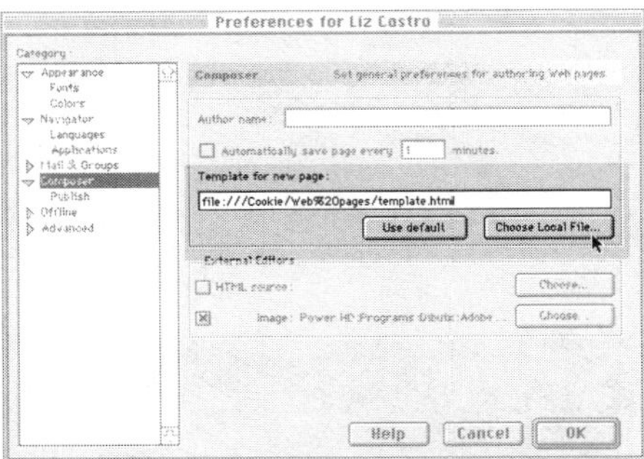

Figure 17.19 *Click the Choose Local File button in the middle of the dialog box.*

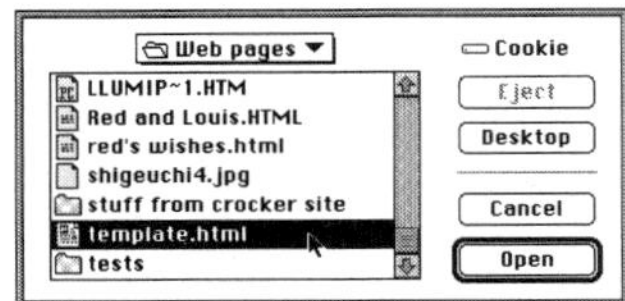

Figure 17.20 *Locate the desired template file on your hard disk and click Open.*

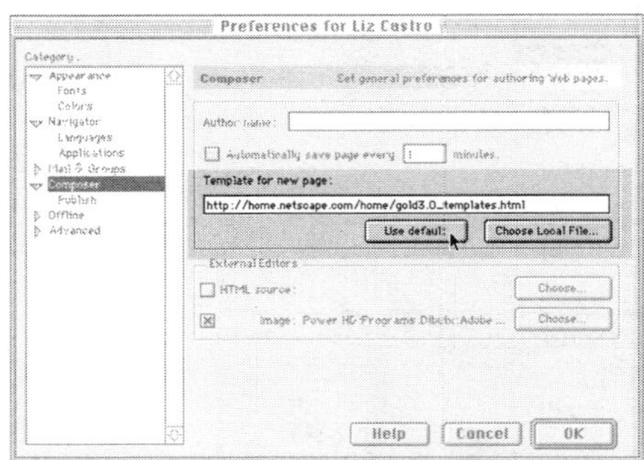

Figure 17.21 *Click the Use default button to use Netscape's templates again.*

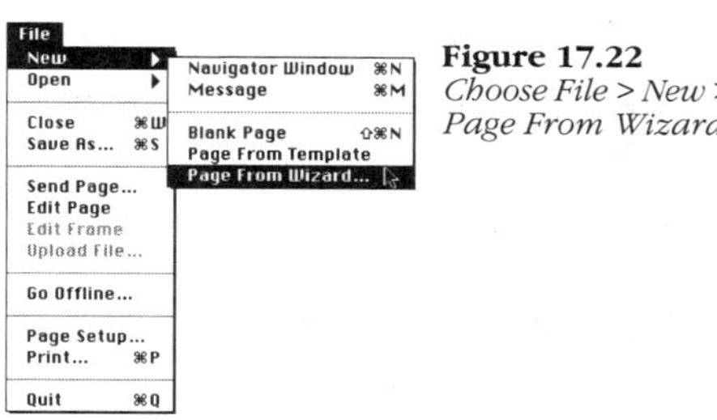

Figure 17.22 *Choose File > New > Page From Wizard.*

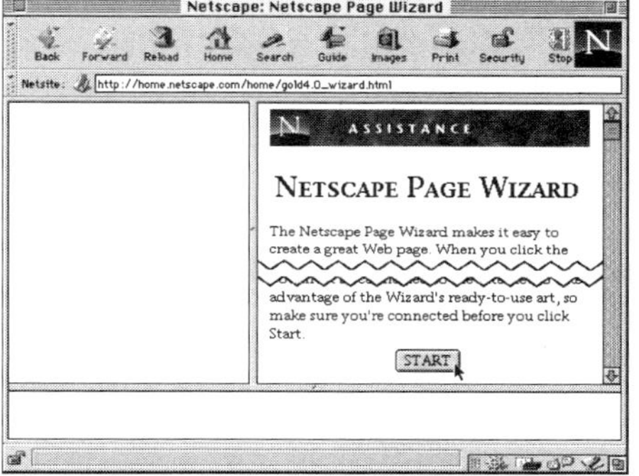

Figure 17.23 *Netscape's Page Wizard is a set of frames. Scroll down in the first frame (showing) and click Start to begin your page.*

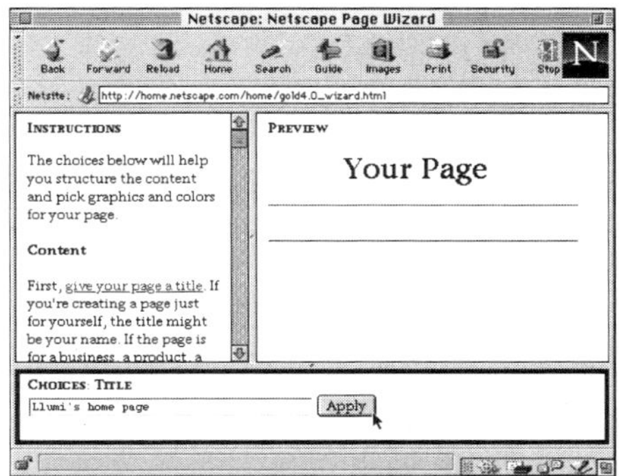

Figure 17.24 *The left frame guides you through the page creation process. When you click on a step, the lower frame offers options from which to choose, or a text box in which you can enter information. The right frame displays a preview of your page.*

Opening a new page with the Page Wizard

Netscape has also set up a special script that takes information entered into a form and converts it into a Web page. You can then use the generated Web page as is or modify it further as desired.

To open a new page with the Page Wizard:

1. Open your Internet connection.
2. Choose File > New > Page From Wizard **(Figure 17.22)**. Netscape's Page Wizard is displayed in Navigator.
3. In the upper-right frame, read the text and then scroll down to the bottom and click Start **(Figure 17.23)**. The introduction and page creation guide appear in the left frame.
4. Under Content, click the "give your page a title" link. The bottom frame displays a text box in which you can type your page's title **(Figure 17.24)**.
5. Enter a title in the bottom frame and click Apply. The new title is previewed in the upper-right frame.
6. Scroll down to the next section in the left frame. Continue using the links in the left frame and the corresponding options in the bottom frame to design your page. When you're finished, you'll find a Build button at the bottom of the left frame. Click it. The completed page is displayed in the Navigator window **(Figure 17.25)**.
7. Choose File > Edit Page to view the new page in the Composer window **(Figure 17.26)**.

8. Edit the page, if necessary **(Figure 17.27)**.

9. Choose File > Save to save the changes periodically *(see page 230)*.

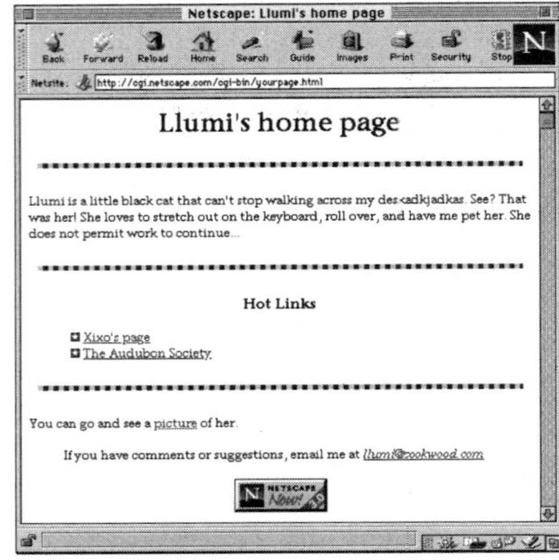

Figure 17.25 *Your page is generated from the responses given on the form. Notice the ubiquitous Netscape logo automatically inserted at the bottom of the page.*

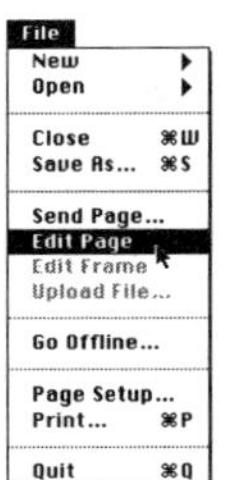

Figure 17.26 *Choose File > Edit Page to open the generated page in the Composer window.*

✔ Tips

- Be careful to choose a background pattern that contrasts enough with the text color so that people can read your page.
- If you don't like the way the page comes out, while you're still in the Navigator window, click the Back button, change the desired options (everything will be just as you left it), and click Build again.
- Netscape inserts its own logo (currently an old logo from Netscape 3) at the bottom of every page created with the Page Wizard. If you don't feel like doing your part to advertise Netscape's stock, just erase it once you're in the Composer window.
- You have to be connected to the Internet to use the Page Wizard.

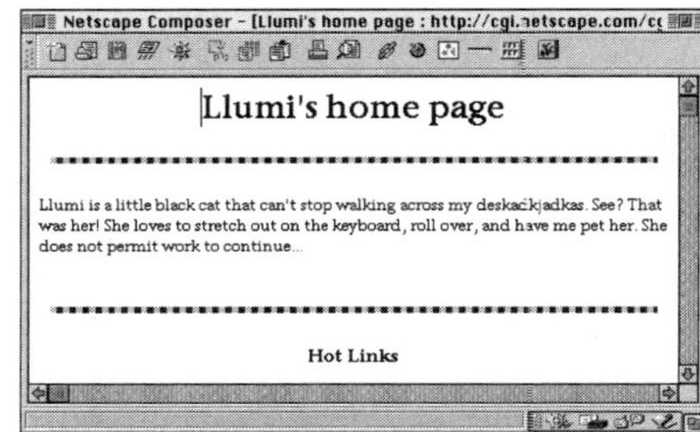

Figure 17.27 *You can polish the generated page in the Composer window.*

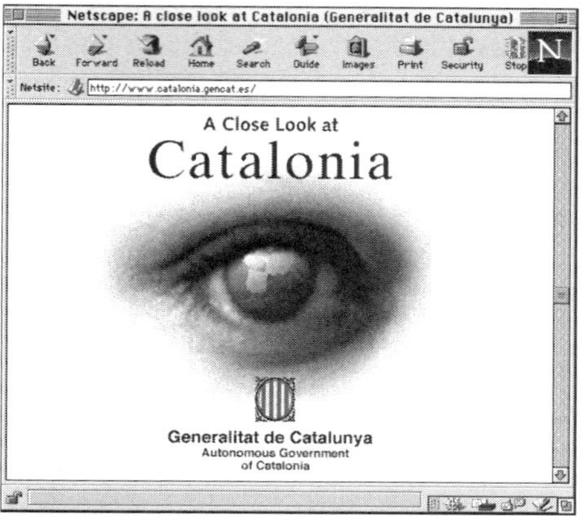

Figure 17.28 *Navigate to the page that you wish to edit.*

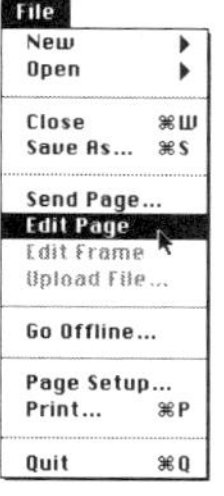

Figure 17.29 *Choose File > Edit Page.*

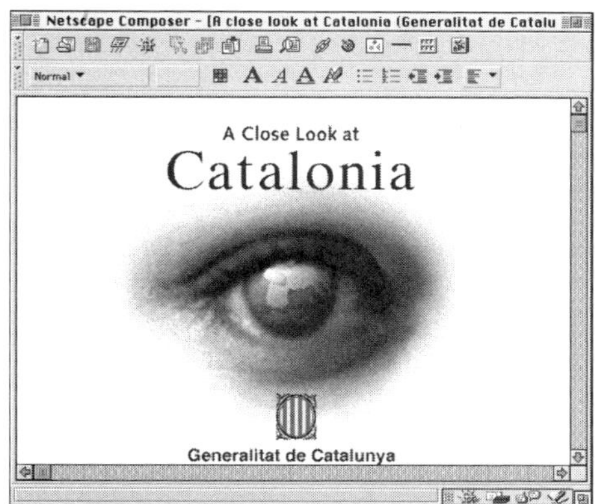

Figure 17.30 *The page is displayed in the Composer window. You can make any changes you like.*

Editing a page from the Web

You may open pages that you find on the Web in the Composer window and edit them to create new pages. This is a good way to learn different Web page construction techniques, although you should keep in mind that the images and text you find may be copyrighted, and at any rate, should not be used in your Web page without permission.

To edit an existing page:

1. Navigate to the page that you wish to edit **(Figure 17.28)**.
2. Choose File > Edit Page **(Fig. 17.29)**. The page appears in the Composer window **(Figure 17.30)**.
3. Make changes as desired.
4. Choose File > Save when you're ready to save changes to your new page *(see page 230)*.

✔ Tip

- You shouldn't copy any text or images from another page without permission. Besides being against the law, it's pretty slimy. Instead, use other pages as a source of inspiration. Then write your own text and draw or scan your own pictures.

Editing a saved file

You don't have to go out on the Web to find a page to copy. You can open any HTML file that you have previously created or saved—indeed *any* text file—in the Composer window.

To edit a saved file:

1. Make sure the saved file is either an HTML or text-only document. In both cases, it must carry either the .htm or .html extension.
2. Choose File > Open > Page in Composer **(Figure 17.31)**. The Open dialog box appears.
3. Choose the desired file and click Open **(Figure 17.32)**. The file appears in the Composer window **(Fig. 17.33)**.

✓ Tips

- To convert any existing word processor document into a Web page, first save it as Text only with the .htm or .html extension. Then open it in the Composer window.
- You are not limited to documents created with Composer. Any text document will do.
- If you open a text document with no extension or with the .txt extension, Netscape annoyingly puts all the text in each paragraph on one very long line and formats it in Formatted style. Add the .htm or .html extension (by typing it at the end of the file name, in the Finder) to the text file, and Netscape will wrap long lines correctly and format the text as Normal.

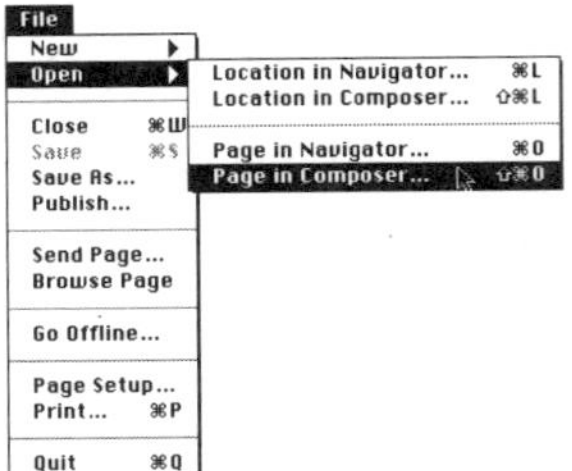

Figure 17.31 *Choose File > Open > Page in Composer.*

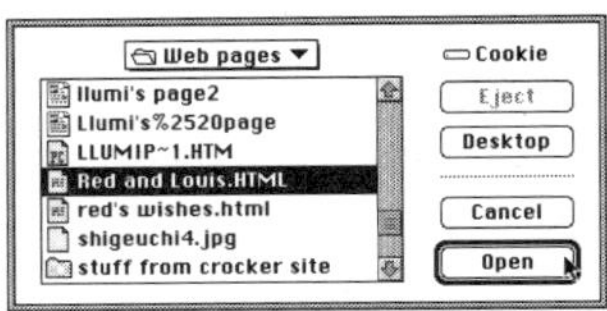

Figure 17.32 *Find the file on your hard disk that you wish to edit and click Open. You can open any text file. However, Netscape interprets text files with the .htm or .html extension more accurately.*

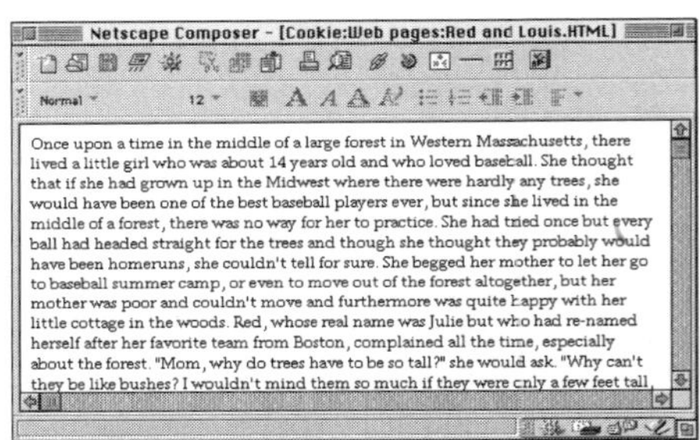

Figure 17.33 *Once the text file is in the Composer window, you can format it and add images and links.*

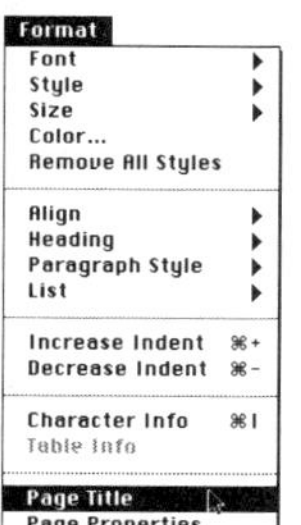

Figure 17.34 *Choose Format > Page Title. (You could also choose Page Properties. The two commands have the same effect in this case.)*

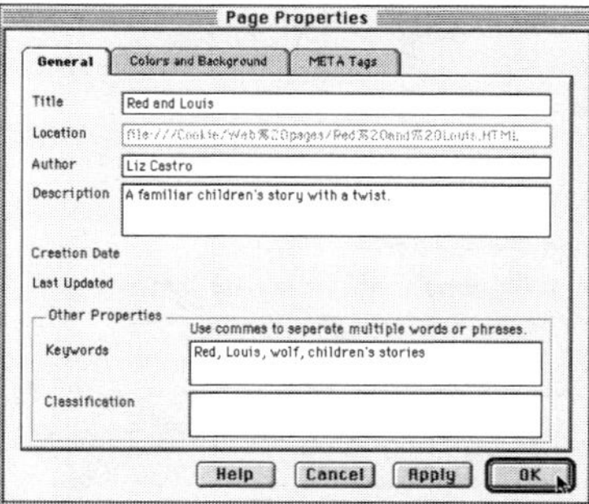

Figure 17.35 *In the General tab of the Page Properties dialog box, fill in the fields and then click OK. (You can add the Author name in the Composer panel of the Preferences dialog box (see page 328) so that you don't have to enter it manually each time.)*

Figure 17.36 *The new title appears in the title bar. The other added data is stored internally.*

Adding a title and keywords

The title and keywords of a page, and to lesser degree, the author, description, and classification, are used by search services to categorize Web pages. By creating a descriptive title and inserting specific keywords, you make it easier for people to find your page.

To add a title and keywords:

1. With the Composer window active, choose Format > Page Title **(Figure 17.34)**. The Page Properties dialog box appears.
2. Click the General tab, if necessary.
3. Enter a title for your page **(Fig. 17.35)**. Make it short (less than 60 characters) and descriptive.
4. If desired, enter your name in the Author field and a short description in the Description field.
5. In the Keywords field, type three or four important words that appear on your page or that your page is about.
6. If desired, type a category in the Classification field.
7. Click OK to save the changes. The new title appears in the title bar **(Figure 17.36)** The other information is saved internally.

✔ Tip

- AltaVista, among others, uses the description when listing pages that match a user's search criteria (instead of the first few lines of the page). It indexes the keywords in order to facilitate searches of those words. For details, see *http://altavista.digital.com/av/content/addurl_meta.htm.*

Saving your Web page

It's important to save your Web pages frequently while creating them.

To save your Web page:

1. With the Composer window active, choose File > Save **(Figure 17.37)**.
2. If you have not saved the file before, the Save As dialog box will appear. Enter a name and location for the document **(Figure 17.38)**.
3. Click Save. The document is saved and the new file name appears in the title bar **(Figure 17.39)**.

Figure 17.37 *Choose File > Save.*

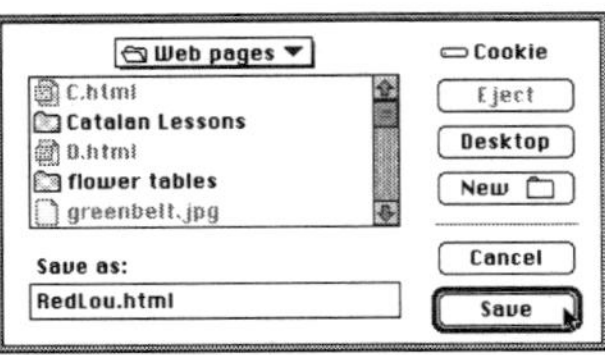

Figure 17.38 *Give the file a name, choose a location, and click Save.*

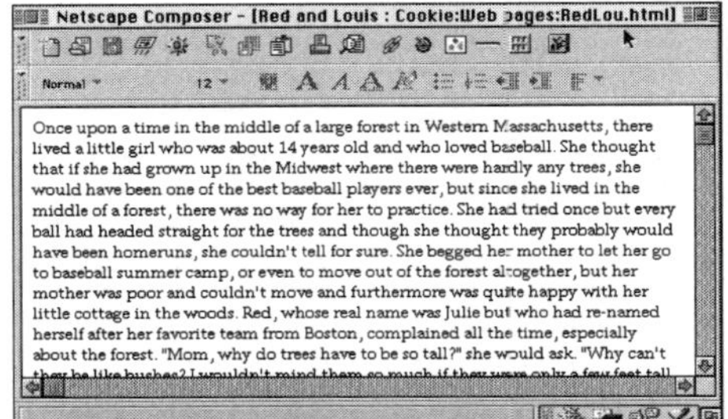

Figure 17.39 *The new file name appears in the title bar.*

✔ Tips

- You can have Composer save your file automatically every few minutes. For more information, consult *Saving pages automatically* on page 231.
- After you've saved the document once, choose Save to save additional changes and Save As to save the document with a new name or location.
- You can also save a Web page by clicking the Save button on the Composition toolbar.
- If you close a page without saving the changes, Composer will give you a chance to save the page.

Figure 17.40 *Choose Edit > Preferences.*

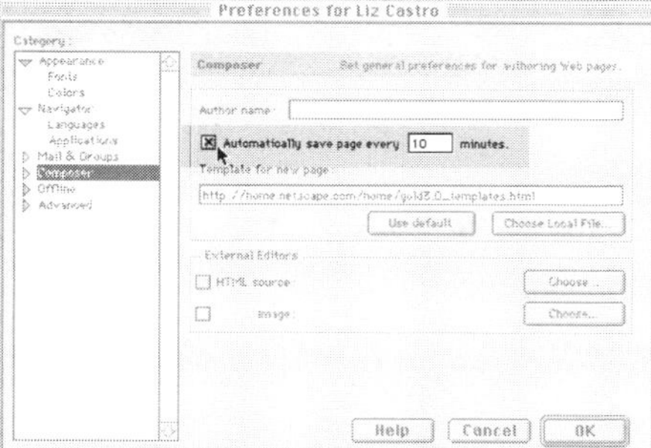

Figure 17.41 *Check the box next to the option and enter how often you want the page to be saved.*

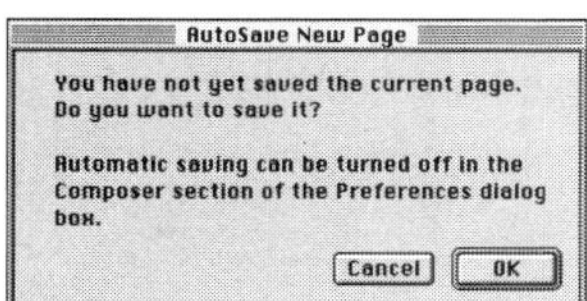

Figure 17.42 *If you haven't yet named your page, this alert will appear and give you the chance to do so. Click OK and then enter the name in the dialog box that appears.*

Saving pages automatically

If you get really into designing and writing your Web page, you may forget the most important thing: making sure it doesn't dissolve into bits by saving it regularly. Luckily, you can set Composer up to save your pages automatically, at regular intervals.

To save pages automatically:

1. Choose Edit > Preferences **(Figure 17.40)**. The Preferences dialog box appears.
2. Click Composer in the list at the left if it's not already selected. The Composer preferences are displayed.
3. Near the top of the dialog box, check the Automatically save page every xx minutes box and enter the desired number of minutes **(Figure 17.41)**.
4. Click OK to close the Preferences dialog box.

✔ Tips

- You have to restart Communicator for the changes to take effect.
- The automatic saving setting affects all Composer pages. If the page doesn't yet have a title, Composer will ask you for one **(Figure 17.42)**.
- Once Composer saves changes, you can't revert to an earlier version. Therefore, you may *not* want to use the automatic save feature.

Viewing paragraph marks

Composer lets you view paragraph marks in order to more easily determine where you are and where you wish to make changes.

To view paragraph marks:

Choose View > Show Paragraph Marks **(Figure 17.44)**. After you've chosen the option, you'll see small rectangles at the end of each paragraph **(Figure 17.45)**. Choose View > Hide Paragraph Marks to make the rectangles disappear.

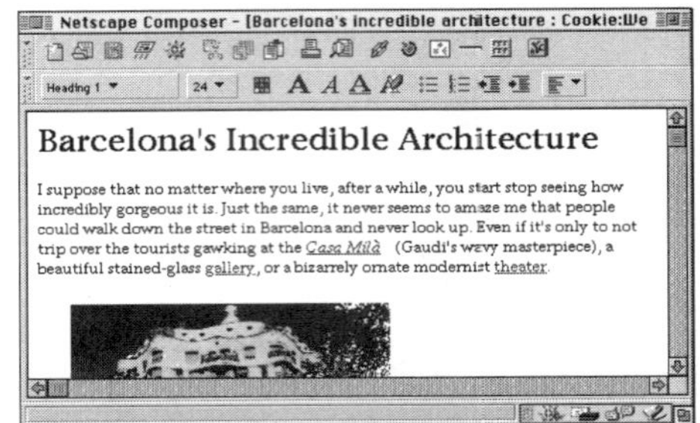

Figure 17.43 *By default, the returns at the end of each paragraph are invisible.*

Figure 17.44 *Choose View > Show Paragraph Marks.*

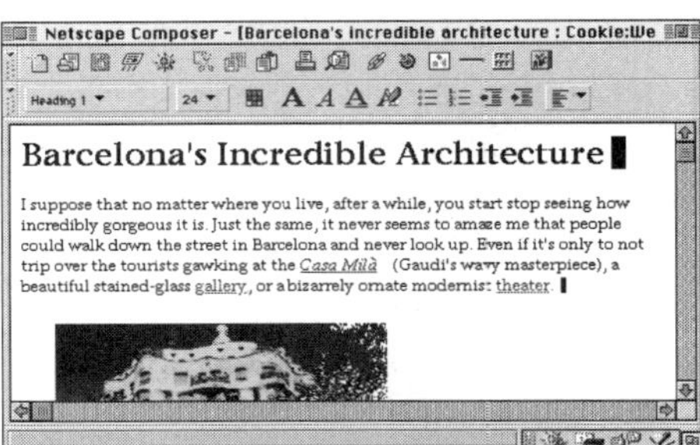

Figure 17.45 *Individual paragraphs are identified by a black rectangle after the last word in the paragraph, as shown after* Architecture *in the title and* theater *in the first paragraph.*

18 Formatting a Web Page

A Web page is just a regular word processing document. Its formatting is added with special tags that enable you to save the page in text-only format. This means that the document can be read by almost any computer. Although you could write the tags, called HTML, with any word processor (even SimpleText), the Composer component of Netscape Communicator has one important advantage: instead of showing the tags, it shows you the actual formatting.

HTML was designed to be a universal language, equally intelligible from a PC as from a Mac, or even a Unix computer. For that reason, there are limits to the number of ways you can format your page in the Composer window. For example, you can't control kerning and tracking, or stretch text to distort its width or height.

Choosing a font for text

Much to Web page designers' delight, you can finally specify a font for the text on a Web page. However, it is wise to remember that you can't specify what fonts your viewers buy and download to their hard disk. If they don't have your font, one that you might not like nearly as well may be the replacement.

To have some control over what font is used without having to worry about what fonts your users own, you can choose simply between Variable Width (Times, Arial, etc.) and Fixed Width fonts (Courier).

To choose a font for text:

1. Select the text that you want to change **(Figure 18.1)**, or place the cursor where you want to type new text.

2. Choose Format > Font > and then the font name in the submenu **(Figure 18.2)**. Or choose Variable Width or Fixed Width to choose just the *type* of font. The text is displayed in the desired font **(Figure 18.3)**.

✔ Tip

- Don't be misled by the display font in *your* Composer or Navigator windows. The font that you choose for displaying pages in the Fonts preferences dialog box only affects pages viewed on *your* computer. To apply a font to the page, use the steps outlined above.

Figure 18.1 *Select the text that you want to change.*

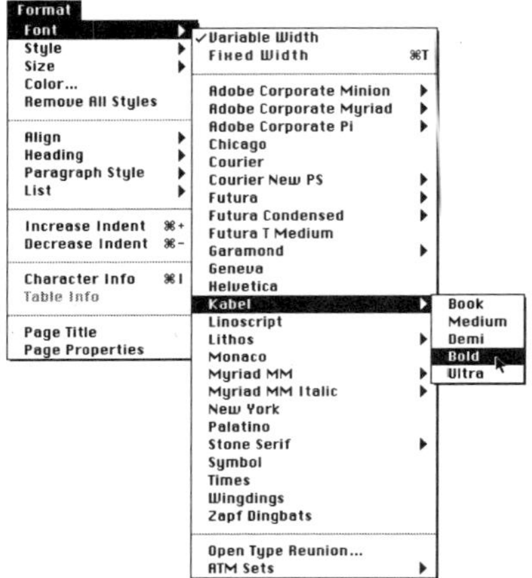

Figure 18.2 *Choose the desired font in the Font submenu.*

Figure 18.3 *The selected text is shown in the chosen font—in this case, Kabel.*

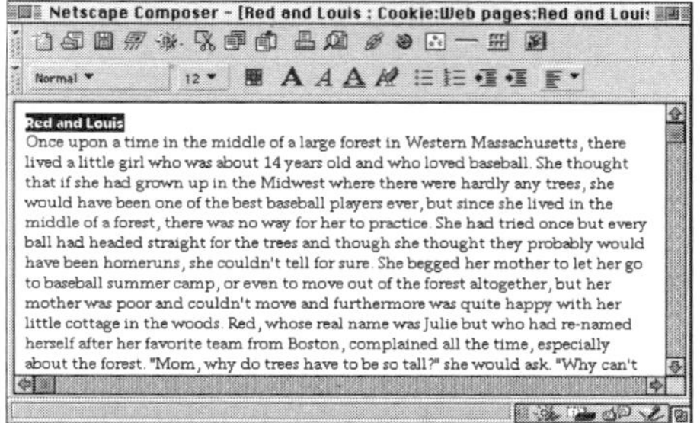

Figure 18.4 *Select the text that you want to change.*

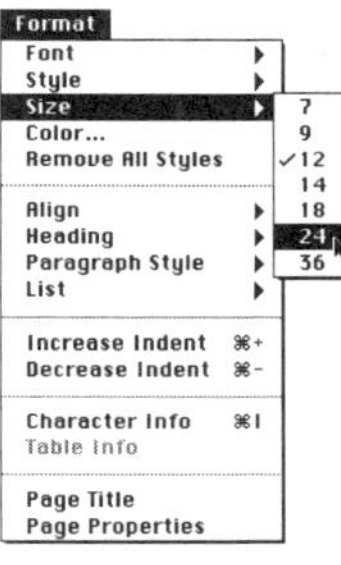

Figure 18.5 *Choose Format > Size and then the desired relative point size.*

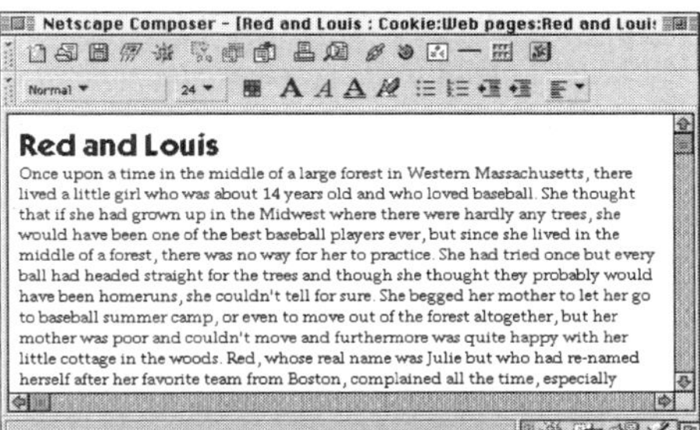

Figure 18.6 *The title now stands out better.*

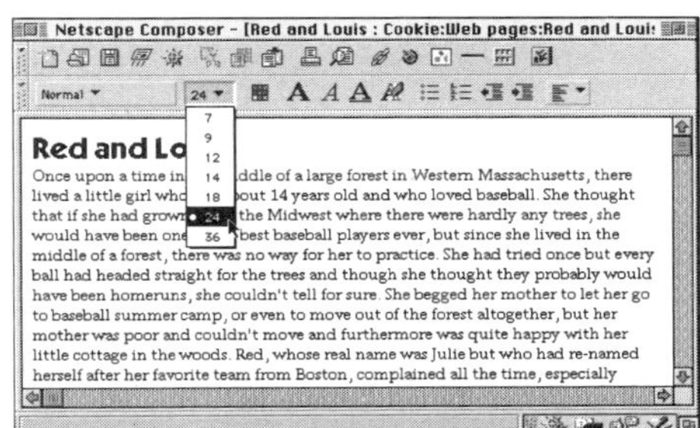

Figure 18.7 *You can also apply a new size by choosing it in the Size pop-up menu on the Formatting toolbar.*

Changing the size of text

You may change the size of certain words to give them emphasis.

To change the size of text:

1. Select the character(s) that you wish to make larger or smaller **(Fig. 18.4)**.
2. Choose Format > Size > and then a relative size in the submenu that appears **(Figure 18.5)**. The text is changed **(Figure 18.6)**.

✔ Tips

- You can also change the size of the text with the Size pop-up menu on the Formatting toolbar **(Figure 18.7)**.
- The sizes you choose all depend on the font and size that your reader has chosen to view your page with *(see page 28)*.
- Changing the size of an individual letter may change the spacing (leading) of the entire line. There's no simple solution. (The hard solution is to insert an *image* of the opening letter and wrap the text around it—see page 256.)

Adding basic character formatting

As in word processors and page layout software, character formatting means any style that can be added to a single character or word. *Basic* character formatting means bold, italic, underlined, fixed width, strikethrough, superscript, subscript, and blinking **(Figure 18.8)**. You can also create text that is not separated by line breaks *(see page 250)*.

Figure 18.8 *All character styles except* Blink *are displayed properly in the Composer window. To see blinking text, you have to view the file in the Navigator window.*

To add basic character formatting:

1. Select the character(s) you wish to modify **(Figure 18.9)**.

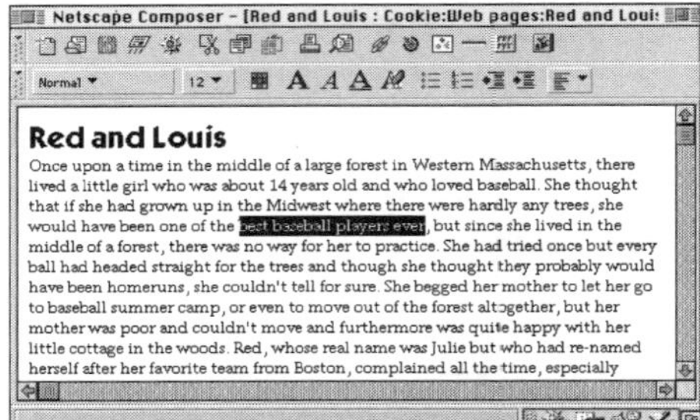

Figure 18.9 *Select the letters or words that you wish to format.*

2. Choose Format > Style and then choose the desired style in the submenu **(Figure 18.10)**. The changes are applied to the text immediately **(Figure 18.11)**.

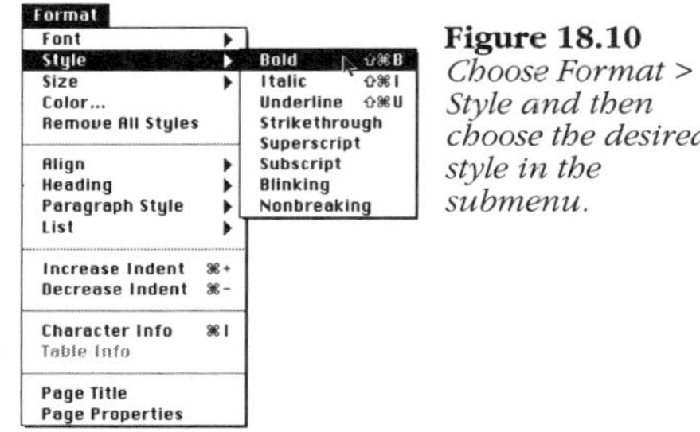

Figure 18.10 *Choose Format > Style and then choose the desired style in the submenu.*

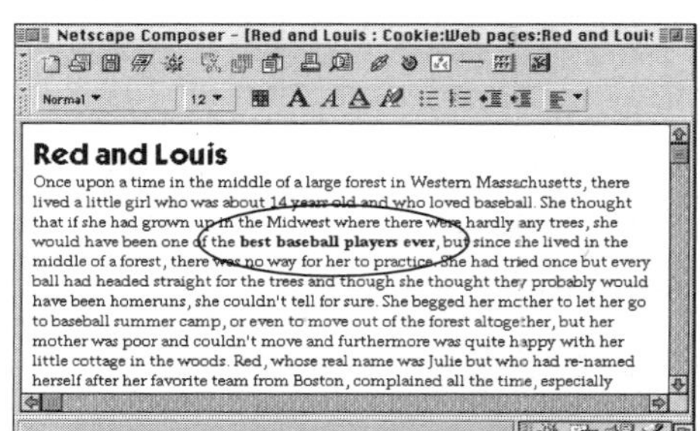

Figure 18.11 *The selected words now appear in bold formatting.*

✔ Tips

- If you don't select anything before applying styles, the formatting will be applied to the next thing you type.
- You can also apply character formatting by checking an option in the Style section of the Character tab of the Format dialog box *(see page 238)*.
- Apply bold, italic, and underlined formatting by clicking the corresponding buttons on the Formatting toolbar: **A**, *A*, or A, respectively.
- Unfortunately, Composer only uses *physical* formatting like bold and italic. To apply *logical* formatting like emphasis or strong, you must add the HTML tag manually. For more information, consult *Adding HTML tags manually* on page 296.

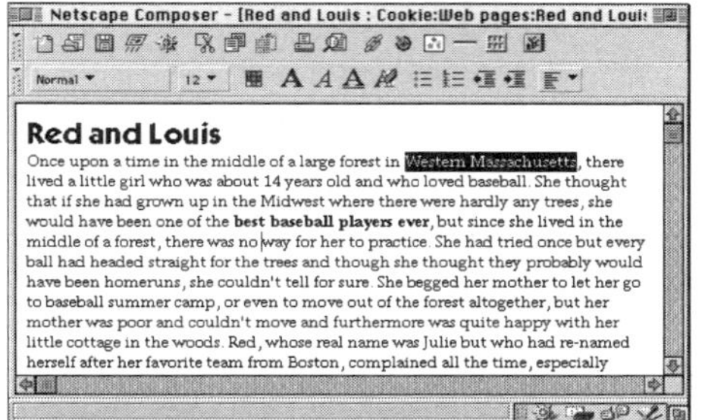

Figure 18.12 *Select the letters or words that you wish to change*

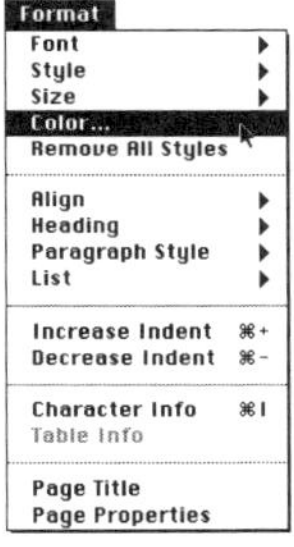

Figure 18.13 *Choose Format > Color.*

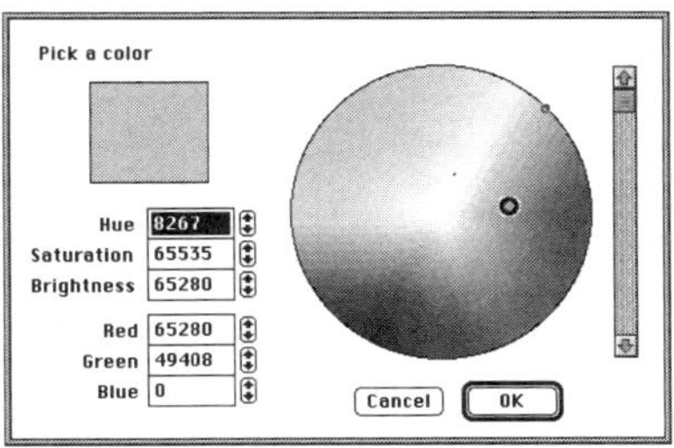

Figure 18.14 *Click the desired color in the color wheel and click OK.*

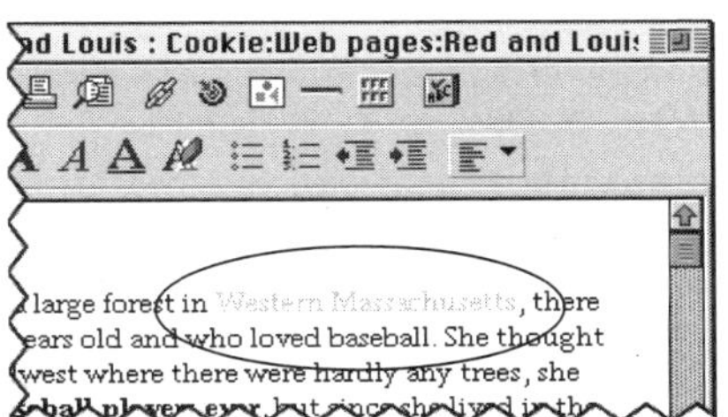

Figure 18.15 *The text is changed to the selected color.*

Changing the color of text

You should be a little careful about changing the color of the text on your Web page. First of all, some colors already have standard uses, like blue for links and purple for visited links. Secondly, the colors should have good contrast with the background color or image. Finally, keep in mind that not all of your readers will have color screens (or that they may choose to view pages with their own colors) and may not benefit from your efforts.

To change the color of text:

1. Select the character(s) that you wish to change the color of **(Figure 18.12)**.
2. Choose Format > Color **(Fig. 18.13)**. The Color dialog box appears.
3. Click the desired color for the text and click OK **(Figure 18.14)**. The text changes color **(Figure 18.15)**.

✔ Tips

- You can also change the color of text by using the Font Color button on the Formatting toolbar.
- Remove color formatting by choosing Format > Remove All Styles or by clicking the Remove All Styles button on the Formatting toolbar. For more information, consult *Clearing character styles* on page 239.

Changing the color of text

Applying many character styles at once

Although there are about twelve ways to apply character formatting (OK, maybe four), one of the nicest is through the Character tab of the Format dialog box, since you can apply several styles at once, see the changes without closing the dialog box, modify the options, and try again and again until you're satisfied with the results.

To apply many character styles at once:

1. Select the character(s) that you wish to modify **(Figure 18.16)**.
2. Choose Format > Character Info **(Figure 18.17)**. The Format dialog box appears.
3. Click the Character tab to see the Character attributes, if necessary.
4. Check the desired character styles, and select a size, font, and color for the text **(Figure 18.18)**.
5. If desired, click Apply to apply the changes without closing the dialog box. You may then check or uncheck the desired options, and click Apply again until you are satisfied.
6. Click OK (or Close if you've already applied the changes) to close the Format dialog box. All the changes are applied **(Figure 18.19)**.

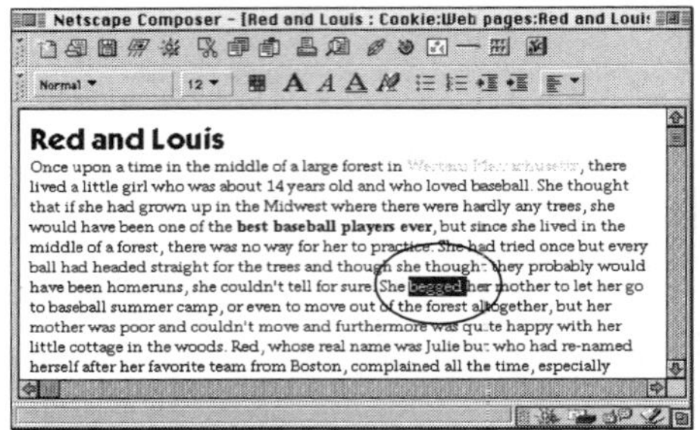

Figure 18.16 *Select the text you wish to change.*

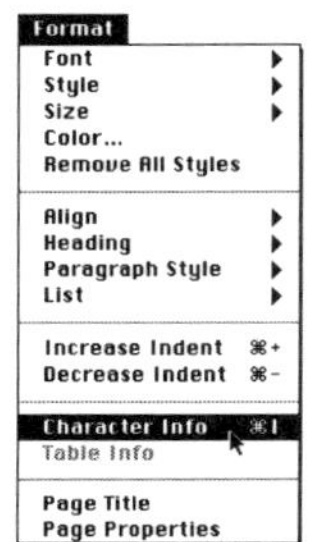

Figure 18.17 *Choose Format > Character Info.*

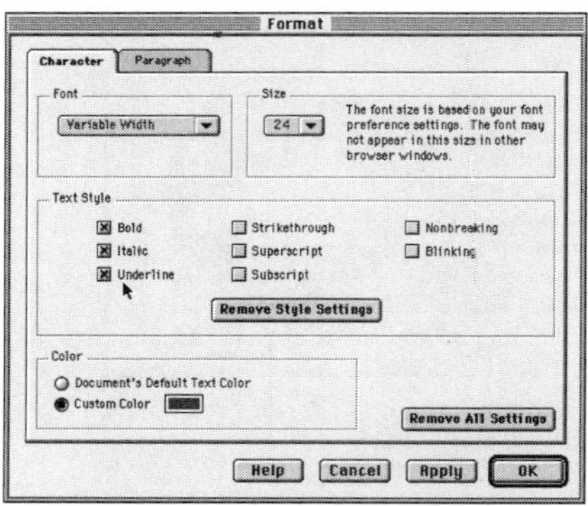

Figure 18.18 *Choose the desired character styles in the Character tab of the Format dialog box*

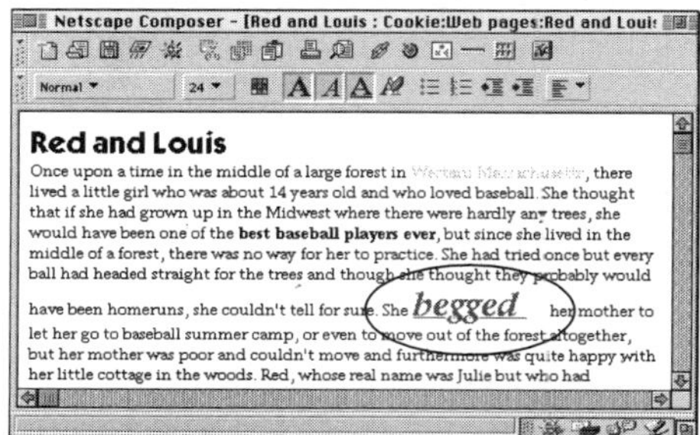

Figure 18.19 *All of the chosen styles are applied to the selected text.*

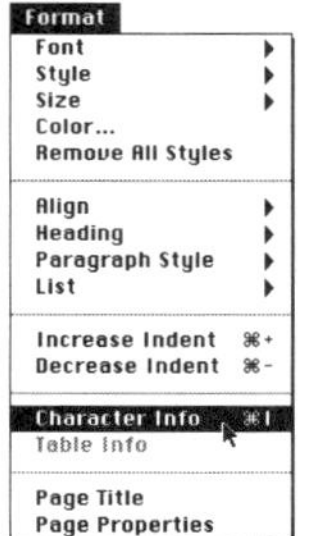

Figure 18.20 *Choose Format > Character Info.*

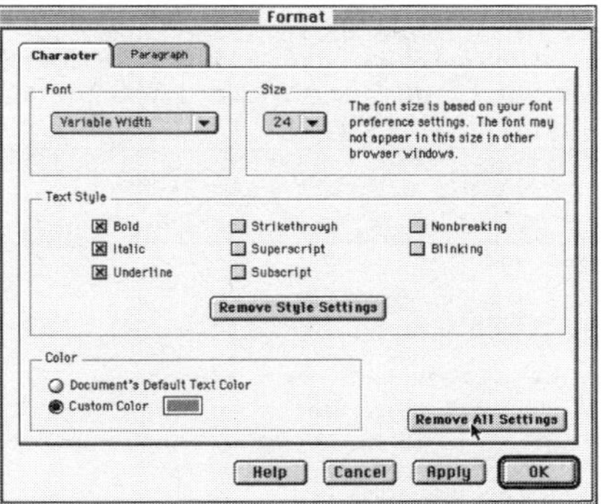

Figure 18.21 *Click Remove Style Settings to remove all the basic character styles. Click Remove All Settings to reset all the styles in this dialog box*

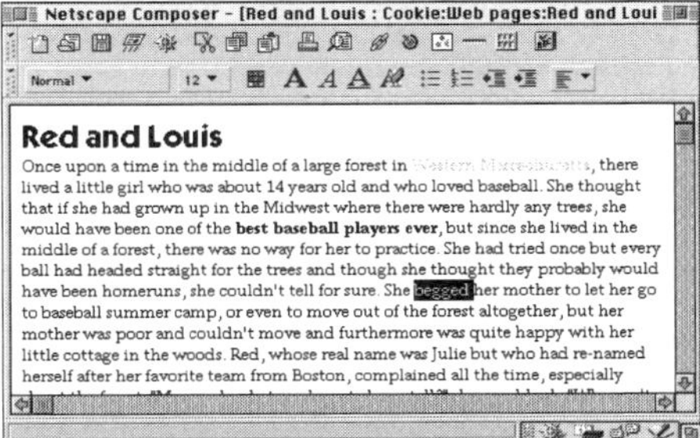

Figure 18.22 *All of the formatting is removed from the selected text.*

Clearing character styles

Sometimes it's easy to go overboard with character formatting. Luckily, it's easy to get rid of. Composer has two commands for clearing character styles. One eliminates only the basic character styles like bold and italic while the other eliminates all possible character styling, including size, color, and font face.

To clear character styles:

1. Select the desired text and choose Format > Character Info **(Fig. 18.20)**. The Format dialog box appears.
2. Click the Character tab to see the Character attributes, if necessary.
3. To eliminate basic style settings (that is, the ones in the Text Style section of the dialog box) click Remove Style Settings. To eliminate all character formatting, click Remove All Settings **(Figure 18.21)**.
4. Click Apply to apply the changes without closing the dialog box.
5. Click OK (or Close if you've already applied the changes) to close the dialog box. The formatting is removed **(Figure 18.22)**.

✔ Tip

- Another way to "unformat" text is by clicking the Remove All Styles button on the Formatting toolbar or selecting Format > Remove All Styles.

Using paragraph styles

Paragraph styles, by definition, affect all of the text in the paragraph containing the cursor, regardless of what is actually selected. In Composer, and indeed in HTML in general, the styles are already defined and each browser on each platform interprets them in its own way. This way, you can distinguish one paragraph from another and organize your information without restricting your page to a particular platform.

To use paragraph styles:

1. Decide how you want to organize your information. Divide your page into sections, with descriptive headings. Apply the Heading styles *(see page 241)* to section heads **(Figure 18.23)**.
2. Use the List Item for lists. There are several kinds: Numbered, Unnumbered (unordered), Directory, Menu, and Description **(Figure 18.24)**. Lists are described more fully on page 242.
3. The Formatted style (known as *Preformatted* in regular HTML lingo) is for fixed width text like handmade tables **(Figure 18.24)** or ASCII images. All spaces are maintained and the text is displayed in a fixed width font like Courier *(see page 247)*.
4. Use the Address style *(see page 248)* to format your name and e-mail address as a signature at the bottom of the page **(Figure 18.24)**.
5. Use Description Title and Description Text to format the pairs of entries in Description lists.

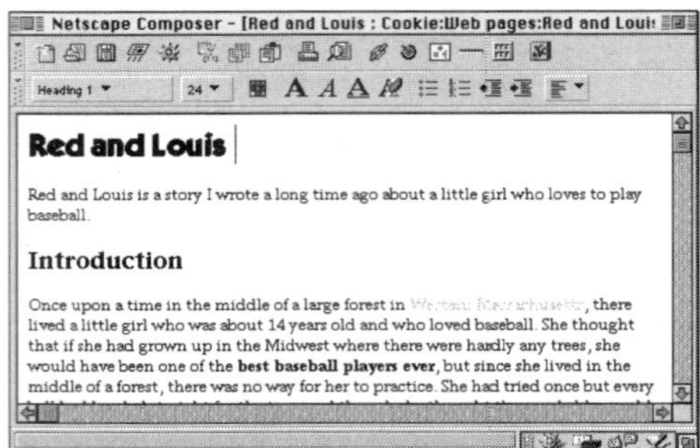

Figure 18.23 *In this page,* Red and Louis *is formatted with Heading 1,* Introduction *is formatted with Heading 2, and the rest of the text is Normal.*

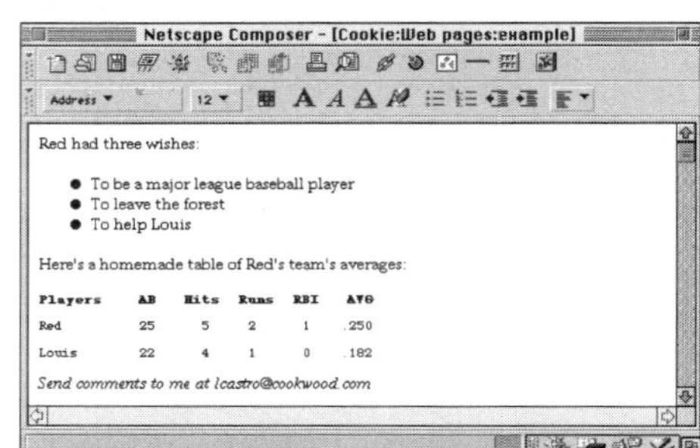

Figure 18.24 *Here we have an unordered list, with round bullets, and a table made from formatted text (that is, fixed width text). At the bottom of the page is the author's name, formatted with Address.*

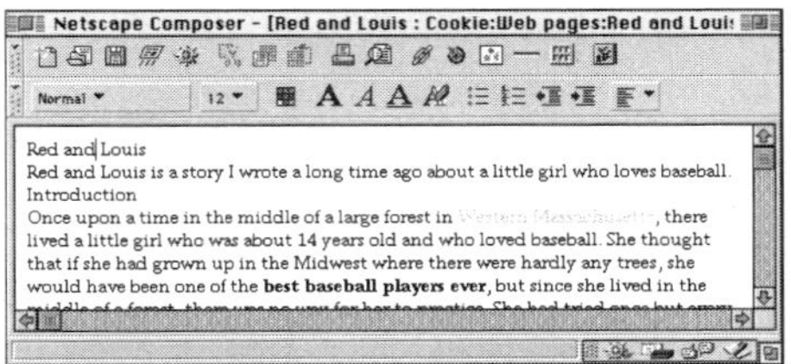

Figure 18.25 *Place the cursor in the paragraph that you want to make into a heading in this example.*

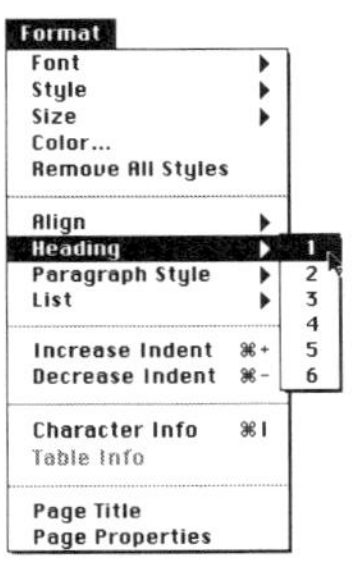

Figure 18.26 *Choose Format > Heading and then the level of heading desired.*

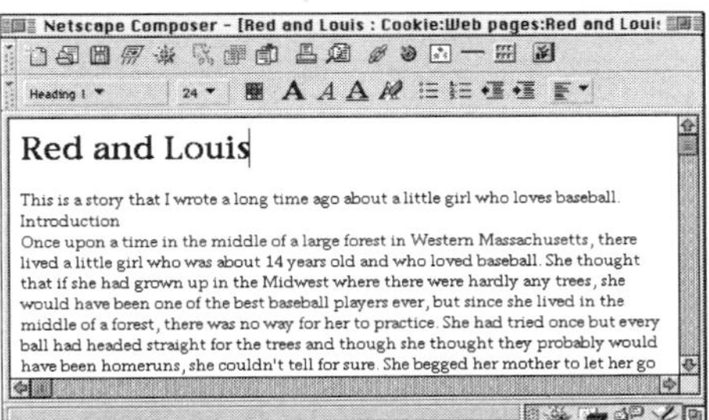

Figure 18.27 *The selected paragraph is displayed in Heading 1 style.*

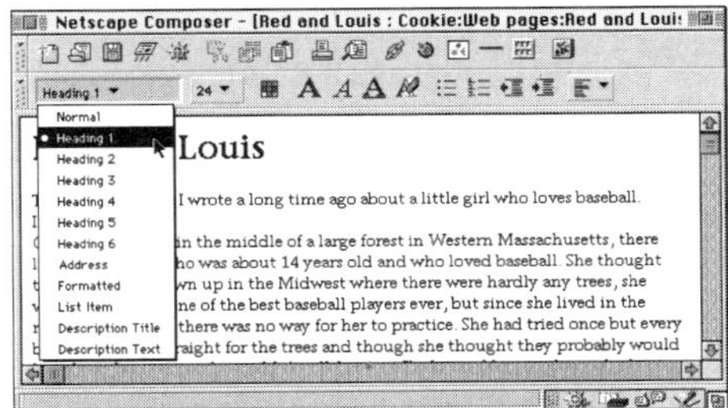

Figure 18.28 *You can also choose the desired heading style from the pop-up menu on the Formatting toolbar.*

Creating headings

Headings divide your page into visible units. They make it easy for your visitors to find information and to navigate around your page.

To create a heading:

1. Place the cursor in the paragraph that you want to make into a heading **(Figure 18.25)**. You don't have to select anything, nor does there have to be any text already typed in.
2. Choose Format > Heading and then the number of the level of heading desired **(Figure 18.26)**. The higher the number, the larger the font size used. The text is displayed with the chosen format **(Figure 18.27)**.

✔ Tips

- You can also choose a heading from the Paragraph style pop-up menu on the Formatting toolbar **(Fig. 18.28)**.
- Or choose Format > Character Properties. Then, click the Paragraph tab. Finally, choose a heading in the Paragraph style pop-up menu. That seems like a lot of work, but I suppose it could be useful if you wanted to change several paragraph attributes at once *(see page 249)*.

Creating lists

Creating a list can be as easy as clicking a button. Or you can tweak your list with special numbering and bullet schemes.

To create a list:

1. Place the cursor in the paragraph that you want to convert into a list item **(Figure 18.29)**. There doesn't have to be text in it yet.
2. Select Format > List and then choose the type of list from the submenu **(Figure 18.30)**. The selected paragraph is converted into a list item of the type selected in the submenu **(Figure 18.31)**.
3. If you want to choose a special numbering or bulleting system, choose Format > Character Info **(Fig. 18.32)**. The Character tab of the Format dialog box appears.
4. Click the Paragraph tab to see the Paragraph attributes **(Figure 18.33)**. The Paragraph Style will already show List Item. Choose List in the Additional Style pop-up menu if it's not already selected.
5. In the List section, which is now active, the type of list you chose in the submenu should be showing. You can modify it here if you've changed your mind.
6. For unnumbered lists, you can select what kinds of bullets should be used from the Bullet Style pop-up menu. If you've created a Numbered list, you can decide what kind of numbering to use with the Number Style pop-up menu. Then choose an initial number for the list in the Starting number text box.

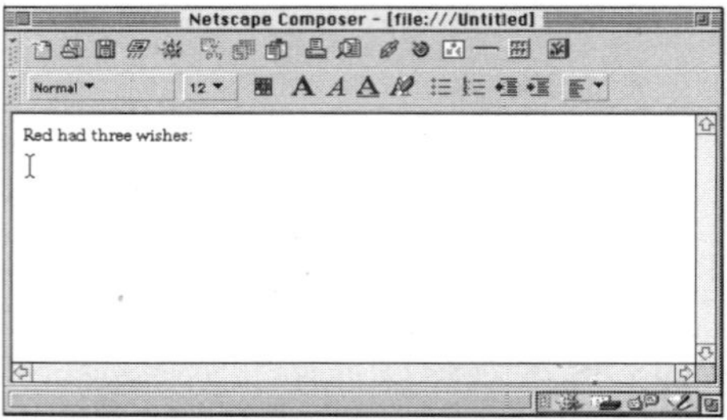

Figure 18.29 *Click in the paragraph where you want to create a list. You needn't type anything.*

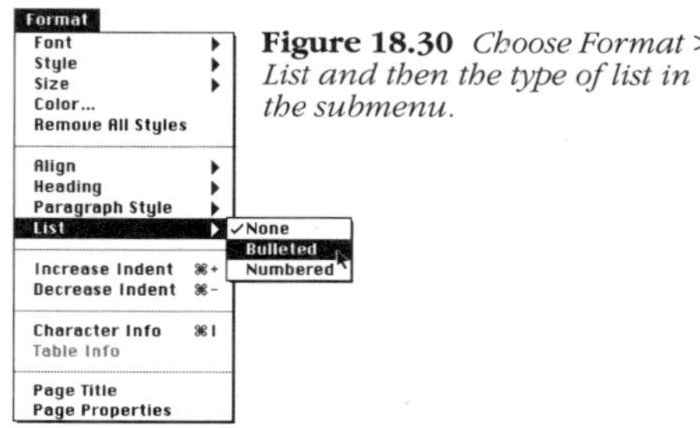

Figure 18.30 *Choose Format > List and then the type of list in the submenu.*

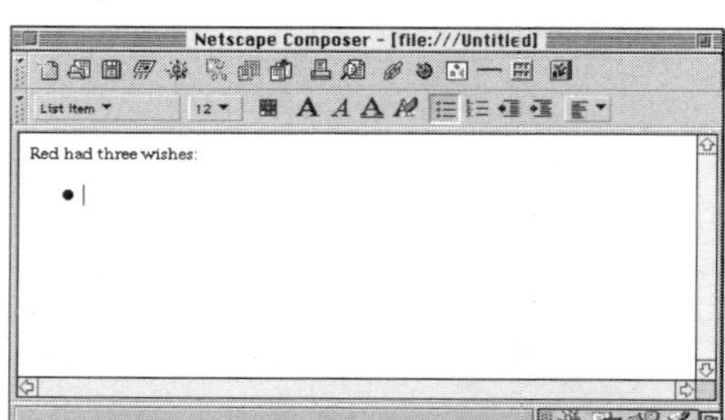

Figure 18.31 *You can tell by the bullet that the paragraph is formatted as a list.*

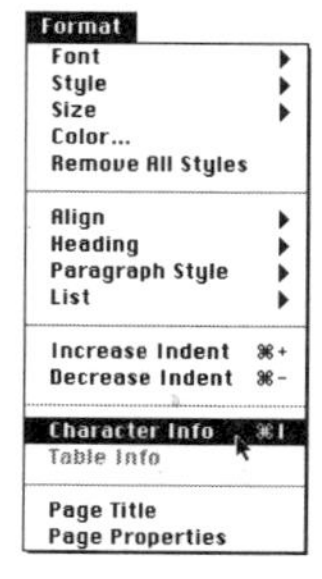

Figure 18.32 *Choose Format > Character Info.*

Creating lists

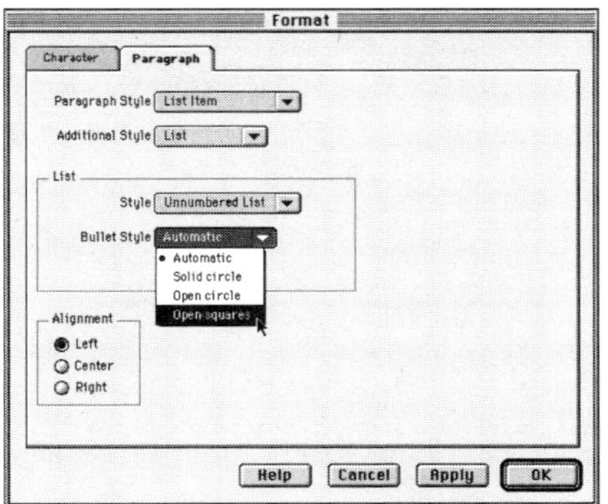

Figure 18.33 *Choose List in Additional Style and select the type of list in the Style menu. Then choose a bullet or number style. (If you're working on a Numbered list, the Starting Number text box will appear which you can use to set the first number in your list.) Finally, click OK.*

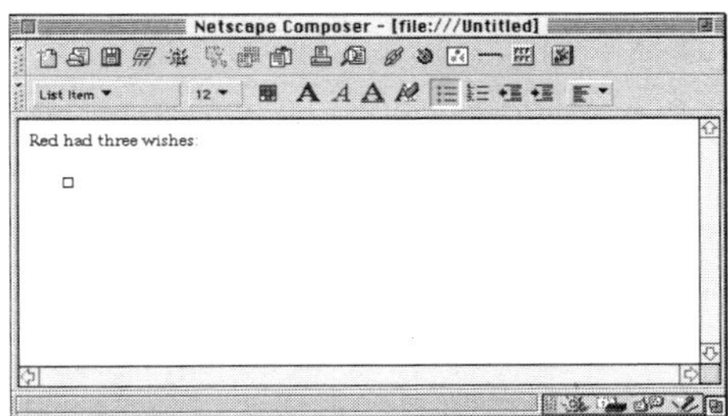

Figure 18.34 *The bullet is replaced by the open square we selected in the dialog box in Figure 18.33.*

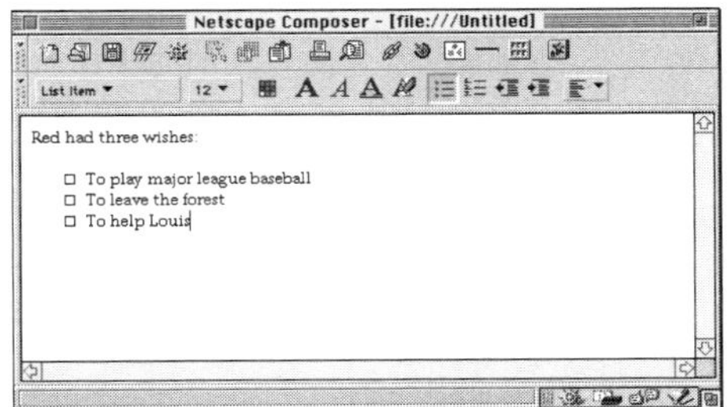

Figure 18.35 *Type the list, placing a return after each item. You could just as easily type the list first and then format it using the same steps.*

7. If desired, click Apply to apply the changes without closing the dialog box. Make additional changes and apply them until you are satisfied.

8. Click OK (or Close if you've previously applied the changes) to close the dialog box. The changes will be applied **(Figure 18.34)**.

9. Type the contents of the list if you haven't done so already, adding a return after each list item **(Fig. 18.35)**.

✔ Tips

- You can use the Bullet List button or the Numbered List button on the Formatting toolbar to change a list from one format to the other.
- To finish the list and go back to normal text, press Return, and then choose Format > List > None. The empty line will return to Normal style and you can keep typing from there. If you simply choose Normal in the pop-up menu on the toolbar, you'll get *indented normal* and will have to click the Decrease Indent button on the Formatting toolbar to make it completely normal.
- If you format a lone paragraph by choosing List Item in the pop-up menu, it turns into a sort of orphan list, with a small bullet. That command works best on new lines that follow an existing list.
- The numbers in a numbered list do not appear until you browse the page. Until then, they are shown as ##. All initial letters appear as a lowercase *a* or a capital *A*, depending on the option chosen in the Number Style pop-up menu.

Aligning text

You can align the text on your page to the left or to the right, or you can center it. By default, all paragraphs are aligned to the left.

To align text:

1. Click anywhere in the paragraph you wish to align **(Figure 18.36)**. You don't have to select anything.

2. Choose Format > Align and then Left, Center, or Right **(Figure 18.37)**.
   The text is aligned as specified **(Figure 18.38)**.

✔ Tip

- You can also align text by choosing an option in the Alignment pop-up menu on the Formatting toolbar **(Figure 18.39)**.

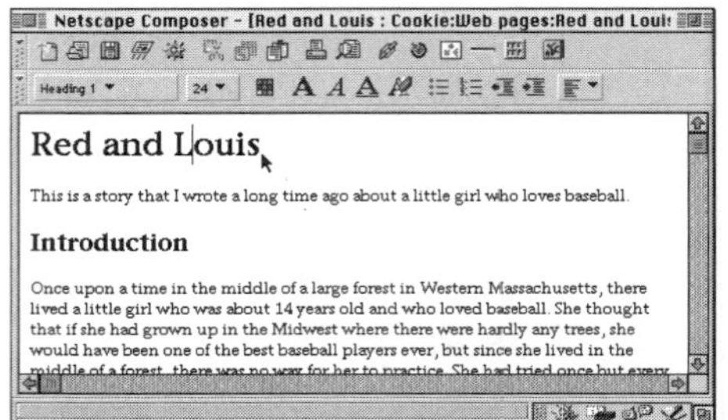

Figure 18.36 *Click anywhere in the paragraph whose alignment you wish to change.*

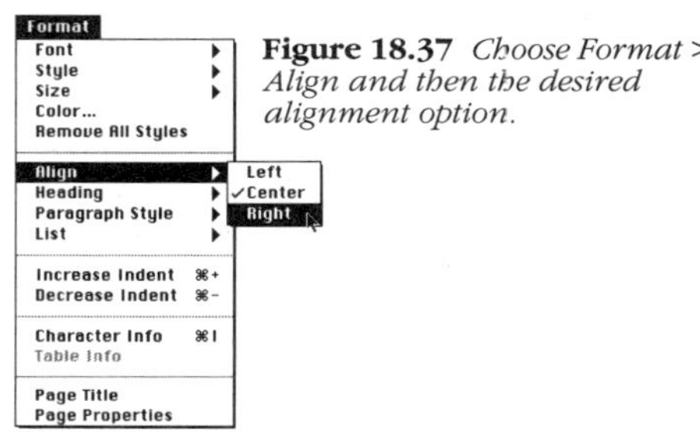

Figure 18.37 *Choose Format > Align and then the desired alignment option.*

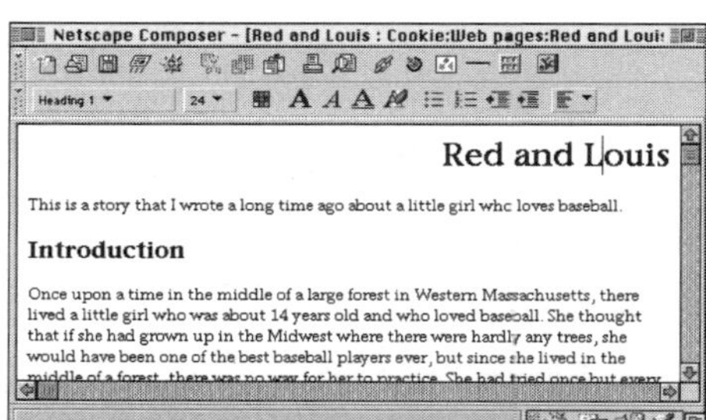

Figure 18.38 *The paragraph is aligned to the right.*

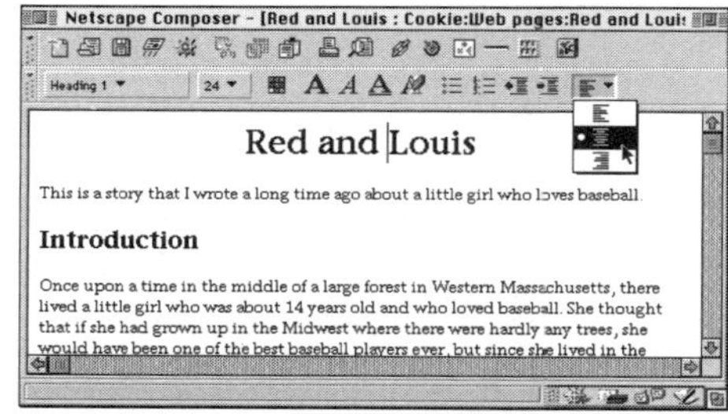

Figure 18.39 *You can also choose an alignment option from the pop-up menu.*

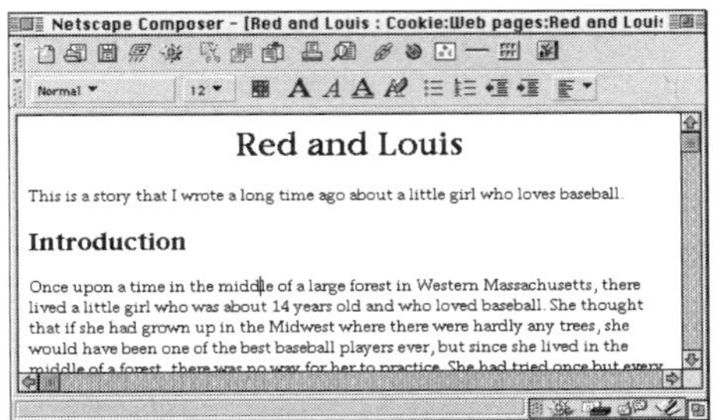

Figure 18.40 *Click anywhere in the paragraph that you want to indent (in this case, in the bottom paragraph, in the word* middle*).*

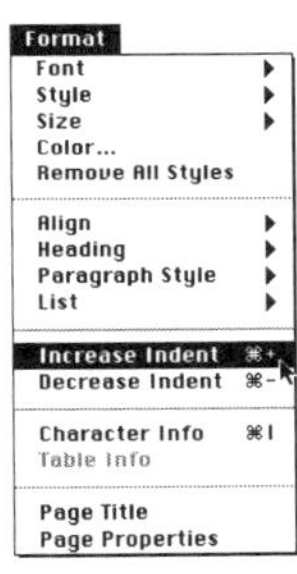

Figure 18.41 *Choose Format > Increase Indent.*

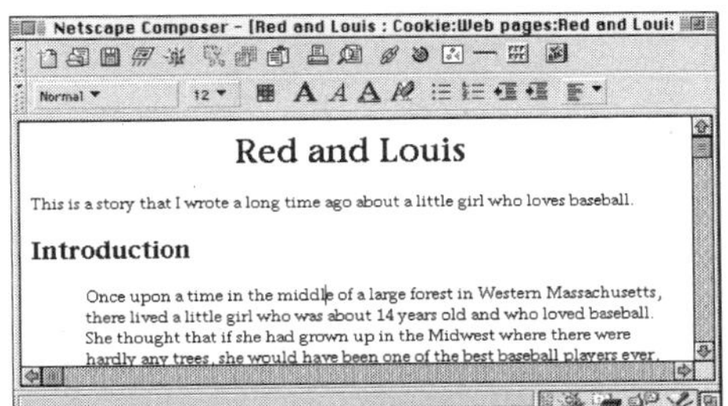

Figure 18.42 *The entire paragraph is indented.*

Indenting a paragraph

HTML does not accept multiple spaces or returns. If you try and type two spaces, the program will simply ignore you. However, Composer lets you indent an entire paragraph, with a device that approximates a tab.

To indent a paragraph:

1. Place the cursor anywhere in the paragraph that you want to indent **(Figure 18.40)**. You don't have to select anything.
2. Choose Format > Increase Indent **(Figure 18.41)**. The paragraph is indented toward the right **(Figure 18.42)**.

When you remove an indent from a paragraph, the whole paragraph is shifted back toward the left.

To remove an indent:

1. Place the cursor anywhere in an indented paragraph.
2. Choose Format > Decrease Indent. The indent disappears and the paragraph is moved to the left.

✓ Tip

- Or use the Increase Indent button or the Decrease Indent button on the Formatting toolbar.

Creating a block quote

A block quote is a special device used on Web pages to call attention to a short paragraph. In Navigator, block quotes are formatted in the variable width font *(see page 313)* and are indented from both margins.

To create a block quote:

1. Click anywhere in the paragraph that you wish to make into a block quote **(Figure 18.43)**. It doesn't matter if the paragraph has any text in it yet.
2. Choose Format > Character Info. The Format dialog box appears.
3. Click the Paragraph tab to see the Paragraph attributes.
4. Choose Block Quote in the Additional Style pop-up menu **(Figure 18.44)**.
5. Click OK. The selected paragraph is changed to block quotes **(Figure 18.45)**.

✓ Tips

- You can combine block quotes with any other principal paragraph style. Use the Paragraph panel of the Format dialog box.
- In many browsers, block quotes are displayed in a fixed width font at a smaller size.

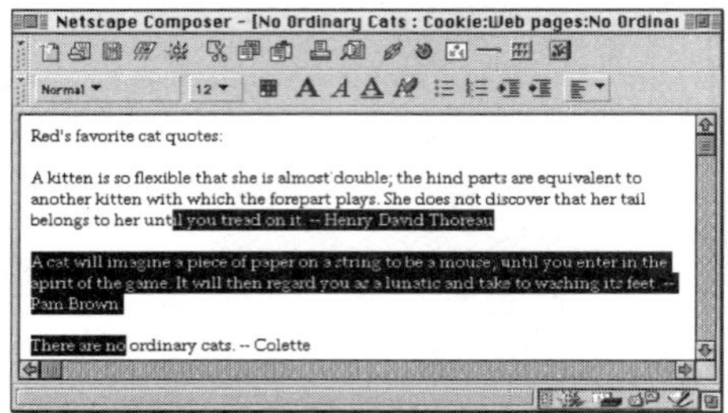

Figure 18.43 *Select the paragraph(s) that you wish to convert to block quotes. (You don't have to select entire paragraphs.)*

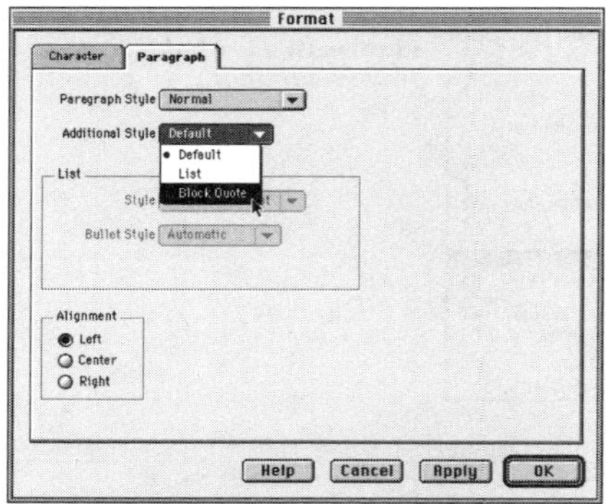

Figure 18.44 *Choose any style you want in the Paragraph Style pop-up menu. Then choose Block Quote in the Additional Style pop-up menu.*

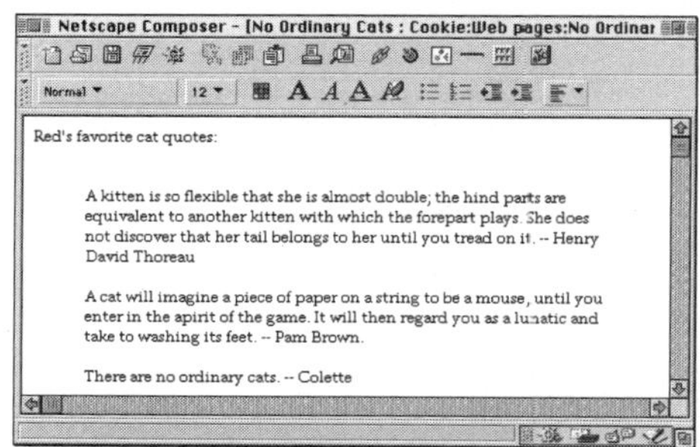

Figure 18.45 *Netscape's browser indents the block quotes on both sides. Other browsers use a smaller font, and/or italics, for block quotes.*

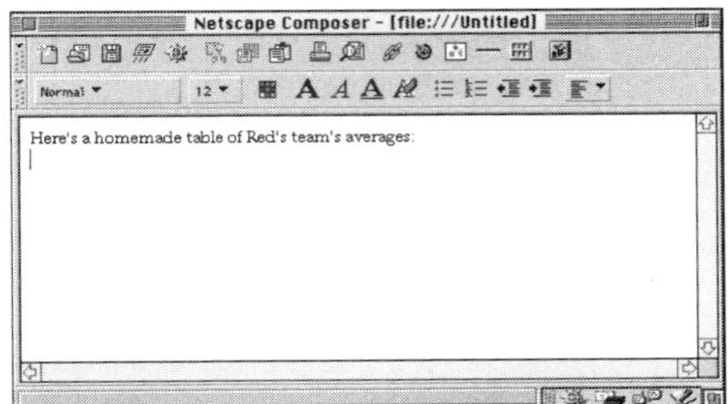

Figure 18.46 *Click in the paragraph that you want to format as preformatted text.*

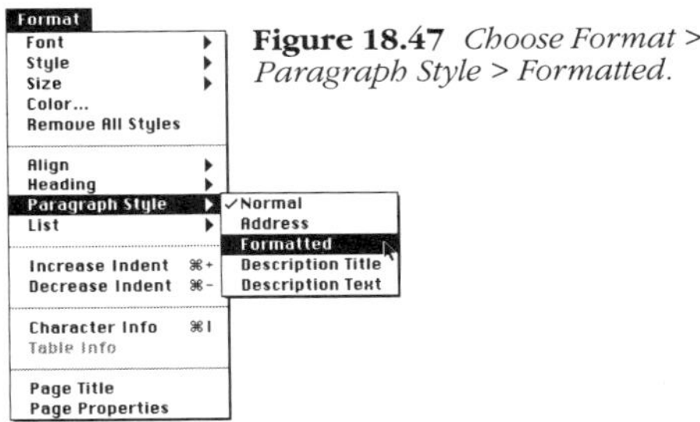

Figure 18.47 *Choose Format > Paragraph Style > Formatted.*

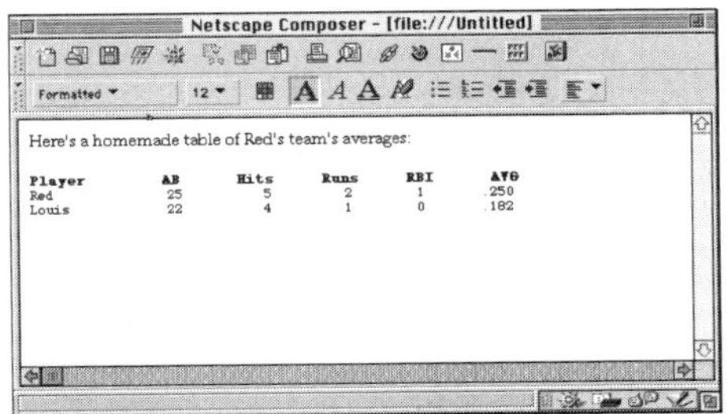

Figure 18.48 *Here is a table created with preformatted text.*

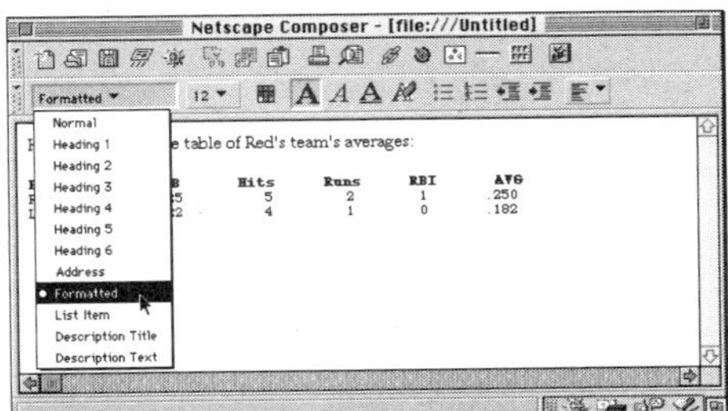

Figure 18.49 *You can also choose Formatted in the Paragraph style pop-up menu on the Formatting toolbar.*

Creating preformatted text

In the old days of Web design (say, two years ago), one special way to display text was to add extra spaces by hand and to use a monospaced font. It sounds pretty ugly, but it was (and still is) particularly useful for tables and ASCII images—and these can be displayed in *any* browser, including the text-only Lynx. In HTML parlance, that text was called *preformatted.* For some reason I fail to understand, Composer uses the much more ambiguous *formatted* to refer to this kind of text (What about bold text? Isn't it formatted? Not according to Netscape). And although hardly any browsers have trouble with real tables, preformatted ones remain *universally* accepted.

To create preformatted text:

1. Click anywhere in the paragraph that you wish to make into preformatted text. It doesn't matter if the paragraph has any text in it yet **(Figure 18.46)**.
2. Choose Format > Paragraph Style > Formatted **(Figure 18.47)**. The selected paragraph is displayed in a monospaced font and all spaces and returns it contains are maintained **(Figure 18.48)**.

✔ Tip

■ You can also create preformatted text by choosing Formatted from the Paragraph style pop-up menu on the Formatting toolbar **(Figure 18.49)**.

Creating an address line

The address format is one of the oldest, rather superfluous traditions for Web pages that has not yet been abandoned. It is simply a special format for the line that contains the e-mail address of the creator of the Web page.

To create an address line:

1. Click anywhere in the paragraph that you wish to make into an address line **(Figure 18.50)**. It doesn't matter if the paragraph has any text in it yet.

2. Choose Format > Paragraph Style > Address **(Figure 18.51)**. The selected paragraph is changed to an address **(Figure 18.52)**.

✔ Tips

- Whether or not you use the address format, it's a great idea to include your e-mail address on each page of your site so that your visitors can contact you with comments, corrections, and suggestions.

- You can also choose Address from the Paragraph style pop-up menu on the Formatting toolbar **(Figure 18.53)**.

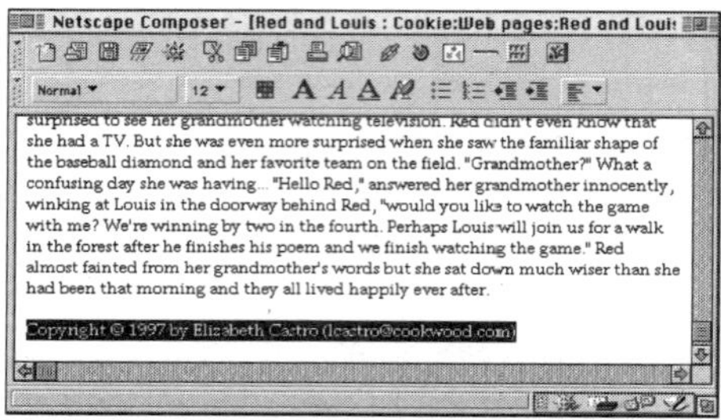

Figure 18.50 *Select the line you want to format as an address.*

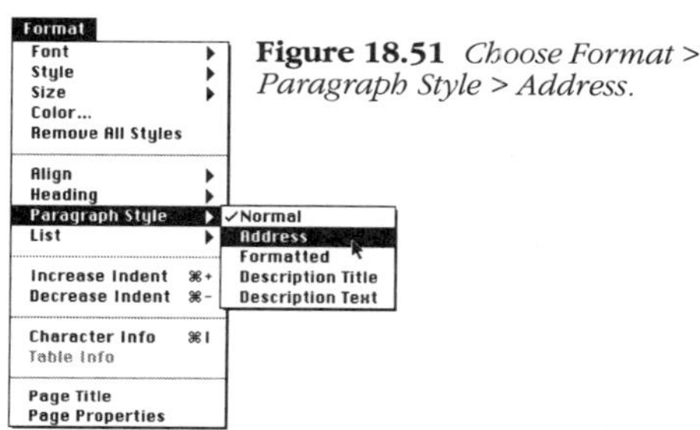

Figure 18.51 *Choose Format > Paragraph Style > Address.*

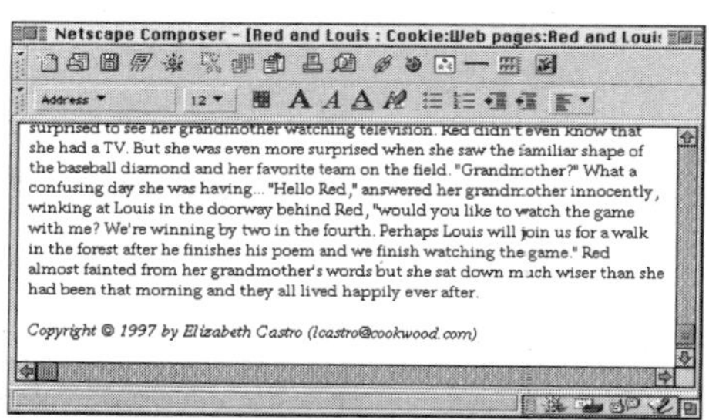

Figure 18.52 *Address lines are generally displayed in italics.*

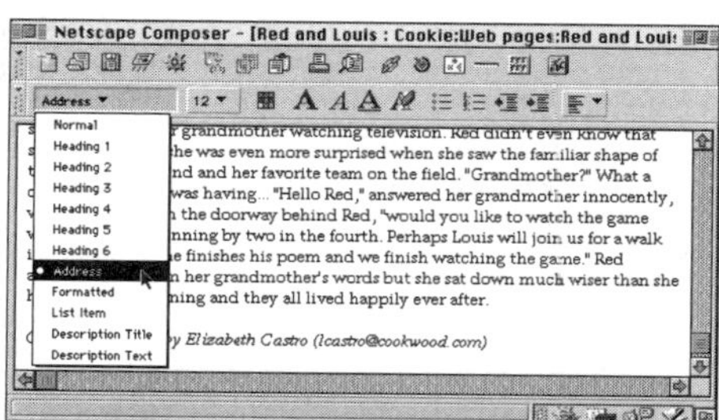

Figure 18.53 *You can also choose Address in the Paragraph style pop-up menu on the Formatting toolbar.*

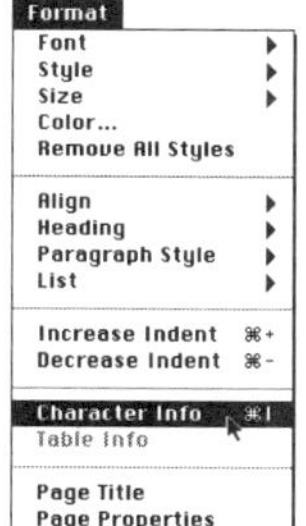

Figure 18.54 *Choose Format > Character Info.*

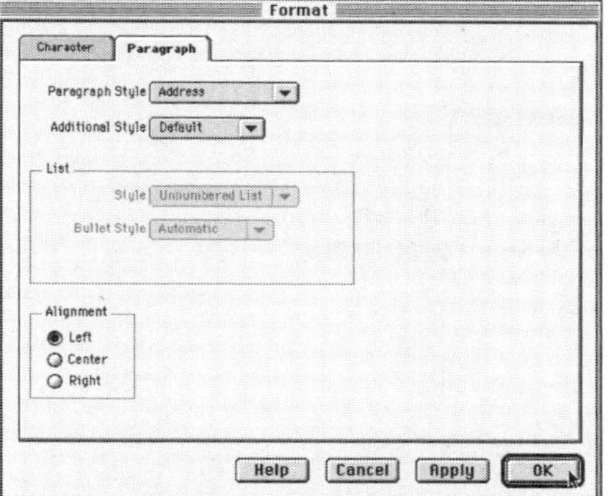

Figure 18.55 *In the Paragraph tab of the Format dialog box, select the desired attributes and then click Apply or OK.*

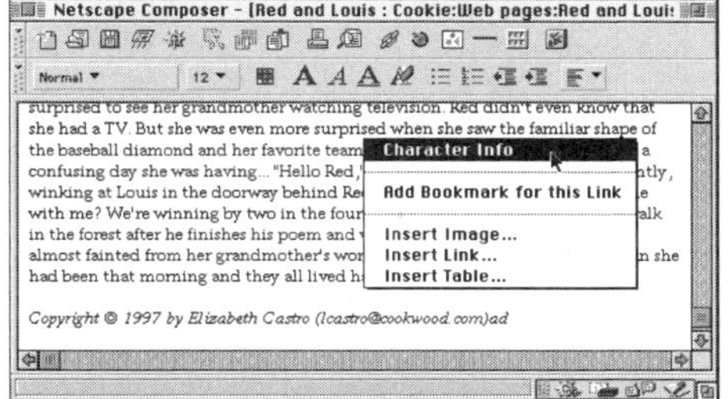

Figure 18.56 *You can also click and hold anywhere in the Composer window until the pop-up menu appears. Then choose Character Info.*

Applying many paragraph features at once

Although it's a bit easier to select the desired paragraph styles from the toolbar or the menu, the Paragraph tab of the Format dialog box lets you apply several paragraph characteristics at once.

To apply several paragraph features at a time:

1. Place the cursor in the paragraph that you wish to modify. You don't need to select anything.
2. Choose Format > Character Info **(Figure 18.54)** to view the Format dialog box.
3. Click the Paragraph tab to see the Paragraph attributes.
4. Choose the desired paragraph style, additional style, list styles, as well as an alignment **(Figure 18.55)**.
5. Click Apply to apply the changes without closing the dialog box. Make changes in the selections and click Apply again until you are satisfied.
6. Click OK (or Close if you've already applied the changes) to close the dialog box. The styles are applied.

✔ Tips

- How do you eliminate styles? Since all paragraphs must have some style, simply apply a different one. The Normal style is closest to none.
- You can also make the Format dialog box appear by clicking and holding anywhere in the Composer window and then choosing Character Info in the pop-up menu **(Figure 18.56)**.

Keeping text on the same line

Composer lets you format text so that it all stays on the same line—no matter what. Although this might be useful to keep headings intact and powerful, keep in mind that part of your text may be hidden if the user's window isn't wide enough to accommodate the line of text.

To keep a long line together:

1. Click in the Composer window where you wish to enter the nonbreaking space **(Figure 18.57)**.
2. Choose Format > Style > Nonbreaking **(Figure 18.58)**. The text will be displayed all on one line **(Figure 18.59)**.

✓ Tips

- Some browsers do not recognize nonbreaking spaces. They will divide words and eliminate the spaces as always.
- You can also format nonbreaking text with the Character tab of the Format dialog box.

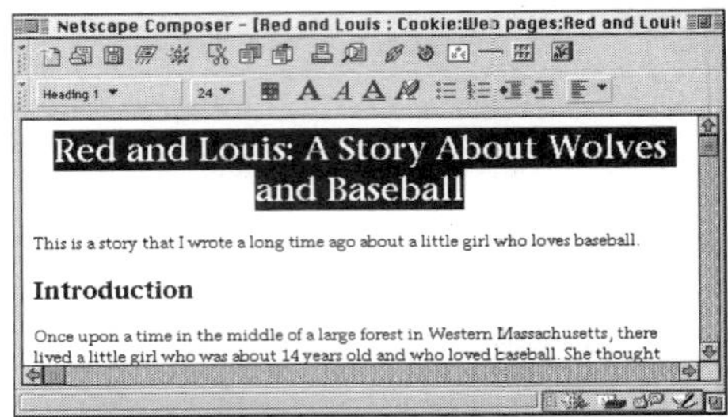

Figure 18.57 *Select the text that you want to display all on the same line.*

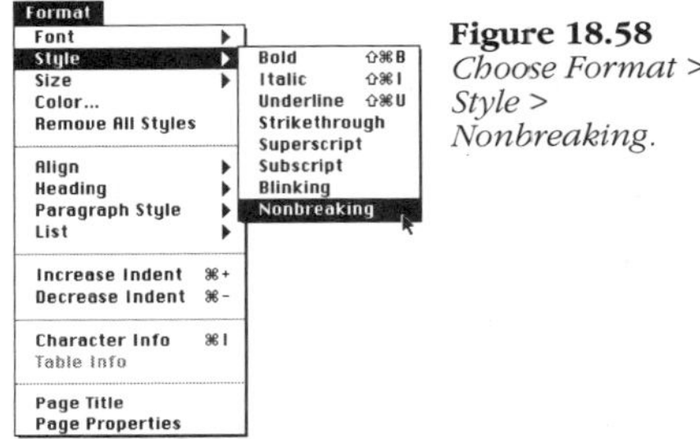

Figure 18.58 *Choose Format > Style > Nonbreaking.*

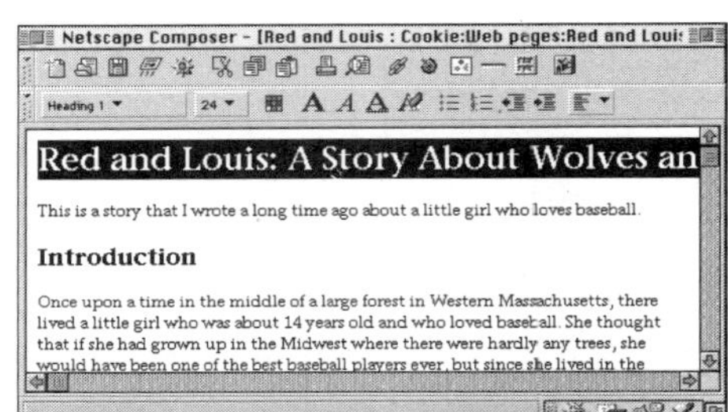

Figure 18.59 *Remember that although you can force a line to display all together on one line, you can't force your user to make the window big enough to read it.*

Adding Images to a Page

19

Perhaps the greatest appeal of the World Wide Web and of HTML documents in particular is that they can contain colorful images. You can insert a photo of your cat on your personal home page, or a representation of your company's logo on your business page. And you can add images to link definitions, making buttons that take your reader to their next destination.

Image formats

Because the Web is accessed by all different kinds of computers, the graphics you use in your Web page must be in a format that each of these operating systems can recognize. The two most widely used formats are JPEG and GIF.

GIF, or Graphics Interchange Format, was developed by CompuServe. LZW, the compression it uses, reduces the size of images with large blocks of the same color—common in computer generated art. In addition, LZW is *lossless* compression. You can compress, uncompress, and recompress the image without any loss in quality.

The JPEG compression scheme is ideal for photographs and other "natural" color images. JPEG compressed images may have millions of colors, and their file size is determined primarily by their image size, not their number of colors.

However, JPEG is *lossy* compression—deciding that the eye cannot distinguish as many colors as are in your original image, it may eliminate them permanently to save space. Uncompressing the image will not restore the lost data.

Inserting an image

Images add interest to your pages. They also make it slower to view. If you add too many images, readers will get frustrated with the download time. If you add too few, they may be bored. Balance is key.

To insert an image:

1. Click in the Composer window where you wish to insert the image **(Figure 19.1)**.
2. Choose Insert > Image **(Figure 19.2)**. The Image tab of the Format dialog box appears.
3. Next to the text box under Image File Name or Location, click Choose File **(Figure 19.3)**.
4. Locate the image that you wish to insert. Click Open. The image's file name appears in the Image tab of the Format dialog box **(Figure 19.4)**.
5. Click OK. The image appears in the Composer window **(Figure 19.5)**.

✔ Tips

- You can drag an image from Navigator (but not from Composer!) or from the Desktop directly to an open Composer window.
- Double click an image to open the Image tab of the Format dialog box. Or select the image and click the Image button on the Composition toolbar.
- By default, Composer copies the image to the folder that contains the Web page *when you save the page.* If you don't want to copy the image, check the Leave image at the original location box in the Image tab of the Format dialog box.

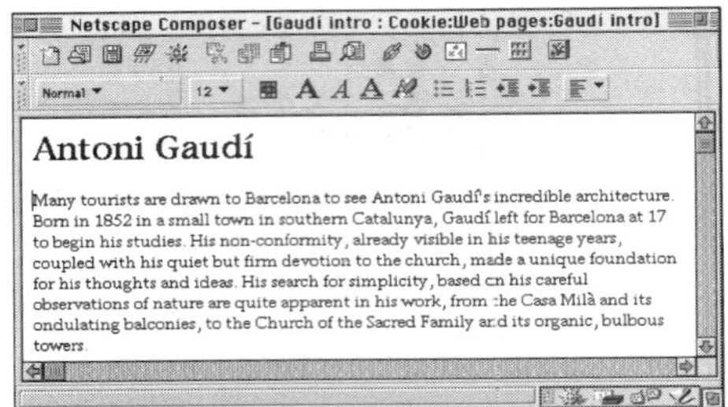

Figure 19.1 *Click in the Composer window where you wish the image to appear.*

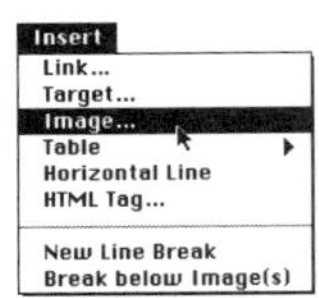

Figure 19.2 *Choose Insert > Image.*

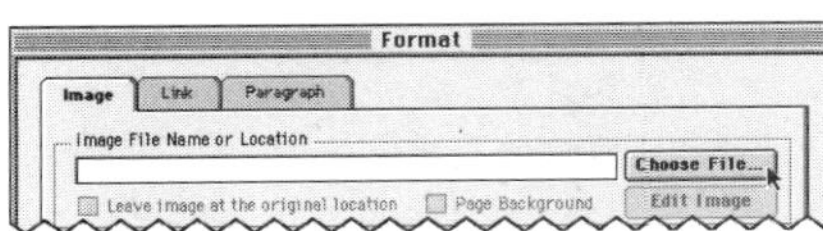

Figure 19.3 *Click Choose File next to the Image File Name text box. (Or enter the file name manually.)*

Figure 19.4 *The file name appears in the Image tab of the Format dialog box. Click OK.*

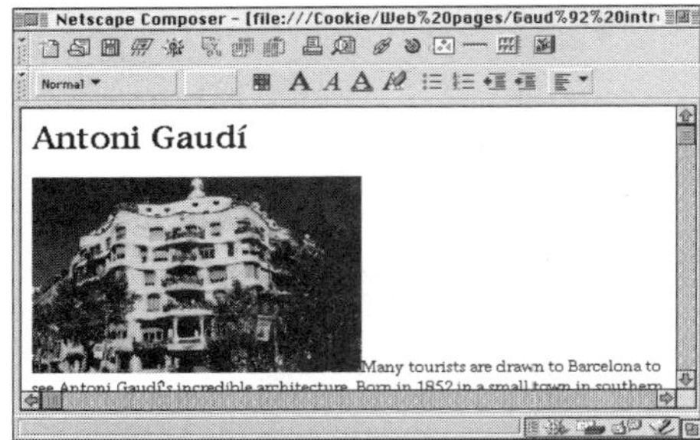

Figure 19.5 *The image appears in the Composer window at the insertion point, displacing text as necessary.*

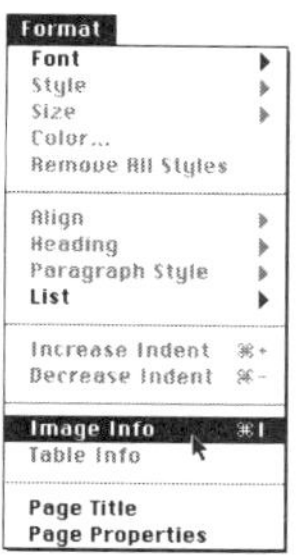

Figure 19.6 *Select the image and then choose Format > Image Info.*

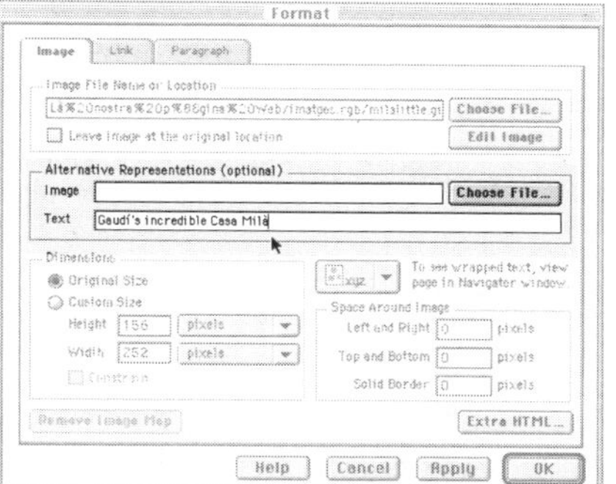

Figure 19.7 *Type the alternate text in the Text box under Alternative Representations.*

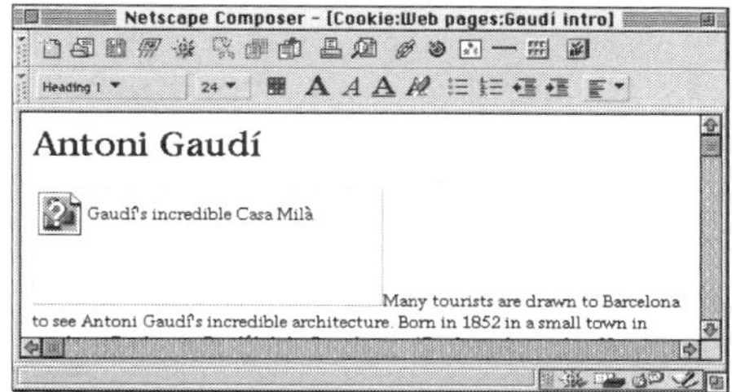

Figure 19.8 *Navigator users who have deactivated the Auto Load Images option and users of non-graphical browsers won't see the images, but will see the alternate text instead.*

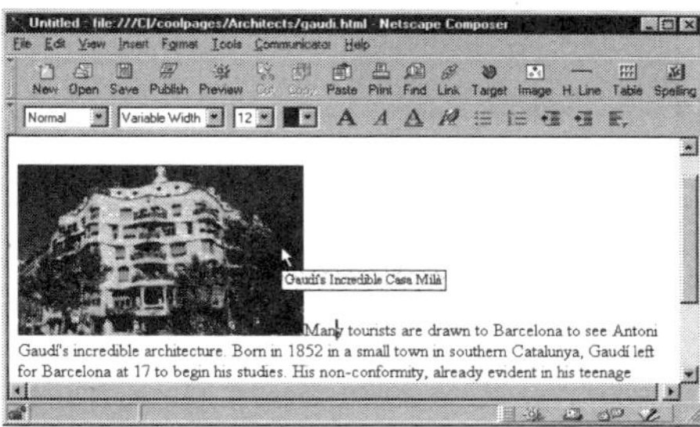

Figure 19.9 *Alternate text shows up as a label for Windows users when they pass the cursor over the image.*

Using alternate text

It's important to remember that not everyone who browses the World Wide Web uses Navigator to do it. Unix users, for example, typically use a program called Lynx, that does not show images at all. And users with a slow modem or computer may disable image viewing to speed up their browsing *(see page 43)*. In order to communicate what the images contain to those users who can't see them on the page, you can use alternate text which appears when the images don't.

To use alternate text:

1. If you are inserting a new image, follow steps 1–4 on page 252. Or select an existing image and choose Format > Image Info **(Figure 19.6)**. The Image tab of the Format dialog box appears.
2. Under Alternative Representations, type the text that should appear when loading an image, when a Windows user passes the cursor over the image, instead of images when these are not loaded, and in text-only browsers **(Figure 19.7)**.
3. Click OK. Alternate text appears when the image is not found **(Fig. 19.8)**.

✔ Tips

- Entice users who disable automatic image loading in order to save time by using *descriptive* alternate text.
- Alternate text is a must with navigational buttons. Otherwise, some users may not be able to navigate your page.
- Windows users see alternate text in the form of a tool tip when they pass the cursor over the image **(Figure 19.9)**.

Using low resolution images

Low resolution images with fewer colors load faster than high resolution images with more colors. You can specify a low resolution version of your image to load immediately while the high resolution is coming in slowly. This way, your reader has the best of both worlds: instant feedback and then, beautiful images.

To use a low resolution image:

1. If you are inserting a new image, follow steps 1–4 on page 252. Or select an existing image and choose Format > Image Info. The Image tab of the Format dialog box appears.
2. In the Image text box under Alternative Representations, type the path and file name of the low resolution version of the image, or click Choose File to locate it on your hard disk **(Figure 19.10)**.
3. Click OK. When a user jumps to your page, the low res version of the image is quickly loaded **(Figure 19.11)** before being replaced by the high resolution image **(Figure 19.12)**.

✔ Tips

- The low resolution image should have the same height and width as the high res image.
- You can create one single low resolution image and use it as the low res image for all the images on your page.

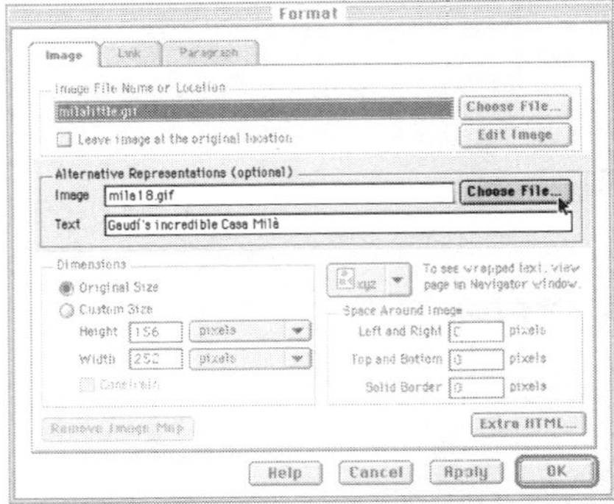

Figure 19.10 *In the Image text box under Alternative Representations, type the file name and path of the low resolution version of your image. Or click Choose File to locate the file on your hard disk.*

Figure 19.11 *When the user jumps to your page, the low resolution version of your image is quickly loaded. It doesn't look great, but it gives an idea of what's to come.*

Figure 19.12 *The high resolution image takes longer to load in, and gradually replaces the low resolution version.*

Image size

If you've wandered a bit around the Internet, you are sure to have experienced The Page From Hell. The designer was so anxious to show you every image he's ever created, that he placed them all on the same page. And no small images either—these are 24-bit color images. You're still on a 14.4 modem, but that's no excuse to make you wait this long to see the page. After a minute or two staring at the progress indicator at the bottom of the browser, you bag, and surf to a friendlier page.

When you construct *your* page, keep it under 30K—including images. It will take your users with 14.4 modems, not to mention those who are still on 9600s, about a second to load each K of data, for a total of 30 seconds. That's about how long you can expect anyone to wait.

If you want to include larger images, you have several options. First, you can use a miniature version, or icon, of the image on your page that links the user—if they so choose—to the full image. Next, you can create a low resolution version of the image that loads almost immediately and allows the user to browse the text areas of your page while the high resolution image is loading *(see page 254)*. Finally, you can interlace the image which also lets the user browse almost immediately as the image gradually comes into focus. If your pages are still very slow, try dividing your images among several pages.

Why the resolution is not so important

Since most monitors display everything at 72 or 96 dpi, there is no reason to save your images with a higher resolution, unless you want your users to be able to download and print your images at the other end. Generally, that's not necessary, and the higher resolution only guarantees longer download times.

Why the number of colors *is* so important

Although many monitors can show thousands or even millions of colors on the screen at once, the vast majority of users are limited to 256 colors. This means that if you create several images and each uses its own set of 256 colors, the images will not appear correctly. Therefore, if you plan to include several images on a single page, you need to be careful to either limit each image to 50 or so colors, or to use the same set of colors for all the images. Many image editing programs can limit colors to the "Netscape-safe palette" for you.

In addition, the fewer the colors in your image, the smaller the file size, and thus the faster the download time. To create a fast, friendly Web page, keep your color count down to a minimum.

Wrapping text around images

Letting text flow around images is an easy way to make a visually interesting page.

To wrap text around images:

1. If you are inserting a new image, follow steps 1–4 on page 252. Or select an existing image and choose Format > Image Info. The Image tab of the Format dialog box appears.
2. Choose the desired text wrap option (either to the right of the image or to the left of the image) from the bottom of the Alignment menu in the bottom right section of the Image tab of the Format dialog box **(Figure 19.13)**.
3. Click OK to close the dialog box. Text wrap is not shown in the Composer window **(Figure 19.14)**.
4. To view the results, choose File > Browse Page or click the Preview button on the Composition toolbar. In the Navigator window, the text is shown wrapped around the image **(Figure 19.15)**.

✔ Tips

- Click and hold down over the image and choose Image Info from the pop-up menu that appears to open the Image tab of the Format dialog box.
- Insert an image *before* (that is, above or to the left of) the text you want to wrap around it.
- You can also regulate the amount of space between the image and the text. For more information, consult *Adding space around an image* on page 258.

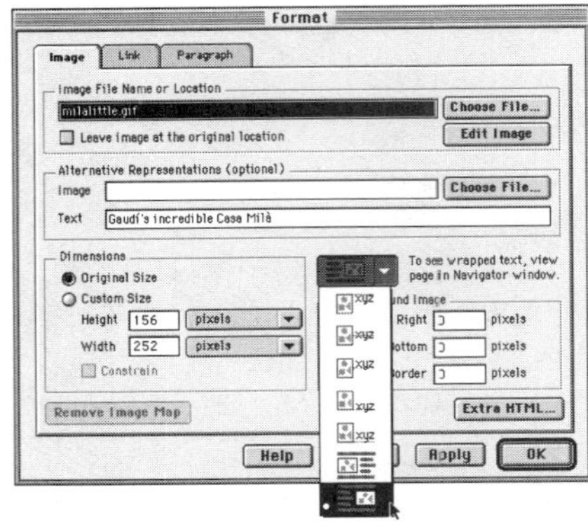

Figure 19.13 *Choose one of the two text wrap options in the Alignment pop-up menu in the Image tab of the Format dialog box.*

Figure 19.14 *Text wrap is not shown in the Composer window.*

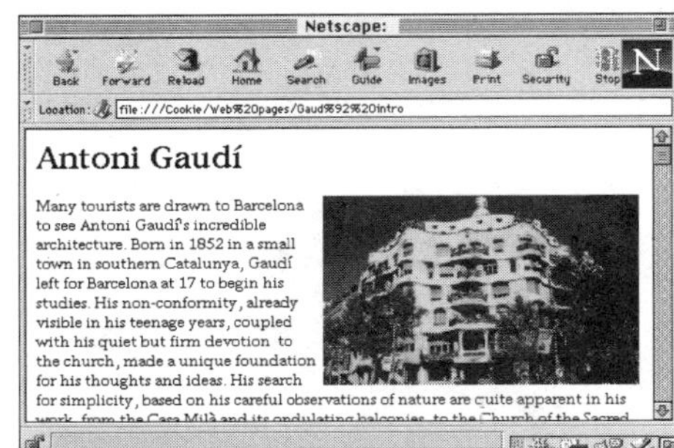

Figure 19.15 *Choose File > Browse Page to view the page in the Navigator window where the text wrap is visible.*

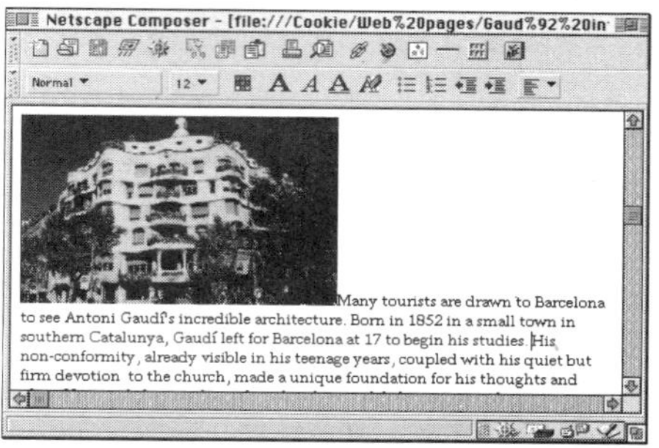

Figure 19.16 *Place the insertion point where you want to stop the text from wrapping. Here, the cursor is in front of "His non-conformity..." in the third line.*

Figure 19.17 *Choose Insert > Break below Image(s).*

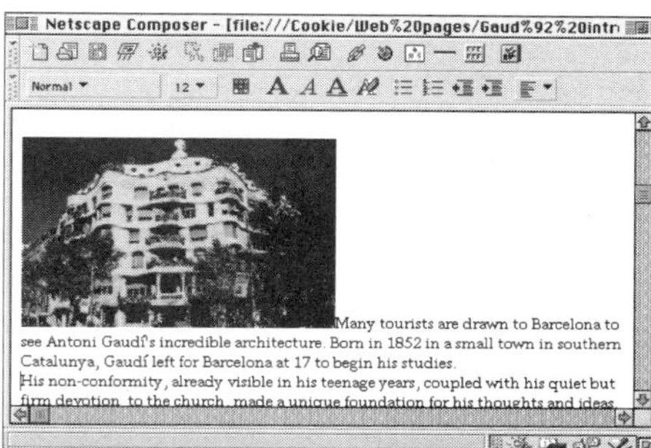

Figure 19.18 *Since text wrap is not visible in the Composer window, it's hard to see how the break affects the final look of the page.*

Figure 19.19 *In the Navigator window, the break makes the text stop flowing until it reaches the end of the image.*

Stopping text wrap

Once you tell Composer to wrap text around an image, it does so until it runs out of text—or encounters a break. You can insert a manual break, as needed.

To stop text wrap:

1. Place the insertion point where you want the text to stop wrapping **(Figure 19.16)**.
2. Choose Insert > Break below Image(s) **(Figure 19.17)**. In the Composer window, you will see a line break **(Figure 19.18)**.
3. Choose File > Browse Page. In the Navigator window, the text will stop flowing at the break and won't begin again until below the image **(Figure 19.19)**.

✔ Tip

- Navigator 3 and 4 for Macintosh have a rather serious bug: they do not properly display a break after images when the text is wrapped to the right of an image. Other browsers do display the break correctly.

Adding space around an image

When you wrap text around images, the image is sometimes squashed or crowded by the text. You can remedy this effect by adding extra space around the image.

To add space around an image:

1. If you are inserting a new image, follow steps 1–4 on page 252. Or select an existing image and choose Format > Image Info. The Image tab of the Format dialog box appears.
2. Enter the amount of space, in pixels, that you wish to leave around the image in the Left and Right and Top and Bottom text boxes in the Space Around Image section **(Figure 19.21)**.
3. Click OK to close the Format dialog box. Although the added space is theoretically visible in the Composer window, you can get a better picture in the browser where the text is wrapped as well.
4. Choose File > Browse Page or click the Preview button on the Composition toolbar. You may be asked to save the page. Click OK to do so. The page is shown as it will appear on the Web **(Figure 19.22)**.

✓ Tip

- Unfortunately, in Composer (or indeed in HTML), there's no way to add space on just one side of an image (e.g., the text side). One solution is to add the space in Photoshop, and then make it transparent.

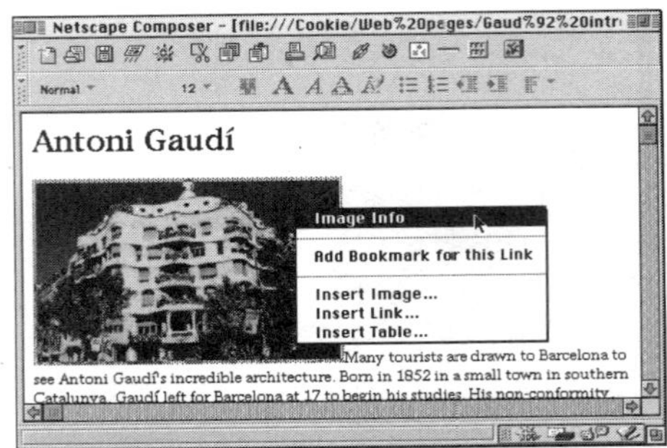

Figure 19.20 *Another way to make the Image tab of the Format dialog box appear is to click and hold down over the image and choose Image Info in the pop-up menu that appears.*

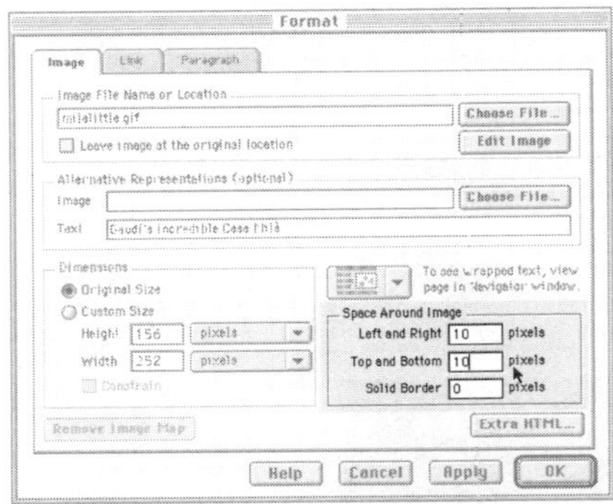

Figure 19.21 *Enter the amount of space, in pixels, that you want to create around the image.*

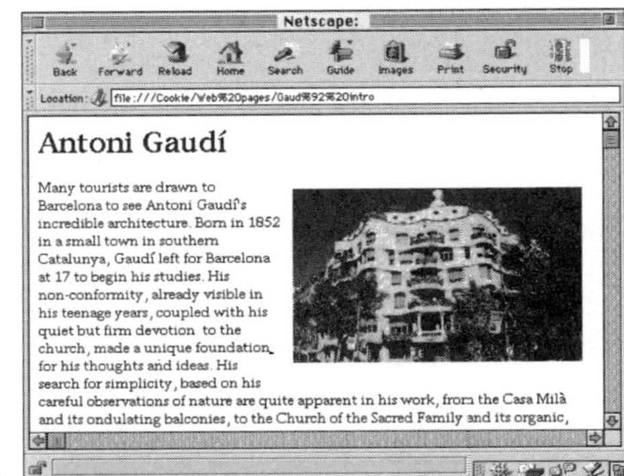

Figure 19.22 *Now the image is not jammed up next to the text. Notice also how space has been added to all sides of the image. Compare this illustration with Figure 19.15 on page 256.*

Figure 19.23 *Double click an image to open the Image tab of the Format dialog box.*

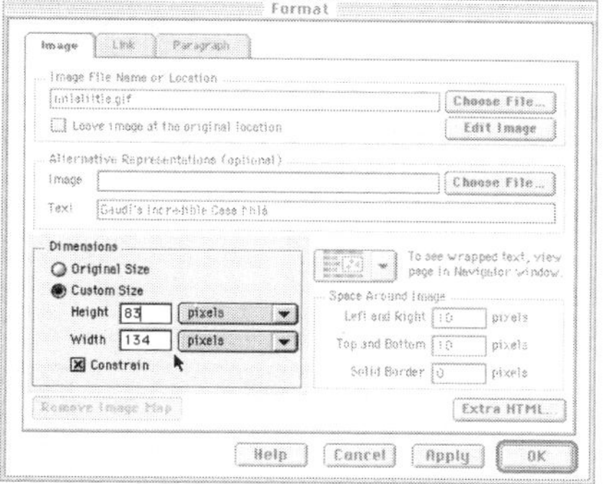

Figure 19.24 *Enter the desired size, in pixels, for the image in the Dimensions area.*

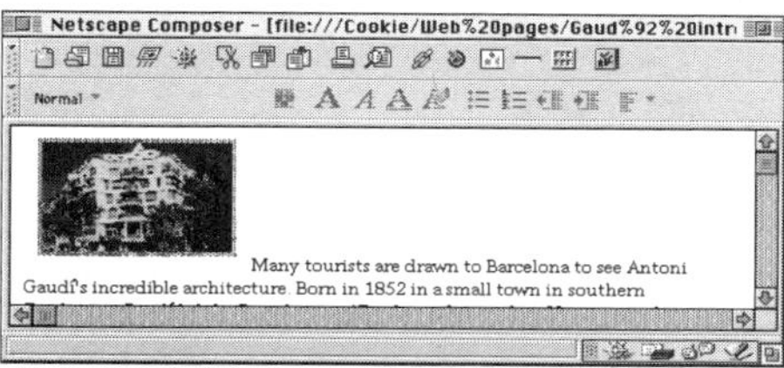

Figure 19.25 *In this example, the image has been reduced to half its size.*

Figure 19.26 *You can distort an image by entering non-proportional dimensions.*

Changing an image's display size

One of the advantages of using Composer is that it automatically includes the size of the image in your Web page, according to the image's real dimensions. This allows the browser to allocate the necessary space for the image as it is downloaded and to display the surrounding text immediately. You can also use the size coordinates to change the display of the image on the page.

To change an image's display size:

1. If you are inserting a new image, follow steps 1–4 on page 252. Or select an existing image and choose Format > Image Info. The Image tab of the Format dialog box appears.
2. Click Custom Size under Dimensions.
3. If desired, check Constrain to maintain the image's original proportions.
4. Enter the desired size for the image in the Dimensions area **(Figure 19.24)**.
5. Click OK (or Close if you've already applied the changes) to close the Format dialog box. The changes are shown immediately in the Composer window **(Figure 19.25)**.

✔ Tips

- To return an image to its original size, click Original Size in the Image tab of the Format dialog box.
- You can distort an image by entering non-proportional dimensions **(Figure 19.26)**.

Creating a border around an image

To set off an image from the surrounding elements on the page, you can create a border around it.

To create a border around an image:

1. If you are inserting a new image, follow steps 1–4 on page 252. Or select an existing image and choose Format > Image Info. The Image tab of the Format dialog box appears.
2. Enter the width of the border, in pixels, in the Solid Border text box in the Space Around Image area **(Figure 19.27)**.
3. If desired, click Apply to apply the changes without closing the dialog box. Adjust the width and click Apply again until you are satisfied with the results.
4. Click OK (or Close if you've already applied the changes) to close the Format dialog box. The border is shown immediately in the Composer window **(Figure 19.28)**.

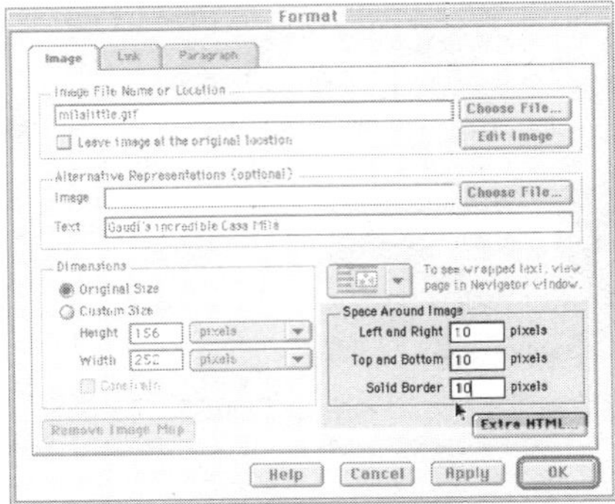

Figure 19.27 *Enter the border thickness in pixels.*

Figure 19.28 *The image appears with a 10-pixel wide border.*

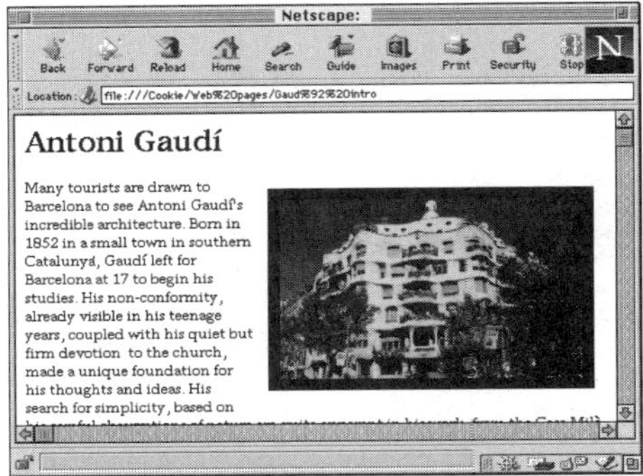

Figure 19.29 *Depending on the image and the background color, the black border may or may not be effective in the Navigator window. Until Composer gives you a way to change the border's color, you may only want to use it around light-colored objects.*

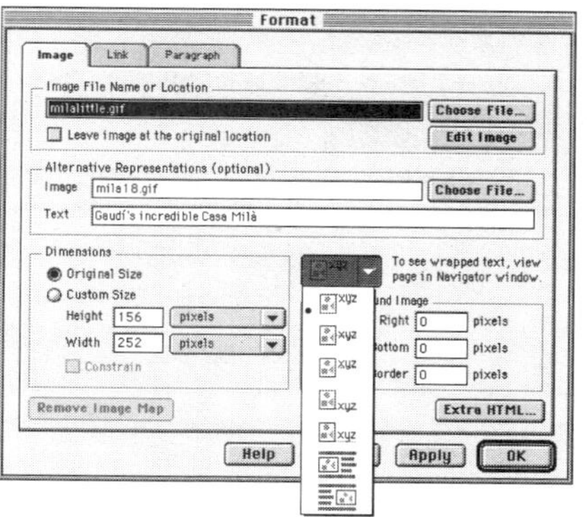

Figure 19.30 *Select an alignment option (one of the first five icons in the Alignment pop-up menu) in the Image tab of the Format dialog box.*

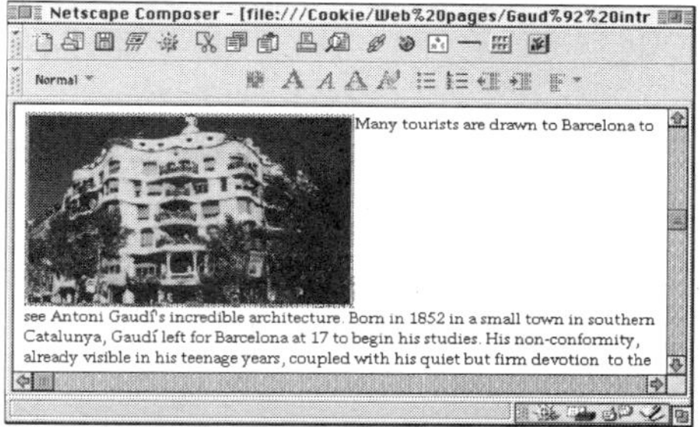

Figure 19.31 *This image is aligned with the top line of text (the first Alignment option, as shown in Figure 19.30). Notice that only the first line of text is affected.*

Figure 19.32 *The middle of this image is aligned with the middle of the first line of text (which is the second Alignment option).*

Aligning images

Images can be aligned in several different ways, depending on what effect you're trying to create. The only thing you can't do is align an image and wrap text around it at the same time.

To align an image:

1. If you are inserting a new image, follow steps 1–4 on page 252. Or select an existing image and choose Format > Image Info. The Image tab of the Format dialog box appears.
2. Choose one of the first five options in the Alignment pop-up menu **(Figure 19.30)**. (The last two are for text wrap—see page 256.)
3. If desired, click Apply to apply the changes without closing the dialog box. Choose a different alignment option and click Apply again until you are satisfied with the results.
4. Click OK (or Close if you've already applied the changes) to close the Format dialog box. The image is immediately aligned in the Composer window **(Figure 19.31)**.

✓ Tips

- The alignment option you choose only affects the first line of text.
- If you have several images on the same line, you can align them in different ways.
- For more information about wrapping text around images (using the last two icons in the Alignment section), consult *Wrapping text around images* on page 256.

Adding a horizontal line

Horizontal lines are amazingly useful for dividing Web pages into intelligible chunks of information. Composer lets you control the size, width, and shading of horizontal lines.

To add a horizontal line:

1. Click in the Composer window where you wish to insert the horizontal line **(Figure 19.33)**.
2. Choose Insert > Horizontal Line **(Figure 19.34)**. The default style line is inserted **(Figure 19.35)**.
3. If desired, change the line as described on page 263.

✔ Tips

- You can also insert a new horizontal line by clicking the Insert Horizontal Line button on the Composition toolbar.
- Eliminate a horizontal line by selecting it and pressing Backspace.

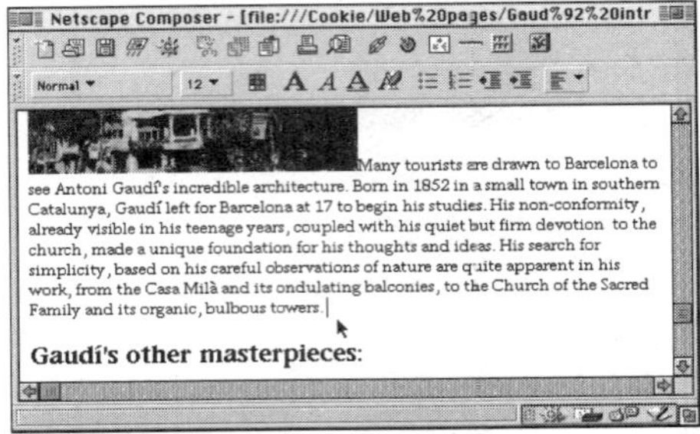

Figure 19.33 *Click in the Composer window where you wish the line to appear.*

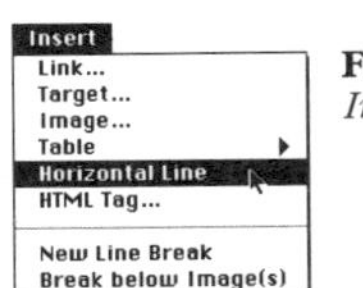

Figure 19.34 *Choose Insert > Horizontal Line.*

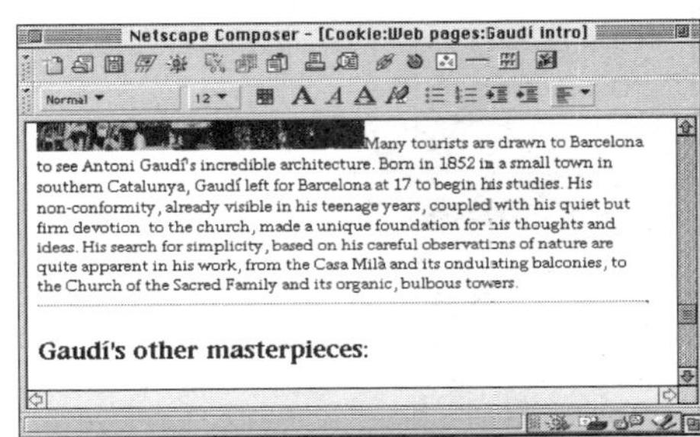

Figure 19.35 *The default horizontal line is 2 pixels high, 100% as wide as the window, and uses 3-D shading (at least in Netscape's Navigator window).*

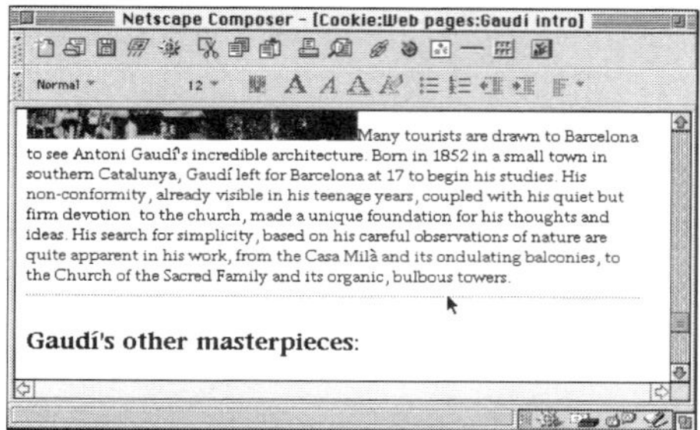

Figure 19.36 *Click the line to select it. (It's hard to tell when you have selected. You'll know you've done it right if you can complete step 2.)*

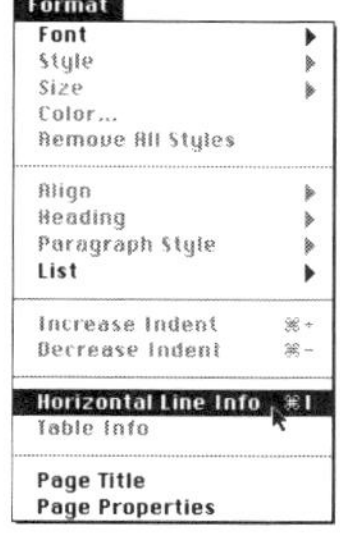

Figure 19.37 *Choose Format > Horizontal Line Info.*

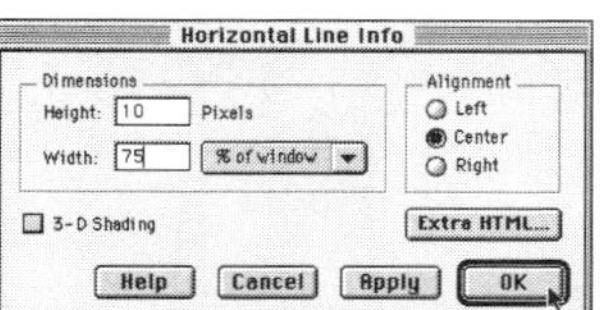

Figure 19.38 *Choose the desired options for the horizontal line and click OK.*

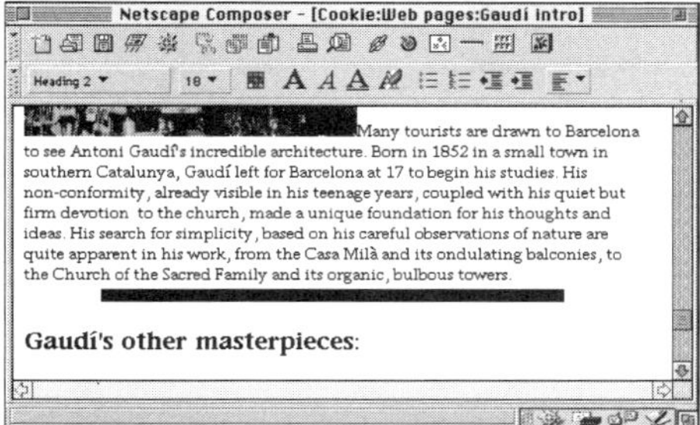

Figure 19.39 *This line is 10 pixels high, 75% of the width of the window, and centered. It does not use 3-D shading.*

Changing a horizontal line

Composer has added several options to its horizontal lines. You can adjust a line's thickness (height), width (both as a percentage of the window width and in absolute pixels), alignment, and shading.

To change a horizontal line:

1. Select the line **(Figure 19.36)** that you want to change.
2. Choose Format > Horizontal Line Info **(Figure 19.37)**. The Horizontal Line Info box appears.
3. Choose a height (thickness), in pixels, for the line **(Figure 19.38)**.
4. Enter a number for the width of the line, either as a percentage of the total window size, or in absolute terms, in pixels.
5. If you've chosen a line width that is narrower than the window width, choose an alignment.
6. If desired, choose 3-D shading for the line or leave it in black and white.
7. Click OK to save the changes. The results are shown in the Composer window **(Figure 19.39)**.

✔ Tip

- There are several other ways to open the Horizontal Line Info dialog box: double click a horizontal line, select it and click the Horizontal Line button on the Composition toolbar, or click and hold it and choose Horizontal Line Info in the pop-up menu.

Choosing custom colors

You can set your own default colors for text, new links, active links, and visited links. Although it's rather in vogue to use garish colors on the Web, keep in mind that it also makes the page hard to read.

To choose a page's colors:

1. Choose Format > Page Properties **(Figure 19.40)**. The Page Properties dialog box appears.
2. Click the Colors and Background tab to make it active **(Figure 19.41)**.
3. Click Use Custom Colors.
4. Click a color box next to each type of text that you want to change.
5. Choose the desired color in the Color Picker dialog box that appears **(Figure 19.42)**.
6. Repeat steps 4–5 for each color.
7. Click OK.

✓ Tips

- Choose preset combinations of colors in the pop-up menu. Remove your color choices by choosing Netscape Default Colors in that menu.
- Click Apply these settings to all new blank pages to use these same colors in all the pages you create from now on.
- If you never touched the colors, no color settings would be saved with your page and the user might change them. To ensure that the default color settings are saved with your page even if you don't change the colors, click the Use Custom Colors radio button (and then leave the colors alone if you like).

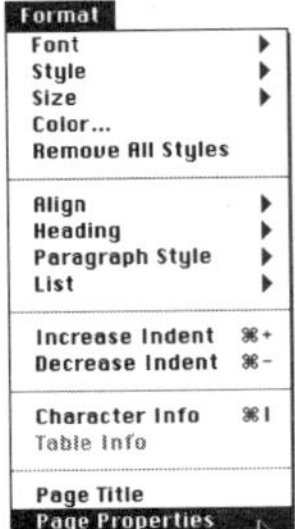

Figure 19.40 *Choose Format > Page Properties.*

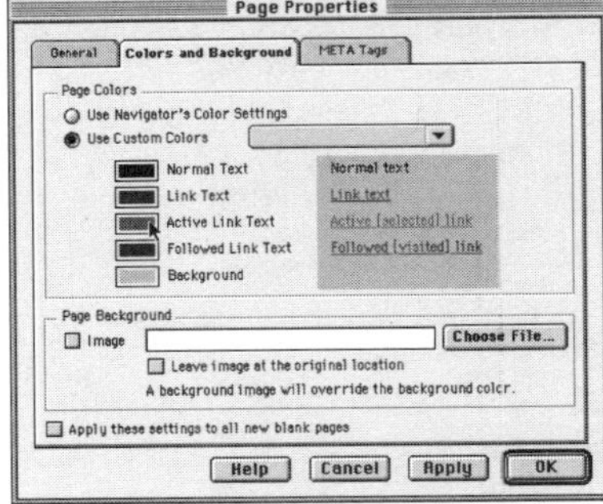

Figure 19.41 *Click a color next to a text element to change it.*

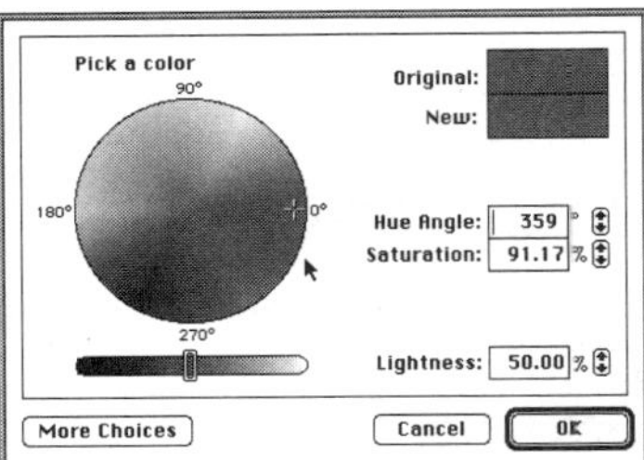

Figure 19.42 *Choose the desired color in the Color Picker dialog box.*

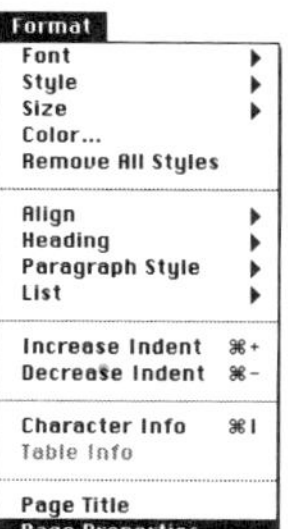

Figure 19.43 *Choose Format > Page Properties.*

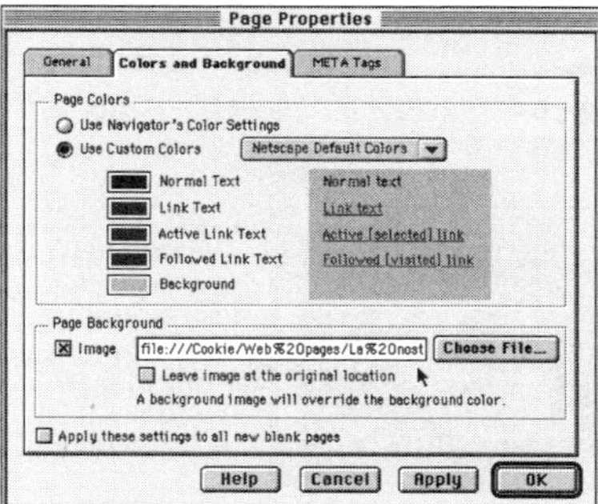

Figure 19.44 *Click Choose File next to the Image text box in the Page Background section. Choose a background image from your hard disk.*

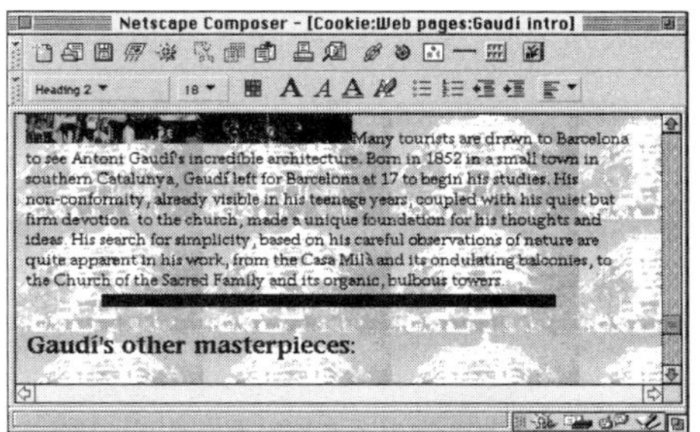

Figure 19.45 *It's difficult to choose a background that doesn't distract from your text.*

Adding a background image

You can also choose a color or an image for the background.

To choose an image for the background:

1. Choose Format > Page Properties **(Figure 19.43)**. The Page Properties dialog box appears.
2. Click the Colors and Background tab to make it active, if necessary.
3. In the Page Background section, check Image and then click Choose File to choose a background image **(Figure 19.44)**.
4. Composer automatically copies the chosen image to the same directory as the Web page when you save. If you don't wish to save a copy of the image in that directory, check the Leave image at the original location box.
5. Click OK to close the dialog box. The changes are applied **(Figure 19.45)**.

✓ Tips

- If the image is smaller than the page, it will be tiled to fill the background.
- If you choose a background color *(see page 264)* before choosing a background image, both will be used.

Editing images

Often it becomes necessary to modify or adapt an image to better suit the page. You can quickly open the image in an editing program from within Composer.

To edit images:

1. Select the image and choose Format > Image Info. The Image tab of the Format dialog box appears.
2. Click Edit Image at the top of the dialog box **(Figure 19.46)**. The image is opened in the editing program of your choice **(Figure 19.47)**.
3. Make the necessary changes and then choose File > Save.

To specify the image editing program:

1. Choose Edit > Preferences and then click Composer in the Category list, if necessary.
2. In the External Editors section, click Choose next to Image **(Fig. 19.48)**.
3. Locate the desired editing image program on your hard disk and click Open **(Figure 19.49)**. The path to the program will be listed next to the Image option at the bottom of the Composer panel of the Preferences dialog box.

✔ Tip

- If you have not already chosen an image editing program upon clicking Edit image, Composer will give you a chance to locate one.

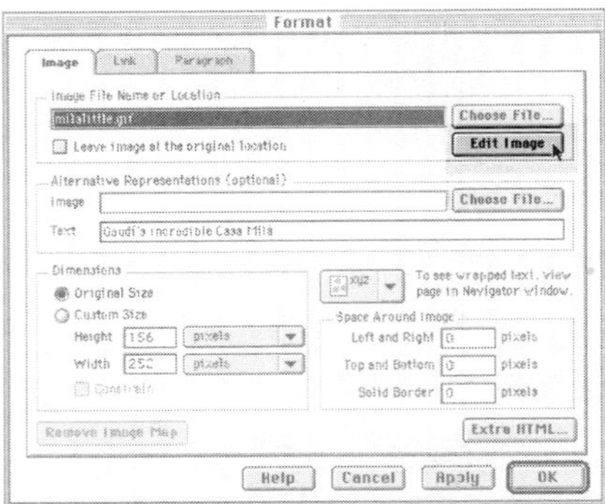

Figure 19.46 *Click Edit Image in the Image tab of the Format dialog box.*

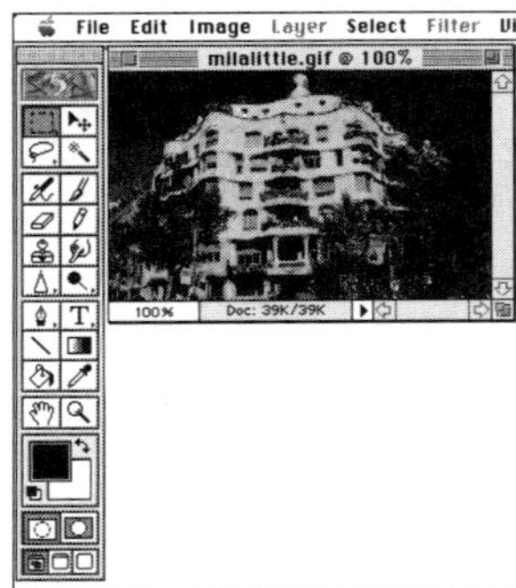

Figure 19.47 *The image is opened in the chosen image editing program, Adobe Photoshop, in this case.*

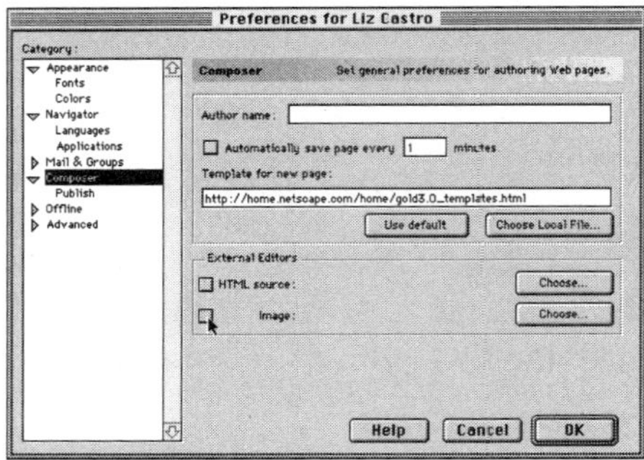

Figure 19.48 *Click Image under External Editors to designate the image editing program that you wish to use.*

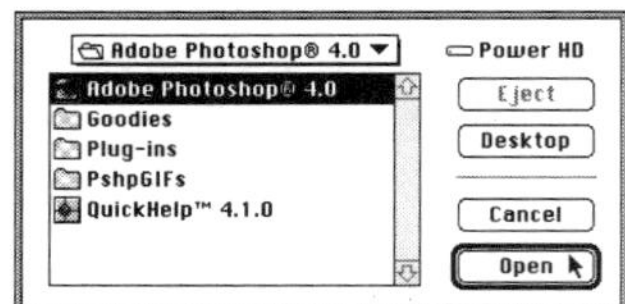

Figure 19.49 *Click Image under External Editors to designate the image editing program that you wish to use.*

Creating Links in a Page

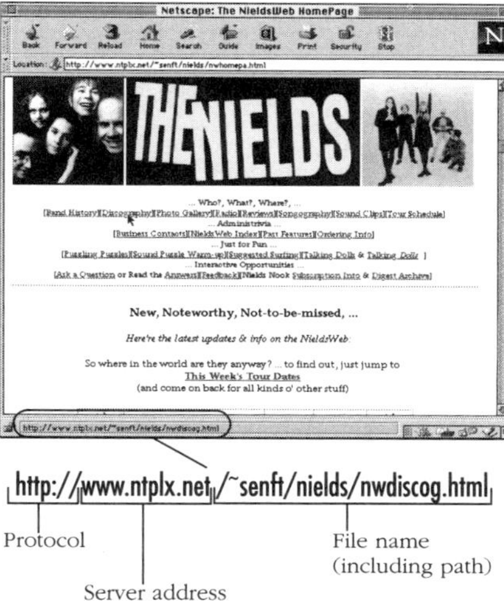

Figure 20.1 *Place the pointer over a link and its URL becomes visible in the status bar at the bottom of the window. If the Location bar is visible, it will display the URL of the page you're* currently *viewing.*

As discussed in Chapter 3, *Surfing the Web*, a Web page can contain dynamic connections with other Web pages, enabling users to jump from one page to another in search of information. These connections are called *links*.

A link can bring the user to the top of a Web page or to a specific section of that page, to an FTP or Gopher site, to a newsgroup, or even to an e-mail address. The Web page designer decides where the link will go.

Links and URLs

Links are made out of URLs, or *Uniform Resource Locators*. The URL is an address that gives the exact location on the Internet of a link's destination. A URL is comprised of a protocol, a server name, and a file name, including the path. The protocol defines what kind of connection will be made (Web, FTP, Gopher, Mail, etc.). The server name is the official name, or IP address, of the server that contains the desired file. The file name is the exact name, including the path indicating its location on the server, of the desired file.

Every single piece of information on the Internet—every page, every image, every file—has a unique URL. Thus, when a user clicks a link, Navigator knows exactly where to go to find the information and display it.

In addition to the URL, a link has *display text*, that is, the text that will be underlined and in blue (in most cases) and that indicates the content of the link to the user.

Copying a link from another source

The pages you find on the Web already contain many interesting links, to other pages, FTP and Gopher sites, e-mail addresses, and discussion groups. You may also find good links in e-mail you receive or in news postings. Or you may wish to include links from your Bookmarks collection. You can copy any link you find and insert it on your own page.

To copy a link from another source:

1. Open the page you are designing in the Composer window **(Fig. 20.2)**.
2. Open the Navigator, Messenger, Collabra, or Bookmarks window and the document that contains the link you wish to copy **(Figure 20.3)**.
3. Organize the two windows on your screen so that the link is visible in the source window and a piece of the Composer window is also visible.
4. Click the link and drag it to the Composer window **(Figure 20.4)**.
5. Click the Composer window to make it active. The link is added at the insertion point **(Figure 20.5)**. The display text is the same as it was on the original page.
6. If desired, select the display text and change it to something more descriptive or specific **(Figure 20.6)**.

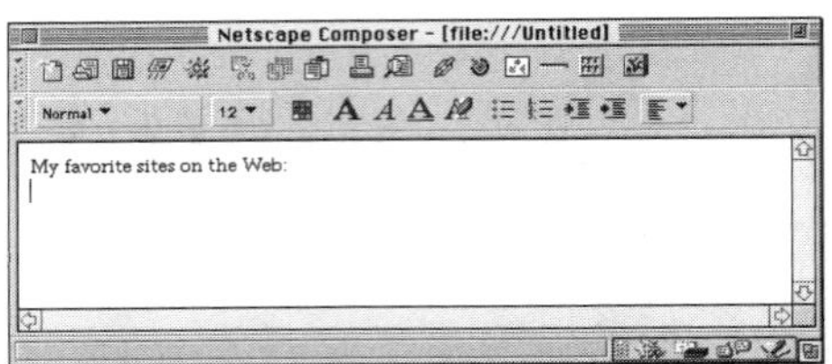

Figure 20.2 *Open the page you are designing in the Composer window.*

Figure 20.3 *In the Navigator window, navigate to the page that has the link you want to copy.*

Figure 20.4 *Drag the link from the Navigator window to the Composer window.*

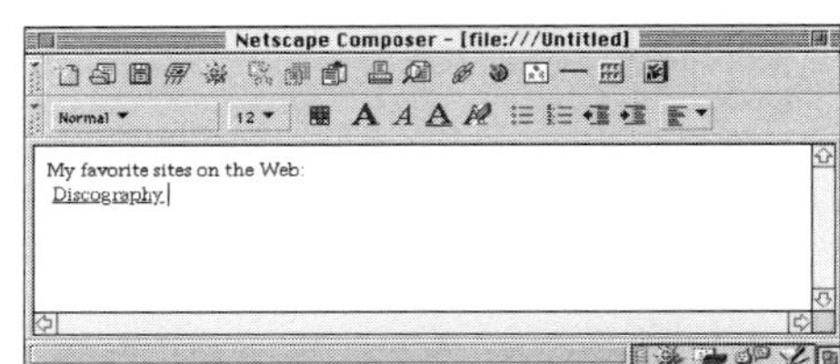

Figure 20.5 *The link is added to the page in the Composer window, with the same display text it had on the original page.*

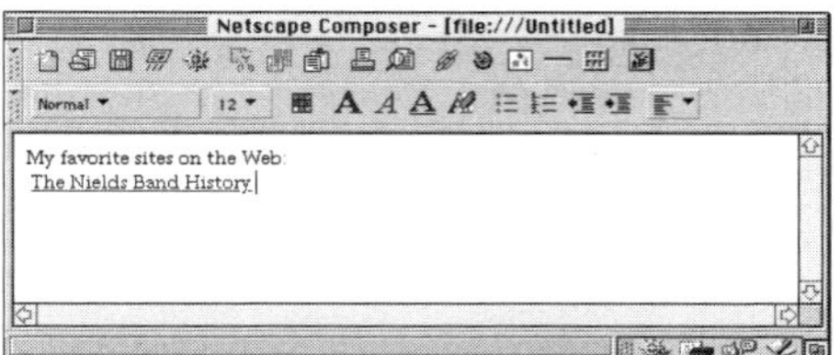

Figure 20.6 *Select the link and type over it to change the display text to something more intelligible, if necessary. Sometimes, in order to maintain the link information, it's necessary to select only a part of the text, type the new text, and then delete the remaining old text.*

Figure 20.7 *To copy a link of the page you're currently browsing and not a link it contains, drag the page proxy icon (at the left of the Location text box) to the Composer window.*

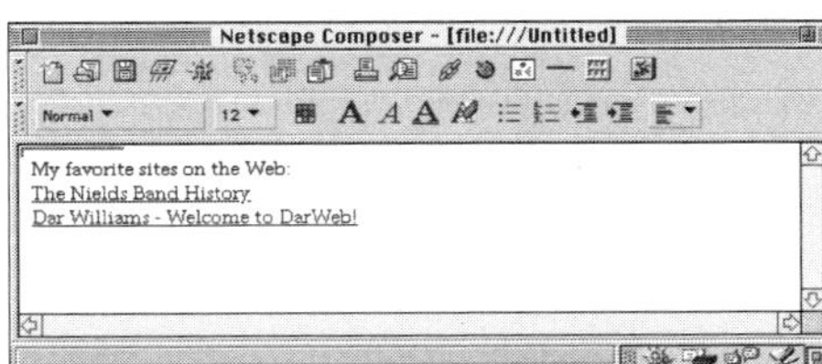

Figure 20.8 *When you use the page proxy icon, the title of the page you're browsing is used as display text for the link.*

✔ Tips

- To insert a link to the *current* page showing in the browser, whether it be a remote page on another server or a local file on your hard disk, drag the page proxy icon at the left of the Location text box to the desired spot in the Composer window **(Figures 20.7 and 20.8)**.
- You can also drag a page from the Desktop to the Composer window to create a link to the page. Keep in mind that the URL used is an absolute address. That is, it references the file on your hard disk and will need to be changed once you publish the page on a remote server.
- If the Composer window isn't hidden by the document that contains the link, you'll be able to see the insertion point and choose where you want to "drop" the copied link.

Creating a link manually

If the link doesn't already exist on another page or if you want to create a link without browsing the page (perhaps you don't want to open your Internet connection), you can type the link's URL manually.

To create a link manually:

1. Click in the Composer window where you want the link to appear.
2. Choose Insert > Link **(Figure 20.9)**. The Link tab of the Format dialog box appears.
3. Type the display text in the Linked Text box **(Figure 20.10)**.
4. Type or copy the URL for the link in the Link To box. If the link is to a local page on your hard disk, click Choose File and locate the desired page.
5. Click OK. The link appears in the Composer window **(Figure 20.11)**.

If the display text already exists and you simply want to add a link to it, there is an easier way.

To create a link manually from existing text:

1. Select the text that you want to make a link out of **(Figure 20.12)**.
2. Choose Insert > Link. The Link tab of the Format dialog box appears with the display text automatically inserted **(Figure 20.13)**.
3. Type the URL for the link or click Choose File if the link is to a local file on your hard disk **(Figure 20.14)**.
4. Click OK. The selected text is now a link **(Figure 20.15)**.

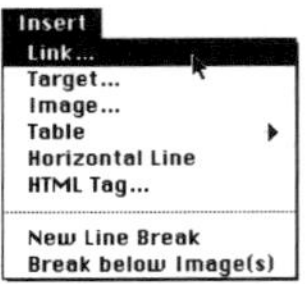

Figure 20.9 *Click in the Composer window where you want the link to appear and choose Insert > Link.*

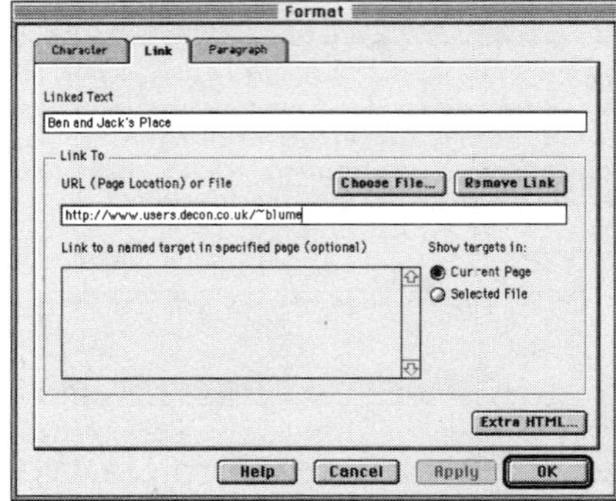

Figure 20.10 *Type the display text in the Linked Text box and the URL for the link in the Link To text box. Then click OK.*

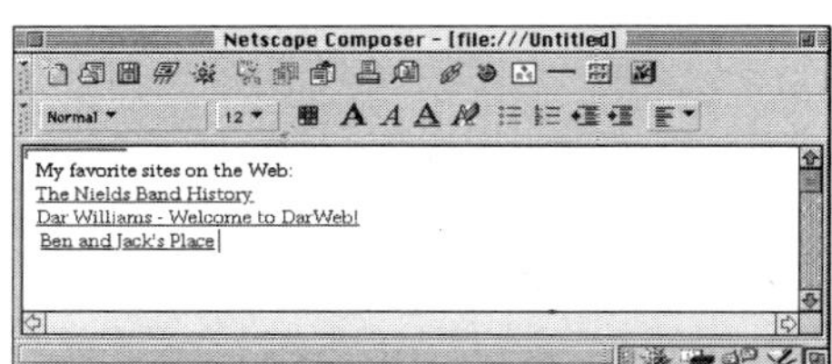

Figure 20.11 *The link appears in the Composer window.*

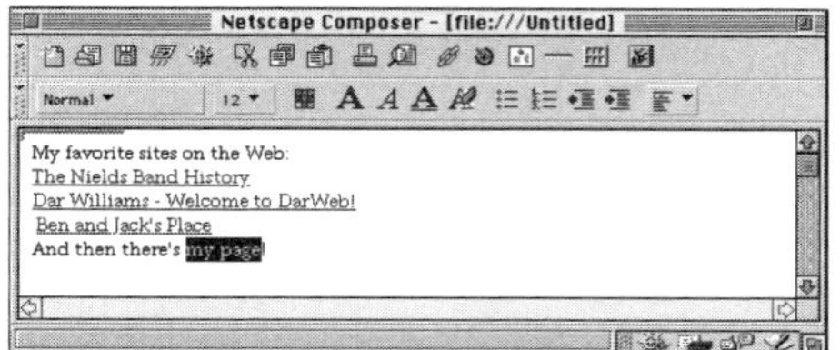

Figure 20.12 *Select the desired text.*

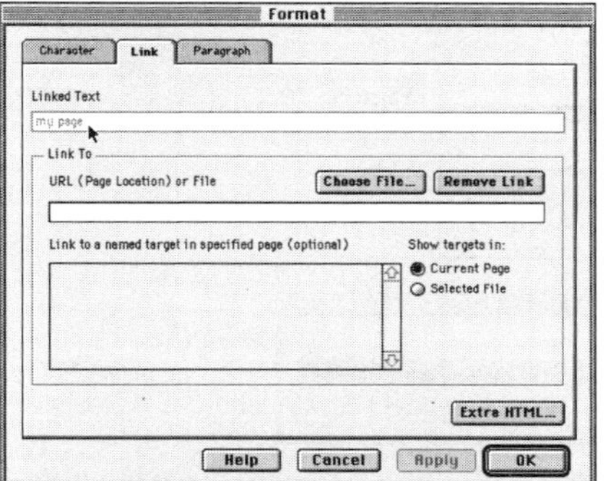

Figure 20.13 *The selected text is automatically entered as display text, and cannot be modified in this dialog box (though you can change it on the page itself).*

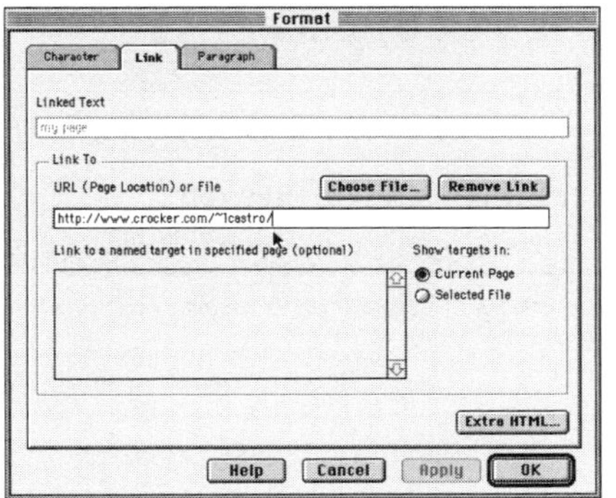

Figure 20.14 *Type or copy the URL for the link.*

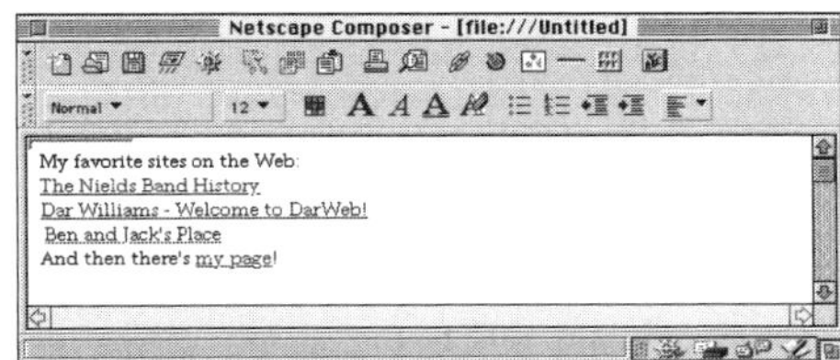

Figure 20.15 *The selected text is converted into a link.*

✔ Tips

- You can insert any kind of URL in the Link To box, including URLs for Web pages, FTP or Gopher sites, e-mail addresses, and newsgroups or newsgroup postings. Links to Web sites should be in the form: **http://www.site.com/path/page.html**. Links to FTP sites should resemble **ftp://ftp.site.com/path/**. Links to Gopher sites should look like **gopher://gophersite.edu/path/**. The format for links to e-mail addresses is **mailto:name@site.com**. The format for links to newsgroups is **news:newsgroup.name**.
- If you don't type any display text in the Linked Text box, Composer uses the URL address as display text.
- You can also click the Link icon on the Composition toolbar to insert a link at the insertion point.
- To avoid typos, you can copy a URL from an existing link in the Navigator window and then paste it into the Link tab of the Format dialog box.

Creating a target

The simplest kind of link brings the user to the *top* of a Web page. If you want a link to bring the user to a *specific part* of the page, you have to create a target and then point the link at that target.

To create a target:

1. Select the text in the Composer window that you want to appear at the top of the Navigator window when the user clicks the link **(Figure 20.16)**. This is the *target.*
2. Choose Insert > Target **(Fig. 20.17)**. The Target dialog box appears.
3. The text box automatically contains the text you selected in step 1. Either accept that word or type another that identifies this section of the Web page you are designing, and click OK **(Figure 20.18)**.
4. A small target icon appears next to the selected text **(Figure 20.19)**. You can now create a link that connects to this target.

✔ Tips

- To create a link that points to the target, consult *Linking to a target on the same page* on page 273 or *Linking to a target on a different page* on page 274.
- The target icon is not visible when the page is viewed in a browser.
- You can also insert a target by clicking the Target button on the Composition toolbar.

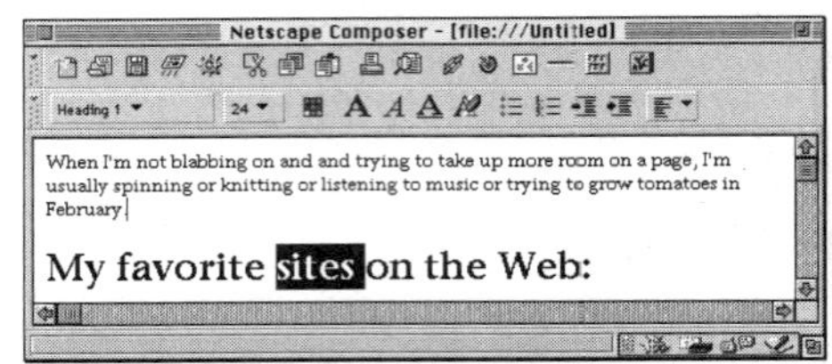

Figure 20.16 *Click in the area that should appear at the top of the page when the user clicks the targeted link.*

Figure 20.17 *Choose Insert > Target.*

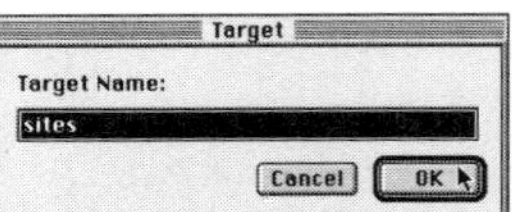

Figure 20.18 *Any text selected at the beginning is automatically entered in the Target dialog box. You may accept this text as the target name or enter your own. The target's name does not affect the Web page in any way.*

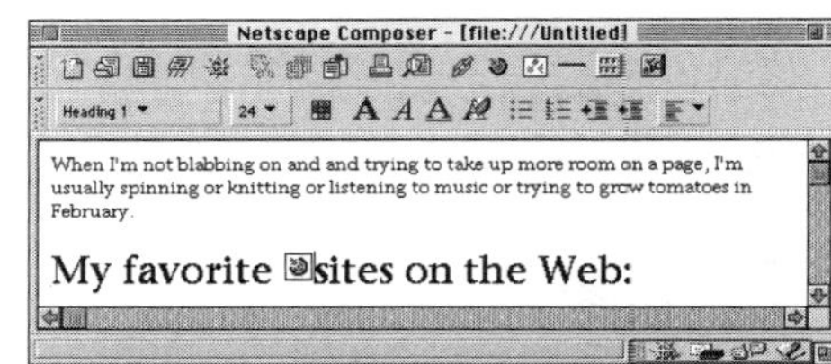

Figure 20.19 *A target icon is inserted next to the selected text.*

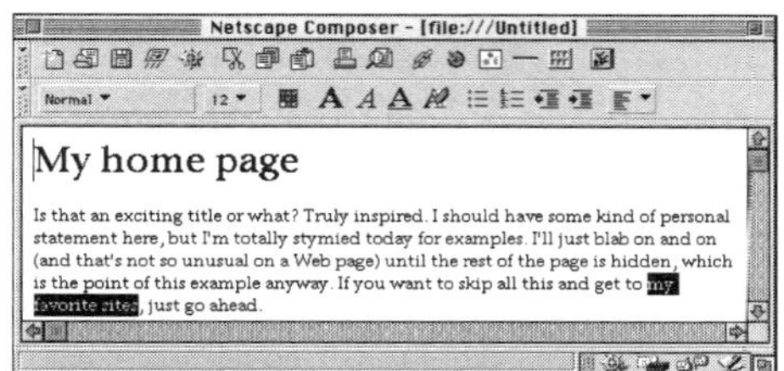

Figure 20.20 *Select the text that you want to convert into a link (or click where you wish to insert a link).*

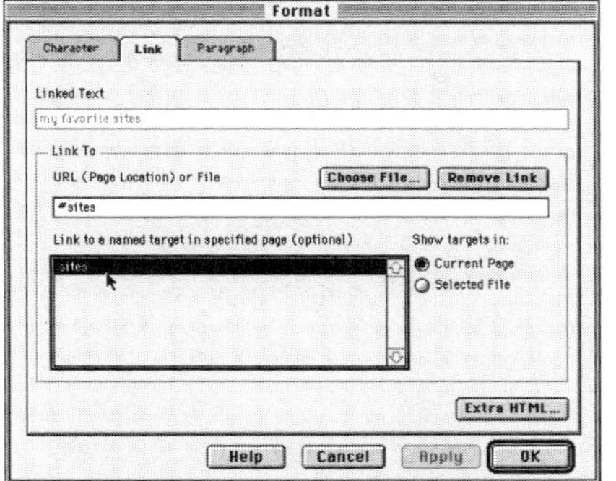

Figure 20.21 *In the Link tab of the Format dialog box, click Current Page and then select the desired target for the link in the list.*

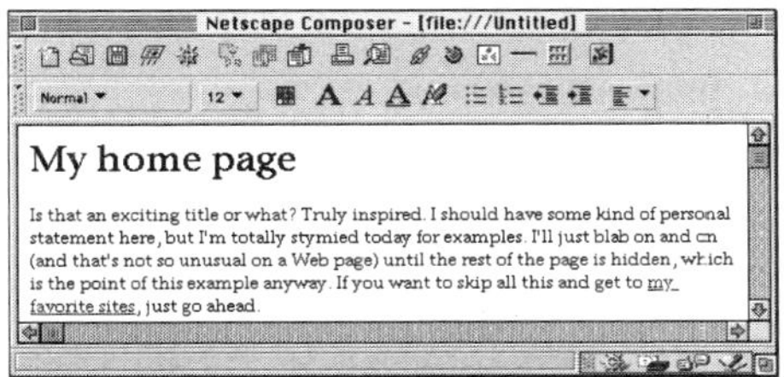

Figure 20.22 *The targeted link is created.*

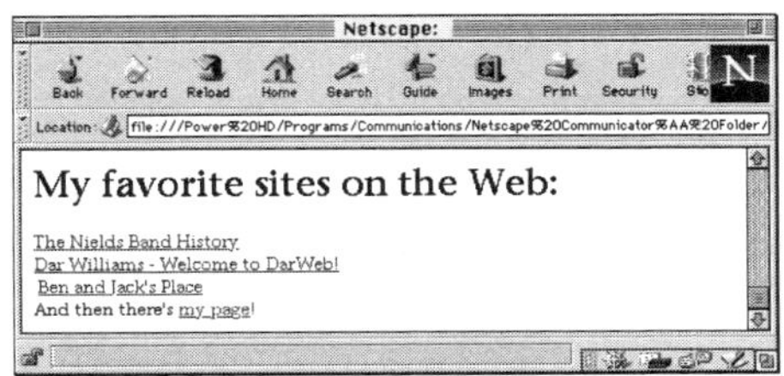

Figure 20.23 *When the user clicks the targeted link, the corresponding section of the page is displayed at the top of the browser.*

Linking to a target on the same page

If you have a particularly long Web page, you can create a kind of table of contents at the top of the page. Then use targets to set up each entry as a link to the section farther down on the page.

To create a link to a target on the same page:

1. Click in the Composer window where you want to create the link. If desired, select the text you want to convert into display text for the link **(Figure 20.20)**.
2. Choose Insert > Link. The Link tab of the Format dialog box appears.
3. If necessary, type the display text in the Linked Text area.
4. Choose the desired target in the scroll list in the Link To area. The target name appears, preceded by a pound sign (#), in the text box **(Fig. 20.21)**.
5. Click OK. The link appears in the Composer window **(Figure 20.22)**.

✔ Tips

- You can also access the Link tab of the Format dialog box by clicking the Link button on the Composition toolbar.
- If you select text before choosing the Link command, the selected text is automatically entered as display text.

Linking to a target on a different page

Once you've created a target in one of your Web pages, you can create a link to it. The link can be on the same page (as in a table of contents) or from another page. Since you can't create targets in e-mail addresses, FTP or Gopher sites, or newsgroups or postings, a link to a target must be to a Web page.

To create a link to a target on a different page:

1. Click in the Composer window where you want to create the link **(Figure 20.24)**. If desired, select the text you want to convert into display text for the link.
2. Choose Insert > Link. The Link tab of the Format dialog box appears **(Figure 20.25)**.
3. Enter the URL for the desired link.
4. Click Selected File under Show targets in. The targets are listed in the box at left **(Figure 20.26)**.
5. Select the desired target. The target's name is appended to the URL, together with a pound sign (#).
6. Click OK to save the changes.

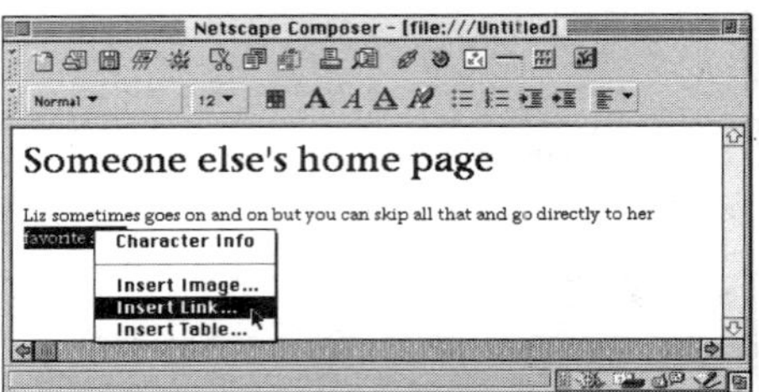

Figure 20.24 *Select the text that you want to convert into a targeted link. Either click and hold and choose Insert Link (as shown here), or choose Insert > Link.*

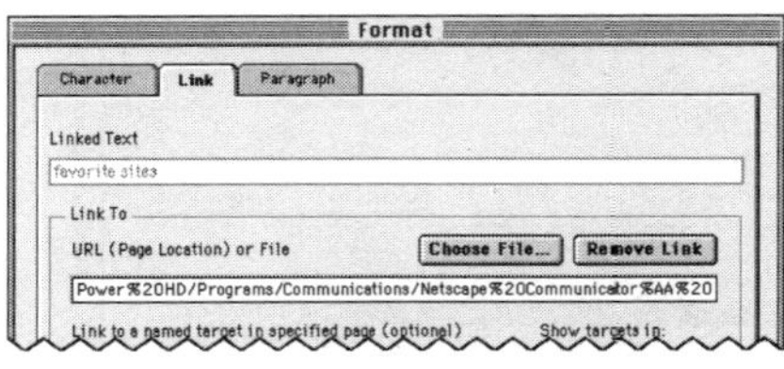

Figure 20.25 *Type the URL of the link page or click Choose File to select a link page on your hard disk.*

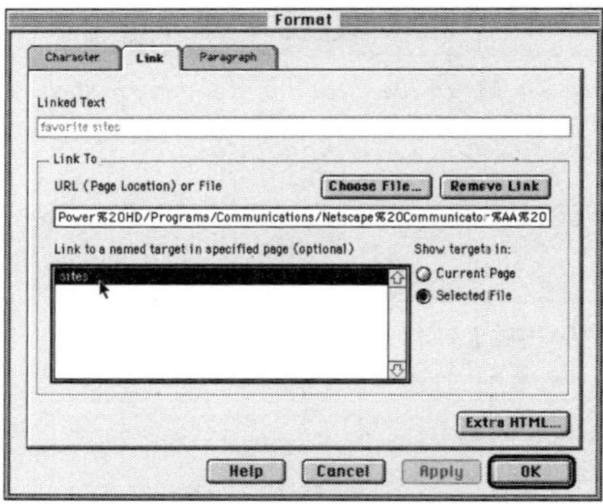

Figure 20.26 *Click Selected File under Show targets in. Then select a target from the list. When you choose a target, its name is appended to the URL, separated by a # sign.*

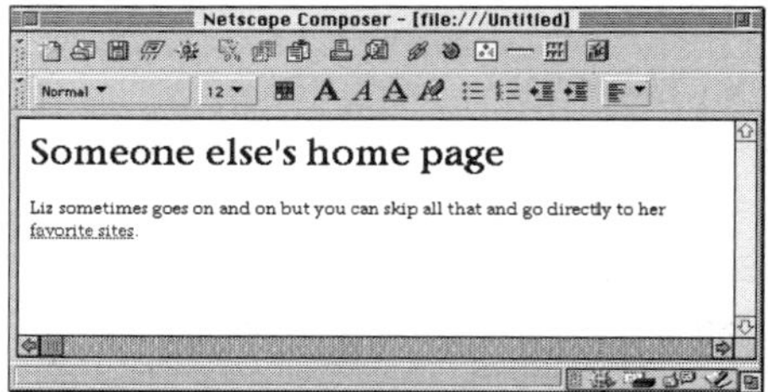

Figure 20.27 *The targeted link is created. When the user clicks the targeted link, the corresponding section of the page is displayed (Figure 20.23).*

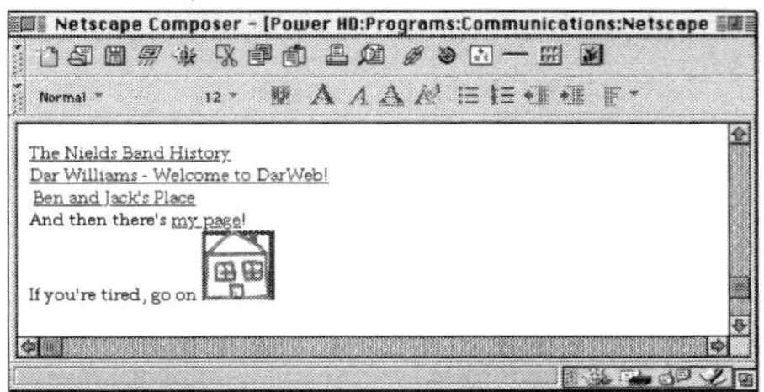

Figure 20.28 *Add an image to the page and select it.*

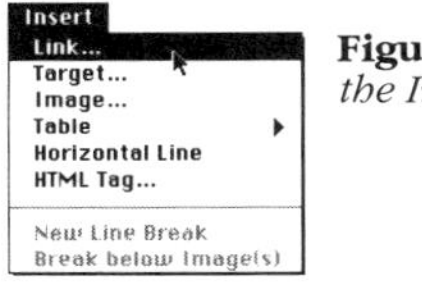

Figure 20.29 *Choose Link in the Insert menu.*

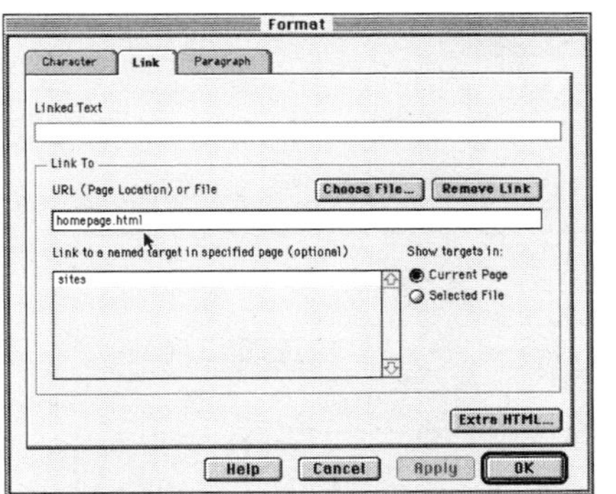

Figure 20.30 *Type or copy the URL in the Link To text area. Choose a target if desired.*

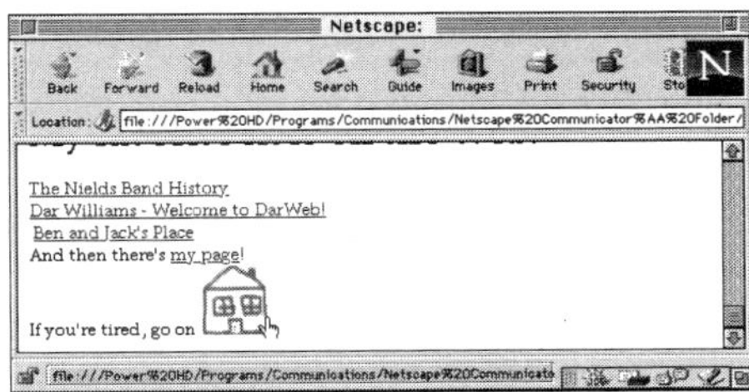

Figure 20.31 *The image is now a link. When the user passes the pointer over the linked image, the pointer turns into a hand and the link's destination is revealed in the status area.*

Creating a link with an image

To add navigational buttons to your page, you have to first insert an image and then make it into a link.

To create a link with an image:

1. Add the image to the page in the Composer window *(see page 252)* and select it **(Figure 20.28)**.
2. Choose Insert > Link **(Figure 20.29)**. The Link tab of the Format dialog box appears.
3. Type the URL for the link in the Link To text box, or click Choose File if the link is to a local file on your hard disk **(Figure 20.30)**.
4. Select a target for the link, if desired *(see page 273)*.
5. Click OK to close the Link tab of the Format dialog box. The image is now a link **(Figure 20.31)**.

✔ Tips

- Double click the image and then click the Link tab in the Format dialog box to view the link attributes.
- Or, you can select the image and then click the Link button on the Composition toolbar to open the Link tab of the Format dialog box for the image.

Changing or removing a link

As you design a Web page, you will find that every so often you need to update a link or add a target to it—or get rid of it.

To change or delete a link:

1. Select the link you want to change **(Figure 20.32)**.
2. Choose Format > Link Info **(Figure 20.33)**. The Link tab of the Format dialog box appears.
3. Change the URL or target *(see page 272)* or click Remove Links to make the link regular text **(Figure 20.34)**.
4. Click OK to save the changes.

✔ Tips

- You can also click and hold over a selected link and then choose Link Info to open the Link tab of the Format dialog box **(Figure 20.35)**.
- To change a link's display text, select the text and type something else.
- To eliminate a link *and* its display text, select it and press Delete.
- To change a target's name, double click the target, select it and choose Format > Target Info, click and hold and choose Target Info in the pop-up menu, or click the Target button on the Composition toolbar. The Target dialog box appears.

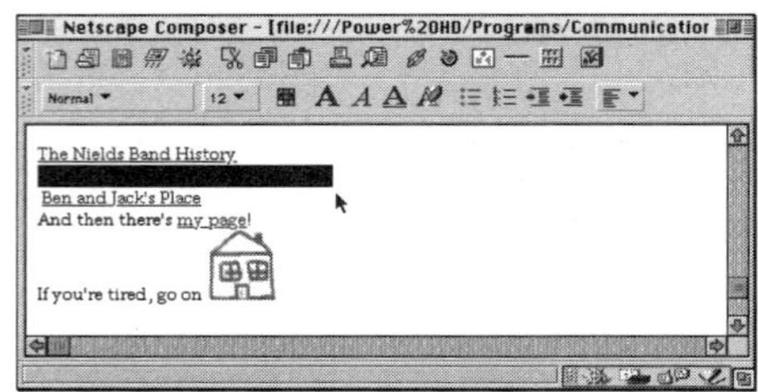

Figure 20.32 *Select the link you want to change.*

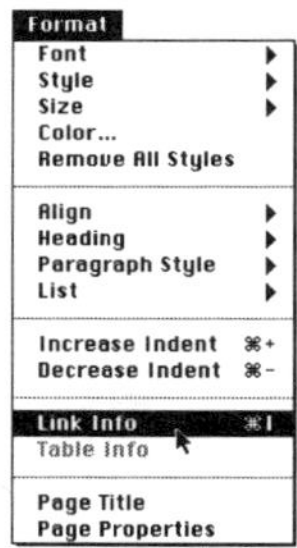

Figure 20.33 *Choose Format > Link Info.*

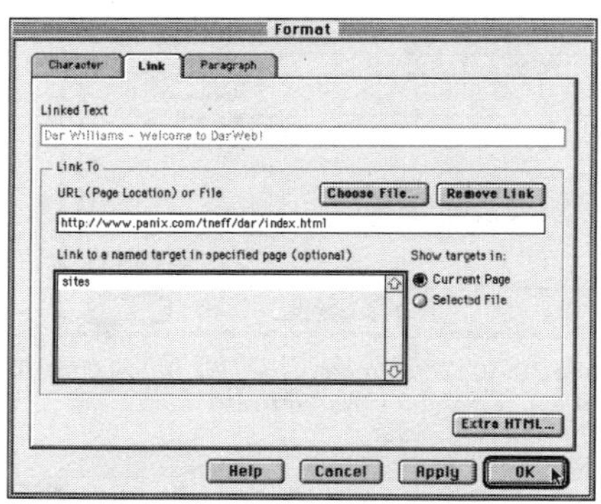

Figure 20.34 *Make any necessary changes to the URL or to the target. Or click Remove Link to remove the link information from the text. Click OK to save the changes.*

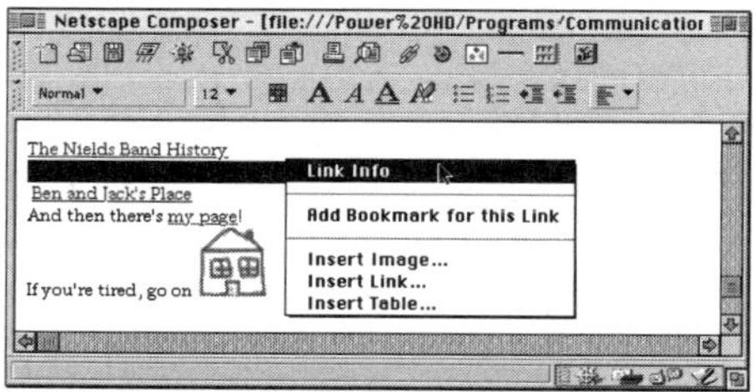

Figure 20.35 *You can also click and hold down a selected link and then choose Link Info in the pop-up menu to access the Link tab of the Format dialog box.*

21 Creating Tables

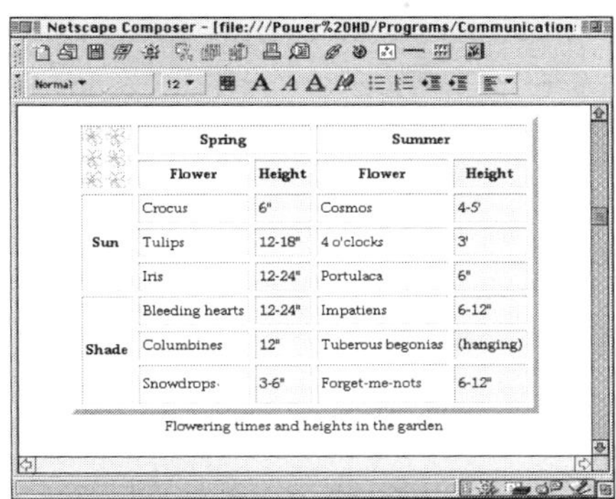

	Spring		Summer	
	Flower	Height	Flower	Height
Sun	Crocus	6"	Cosmos	4-5'
	Tulips	12-18"	4 o'clocks	3'
	Iris	12-24"	Portulaca	6"
Shade	Bleeding hearts	12-24"	Impatiens	6-12"
	Columbines	12"	Tuberous begonias	(hanging)
	Snowdrops	3-6"	Forget-me-nots	6-12"

Figure 21.1 *Detailed lists are often best displayed in a table.*

Detailed lists with categorized information are infinitely easier to understand in table format. Composer *almost* makes them easy to create—certainly much easier than constructing them by hand.

If you are worried about users who use browsers that don't understand tables, you might consider creating hand-spaced tables with preformatted text *(see page 240)*. Tables made with preformatted text can be read by *any* browser.

Creating a new table

You can create a new table in any part of your Web page. The table will appear at the insertion point.

To create a new table:

1. Click on the page where you wish to insert the table **(Figure 21.2)**.
2. Choose Insert > Table > Table **(Figure 21.3)**. The Insert Table dialog box appears **(Figure 21.4)**.
3. Define how many rows and columns the table should have by entering numbers in the Number of Rows and Number of Columns boxes.
4. If desired, further define the appearance of the table as described in the rest of this chapter.
5. Click OK. The empty table is added to your page **(Figure 21.5)**.

✔ Tips

- For information on filling your table, consult *Entering text in a table* on page 281.
- You can also insert a table by clicking the Table button on the Composition toolbar or by clicking and holding down the mouse button and choosing Insert Table in the pop-up menu that appears.

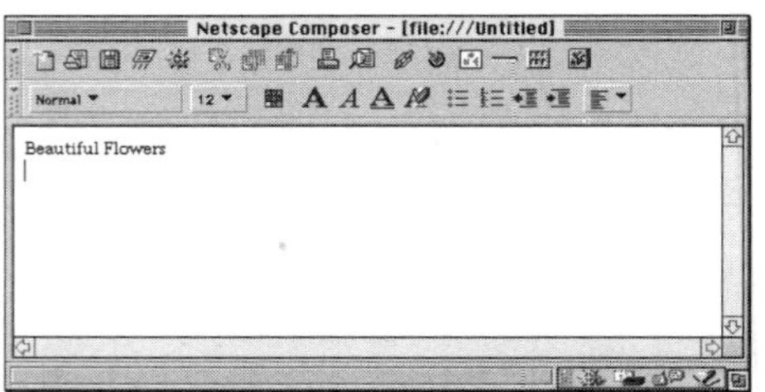

Figure 21.2 *Click in the part of your page where you wish to insert the table.*

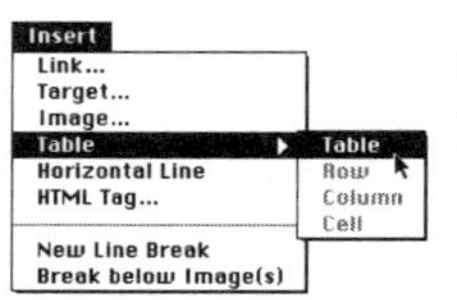

Figure 21.3 *Choose Insert > Table > Table.*

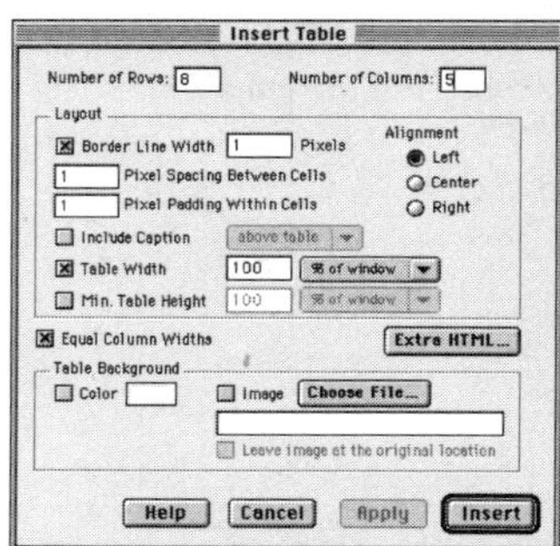

Figure 21.4 *Enter the desired values in the Insert Table dialog box and then click OK to insert the table in your page.*

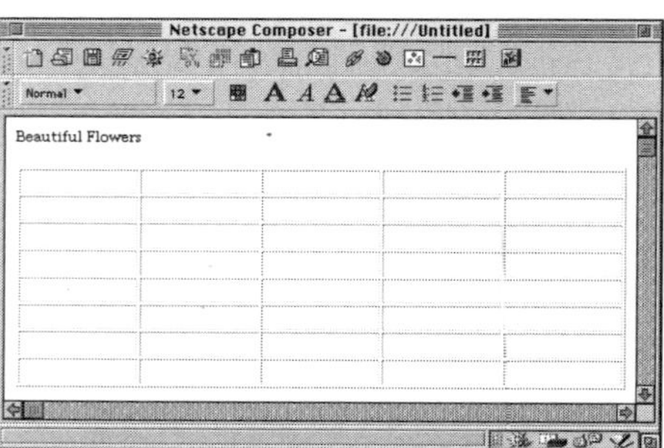

Figure 21.5 *The empty table appears on your page.*

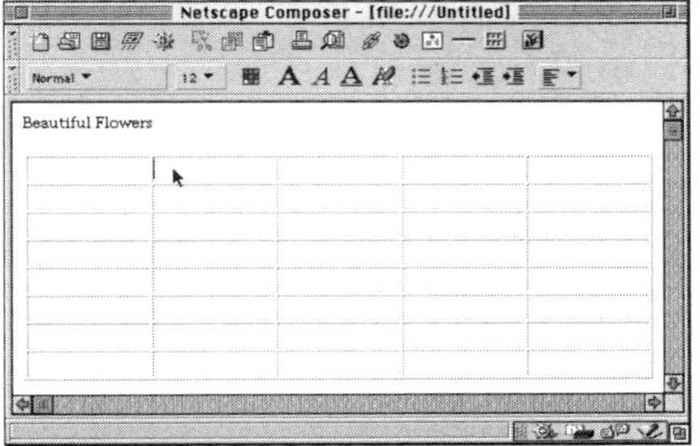

Figure 21.6 *Click in the cell that should span more than one column (or row).*

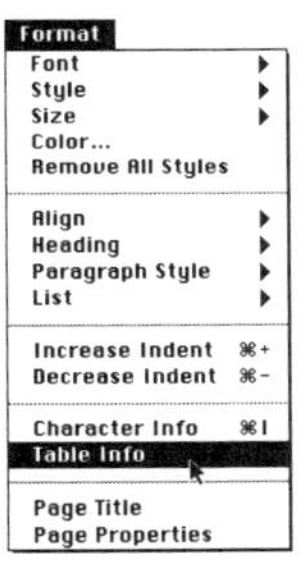

Figure 21.7 *Choose Format > Table Info.*

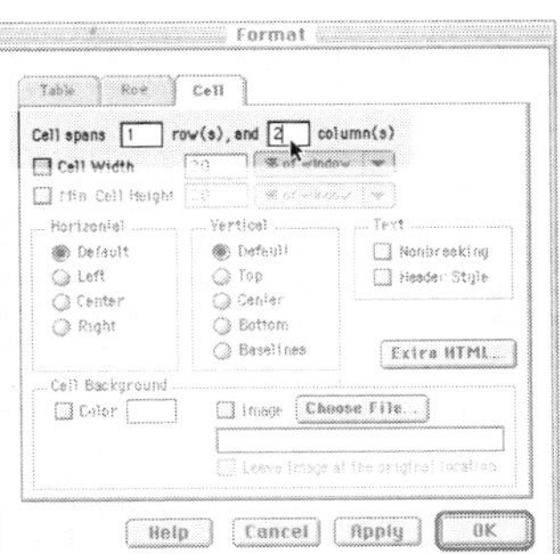

Figure 21.8 *Enter the number of rows or columns the cell should span at the top of the Cell tab.*

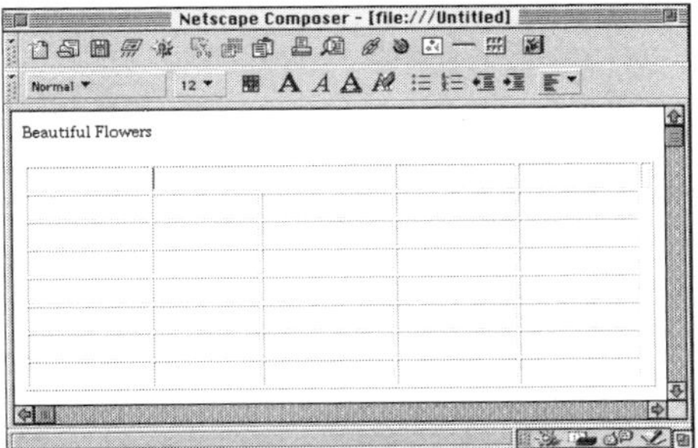

Figure 21.9 *The selected cell now spans two columns. Meanwhile, an extra cell is pushed out to the right and will have to be deleted.*

Spanning a cell over columns or rows

If you have a lot of information that you wish to convey with a table, you can divide a table header into several categories by having it span several columns (or rows), and adding more specific headers in the row below (or column to the right).

To span a cell over several rows and/or columns:

1. Click in the desired cell **(Figure 21.6)**.
2. Choose Format > Table Info **(Figure 21.7)** and click the Cell tab in the Format dialog box that appears.
3. Enter the number of rows and columns that the cell should span next to Cell spans **(Figure 21.8)**.
4. If desired, click the Apply button to see how the changes affect the table. Repeat step 3 and click Apply until you are satisfied with the results.
5. Click OK to close the dialog box. The cell spans the appropriate number of columns or rows, displacing existing cells as necessary **(Figure 21.9)**.

✔ Tip

- When you make a cell span more than one row or column, you may find there are extra cells that need to be deleted. For more information, consult *Adding or deleting cells, rows, or columns* on page 280.

Adding or deleting cells, rows, or columns

Unless you completely design the table on paper before opening Composer, it's almost impossible to know exactly how many cells, rows, or columns you'll need. Luckily, you can add and delete them as you go along.

To add parts of a table:

1. Click in the table where the new cell, row, or column should be inserted.
2. Choose Insert > Table > and then Row, Column, or Cell. The desired element is inserted.

To delete parts of a table:

1. Click in the undesired element **(Figure 21.10)**.
2. Choose Edit > Delete Table > and then Table, Row, Column, or Cell. The selected part disappears **(Figure 21.11)**.

✔ Tips

- As shown in Figure 21.12, you can also click and hold down over an element and then choose Delete Table, Row, Column, or Cell in the pop-up menu that appears.
- There is no warning when you delete part of a table. Choose Undo in the Edit menu (Command-Z) right away to get it back. You only get one chance.
- Elements are added to the right or below the current item. Thus, the only way to add a cell *before another* is to create a new cell below or after it and then copy and paste the contents into the new location.

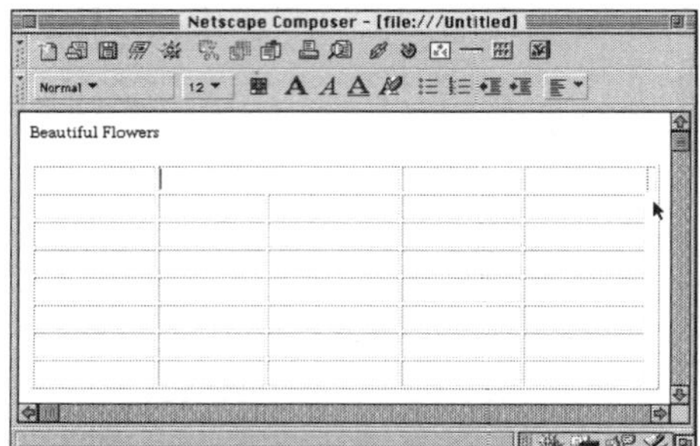

Figure 21.10 *Select the cell that you wish to delete. In this example, we'll remove an extra cell that was created when we spanned the top cell in the second column.*

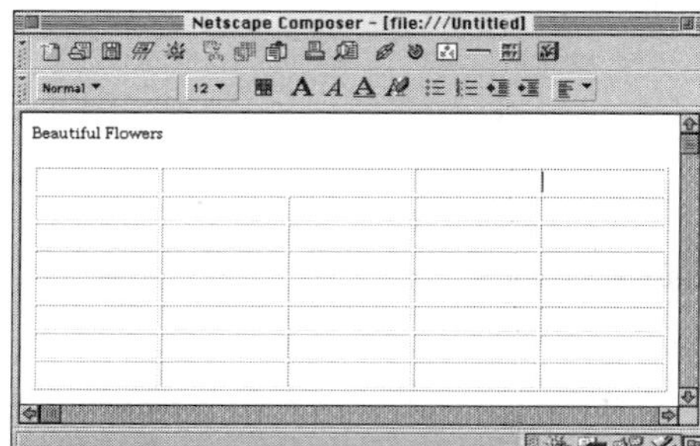

Figure 21.11 *The extra cell disappears.*

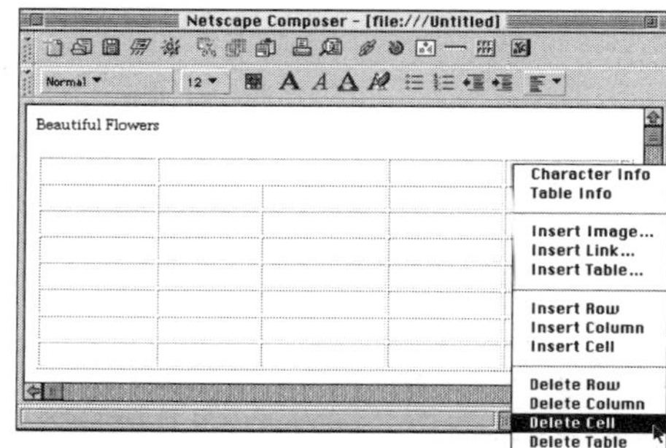

Figure 21.12 *Choose Delete Cell in the pop-up menu.*

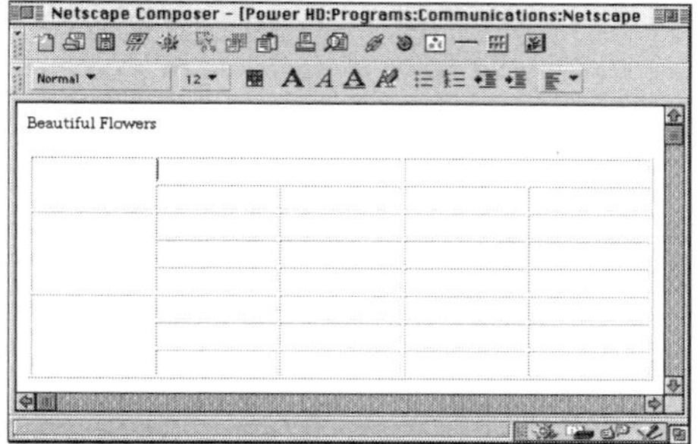

Figure 21.13 *Once you've adjusted the cells so that they span the desired number of rows or columns, you're ready to enter text in the table. Simply click in the desired cell and type.*

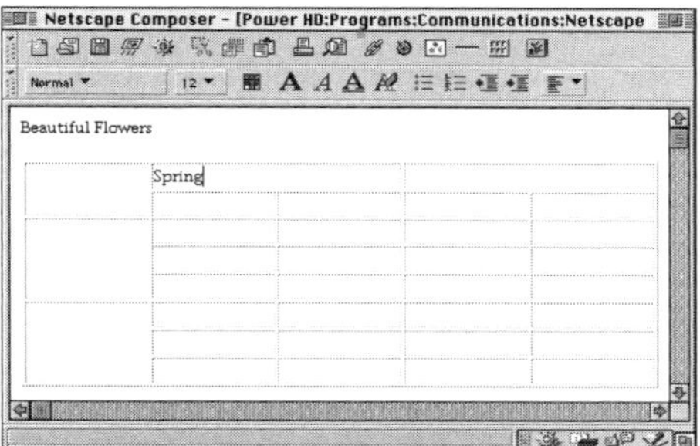

Figure 21.14 *By default, the text will appear aligned to the left and at the same size and style as regular body text (Normal).*

Entering text in a table

Since you can't create a table out of existing text, you'll have to enter text in the table after creating it.

To enter text in a table:

1. Click in the cell in which you wish to enter information **(Figure 21.13)**.
2. Type the desired contents. The cell automatically expands to fit the text **(Figure 21.14)**.
3. Use the Tab key to move to the next cell.
4. Repeat steps 2 and 3 until the table is complete.

✔ Tip

- You may add new cells, rows, or columns at any time. For more information, consult *Adding or deleting cells, rows, or columns* on page 280.

Formatting a table's headers

Although you can manually add physical formatting like bold and italics to distinguish a table's headers from its contents, you're better off formatting them as real headers. This way, any browser that understands tables will be able to interpret and distinguish the headers correctly.

To format a table's headers:

1. Click in the cell that contains the header text **(Figure 21.15)**.
2. Choose Format > Table Info and then click the Cell tab in the Format dialog box that appears.
3. Click Header Style in the Text section in the middle of the dialog box **(Figure 21.16)**.
4. If desired, click the Apply button at the bottom of the dialog box to see the changes.
5. Click OK to close the dialog box and save the changes **(Figure 21.17)**.

✔ Tips

- You can only format one cell at a time. If you select more than one, only the first cell is affected.
- Different browsers may display headers in different ways.

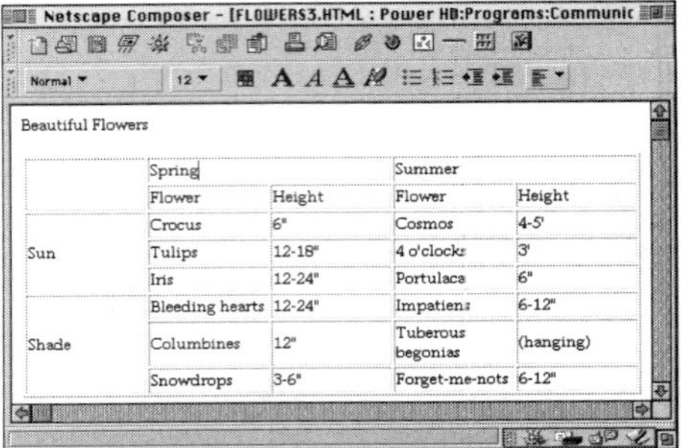

	Spring		Summer	
	Flower	Height	Flower	Height
Sun	Crocus	6"	Cosmos	4-5'
	Tulips	12-18"	4 o'clocks	3'
	Iris	12-24"	Portulaca	6"
Shade	Bleeding hearts	12-24"	Impatiens	6-12"
	Columbines	12"	Tuberous begonias	(hanging)
	Snowdrops	3-6"	Forget-me-nots	6-12"

Figure 21.15 *Click in the cell that you wish to define as a table header.*

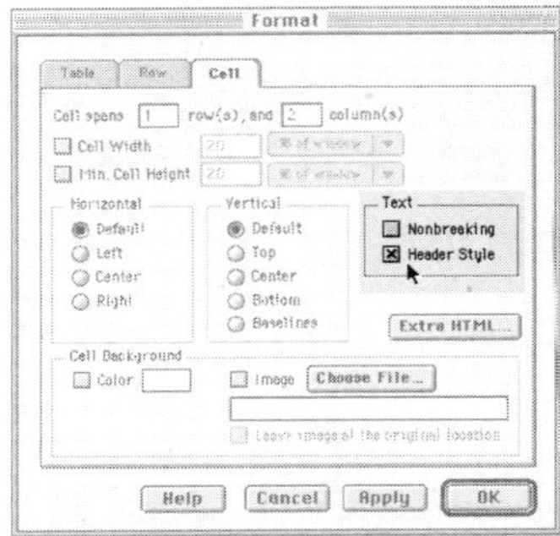

Figure 21.16 *In the Cell tab of the Format dialog box, check the Header Style box in the Text section.*

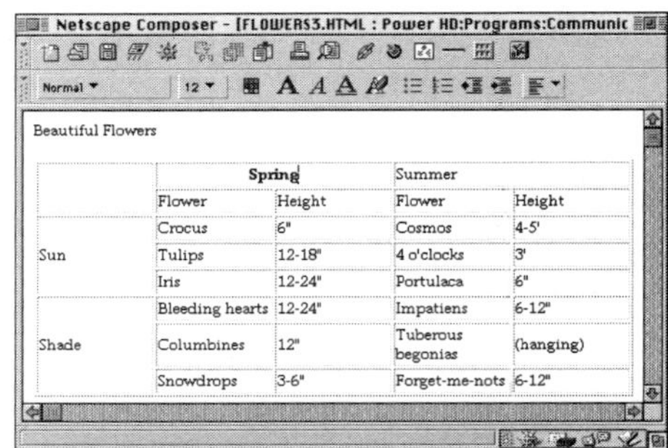

	Spring		Summer	
	Flower	Height	Flower	Height
Sun	Crocus	6"	Cosmos	4-5'
	Tulips	12-18"	4 o'clocks	3'
	Iris	12-24"	Portulaca	6"
Shade	Bleeding hearts	12-24"	Impatiens	6-12"
	Columbines	12"	Tuberous begonias	(hanging)
	Snowdrops	3-6"	Forget-me-nots	6-12"

Figure 21.17 *Netscape 4 for Macintosh displays header cells in boldface and centered. Version 3 displayed them in boldface but aligned to the left.*

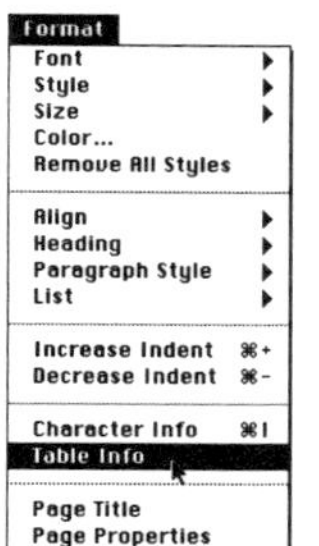

Figure 21.18 *Choose Format > Table Info.*

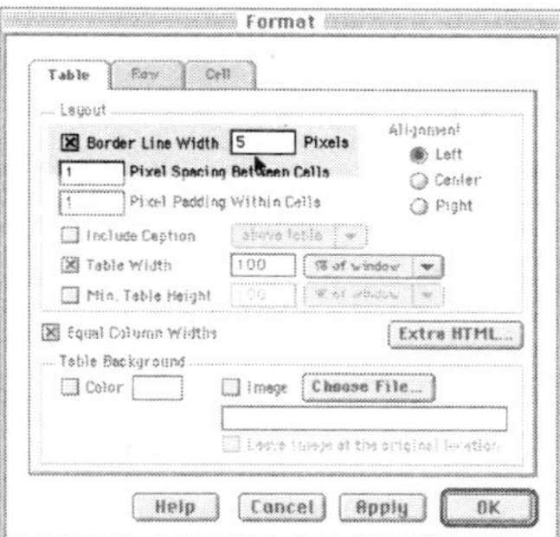

Figure 21.19 *Enter the desired width in pixels in the Border line width box in the Table tab of the Format dialog box.*

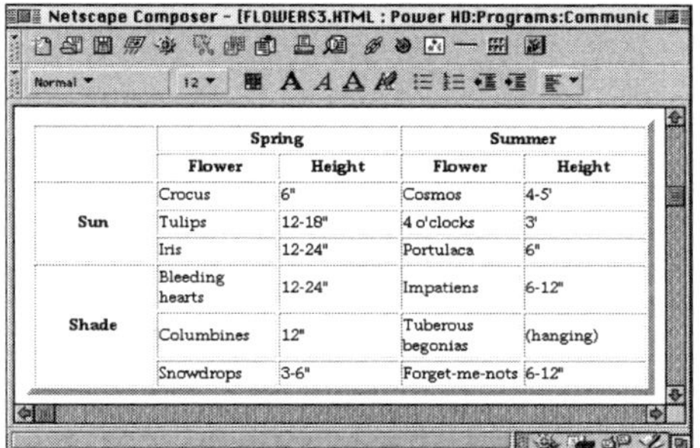

	Spring		Summer	
	Flower	Height	Flower	Height
Sun	Crocus	6"	Cosmos	4-5'
	Tulips	12-18"	4 o'clocks	3'
	Iris	12-24"	Portulaca	6"
Shade	Bleeding hearts	12-24"	Impatiens	6-12"
	Columbines	12"	Tuberous begonias	(hanging)
	Snowdrops	3-6"	Forget-me-nots	6-12"

Figure 21.20 *Netscape shades the border, according to the background color. Other browsers may display the border differently.*

Defining a table's border

Giving your table a border helps separate it from the rest of the text.

To define a border:

1. Click anywhere in the table to select it.
2. Choose Format > Table Info **(Figure 21.18)** and click the Table tab to see the general table attributes.
3. Enter the desired width for the border, in pixels, next to Border Line Width near the top of the dialog box **(Figure 21.19)**.
4. If desired, click Apply to see the effect of the changes. Make further changes as desired until you're satisfied.
5. Click OK to save the changes and close the dialog box **(Figure 21.20)**.

✔ Tips

- To eliminate the border, enter a value of 0 in the Border line width box.
- You can define the width of the border when you initially create the table.
- It doesn't matter where you place the insertion point. Changing the border affects the entire table.

Adding a caption

A caption gives a short description of a table's contents. By adding this information in the form of a caption, it will always be related and connected to the table, regardless of the browser used to view it.

To add a caption:

1. Click anywhere in the table to select it **(Figure 21.21)**.
2. Choose Format > Table Info and then click the Table tab to see the general table attributes.
3. Check the Include Caption box **(Figure 21.22)**.
4. In the pop-up menu, select above table or below table to determine the position of the caption.
5. Click Apply to see the effect of the changes. Change the options and click Apply again until you are satisfied.
6. Click OK to save the changes and close the dialog box. A dotted box appears for the caption.
7. Type the caption **(Figure 21.23)**.

✔ Tips

- Different browsers display captions in different ways. While Navigator centers captions and divides the lines to fit the table's width, Mosaic displays captions in boldface and aligns them to the left.
- If your table already contains a caption, you can use this technique to move the caption above (or below) the table.

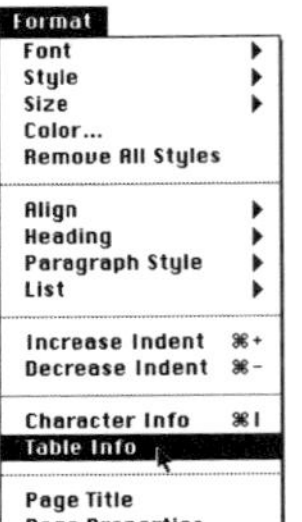

Figure 21.21 *Select the table and choose Format > Table Info.*

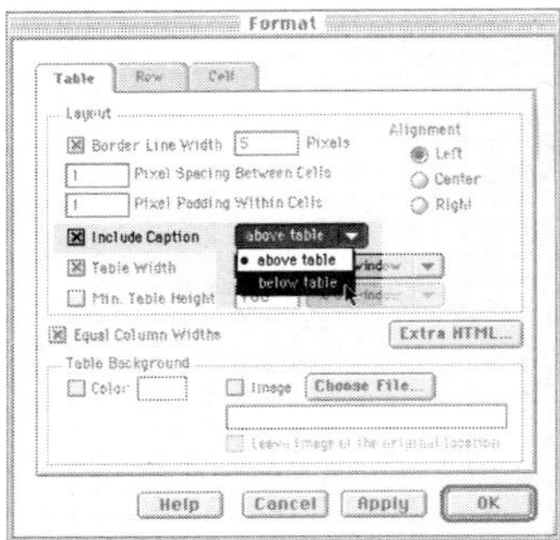

Figure 21.22 *Check the Include Caption check box and then select either above table or below table in the pop-up menu to determine the caption's position.*

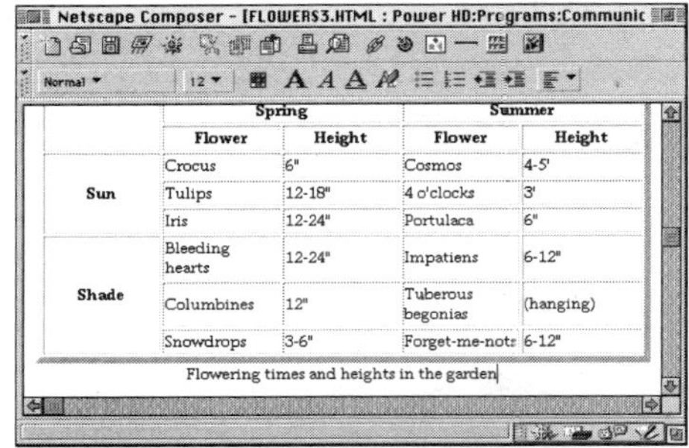

	Spring		Summer	
	Flower	Height	Flower	Height
Sun	Crocus	6"	Cosmos	4-5'
	Tulips	12-18"	4 o'clocks	3'
	Iris	12-24"	Portulaca	6"
Shade	Bleeding hearts	12-24"	Impatiens	6-12"
	Columbines	12"	Tuberous begonias	(hanging)
	Snowdrops	3-6"	Forget-me-nots	6-12"

Flowering times and heights in the garden

Figure 21.23 *Once you close the Format dialog box, the insertion point will be automatically placed in the caption area. Type the caption.*

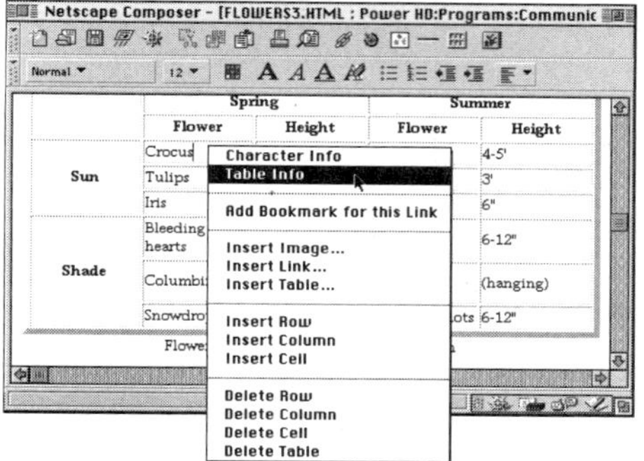

Figure 21.24 *Another way to access the Format dialog box is to click and hold over the table and then choose Table Info in the pop-up menu.*

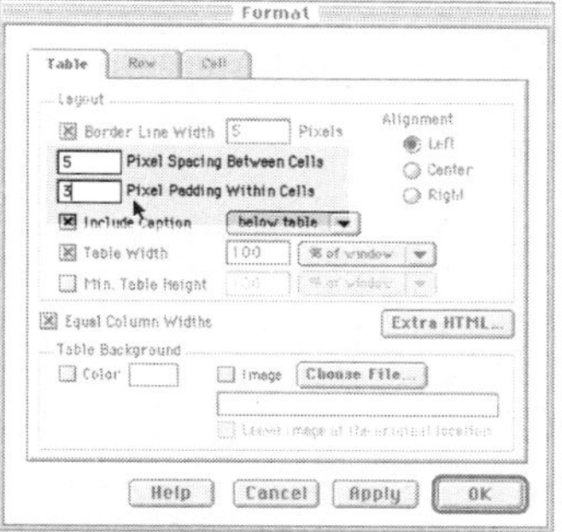

Figure 21.25 *In the Table tab of the Format dialog box, enter the desired values in the Pixel Spacing Between Cells and Pixel Padding Between Cells boxes to determine the amount of space that should be added between and inside the cells, respectively.*

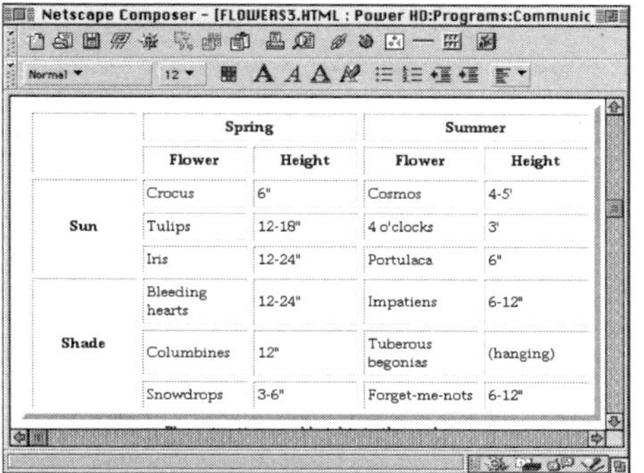

	Spring		Summer	
	Flower	Height	Flower	Height
Sun	Crocus	6"	Cosmos	4-5'
	Tulips	12-18"	4 o'clocks	3'
	Iris	12-24"	Portulaca	6"
Shade	Bleeding hearts	12-24"	Impatiens	6-12"
	Columbines	12"	Tuberous begonias	(hanging)
	Snowdrops	3-6"	Forget-me-nots	6-12"

Figure 21.26 *Increasing the cell spacing thickens the borders between cells; increasing cell padding adds invisible space between the contents of the cells and the cells' borders.*

Spacing and padding cells

Cell spacing is the amount of space between individual cells. You can sometimes make a table easier to read by adjusting the cell spacing.

To add cell spacing or padding:

1. Click anywhere in the table to select it.
2. Select Format > Table Info and then click the Table tab.
3. In the Pixel Spacing Between Cells box, enter the amount of space that should appear between one cell and the next **(Figure 21.25)**.
4. In the Pixel Padding Between Cells box, enter the amount of space that should appear between the cell's contents and its border.
5. Click the Apply button to see the changes. Make additional changes and click Apply until you're satisfied with the results.
6. Click OK to close the dialog box and save the changes to the table **(Figure 21.26)**.

✔ Tips

- The alignment options *(see page 287)* consider the cell padding as the actual cell limits, and thus may give unexpected results.
- The default value for cell spacing is 2 pixels. The default value for cell padding is 1 pixel.

Changing the table's width and height

Every person who jumps to your page on the Web may see your table at a different size, depending on the size of the window he or she is using. You can set a minimum height and width for the table, if desired.

To change the width and height of a table:

1. Select the table and choose Format > Table Info **(Figure 21.27)**. Click the Table tab to see the general table attributes.
2. Check the Table Width and/or Min. Table Height boxes to activate them **(Figure 21.28)**.
3. Enter the desired values in pixels or as a percentage of the browser window size.
4. Click OK to save the changes **(Figure 21.29)**.

✔ Tip

- You can't make the table too small for its contents. If you try, Composer will ignore you. Most browsers will expand the table as necessary, regardless of the measurements you've specified, so that the entire contents can be seen.

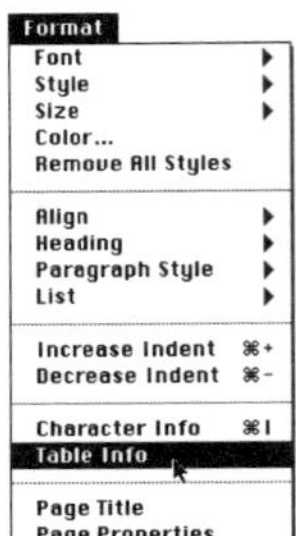

Figure 21.27 *Select the table and choose Format > Table Info.*

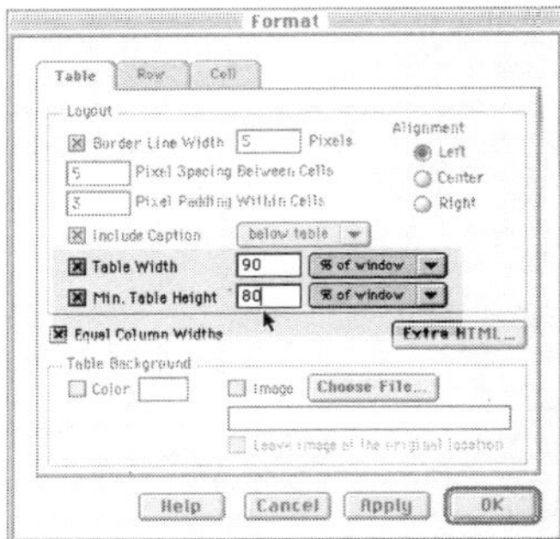

Figure 21.28 *Check the Table Width box and enter the desired value in pixels or as a percentage of the browser window's size.*

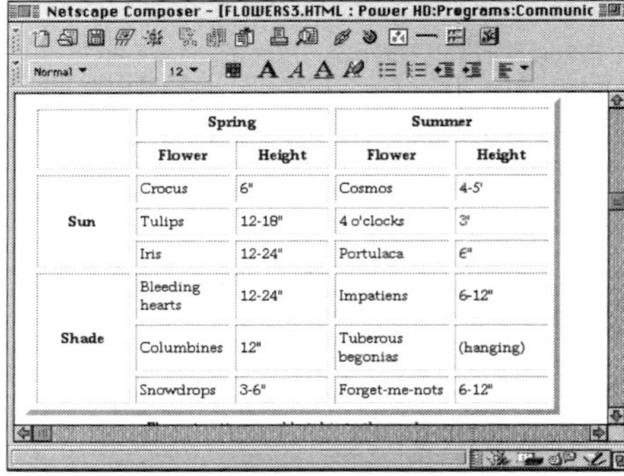

	Spring		Summer	
	Flower	Height	Flower	Height
Sun	Crocus	6"	Cosmos	4-5'
	Tulips	12-18"	4 o'clocks	3'
	Iris	12-24"	Portulaca	6"
Shade	Bleeding hearts	12-24"	Impatiens	6-12"
	Columbines	12"	Tuberous begonias	(hanging)
	Snowdrops	3-6"	Forget-me-nots	6-12"

Figure 21.29 *The table occupies only 90% of the window's width now.*

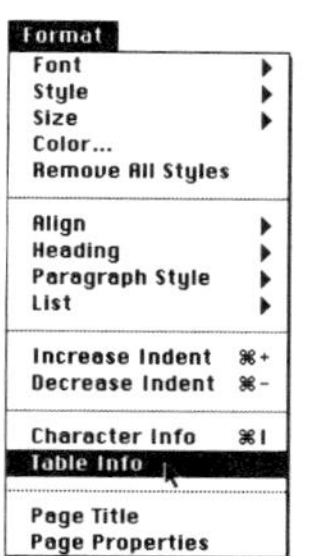

Figure 21.30 *Select the table and choose Format > Table Info.*

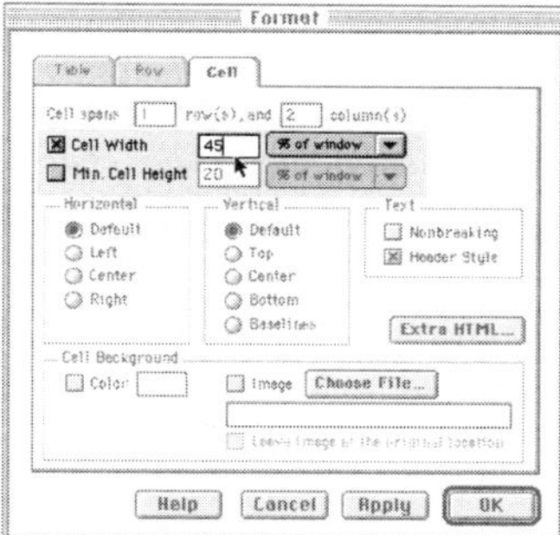

Figure 21.31 *In the top section of the Format dialog box's Cell tab, enter the desired cell width in pixels, or as a percentage of the entire table size.*

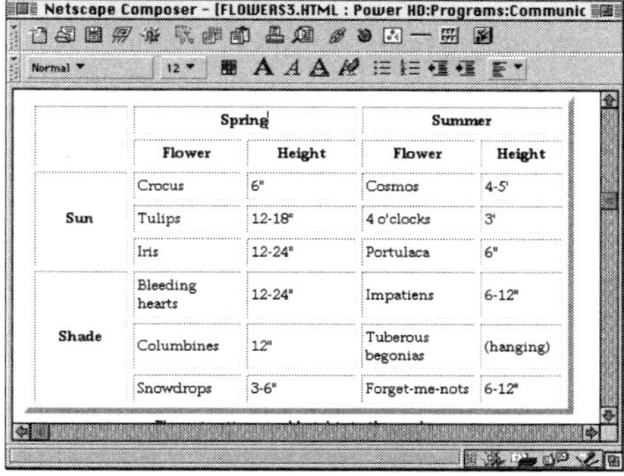

Figure 21.32 *The "Spring" cell is now better proportioned with respect to the rest of the table, although further adjustments probably wouldn't hurt.*

Changing a cell's width and height

You may wish to adjust the height and width of individual cells to make the table more attractive. Although browsers make an effort to size the elements accordingly, sometimes the results are wanting.

To change an individual cell's height and width:

1. Select the desired cell and choose Format > Table Info **(Figure 21.30)**. Click the Cell tab in the Format dialog box that appears.
2. In the Cell tab, check the Cell Width and/or Min. Cell Height boxes to activate them **(Figure 21.31)**.
3. Enter the desired values in pixels or as a percentage of the total table size.
4. Click OK to save the changes **(Figure 21.32)**.

✔ Tip

- You can't make a cell too small for its contents. Most browsers will expand each cell of a table as necessary, regardless of the measurements you've specified, so that the entire contents can be seen. However, the contents may be divided into separate lines. To keep the entry all on one line, consult *Controlling line breaks in a cell* on page 291.

Making equal size columns

Composer automatically divvies up the available space equally between all the columns in your table. However, if you have a column that doesn't need as much space, like the flower heights in the example, you may want to turn off this option.

To make equal size columns:

1. Select the table and choose Format > Table Info. Click the Table tab to see the general table attributes.
2. Check Equal Column Widths in the middle of the dialog box **(Figure 21.34)**.
3. Click the Apply button to see the changes. Make additional changes and click Apply until you're satisfied with the results.
4. Click OK to close the dialog box and save the changes to the table **(Figure 21.35)**.

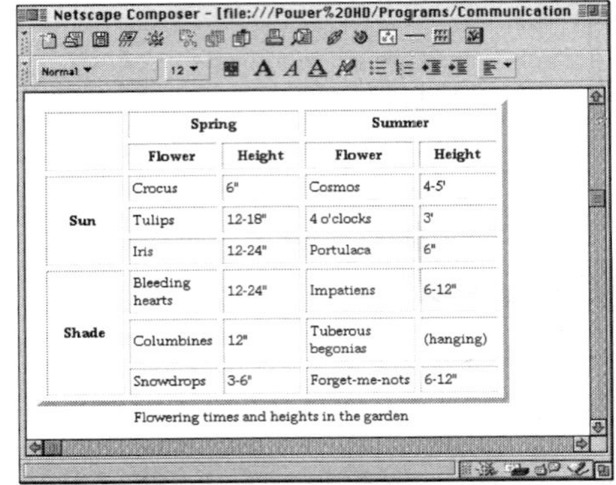

	Spring		Summer	
	Flower	Height	Flower	Height
Sun	Crocus	6"	Cosmos	4-5'
	Tulips	12-18"	4 o'clocks	3'
	Iris	12-24"	Portulaca	6"
Shade	Bleeding hearts	12-24"	Impatiens	6-12"
	Columbines	12"	Tuberous begonias	(hanging)
	Snowdrops	3-6"	Forget-me-nots	6-12"

Figure 21.33 *The Equal Column Widths option, activated by default, is not great for tables with very narrow columns, like this one.*

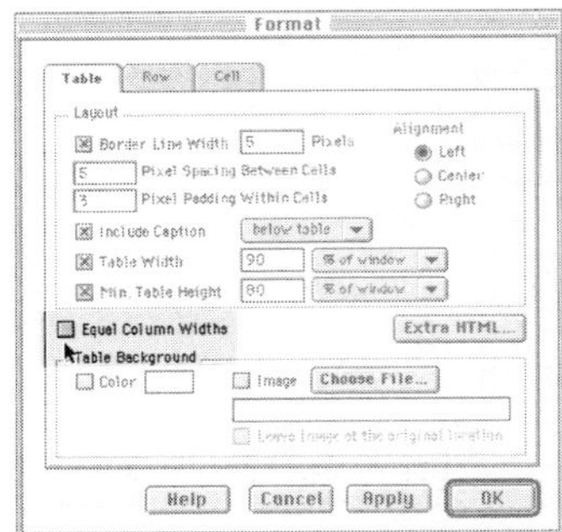

Figure 21.34 *Deselect the Equal Column Widths option to have each browser adjust individual column widths according to the contents of each column.*

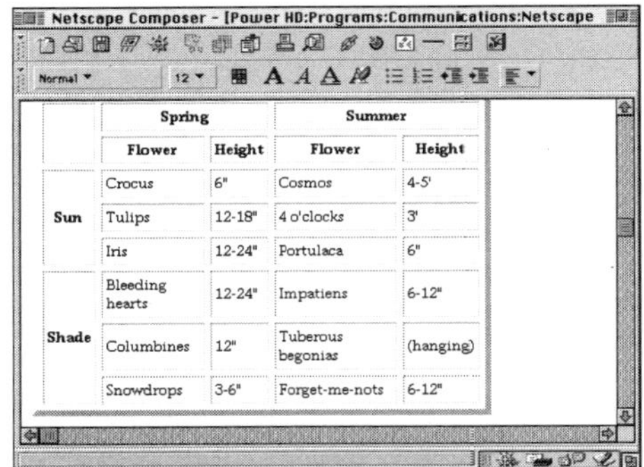

	Spring		Summer	
	Flower	Height	Flower	Height
Sun	Crocus	6"	Cosmos	4-5'
	Tulips	12-18"	4 o'clocks	3'
	Iris	12-24"	Portulaca	6"
Shade	Bleeding hearts	12-24"	Impatiens	6-12"
	Columbines	12"	Tuberous begonias	(hanging)
	Snowdrops	3-6"	Forget-me-nots	6-12"

Figure 21.35 *The Height columns are now much narrower, and better fit their contents.*

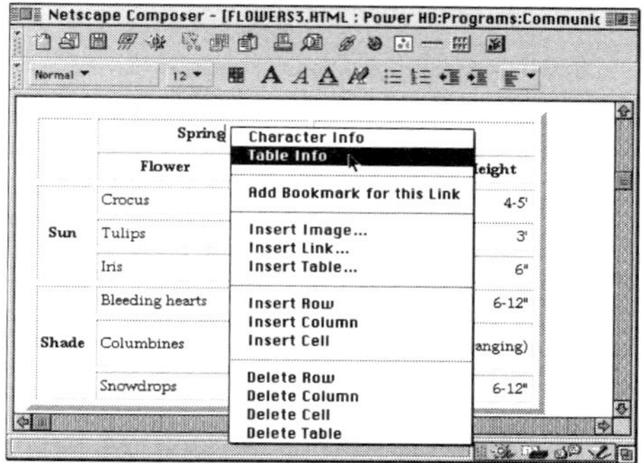

Figure 21.36 *Click and hold over the table and choose Table Info in the pop-up menu to make the Format dialog box appear.*

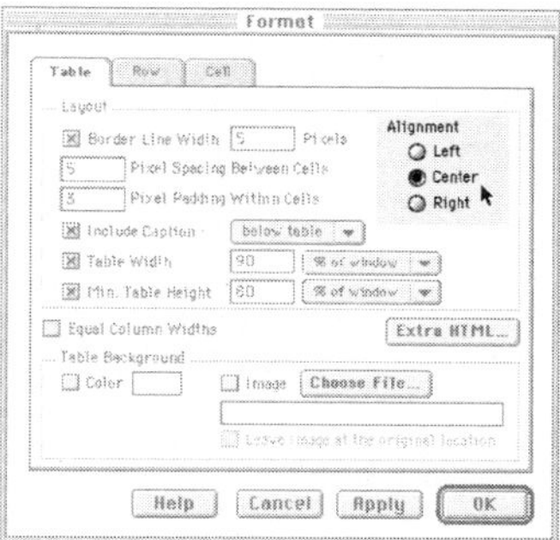

Figure 21.37 *Choose an alignment option from the right side of the Table tab of the Format dialog box.*

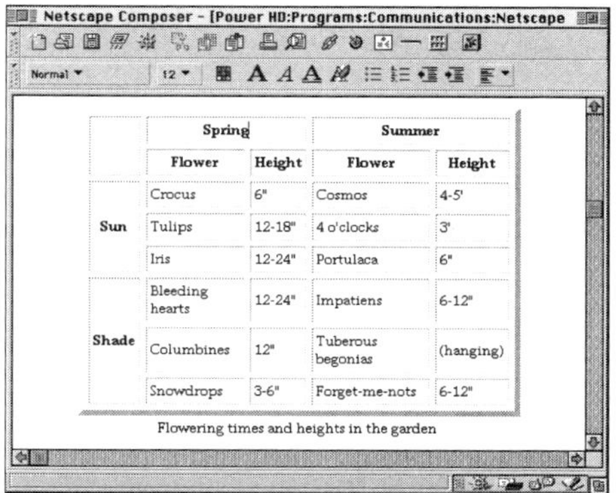

Figure 21.38 *The table is now centered in the window.*

Aligning a table

You can choose to center your table in the middle of the page, or to align it to the left or right.

To align a table:

1. Select the table and choose Format > Table Info. Click the Table tab to see the general table attributes **(Figure 21.37)**.
2. Click the desired alignment option in the Alignment section at the top of the dialog box.
3. Click the Apply button to see the changes. Make additional changes and click Apply until you're satisfied with the results.
4. Click OK to close the dialog box and save the changes to the table. The table is aligned **(Figure 21.38)**.

Aligning the table's contents

Different browsers may show the contents of the cells in a table in their own way, by default, which may or may not be how you think the data looks best. To gain a little more control over the alignment of a cell's contents, set the alignment for each cell individually or by row.

To align a cell's contents:

1. Click in the desired cell to select it **(Figure 21.39)**, choose Format > Table Info, and then click the Cell tab, if necessary.
2. Select both a horizontal and vertical alignment in the alignment sections **(Figure 21.40)**.
3. If desired, click Apply to see the changes and then adjust the options until you are satisfied.
4. Click OK to close the dialog box and save the changes **(Figure 21.41)**.

To align all the cells in a row:

1. Click in the desired row to select it.
2. Choose Format > Table Info and then click the Row tab.
3. Select both a horizontal and vertical alignment at the top of the dialog box.
4. If desired, click Apply to see the changes.
5. Click OK to close the dialog box. All of the cells in the selected row will be aligned in the same way according to the options chosen in step 3. (You can't align a whole *column* at once.)

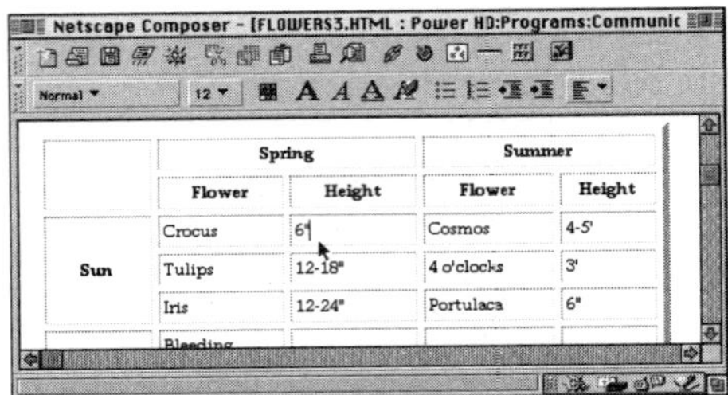

Figure 21.39 *Click in the cell that you wish to align.*

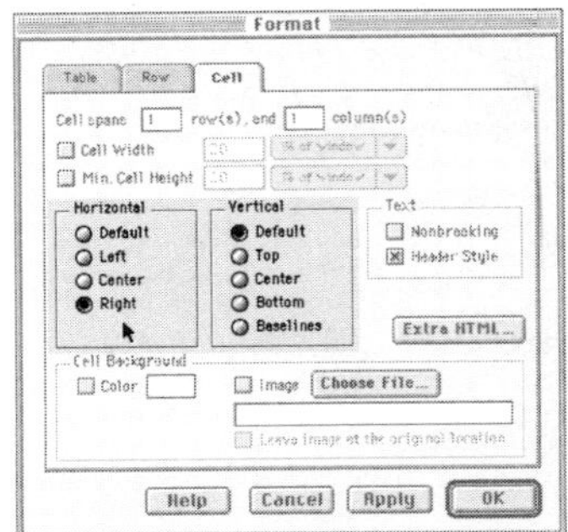

Figure 21.40 *Choose an alignment option in the Horizontal and Vertical sections of the Cell tab of the Format dialog box.*

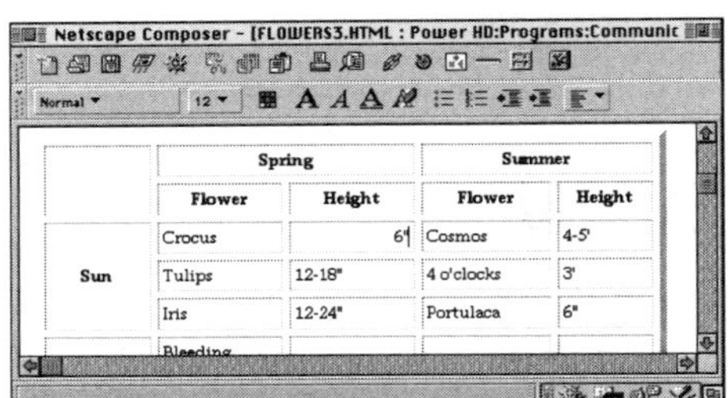

Figure 21.41 *The contents of the cell are aligned to the right.*

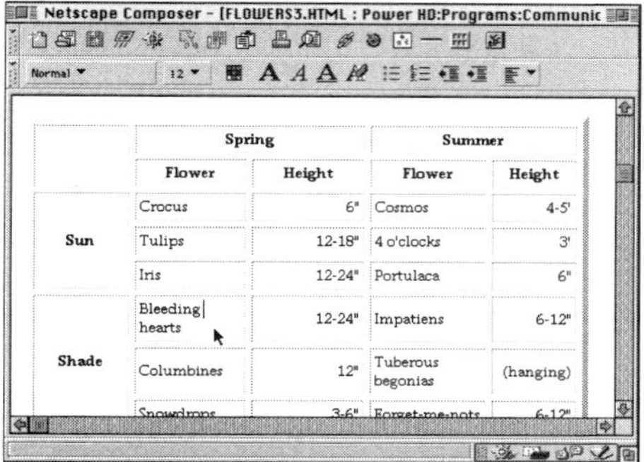

Figure 21.42 *Click in the cell whose contents you wish to display on one line.*

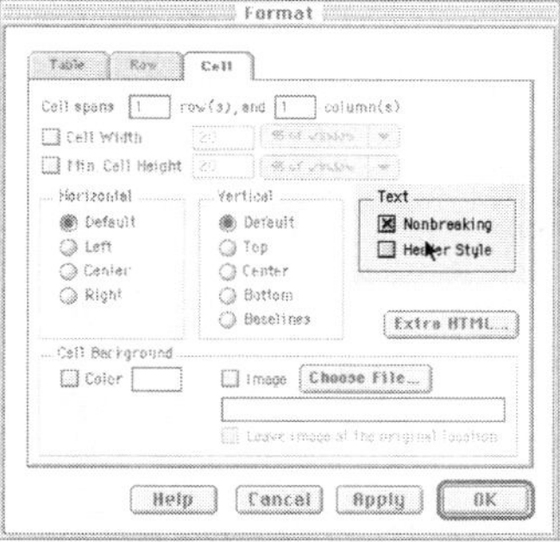

Figure 21.43 *Check the Nonbreaking box in the Text section of the Cell tab of the Format dialog box.*

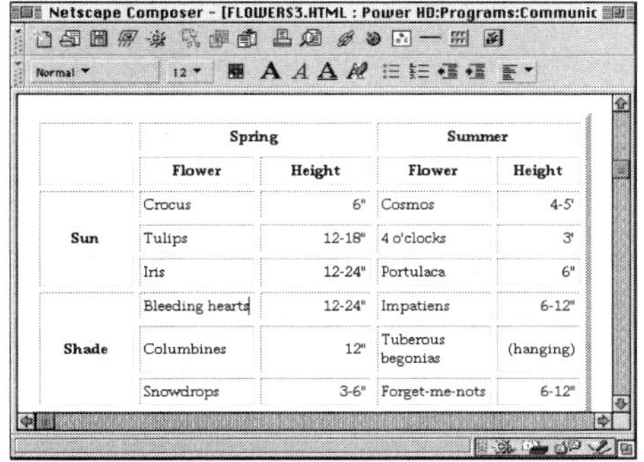

Figure 21.44 *The table and cell widths are adjusted so that the cell's contents fit on a single line.*

Controlling line breaks in a cell

Unless you specify otherwise, a browser will divide the lines of text in a cell as it decides on the height and width of each column and row. With Composer, you can set certain cells so that the contents are not divided.

To control the line breaks in a cell:

1. Click in the cell whose text you want to display all on one line **(Fig. 21.42)**.
2. Choose Format > Table Info and then click the Cell tab.
3. Check the Nonbreaking box in the Text section **(Figure 21.43)**.
4. Click Apply to apply the changes or OK to close the dialog box and save the changes. The contents of the chosen cell are displayed on one line and the table is adjusted accordingly **(Figure 21.44)**.

Changing the color of a table, row, or cell

You can change the color of the entire table or just of an individual cell or row of cells to make important information stand out (or distract the user, as you prefer).

To change the color of a table, row, or cell:

1. Click anywhere in a table, row, or cell to select it, choose Format > Table Info, and then click the tab that corresponds to the part of the table you wish to modify: Table, Row, or Cell.
2. Check the Color option and then click the swatch in the Table, Row, or Cell Background section near the bottom of the dialog box **(Figure 21.45)**. The Color picker dialog box appears.
3. Click on the desired color **(Figure 21.46)**.
4. Click Apply to see the changes right away. Make further changes and click Apply until you're satisfied with the results.
5. Click OK to close the dialog box and save the changes **(Figure 21.47)**.

✔ Tips

- Not everyone has a color monitor. Be sure you choose colors that have a high enough contrast to be effective on grayscale monitors.
- Cell colors override row colors which, in turn, override colors specified for the entire table. Images, on the other hand, override all colors *(see page 293)*.

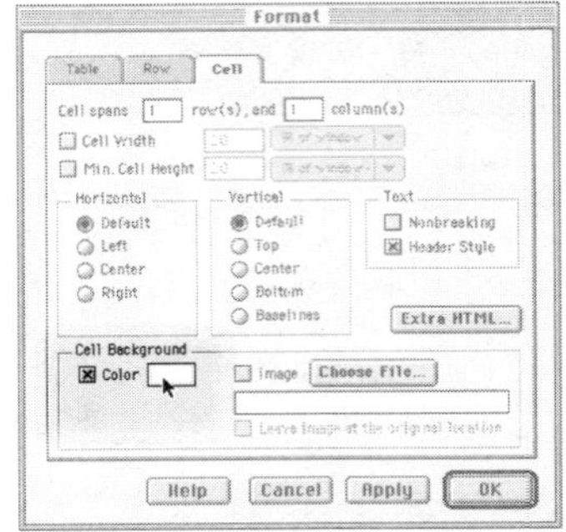

Figure 21.45 *Check the Color box at the bottom of the Format dialog box and then click the Color swatch.*

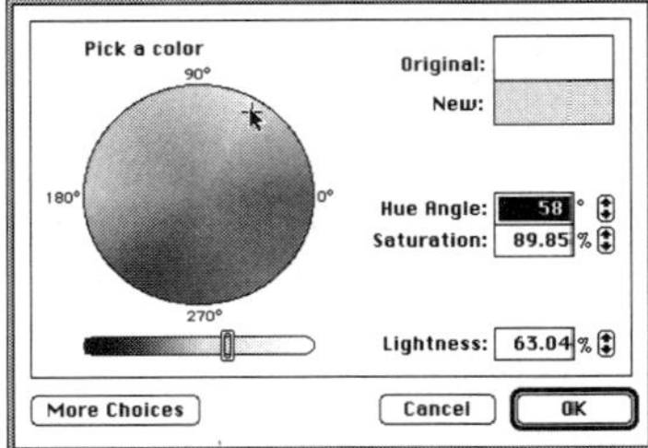

Figure 21.46 *Choose the desired color from the Color picker dialog box.*

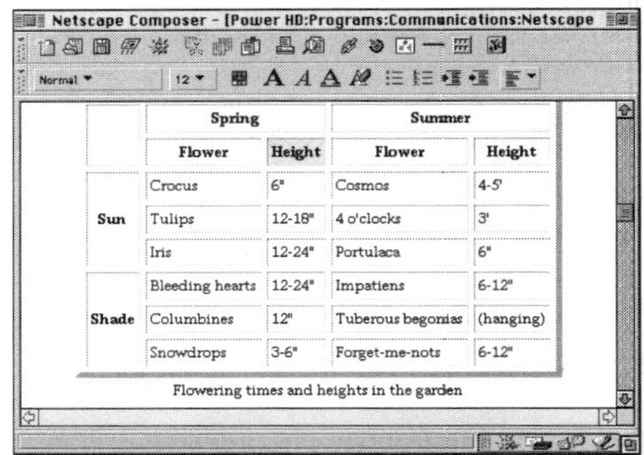

	Spring		Summer	
	Flower	Height	Flower	Height
Sun	Crocus	6"	Cosmos	4-5'
	Tulips	12-18"	4 o'clocks	3'
	Iris	12-24"	Portulaca	6"
Shade	Bleeding hearts	12-24"	Impatiens	6-12"
	Columbines	12"	Tuberous begonias	(hanging)
	Snowdrops	3-6"	Forget-me-nots	6-12"

Flowering times and heights in the garden

Figure 21.47 *The selected element's background color is changed.*

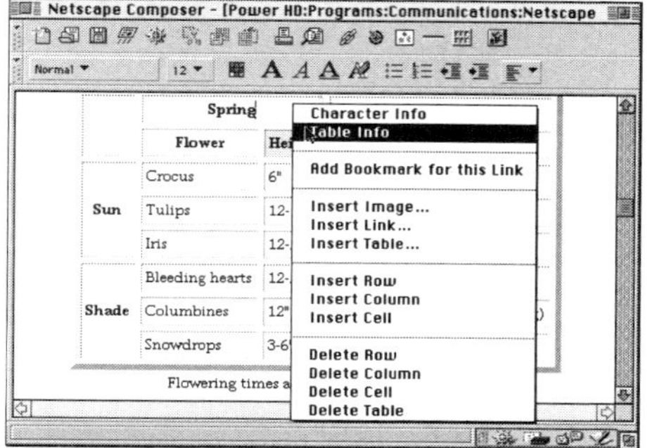

Figure 21.48 *Click and hold over the table and choose Table Info in the pop-up menu.*

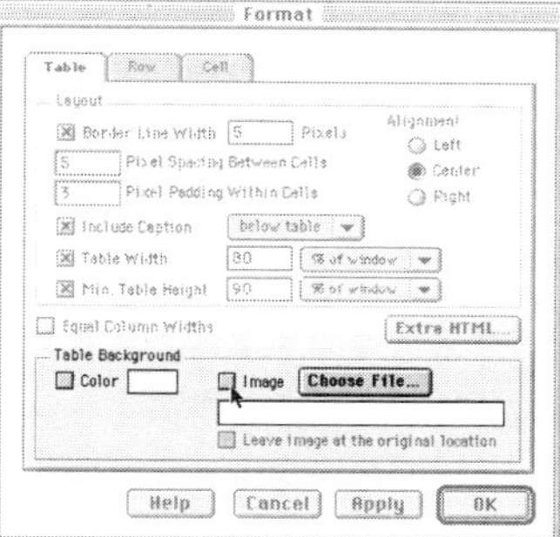

Figure 21.49 *Click Image in the Table Background section at the bottom of the dialog box.*

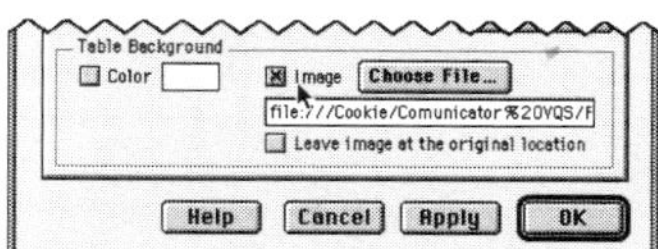

Figure 21.50 *Once you've chosen a file, its URL appears under Image in the text box.*

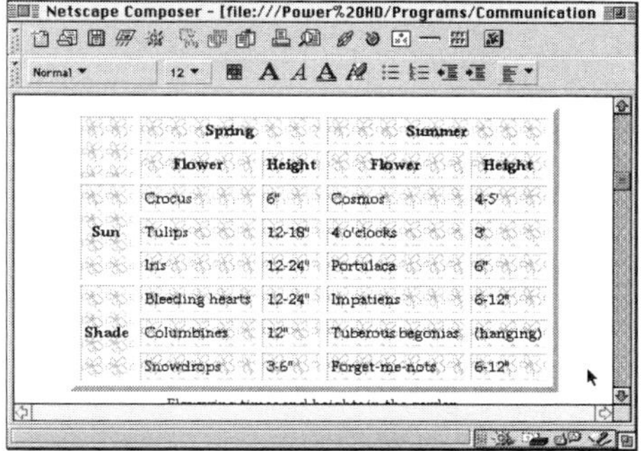

Figure 21.51 *The selected element's background image is changed.*

Adding an image to the table

You can create an image to use as a backdrop to a cell, row, or to the entire table. Keep in mind, however, that images can make the text very difficult to read.

To add an image to the table:

1. Click anywhere in a table, row, or cell to select it **(Figure 21.48)**, choose Format > Table Info, and then click the tab that corresponds to the part of the table you wish to modify: Table, Row, or Cell.
2. Click the Image option in the Table, Row, or Cell Background section near the bottom of the dialog box **(Figure 21.49)**. A dialog box automatically appears from which you can choose the image file.
3. Locate the image file on your hard disk and click Open. The file's URL is stored in the Format dialog box **(Figure 21.50)**.
4. Click Apply to see the changes right away. Make further changes and click Apply until you're satisfied with the results.
5. Click OK to close the dialog box and save the changes **(Figure 21.51)**.

✔ Tips

- Any image you choose overrides any colors already specified *(see page 292)*.
- The images you've specified for a cell will override those that you've chosen for a row, while the images you've specified for a row override those that you've picked for the entire table.

Advanced Page Design

22

Advanced is a relative term, of course. While the topics discussed in this chapter may be advanced for those new to Composer and to designing Web pages in general, seasoned HTML writers would be hard pressed to agree.

HTML, or HyperText Markup Language, is the stuff that pages are made of. It looks a little bit like WordPerfect formatting in the early days of computers: to make something bold you had to add <B> in front of the word. On screen it looked terrible, but once printed, it *almost* made the tags worthwhile.

Composer is great for basic page design. Like early versions of PageMaker, it lets you create simple pages without much technical knowledge. For example, it makes inserting images and adding special attributes to them (like alignment or size) very simple. And it is much more careful about its end brackets than any human could ever be.

However, Composer has many limitations. For example, you cannot apply logical formatting such as emphasis or strong. You cannot create forms or frames. And, Netscape inserts information about its own company on every page you create, which you may or may not like.

The trick is to take advantage of both worlds. Use Composer as a foundation, and then create additional features manually, as described in this chapter.

Adding HTML tags manually

Thankfully, you are not limited to the tags that Composer can insert through its commands and buttons. You can add any HTML tag you like manually, whether or not Composer (or Navigator, for that matter) recognizes it. This gives you the flexibility to expand as HTML expands, without having to wait until Composer catches up.You can also add HTML attributes to the code that Composer creates. For more details, consult *Adding extra HTML* on page 298.

To add an HTML tag manually:

1. Place the cursor where you wish to insert the opening HTML tag **(Figure 22.1)**.
2. Choose Insert > HTML Tag **(Figure 22.2)**. The HTML Tag dialog box appears.
3. Type a single HTML tag in the text area **(Figure 22.3)**. Composer automatically checks to see if you have typed an end bracket (>) and that you have enclosed necessary attributes in quotation marks.
4. If desired, click Verify to have Netscape check if your HTML tag is standard HTML.
5. Click OK. A big yellow tag with a less than sign appears in the Composer window **(Figure 22.4)**.
6. If necessary, click where you wish to insert the closing HTML tag and repeat steps 2–5 **(Figures 22.5, 22.6, and 22.7)**.
7. Browse the page to view the effects of the HTML tag **(Figure 22.8)**.

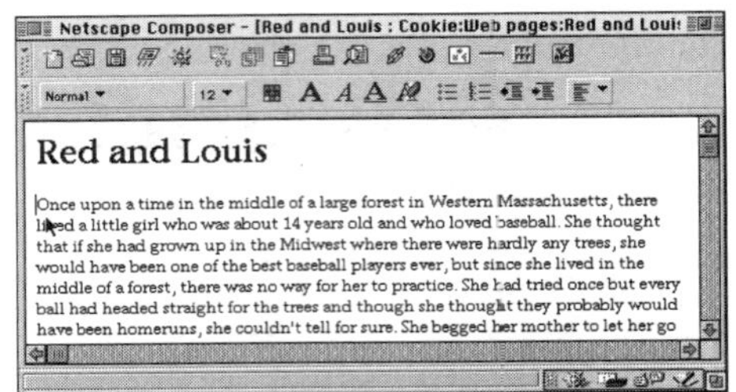

Figure 22.1 *Click where you want to insert the HTML tag manually.*

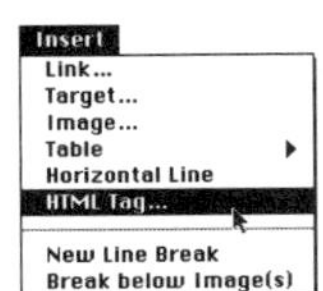

Figure 22.2 *Choose Insert > HTML Tag.*

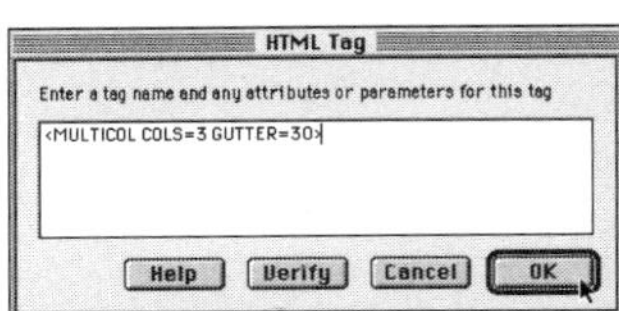

Figure 22.3 *Type one single tag (and any attributes) in the HTML Tag dialog box. Click OK to close the dialog box.*

Figure 22.4 *The HTML tag is shown with a big, yellow tag.*

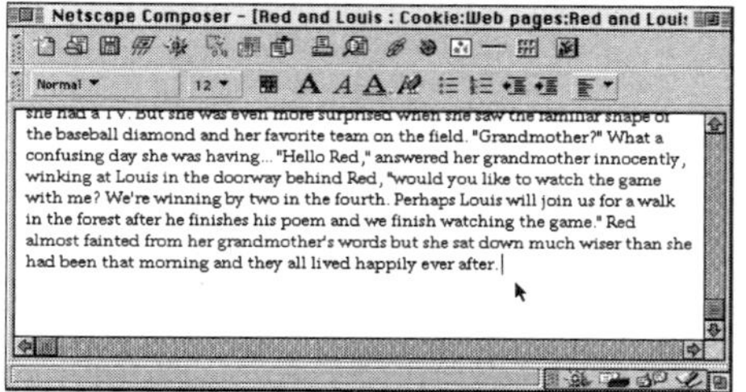

Figure 22.5 *To insert the closing tab, click in the Composer window where you wish to put it.*

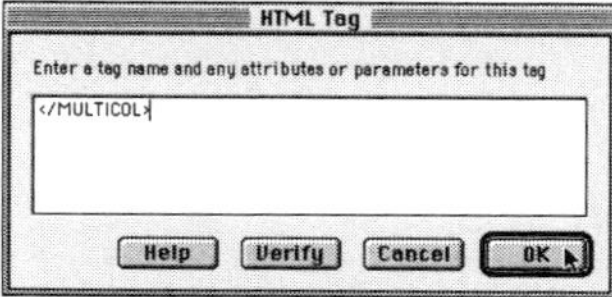

Figure 22.6 *Type the closing tag in the HTML Tag dialog box and click OK.*

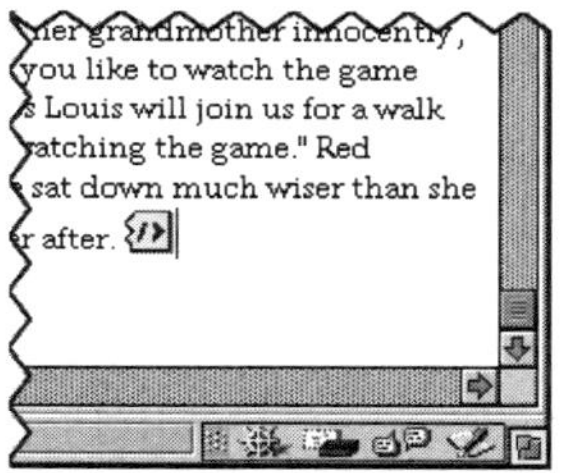

Figure 22.7 *The closing tag symbol displays a forward slash and greater than sign, to distinguish it from an opening tag.*

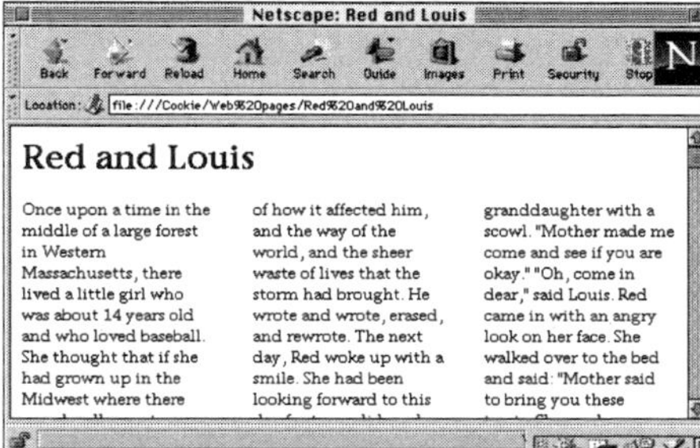

Figure 22.8 *The HTML tag is correctly interpreted in the Navigator window. These are multiple columns!*

✔ Tips

- For a listing of exactly what Composer can do on its own, consult *How Composer translates into HTML* on page 342.
- Here are some things you might want to add manually: multiple columns, margins, indents, spacers, client-side image maps, internal sound, external video, applets, counters, and comments. For the exact coding, you might want to try another book of mine: *HTML for the World Wide Web, 2nd Edition: Visual QuickStart Guide,* also published by Peachpit Press.
- I don't recommend adding forms or frames to your page with Composer. Besides the fact that the program has a hard time dealing with those features and bombs a lot, it's just not worth the hassle. Use a text editor or full-fledged word processor *(see page 299).*
- You can only insert one tag at a time. For tags that have opening and closing versions, you'll have to insert the opening tag, type the affected text, and then insert the closing tag.
- If Composer can't create the tag, it probably can't view the result either. Preview the page in Navigator or some other browser.
- To add HTML to an existing element created with Composer, consult *Adding extra HTML* on page 298.
- Click and hold over the big yellow tags and then choose HTML Tag Info to access the HTML Tag dialog box and make any necessary changes.

Adding extra HTML

Sometimes it's easier to let Composer create an element and then add HTML code to that element. For example, you could create a link with Composer and then manually add the HTML code to open the link in a new window.

To add extra HTML to a tag created with Composer:

1. Open the Format dialog box for the element in question **(Figure 22.9)**.
2. Click the Extra HTML button **(Figure 22.10)**. The Extra HTML dialog box appears.
3. Type the HTML attributes or JavaScript that you wish to add to the existing tag **(Figure 22.11)**.
4. Click OK to close the Extra HTML box and then OK to close the Format dialog box. You probably won't be able to see the difference in the Composer window, but the added code should work properly in a browser, maybe even in Navigator.

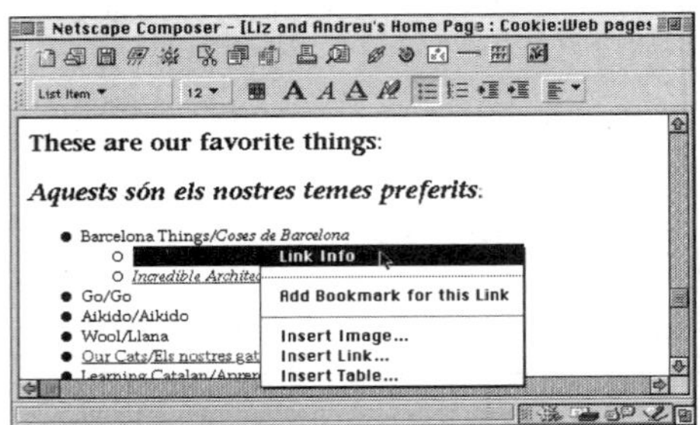

Figure 22.9 *Click and hold over the link and then choose Link Info from the pop-up menu that appears.*

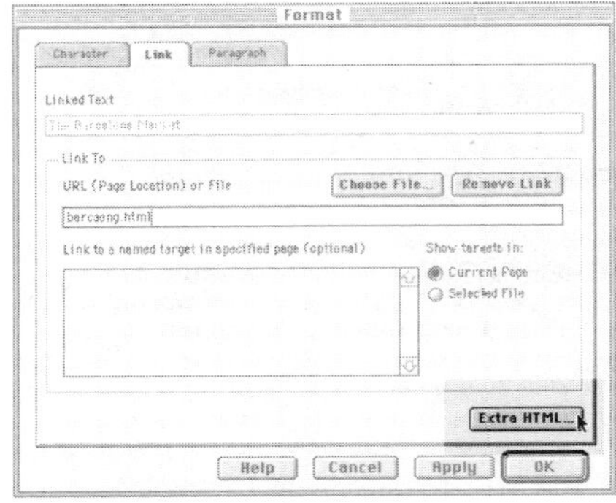

Figure 22.10 *In the Format dialog box, click the Extra HTML button.*

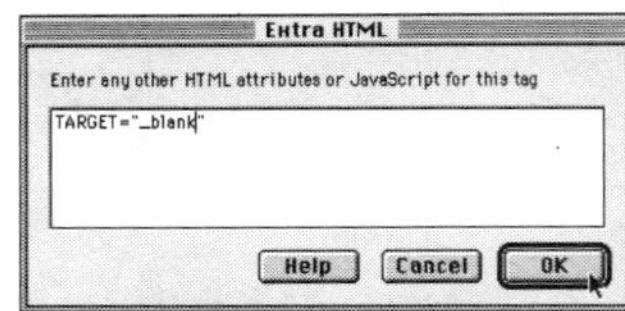

Figure 22.11 *Type the extra HTML code in the dialog box.*

✓ Tips

- To add an entire tag manually, consult *Adding HTML tags manually* on page 296.
- You can add extra HTML to links, images, tables, and horizontal lines.
- For more help on the exact coding to add, you might want to consult another book of mine: *HTML for the World Wide Web, 2nd Edition: Visual QuickStart Guide,* also published by Peachpit Press.

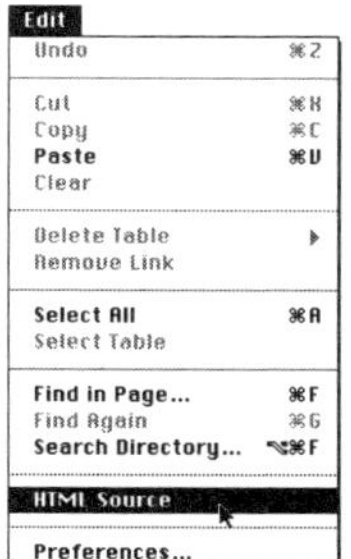

Figure 22.12 *With the page in the Composer window, choose Edit > HTML Source.*

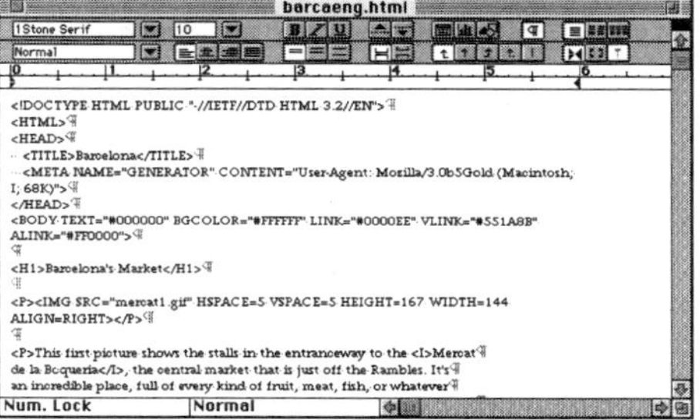

Figure 22.13 *The page's HTML coding is displayed in the designated program (this is Microsoft Word).*

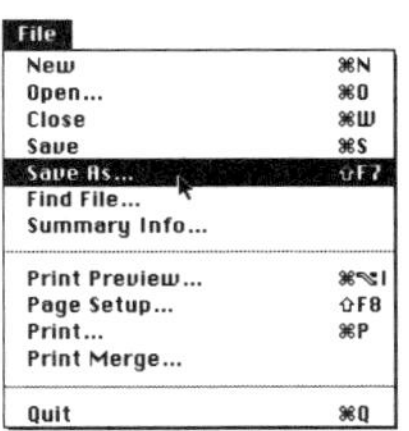

Figure 22.14 *Choose File > Save As in the text editor.*

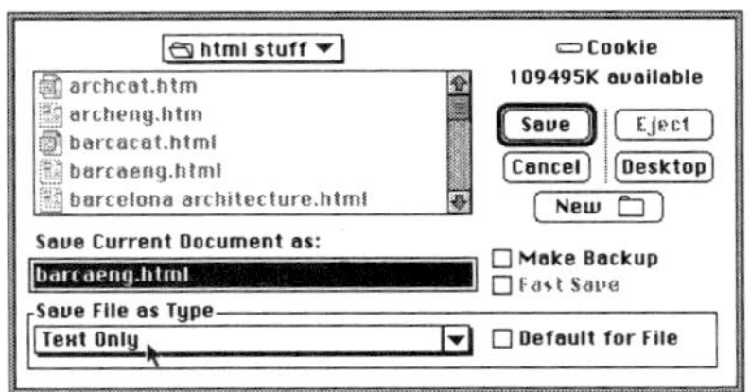

Figure 22.15 *Make sure you save the file in Text Only format with the .htm or .html extension.*

Editing HTML tags externally

You can look at the HTML tags on your page by opening the page with any text editor. Once in the text editor, you can remove Netscape's annoying, automatic self-identification tags and add features that Composer does not support.

To edit HTML tags externally:

1. From Composer, choose Edit > HTML Source **(Figure 22.12)**. Composer launches the program you've specified for editing HTML *(see page 300)* and opens the page **(Figure 22.13)**.
2. Make any desired changes.
3. Choose File > Save As in the text editor **(Figure 22.14)**.
4. Choose the Text Only format and give the file either the .htm or .html extension **(Figure 22.15)**. Otherwise, browsers won't recognize the file.

✔ Tips

- Of course, you don't even have to open Communicator to edit your HTML tags manually. Simply open the text editor (SimpleText will do fine, though you can use a fancier word processor if you prefer) and then open the HTML document.
- To choose the text editor, consult *Specifying a program for editing HTML tags* on page 300.
- If you haven't chosen a text editor before attempting to edit the HTML externally, Composer will give you a chance to select a suitable program.

Specifying a program for editing HTML tags

Since HTML documents are always saved in text-only (ASCII) format, you can use virtually any word processor—from SimpleText to NisusWriter—to edit HTML tags. You can specify which program you'd like to use, and Communicator will launch it automatically when you decide to edit the tags manually *(see page 299)*.

To specify a program for editing HTML tags:

1. Choose Edit > Preferences **(Figure 22.16)**.
2. Click Composer in the Category list.
3. In the External Editors section, click Choose next to HTML source **(Figure 22.17)**. An Open dialog box appears.
4. Locate the desired text editor on your hard disk and click Open **(Figure 22.18)**. The path to the program now appears next to HTML source in the Composer panel of the Preferences dialog box **(Fig. 22.19)**.
5. Click OK to close the dialog box.

✔ Tip

■ You can also choose a program for editing images externally *(see page 266)*.

Figure 22.16 *Choose Edit > Preferences.*

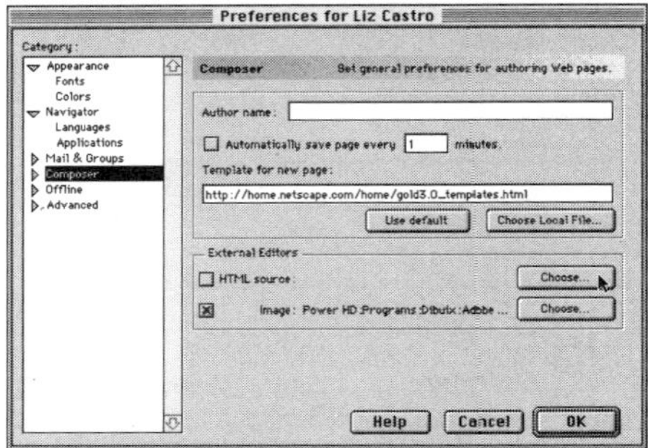

Figure 22.17 *Click Choose next to HTML source in the Composer panel of the Preferences dialog box.*

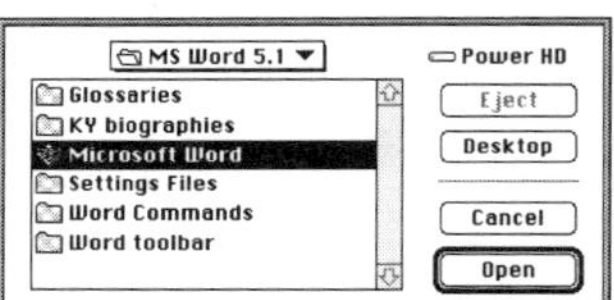

Figure 22.18 *Choose the text editor that you want to use and click Open.*

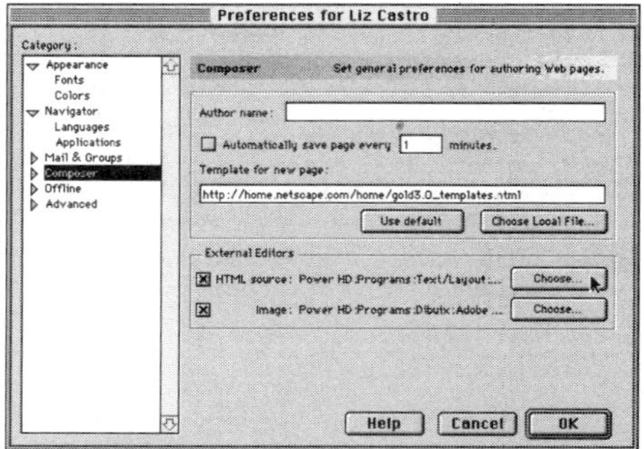

Figure 22.19 *The path to the chosen text editor is shown next to HTML source in the Composer preferences dialog box.*

23 Publishing a Page

Once you've finished designing your page, you have to make it accessible to your public. First you should test your page and make sure all your images appear as they should, that your text is formatted properly, and that your links lead where you intended.

Then you're ready to transfer the files to your server. Composer boasts a one-step publishing command that copies a page and its associated images to a given location on a remote server.

Once your page is up and running, you'll want to put out the word so that people know how to find it.

Testing your page

You should always test your Web pages in at least one browser, if not more. It is not necessary to connect to the server to test your pages. Instead, open and check the pages from your hard disk.

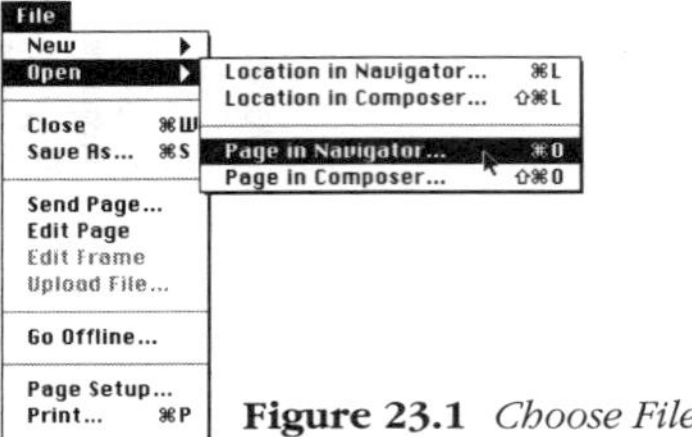

Figure 23.1 *Choose File > Open > Page in Navigator.*

To test your pages:

1. Open a Navigator window and choose File > Open > Page in Navigator **(Figure 23.1)**. The Open dialog box appears.

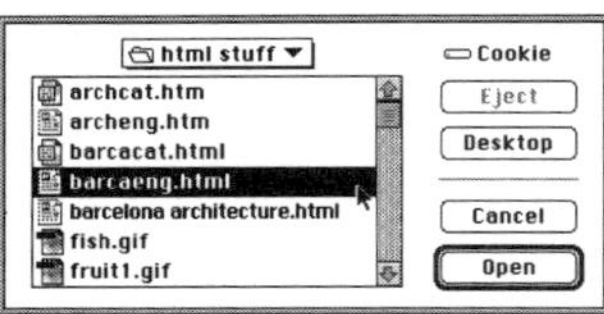

Figure 23.2 *Choose the page on your hard disk that you wish to test and click Open.*

2. Choose the file on your hard disk and click Open **(Figure 23.2)**.

3. Go through the whole page and make sure it looks exactly the way you want it to **(Figure 23.3)**. For example:

   Is the formatting what you wanted?

   Does each of your links lead to the correct destination?

   Are your images aligned properly?

   Have you included your name and e-mail address (preferably in a link, and/or formatted with Address) so that your users can contact you with comments and suggestions?

Figure 23.3 *Read the page over, checking for spelling and formatting errors. Do the images appear as desired? Do the links go where they should?*

4. In Navigator, choose File > Edit Page to switch to Composer **(Figure 23.4)**. The page appears in the Composer window **(Figure 23.5)**.

5. Make any necessary changes.

6. Choose File > Save to save the changes **(Figure 23.6)**.

Testing your page

Figure 23.4 *From the Composer window, choose File > Edit Page.*

Figure 23.5 *In the Composer window, make any necessary corrections.*

Figure 23.6 *Choose File > Save to save the corrections made to your Web page.*

7. Choose File > Browse Page or click the Preview button on the Composition toolbar to switch from Composer to Navigator in order to view the changes.

8. Repeat steps 1–7 until you are satisfied with your pages. Don't get discouraged if it takes several tries.

9. View your page with other browsers to make sure your page will be attractive no matter what browser your readers use.

10. Transfer the files to the server, if you haven't done so already *(see page 304)*.

11. Test all your links again to make sure that they work correctly from the server.

✔ Tips

- Use several browsers (Microsoft Internet Explorer, Mosaic, Lynx, etc., and perhaps several versions of each) to test your pages. You never know what browser your user is going to view your pages with.
- You can test the links locally by clicking them as long as the destination documents are in the same relative position on your computer. In other words, if two pages will be in the same directory on the server, they should be in the same directory on your hard disk. The same rule applies to images, sounds, and any other associated files. The only things that won't work locally are CGI scripts and server-side image maps.

Publishing your page

Composer has a special publishing option that automatically transfers all of the files in your Web site to your server so that your public has access to them.

To publish your page:

1. Open a connection to the Internet if you're not already connected.
2. Open the page in Composer that you want to publish.
3. In Composer, choose File > Publish **(Figure 23.7)**. The Publish Page dialog box appears. The page's title and file name are automatically entered at the top of the dialog box.
4. Enter the location on the server—that is, the URL—where the principal file should be copied **(Figure 23.8)**. If you're not sure what to type here, ask your Internet service provider. Typically, it will be the FTP address of your Web site on the server plus the name of the file you're uploading.
5. Enter your user name and password. If desired, click Save Password so that you don't have to enter it each time you publish a page.
6. In the bottom section, if you want to upload the images, sounds, and other auxiliary files for this one page, check Files associated with this page. If you are publishing more than one page, to include the auxiliary files from all of them, check All files in page's folder.

Figure 23.7 *With the Composer window active and the page you want to publish showing, choose File > Publish.*

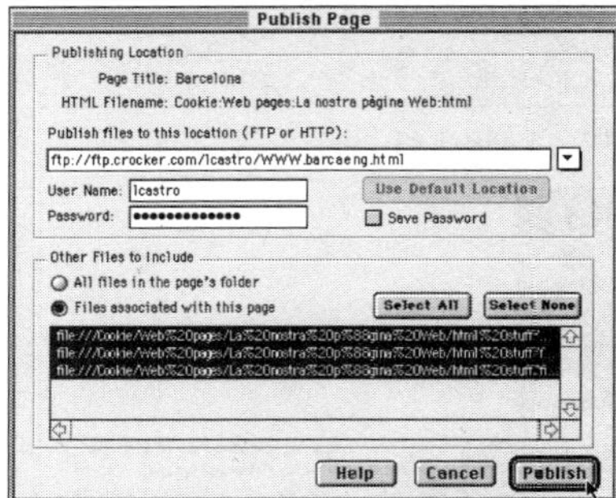

Figure 23.8 *At the top of the Publish Page dialog box, the file name and title of the page are automatically entered. Type the destination URL of the main file you want to publish. You can also choose to publish the auxiliary files (images, sound files, etc.) which will be listed in the list at the bottom of the dialog box.*

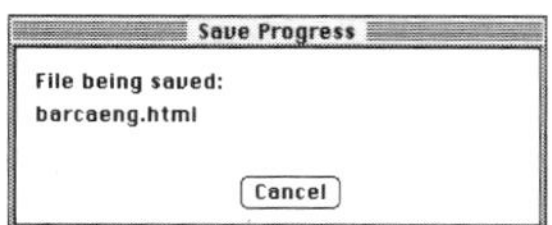

Figure 23.9 *As the files are published, a dialog box gives you a progress report.*

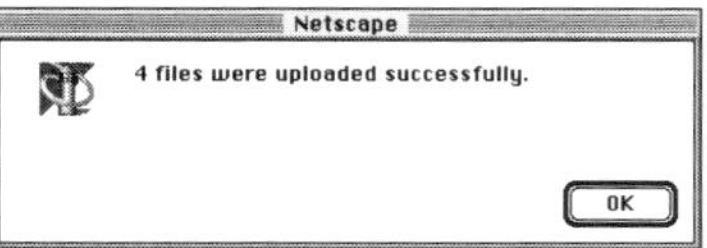

Figure 23.10 *When Composer has finished publishing your files, it will give you this message, showing just how many files were uploaded.*

Figure 23.11 *Once the files have been published to the server, it's a good idea to connect to the Internet and check the newly uploaded pages.*

7. The images from the current document (or all the images in the current page's folder) appear in the scroll list. Click the files that you want to copy to the server, or use the Select None and Select All buttons as necessary. Your readers will only be able to see the images on a page if you copy them to the server.
8. Click Publish to send the files to the server. As the selected page and the additional files listed in the scroll box are copied, a dialog box keeps you apprised of the progress **(Fig. 23.9)**.
9. An alert assures you that you have successfully published the page **(Figure 23.10)**
10. Once the page is published, surf to it with Navigator **(Figure 23.11)**.

✔ Tips

- The default publishing location is specified in the Publish panel of the Preferences dialog box *(see page 306)*. You can either accept the default, choose a different location from the pop-up menu, or type in a new location.
- The principal page to be published is always the one active in the Composer window when you chose File > Publish.
- If you are wary of automatic gadgets, publish your pages manually with FTP. For more information, consult *Uploading a single file* on page 59.
- If you check the Save Password option as described in step 5, be aware that any person with access to your computer will be able to publish documents to your FTP site.

Setting up a default publishing location

Generally, one always publishes to the same location on the server. You can define that location so that you don't have to enter it manually during each publishing session.

To set up a default publishing location:

1. Choose Edit > Preferences **(Figure 23.12)**.
2. Click Publish in the Category list to see the Publish preferences.
3. In the Default publishing location section, enter an FTP or Web address where you want to publish your pages **(Figure 23.13)**. If you're not sure what address to use, contact your Internet service provider.
4. Click OK to save the changes.

Figure 23.12 *Choose Edit > Preferences.*

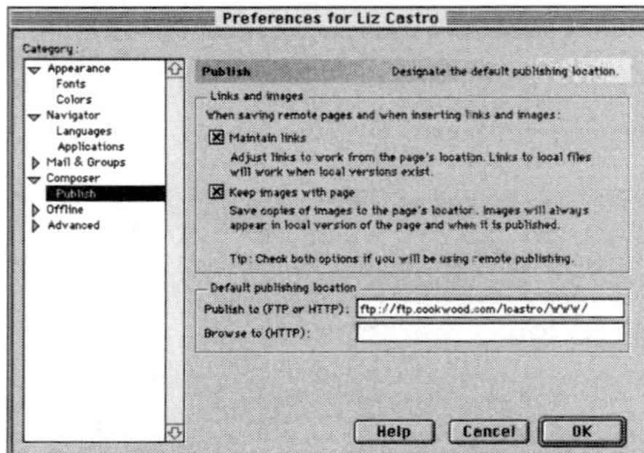

Figure 23.13 *Enter the location where you publish most of your pages in the Publish to text box.*

✔ Harrumph!

- Now what is the *Browse to* box for, you may wonder? After publishing a page, Netscape for Windows users are given the option of automatically jumping to their most often browsed page, which they've entered here in the Preferences dialog box. They don't give Netscape for Macintosh users that option. But they still let you specify where you might have liked to browse if you had been given the opportunity. Gee.

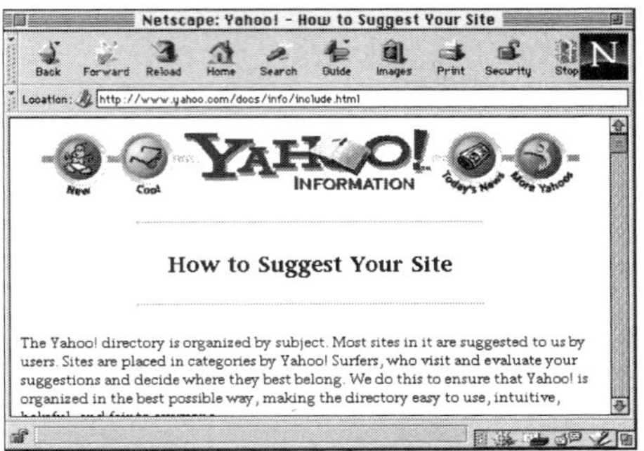

Figure 23.14 *Read Yahoo's instructions for adding or changing a link to your site.*

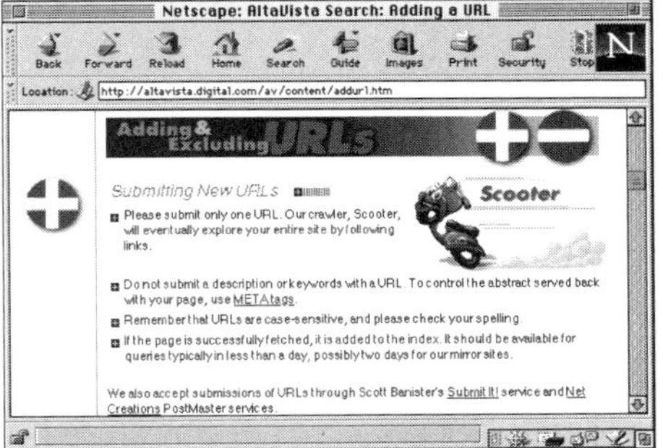

Figure 23.15 *Add your URL to AltaVista so that your page comes up when a user makes a relevant search.*

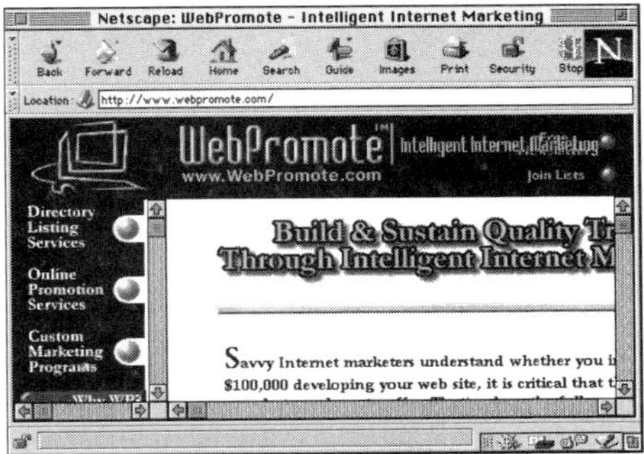

Figure 23.16 *Commercial services like WebPromote can provide marketing for your page—for a fee.*

Advertising your site

With the growing popularity of the Web, there has come an explosion in services for both Web page publishers (that's you!) and their audiences. There are many ways to get the word out about your page. Here are some starters.

To advertise your site:

- Use the forms at free Web indexing services like Yahoo! **(Figure 23.14)** and AltaVista **(Figure 23.15)**.

  Yahoo!: *http://www.yahoo.com/docs/info/include.html*

  AltaVista: *http://altavista.digital.com/av/content/addurl.htm*

  (There are no spaces in either of these URLs.)

- Pay a company to advertise your page for you. One such company is WebPromote *(http://www.webpromote.com)*, but there are many others **(Figure 23.16)**.
- Post a note in the moderated newsgroup *comp.infosystems.www.announce* or the unmoderated *comp.internet.net-happenings* or in discussion groups that have similar interests as your Web site.
- Send e-mail to your associates and friends. You can include the URL for your site in all your correspondence with a signature *(see page 170)*.
- Send e-mail to the creators of other sites with similar interests or topics.
- Check out Don Sellers' book *Getting Hits*, also published by Peachpit Press, for more tips on getting your Web page noticed.

Part V: Preferences

Appearance Preferences

24

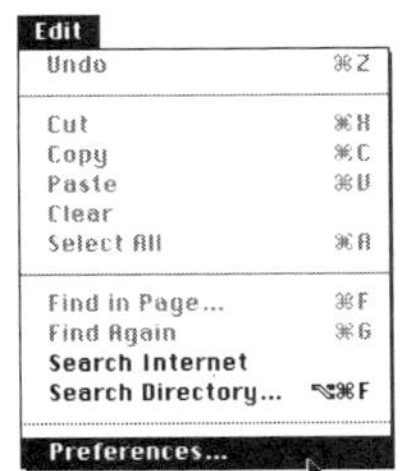

Figure 24.1 *Choose Edit > Preferences.*

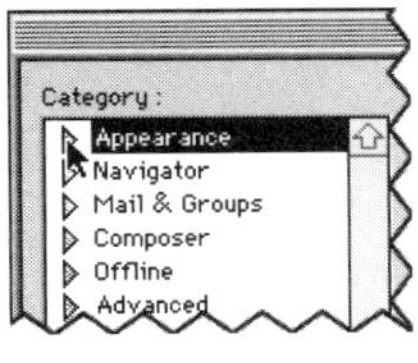

Figure 24.2 *Click on the arrow next to Appearance to expand it and see the sections it contains.*

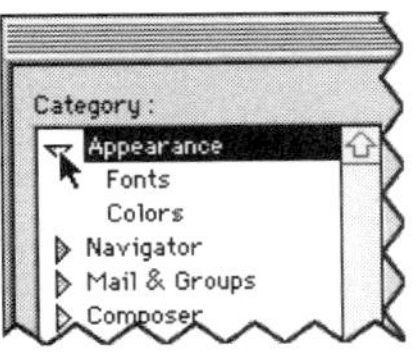

Figure 24.3 *The Appearance category has three sections (Appearance, Fonts, and Colors) that can be accessed by clicking the corresponding name.*

The settings in the Appearance section of the Preferences dialog box let you specify which component you want to start with, how you want to display the toolbars, which fonts you want to use, and which colors you want to use for different elements in Navigator.

To access the Appearance preferences, choose Edit > Preferences **(Figure 24.1)** and then click on the arrow next to the word Appearance to see all three sections it contains **(Figures 24.2 and 24.3)**. Finally, click one of the sections (Appearance, Fonts, or Colors) to access its settings. Each is described in detail on the following pages.

Once you've made the desired changes to the settings, click OK to save the changes, or Cancel to leave the dialog box without saving them. Click Help to access Communicator's Help file.

Appearance

Click the Appearance tab in the Preferences dialog box to show the Appearance preferences. Use the Appearance preferences to control the appearance of the toolbar and which part of Communicator you launch upon start up.

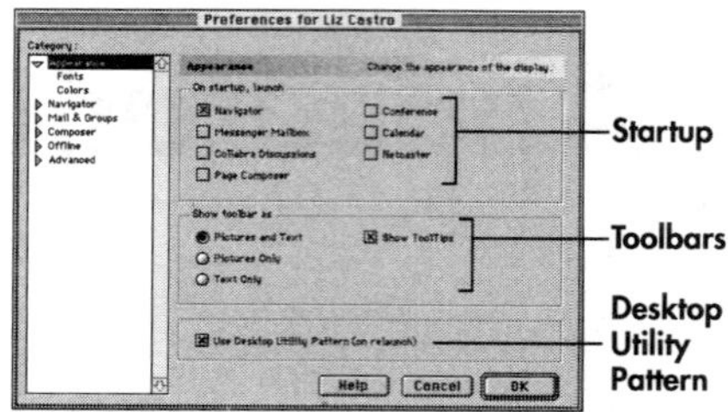

Startup

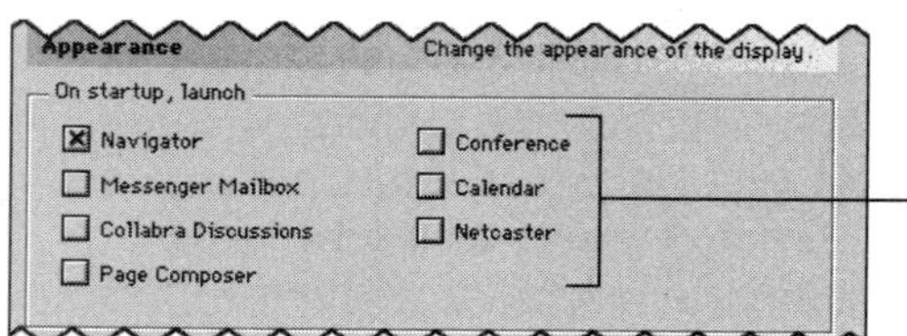

You may check more than one component, but make sure you check at least one—and one that you really have installed on your computer. For instance, if you are not sure whether you have Netcaster or not, don't check it by itself, or Communicator may give you trouble opening the program.

Click **Navigator** so that the first window you see when entering Communicator is the Navigator window.

Click **Messenger Mailbox** to start with the Inbox window (and automatically check your mail).

Click **Collabra Discussions** to start with the Message Center window, from where you can also access the mail functions.

Click **Page Composer** to start with a blank page in Composer that you can use to create your own page.

Click **Conference** to start with Conference, so you can make direct calls to individuals.

Click **Calendar** to start with Calendar, which may need to be installed separately.

Click **Netcaster** to start with Netcaster, which may need to be installed separately.

Toolbars

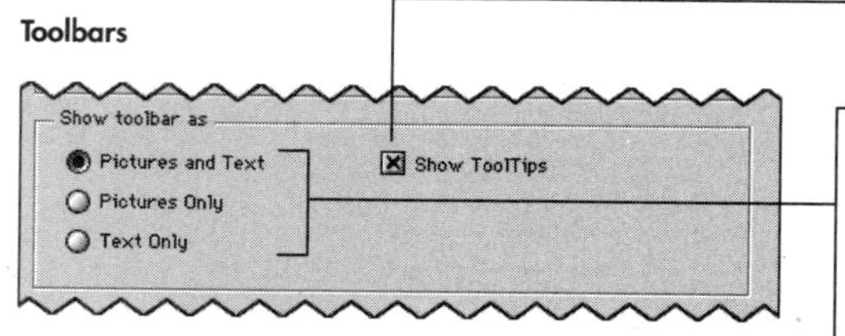

Although the section title is Show toolbar as, *it affects the two toolbars: Navigation and Location.*

Click **Show ToolTips** to have Communicator show you a button's name when you point at it with the cursor.

Choose **Pictures and Text** to see the toolbar icons with the command name label underneath.

Choose **Pictures Only** to use smaller icons, with no labels.

Choose **Text Only** to see only the command name labels on the buttons. This option saves the most space.

Desktop Utility Pattern

Click **Use Desktop Utility Pattern** to have Communicator display the background of the windows themselves with the pattern used for the Desktop.

Fonts

Click the Fonts category in the Preferences dialog box to display the Fonts preferences. Use the Fonts preferences to choose the default font encoding for the documents you browse, as well as the particular fonts that should be used.

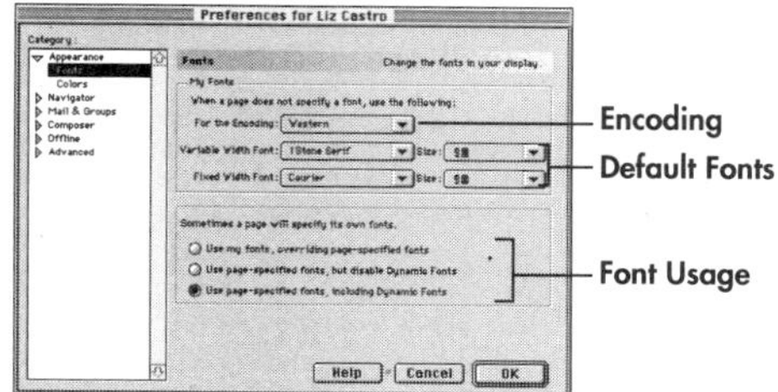

Encoding and Default Fonts

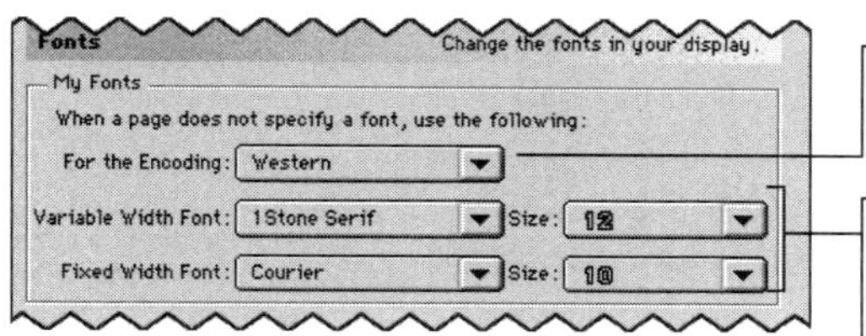

Choose an **encoding** that matches the alphabet of the documents you will read. An encoding describes the relationship between characters and their hexadecimal representations.

Most of the text you see in a document will be displayed with the **variable width font** chosen here. You may also choose a **size** for the text.

The text displayed in entry forms and other special parts of a page is displayed with the **fixed width font** chosen here. (See *Controlling text in the Navigator window* on page 28.)

Font Usage

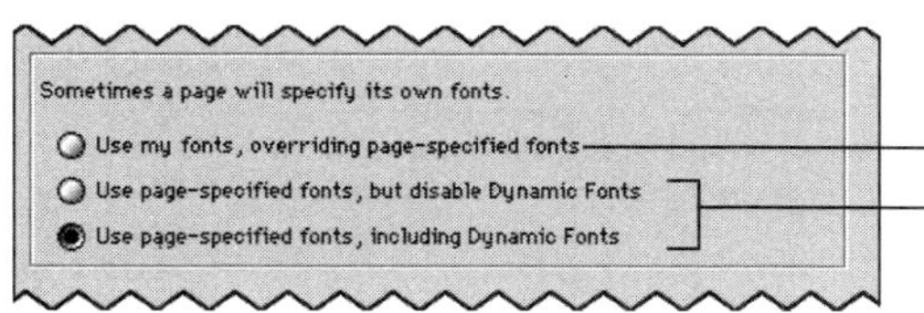

As it becomes easier for designers to specify particular fonts for Web pages, it may in fact become necessary to disable them in order to browse pages more quickly. Keep in mind, however, that fonts usually add spice and interest to a page. It is a matter of balancing how long you're willing to wait with what you hope to see.

Use this option to **speed up the viewing** of the pages at the expense of not viewing the fonts specified in the documents.

Choose one of these two options to attempt to display the page with the **fonts specified by the designer**. The bottom option will download necessary fonts to ensure that the document appears precisely as designed. The middle option attempts to use the designer's fonts, but if they are not available, will make a substitution. (See *Controlling text in the Navigator window* on page 28.)

Colors

You have some control over the colors used on the pages you browse. You can choose a different color for new and visited links and for regular text. For the background, choose either a color or an image. Finally, you can make these choices override the options used in any individual Web page.

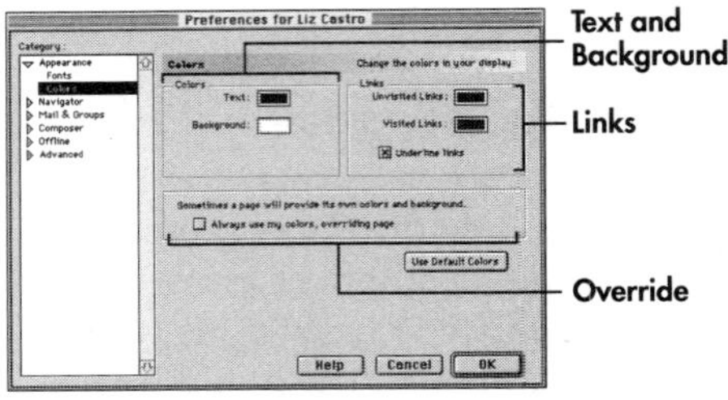

Text and Background

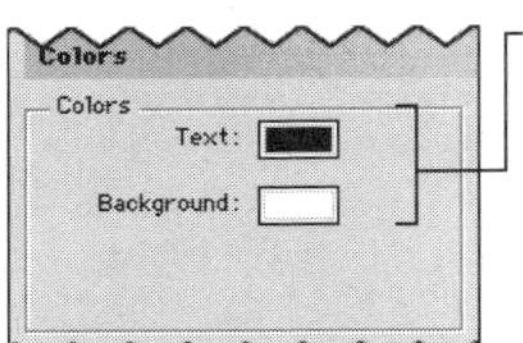

You may choose a special **color for the text and for the background** of all the pages you browse.

Links

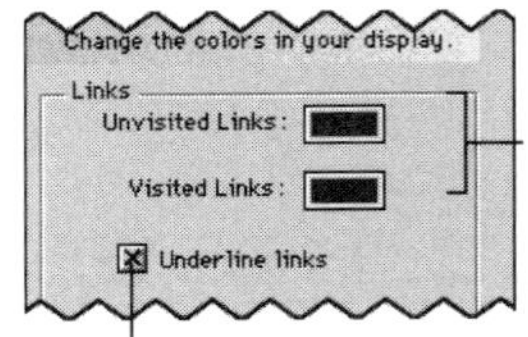

Click here to **underline** the links, which makes link recognition easier on monochrome monitors.

You can choose **your own colors for links** you haven't visited (Unvisited Links) and for links you have visited (Visited Links). Simply click on the color swatch and choose a color in the dialog box that appears and click OK. The new color will be shown in the swatch.

Override

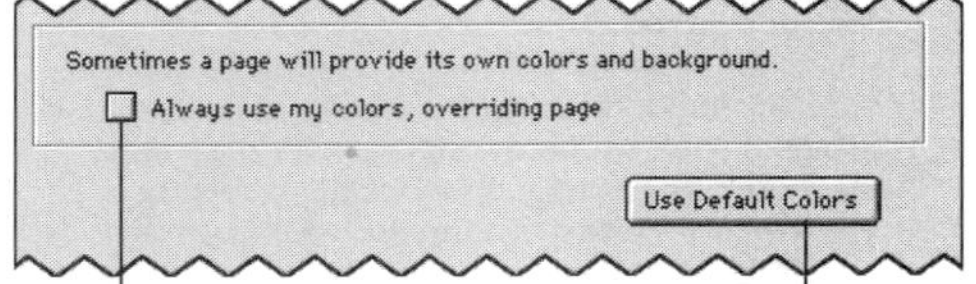

Some Web page designers define their own colors for text, links, and background. You can choose to override their choices.

Click **Always use my colors, overriding page** if you want your colors (chosen in the upper part of the dialog box) to take precedence over a particular Web page designer's fancy. For example, if you're having trouble reading a page because the Web designer chose non-contrasting colors or a busy background, you can go back to normal colors by using this option.

Click here to use Communicator's **default colors** (the default background color is grey).

Navigator Preferences

25

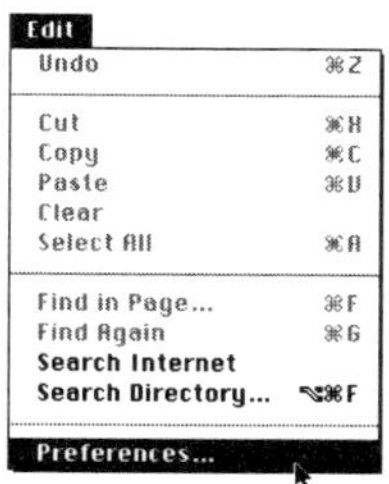

Figure 25.1 *Choose Edit > Preferences.*

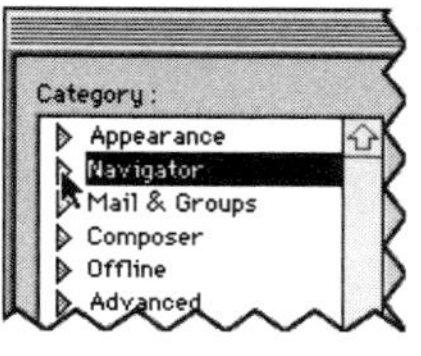

Figure 25.2 *Click on the arrow next to Navigator to expand it and see the sections it contains.*

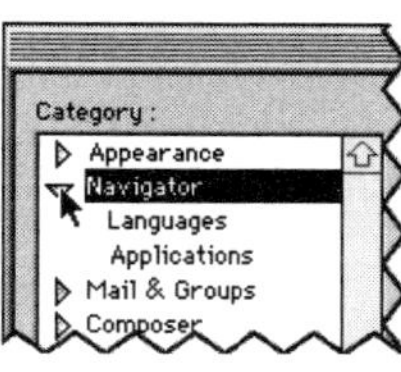

Figure 25.3 *The Navigator category has three sections (Navigator, Languages, and Applications) that can be accessed by clicking on the corresponding name.*

The settings in the Navigator section of the Preferences dialog box let you specify which page Navigator opens upon startup, where your home page is located, which applications handle the different types of files, and the language scheme for viewing text in the Navigator window.

To access the Navigator Preferences, choose Edit > Preferences **(Figure 25.1)** and then click on the arrow next to the word Navigator to see all three sections it contains **(Figures 25.2 and 25.3)**. Finally, click one of the sections (Navigator, Applications, or Languages) to view the corresponding settings. Each section is described in detail in the following pages.

Once you've made the desired changes to the settings, click OK to save the changes, or Cancel to leave the dialog box without saving them. Click Help to access Communicator's Help file.

Navigator

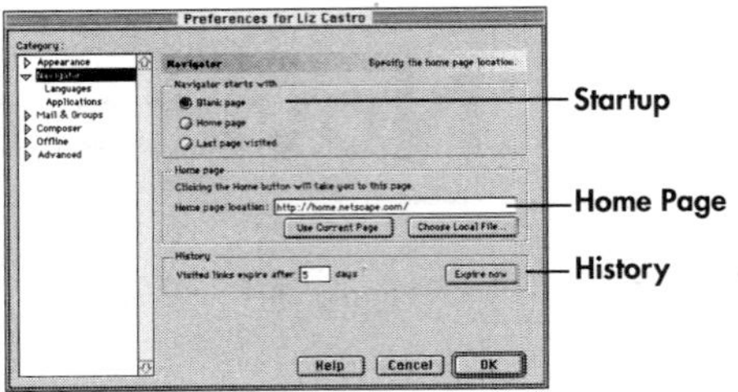

Click Navigator in the Category list of the Preferences dialog box to display the Navigator preferences. You can choose the type of page displayed upon starting up Navigator, the location of your home page (not Netscape's home page), and the number of days that the addresses in the History window are remembered.

Startup

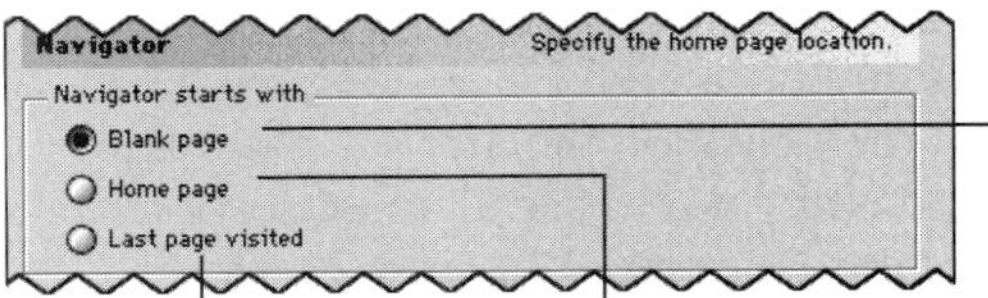

Use **Blank page** to open Navigator with a clean, blank window.

Choose **Last page visited** to start Navigator with the page you ended up in on your last surfing session.

Click **Home page** to display a given page of your choice that you access frequently. Choose the page in the Home page section of the dialog box, described below.

Home Page

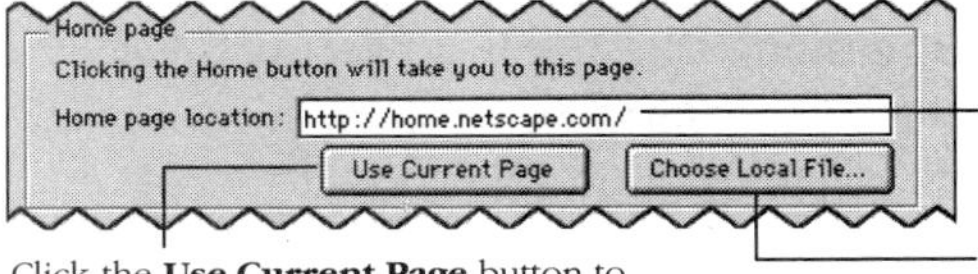

Type in the **URL** of the page that you want to use as your home page.

Click the **Use Current Page** button to use as your home page whatever page you happen to be in at that precise moment.

If the page you intend to use is on a local hard disk, click **Choose Local File**, locate the HTML file on your hard disk, and click Open.

History

Links change color when you click them. Enter the **number of days** you want to show the links as visited. After that, the links will be displayed as not yet visited (generally, in black).

Click **Expire now** to immediately return all links to their unvisited status (which are generally displayed in black).

Languages

Click Languages in the Category list in the Preferences dialog box to see the Language preferences. When a page on the Web is available in more than one language, you can tell the server what language(s) you prefer to browse by creating an "accept list" of languages.

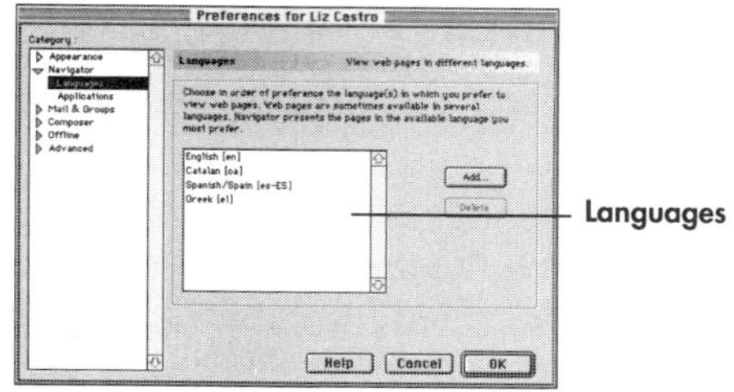

Languages

You can create a priority list of languages in which you prefer files to be downloaded or viewed through the Accept list. Then Navigator advises the server of the desired languages and if the server understands, it gives you access to the appropriate language version.

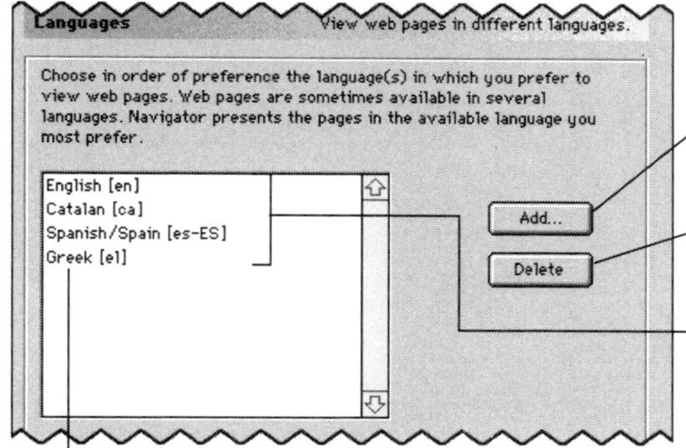

Click **Add** to go to the Add Languages dialog box, where there is a list of languages from which you can choose. *(See below).*

Select a language from the list and click **Delete** to disregard it as an option for viewing. text.

Languages at the top of the list are given priority over languages farther down the list. Select a language and **drag it up and down** to change its priority.

The acceptable languages are listed in order of preference.

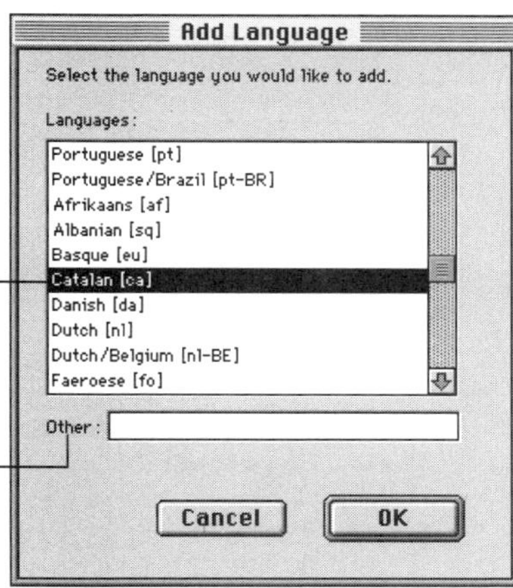

Select a language in the **Languages** list to add it to the accept list.

If the desired language or region does not appear in the list, type it in the **Other** field to add it to the accept list. The first tag should be a two letter ISSO 639 language abbreviation. The second two letters should be an ISO 3166 country tag.

Applications

Click Applications in the Category list in the Preferences dialog box to see the Applications preferences. You can choose which helper applications should be launched for the files Navigator encounters out on the Web, or if the files should simply be saved without launching any program.

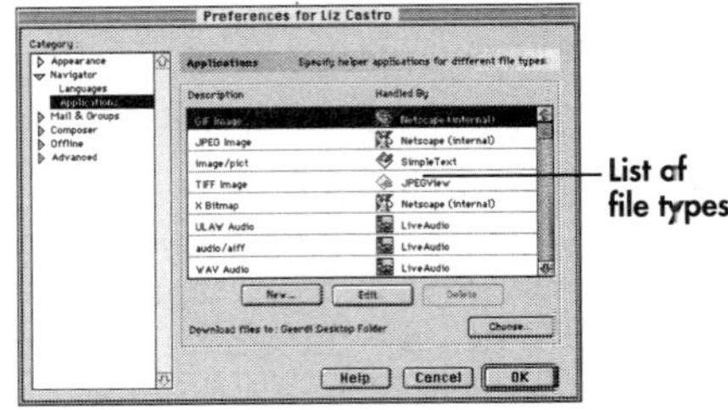

List of file types

List of file types

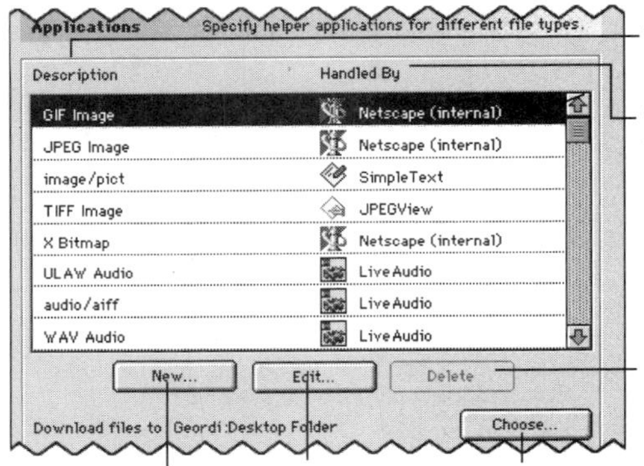

The **Description** column gives the name of the file type.

The **Handled By** column tells you which application is currently handling that kind of file.

Click **Delete** to delete the file type and its description from the list (it is in grey because internally handled file types cannot be eliminated).

Click **New** to create a file type for a kind of file not already in the list *(see Edit/New Type below).*

Click a file type and click **Edit** to change its options in the Edit Type dialog box *(see Edit/New Type below).*

Click **Choose** to specify the folder on your hard disk where you wish to download that kind of file.

Edit/New Type

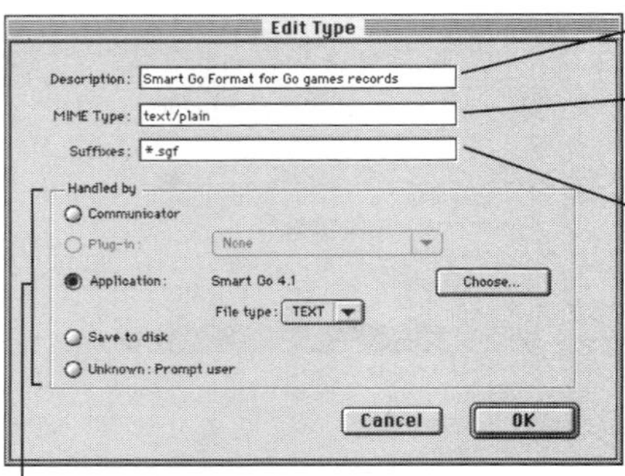

Enter a **description** of the file type, something that gives you a hint as to what kind of file you are dealing with.

Enter the **MIME type** for the files that you wish to define. The MIME type is a standardized way to classify file types on the Internet.

Enter the **file suffixes** of the files that you wish to define as the selected File type. The suffix indicates what kinds of files are included in the File type.

You tell Navigator what you want it to do with each kind of file it finds. You can view the file directly (if Navigator can), use a Plug-in to handle it, launch a helper application that opens the files, save the file, or have Navigator ask you what to do with it.

Choose **Communicator** to view the file in Navigator, when possible.

Choose **Plug-in** to have a specific Plug-in handle that kind of file.

Choose an **application** on your hard disk that you want to handle the specific file type. Click Choose and locate the program you wish to use.

Choose **Save to disk** to have Navigator automatically save the files with this extension to your hard disk.

Click on **Unknown: Prompt user** to decide what to do with each file type individually.

26

Mail and Groups Prefs

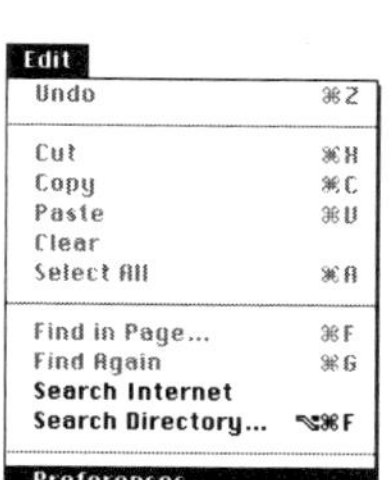

Figure 26.1 *Choose Edit > Preferences.*

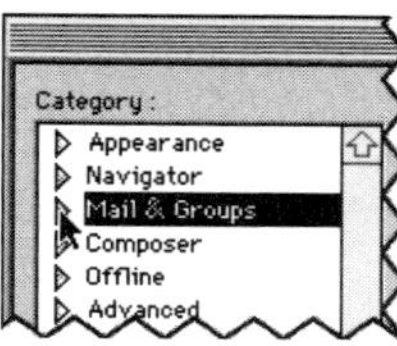

Figure 26.2 *Click on the arrow next to Mail & Groups to expand it and see the sections it contains.*

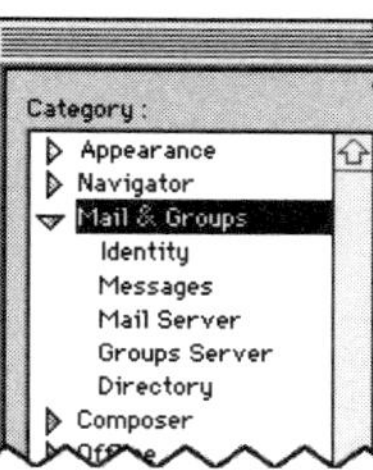

Figure 26.3 *The Mail & Groups category has six sections (Mail & Groups, Identity, Messages, Mail Server, Groups Server, and Directory) that can be accessed by clicking the corresponding name.*

The settings in the Mail & Groups sections of the Preferences dialog box control many different aspects of the mail and discussion groups windows.

To access the Mail & Groups preferences, choose Edit > Preferences **(Figure 26.1)** and then click on the arrow next to Mail & Groups to see all six sections it contains **(Figures 26.2 and 26.3)**. Finally, click one of the sections (Mail & Groups, Identity, Messages, Mail Server, Groups Server, or Directory) to access its settings. Each is described in detail in the following pages.

Once you've made the desired changes to the settings, click OK to save the changes, or Cancel to leave the dialog box without saving them. Click Help to access Communicator's Help file.

Mail & Groups

Click Mail & Groups in the Category list in the Preferences dialog box to change the way messages appear. You can choose the font that messages should be displayed in, the style and size of quoted sections, the way the windows are reused, and whether you want Communicator to warn you with a sound when new messages arrive.

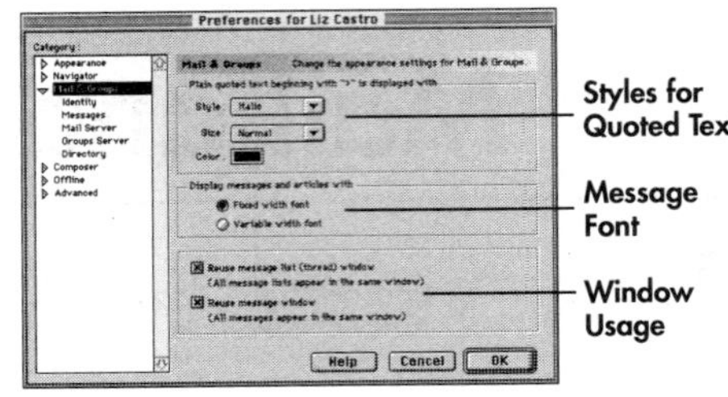

Styles for Quoted Text

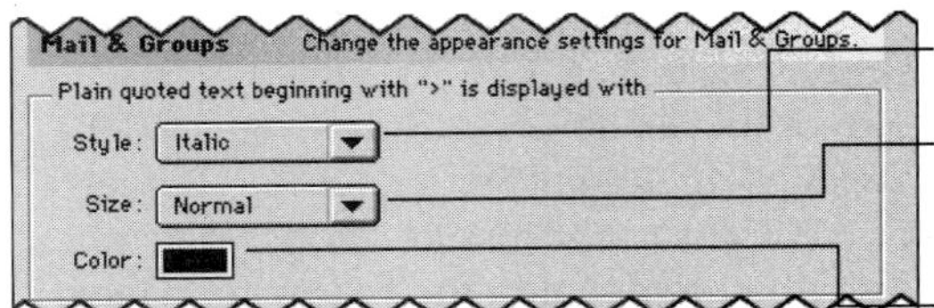

Many messages contain text from earlier correspondence. You can format that text with a special style and size to set it apart from the current message's contents.

Select Regular, Bold, Italic or Bold Italic from the **Style** pop-up menu to format quoted text with the corresponding style.

Select Normal from the **Size** pop-up menu to keep the quoted text at the same size as regular text. Choose Bigger or Smaller to change the relative size of quoted text.

Click on the **Color** swatch and select a color from the dialog box that appears to distinguish quoted text from the surrounding message.

Message Font

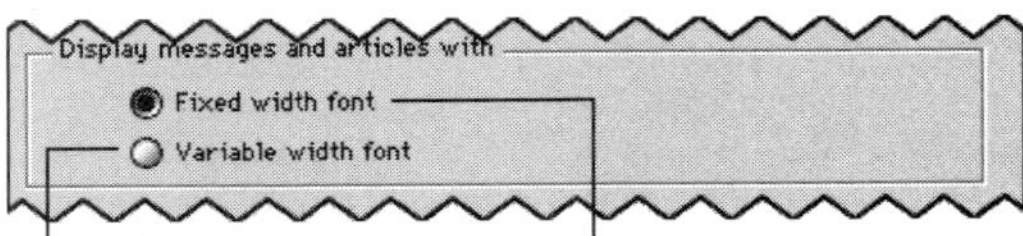

Click **Variable width font** to use the font defined next to "Variable Width Font" in the Fonts section of the Preferences dialog box *(see page 313).*

Click **Fixed width font** to use the font defined next to "Fixed Width Font" in the Fonts section of the Preferences dialog box *(see page 313).*

In the Fonts preferences section (page 313), you chose a specific font for proportional text and another for fixed font text. Here, you can choose which of those fonts should be used for displaying messages.

Window Usage

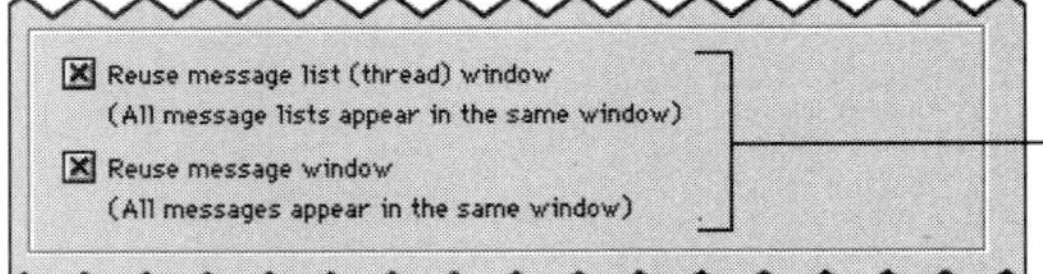

To fight window clutter, check both these options. The first means that each time you double click a folder in the Message Center, it opens in the same Message List window. The second means that each time you double click a message, it opens in the same Message window. Uncheck these options to use a new Message List or Message window each time you double click.

Mail & Groups

Identity

Click Identity in the Category list under Mail & Groups to enter information about yourself, including your name, e-mail address, the e-mail address where you want to receive replies, and the name of your organization. You can also specify a signature file that will be appended to every outgoing message.

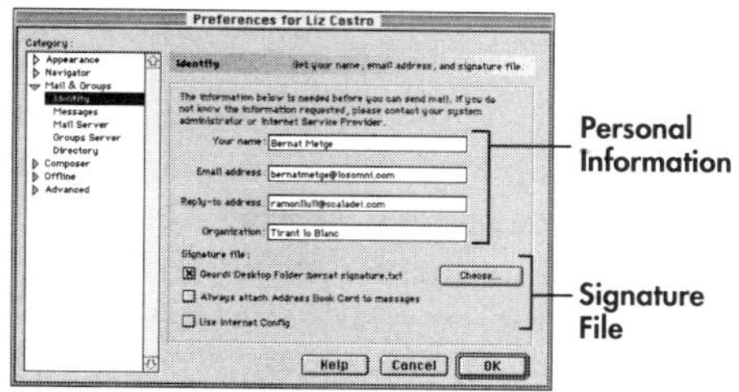

Personal Information

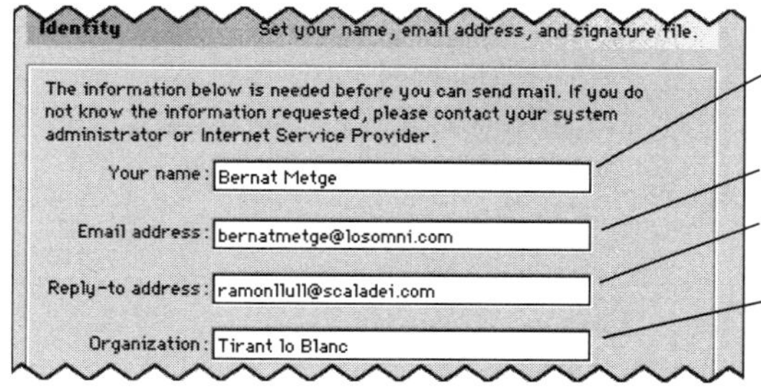

All of the information you type here appears on each message you send out.

Type **your name** as you wish it to appear on every outgoing message.

Type your **e-mail address**.

Type the address where you want **replies** to be sent.

Type the name of your **organization**. If you don't type anything here, Communicator will use the name of your Internet Service Provider in all outgoing correspondence.

Signature File

You can create a text file and then have Communicator automatically add it the end of each message you send. Most signatures include the writer's name, e-mail address, sometimes their postal address, and a cute quote. The only requirement is that it be saved in Text Only format.

Click **Choose** to locate your signature file (any text file) on the hard disk. For more information on signatures, consult *Creating a signature file* on page 169.

Click **Always attach Address Book Card to messages** to add the personal information included in your card to every message you send.

Click **Use Internet Config** if you want Communicator to get your identity information from the Internet Configuration System (or Internet Config), which stores your identity and server information and makes it available to many different Internet client programs, including Communicator, Eudora, and Archie, among others. For information, check out the FAQ at *http://www.quinn.echidna.id.au/Quinn/Config/IC_FAQ.html.*

Messages

The Messages category under Mail & Groups in the Preferences dialog box allows you to specify message properties such as automatic quoting, HTML-awareness, the length of the lines, and the way in which copies of messages are sent and copied.

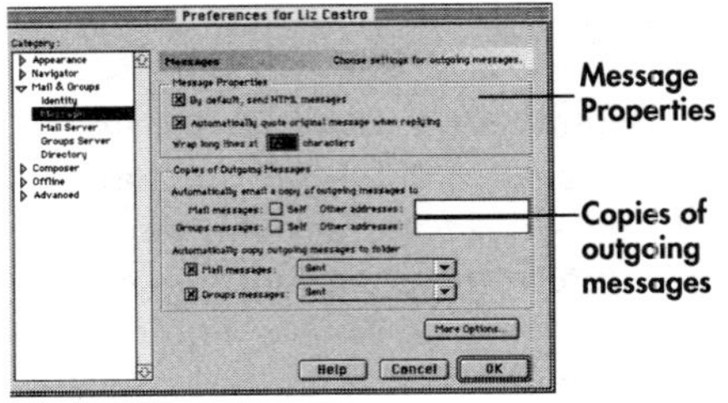

Message Properties

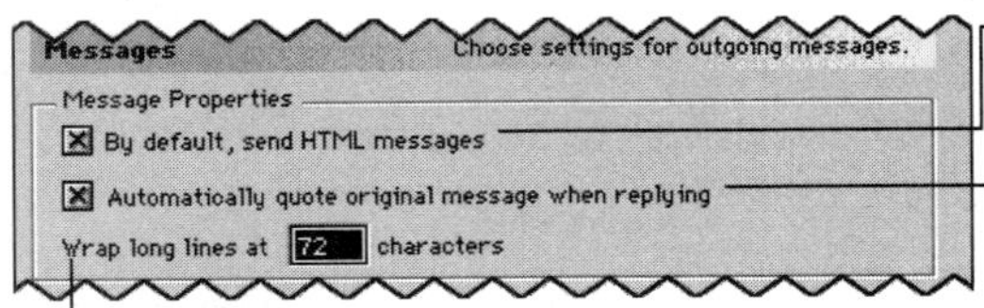

Click here to send messages with **HTML** formatting. For more information, consult *Adding images, links, and formatting* on page 154.

Select this option to have the message you are responding to **automatically quoted** in your reply.

Enter the number of characters to indicate how long you want **message lines** to be.

Copies of outgoing messages

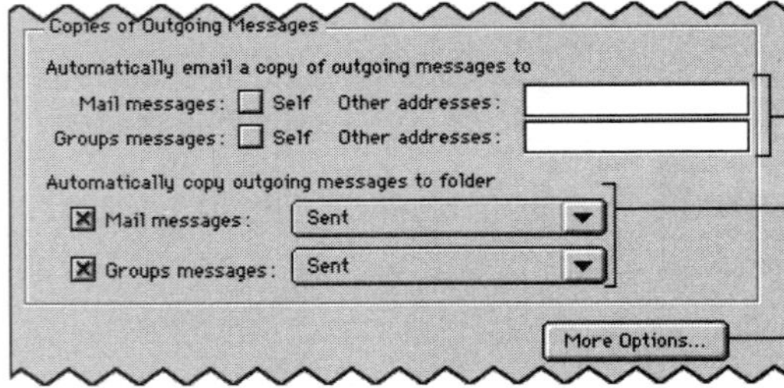

Type an e-mail address in **Mail messages** or **Groups messages** to send a copy of all outgoing messages to that address. Or click **Self** to send them to the address entered in the Identity preferences *(see page 321)*

Select a folder from the pop-up menus **Mail messages** and **Groups messages** to indicate where you want to save a copy of all outgoing messages.

Click **More Options** to access the More Messages Preferences dialog box *(see below)*.

More Messages Preferences

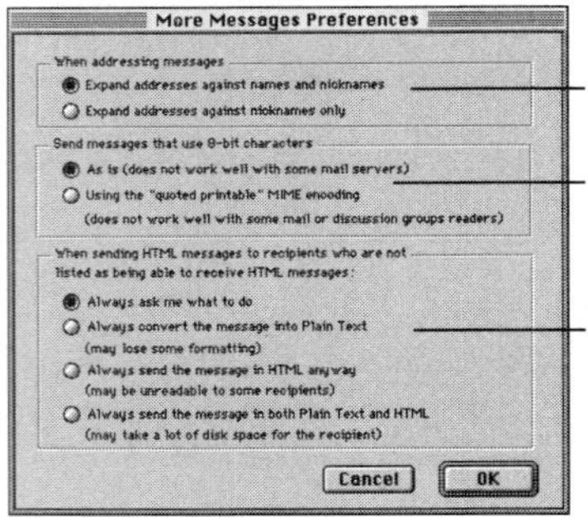

The first option uses both **names and nicknames** to look up e-mail addresses. The second uses only nicknames, in case some of the names and nicknames are the same.

Click **As is** for widest compatibility with e-mail servers in the US and Europe. Click the other option to make Communicator send messages with **MIME encoding**.

Not everyone uses Communicator to read their mail. Choose one of these options to help ensure that everyone can read your messages. From top to bottom, either have Communicator **ask you**, send messages in **plain text** (and lose HTML formatting), send messages in **HTML** (risking some recipient's ability to read them), or in **both** HTML and plain text (taking up more disk space).

Mail Server

Click Mail Server under Mail & Groups in the Category list of the Preferences dialog box to enter essential information for sending and receiving mail, including your user name, the name of the outgoing and incoming mail servers and whether the messages should be left on the server or not.

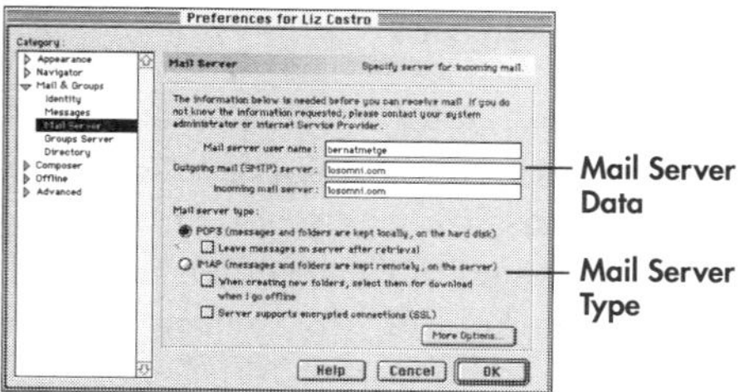

Mail Server Data and Mail Server Type

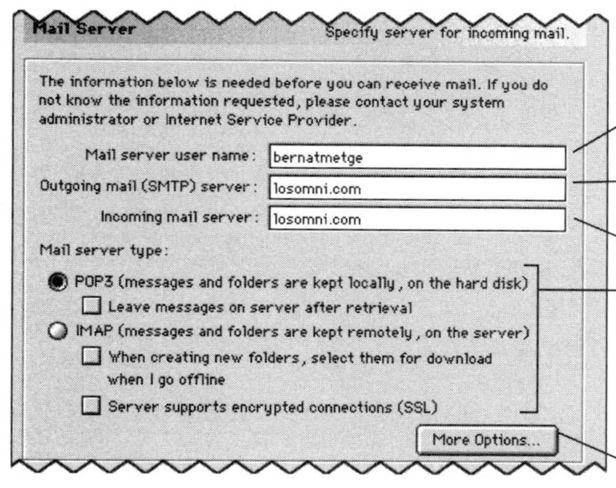

You won't be able to send or receive mail until you fill in this important data. If you are not sure what to put in, ask your Internet service provider.

Type your **user name** here. This is the part of your e-mail address before the @ symbol.

Type the name of your **outgoing mail server** here.

The name of your **incoming mail server** goes here.

Choose the appropriate type of server (**POP3** or **IMAP**). Ask your ISP if you're not sure.
Click **Leave messages on server after retrieval** if you use Communicator on two computers and want to archive all the messages on one machine while reading them on both.

Click **More Options** to access advanced options related with mail and mail servers *(see below)*.

More Mail Server Preferences

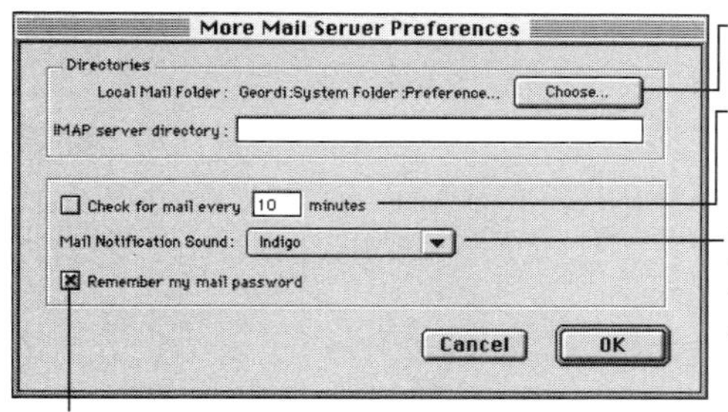

Click **Choose** to select a local folder where you want to store all your mail.

Enter a number of **minutes** to determine how often Communicator should check to see if you have mail.

Choose a **notification sound** so that Communicator beeps when you have new mail. You can choose, besides the usual sounds found in the System, a couple of phone sounds.

Click **Remember my mail password** so that you don't have to enter your password each time you check your mail. Of course, if somebody else has access to your computer, they'll be able to use your e-mail account.

Groups Server

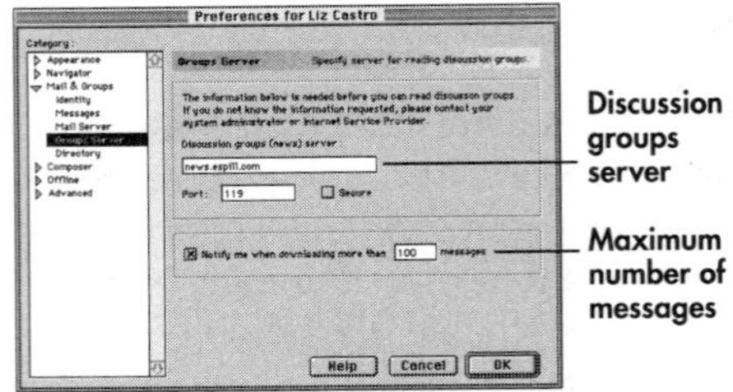

Click Groups Server in the Category list under Mail & Groups to specify the name of your discussion group server (ask your Internet service provider), the directory where your discussion group settings should be stored, and how many messages you want to retrieve at a time.

Discussion groups server

Enter the name of your **discussion groups server** here. Ask your ISP if you're not sure.

Click **Secure** to connect to a secure discussion group servers. Otherwise, you won't be able to access it—whether you need a password or not.

If necessary (usually, it's not) enter the **port** number. If you are not sure, ask your ISP. Generally, the default port number works fine.

You won't be able to read messages on discussion groups until you fill out the information in this area. If you need help, contact your Internet service provider.

Maximum number of messages

Click here and enter the **number of messages** that you want to receive at a time before Communicator warns you about it.

Directory

The Directory category under Mail & Groups is for storing the name and address of the directories of addresses that you use when you search for information about someone on the Internet. To know more about how to look for someone's e-mail address, consult *Searching for an address* on page 177.

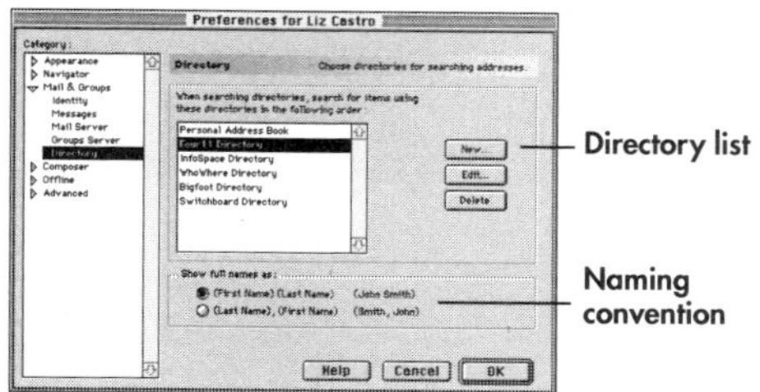

Directory list

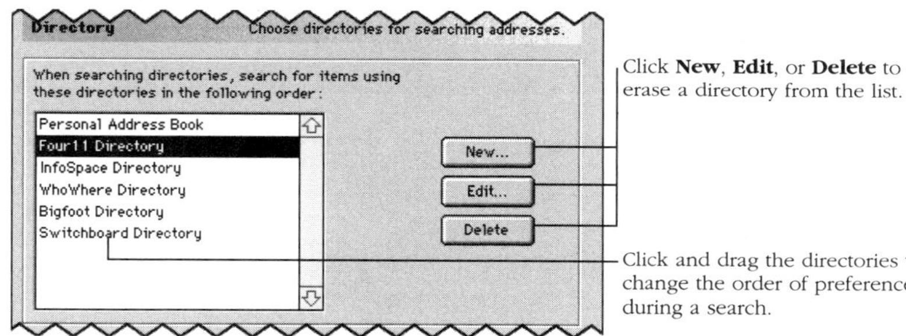

Click **New**, **Edit**, or **Delete** to create, modify, or erase a directory from the list.

Click and drag the directories **up and down** to change the order of preference of a directory during a search.

Naming convention

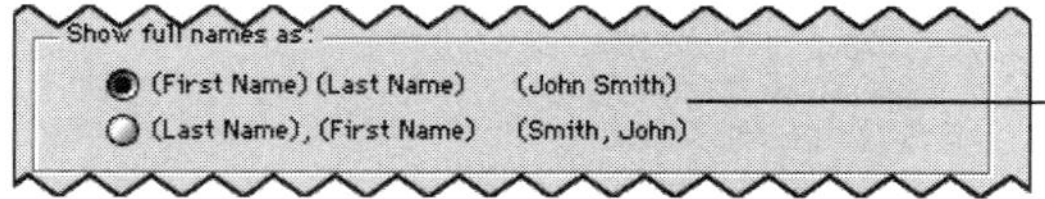

Select one of these options to choose how **names** should be displayed.

27 Composer Preferences

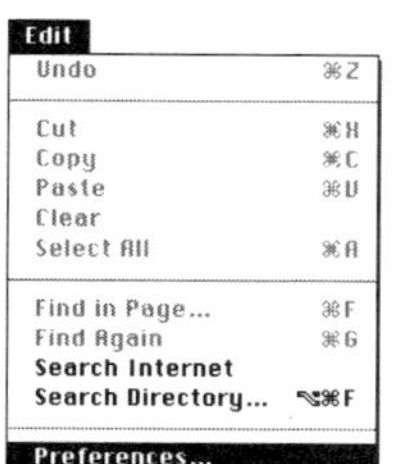

Figure 27.1 *Choose Edit > Preferences.*

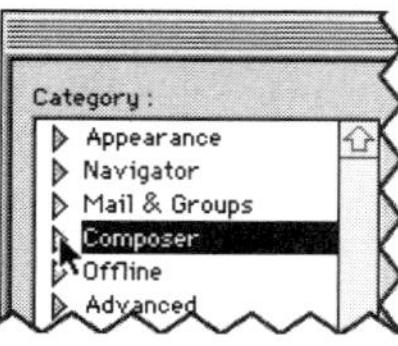

Figure 27.2 *Click on the arrow next to Composer to expand it and see the sections it contains.*

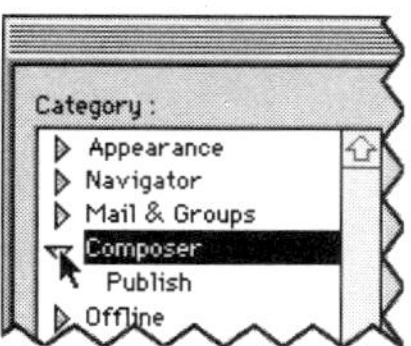

Figure 27.3 *The Composer category has two sections (Composer and Publish) that can be accessed by clicking on the corresponding name.*

The settings in the Composer sections of the Preferences dialog box control how documents are created and how they're published.

To access the Composer preferences, choose Edit > Preferences **(Figure 27.1)**. In the Preferences dialog box that appears, click the arrow next to Composer to view both sections **(Figures 27.2 and 27.3)**. Finally, click one of the section's names (Composer or Publish) to access those settings. Each section is described in detail in the following pages.

Once you've made the desired changes to the settings, click OK to save the changes, or Cancel to leave the dialog box without saving them. Click Help to access Communicator's Help file.

Composer

Click on the Composer section to change the default author's name and to choose external text and image editors.

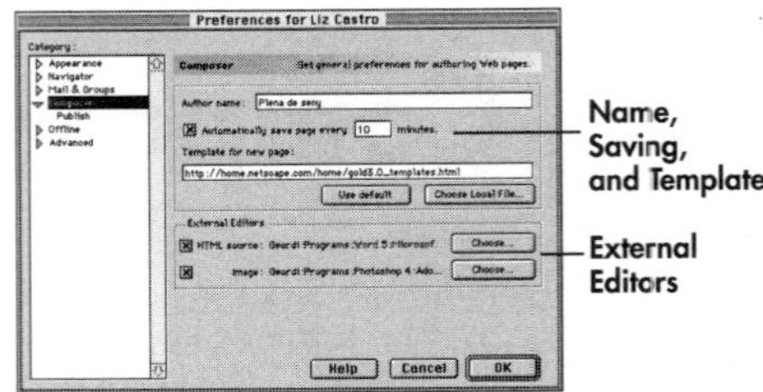

Name, Saving, and Template

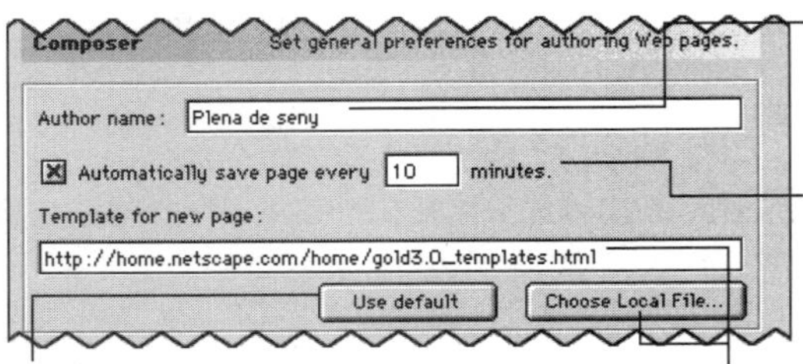

The **Author name** identifies the pages you create. The information does not appear on the Web page when viewed with a browser, but instead is inserted into the HTML tags and can be used by search services.

Enter a number in the **Automatically save page every xx minutes** text box to have Communicator save your file periodically as you work.

Click **Use default** to use Netscape's default templates at Netscape's Web site.

When you choose Open > New > Page from Template, Navigator loads the page specified here. You can create your own **template** and either type the path to it here or click **Choose Local File** to locate it in your hard disk.

External Editors

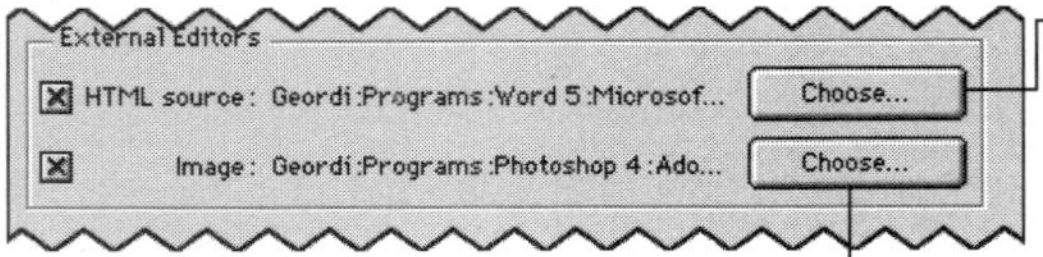

Click **Choose** to locate on your hard disk the text editor that you would like to use, in addition to Composer, for **viewing and modifying HTML tags**.

Communicator gives you a shortcut to the programs you use most often for editing HTML tags and images.

Click **Choose** and locate the image editor (like Adobe Photoshop) that you would like to use for **editing images**.

Publish

Click Publish in the Category list to determine how Composer treats links and images in your pages, and to specify the location of the server where your page and its associated images should be copied when you publish them. For more details on publishing, consult *Publishing your page* on page 304.

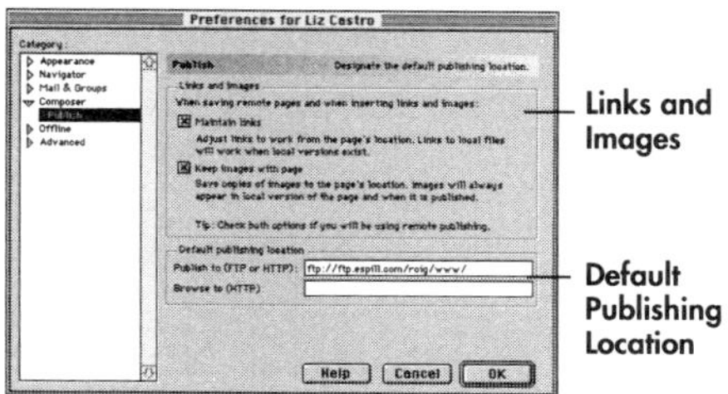

Links and Images

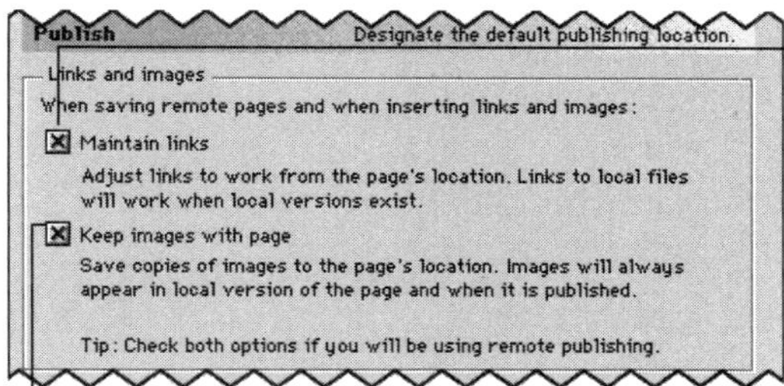

Choose **Maintain links** to have Communicator convert absolute links into relative ones on the pages that you copy from the Web. This will enable the links to continue to work correctly when you open them locally (from your hard disk).

Check **Keep images with page** if you want Communicator to copy all the images inserted on a page to the same directory on your hard disk that contains the Web page itself.

Default Publishing Location

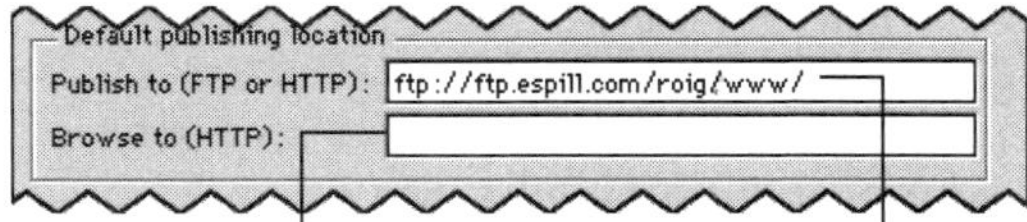

Specify where your pages should be published when you choose File > Publish.

This looks like a bug. In the Windows version of Communicator, when you've finished publishing a page, Composer offers to take you to your **default *browsing* location** which you specify here. However, the Macintosh version does not offer that option; this is just a remnant *(see page 306)*.

In the **Publish to (FTP or HTTP)** field, type the URL of the FTP or Web site where you wish to publish your files. If you're not sure, ask your Internet service provider. For more information, consult *Setting up a default publishing location* on page 306.

Offline Preferences

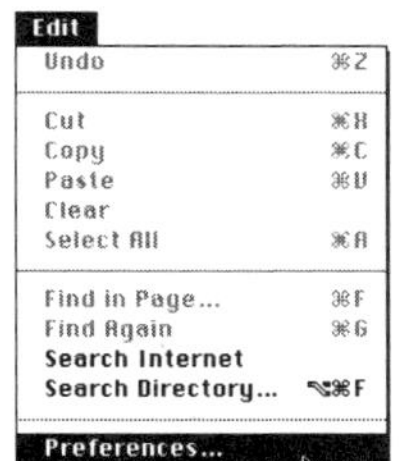

Figure 28.1 *Choose Edit > Preferences.*

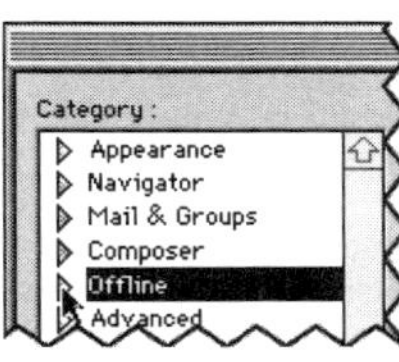

Figure 28.2 *Click on the arrow next to Offline to expand it and see the sections it contains.*

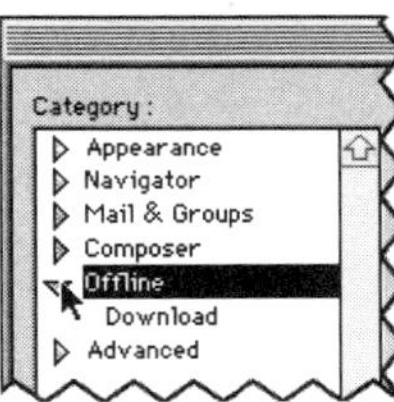

Figure 28.3 *The Offline category has one other Subcategory, Download, that can be accessed by clicking on the corresponding name.*

The settings in the Offline section of the Preferences dialog box control whether you start up Communicator in online or offline mode, and from which discussion groups you download messages for offline work. To know more about working offline, consult *Downloading mail for offline reading* on page 123 and *Getting news messages for reading offline* on page 134.

To access the Offline preferences, choose Edit > Preferences **(Figure 28.1)** and then click on the arrow next to the word Offline to see both of its sections **(Figures 28.2 and 28.3)**. Finally, click the name of one of the sections (Offline or Download) to access its settings. Each section is described in detail in the following pages.

Once you've made the desired changes to the settings, click OK to save the changes, or Cancel to leave the dialog box without saving them. Click Help to access Communicator's Help file.

Offline

Click on the Offline section to choose whether you start up in offline or online mode, or if you wish the program to ask you first. In Offline mode, you cannot surf the Web, get new messages, or update Netcaster channels. (Personally, I think going offline is rather pointless.)

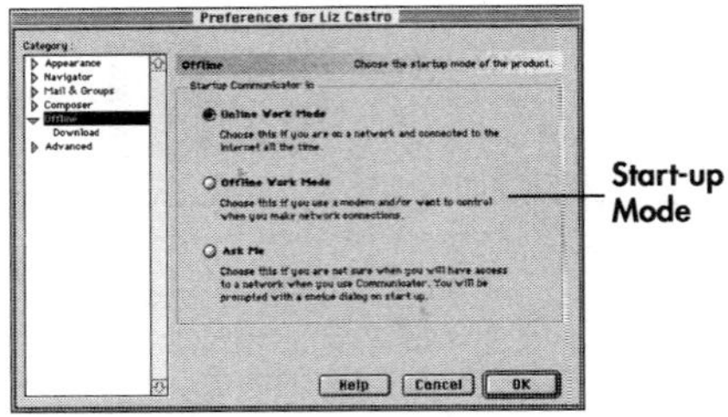

Start-up Mode

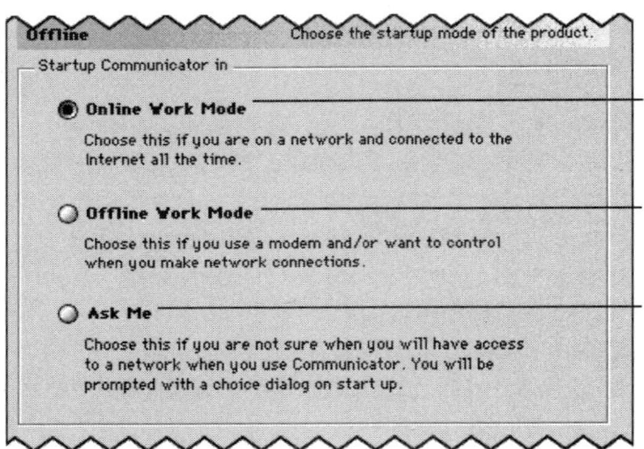

Click **Online Work Mode** to start up Communicator in online mode. If you start up with Navigator, it goes directly to the home page specified in the Appearance preferences *(see page 312)*.

Click **Offline Work Mode** to start up Communicator in offline mode. You'll need to choose File > Go Online to be able to access Web pages, e-mail and discussion groups.

Choose **Ask Me** to have Communicator present you with a dialog box each time you launch the program, in which you can choose to start in Online or Offline work mode.

Download

Click Download in the Category list of the Preferences box to specify which messages to download when choosing File > Go Offline or File > Go Online.

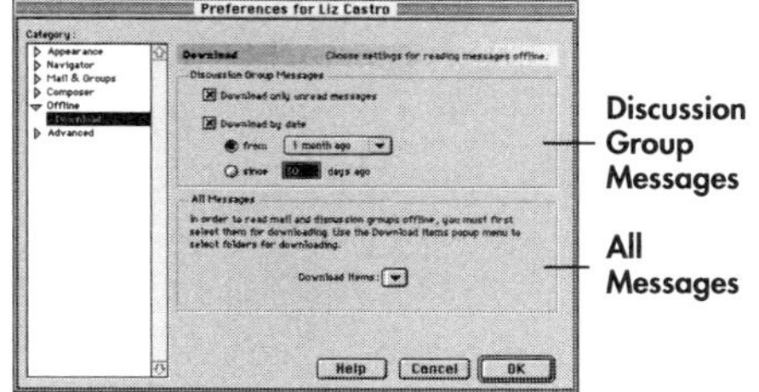

Discussion Group Messages

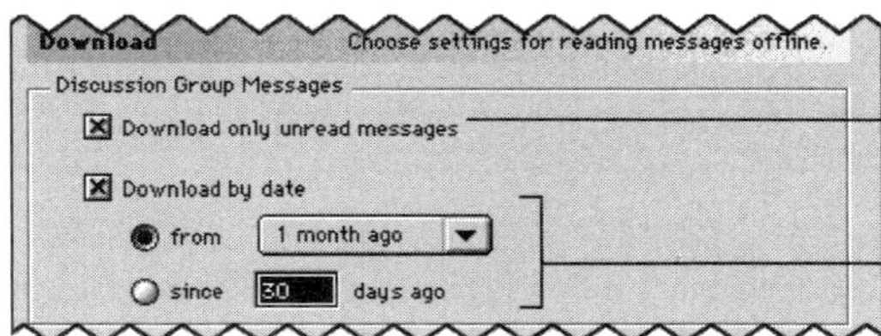

Click **Download only unread messages** to get just the messages that you have not yet read when downloading discussion group messages.

Click **Download by date** and choose a time frame within which you want to download messages.

All Messages

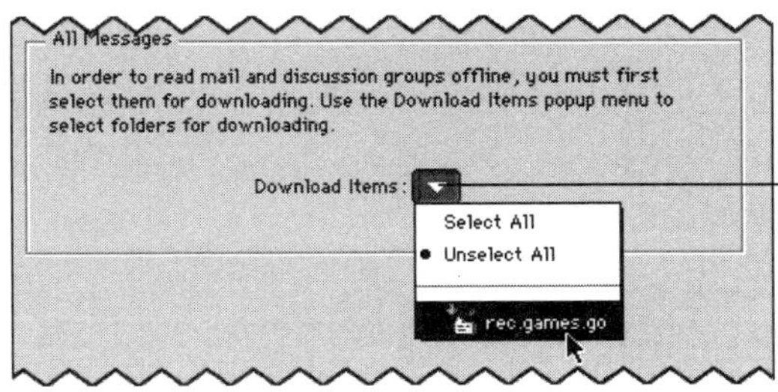

Click **Download Items** and, in the menu that appears, choose the discussion groups from which you want to download messages for offline reading. For more information, consult *Getting news messages for reading offline* on page 134.

Advanced Preferences

Edit
Undo ⌘Z
Cut ⌘X
Copy ⌘C
Paste ⌘V
Clear
Select All ⌘A
Find in Page... ⌘F
Find Again ⌘G
Search Internet
Search Directory... ⌥⌘F
Preferences...

Figure 29.1 *Choose Edit > Preferences.*

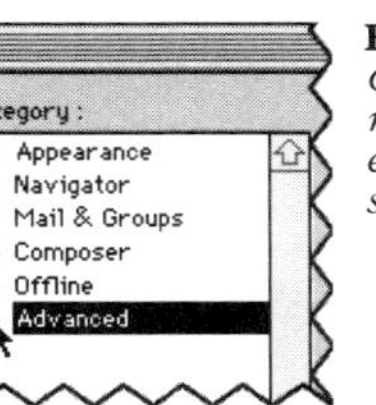

Figure 29.2 *Click on the arrow next to Advanced to expand it and see the sections it contains.*

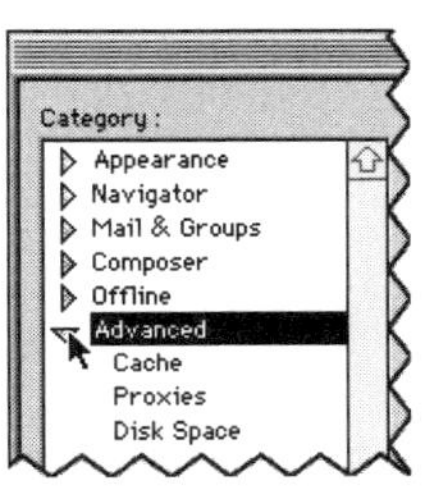

Figure 29.3 *The Advanced category has four sections (Advanced, Cache, Proxies, and Disk Space) that can be accessed by clicking on the corresponding name.*

The settings of the Advanced preferences category control how Communicator works over a network and how it manages memory and disk space.

To view the Advanced preferences, choose Edit > Preferences **(Figure 29.1)** and then click the arrow next to Advanced in the Preferences dialog box to see the four sections it contains **(Figures 29.2 and 29.3)**. Finally, click one of the section names (Advanced, Cache, Proxies, or Disk Space) to view its settings. Each section is described in detail on the following pages.

Once you've made the desired changes to the settings, click OK to save the changes. Click Cancel to close the dialog box without saving changes. Click Help to access Communicator's Help file.

Advanced

The Advanced category controls a variety of options, including enabling Java, downloading images automatically, enabling style sheets, and how you want to treat those pesky little creatures that thrive these days on the Internet: cookies.

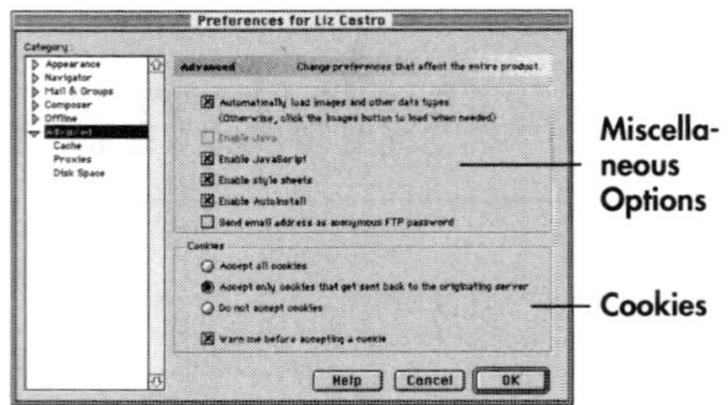

Miscellaneous Options

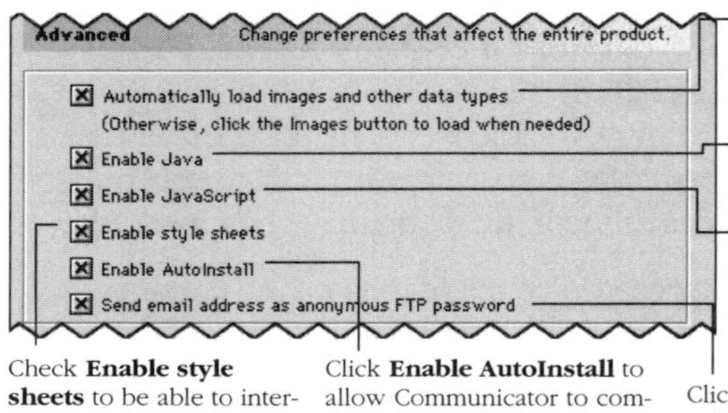

Click **Automatically load images** to see all the images in all the Web pages you visit. If you uncheck it, you'll have to load images manually with the Images button *(see page 43)*.

Check **Enable Java** if you want to be able to execute Java applets.

Check **Enable JavaScript** to be able to interpret JavaScript code that has been embedded in a page's HTML code. Although enabling both Java options may not be 100% secure, some pages will not display properly unless you do.

Check **Enable style sheets** to be able to interpret correctly the fonts specified with style sheets.

Click **Enable AutoInstall** to allow Communicator to complete the installation process of additional components with Smart Update.

Click this option to automatically send your e-mail address to an **FTP** site that accepts **anonymous** connections.

Cookies

You may choose to automatically **accept all cookies** (you'll be bothered the least, but you may be sharing more information than you intend over the Internet), **accept only those cookies that are sent back to the originating server** (thereby reducing the risk that your information is sent all over creation), or decide **not to accept cookies** (which may make it impossible to use those sites that need to be able to recognize who you are).

If you choose any of the options that accept cookies, you can also check this option to have Communicator **warn** you with an alert about the site sending you a cookie. Usually there is some kind of hint about what the cookie is about, or at least who is sending it.

Cookies are files that the server stores on your computer so that it can recognize you the next time you surf to that site. Some companies use cookies only for their own sites or domains and are relatively inoffensive. Other companies may collect marketing information gleaned from cookies—like where you've been surfing—and share it with other companies.

Advanced

Cache

Click the Cache category to change the settings for the Disk cache, to change the directory, and to decide how often Communicator should compare a page saved in cache with the actual page on the server.

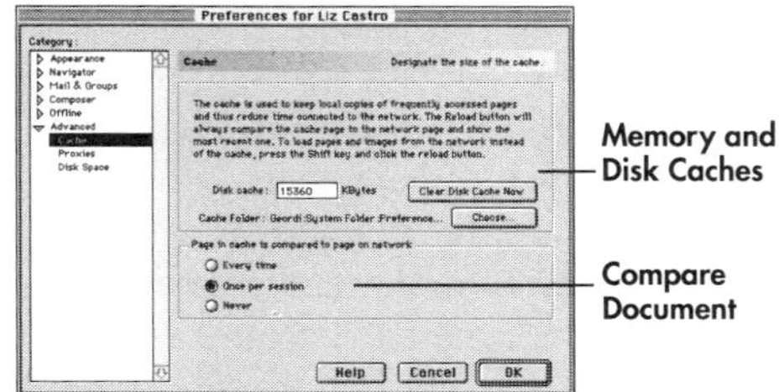

Memory and Disk Caches

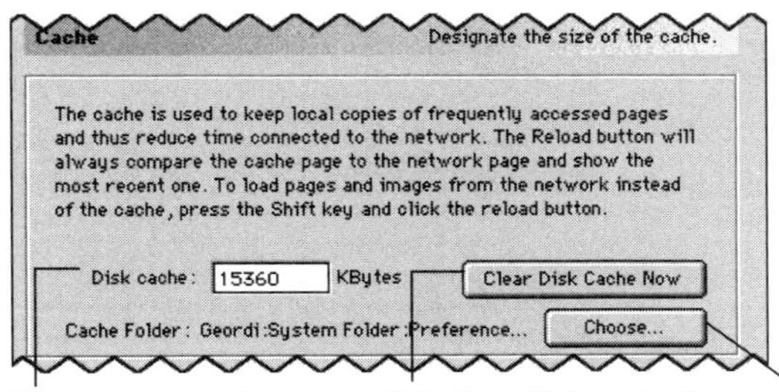

Navigator saves many of the pages and images that you browse in its Memory and Disk Caches. Once a page or image is stored in a cache, it takes much less time to display. Navigator organizes the Cache when you exit the program. If it seems to take too long, try reducing the size of the Disk Cache.

Type a number in the text box to **set the size** of the Disk (storage) cache. The number here is twice the default.

Click **Clear Disk Cache Now** to erase all the pages and images in the disk cache and make more space available on your hard disk.

Click **Choose** and select the folder where you want the disk cache to **store the pages** and images that you browse.

Compare Document

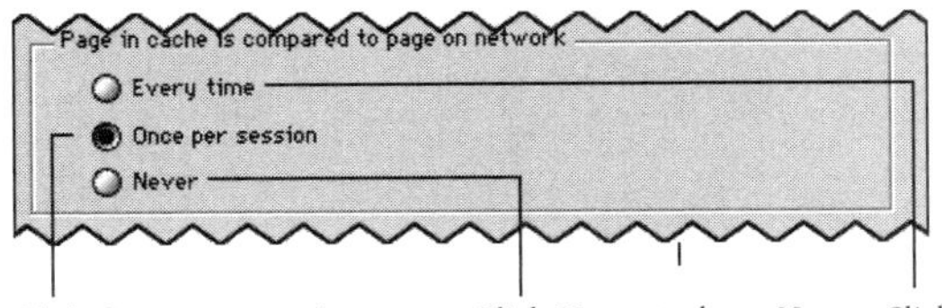

Pages on the Web are incredibly dynamic. Think of all the pages you've seen "under construction." You can have Navigator compare the document you have saved in cache with the current version once each time you open Navigator, every time you look at the page, or never.

Click **Once per session** to have Navigator compare the cached version with the real page on the server only the first time you access the page during a session with Navigator.

Click **Never** to have Navigator always use the cached version without checking for changes.

Click **Every time** to make Navigator compare the cached version with the server each time you browse the page. If you select this option, it doesn't make sense to have a big cache *(see above)*.

Cache

Proxies

Click the Proxies category to change how Navigator interacts with proxy software. In situations where a firewall protects internal computer networks from external access, Navigator needs proxy software to get by the firewall to remote servers without compromising security.

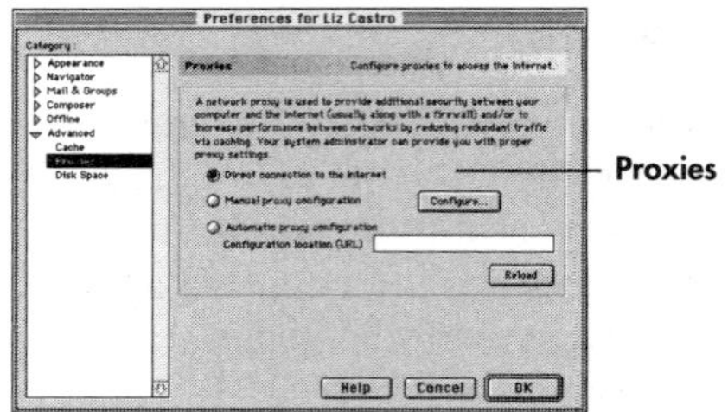

Proxies

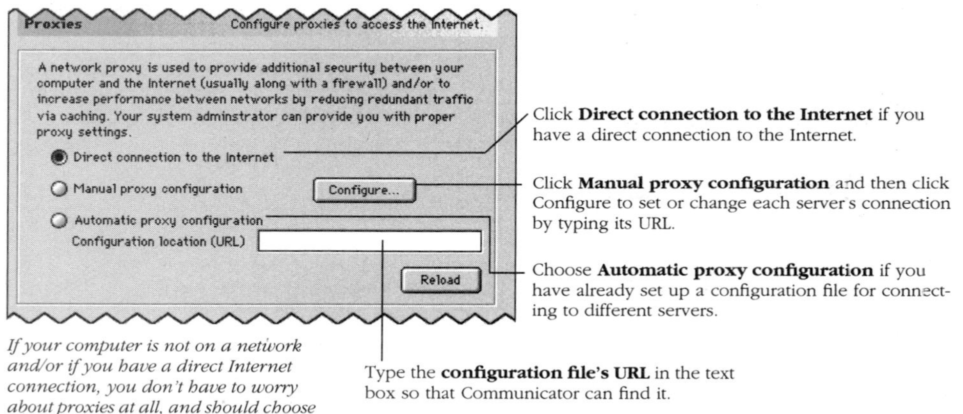

Click **Direct connection to the Internet** if you have a direct connection to the Internet.

Click **Manual proxy configuration** and then click Configure to set or change each server s connection by typing its URL.

Choose **Automatic proxy configuration** if you have already set up a configuration file for connecting to different servers.

Type the **configuration file's URL** in the text box so that Communicator can find it.

If your computer is not on a network and/or if you have a direct Internet connection, you don't have to worry about proxies at all, and should choose ***Direct connection to the Internet***.

Disk Space

Click the Disk Space category in the Preferences dialog box to specify the maximum size of e-mail messages and how long messages from discussion groups are kept.

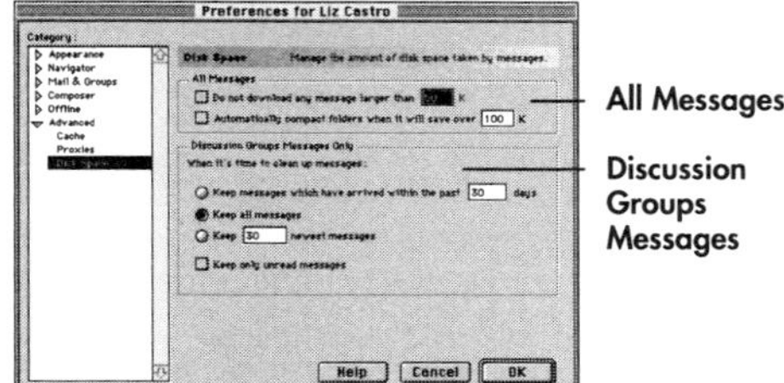

All Messages

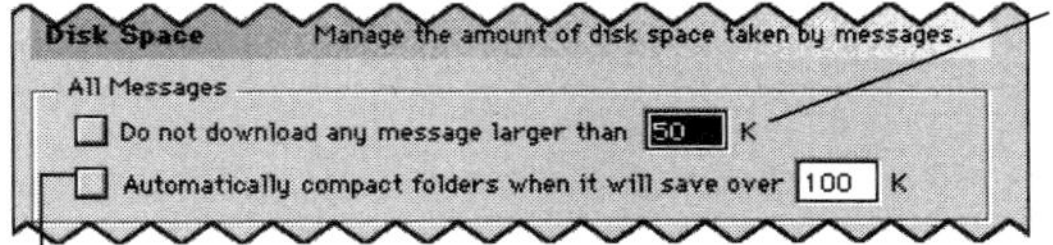

Click this option and enter a number here to determine **how big a message** you are willing to receive. If you do not select this option, there is no limit to the size of messages.

Click this option to **compact folders** to save disk space. (Space is wasted when messages are moved from folder to folder.) A low number allows for more frequent compacting.

Discussion Groups Messages

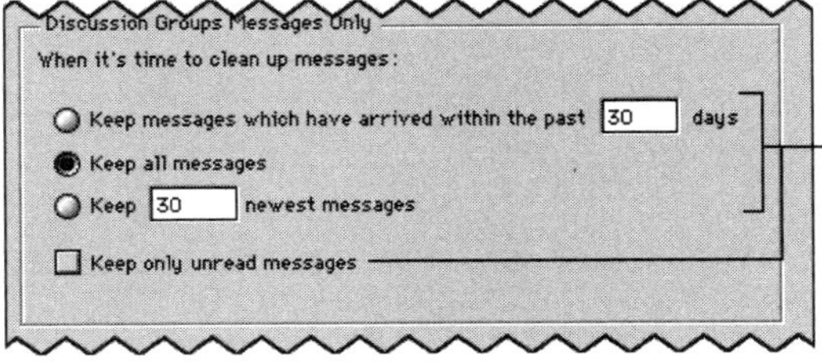

Select one of these options to decide how to manage old messages from discussion groups.

Composer vs. HTML

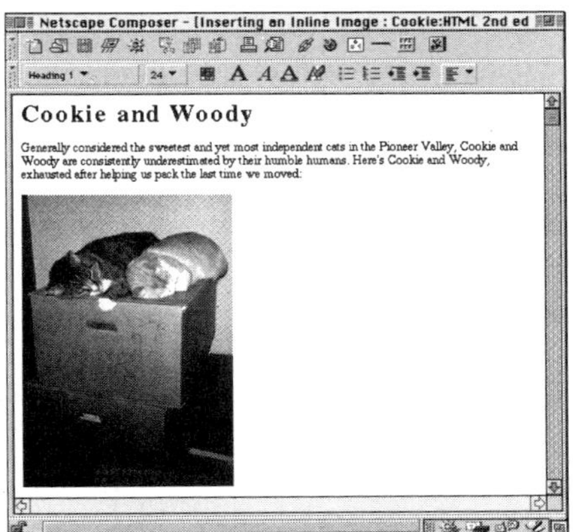

Figure A.1 *Navigate to the page whose HTML codes you wish to view.*

Figure A.2 *Choose Edit > HTML Source.*

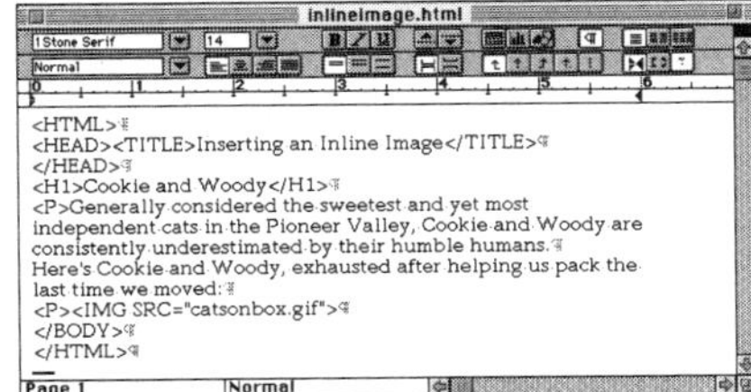

Figure A.3 *The HTML codes for the page are shown in a new window in the program specified (in this case, Word).*

As you go about designing your page, you may want to know how Composer converts the page's elements and formatting into HTML. If you are familiar with HTML, this information may help you determine how other browsers will display your page.

Viewing and editing a page's HTML

One way to see how Composer converts its pages into HTML is to look at your own. Or perhaps you want to study someone else's page and see how they achieved a particular effect. You can also make changes to the HTML code directly.

To view or edit a page's HTML:

1. Open the page in Composer **(Figure A.1)**.
2. Choose Edit > HTML Source **(Figure A.2)**. The HTML that makes up the current page is displayed in the program of your choice **(Figure A.3)**.

✓ Tips

- You can also view HTML code from Navigator *(see page 45)*.
- If you do make changes to the HTML code, be sure and save the document in text-only format with the .htm extension.
- One nice thing to edit out is the information about Netscape on your page.

How Composer translates into HTML

Use the following table to see how individual formatting commands in Composer are translated into HTML code. Note that most default values are not translated at all even if they have a command in Composer. Also, some Composer commands actually *remove* HTML coding. Both of these cases are denoted in the table with a long hyphen (—). Only the HTML codes that Composer can produce are listed here. For more information on inserting HTML codes not supported by Composer, consult *Adding HTML tags manually* on page 296.

COMMAND NAME IN COMPOSER	HTML CODE USED	COMPATIBILITY
Document Properties		
General		
Creation of page (automatic)	<html>	HTML 3.2
Header area (automatic)	<head>	HTML 3.2
Title	<title>	HTML 3.2
Author	<meta name="Author" content="xxx">	HTML 3.2
Description	<meta name="Description" content="xxx">	HTML 3.2
Generator (automatic)	<meta name="Generator" content="User-Agent: Mozilla/ 4.01 [en] (Macintosh; I; 68K) [Netscape]key">	HTML 3.2
Keywords	<meta name="KeyWords" content="xxx">	HTML 3.2
Classification	<meta name="Classification" content="xxx">	HTML 3.2
Appearance		
Body area (automatic)	<body>	HTML 3.2
Normal Text (color)	text="#rrggbb"	HTML 3.2*
Link Text (color)	link="#rrggbb"	HTML 3.2*
Active Link Text (color)	alink="#rrggbb"	HTML 3.2*
Followed Link Text (color)	vlink="#rrggbb"	HTML 3.2*
Background Solid Color	bgcolor="#rrggbb"	HTML 3.2*
Background Image file	background="image.gif"	HTML 3.2*

*HTML Code used: n=any number (when describing width or height it can be either the number of pixels or a percentage of window size); #rrggbb=a color represented by giving the R, G, and B components in hexadecimals; indents indicate attributes that may be added, if desired, to the tag directly preceding it. Compatibility: HTML 3.2=part of standard HTML, up to version 3.2; *=not part of HTML 2 and probably not recognized by older browsers, N=Composer only*

COMMAND NAME IN COMPOSER	HTML CODE USED	COMPATIBILITY
Character Styles		
Color		
Document's default color	—	
Custom color	<font color="#rrggbb">	HTML 3.2*
Style		
Font	<font face="fontname">	HTML 3.2
Remove all styles	—	
Bold	<b>	HTML 3.2
Italic	<i>	HTML 3.2
Underline	<u>	HTML 3.2
Fixed width	<tt>	HTML 3.2
Strikethrough	<strike>	HTML 3.2*
Superscript	<sup>	HTML 3.2
Subscript	<sub>	HTML 3.2
Blinking	<blink>	N
Nonbreaking	<nobr>	HTML 3.2
Size		
Pop-up menu	<font size=n>	HTML 3.2*
Paragraph Styles		
General		
Header 1, Header 2, etc.	<h1>, <h2>, *etc.*	HTML 3.2
Address	<address>	HTML 3.2
Formatted	<pre>	HTML 3.2
List item	<li>	HTML 3.2
Description Title	<dt>	HTML 3.2
Description Text	<dd>	HTML 3.2
Increase Indent	<ul>	HTML 3.2
Decrease Indent	—	
Block Quote	<blockquote>	HTML 3.2
Align Left	—	
Align Right	<div align=right>	HTML 3.2*
Align Center	<center>	HTML 3.2

*HTML Code used: n=any number (when describing width or height it can be either the number of pixels or a percentage of window size); #rrggbb=a color represented by giving the R, G, and B components in hexadecimals; indents indicate attributes that may be added, if desired, to the tag directly preceding it. Compatibility: HTML 3.2=part of standard HTML, up to version 3.2; *=not part of HTML 2 and probably not recognized by older browsers, N=Composer only*

How Composer translates into HTML

COMMAND NAME IN COMPOSER	HTML CODE USED	COMPATIBILITY
Lists		
Numbered List	<ol>	HTML 3.2
Number Style	type=	HTML 3.2*
Automatic	—	
1, 2, 3	—	
A, B, C	A	HTML 3.2*
I, II, III	I	HTML 3.2*
a, b, c	a	HTML 3.2*
Starting Number	start=n	HTML 3.2*
Unnumbered (Bulleted) List	<ul>	HTML 3.2
Bullet Style	type=	HTML 3.2*
Automatic	—	
Solid circle	disc	HTML 3.2*
Open circle	circle	HTML 3.2*
Solid square	square	HTML 3.2*
Description List	<dl>	HTML 3.2
Links		
Link	<a href="url.#target">display text</a>	HTML 3.2
Target	<a name="targetname">targeted text</a>	HTML 3.2
Images		
Image	<img src="image.gif">	HTML 3.2
Alternative representations		
Image	lowsrc=	N
Text	alt=	HTML 3.2
Alignment		
xyz	align=texttop	HTML 3.2*
xyz	align=center	HTML 3.2*
xyz	align=abscenter	HTML 3.2*
xyz	—	
xyz	align=bottom	HTML 3.2*

*HTML Code used: n=any number (when describing width or height it can be either the number of pixels or a percentage of window size); #rrggbb=a color represented by giving the R, G, and B components in hexadecimals; indents indicate attributes that may be added, if desired, to the tag directly preceding it. Compatibility: HTML 3.2=part of standard HTML, up to version 3.2; *=not part of HTML 2 and probably not recognized by older browsers, N=Composer only*

How Composer translates into HTML

COMMAND NAME IN COMPOSER	HTML CODE USED	COMPATIBILITY
Text wrap		
[icon]	align=left	HTML 3.2*
[icon]	align=right	HTML 3.2*
Dimensions		
Height	height=	HTML 3.2*
Width	width=	HTML 3.2*
Space around image		
Left and right	hspace=	HTML 3.2*
Top and bottom	vspace=	HTML 3.2*
Solid border	border=	HTML 3.2*
Horizontal Lines		
Horizontal lines [icon]	<hr>	HTML 3.2
Height	*none if 2, otherwise,* size="n"	HTML 3.2*
Width	width="n" *or* width ="n%"	HTML 3.2*
Align	align=	HTML 3.2*
Left	left	HTML 3.2*
Center	—	HTML 3.2*
Right	right	HTML 3.2*
3d shading	*none when checked*; noshade *when unchecked*	HTML 3.2*
Tables		
General		
Table [icon]	<table>	HTML 3.2
Border line width	border=n	HTML 3.2*
Cell spacing	cellspacing=n	HTML 3.2*
Cell padding	cellpadding=n	HTML 3.2*
Table width	width="n" *or* width="n%"	HTML 3.2*
Table min. height	height="n" *or* height="n%"	HTML 3.2*
Table color	bgcolor="#rrggbb"	HTML 3.2*
Include caption	<caption>	HTML 3.2
above	—	
below table	align=bottom	HTML 3.2*

*HTML Code used: n=any number (when describing width or height it can be either the number of pixels or a percentage of window size); #rrggbb=a color represented by giving the R, G, and B components in hexadecimals; indents indicate attributes that may be added, if desired, to the tag directly preceding it. Compatibility: HTML 3.2=part of standard HTML, up to version 3.2; *=not part of HTML 2 and probably not recognized by older browsers, N=Composer only*

COMMAND NAME IN COMPOSER	HTML CODE USED	COMPATIBILITY
Rows		
Table row	<tr>	HTML 3.2
Alignment—horizontal	align=	HTML 3.2
Left	left	HTML 3.2
Center	center	HTML 3.2
Right	right	HTML 3.2
Alignment—vertical	valign=	HTML 3.2*
Top	top	HTML 3.2*
Center	center	HTML 3.2*
Bottom	bottom	HTML 3.2*
Baselines	baseline *(no s)*	HTML 3.2*
Row color	bgcolor="#rrggbb"	HTML 3.2*
Cells		
Cell (automatic)	<td>	HTML 3.2
Header style	<th> *(instead of <td>)*	HTML 3.2
Cell spans		
rows	rowspan="n"	HTML 3.2
columns	colspan="n"	HTML 3.2
Alignment	*(see Rows above)*	
Wrap text	*nothing if checked;* nowrap *if not checked.*	HTML 3.2*
Cell width	width="n" *or* width="n%"	HTML 3.2*
Cell min. height	height="n" *or* height="n%"	HTML 3.2*
Cell color	bgcolor="#rrggbb"	HTML 3.2*

*HTML Code used: n=any number (when describing width or height it can be either the number of pixels or a percentage of window size); #rrggbb=a color represented by giving the R, G, and B components in hexadecimals; indents indicate attributes that may be added, if desired, to the tag directly preceding it. Compatibility: HTML 3.2=part of standard HTML, up to version 3.2; *=not part of HTML 2 and probably not recognized by older browsers, N=Composer only*

Index

A

B

C

Index

D

E

F

Index

I

J

K

L

M

N

T

U

V

W

Y